Legal Studies in International, European and Comparative Criminal Law

Volume 10

The main purpose of this book series is to provide sound analyses of major developments in national, EU and international law and case law, as well as insights into court practice and legislative proposals in the areas concerned. The analyses address a broad readership, such as lawyers and practitioners, while also providing guidance for courts. In terms of scope, the series encompasses four main areas, the first of which concerns international criminal law and especially international case law in relevant criminal law subjects. The second addresses international human rights law with a particular focus on the impact of international jurisprudences on national criminal law and criminal justice systems, as well as their interrelations. In turn the third area focuses on European criminal law and case law. Here, particular weight will be attached to studies on European criminal law conducted from a comparative perspective. The fourth and final area presents surveys of comparative criminal law inside and outside Europe. By combining these various aspects, the series especially highlights research aimed at proposing new legal solutions, while focusing on the new challenges of a European area based on high standards of human rights protection.

As a rule, book proposals are subject to peer review, which is carried out by two members of the editorial board in anonymous form.

Stefano Ruggeri • Antonella Falcone •
Viviana Di Nuzzo
Editors

Third Parties in Criminal Proceedings

A Comparative Law Study

Springer

Editors
Stefano Ruggeri
Law Department
University of Messina
Messina, Italy

Antonella Falcone
Law Department
University of Messina
Messina, Italy

Viviana Di Nuzzo
Law Department
University of Messina
Messina, Italy

ISSN 2524-8049 ISSN 2524-8057 (electronic)
Legal Studies in International, European and Comparative Criminal Law
ISBN 978-3-031-73969-9 ISBN 978-3-031-73970-5 (eBook)
https://doi.org/10.1007/978-3-031-73970-5

This Springer imprint is published by the registered company Springer Nature Switzerland AG
The registered company address is: Gewerbestrasse 11, 6330 Cham, Switzerland

Contents

Introduction. The Role and Protection of Third Parties in Criminal Proceedings: Old and New Challenges for Fundamental Rights and Procedural Safeguards

Viviana Di Nuzzo and Antonella Falcone

Abstract This Chapter introduces the topic we are dealing with and discuss briefly the main aspects of the role and protection of third parties. The increasing expansion and extension of criminal proceedings, which are capable of reaching numerous individuals and infringing upon their rights due to the use of digital instruments, call for the need to examine which fundamental rights of third parties can be limited, the legal requirements to carry out such a restriction and the procedural safeguards recognised to the addressed subjects. However, in order to do so, a preliminary definition of the very concept of third parties is essential. But, since the thirdness is a relativistic concept that presupposes two other parties, we cannot address such an issue without examining the assets of formal participants in criminal proceedings. This is the reason why the book adopts a two-levels comparative approach: firstly, the comparative method deals with selected national legal orders in order to understand the kind of involvement and the safeguards of third parties in domestic procedural activities; secondly, the comparative analysis is carried out also with regard to international and supranational Courts, which are attentive and responsive to the urge of strengthening the protection of categories of people different from the formal parties.

1 Preliminary Issues

This book examines the role and protection of third parties in the criminal justice system, thus presenting a modest contribution to the discourse on this complex and often overlooked topic in both domestic and international legal discussions. Before delving into the core aspects of the research, however, it is essential to provide a

V. Di Nuzzo · A. Falcone (✉)
Present Address: Law Department, Messina University, Messina, Italy
e-mail: vidinuzzo@unime.it; antonella.falcone@unime.it

A. Falcone
Law Department, Messina University, Messina, Italy

S. Ruggeri et al. (eds.), *Third Parties in Criminal Proceedings*, Legal Studies in International, European and Comparative Criminal Law 10,
https://doi.org/10.1007/978-3-031-73970-5_1

comprehensive overview on this subject matter. This helps frame the various issues addressed in the following Chapters.

In this regard, it is worth recalling that, in recent years, significant developments in the field of criminal justice have raised several issues about the structural and ideological foundations of criminal procedural systems. These changes underscore the need to acknowledge, both nationally and internationally, the interests of individuals other than suspects and defendants, such as victims, their families, and witnesses, who more and more claim effective powers of participation in criminal proceedings.[1]

Upon closer examination, the extension of such a protection stems from the nature of the modern criminal justice, which has the potential to interfere with the fundamental rights of an increasingly broad category of people, including individuals who may be directly or indirectly involved in criminal proceedings. Indeed, even when these persons are not formally suspected or accused, they may find themselves 'trapped' in criminal proceedings, thus making them ever and ever vulnerable subjects.[2] Against this background, it is of utmost importance to provide them with means through which they can claim the infringement of their rights. As we all know, while many persons may be involved in criminal proceedings, from the investigative phase to the trial one, only a select few ones, such as the accused and the public prosecutor, can however formulate claims or are the subjects against whom criminal or civil claims are brought. A few examples, that are be further reported in the contributions, allow us to better understand the extent of the problem.

[1] In this context, as it is showed by Orlando, the European Court of Human Rights (ECtHR) has played a key role in advocating for this acknowledgment by protecting those who claim breaches of rights enshrined in the European Convention on Human Rights (ECHR). Similar solutions can also be found at the national and supranational levels. Along these lines, see the comparative analysis carried out by Di Nuzzo, Falcone, in this volume.

[2] As highlighted in all the national Reports, the concept of vulnerability shows its relevance in the case of vulnerable subjects called to make a contribution in criminal proceedings. Indeed, the notion of vulnerability has been examined in various fields of knowledge. The term's indeterminate nature has allowed for its versatile application in a wide range of contexts, including the legal one, where it has found its own space and relevance. Cf. Giolo and Pastore (2018). When attributing the condition of vulnerability any entity—an individual, a market, or a territory –, we identify both internal factors, *i.e.*, those intrinsic characteristics of the entity at stake that determine fragility and external factors, *i.e.*, those elements linked to the external context that imply a greater exposure to the risk of suffering harm (such as in the case of social, economic, and political factors that can aggravate a situation of vulnerability). As far as we are concerned, some individuals are considered 'vulnerable' under criminal law for various reasons: they may suffer from physical or psychiatric conditions, be in specific physical conditions (such as pregnancy) or be drug addicted. Vulnerability also extends to minors, those who do not speak the language of the proceedings, victims of certain crimes or criminal contexts, and those in economic distress. In such instances, vulnerability therefore results from both physical or biological characteristics or from social or criminal causes and contexts. However, the lack of any external consideration for a particular subject who is directly or indirectly affected by the criminal process, as well as the absence of any power of participation in the proceedings, exposes that subject to an unacceptable *vulnus*. All this highlights the need to extend the notion of vulnerability to include individuals who are traditionally not considered as such, as in the case of third parties.

A case in point, as widely dealt with by almost all the authors, involves those persons whose goods and assets, without any formal accusation being raised against them, may be searched, frozen, seized, and confiscated. Moreover, significant interference is particularly evident with the use of Information and Communications Technologies (ICTs), which has expanded the range of targets of the investigative measures, such as wiretapping or interceptions of communications. These individuals, who are neither suspected nor accused of any crimes, often lack adequate and effective protection against the risk of abuse of such measures. We refer specifically to the possibility of deleting files related to the interceptions or any instrument allowing a third party to promote *ex post* supervision of the lawfulness of the investigative operations.[3] Furthermore, it often happens that only the parties directly involved in the ongoing proceeding have the right to be informed once the operations have been concluded. Indeed, 'third parties' are typically excluded from the proceedings, as they are not entitled to receive any notices and may never be aware that they have been intercepted. There is also no guarantee that individuals other than the formal parties will be made aware of the interceptions. This lack of knowledge is directly linked to the effectiveness of available remedies, thereby hindering the protection against any possible abuse.

The increasing use of new investigative tools, such as drones and digital searches, raises even greater concern. This trend has created a critical scenario where criminal proceedings indiscriminately threaten everyone's daily life and freedoms. Moreover, these problems are aggravated in cross-border cases, where coercive investigative measures are necessary for international cooperation but often neglect the protection of fundamental rights for all involved.[4] This setting underscores the urgent need for safeguards to protect individuals' rights in both domestic and international contexts.

These introductory examples have shown that individuals other than suspects, accused, offenders, and victims may seek recognition of their interests affected by the criminal proceedings. Furthermore, these subjects request the incorporation of their interests into criminal procedural law as part of the broader public interest that has traditionally governed the administration of criminal justice. Consequently, the infringement of private rights and freedoms, as enshrined in the most significant Charters and Conventions on Human Rights, as well as in domestic Constitutions, demands an appropriate discussion about solutions aimed at clarifying the hierarchy

---

[3] Along these lines, see the recent case of the ECtHR, 23 May 2024, *Contrada v. Italia* (No. 4), Appl. no. 2507/19, which ruled against Italy for failing to provide procedural safeguards for extraneous persons to the investigative proceedings. If present, these would allow them to make recourse to the judicial authorities to effectively verify the lawfulness and necessity of such measures and to obtain adequate compensation. In light of this, the ECtHR stated that Italian law does not meet the requirement of the "quality of the law" and is unable to limit "interference" to what is "necessary in a democratic society". This judgement is noteworthy as it sheds light on the third party's right to assert the unlawful interference in their personal sphere. Furthermore, this decision draws a clear difference between a third party directly intercepted and that incidentally intercepted in the context of operations regarding other suspects. Read, on this topic, Malino, Foti, in this volume, para. 4.3 and Orlando, in this volume, para. 4.

[4] See Falcone, in this volume, paras. 3.1, 3.2, 4 and 5.2.

of competing rights and interests of each person involved in criminal justice and limiting the interferences on the basis of the necessity and proportionality principles.[5] In other words, these issues pertain to achieving a trade-off in the often unbalanced relationship between protecting human rights and meeting the needs inherent in criminal proceedings.[6] Indeed, a common feature of all contributions in this book is stressing how the reach of such a balance is crucial to ensure that the pursuit of justice does not come at the expense of fundamental rights and freedoms.[7]

However, adopting a human rights-oriented approach requires a fundamental shift in how criminal proceedings are conceived. Traditionally viewed as a

[5] As national Reports on France, Hungary, Spain, Portugal, Italy, and Brasil have shown, these principles have gained relevance in different legal systems that are quite distant from each other. Indeed, the proportionality test has been chosen as a 'universal model' applicable by national and European courts when assessing the legitimacy of interference by public authorities in relation to the limitation of rights and freedoms. With regard to the proportionality, it may be useful for the sake of this study to remind us how this principle has been interpreted over the years. Firstly, it has been regarded as a general method for granting adequate protection of individual rights in the field of criminal proceedings. Secondly, it has been considered as a goal, serving as a useful parameter for verifying the fairness of the solution adopted in a concrete case. Along these lines, see Caianiello (2014), p. 145, who underscores that the increasing Europeanisation of criminal law has made the principle a pillar of EU law, as it is at the centre not only of the authority-individual relationship but also of the relationship between EU power and the power of Member States. According to Caianiello, the principle at stake has been also incorporated into the case-law of the European Court of Justice to the extent that it has become a 'supra-principle' underpinning the entire legal construction of the European Union, and a 'meta-principle', *i.e.*, a key parameter for the interpretation and application of other fundamental rights recognised by the EU legal system. This aspect is further analysed by Falcone, in this volume. It is important to anticipate that proportionality is also recognised as a principle within the ECHR system, thanks to the case law of the Strasbourg Court, since, as it has been demonstrated by Orlando, in this volume, it generally serves as a limitation on the discretion granted to Member States in implementing the rights and freedoms of the Convention. Moreover, over time, proportionality has become a benchmark for verifying the effective protection of all the fundamental rights provided by the Convention. See, on this topic, Bachmaier Winter (2021). Nonetheless, the following Chapters show that the recourse to the proportionality principle is somewhat misleading. Thus, as observed by Negri (2020), p. 3 ff. as well as proved by national Reports, such a principle, originally conceived as a guarantee for the individual against the risk of being subjected to measures restricting personal freedoms, is now facing challenges due to the power of technological evolution and the emergence of major crime phenomena. According to this author, one possible way to counter this trend could be to combine the principles of proportionality and legality. This could be achieved, for instance, by introducing subsidiarity clauses that make it more difficult to select coercive measures that are particularly detrimental to individuals.

[6] It should be underlined that nowadays the use of intrusive methods and investigations that invoke a state of exception is often accompanied by sympathetic thoughts regarding victims and calls for zero tolerance towards crime and criminals, thus posing risk to the *Rechtsstat*. Cf. Delmas-Marty (2007), p. 21 ff. The aforementioned approach overlooks the safeguarding of other individuals, who may be more or less vulnerable, but whose interests are equally deserving of protection.

[7] Proportionality and necessity are tools aimed at balancing values that are equally important since they determine whether the public interest or a conflicting individual right better serves the community's shared ultimate goals in each case. Cf. Negri (2020), p. 6.

two-party contest between the authority and the accused,[8] there is now a need to transition towards a more participatory model of criminal justice.[9] This change necessitates a preliminary definition of the term 'third party', thus explaining why all the contributions firstly deals with the understanding of this concept. Indeed, one possible reason for the limited attention this topic has received from criminal justice scholars is the difficulty in precisely identifying third parties within the context of criminal proceedings. In this light, it is crucial to understand the extent to which we can resort to using this category. In some situations, the 'third party' affected or involved could encompass all members of society, making it difficult to distinguish third parties as everyone is directly impacted by investigative activities, procedures, or measures. This circumstance is not far from reality, as mass surveillance for intelligence and preventive purposes can now reach into everyone's life and personal sphere.

In light of all this, the significance of this subject matter lies in its potential to rethinking fundamental categories of criminal justice, including the notion of thirdness and the meaning of both subjects and parties in criminal proceedings. These concepts will be further depicted in the following paragraphs.

2 The Different Meanings of Thirdness in the Legal Discourse: A Brief Overview

To effectively address the topic at hand, it is essential to first explore the significance of the term 'thirdness', which forms the foundation of our analysis. Upon closer examination, indeed, this concept is not unfamiliar in legal discourse, since it appears in various contexts including legal philosophy, civil, administrative, and notably, in criminal law.

Although this notion is further analysed in this volume,[10] it may be useful to preliminary note that the notion 'thirdness' normally pertains to both neutrality and impartiality, which are crucial qualities of the adjudicating body.[11] Pursuant to this

---

[8] It is worth mentioning that also legal philosophy often employs a triadic structure to analyse relationships and interactions. This structure includes the two primary parties (*e.g.*, in civil law, plaintiff and defendant) and a third 'entity' (*e.g.*, judge, mediator, or societal norms) that helps to balance, mediate, or adjudicate their interactions. This contrasts with a dyadic perspective, which can be overly simplistic. On this topic, cf. Condello, Ciaccio, in this volume.

[9] In fact, the possibility of participating in criminal proceedings effectively does not depend solely and exclusively on economic means and instruments in the broader cultural sense, but on whether and how the powers of participation are distributed among those entitled to taking part.

[10] See, in particular, Ruggeri and Condello, Ciaccio.

[11] The notion of 'thirdness' in legal philosophy extends beyond its application in criminal proceedings to a broader theoretical framework. It is rooted in the idea of introducing a third element that influences the relationship between two primary entities. The philosophical reconstruction of the notion of 'thirdness' is further deepened by Condello, Ciaccio, in this volume, paras. 2 ff.

approach, 'thirdness' denotes the presence of a neutral entity in a legal relationship—a subject that is unrelated or has no shared interest with the other individuals involved in the case –. In criminal proceedings, for instance, the judge occupies a key position by ensuring a proper trade-off between the prosecution and the defence.[12] Thus, the trial is structured as a triangular relationship involving the defendant (or defence counsel), the prosecution, and the judge. This judge's 'thirdness' must be both personal and institutional, that is to say, he/she must have no personal interest in the outcome of the case and must avoid any bias stemming from public or institutional interests.[13] In this light, 'thirdness' is therefore a quality that is undoubtedly essential to guarantee the full respect of the fundamental principles of any criminal proceedings, such as the equality of arms and cross-examination, in order to be consistent with the participatory model advocated by international and supranational human rights courts.

Also, to delve deeper into the notion of 'thirdness' in criminal proceedings, it is important to recognise the role of the media and public interest. Therefore, it may be useful to note that media serves as a crucial mean for informing the public about ongoing proceedings, shaping public perception, and influencing the discourse surrounding justice. Through their reporting, the media can highlight key aspects of trials, legal arguments, and outcomes, thereby playing a significant role in how justice is perceived by society.[14] Public interest, on the other hand, encompasses the broader societal concern and attention given to criminal cases. Indeed, it can influence decisions made by legal authorities, including prosecutors, judges, and juries, as they face the complexities of each case. Doubtless, the alignment of legal

---

Without anticipating too much, these authors state that 'thirdness' in legal philosophy is tied to hermeneutics, the theory and methodology of interpretation. Indeed, legal interpretation involves understanding the law not just in its literal sense but also considering the context, purpose, and underlying principles. This interpretative process often involves a third perspective that mediates between the text of the law and its application. Also, this reminds us of that thirdness can represent the influence of social and moral norms on legal reasoning and decision-making. As it is further explained, these norms act as a third element that informs and constrains the behavior of individuals and institutions, ensuring that the law reflects societal values and ethical standards.

[12]For the sake of completeness, we should remember that the concept of 'thirdness' is quite different in the field of the public administration. Since the public administration undergoes the direction and control of the political power, which identifies the relevant public interests, defines the extent to which they are to be pursued and, if necessary, balances their application, the requirement of neutrality must therefore be different from what is discussed in relation to the judiciary.

[13]As Condello and Ciaccio argue, in legal philosophy, 'thirdness' is conceived as an essential element for balancing competing interests and rights. Any legal system, as a third entity, is called upon to mediate between the rights of individuals (*e.g.*, freedom of speech) and the interests of the community (*e.g.*, public order). Thus, this balancing activity often requires introducing a third perspective that weighs and reconciles these interests.

[14]On the role of media as watchdog of democracy, see ECtHR, *Goodwin v. United Kingdom*, 27 March 1996, app. No. 17488/90, para. 39.

outcomes with public expectations and perceptions can impact the legitimacy and fairness of criminal justice proceedings.[15]

However, the concept of 'thirdness' has not received sufficient analysis in legal discourse, typically being limited to discussions about the role of the judge. Doubtless, a somewhat reductionist approach. A more comprehensive understanding can be attained by expanding the scope of the inquiry. To do so, a preliminary distinction between the approach of the subjectivity in substantive and procedural criminal law should be taken into consideration. Along these lines, it worth noting that in substantive criminal law committing an act alone does not suffice to constitute an offense, since there must also be a psychological link (*i.e.*, subjective element) between the offender and the criminal activity. Hence, this principle excludes the strict liability for other individuals who do not contribute actively and voluntarily in the criminal act. Despite this, criminal activities can potentially involve 'third parties' in different ways. For instance, a person other than the perpetrator or law enforcement—a third party—may come into possession of evidence or proceeds of crime. Also, criminal sanctions can affect third parties who are not criminal responsible (*e.g.*, companies in the event of corporate liability deriving from criminal activity). Interestingly, third parties can play a key role in the context of restorative justice, in which communities can participate to the programme and promote the restoration of the harm caused by the crime.

Against this background, the concept of 'thirdness' within the criminal proceedings seems to pertain to the involvement and role of individuals or entities beyond the primary parties—the prosecution and the defence –. This understanding of thirdness encompasses various participants in the proceedings, each with distinct roles, rights, and interests. Here are some examples of individuals to whom the concept of thirdness may apply: (*i*) victims, when they do not hold the formal *status* of a party, (*ii*) accused and victims' next of kin, (*iii*) witnesses and experts, (*iv*) and other involved parties.

Starting with the victim of crimes, he/she plays a pivotal role in criminal proceedings, since this subject has a substantial interest in the final decision and is also capable of contributing through statements. Ensuring recognition and protection of victims' rights is therefore crucial to adequately representing and addressing their interests.

Witnesses and experts also serve as third parties by providing testimony and vital information that can significantly influence trial outcomes. Safeguarding their protection and ensuring the integrity of their testimony are essential for the fairness of proceedings. Indeed, specific measures are often implemented to shield witnesses and vulnerable victims who are called to testify from intimidation or retaliation and risk of secondary victimisation.

[15] Cf., on this topic, Manes (2022) and Larivière (1994). Thus, understanding the interplay between the media, public interest, and the dynamics of criminal proceedings may provide a comprehensive view of 'thirdness' in the context of justice administration. Furthermore, it underscores the multidimensional nature of participation and influence beyond the immediate parties directly involved in the criminal proceedings.

Moreover, individuals indirectly affected by criminal proceedings, such as family members of victims or accused, can also be considered third parties. Additionally, those whose privacy or property rights are impacted by investigative measures, such as wiretapping or searches, fall into this category.[16] Furthermore, there are other third parties who may contribute to criminal proceedings in different ways, including translators, interpreters, and legal aides. Although not being part of the prosecution or defence parties, these individuals play pivotal roles, and their rights and responsibilities must be recognised and protected to ensure a fair and comprehensive criminal proceeding.

Having identified these individuals broadly, it is important to consider the role they currently hold within the criminal proceedings. Therefore, reflecting on the concept of 'party' will be relevant in understanding their legal standing in the proceedings.

3 Formal Parties, Substantial Parties, Third Parties

Next Chapters show that the traditional structure of criminal proceedings generally implies that the status of formal parties is recognised to the main subjects involved in the procedure, namely the public prosecutor and the accused, without which a criminal trial is not even conceivable. In addition, other subjects are entitled to become formal parties due to the existence of a specific interest, normally linked to the financial restoration that must be paid in case of a decision that states on the civil liability of the accused.

However, things are particularly different in the course of criminal investigations, in which the categories of subjects involved in this stage are a sort of anticipated projection of the parties that will participate in the trial phase. As we can clearly see in the national Reports, in this preliminary moment of criminal proceedings, investigative bodies have the power to adopt several coercive measures that infringe upon the fundamental rights of the accused, the victims and even third parties. Even if in this stage we cannot properly discuss about formal parties, a growing array of ever newer investigative measures, developed through ICTs, may produce a significant involvement of individuals other than suspects and victims, whose fundamental rights can be prejudiced directly or fortuitously by coercive measures adopted in this moment.

The possibility for third parties to be addressed by procedural activities has been demonstrated across all the stages of criminal proceedings at various levels (international, supranational, national) and in domestic jurisdictions presenting different

[16] Beyond individual participants, institutions, and legal frameworks themselves can embody thirdness. For instance, oversight bodies or human rights organisations may play a pivotal role in monitoring the fairness and legality of criminal proceedings, advocating for reforms, and protecting the rights of involved parties. See, also, Beltrán Montoliu, in this volume, para. 7 with regard to the intervention of *amicus curiae* before the ICC and Vasconcellos, Lucchesi, in this volume, para. 7.

legal traditions and approaches.[17] However, the most sensitive response to such a complex topic results from the decisions provided by international and supranational courts, which constantly attempt to strike a proper balance between, on one hand, fundamental liberties and rights (particularly, personal freedom, liberty and secrecy of communication and correspondence, liberty of speech and privacy and intimacy of the domicile and the informatic systems) and, on the other hand, the general interest to public security.[18]

As Gascón Inchausti and Schumann Barragán have shown in their Report, concerning the restriction on fundamental rights by means of digital measures of investigation, in 2015 the Spanish legislator proved to be aware of the risks linked to the use of technological instruments for investigative purposes, by amending the domestic Code of Criminal Procedure and introducing some legal provisions that require the investigative judge to explicitly give reasons of the conditions that justify the interference with third parties' rights.[19]

Moreover, not only in the course of the investigative phase can third parties have their rights restricted, but also this could happen alongside all the criminal proceedings and for multiple goals, with the consequence that these subjects, from being extraneous, became informal participants of the proceeding and hold a role that has been no classified nor described in its essence.[20] However, once they have been involved in the criminal proceedings, they bear some kind of interest that must be recognised and safeguarded. Along these lines, from the perspective of international and supranational courts, the recognition of procedural safeguards for third parties can be justified on the grounds of their substantial interest in the final decision of criminal proceedings or their involvement in certain procedural activities. Indeed, we have already seen that, for the purpose of this study, we can consider third parties as non-formal participants who may be involved in criminal proceedings for multiple different reasons (persons intercepted directly or fortuitously,[21] persons whose goods have been seized or confiscated, witnesses, and so on).

In addition to this, it has been observed that the non-recognition of formal participatory rights to third parties is due to the absence of a clear and precise

---

[17] The comparative constitutional analysis on the safeguards of third parties in criminal proceedings is carried out by La Fauci, in this volume. The author specifically focuses on the regulations that have been adopted by the jurisdictions whose legal systems have been analysed in in this book, stressing their merits and limitations and the way such provisions could be modified in order to protect these subjects' rights.

[18] Cf. ECtHR, *Big Brother Watch and Others v. the United Kingdom*, judgment of 25 May 2021, Appl. Nos. 58170/13, 62322/14, and 24,960/15. CJEU, 8 April 2014, *Digital Rights Ireland and Seitlinger and Others*, joined cases C-293/12 and C-594/12.

[19] The Report on Spain has underlined that domestic legislation on investigative measures base on the recourse to communication technologies requires the judge to give reasons about the connection existing between the ongoing investigation and the third party concerned.

[20] As underlined above, the concept of thirdness has been always discussed, above all in legal philosophy, with only regard to the role of the judge.

[21] ECtHR, *Amann v. Switzerland*, judgment of 16 February 2000, Appl. No. 27798/95, para. 61.

definition or specific indications regarding their status in either domestic or international and supranational law.

In this book, we see that, depending on the nature of their participation, third parties can be distinguished in some different categories: *(a)* subjects of the criminal proceedings other than formal participants[22]; *(b)* persons whose fundamental rights are limited by pre-trial measures and procedural activities[23]; *(c)* persons whose knowledge and contribution are essential to the fact-finding process (witnesses and experts).[24] These categories clearly emerge from the national Reports and the Chapters concerning the case law of ECtHR, CJEU and IACtHR, which shall also pay attention to the interests of victims, whose participation has been improved also before the ICC, even though their role in criminal justice has been always controversial. Indeed, the person who suffered the consequences of the crime has a peculiar role, since this subject, according to domestic legal orders, can become a formal party with a different range of powers, depending on the legal instruments provided by national legislations: for example, in Spain, Portugal, Brasil and France, victims are allowed to bring charges privately or in conjunction with the Public Prosecutor's Office, while in Italy they can only bring a civil law action in the criminal proceeding aiming at obtaining a financial restore. Even if the injured person bears a substantial interest in the development of the criminal proceedings and in its outcome, he/she can also choose to remain extraneous to the trial, thus confining themselves to the status of third party.[25] In these cases, the injured party has the only possibility to contribute to the proceedings through their statements, as any other witness.

However, criminal investigations and trials increasingly necessitate the involvement of individuals other than the formal participants in order to collect evidence and ascertain the criminal liability and, more importantly, can negatively impact on the rights or interests of those subjects included in various procedural activities. In this context, several new categories of third parties have emerged, as it is highlighted in all national Reports and in the analysis of supranational and international law.

In all these cases there is an urgent need to afford adequate safeguards to the rights and interests of such subjects, safeguards that can be provided in different stages and ways. First of all, protecting the rights of the persons concerned implies that the law, at both national and supranational or international levels, should limit

[22]In a strict sense, this concept relates to specific natural or legal persons other than formal participants in the criminal process, who are granted some procedural powers which are equivalent or similar to those of formal participants (access to the materials of the case, *ius postulandi*, etc.).

[23]Adopting a human rights perspective, *i.e.*, a viewpoint oriented towards the degree of intrusiveness of procedural measures in the sphere of fundamental rights, we may broaden the notion of 'third parties' by extending it to people that, even though criminal investigations are not addressed against them, may be indirectly affected by procedural activities (*e.g.*, the family members of undercover agents or people under a special protection programme).

[24]The need to protect witnesses or vulnerable victims can determine some risks for the defendant's rights, since they may be heard by means of special measures in order to avoid any further prejudice to their safety while avoiding their contact with the accused.

[25]Cf. Di Nuzzo, Falcone, in this volume, paras. 3 ff.

the most invasive measures involving third parties, while providing specific conditions under which the proceeding authorities can interfere with their fundamental rights in the light of the principle of proportionality and only when such measure is strictly necessary.

Secondly, the safeguard of a judicial scrutiny appears to be the most adequate to verify whether the legal requirements are met, as underlined by Orlando. The moment in which the judge (or, alternatively, an independent and impartial administrative authority)[26] is called to verify the existence of the conditions under which the measure is carried out can precede or follow the operations, but the results can be sensitively different. Indeed, whenever the judicial control is performed *ex ante* and in compliance with the legal requirements may lead to an evaluation of not-necessity or not-proportionality of the requested measure, resulting in the refusal of the judicial body to authorise the interference with fundamental rights of third parties.

After the coercive measures have been carried out, however, the addressee—regardless their status of suspect or person on which any suspicion of guilt has been raised—must be granted with procedural powers in order to challenge the lawfulness of the intrusion in their private lives and, bearing in mind this purpose, a system of information and notification is indispensable, as underlined by ECtHR and CJEU in cases regarding mass surveillance and bulk interception of communications.[27]

Nonetheless, in the field of investigative measures the protection afforded to third parties is still quite weak and some domestic legislation lacks specific provisions to ensure adequate safeguards for the individuals concerned, particularly when intrusive technologies are used to gather large amounts of information quickly and the number of affected individuals cannot be predetermined.

In addition to this, the extraneity to criminal proceedings often impede third parties to defend their interests, since they have no access to adequate and effective legal remedies.

As the comparative analysis of the national legal systems has shown, the situation is pretty different when it comes to the owners of goods and assets seized or confiscated. In such cases, the comparative analysis of domestic jurisdictions has demonstrated that national legislations have taken into account the property rights of these persons, who are granted with some specific participatory powers, generally with the purpose of obtaining the restitution, which seem quite equivalent to the ones

[26] The case law of the ECtHR does not consider the preventive judicial control as a 'necessary requirement', thus also accepting the supervision of an independent body which should be informed of both the purpose of the interception and the bearers or communication routes likely to be tapped. See Orlando, in this volume, para. 4.

[27] ECtHR, *Big Brother Watch and Others v. the United Kingdom*, para. 358: "Regardless of whether material was acquired through targeted or bulk interception, the existence of a national security exception could deprive a notification requirement of any real practical effect. The likelihood of a notification requirement having little or no practical effect will be more acute in the bulk interception context, since such surveillance may be used for the purposes of foreign intelligence gathering and will, for the most part, target the communications of persons outside the State's territorial jurisdiction. Therefore, even if the identity of a target is known, the authorities may not be aware of his or her location".

recognised to the main parties of the proceedings. This consideration shows once again that a more participatory model of criminal justice is possible by providing third parties with some procedural powers (such as the right to be fairly heard or take part in court activities) necessary to effectively shield their own interests in particular stages (for example to take part in the decision whether or not to charge) or procedural activities.

In this sense, this book has made it clear that the traditional way of intending the participation in criminal proceedings, based on the recognition of a formal status described by the law, is not sufficient anymore to ensure the satisfaction of all the interests involved in criminal justice, as deeply underlined by Ruggeri. Furthermore, the concept of personal participation in criminal proceedings cannot be referred exclusively to the accused, as it has been conceived until now, but must be deformalised and extended to all those persons that bear a substantial interest in the final decision or whose fundamental rights have been limited in such context. Maybe the time has come to consider as participants all those individuals who bear substantial interests and are concerned within specific procedures (arrest proceedings, remand proceedings, procedures on communication intercepts, etc.), while, at the same time, providing them with the necessary participatory rights for protecting their private sphere. In this way, what is mostly enhanced is not the formal quality provided to someone, but the effectiveness of their substantive participation in the different stages or in specific procedural activities.

4 Object, Methods and Aims of the Study

The outcome of this book is the result of a joint effort by all contributors. Through the process of cross-checking and the exchange of peer reviews, indeed, each contributor has not only enhanced their own Chapters but also gained insight into realities they were previously unaware of.

This research, however, not only has a diagnostic objective but also strives to provide a reconstruction of this problematic area of thirdness, formal and substantial participation, which constitute the main lines of this study, in accordance with the modern, human rights-oriented concept of criminal justice.

Indeed, as we can see from the brief considerations made hitherto, the question of who third parties are in the context of criminal justice and of the protection they deserve is among the most complex ones. Legal scholarship has borrowed the category of thirdness from other legal fields, such as civil law or administrative law, without having ever defined and contextualised it with specific regard to criminal procedure law.

In order to understand who may be considered as third parties in criminal proceedings, this book presents various levels of analysis, which have contributed to a systematic study of the various roles that persons who are not addressed by suspicion of guilt can take on during the entire proceeding.

First of all, a detailed examination of six jurisdictions provides an in-depth overview of their legal principles, rules, case law and practices, which allows us to understand how the protection of third parties works in these legal orders. The study focuses on five civil-law jurisdictions within the EU to analyse the impact and extent of supranational law on national legislation and the implementation of European Union provisions. In addition, Brazilian legislation is included in this research as a non-EU example that has been mostly influenced by Italian, Spanish and Portuguese law.

Secondly, we decided to conduct a comparative analysis of these selected legal systems by examining legal principles, rules, and practices across six different jurisdictions. Indeed, the national legislation under review display significant differences in the role of the judiciary during the investigative stage, which has been recognised as a crucial aspect for this study. For instance, while France, Hungary, Portugal, and Spain have an investigating judge leading the investigation alongside the Public Prosecutor's Office, Italy and Brazil feature a judge who only intervenes when the public prosecutor requested the authorisation for some investigative activities. This difference in approach can help assess which mechanisms are most effective for protecting third parties during criminal inquiries and how judicial oversight can safeguard their interests during this particularly intrusive phase of criminal proceedings. This comparative approach aims to identify similarities, differences, and best practices in protecting third parties in criminal justice systems. For this reason, the comparative analysis includes various stages of criminal proceedings, from investigation to trial and beyond, since the involvement of third parties can happen in different moments and in multiple manners. This method helps determine which procedural activities are most likely to interfere with third parties, the reasons and limitations for such involvement, and, above all, the protection they receive. Studying different approaches to third-party safeguards across these stages permits to assess how national laws align with evolving social values, such as digital privacy, and meet international and supranational legal requirements.

Alongside the study of the reported domestic jurisdictions and the comparative analysis among them, there is another level of research regarding third parties' protection. Indeed, specific attention has been paid to supranational and international law, particularly the EU legal framework, the ECtHR case law, the IACtHR system and the setup of criminal proceedings before ICC. For what concerns the latter, a deep analysis of victims' participation in ICC criminal proceedings has discovered that these subjects are allowed to present their opinions and observations, once they have acquired the victim status.[28] The victims' participation in the field of international criminal proceedings presents peculiar features, since they are not considered as partied in a strict sense, but are granted with some participatory rights, and they also have a primary role during the reparation phase, which includes restitution, compensation, and rehabilitation. In this regard, one of the most important results of

[28] The status of victim before the ICC is granted to natural persons who have suffered harm directly caused by a crime under the Court's jurisdiction. Cf. Beltrán Montoliu, in this volume, paras. 2 ff.

this book is that this unique and *sui generis* status makes it difficult to classify their participation as that of a third party at various levels.[29]

Furthermore, the European and Interamerican Courts of human rights have been showing a true consideration of the fundamental rights and interests presented by not only victims but also third parties in the context of criminal proceedings. It is remarkable to note that while national criminal justice systems are often more sensitive to the position of the investigated person or the one charged with criminal accusation, the supranational and international Courts have tried to rebalance all the positions at stake in order to ensure a trial which is truly fair for all the subjects involved, while recognising the access to adequate and effective remedies to individuals whose rights have been infringed upon by procedural activities.

These multilevel analysis and comparison are intended to clarify who third parties are (or can be) in the complex experience of criminal justice, which has been studied until now with a dichotomic structure based on the contrast between the Public Prosecutor's Office and accused person. The urge to define who third parties are finds its roots in the necessity to provide them with adequate safeguards and procedural powers, when this is necessary in order to allow them to defend their interests. In times where the reach of criminal proceedings is unpredictable, primarily due to the recourse to digital investigative measures, the general theory of formal participation does not fit anymore the needs of post-modern criminal justice and must be updated with the aim of adapting it to the fast-evolving social values and to the increasing possibility that numerous persons can be involved in a single criminal proceeding. Indeed, once this happens, by virtue of their knowledge, their connection with the crime or the accused or for any other reason, they must be safeguarded through protective measures (when necessary) or by affording specific legal remedies to claim the legitimacy of the interference with their fundamental rights. In the light of this, the recognition of a multisubject theory regarding the participation is only the first step to build a fair and comprehensive approach to the complex developments that are rapidly occurring in criminal justice worldwide. Further studies will be necessary to deal with such a new and challenging topic.

References

Bachmaier Winter L (2021) Proportionality, mass surveillance and criminal investigation: the Strasbourg court facing big brother. In: Billis E, Knust N, Rui JP (eds) The principle of proportionality in crime control and criminal justice. Hart Publishing, Oxford, pp 317–335

Caianiello M (2014) Il principio di proporzionalità nel procedimento penale. Diritto penale contemporaneo 3-4:143–163

[29] Cf. also Malino, Foti, in this volume, who describe the victim as a '*sui generis*' subject, since they can become a formal participant in Italian criminal proceedings only when claiming for civil damages. Similarly, see both Falcone and Orlando, in this volume, who underline the hybrid role of victims within the EU and ECHR legal systems.

Delmas-Marty M (2007) Il paradigma della guerra contro il crimine: legittimare l'inumano? Studi sulla questione criminale 2: 21-37
Giolo O, Pastore B (2018) Vulnerabilità. Analisi multidisciplinare di un concetto. Carocci, Roma
Larivière DS (1994) Il circo mediatico-giudiziario. Liberilibri, Macerata
Manes V (2022) Giustizia Mediatica. Gli effetti perversi sui diritti fondamentali e sul giusto processo. Il Mulino, Bologna
Negri D (2020) Compressione dei diritti di libertà e principio di proporzionalità davanti alle sfide del processo penale contemporaneo. Rivista Italiana di Diritto e Procedura Penale 1:3–35

Part I
Third Parties in Domestic Criminal Justice

Report on Brazil

Vinicius Gomes de Vasconcellos and Guilherme Brenner Lucchesi

Abstract This work describes the main aspects concerning the participation of third parties in the Brazilian criminal procedure. Based on a brief explanation of the general characteristics of Brazilian criminal justice, it defines the defendants and the prosecution as parties to the criminal process (in general, represented by the Public Prosecutor's Office and, exceptionally, the victim by his lawyer), and characterizes as third parties subjects with procedural powers, such as assistants to the prosecution (commonly victims of crimes) and holders of property constrained as a result of investigations and/or criminal proceedings, addressing specific issues rising upon the intervention of third parties under Brazilian Criminal Procedural Law, mainly their procedural powers during investigations, trial and appeals.

1 Introduction. General Features of Brazilian Criminal Justice

Initially, in a general view, the Brazilian criminal procedure system is described by most Brazilian legal scholars as mixed, because it is structured with an inquisitive preliminary investigation stage and, later, an adversarial trial stage.[1] In another sense, there is a critical perspective of some authors that argues that the procedure is, in fact, essentially inquisitorial, since the judge is allowed to produce evidence *ex*

[1] Nucci (2018), p. 50; de Mendonça (2014), p. 64.

V. G. de Vasconcellos (✉)
Instituto Brasileiro de Ensino, Desenvolvimento e Pesquisa – IDP/DF, Brasília, Brazil

Universidade Católica de Brasília, Taguatinga, Brazil

Universidade de São Paulo, São Paulo, Brazil
e-mail: vinicius.vasconcellos@usp.br

G. B. Lucchesi
Universidade Federal do Paraná, Curitiba, Brazil
e-mail: lucchesi@ufpr.br

S. Ruggeri et al. (eds.), *Third Parties in Criminal Proceedings*, Legal Studies in International, European and Comparative Criminal Law 10,
https://doi.org/10.1007/978-3-031-73970-5_2

officio[2] and does not set out yet a clear separation between the investigative and the trial phases.[3] However, in constitutional terms, it is stated that the Federal Constitution of 1988 consolidated an accusatorial system, by determining in Article 129(I), that the Prosecution Office (*'Ministério Público'*, hereinafter MP) is solely responsible for bringing a public action when a crime is committed.[4]

So, in strict terms, the persons that hold the formal status of parties in the criminal procedure are the defendants and the prosecution (in general, the Public Prosecutor, or, in some rare cases, the victim by its lawyer).

Generally, a criminal accusation is initiated by the public prosecutor.[5] In such cases, it is stated that the principle of mandatory prosecution is in force in Brazil, so that, provided there is sufficient evidence to indicate the occurrence of a crime (probable cause), criminal proceedings must be initiated by the prosecutor.[6] That is, in the majority and traditional view, there would be no choice or discretionary powers for the MP.[7]

---

[2] Under the terms of Article 156 of the Brazilian Code of Criminal Procedure (CCP), the judge may: "*I—order, even before the opening of the criminal trial, the anticipated production of evidence deemed urgent and relevant, observing the necessity, adequacy and proportionality of such measure*" and "*II—determine, in the course of the trial, or before the decision, measures to be taken to settle any doubt on a relevant matter*".

[3] According to Articles 12 and 155 of the Brazilian CCP, the investigative dossier must be fully annexed to the case file and the judge may consider its elements in the sentence, although this cannot be sufficient grounds for conviction at its own: "Art. 12. The police investigative dossier must be annexed to the accusation, whenever it serves as basis for it"; "Art. 155. *The judge will form his conviction by the free assessment of the evidence produced in the adversarial proceeding and cannot base his decision solely on the elements gathered in the investigation, except for precautionary, non-repeatable and anticipated evidence*". We must point that the Law 13.964/2019 has made some important changes in this aspect, like creating the "judge of guarantees" and setting the separation of the investigatory and the trial dossiers, which we will explain in the next paragraphs. But this changed have been suspended by a provisional decision of the Brazilian Supreme Court. In August 2023, the Supreme Court finalized the judgment regarding the constitutionality of the "judge of guarantees", ruling that it must be implemented in the Brazilian system 12–24 months. However, the Court declared the unconstitutionality of significant parts of the reform, such as the Article that mandated the separation between the files of the police investigation and the process. Thus, although there is a substitution of the judge between the phases, the trial judge will have full access to the acts of the investigation. Claiming to be an inquisitive system: de Coutinho (1998), p. 28; Lopes Jr. (2012), pp. 134–135.

[4] The Supreme Federal Court has a firm position in favor of adopting an accusatory system, with the separation of the functions of accusation and judging, although, as a rule, does not prohibit the judge's initiative to produce evidence *ex officio*. For an exposition of such precedents: Vasconcellos (2015).

[5] de Mendonça (2014), p. 65.

[6] Jardim (1998), pp. 92–99; Fernandes (2005), p. 263; Batista (1992), p. 210. The majority of researchers argues that Brazilian CCP imposes the principle of mandatory prosecution in Articles 42 ("The prosecutor will not be able to dismiss the accusation") and 576 ("The prosecutor will not be able to withdraw the appeal that has been filed").

[7] Recently, Law 12.850/2013 regulated an innovative hypothesis for the prosecutor "not offering the accusation" in specific cases of cooperation agreement, when the defendant is the first to collaborate with Justice and not the head of the criminal organization [Art. 4(4)].

Concerning the judicial phase, the trial is normally carried out in the first instance by a single judge.[8] A jury would only be called in exceptional circumstances, that is for intentional crimes against life, like murder or abortion.[9] The ordinary Brazilian criminal procedure is eminently written, with a moment of orality in the "trial hearing", when witnesses, experts and defendants are questioned (Art. 400 CCP). However, in general, all other acts are written and, as already explained, the elements produced in the preliminary investigation can also be considered by the judge in the sentence.

1.1 Formal Participants in Criminal Proceedings

According to Brazilian legal scholars, "parties are the persons who participate in the adversary hearing before the State Judge", that is, "the one who, by himself or through an attorney, comes to assert a claim to jurisdictional protection, filing suit (complainant), as well as the person involved in the claim (defendant)".[10] So, the parties in criminal proceedings are different to those in other types of actions (such as a writ of *habeas corpus* or an action to vacate an unappealable criminal conviction[11]). In a conviction proceeding, on the one hand, "the parties shall be: actively, in public initiative criminal actions, the prosecutor and, in private criminal actions, the victim, his attorney or his successors".[12] On the other hand, the defendant will be the active subject of the criminal offense, that is, the perpetrator. In other types of actions, the perpetrator is classified as a party, but the MP is not always formally defined as a party.[13] For instance, in a writ of *habeas corpus*, the petitioner can be anyone and the arrestee will be the offender. However, the MP only makes its statements in an opinion, in the position of *custos legis*.

In these terms, even in relation to the performance in the criminal proceeding, the position of the MP and its possible impartiality regarding the issue under analysis is discussed. Traditionally, it is said that the MP, even in criminal proceedings, adopts the position of *guardian of the law*, since it is a state agency that impartially seeks the truth.[14]

---

[8] According to the Constitution of Brazil of 1988 (Articles 102 and 105, for instance), there are hypotheses of 'privileged jurisdiction' (like parliamentary immunity), in which people occupying functions relevant to the State are directly judged by Court boards, such as State Appellate Courts or even in the Supreme Court.

[9] Art. 74(1) CCP. Available at: http://www.planalto.gov.br/ccivil_03/decreto-lei/Del3689Compilado.htm. Access in: Oct. 16th, 2021.

[10] Dinamarco et al. (2020), p. 362.

[11] In Brazilian criminal procedure, the "action for criminal revision", or simply "criminal revision", is an action to vacate an unappealable criminal conviction.

[12] Zanoide de Moraes (2000), p. 241.

[13] On this topic: Tucci (2011), pp. 137–138.

[14] Cintra et al. (2008), pp. 319–321.

Still, in a critical view, *the impossibility of conceiving the Prosecution Office as an impartial party* in criminal justice is sustained.[15] Thus, Montero Aroca clarifies that.

> leaving aside the contraditio in terminis that implies qualifying a party as impartial, it happens that not even for reasons that underlie the essence of its function can the MP be characterized as an 'impartial party'.[16]

Furthermore, such a view restricts the possibility of persuading the judge with a defensive case.[17]

Therefore, in criminal justice, as a rule the prosecutor adopts an incriminatory viewpoint, which is clearly manifested in the filing of the accusation.[18] Any different understanding, for example, with a request for acquittal or to dismiss the charges of the police investigation, does not result from an alleged impartiality of the prosecutor, but from his strict submission to the rule of law[19]: requesting someone's conviction without sufficient evidence, beyond reasonable doubt, represents an evident abuse of the power to accuse, entailing the inherent illegality of such conduct.

1.2 Third Parties to Criminal Proceedings

The CCP provides no legal definition of "third parties". It does, however, grant procedural powers to certain individuals, such as assistants to the prosecution[20] and third-party owners of assets that have been seized or otherwise attached during investigations and/or criminal proceedings, be they natural persons or corporations.

Concerning the prosecution's assistant, as noted above, victims are not parties *per se* in Brazilian criminal procedure. In most cases with identifiable victims,[21] they

---

[15] Vasconcellos (2016).

[16] Montero Aroca (2008), p. 122 (our translation).

[17] "*Conceiving the Prosecution Office as an impartial party means making the dialectic of parts unfeasible, or, at least, making the opposition between thesis and antithesis something artificial or merely formal. In the accusatory proceeding, in which the dialectical relationship between the parties is emphasized, the Prosecution Office must be a true party, that is, a partial party*". [Badaró 2020, p. 334] (our translation).

[18] "*When formulating the charge, although it is seeking a judicial settlement on the occurrence or not of the criminal fact attributed to the accused, the Prosecution Office has already been previously convinced of the culpability and will seek to prove it*". [Badaró 2003, p. 220].

[19] Badaró (2003), p. 225.

[20] For the purposes of this Article, the term *Assistant to the Prosecution* refers to the victim's (or their legal representative's) assistance of the public prosecution through private counsel. It does not refer to cases tried solely by the victim or their legal representative, which also exist in Brazil, but where the private prosecution acts as a proper party to the proceedings. (Ziyade 1993, p. 23).

[21] "*There is a very wide variety of criminal offenses that, apparently, do not reveal the existence of specific or individual victims, such as homicide, bodily harm, theft, etc. This category, which the*

may be listed by the prosecution to be heard during trial, subject to cross-examination, but they are not legally considered *witnesses* for the prosecution.[22] Like witnesses, victims are compelled to appear before Court, and may not refuse to be heard, except when asserting some sort of *privilege.*[23] Victims, however, are not subject to criminal penalties under *false testimony,*[24] although their conduct may amount to crimes such as *libelous accusation,*[25] if it is proven that the presumed victim's untrue statements gave cause to the defendant's indictment. Victims also have the power to request that they be heard outside the presence of the defendant, to prevent revictimization or any form of harassment[26]; this, however, does not exclude defense counsel from the proceedings, as even the victim's testimony is subject to cross-examination. Given that many crimes also result in civil damages, victims may also request compensation for material and moral damages after proceedings.[27]

Anglo-American doctrine designates as crimes without victims, and in the suggestive expression of Figueiredo Dias, it is called crimes without especially offended persons. Infractions against the environment and white-collar criminality emerge as a very clear hypothesis of this category of victims who are not personally identified since they constitute the mass of offended indistinctly. The same can be said in relation to certain offenses committed against public safety, public peace, public administration, etc. In all these types of illicit activities, it can be said that the victim is considered to be something abstract insofar as natural persons are not indicated in the legal types of crime". Dotti (2012), p. 855.

[22] A witness is someone who "not being a party or an individual interested in the outcome of the procedure, may be heard before the Court on past facts relevant to the procedure that have been perceived by their senses". The victim "is interested in the result of the procedure. Because of this the victim cannot be considered a witness, who, by definition, is an uninterested third party". From a terminological viewpoint, the drafters of the CCP were careful as to distinguish victims from witnesses since a victim "gives a statement" (Art. 201 CCP) while the witness "gives testimony" (Art. 204 CCP). Badaró (2020), pp. 553–556.

[23] According to Jesus and Estefam (2020), p. 267, the witness may be excused from the duty to testify due to marriage or kinship (Art. 206 CCP,), as well as when the witness is subject to duty of secrecy due to function, ministry, office, or profession, except when excused by the interested party (Art. 207, CCP).

[24] Brazilian Criminal Code ("*Código Penal*", henceforth CP) Art. 342. The crime of false testimony does not include a "false oath" as attendant circumstance to the crime, referring only to false statements or undue omissions by a witness, expert, accountant, translator, or interpreter, and does not include the defendant or the victim, who, by definition, cannot commit the crime of false testimony, as they may not be properly regarded as "witnesses" (Busato 2017), p. 751.

[25] Art. 328 CP.

[26] "*The victim may not refuse to appear before the Court (Art. 201 § 1°), under penalty of issuance of a bench warrant (including in the investigation stage). They may, however, request the defendant be removed from the courtroom during their declaration if [the defendant's] presence might influence their state of mind when deposed (Art. 217 CCP)*", Lopes Jr. (2020), p. 726. Furthermore, the CCP provides the possibility of declaring secrecy on the victim's personal records, to prevent their exposure [Art. 201(6) CCP] [Pacelli 2020, p. 546], as well as the possibility of referring the victim to psychological, legal and health care at the expense of the State [Art. 201(5) CCP).

[27] On the victim's possibility to obtain civil reparation for damages suffered, see Greco Filho (2010), pp. 194–195.

In all cases where a victim is identified, they may retain private counsel[28] to appear as assistant to the prosecution in criminal proceedings (Art. 268 CCP). This is generally done to influence the decision-making process, aiming to strengthen a claim for civil damages[29] or to secure retribution for the offense. The prosecution must be heard before a victim or their representative is admitted as assistant (Art. 272 CCP), however, the decision is made by the judge alone and is not subject to appeal (Art. 273 CCP).

The assistant to the prosecution, although not a formal party to the proceedings, is awarded procedural powers, such as the authorization to propose means of evidence, question witnesses for the prosecution and the defense (direct and cross-examination), participate in the oral and/or written debates, and present arguments in the prosecution's appeals (Art. 271 CCP). Exceptionally, the assistant may also appeal in their own name if the MP does not appeal the acquittal or any other sentence favorable to the defense in a timely manner (Art. 598 CCP).

In broader sense, other persons affected by criminal investigations may also have claims in the course of proceedings. For instance, witnesses have a right to access court records[30] and may be accompanied by counsel in trial or pre-trial hearings.[31] Also, in cases involving physical, psychological, sexual, or institutional violence,[32] where a witness is a child or adolescent, they have a right to a "damage-free deposition", to be interviewed by a social worker or other professional under

[28] Except where the victim or their representative (Art. 31 CCP: in cases of death or legal absence, the victim may be represented by their spouse, ascendant, descendant or sibling) themselves are admitted to the bar, no *pro se* representation is admitted due to lack of *ius postulandi.*

[29] Under Brazilian Law, assistance to the prosecution is not to be confused with the "*parte civile*" of Italian Criminal Procedure, *i.e.*, whose objective is solely to secure the efficiency of a civil claim for damages caused by the crime [Lozzi (2008), p. 130]. The justification for the admission of the victim as assistant to the prosecution is based on more than their interest in reparation, being based on the correct application of justice to the offender, collaborating with the Public Prosecutor and make up for any omissions by the State. Differently from the *parte civile*, the function of the assistant is not to defend their own right to reparation, but to serve as an auxiliary to the prosecution [Frederico Marques 1961, p. 249]. The legislative history of the CCP favors this interpretation, as the framers expressly refrained from adopting the "ambiguous institute" of the *parte civile* in Criminal Procedure (*Exposição de Motivos*, item VI).

[30] The Brazilian Superior Court of Justice (*Superior Tribunal de Justiça*, henceforth "STJ") has held that "*the victim's access to the evidence already documented in the ongoing police investigation is relevant, as well as knowledge about any obstacles to the continuity and completion of the investigative work, and their collaboration may be useful for the police authority to reach a successful conclusion and, effectively, fulfil its constitutional mission*" (STJ, RMS 55.790/SP, Realtor: Min. Jorge Mussi, 06.12.2018). During proceedings, the victim shall be notified of the defendant's arrest and release, the appointment of hearing dates, the ruling on the case and respective appellate rulings that maintain or modify the decision [Art. 201(2) CCP].

[31] The victim may pose questions to witnesses under Art. 271 CCP, but only when admitted as assistant to the prosecution and duly represented by an attorney. *Pro se* representation in Brazil is contingent on admission to the Bar, since only an attorney possesses *ius postulandi* [Machado 2009, p. 89].

[32] As defined under Law No. 13341/17, Art. 4.

direction of the Judge, allowing the witness to provide a free narrative of the facts, subject to clarification questions submitted by the parties, but asked by the professional to the child witness.[33]

2 Fundamental Rights and Safeguards of Third Parties

The Brazilian legal system stipulates rights and guarantees to citizens and parties to judicial procedures that may be applied to third parties as defined in Sect. 1.2, above. These safeguards are important corollaries to the procedural aspects described in the following sections.

2.1 Constitutional Law

Under the Brazilian Constitution, the Brazilian Federal Republic is founded on the bedrock principle of human dignity [Art. 1(III)], understood as the intrinsic and distinctive quality recognized in every human being that makes them deserving of the same respect and consideration by the State and the community.[34] In this sense, all third parties have a fundamental right to seek defense of their human dignity.

The Constitution, furthermore, establishes a series of fundamental individual rights and guarantees in Art. 5, among which are the right to privacy (Art. 5, X[35]), the right to property (Art. 5, XXII[36]), the right to judicial review (Art. 5, XXXV[37]), the non-transcendence of criminal penalties (Art. 5, XLV[38]), the right to due process,

---

[33] Law No. 13341/17, Arts. 7–12. Damage-free depositions were first adopted by the second Children and Youth Court of the District of Porto Alegre "having as its main objective the psychological protection of child and adolescent victims, avoiding their revictimization by successive testimonies, in the administrative, police and judicial spheres" [Malan and Mirza 2020, p. 199]. *"[T]his procedure consists of hearing the victim in a less intimidating environment and more conducive to questioning, that is, in the presence of only the judge (or not even the judge, if necessary!), a social worker and a clerk. [...] Law No. 13431/17, in addition to regulating this procedure in Articles 7 et seq also extended it to other situations of violence (not only of a sexual nature) perpetrated against children or adolescents as well as when they are witnesses*". [Pacelli 2020, pp. 545–546].

[34] Sarlet (2009), p. 67.

[35] "X—the privacy, private life, honor and image of persons are inviolable, and the right to compensation for property or moral damages resulting from their violation is ensured".

[36] "XXII—the right of property is guaranteed".

[37] "XXXV—the law shall not exclude any injury or threat to a right from the consideration of the Judicial Power".

[38] "XlV—*no punishment shall go beyond the person of the convict, and the obligation to compensate for the damage, as well as the decreeing of loss of assets may, under the terms of the law, be extended to the successors and executed against them, up to the limit of the value of the assets transferred*".

including the guarantees to an adversarial proceeding[39] and full defense (Art. 5, LIV and LV[40]), and finally the right to assistance where the Public Prosecutor fails to bring charges in a timely manner (Art. 5, LIX[41]).

In criminal procedure, it may be thus said that third parties have a right to request before the competent Court the review of any rulings that affect their privacy, liberty, or property, including any rulings or pre-trial measures that freeze or seize their assets, or in any manner infringe on their constitutional rights. Furthermore, the Constitution expressly recognizes the victim's standing to act in criminal proceedings, be it as a proper party or, implicitly, assisting the prosecution to obtain a favorable ruling.

2.2 Domestication of International Law

Adding to the constitutional procedural guarantees, the American Convention on Human Rights—Pact of San José, Costa Rica—provides judicial safeguards for parties in general and to criminal defendants, especially, in Articles 7 and 8.

Regarding third parties, the main procedural rights are the right to a trial within reasonable time [Article 8(1)[42]], the right to public records [Article 8(5)[43]], the right to reparation in case of judicial error [Article 10[44]], and the right to judicial protection [Article 25(1)[45]].[46]

---

[39]When ensuring an "adversary system", the Constitution simply affords litigants the right to information and reaction (*contraditório*) of the adverse party's arguments and evidence, *i.e.* "bilateral awareness of procedural acts and terms and the possibility of contradicting them" (Almeida 1937, p. 110). See Badaró (2020), pp. 60–61. However, despite the existence of adversary proceedings, Brazil's criminal justice system is defined as inquisitorial due to the Courts' powers of instruction ("*gestão da prova*") in criminal trials (de Coutinho 1998, pp. 166–167).

[40]"LIV—no one shall be deprived of freedom or of his assets without the due process of law"; "LV—litigants, in judicial or administrative processes, as well as defendants in general are ensured of the adversary system and of full defense, with the means and resources inherent to it".

[41]"LIX—private prosecution in the cases of crimes subject to public prosecution shall be admitted, whenever the latter is not filed within the period established by law".

[42]"*Every person has the right to a hearing, with due guarantees and within a reasonable time, by a competent, independent, and impartial tribunal, previously established by law, in the substantiation of any accusation of a criminal nature made against him or for the determination of his rights and obligations of a civil, labor, fiscal, or any other nature*». This means more than simply a "speedy trial [Lopes Jr. and Badaró 2006, p. 17].

[43]"Criminal proceedings shall be public, except insofar as may be necessary to protect the interests of justice".

[44]"Every person has the right to be compensated in accordance with the law in the event he has been sentenced by a final judgment through a miscarriage of justice".

[45]"*Everyone has the right to simple and prompt recourse, or any other effective recourse, to a competent court or tribunal for protection against acts that violate his fundamental rights recognized by the constitution or laws of the state concerned or by this Convention, even though such violation may have been committed by persons acting in the course of their official duties*".

[46]See Badaró (2020), pp. 43–48.

These rights are incorporated into Brazilian Law with supra-legal status—*i.e.*, below the constitutional text but above ordinary laws—, superseding any legal text that conflicts with the protection awarded to litigants.[47]

3 Third Parties in Criminal Inquiries

The first phase of criminal prosecution, although not mandatory, is the preliminary investigation. Strictly speaking, it is not considered a procedural stage, but preparatory,[48] and may occur in various forms, such as police inquiry, public civil inquiry, direct investigation by the Prosecution, Parliamentary Investigative Commission, etc.[49] The investigation is essentially carried out in written records, with limited publicity, and its function is to prepare a possible accusation to be filed for the initiation of the trial, as well as to obtain unreproducible evidence.[50] However, in a broad view, it can be stated that "the function of avoiding unfounded accusations is the main objective of preliminary investigation, because in reality, avoiding unfounded accusations means clarifying the fact".[51]

In the investigation phase, there are no persons that hold the status of parties, as it is not considered a criminal proceeding with an established judicial relation between the judge, the defense, and the prosecution. The exercise of the right of defense during the investigative stage is partially restricted. Although in recent years the performance of the attorney and his access to the dossier file has been progressively ensured,[52] there is still no regulation on defensive investigation and the possibility of production of defensive evidence at such stage is limited.[53]

Generally, the investigation takes place through a police inquiry and here we point out a peculiar characteristic of the Brazilian criminal procedure: the figure of the chief of police ("*delegado de polícia*"). He or she is a senior police officer responsible for conducting the police inquiry and therefore guiding it, with a

[47] STF, Pleno, RE 466.343/SP, Relator: Min. Cezar Peluso, 22.11.2006. See Badaró (2020), p. 47.

[48] Fernandes (2005), p. 35.

[49] Badaró (2017), p. 121.

[50] Fernandes (2005), p. 75.

[51] Lopes Jr. and Gloeckner (2014), pp. 107–108.

[52] For instance, the Supreme Federal Court's *Súmula Vinculante* no. 14 ("It is right of the attorney, in the interest of the defendant, to have broad access to evidence that, already documented in an investigative procedure conducted by the police, concern the exercise of the right of defense") and the modification brought by Law 13.245/2016, which expanded the attorney's performance in the police inquiry (Available at: http://www.planalto.gov.br/ccivil_03/_ato2015-2018/2016/lei/L13245.htm. Access on 15.10.2018.

[53] On such a scenario, see Saad (2004), pp. 198–205; Choukr (2001), pp. 124–132; Tucci (2011), pp. 303–304; Lopes Jr. and Gloeckner (2014), p. 468.

"relative discretionary power to determine the collection of evidence throughout the investigation".[54]

There are no maximum terms or deadlines in the Brazilian Code of Criminal Procedure (CCP) for the investigations, which may last for months or even years. At the end, the chief of police presents a report of the investigation, which is sent to the prosecutor, who will decide whether to bring charges or move to dismiss the investigation.[55] Therefore, the police authority, in legal terms, has no discretion to decide what to investigate or dismiss, because everything must be submitted to the Court to decide.[56]

There is some debate on the role of the MP in relation to the police inquiry. It is argued that, being responsible for the accusation, the prosecutor must also oversee the investigations, thus having greater control over the direction of the police inquiry. However, especially in the face of resistance from the chief of police, the power of the prosecutor in relation to police investigation and the independence of the chief of police is still controversial.[57] On the other hand, the Brazilian Federal Supreme Court (*Supremo Tribunal Federal*, hereinafter STF) declared the constitutionality of investigations carried out directly by the MP, without any activity by the police.[58]

The role of the Judiciary in the preliminary investigation phase is essentially to safeguard fundamental rights and limit state investigative powers. Prosecutors and the police cannot make arrests, except *in flagrante delicto*, or engage in invasive investigative means such as telephone tapping or search and seizure without judicial authorization with a warrant. Therefore, any measure to that effect is submitted to the judge with jurisdiction over the case.[59]

It is noteworthy that until recently the CCP did not have the position of the judge of guarantees and that the jurisdiction of the trial judge is determined by the criterion of "*prevenção*", *i.e.*, the same judge who followed the investigation and eventually decided on precautionary or investigative measures, was still responsible for the trial and subsequent decision.[60] In December 2019, Law No. 13964/19 amended the CCP to create the position of the judge of guarantees, determining that he is responsible for decision-making acts in the investigative phase and, consequently, prohibited to

[54] de Mendonça (2014), p. 66.

[55] Badaró (2017), pp. 145–150. Law No. 13964/19 has modified the systematic regarding dismissal of investigations, as it changed CCP Art. 28, defining that the prosecutor may dismiss an investigation without submitting it to judicial control, as it would be reviewed by the Public Prosecution Service itself. However, this modification has been suspended by the Brazilian Supreme Court without a definitive ruling.

[56] Art. 17, CCP: "The police authority may not have the inquiry files dismissed".

[57] Concerning such debate, see Lopes Jr. and Gloeckner (2014), pp. 243–249.

[58] STF, RE No. 593.727/MG, Relator: Min. Cezar Peluso, Relator p/ acórdão: Min. Gilmar Mendes, 14.05.2015.

[59] Lopes Jr. and Gloeckner (2014), pp. 258–260.

[60] On the judge's impartiality and the guidelines to stablish jurisdiction, see Maya (2011).

judge the merits of the criminal trial afterwards.[61] However, this amendment was suspended by the STF, in a provisional decision taken by one of the Judges. In August 2023, the Supreme Court finalized the judgment regarding the constitutionality of the "judge of guarantees", ruling that it must be implemented in the Brazilian system 12–24 months. The Court declared the unconstitutionality of significant parts of the reform, such as the Article that mandated the separation between the files of the police investigation and the process. Thus, although there is a substitution of the judge between the phases, the trial judge will have full access to the acts of the investigation.

During preliminary investigations, there are relevant procedural acts that may affect third parties. Firstly, concerning victims, they play a special role in initiating police investigations, since their complaint will notify the authorities of the occurrence of the crime [Art. 5(II) CCP][62] In most crimes, however, investigations are not contingent on the victim's compliant, and may be initiated *ex officio* by the police authority (CCP Art. 5, I), especially upon *flagrante delicto* arrests. These cases coincide with unconditional public prosecution, where the MP is able to bring charges whenever it takes notice of the occurrence of a crime. In other cases, exceptionally, where public prosecution depends on representation by the victim or even in cases where prosecution is exclusively private (see *infra* para. 6), investigations may not be initiated without representation by the victim or their legal representative [Art. 5(5 and 6) CCP]. During investigations, the victim can contribute to police work by requesting actions and other investigative measures (Art. 14 CCP). It is possible for the victim to conduct a private internal investigation, sharing their work product with the police authority,[63] however, any privately obtained evidence will only be used in the official investigation at the police authority's discretion (Art. 14 CCP *in fine*).

Secondly, even during investigations, without formal charges, the police or the MP may seek pre-trial seizure of assets against the alleged offender, and these measures may affect third parties, such as spouses and other family members, *bona fide* third parties that may have entered into business with the alleged offender, and legal entities, such as corporations in which the alleged offender is a stakeholder.[64] These measures and the respective challenges by third parties are described below, in Sect. 5. It is relevant, however, to state that these restrictive orders during

[61] Available at: http://www.planalto.gov.br/ccivil_03/_ato2019-2022/2019/lei/L13964.htm. Access on 26.12.2019.

[62] *Notícia de crime* or *notitia criminis*. Under Art. 5 CCP, the complaint will contain, whenever possible: (a) a narration of the fact, with all its circumstances; (b) an identification of the offender (or his characteristic signs that will allow identification) and the reasons that led to identify this person as the presumptive offender; and (c) a list of witnesses to the fact, indicating their profession and place of residence.

[63] See da Silva (2021), p. 75 et seq; Araujo (2019), p. 93 et seq.

[64] We define "stakeholder" in broad terms, referring to a formal condition of partner or shareholder, but even cases where the party occupies a position of upper management, as a board member or officer.

investigations are meant to be exceptional, and subject to reversal in case formal charges are not brought within 60 days [Art. 131(I) CCP] or within 90 days when involving crimes against the public treasury (Decree-Law[65] No. 3240/1941 Art. 2(1)]. However, Brazilian courts have rendered this provision ineffective, in many cases recognize that the complexity of the facts under investigation justify the extension of the 60 (or 90) day period[66] or that the restricted assets are subject to forfeiture upon future conviction.[67]

Finally, as stated above in para. 1.2, witnesses are afforded special rights during investigations, such as the right to access the investigative records[68] and, in special cases, the right to be heard in a "damage free deposition» that involves violent crimes against children or adolescents".[69]

4 Scientific Developments, New Technologies and the Safeguards of Third Parties

Given the expansion of technological innovations in criminal investigations, we can notice the increasing risk of the impacts on the fundamental rights of the parties involved in the case and also of third parties. For instance, wiretapping, searches on servers and computers or even the use of malware (*trojans*) bring new complexities to restricting access to data which may lead to undue access to privileged or third-party information.[70]

However, the Brazilian system does not have a specific regulation in criminal matters on digital evidence, nor its criteria or limits.[71] Documental and expert evidence on electronic media are produced in compliance with the traditional evidence regime, considering the terms of the Brazilian Code of Criminal Procedure (CCP) with original wording from 1941. This scenario is criticized by some scholars, who point out the insufficiency of the current legislation and the need for

[65] Decree-laws were executive acts authorized by Brazil's authoritarian constitutions of 1937 and 1946 (under the regime of Institutional Act 5/1968) that usurped legislative functions, that differ from executive orders since decree-laws were not subject to congressional approval. These acts were abolished by the democratic 1988 Constitution, but the enacted texts have since been considered valid through constitutional reception, as is the case of the CCP itself (Decree-Law No. 3689/1941).

[66] STJ, 5T, REsp No. 1.749.472 AgRg, Relator: Min. Jorge Mussi, 04.04.2019. An outlier ruling by the STJ has recognized that constrictions lasting over 2 years are unreasonable (STJ, 6T, AREsp 1.685.251 AgRg, Relator: Min. Sebastião Reis Júnior, 23.03.2021), however there are no precedents reversing seizures immediately upon exceeding the legal 60-day limit.

[67] STJ, 5T, AREsp No. 1.082.970 AgRg, Relator: Min. Joel Ilan Paciornik, 25.09.2018.

[68] See *supra* notes 35–36 and accompanying text.

[69] See *supra* notes 37–38 and accompanying text.

[70] In the topic, among the Brazilian production: Mendes (2020).

[71] In the same sense: Soares (2016).

modification, in accordance with the characteristics of "digital evidence", such as immateriality, volatility and duplicating susceptibility.[72]

Recently, modifications have been made to the CCP in order to expand the power of investigating authorities to request information and data related to victims or suspects from public or private companies. Such measure is authorized, even without the need for judicial control, only for registration data (name, address, etc.) or geolocation, exclusively in prosecution of crimes related to human trafficking (Articles 13-A and 13-B, inserted in the CCP by Law 13.344/2016).[73]

In terms of data protection, the General Data Protection Law (Law 13.709/2018) was recently approved, which structured a detailed system for the protection of personal data in Brazil. However, such legislation expressly excludes its applicability in relation to data used for public security purposes [Art. 4 (III)(a)]. In view of the absence of specific rules about the use of data for criminal purposes, legal scholars debate the subsidiary application of Law 13.709/2018, as far as possible, while there is no specific legislation.[74] Therefore, there is a relevant omission in the Brazilian legal system, which highlights the importance of conforming to new technologies.

In any case, some topics have been debated and involve the protection of third-party interests. In a controversial case that investigates the murder of a city councilor in Rio de Janeiro, the judge ordered Google to provide information on who went through certain parts of the city, based on search and access data in its applications. The measure generically covered several people, even non-investigated, that is, unspecified third parties. When analyzing Google's appeal, the Superior Court of Justice upheld the order for the disclosure of confidential static data referring to the identification of application users in a given geographic perimeter, but not the content of their communications.[75]

The Superior Court of Justice has also ruled that it is admissible to set a daily fine (*astreintes*) against third parties due to the delay or non-compliance with an order issued by a judge in criminal proceedings. In this case, it was determined that Facebook would provide data in relation to an investigation for offensive posts, which was done 10 days late in relation to the deadline set by court. Therefore, the

[72] Vaz (2012), pp. 66–70; Jezler Jr (2019), pp. 18–20; Costa and Leonardi (2011).

[73] "Article 13-A. *In the crimes provided in Articles 148, 149 and 149-A, in §3 of Article 158 and in Article 159 of Decree-Law no. 2.848, of December seventh, 1940 (Penal Code), and in Article 239 of Law no. 8.069, of July 13th, 1990 (Statute of Children and Adolescents), the prosecutor or the police chief may request data and information from any public authority or private companies records of the victim or suspects.* Article 13-B. *If necessary for the prevention and repression of crimes related to human trafficking, the prosecutor or the police chief may request, upon judicial authorization, the telecommunications and/or telematic service providers to immediately make available the appropriate technical means—such as signs, information and others—that allow the location of the victim or suspects of the ongoing crime*".

[74] Abreu (2021), p. 598. On this topic, also: Gleizer et al. (2021).

[75] Available at: https://www.stj.jus.br/sites/portalp/Paginas/Comunicacao/Noticias/26082020-Terceira-Secao-rejeita-recurso-da-Google-contra-fornecimento-de-dados-no-caso-Marielle-Franco.aspx. Access on 30 September 2021.

judge imposed the amount of the fine on the company, which was upheld by the Court.[76]

5 Pre-trial Measures and the Protection of Fundamental Rights of Third Parties

The CCP established provisional measures to secure the material accessory effects of criminal convictions provided in Art. 91 of the Brazilian Penal Code: the forfeiture of criminally obtained assets and the obligation to repair damage caused by the crime. These provisional measures are called "assurance measures"[77] or "property precautionary measures".[78]

For these measures, Brazil adopts a model of *nummerus clausus* provisions and strict definition that do not allow ampliation by analogy and a direct correlation to the protective goal of securing the accessory effects of conviction, *i.e.*, asset forfeiture and reparation.

On the one hand, asset seizure (Arts. 125–132 CCP) is intended to secure the forfeiture of proceeds of crime upon conviction, applying to assets "acquired by the defendant with the proceeds of the offense, even if they have already been transferred to a third party" (Art. 125 CCP), provided there is a demonstration of "vehement evidence of criminal origin" (Art. 126 CCP) by the prosecution. If these proceeds are not found or are located abroad, the CCP allows seizure to alternatively apply to an equivalent amount of lawful assets possessed by the defendant [Art. 91(1–2) CCP].

On the other hand, specialization of legal mortgage and attachment (Arts. 134–137 CCP) aim to secure solvency for an eventual reparation of damages caused by the offense and depend on a demonstration of "certainty of the infraction and sufficient evidence that the defendant committed the crime" (Art. 134 CCP). Unlike attachment, these measures apply to the defendant's lawful assets.[79] In particular, the specialization of legal mortgage aims to ensure the right *in rem* provided in the Civil Code, guaranteeing part of the defendant's assets so that the victim may obtain compensation before a civil court.[80] As for attachment, there as two different types provided in the CCP: (i) provisional attachment (Art. 136 CCP), which stands as a precautionary measure to ensure future specialization of legal mortgage, due to the latter measure's complexity; and (ii) subsidiary attachment (CCP Art. 137), which

[76] Superior Tribunal de Justiça, 3ª Seção, Recurso Especial 1.568.445-PR, Rel. Min. Rogerio Schietti Cruz, Rel. Acd. Min. Ribeiro Dantas, j. 24/06/2020.

[77] *Medidas assecuratórias* (CCP Title VI, Chapter VI).

[78] *Medidas cautelares patrimoniais.*

[79] Lopes Jr. (2020), p. 1110.

[80] Saad (2007), p. 176.

applies to goods and chattel[81] when the defendant does not possess sufficient real property to ensure reparation.[82]

Considering the precautionary nature of these assurance measures, the Court may only grant them when there is evidence of *fumus commissi delicti—i.e.,* proof of the existence of the crime and sufficient evidence that the defendant committed the offense[83]—and *periculum in mora—i.e.,* danger of damage or risk to the useful outcome of the procedure.[84]

The victim, whilst considered a third party in the main criminal procedure, may act as a party to the incident seeking assurance measures, since they are the main interested party in recovering proceeds of crime and seeking reparation.[85] Aside from the victim, the MP is also entitled to request a seizure order.[86] However, in the cases of specialization of legal mortgage and attachment, standing is held only by the victim,[87] their heirs or successors or their legal representative (arts. 134 and 137, CCP).

With regard to the recipient of these measures, attachment and specialization of legal mortgage are exclusively aimed at the property of the person responsible for committing the offense, in view of his civil liability, and thus apply *in personam.*[88] Seizure, however, applies *in rem*, falling primarily on the defendant's assets, but may affect assets belonging to third parties when there is a strong indication of

[81] *Bens móveis*, or movable property.

[82] Badaró (2020), p. 1286.

[83] Under Art. 312 CCP, personal precautionary measures (*i.e.*, preventive detention or other subsidiary measures) require demonstration of *fumus commissi delicti* in the following terms: "Art. 312. *Preventive detention may be decreed as a guarantee of public order, economic order, for the convenience of criminal instruction or to ensure the application of criminal law, when there is proof of the existence of the crime and sufficient evidence that the accused committed the act and of danger generated by the state of freedom of the accused*". *Fumus commissi delicti* for the enactment of precautionary property measures must also be understood in this way.

[84] Art. 300 CPC defines *periculum in mora* in the following terms: "Art. 300. Urgent relief will be granted when there are elements that evidence the probability of the right and the danger of damage or risk to the useful outcome of the process".

[85] Standing to request precautionary protective measures is not contingent upon the victim's admission as assistant to the prosecutor, but they must, however, be represented by an attorney to acquire *ius postulandi*. Leite (2011), p. 312.

[86] Art. 126 CCP provides that seizure may be ordered *ex officio* by the Court. However, Art. 282(2) CCP, after Law No. 13964/2019, expressly prohibits *ex officio* precautionary orders, therefore these protective property measures may not be ordered without request by the victim or the MP. Nicolitt (2018), p. 897; Lopes Jr. (2020), p. 1102; Badaró (2020), p. 1286.

[87] Art. 142 CCP provides that the MP is entitled to request the specialization of legal mortgage and attachment in cases where (a) the victim is poor and requires legal aid, or (b) there is interest by the public treasury. However, in case (a), under the 1988 Constitution, legal aid no longer provided by the MP, but rather the Public Defender's Office. Likewise, in case (b), legal representation of the public treasury stands with the municipal, state or federal attorney general or attorney for the treasury (Art. 182 CPC), and not with the MP. See Saad (2007), p. 131; Nicolitt (2018), p. 897.

[88] Pacelli (2020), p. 407.

criminal origin (CCP Art. 125). Even if transferred to others for consideration, criminally derived assets held by third parties are subject to seizure.[89]

The CCP provides for an interplea by the defendant[90] (CCP Art. 130, I) as the primary challenge by the accused against a seizure order. Thus, the seizure's effects may cease if the defendant is able to demonstrate that the property in question is not criminally derived (*e.g.*, acquired prior to the offense), thus rendering a ruling of forfeiture on these assets impossible.[91]

In turn, for cases in which seizure affects property belonging to a third party, the CCP provides for two types of interpleas aimed at overturning the protective measure: a *bona fide* third-party interplea[92] (CCP Art. 130, II) and an outside third party interplea[93] (CCP Art. 129).

The first type of third-party interplea—*bona fide* third-party interplea—is provided in CCP Art. 130, I, and applies to cases in which the acquirer claims to be unaware of and have no evidence to suspect the criminal origin of the asset acquired for consideration and at a fair price.[94] Furthermore, CCP Art. 131, II, allows for seizure to be lifted if the third party to whom the assets were transferred provides a guarantee in an amount sufficient to guarantee the forfeiture of proceeds of crime (CP Art. 91, II, b). This possibility is allowed only for a third party acting in good faith that purchased the seized property that had belonged to the accused.[95]

The second kind of third-party interplea—outside third party interplea—is provided in CCP Art. 129 and it is based on an allegation that the asset under constriction was not purchased with gains from criminal practices, thus rendering the interested third party a stranger to the facts under trial, such as is the case of a partner or joint owner.[96] Third parties who did not acquire the property, but who were somehow affected by the seizure order, may also make use of this type of interplea, such as the defendant's spouse in order to defend their marital share.[97]

As can be seen, the Brazilian criminal procedural system, as a rule, requires that the allegations against seizure be challenged through a proper proceeding by opposing third parties before the same Court that granted the measure. An appeal may be filed against a ruling on third-party interpleas (Art. 593, II, CCP).

Alternative means to challenge orders of seizure directly before appellate courts have also been admitted, however, though an appeal.[98] This, however, is criticized,

---

[89] Leite (2011), pp. 313–314.

[90] *Embargos do acusado.*

[91] Ramos (1998), p. 294.

[92] *Embargos do terceiro de boa-fé.*

[93] *Embargos de terceiro estranho ao processo.*

[94] Lopes Jr. (2020), pp. 1103–1104.

[95] Badaró (2020), p. 1269.

[96] Dezem (2018), p. 522.

[97] Ramos (1998), p. 295.

[98] STJ, 5T, RMS No. 45.707 AgRg, Relator: Min. Felix Fischer, 15.05.2015; STJ, 5T, RMS No. 41.541 AgRg, Relator: Des. Fed. Conv. Leopoldo de Arruda Raposo, 28.09.2015; STJ, 5T,

as a seizure order does not conform to any of the hypotheses authorizing appeal under CCP Art. 593, therefore only an autonomous writ of mandamus would be allowed.[99]

As for orders of specialization of legal mortgage or attachment, no interplea is provided for in the CCP, be it by the defendant himself or a third party, since under CCP arts. 129 and 130 interpleas are only established to challenge orders of seizure. Therefore, orders of specialization of legal mortgage or attachment may only be challenged through appeal[100] or writ of mandamus.[101]

Even after all these means of challenge have been exhausted (by appeal or writ), the decision that orders or maintains assurance measures is, by definition, provisional, and its effects may not last in perpetuity. Therefore, it does not submit to material *res judicata*, which is incompatible with the summary cognition necessary to grant a precautionary order.[102] In turn, given the necessary demonstration of *periculum in mora* for their issuance, the precautionary measures have their stability conditioned to the state in which they were determined — or *rebus sic stantibus*.[103] It is improper, therefore, to refer to *res judicata* in these matters.

6 Third Parties and the Decision to Charge (or to Terminate the Proceedings)

In the Brazilian criminal procedure system, as a general rule, a criminal charge is presented and directed by the MP, without the need for authorization or request from the victim. The types of criminal action are classified as: (1) public initiative criminal action; (2) private initiative criminal action.

On the one hand, the vast majority of crimes provided for in the Brazilian legal system are prosecuted through unconditioned public criminal action, that is, under the responsibility of the MP, without direct influence of the victim on the decision to accuse, which, according to the majority position, adheres to the principle of mandatory prosecution. However, there is constitutional provision (Art. 5, LIX, CF/88) of the "private criminal action subsidiary of the public action",[104] which authorizes the victim to file the accusation, even in crimes of unconditioned public

---

RMS 38.959 AgRg, Relatora: Min. Laurita Vaz, 15.04.2013; STJ, 6T, RMS 28.938, Relatora: Min. Maria Thereza de Assis Moura, 13.12.2012. See also Leite (2011), p. 330; Dezem (2018), pp. 517–522; Choukr (2019), p. 406.

[99] Greco Filho (2010), p. 269; Saad (2007), p. 151.

[100] Choukr (2019), p. 414.

[101] Saad (2007), p. 176.

[102] Wambier and Talamini (2020), p. 414.

[103] Badaró (2020), p. 1217.

[104] Barros (2008), pp. 159–160. See also, Fayet Jr and Varela (2017).

criminal action, when the inertia of the MP is verified.[105] That is, if, after receiving the police investigation files, the MP makes no statement within the prescribed deadline, the victim can initiate and be a party to the criminal proceedings. In this case, the prosecutor will act as a third party, in an oversight and supervision role for the public interest. However, if the MP drops the charges, there is no possibility of "private criminal action subsidiary of the public action".

On the other hand, there are cases of crimes in which the victim has greater power in the decision to initiate the investigation and criminal proceedings. In cases of criminal actions conditioned on a complaint, the victim must authorize the State to initiate criminal prosecution, which occurs through the "complaint" (a formal manifestation by which the victim expresses interest in the prosecution). However, even so, the prosecution and the direction of the case are responsibility of the MP and the victim maintains the role of a third party in the proceeding.

In the case of death or legally declared absence, the right of complaint will pass to the spouse, ascendant, descendant or sibling [Art. 24(1) CCP]. Once the complaint is filed, revocation is possible until the beginning of the criminal proceedings (filing of the accusation by the MP).[106] In cases of crimes related to gender violence, such as bodily injury against women, the Supreme Federal Court ruled that they should not depend on the victim's will, given the circumstantial complexities that may obstruct the proper processing of those cases.[107]

There are also crimes that depend on the victim to initiate their prosecution and, then, they will be part of the process, having an attorney to file for the prosecution.[108] These criminal offenses, such as crimes against honor, are classified as private initiative criminal actions.[109] If the victim dies or is declared absent by a court decision, the right to file the accusation or to continue with the action will pass to the spouse, ascendant, descendant or sibling (Article 31, CCP). Some jurists criticize the hypotheses of private initiative criminal actions, as such crimes involve private interests and would not have dignity for protection under the Criminal Law.[110]

In Brazil, there is no "popular accusation", through which a third person can file a criminal accusation against the perpetrator.[111] Therefore, citizens in general can

---

[105] Article 29 CCP. The private criminal action will be admitted in crimes of public action, if the latter is not brought within the legal deadline, being up to the Prosecution Office to amend the complaint, reject it and offer a substitute accusation, intervene in all terms of the proceeding, provide evidence, file an appeal and, at any time, in the case of negligence by the victim, resume the action as the main party.

[106] Art. 25 CCP. The complaint shall be irrevocable, once the accusation has been filed.

[107] STF, ADC 19, Plenário, rel. Min. Marco Aurélio, j. 9.2.2012.

[108] If the victim cannot afford the costs, the judge must appoint an attorney (Art. 32 CCP).

[109] Article 30 CCP. The victim or whoever has the capacity to represent him or her shall be responsible for bringing the private action.

[110] On this topic: Almeida (2017) and Schott (2008).

[111] Exceptionally, the Consumer Protection Code (CDC) authorizes, in crimes against consumer relations, subsidiary criminal complaints filed by entities and bodies of the Public Administration, directly or indirectly, even if without legal personality, specifically intended for the defense of

report a crime to the authorities,[112] but the opening of investigations or prosecution invariably depends on the initiative of the MP or the victim, in the rare cases of private initiative criminal actions.

In the ordinary procedure, the police authority will draft a report at the conclusion of the investigation, expressing its perception of what was investigated, which facts are proven, if there was any crime and which was it, in addition to who committed it. Then, the records of the investigation are sent to the court and a term is opened for the MP's statement in cases of public initiative criminal action. The conclusion presented by the chief of police in the report does not bind the MP, which may offer the accusation, request further investigations or dismiss the case.

As previously said, if the MP does not file the accusation in situations of public initiative criminal action and dismisses the case, the victim cannot bring the private criminal action subsidiary of the public action, as it is only applicable in the face of inertia of the MP. In the original system of the Brazilian CCP, the prosecutorial decision to dismiss the case may be controlled by the judge, who could disagree and refer the matter for internal review in the MP.[113] However, Law 13.964/2019 amended Art. 28 of the CCP, suppressing judicial control, so that the prosecutor would no longer request that the judge dismiss the case, but would do it directly, which could be reviewed internally by the MP at the victim's request or automatically.[114] Such provision, however, was interpreted by the Federal Supreme Court as upholding judicial oversight, while also ensuring the participation of the victim.[115]

---

interests and rights protected by the CDC, and associations legally constituted for at least 1 year and which include among their institutional purposes the defense of the interests and rights protected by the CDC, with the assembly authorization being waived (Art. 80, Law no. 8.078/1990). Currently, the draft of a new Electoral Code (PLP 112/2021) is under debate in Congress and one of the innovations would be the possibility of a subsidiary popular initiative in electoral crimes.

[112] Art. 27 CCP. Any person of the people may provoke the initiative of the Prosecution Office, in cases of public action, providing written information on the fact and possible perpetrator and indicating the time, place and evidentiary elements.

[113] CCP, original wording, "Article 28. *If the Prosecution Office, instead of filing the accusation, requests the dismiss of the police investigation or any pieces of information, the judge, if the reasons invoked are unfounded, will send the investigation report or pieces of information to the Attorney General, and the latter will file the accusation, designate another prosecutor to file it, or insist on the dismissing, which only then will the judge be obliged to attend*".

[114] According to Law 13.964/19, "Article 28. *Once the police investigation or any information of the same nature has been dismissed, the Prosecution Office will notify the victim, the investigated and the police authority and will send the records to the prosecution body of review for approval, in the form of the law. § 1° If the victim, or his legal representative, does not agree with the dismissing of the police investigation, he or she may, within 30 (thirty) days of receiving the communication, submit the matter for review by the competent instance of the prosecution body, as provided for by the respective organic law. § 2° In criminal proceedings relating to crimes committed to the detriment of the Union, States and Municipalities, the review of the police investigation dismissing may be brought about by the head of the body responsible for its judicial representation*".

[115] Supreme Federal Court, Direct Actions for the Declaration of Unconstitutionality n. 6.298, 6.299, 6.300 e 6.305, 23.08.2023.

With the progressive expansion of criminal agreements in the Brazilian criminal procedure, the influence of the victim on the MP's decision in relation to the opportunity for criminal action must also be verified. In relation to the currently existing mechanisms *(transação penal, suspensão condicional do processo, acordo de não persecução penal* and colaboração premiada), although the legislation generally provides for the victim's right to be informed about the agreement,[116] the negotiation takes place between the accused and the MP, without obligation of the victim's participation, who cannot prevent it from happening.

7 Third Parties in Court Proceedings

During the criminal proceeding, in cases of public initiative criminal action, in which the MP files the accusation and directs the prosecution, the victim, although not controlling the performance of the prosecutor, can join the process as an assistant to the prosecution, through an attorney who needs to be authorized by the judge. In case the victim is absent, his/her spouse, ascendant, descendant or sibling may join as assistant.[117] It is not permitted that the codefendant in the alleged criminal act becomes an assistant to the prosecution. The assistant may propose the production of evidence, question witnesses, participate in the oral debate and argue the appeals filed by the MP, or by the assistant himself, in exceptional situations in which he can appeal alone (Art. 271, CCP).

Regarding the role of the prosecution assistant in the proceeding, legal scholars usually have two positions: on the one hand, there are those who claim that the assistant can only protect the victim's patrimonial interests, seeking civil reparation for the damage caused by the crime,[118] on the other hand, it is also argued that the assistant may seek the conviction of the defendant in his/her own interest.[119] This is reflected, for example, in the limits of the appeal that can be filed by the third party.[120] If it is only patrimonial interest, the assistant would not be allowed to appeal to increase the punishment imposed by the judge, as this does not influence the civil compensation to be fixed. However, this position did not prevail, and the Brazilian courts accept that the prosecution assistant can appeal even for the sole purpose of seeking a higher penalty for the defendant.[121]

[116]In relation to the non-criminal prosecution agreement, for example: Art. 28-A(9) CCP: "The victim will be notified of the ratification of the non-criminal prosecution agreement and its non-compliance".

[117]"Art. 268 CCP. In all terms of the public action, the victim, or his legal representative, or any of the persons mentioned in Article 31 in case of absence, may intervene, as an assistant to the Prosecution Office".

[118]Lopes Jr. (2020), p. 569.

[119]Badaró (2020), p. 345.

[120]Barros (2008), pp. 157–158.

[121]STF, *habeas corpus* 71.453, Segunda Turma, Rel. Min. Paulo Brossard, j. 6.9.1994.

The participation of interested third parties in the debate is also possible in cases of relevance to the Supreme Federal Court, for instance, from the joining of *amicus curiae*.[122] These are mechanisms that authorize the contribution of the third party to the resolution of the case, especially when there is a setting of precedent applicable to other similar situations. The *amicus curiae* must be representative and relevant to the topic under discussion in the proceeding, whether or not its participation is accepted by the judge.[123] Traditionally, its role was more common in actions for constitutional review, but it has expanded to other types of proceedings, such as collective writ of *habeas corpus*. This agent may present subsidies to the proceeding, like memorials and oral arguments, but, as a rule, he does not have the legitimacy to appeal, for example.

Finally, a current issue under debate in the Brazilian criminal procedure concerns the participation of other perpetrators of the crime, not charged by the prosecutor in the specific case, either because they benefited from a cooperation agreement or due to a procedural split. In this scenario, although involved in the fact, the other perpetrator is not a co-defendant in the same proceeding, joining it as a third party. In the event of being part of a criminal agreement, the Superior Court of Justice has already ruled that the deponent's situation as a collaborator must be informed to the parties.[124]

Concerning challenges against assurance measures, see above Sect. 5.[125]

8 The Protection of Third Parties in Decision-Making Processes

The protection of third parties in decision-making takes place, especially, considering the victim's monetary interests. In 2008, Law no. 11.719 reformed the Brazilian CCP to increase the accumulation of civil claims through the criminal procedure itself. This change allowed the judge, when issuing a conviction, to set a minimum amount of patrimonial reparation to the victim, as long as this was requested by the prosecution and submitted to debate during the proceeding.[126]

---

[122] On this topic: Medina (2010) and Almeida (2019).

[123] Article 138 of the Code of Civil Procedure (CPC): "*The judge or the rapporteur, considering the relevance of the matter, the specificity of the topic object of the demand or the social repercussion of the controversy, may, by non-appealable decision, ex officio or at the request of the parties or whoever intends to make a statement, request or admit the participation of a natural or legal person, body or specialized entity, with adequate representation, within 15 (fifteen) days of its notification*".

[124] Superior Court of Justice, *habeas corpus* 75.856, 6ª Turma, Rel. Min. Nefi Cordeiro, j. 6.12.2016. On this topic: Vasconcellos (2021), pp. 78–82.

[125] See *supra* notes 95–108 and accompanying text.

[126] Badaró (2020), pp. 248–253.

In addition to the main effect resulting from a conviction—*i.e.*, subjecting the offender to the penalty imposed on him —arts. 91 and 91-A of the Penal Code (CP) establish accessory patrimonial effects arising from the conviction. Among them, the CP provides for the effect of "making certain the obligation to repair the damage caused by the crime" (CP Art. 91, I). It also determines the forfeiture of (a) "the proceeds of crime or any asset or value that constitutes profit earned by the agent from the practice of the criminal act" (CP Art. 91, II, b), (b) assets "equivalent to the proceeds or profits of the crime when they are not found or when they are located abroad" (CP Art. 91, §1), or (c) "property corresponding to the difference between the value of the convict's property and the one that is compatible with its lawful income" (CP Art. 91-A).

With regard to the effects of the conviction in relation to third parties, CP Art. 91, II, b, when determining the forfeiture of proceeds of the crime, expressly reserves the right of the injured party or third party in good faith. Thus, once the acquisition for consideration is proven to be in good faith because the third party did not know, nor was it possible to know, that the purchased property was criminally derived, the purchaser will be entitled to compensation for the loss suffered. In relation to a third party acting in bad faith, in case of awareness of the asset's criminal origin, forfeiture will apply due to collusion.[127]

In turn, regarding CP Art. 91, I, the conviction only ensures the obligation to repair damages, and does not, in itself, impose any restrictive measures on the convicted party's property—except for a precautionary order issued before or during trial.[128] This effect is limited, as the Constitution provided that the penalty shall not exceed the person of the convict.[129]

These property effects of conviction have been established by the Penal Code since its enactment.[130] However, Law No. 13964/2019 introduced extended forfeiture (CP Art. 91-A) as a new effect upon conviction, applying to offenses with a maximum penalty of more than 6 years, leading to forfeiture of assets "corresponding to the difference between the value of the convict's assets and that which is compatible with his lawful income" upon a specific motion by the prosecution.

Basically, extended forfeiture is based on a legal presumption that the property of the convict that exceeds their lawful income is criminally derived. In this case, the burden of proof resides with the convicted party to demonstrate otherwise. Under CP Art. 91-A, § 1, the definition of the "convict's property" is broadened to reach other assets belonging to third parties. This is the case of assets which the convicted party "has the domain over and the direct or indirect benefit of, on the date of the criminal offense or subsequently received" (Art. 91-A, §1, I CP) and assets "transferred to

[127] Essado (2014), p. 83.

[128] See *supra* notes 82–89 and accompanying text.

[129] See *supra* note 43 and accompanying text.

[130] Saad (2007), p. 33. The exception is the forfeiture of "equivalent" assets [CP Art. 91(1)], introduced by Law No. 12.694/2012.

third parties free of charge or upon negligible consideration, from the beginning of the criminal activity" (Art. 91-A, §1, II CP).

Therefore, upon conviction, a third party may suffer the effects of forfeiture if (a) they have acquired the property free of charge or at a price considered to be negligible, or (b) the property, despite being formally owned by a third party, is available and used for the benefit of the convict. To protect property from the effects of extended forfeiture, one may demonstrate the compatibility of property owned with a demonstrated lawful origin, however, part of the literature states that this constitutes an inversion of the burden of proof.[131]

As an effect of the conviction, the loss of custody in relation to descendants may also occur, for example, with an order declaring the.

"incapacity to exercise family power, guardianship or curatorship in intentional crimes punished with imprisonment when committed against another equal holder of the same family power, against a son, daughter or other descendant or against the ward" (Article 92, II, CF/88).

However, the criminal conviction cannot be passed on to third parties,[132] as the Brazilian Constitution of 1988 provides that.

"no punishment shall go beyond the person of the convict, and the obligation to compensate for the damage, as well as the decree of loss of assets may, under the terms of the law, be extended to the successors and executed against them, up to the limit of the value of the assets transferred" (Art. 5°, XLV).

Regarding the evidentiary assessment, the victim's testimonies, especially in sexual crimes, are usually given greater reliability, even admitting the conviction of the defendant exclusively on the basis of the victim's words. This is a complex and debated theme in view of the balance between the interests of the victim in the prosecution of the crime and the presumption of innocence with the standard of proof arising from it.[133]

9 Third Parties in Appeal Proceedings

People normally claim that the Brazilian appeal system has an excessive number of appeals applicable in criminal matters. The Brazilian Constitution of 1988 states that "no one shall be considered guilty before the issuing of a final and unappealable penal sentence" (Art. 5, LVII). Thus, the execution of a sentence can only start after the conclusion of all possible appeals, so that prison before res judicata would only be authorized when motivated in precautionary reasons. This position was recently reiterated in the judgment of ADCs 43, 44 and 54, in which the STF, in a tight vote

[131] de Souza (2020), p. 43.
[132] Martinelli and Bem (2020), pp. 857–858.
[133] Matida (2019).

(6 to 5), declared the constitutionality of Art. 283 of the CCP and prohibited the provisional execution of the sentence after judgment by an Appellate Court.[134]

The conviction or acquittal sentence may be reviewed by an Appellate Court through an "appeal".[135] It is a remedy without major formalities and requirements, which returns all the debated issues of the trial for review, in a written manner and without compliance with the principle of immediacy between the judge and the gathering of the evidence. Although the CCP authorizes the review of evidence in the second degree, such a provision is almost never used in practice. Therefore, the appeal is decided based on the elements produced by the trial judge in the first instance and documented in the case file.[136]

Then there are special (like a cassation of the continental systems)[137] and extraordinary appeals, respectively directed to the Superior Court of Justice (for violation of federal law, such as the CCP, or divergence between Appellate Courts) and to the STF (for violation of the Constitution). Although abstractly it may be filled in any case, these appeals are subject to strict controls, with admissibility requirements that make it difficult for the higher courts to admit the appeals.

The participation of the victim and the prosecution assistant in the appeal stage is limited. According to Article 271 of the CCP, the assistant may brief the appeals filed by the MP, or by himself, when it is restricted to cases of appeal against an acquittal or dismissal, if the MP does not appeal.[138] That is, its legitimacy to appeal is subsidiary and limited.

The Brazilian CCP has an exceptional hypothesis of legitimacy for any citizen to file an appeal against the list of jurors selected annually in each judicial district (Art. 426, first paragraph). This is a case of appeal legitimacy for a third party, any person, even if it is not related to a case under judgment.[139]

With regard to third parties in the appeal relation, codefendants who have not filed the appeal may benefit from any decision favorable to those who filed it. This is called the "extensive effect" of appeals.[140] According to Article 580 of the CCP, "in the event of codefendants (Penal Code, Art. 25), the appeal filed by one, if based on reasons that are not exclusively personal, will benefit the others". That is, if the foundations of the decision can be shared with the other principals, it should be applied to them. However, if the grant of the appeal is motivated by justifications exclusively applicable to the appellant, the extension will not occur.

---

[134] STF, ADCs 43, 44 e 54, Plenário, Rel. Min. Marco Aurélio, j. 7.11.2019.

[135] Batista (1992), pp. 223–224.

[136] Audiovisual recording mechanisms for audiences have been progressively structured, so that the Courts might reproduce the judicial acts by audio and video, but this is still not widespread in Brazil.

[137] Thaman (2019), pp. 949–957.

[138] Badaró (2020), p. 351.

[139] Zanoide de Moraes (2000), p. 395.

[140] Badaró (2021), pp. 197–204.

Concerning challenges against assurance measures and their respective appellate proceeding, see above para. 9.[141]

10 Res Judicata and the Effects of Criminal Judgments Upon Third Parties

Once the court decision has been rendered and the *res judicata* consolidated, there are effects that may affect third parties, especially with regard to possible patrimonial interests. According to Article 63 of the CCP, "when the adverse judgment becomes final, the victim, his/her legal representative or his/her heirs may file for enforcement of the judgment in civil court for the purpose of repairing the damage".

The CCP provides for hypotheses in which the acquittal decision prevents the possible filing of civil action for damages. Depending on the legal basis of the criminal acquittal, civil liability will be prevented or not, so that the adoption of a system of relative separation between the civil and criminal spheres is usually affirmed.

Thus, the law states that "a criminal sentence that recognizes that the act was performed in out of necessity, in self-defense, in strict compliance with a legal duty or in the regular exercise of law" (Article 65) and "notwithstanding the acquittal in the criminal court, the civil action may be filed when the material inexistence of the fact has not been categorically recognized" (Article 66). Therefore, if the criminal acquittal is based on a clear acknowledgment of non-existence of the fact, non-perpetration or participation of the accused or a cause of justification, any civil liability is not feasible. However, if the criminal acquittal, for example, occurs due to insufficient evidence, the civil action may be filed.[142]

In addition, there are limits to the incidence of *res judicata* in relation to third parties that were not part of the original procedural relation. It is stated that the *res judicata*, as a rule, only affects the parties to the proceeding, in compliance to the adversary proceeding.[143] Although the CCP does not have a clear provision, the rule of the Code of Civil Procedure is adopted: "The judgment is *res judicata* to the parties between which it is given, not harming third parties" (Article 506, Law 13.105/2015). However, in view of the extensive effect previously analyzed (Article 580, CCP), an acquittal decision may be applied to the codefendant or, indirectly, even to third parties (others who committed the crime that have not been sued in the same action).[144] The possibility of enforcement against the person civilly liable for

[141] See *supra* notes 103–106 and accompanying text.

[142] "Article 67 CCP. *The following shall not impede the filing of a civil action: I - the dismiss of the police investigation or pieces of information; II - the decision that states the extinction of criminal liability; III - the acquittal that decides that the fact does not constitute a crime*".

[143] Nicolitt (2018), pp. 951–952.

[144] Badaró (2021), pp. 665–666.

the effects of the criminal conviction is also debated, such as an employer in damages related to a crime caused by an employee. Although there is caselaw of the courts admitting it, legal scholars criticize this position due to violation of the adversarial procedure, sustaining the need to open civil proceedings to hold the third party liable.[145]

On the *rebus sic stantibus* effects on orders of seizure, attachment and specialization of legal mortgage and their respective challenges, see Sect. 5 above.[146]

11 Third Parties in Police and Judicial Cooperation in Criminal Matters

Due to globalization, many States deemed it necessary to adopt a joint posture in the face of transnational crime, thus strengthening international judicial cooperation in criminal matters. If the commission of crimes is not restricted to the borders of a single State, it is logical that procedural acts necessary for criminal prosecution not be restricted to a single territory.[147] In this context, international judicial cooperation is conceived as a set of procedural activities carried out by jurisdictional bodies belonging to different sovereign States that converge at the international level in achieving the same purpose.[148]

In the Brazilian legal system, there is no law that covers, in a structured and systemic manner, international judicial cooperation, unlike other countries such as Germany, South Africa, Argentina, the United Kingdom and Switzerland.[149] The CCP regulated this issue in Book V, entitled "On jurisdictional relations with foreign authorities", in which it establishes general (CCP Arts. 780–782) and specific provisions (Arts. 783–790 CCP). Elsewhere, Law No. 9613/1998 (Anti-Money Laundering Act) provides for protective property measures when money laundering offenses are committed abroad, indicating the bases of cooperation and the percentage division of assets (50% for each state).[150]

In civil matters, the Brazilian Code of Civil Procedure[151] allocates an entire chapter to the regulation of international judicial cooperation (CPC Arts. 26–41), which can be applied to criminal proceedings when it does not conflict with the criminal provisions (Art. 3 CCP). In addition, there are executive ordinances that regulate the matter, such as Interministerial Ordinance No. 501/501, enacted by the Ministry of Justice and the Ministry of Foreign Affairs. The Ordinance aims to

145 Grinover (1978), p. 51.

146 See *supra* notes 105–106 and accompanying text.

147 Souza (2015), p. 2.

148 Cervini and Tavares (2000), p. 51.

149 Kleebank (2004), p. 18.

150 Law No. 9613/1998, Art. 8.

151 *Código de Processo Civil.*

standardize the processing of letters rogatory[152] and requests for direct assistance[153] when recipient countries do not have a judicial cooperation treaty with Brazil. In addition, STJ Resolution No. 9/2005 presents important definitions for the procedure to be adopted to comply with requests for cooperation.

The basis of international legal cooperation can be a bilateral or multilateral treaty[154] or the promise of reciprocity.[155] Regarding bilateral international treaties, Brazil has ratified agreements on the matter with the following countries: (i) China (Decree No. 6282/2007); (ii) South Korea (Decree No. 5721/2006); (iii) the United States of America (Decree No. 3810/2001); (iv) Colombia (Decree No. 3895/2001); (v) Peru (Decree No. 3988/2001); (vi) France (Decree no. 3324/1999); (vii) Italy (Decree No. 862/1993); and (viii) Portugal (Decree No. 1320/1994).[156]

With regard to multilateral treaties, Brazil is currently a party to (i) the Inter-American Convention on Mutual Assistance in Criminal Matters, of 23.05.1992, and its optional protocol, of 11.06.1993 (Decree No. 6340/2008); (ii) the United Nations Convention against Corruption (Decree No. 5687, of 01/31/2006); (iii) the United Nations Convention against Transnational Organized Crime (Decree No. 5015/2004) and its three additional protocols (Decrees No. 5017/2004, 5016/2004 and 5941/2006); (iv) the United Nations Convention against Illicit Traffic in Narcotic Drugs and Psychotropic Substances (Decree No. 154/1991); and (v) the Protocol of Mutual Legal Assistance in Criminal Matters—Mercosur (Decree No. 3468/2000).

The substantial number of transnational money laundering cases in Brazil demands an active coordinated approach by Brazilian and American authorities. These jurisdictions' relations are governed by their bilateral agreement on criminal matters (Decree No. 3810/2011), under CCP Art. 1, I. The treaty presents detailed

[152] The letter rogatory is an international legal cooperation mechanism by which the judicial authority of one country requests the judicial authority of another country to carry out the necessary steps for the effective development of procedural relations. There are three types of letters rogatory: (a) ordinary, whose object is the production of procedural acts, such as service of process and notification; (b) instruction, whose object is the collection of evidence; and (c) enforceable, whose object is to carry out restrictive procedural acts. In addition, the letter rogatory can be classified as (a) active, when it is forwarded by the Brazilian judicial authority; or (b) passive, when the request for cooperation arises from a decision issued by a foreign judicial authority for compliance in Brazil. See Bechara (2009), p. 41.

[153] Direct assistance is an instrument of international legal cooperation used when a certain foreign State needs a judicial (or administrative) measure to be obtained in another jurisdiction, regardless of a letter rogatory or the ratification of a foreign judgment. What determines the use of the letter rogatory or direct assistance is the existence of international treaties between the respective States. If there is a treaty, the cooperation mechanism will be direct assistance; if it does not exist, cooperation will be carried out through diplomatic channels by means of a letter rogatory. (Silva 2006, p. 78).

[154] A treaty is the formal agreement concluded between legal persons under public international law and intended to produce legal effects. In Brazil, after going through its internalization process, it becomes effective with the status of ordinary law [Rezek 2011, p. 38].

[155] The promise of reciprocity translates into the requesting State's commitment that it will comply with equivalent measures executed by the requested State, in the same circumstances, if the latter executes the request made by the former (Accioly et al. 2021, item 5.4.3.).

[156] Souza (2015), p. 7.

provisions concerning judicial cooperation in criminal matters, especially evidence, searches and seizure of assets.[157]

Within the scope of international cooperation between police authorities, the International Criminal Police Organization—Interpol stands out, which centralizes one of the oldest mechanisms of aid and assistance at the international level. Currently, Interpol occupies 190 (one hundred and ninety) member countries with the objective of coordinating the work of the police in preventing and combating transnational crime. Interpol's activities are provided for in the United Nations Convention against Illicit Traffic in Narcotic Drugs and Psychotropic Substances—Vienna Convention (Decree No. 154/1991, Art. 7(8)), in the United Nations Convention against Transnational Organized Crime—Palermo Convention (Decree No. 5015/2004, Art. 18(13)), as well as the United Nations Convention against Corruption—Merida Convention (Decree No. 5687/2006, Art. 46(13)).

The subjects of legal cooperation are classified as mediate/indirect and immediate/direct. The immediate/direct subjects are those directly responsible for cooperation, *i.e.*, the States and, depending on the case, the international intergovernmental organizations. The mediate/indirect subjects are the individuals of each State who suffer the effects of the aid or assistance measure—either positively, when the requested measure is granted; or negatively, when the transaction is denied.[158]

Among the mediate subjects, in addition to the parts of the criminal proceedings in progress in the national territory, possible *third parties* may be the target of the effects of the acts carried out through international cooperation. This is the case of offshore corporations, defined as legal entities located outside the country of domicile of their holders created to serve as a *de facto* partnership.[159] Under criminal prosecution, offshore corporations tend to be regarded as legal entities founded abroad with the purpose of committing acts of money laundering,[160] corruption, drug trafficking, tax fraud, and other offenses.

International cooperation is used as means by which the authorities request the "freezing" of assets deposited abroad in bank accounts held by defendants or third parties—*e.g.*, legal entities—to ensure the seizure of amounts arising from criminal activities. It is worth noting, however, that in cases where money laundering offenses are investigated nationally, Law No. 9613/1998—where it provides for "the restriction of assets, rights or values arising from the commission of crimes abroad"—, expressly reserves the right of third parties in good faith from the effects of protective pre-trial measures (AML Act, Art. 8, §1).

According to a report published by the Brazilian Federal Public Prosecutor's Office,[161] in the 2019–2021 biennium, US$ 866 million, € 92 million and CHF 13 million deposited in accounts abroad were frozen through international judicial

---

[157] Aras (2021).

[158] Ramos (2015), p. 6.

[159] Block and Rabello (2015), p. 237.

[160] Xavier (2016), p. 239.

[161] *Ministério Público Federal.*

cooperation — in most cases, deposited in offshore accounts. According to data released by the Federal Prosecution Office, the recovery of assets took place predominantly through judicial cooperation with Switzerland, but there was also cooperation with Monaco, Singapore, Luxembourg, Jersey Islands, the Guernsey Islands, the United States of America, and other jurisdictions.[162]

References

Abreu JS (2021) Tratamento de dados pessoais para segurança pública. In: Mendes L, Doneda L, Sarlet IW, Rodrigues OL Jr, Bioni B (eds) Tratado de Proteção de Dados Pessoais. Forense, Rio de Janeiro
Accioly H, Casella PB, Silva GEN (2021) Manual de direito internacional público, 25th edn. Saraiva, São Paulo
Almeida JC (1937) A contrariedade na instrução criminal. Saraiva, São Paulo
Almeida LS (2017) Desnecessidade dos crimes de ação penal de iniciativa privada originária. Lumen Juris, Rio de Janeiro
Almeida EM (2019) Capacidades institucionais dos amici curiae no Supremo Tribunal Federal: acessibilidade, admissibilidade e influência. Revista Direito e Práxis 10(1):678–707
Aras V (2021) A cooperação jurídica internacional com os Estados Unidos. Blog do Vlad. https://vladimiraras.blog/2021/01/14/a-cooperacao-juridica-internacional-com-os-estados-unidos/
Araujo MA (2019) Investigações empresariais. LiberArs, São Paulo
Badaró GH (2003) Ônus da prova no processo penal. RT, São Paulo
Badaró GH (2017) Processo Penal, 5th edn. RT, São Paulo
Badaró GH (2020) Processo Penal, 8th edn. RT, São Paulo
Badaró GH (2021) Manual dos Recursos Penais, 5th edn. RT, São Paulo
Barros FM (2008) A participação da vítima no processo penal. Lumen Juris, Rio de Janeiro
Batista WM (1992) An overview of Brazilian criminal procedure. Panorama Braz Law:207–232
Bechara FR (2009) Cooperação jurídica internacional em matéria penal: eficácia da prova produzida no exterior. Doctoral Thesis — USP, São Paulo
Block M, Rabello M (2015) Lavagem de dinheiro envolvendo offshores. Revista de Direito Bancário e do Mercado de Capitais 68:237–255
Busato PC (2017) Direito Penal 3. Atlas, São Paulo
Cervini R, Tavares J (2000) Princípios de cooperação jurídica penal internacional no protocolo do Mercosul. RT, São Paulo
Choukr FH (2001) Garantias constitucionais na investigação criminal, 2nd edn. Lumen Juris, Rio de Janeiro
Choukr FH (2019) Código de Processo Penal, 9th edn. D'Plácido, Belo Horizonte
Cintra AC, Grinover AP, Dinamarco CR (2008) Teoria Geral do Processo. 24ed. Malheiros, São Paulo
Costa H, Leonardi M (2011) Busca e apreensão e acesso remoto a dados em servidores. Revista Brasileira de Ciências Criminais 88
da Silva DR (2021) Investigações corporativas e processo penal. Thoth, Londrina
de Coutinho JNM (1998) Introdução aos princípios gerais do processo penal brasileiro. Revista da Faculdade de Direito da UFPR 30:163–198
de Mendonça AB (2014) The criminal justice system in Brazil: a brief account. Res Material UNAFEI 92:63–70

[162] MPF (2021), p. 49.

de Souza LA (2020) Alterações no Código Penal (Art. 2°). In: de Souza LA, Dezem GM (eds) Comentários ao Pacote Anticrime Lei 13.964/2019. RT, São Paulo, pp 21–62
Dezem GM (2018) Curso de Processo Penal. RT, São Paulo
Dinamarco CR, Badaró GH, Lopes BV (2020) Teoria Geral do Processo, 32nd edn. Malheiros, São Paulo
Dotti RA (2012) O problema da vítima. Revista dos Tribunais Online:853–862
Essado TC (2014) A perda de bens e o novo paradigma para o processo penal brasileiro. Master's Dissertation—USP, São Paulo
Fayet N Jr, Varela AG (2017) A ação (penal) privada subsidiária da pública. Livraria do Advogado, Porto Alegre
Fernandes AS (2005) Teoria geral do procedimento e o procedimento no processo penal. RT, São Paulo
Frederico Marques J (1961) Elementos de direito processual penal 2. Forense, São Paulo
Gleizer O, Montenegro L, Viana E (2021) O direito de proteção de dados no processo penal e na segurança pública. Marcial Pons, Rio de Janeiro
Greco Filho V (2010) Manual de processo penal, 8th edn. Saraiva, São Paulo
Grinover AP (1978) Eficácia e autoridade da sentença penal. RT, São Paulo
Jardim AS (1998) Ação penal pública: princípio da obrigatoriedade, 3rd edn. Forense, Rio de Janeiro
Jesus DE, Estefam A (2020) Direito Penal, vol 4, 20th edn. Saraiva, São Paulo
Jezler I Jr (2019) Prova Penal Digital. Empório do Direito, Florianópolis
Kleebank S (2004) Cooperação jurídica por via diplomática: avaliação e propostas de atualização do quadro normativo. Fundação Alexandre Gusmão, Brasília
Leite L (2011) Medidas patrimoniais de urgência no processo penal. Renovar, Rio de Janeiro
Lopes A Jr (2012) Direito processual penal, 9th edn. Saraiva, São Paulo
Lopes A Jr (2020) Direito processual penal, 17th edn. Saraiva, São Paulo
Lopes A Jr, Badaró GH (2006) Direito ao processo penal no prazo razoável. Lumen Juris, Rio de Janeiro
Lopes A Jr, Gloeckner RJ (2014) Investigação preliminar no processo penal, 6th edn. Saraiva, São Paulo
Lozzi G (2008) Lezioni di procedura penal, 7th edn. G. Giappichelli, Torino
Machado AA (2009) Curso de processo penal, 2nd edn. Atlas, São Paulo
Malan DR, Mirza FM (2020) Right of confrontation and protective measures of child and adolescent witnesses. Revista Brasileira de Ciências Criminais 171:187–224
Martinelli JP, Bem LS (2020) Direito Penal. Parte Geral, 5thed edn. D'Plácido, Belo Horizonte
Matida JR (2019) O que deve significar o especial valor probatório da palavra da vítima nos crimes de gênero. Trincheira Democrática 3
Maya AM (2011) Imparcialidade e processo penal da prevenção: da competência do juiz das garantias. Lumen Juris, Rio de Janeiro
Medina D (2010) Amicus Curiae: amigo da corte ou amigo da parte? Saraiva, São Paulo
Mendes C (2020) Tecnoinvestigação. Entre a proteção de dados e a infiltração por software. Juspodivm, Salvador
Ministério Público Federal, Brazil (2021) Pensamento e ação: Procuradoria-Geral da República 2019–2021. MPF, Brasília
Montero Aroca J (2008) Proceso penal y libertad. Ensayo polémico sobre el nuevo proceso penal. Thompson Civitas, Madrid
Nicolitt A (2018) Manual de Processo Penal. D'Plácido, Belo Horizonte
Nucci GS (2018) Curso de Direito Processual Penal, 15th edn. Forense, Rio de Janeiro
Pacelli E (2020) Curso de Processo penal, 24th edn. Atlas, São Paulo
Ramos JGG (1998) A tutela de urgência no processo penal brasileiro. Del Rey, Belo Horizonte
Ramos MA (2015) O Paradigma da soberania e a cooperação jurídica. In: Menezes W, Ramos AC (eds) Direito Internacional Prova e a Nova Cooperação Jurídica Internacional. Arraes, Belo Horizonte, pp 115–133

Rezek JF (2011) Direito internacional público, 13th edn. Saraiva, São Paulo
Saad M (2004) O direito de defesa no inquérito policial. RT, São Paulo
Saad M (2007) As medidas assecuratórias do Código de Processo Penal como forma de tutela cautelar destinada à reparação do dano causado pelo delito. Doctoral Thesis—USP, São Paulo
Sarlet IW (2009) Dignidade da pessoa humana e direitos fundamentais na Constituiçào Federal de 1988, 7th edn. Livraria do Advogado, Porto Alegre
Schott AV (2008) Ação penal (privada) em face da institucionalização do conflito. Juruá, Curitiba
Silva RPM (2006) Cooperação jurídica internacional e auxílio direto. Revista CEJ 32:75–79
Soares G (2016) Investigação criminal e inovações técnicas e tecnológicas. D'Plácido, Belo Horizonte
Souza CY (2015) Cooperação jurídica internacional em matéria penal: considerações práticas. Revista Brasileira de Ciências Criminais 7:297–325
Thaman SC (2019) Appeal and cassation in continental European criminal justice systems. Guarantees of factual accuracy, or vehicles for administrative control? In: Brown DK, Turner JI, Weisser B (eds) The Oxford handbook of criminal process. Oxford University Press, New York
Tucci RL (2011) Direitos e garantias individuais no processo penal brasileiro, 4th edn. RT, São Paulo
Vasconcellos VG (2015) O 'Sistema Acusatório' do Processo Penal Brasileiro: apontamentos acerca do conteúdo da acusatoriedade a partir de decisões do Supremo Tribunal Federal. Direito, Estado e Sociedade 47:181–204
Vasconcellos VG (2016) Lide na justiça criminal? Sobre a importância do conflito de interesses entre as partes processuais e sua irrelevância para a necessidade do Processo Penal. Revista Brasileira de Ciências Criminais 119:165–199
Vasconcellos VG (2021) Colaboração premiada no processo penal, 4th edn. RT, São Paulo
Vaz D (2012) Provas Digitais no Processo Penal: formulação do conceito, definição das características e sistematização do procedimento probatório. Doctoral Thesis—USP, São Paulo
Wambier LR, Talamini E (2020) Curso avançado de processo civil 2, 16th edn. RT, São Paulo
Xavier LP (2016) O direito brasileiro à procura de um conceito: encontros e desencontros com o trust. Doctoral Thesis—UFPR, Curitiba
Zanoide de Moraes M (2000) Interesse e legitimação para recorrer no processo penal brasileiro. RT, São Paulo
Ziyade F (1993) O assistente de acusação. Livraria do Advogado, Porto Alegre

Report from France

Barbara Drevet

Abstract French criminal law has been subject to recent changes to make sure that the rights of third parties to the proceedings are more protected. Most of those changes deal with the rights of third parties having rights on or over the property, to make sure that they can be informed of a decision of confiscation and that they can be heard or appeal the decision.

1 Introduction. General Features of Domestic Criminal Justice

1.1 Formal Participants in Criminal Proceedings

In French criminal procedure, the formal participants can be divided into two categories: the public party and the private parties. On the one side, the public party is the prosecutor, whose job is to initiate and exercise public prosecution for the imposition of penalties.[1] The prosecutor must guarantee the public order and is the first participant in criminal proceedings because she is the one who starts the whole process.

On the other side, the private parties can be subdivided into two parties. First, the most obvious one is the person who committed the offence. Depending on the stage of the criminal proceedings, she will be called suspect, person under judicial examination, *prévenu*[2] or accused[3] but she will always have rights granted

[1] Art. 1(1) CCP.

[2] If she is accused of a misdemeanour.

[3] If she is accused of a crime.

B. Drevet (✉)
University of Clermont-Ferrand, Centre Michel de l'Hospital (UR4232), Clermont-Ferrand, France
e-mail: barbara.drevet@uca.fr

S. Ruggeri et al. (eds.), *Third Parties in Criminal Proceedings*, Legal Studies in International, European and Comparative Criminal Law 10,
https://doi.org/10.1007/978-3-031-73970-5_3

to her.[4] Second, French criminal law gives the victim a status as a party. More precisely, the civil party is a party and she can initiate the public prosecution.[5] In order to be granted the status of civil party, one must have personally suffered from a damage directly caused by the offence.[6] However, French law evolved to grant rights to the victim, even before she has decided to become a civil party: the Preliminary Article of the Code for criminal procedure states that the judicial authority ensures that the victim is informed, and her rights guaranteed during all the criminal proceedings. Article 10-2 CCP provides a detailed list of the victim's rights, such as the right to have any damage repaired, to become a civil party or to have a lawyer.

Consequently, only the prosecutor, the accused and the victim are formal participants in criminal proceedings, in the sense that they are parties to the proceedings.

1.2 Third Parties to Criminal Proceedings

Strictly speaking, a third party would refer to someone who has nothing to do with the criminal proceedings in the sense that she is not a party to the proceedings. However, a criminal case does not only involve formal participants and many other people can be affected by the proceedings or required to participate in them, without being a party.

First, some people can be affected by the criminal proceedings, without being the victim or the accused. It is the case for owners when their property has been used to commit the offense or can be seized as the product of an offense committed by someone else. It is also the case for legally responsible persons, that is to say the person who can be held responsible before a civil jurisdiction. She is the one who will have to compensate damages caused by the offence, even though she is not the accused. This category deals with French civil law and includes for instance parents who are legally responsible for their children; employers responsible for their employees' acts; teachers responsible for their students' acts.[7] In the same way, the insurer, either the victim's or the accused's will be the one paying any money owed. Consequently, all those people are affected by the criminal proceedings and that is why some rights and protection must be granted to them.

Second, and broadly speaking, third party can refer to people who have nothing to do with the offence but who can be indirectly affected by procedural measures, especially during investigations. Their fundamental rights are one of the reasons for the limits surrounding the most intrusive measures.

---

[4] Drevet (2019), p. 93 ff.

[5] Art. 1(2) CCP.

[6] Art. 2 CCP.

[7] For more details on the categories see Ambroise Casterot (2020), pp. 594–597.

Lastly, third party can also relate to the people who are not formal participants to the proceedings but who are required to take part in procedural acts, such as witnesses or experts. Their status is never similar to a party, and they have the duty to help establish the truth. However, they sometimes need to be granted protection, which is especially the case for witnesses.

All of those categories of third parties to criminal proceedings will be explored further when relevant.

2 Fundamental Rights and Safeguards of Third Parties

2.1 Constitutional Law

2021 has been an eventful year regarding the rights and safeguards of third parties. Indeed, no less than three major decisions made by the French *Conseil constitutionnel* deal with confiscation of property and rights of the third party. Those decisions forced the French legislator to intervene to better accommodate the rights of third parties.

The change started with a decision made in April 2021.[8] The case dealt with the additional penalty of confiscation in case of human trafficking. At the time, Article 225–25 CC read that natural or legal persons convicted of this offence also incurred the additional penalty of the confiscation of any or all their property, or, subject to the rights of the owner acting in good faith, of property on which she has rights, of whatever type, movable or immovable, and whether jointly or separately owned. This Article was the object of a priority preliminary ruling on constitutionality to the *Conseil constitutionnel.*[9] It was argued by the claimant that confiscating someone's property without giving her the possibility to participate in the proceedings and to be heard was violating the right to an effective legal remedy and the right to be presumed innocent until proven guilty.[10] The *Conseil constitutionnel*, using Article 16 of the Declaration of the Rights of Man and of the Citizen according to which "any society in which the guarantee of rights is not assured, nor the separation of powers determined, has no Constitution",[11] stated that neither Article 225-25 CC nor any other provisions provided the owner whose quality is known or who claimed such a quality during the proceedings with the possibility to assert her rights and her

[8]Cons. const., 23 April 2021, n° 2021-899 QPC, *Dalloz actualité*, 10 May 2021, obs. Goetz.

[9]In France, the priority preliminary ruling on constitutionality refers to the right for a claimant to argue that a law infringes the rights and freedoms guaranteed by the Constitution and to ask the courts to transfer the case to the *Conseil Constitutionnel* to have the law abrogated (Art. 61-1 of the Constitution).

[10]Cons. const., 23 April 2021, para. 8.

[11]*Ibid.*, para. 10.

good faith before the jurisdiction ordering the confiscation.[12] As a result, the *Conseil constitutionnel* ruled that Article 225-25 CC violated Article 16 of the Declaration of the Rights of Man and of the Citizen. Consequently, the part of Article 225-25 CC reading "or, subject to the rights of the owner acting in good faith" was abrogated.[13] However, the *Conseil constitutionnel* decided to postpone the effect of the decision until the 31st of December 2021[14] to give the legislator time to remedy the situation. As soon as April 2021, it became clear that the general provision on confiscation, Article 131-21 CC, would not last since the same words were used without any effective remedy.[15]

The second decision was made by the *Conseil constitutionnel* in September 2021.[16] This time the case dealt with Article 131-21(3) and (9) CC on confiscation as well as Articles 313-7 (4) on additional penalties in case of fraud and 324-7 on additional penalties in case of money-laundering. They were the object of a priority preliminary ruling on constitutionality, and it was argued that they were violating the right to an effective legal remedy, the rights of the defence and the right to property.[17] Basically, the same grievances were made as the ones against Article 225-25 CC. It is then of no surprise that the *Conseil constitutionnel* ruled in the same way, even using exactly the same sentences than in their April decision.[18] Indeed, the judges stated that neither the provisions against which the claim was made, nor any other provisions provided the owner whose quality is known or who claimed such a quality during the proceedings with the possibility to assert her rights and her good faith before the jurisdiction ordering the confiscation.[19] Consequently, Articles 131-21(3) and (9), 313-7 (4) and 324-7 CC were violating the right to an effective remedy and the rights of the defence and must be declared unconstitutional.[20] However, just as in April, the *Conseil constitutionnel* decided to postpone the effect of the decision until the 31st of March 2022.[21]

Lastly, the third decision made by the *Conseil constitutionnel* in November 2021 sealed the fate of Article 131-21 CC on confiscation.[22] In the case the priority preliminary ruling on constitutionality was about almost all of the provisions of Article 131-21 and it was argued that by authorizing the confiscation of property

---

[12] *Ibid.*, para. 12.

[13] *Ibid.*, para. 13.

[14] *Ibid.*, para. 15.

[15] Hy (2022), p. 66.

[16] Cons. const., 23 September 2021, n° 2021–932 QPC, *Dalloz actualité*, 29 September 2021, obs. Goetz; *D.* 2021. Pan. 2109, obs. Genestet.

[17] Cons. const., 23 September 2021, para. 5.

[18] Comp. Cons. const., 23 April 2021 para. 23 and Cons. const., 23 September 2021, para. 15.

[19] Cons. const., 23 September 2021, para. 15.

[20] *Ibid.*, para. 16.

[21] *Ibid.*, para. 20.

[22] Cons. const., 24 November 2021, n°2021-949/950 QPC, *Dalloz actualité*, 2 December 2021, obs. Dufourq.

belonging to the conjugal community without making it possible for the accused's spouse to be heard by the tribunal, to make observations, be represented by a lawyer or to appeal the decision, Article 131-21 violated Article 16 of the Declaration of the Rights of Man and of the Citizen and the right to property.[23] Again, the *Conseil constitutionnel* stated that no provisions provided the spouse not condemned with the possibility to assert her rights and her good faith before the jurisdiction ordering the confiscation.[24] As a result, the judges ruled that most of Article 131–21 CC violated Article 16 of the Declaration of the Rights of Man and of the Citizen and must be abrogated.[25] Again, the effects of the decision were postponed until the 31st of December 2022 to give the legislator time to remedy the situation. They didn't waste time and passed the Act n° 2021-1729 of the 22nd of December 2021 to rewrite Article 131-21 CC on confiscation and give effective rights to third parties.[26]

2.2 Domestication of International Law

International law does not seem to play a significant role in the protection of rights and safeguards of third parties in French criminal law. ECHR case *Ünsped Paket Servisi San. Ve Tic. A.Ş. v. Bulgarie*[27] is sometimes mentioned by French commentators as having had an influence on the *Conseil constitutionnel's* decisions on confiscation,[28] but nothing clearly indicates that this is the case.

It actually seems that for a long time, French law didn't put much thought into the protection of third parties having rights on or over a property, even though some international instruments did mention that such protection had to be granted. For instance, the Council of Europe Convention on Laundering, Search, Seizure and Confiscation of the Proceeds from Crime stated that when dealing with a request for cooperation, recognition of a judicial decision taken in the requesting Party could be refused if "third parties did not have adequate opportunity to assert their rights".[29] In the same way, the UN Convention against transnational organized crime stated that nothing in Article 12 on confiscation "shall be construed to prejudice the rights of bona fide third parties".[30] Yet, in French law, Article 131–21 CC on confiscation did not provide any protection to third party, nor did any other French instrument.

[23] Cons. const., 24 November 2021, paras. 4–5.

[24] *Ibid.*, para. 13.

[25] *Ibid.*, para. 14.

[26] On those rights see para. 7.1.

[27] ECtHR, *Ünsped Paket Servisi San. Ve Tic. A.Ş. v. Bulgarie*, Judgment of 13 October 2015, Appl. No. 3503/08, para. 38.

[28] Hy (2021) and Fonteix (2022).

[29] Council of Europe Convention on Laundering, Search, Seizure and Confiscation of the Proceeds from Crime, 9 November 1990, Art. 22 (2)(a).

[30] UN Convention against transnational organised crime, Art. 12 para. 8.

2.3 Implementation of EU Law

The main, and probably only, influence of EU law on French criminal law regarding fundamental rights and safeguards of third parties is about confiscation. The implementation of the Council Framework decision 2005 on Confiscation of Crime-Related Proceeds, Instrumentalities and Property[31] led to a change in Article 131-21 CC on confiscation. Indeed, by a law of 2007, the French legislator rewrote Article 131-21 to include third parties' rights on or over the property that was used to commit the offence. As a result, the confiscation of such property could be ordered as a penalty, subject to the third party's rights if she was acting in good faith.[32] However, the provision made a distinction between property that had been used to commit the offence and property that was the object or the product of the offence. Rights of third parties were only provided for in the former case but not in the latter.

It is by using another EU law instrument that the French *Cour de cassation* remedied the situation. Indeed, Directive 2014 of the European Parliament and of the Council on the freezing and confiscation of instrumentalities and proceeds of crime in the European Union states that confiscation "shall not prejudice the rights of *bona fide* third parties".[33] Using that Article, the *Cour de cassation* decided in 2018 that the rights of *bona fide* third parties must be protected, even if the confiscation deals with the product of the offence.[34] By doing so, the judges interpreted Article 131-21 CC in light of the EU Directive and gave more protection to third parties having rights on or over the property confiscated.[35]

Lastly, one must notice that the first decision of the *Conseil constitutionnel* about the unconstitutionality of the French provisions on confiscation intervened only 3 months after the Court of justice of the European Union stated that.

> Article 4 of Framework Decision 2005/212, read in the light of Article 47 of the Charter, must be interpreted as precluding a national law which permits the confiscation, in the context of criminal proceedings, of property belonging to a person other than the person who committed the criminal offence, without the former being afforded an effective remedy.[36]

---

[31] Council Framework Decision 2005/212/JHA of 24 February 2005 on Confiscation of Crime-Related Proceeds, Instrumentalities and Property.

[32] Art. 131-21 CC as it was re-written by the Act n° 2007–297 of the 5 March 2007.

[33] Directive 2014/42/EU of the European Parliament and of the Council of 3 April 2014 on the freezing and confiscation of instrumentalities and proceeds of crime in the European Union, Art. 6 (2).

[34] Crim. 7 November 2018, n°17-87424.

[35] Segonds (2021), p. 95.

[36] CJEU, *OM*, aff. C-393/19, 14 January 2021, para. 68.

3 Third Parties in Criminal Inquiries

3.1 Police and Law Enforcement Investigations

The French Code for criminal procedure distinguishes between two types of police investigations: the flagrancy investigation and the preliminary investigation. Both types of police investigations are carried out under the direction of the prosecutor,[37] which means that the prosecutor directs the activities of the police officers during the investigations.[38] Regarding third parties, two issues can be distinguished, depending on the third party: the person who has rights on or over the property and the witnesses.

3.1.1 Third Parties Having Rights on or Over the Property

Third parties having rights on or over a property can be affected by search and seizures in police and law enforcement investigations. First, according to Article 53 CCP, the flagrancy investigation is only possible in case of a flagrant felony or misdemeanor, that is to say a felony or misdemeanor in the course of being committed, or which has just been committed. The felony or misdemeanor is also flagrant where, immediately after the act, the person suspected is chased by hue and cry, or is found in the possession of articles, or has on or about him traces or clues that give grounds to believe he has taken part in the felony or misdemeanor. In that situation, a flagrancy investigation is possible but cannot exceed 8 days without interruption.[39] By exception, the prosecutor can decide to extend the investigation for 8 more days if it is necessary for the discovery of the truth in relation to a felony or a misdemeanor punished by a sentence of at least 5 years imprisonment.[40]

During the flagrancy investigation, the police officer who is told of a flagrant felony immediately informs the prosecutor, goes forthwith to the scene of the crime, and records any appropriate findings.[41] On the scene of the crime, the police officer can seize the weapons and instruments which were used to commit the felony, or which were designed or intended for its commission, as well as any item which appears to have been the product of this felony.[42] The police officer can also search the home of a person who appears to be involved in the offence or to be in possession of documents, information or articles pertaining to the offence and seize anything

[37] Art. 12 CCP.

[38] Art. 41(2) CCP.

[39] Art. 53(2) CCP.

[40] Art. 53(3) CCP.

[41] Art. 54(1) CCP for the flagrant felony and Art. 67 CCP for the flagrant misdemeanour.

[42] Art. 54(2) CCP for the flagrant felony and Art. 67 CCP for the flagrant misdemeanour.

necessary.[43] In both cases it doesn't matter who the item seized belongs to, so whether a third party is affected by the measure is irrelevant at this point.[44]

Second, according to Article 75 CCP, the preliminary investigation is possible for the three kinds of offenses recognized by the French criminal system: felonies, misdemeanors, and contraventions. If the case doesn't fall into the flagrancy investigation, it can be covered by the preliminary investigation. The main difference with the flagrancy investigation is that the preliminary investigation is by principle not compelling. It means that in order for the police officers to investigate, the person must consent to the investigative measure. Most notably, according to Article 76(1) CCP, searches, house visits and seizures of exhibits may not be made without the express consent, in writing, of the person in whose residence the operation takes place. No reference is made to the involvement of the person in the offence, which means that the search and seizure can take place in the house of someone who is going to be qualified as a third party later.

By exception, the search and seizure can take place without the consent of the person. Indeed, if the needs of an investigation into a felony or a misdemeanor punished by a prison sentence of 5 years or more justify this, the liberty and custody judge may, at the request of the prosecutor, decide, in a written and reasoned decision, that the operations provided for by the present Article will be carried out without the consent of the person in whose residence they take place.[45] Here again there is no reference to the involvement of the person in the offence, which is logical since the aim of the investigation is to identify the people involved. As a consequence, it is possible for a search and seizure to take place in the house of someone who is going to be qualified as a third party later.

It is worth mentioning that the French legislator has introduced a new Title XXIX into the French Code for criminal procedure, named "Special seizures", to improve and facilitate the use of seizure, in order to make the penalty of confiscation more effective.[46] The special seizures are defined by Article 706-141 CCP as the seizures of property assets, intangible assets or seizures not amounting to a dispossession of property. A list of the properties concerned by special seizures is then provided by Articles 706-148 to 706-158. As a result, if the property is one mentioned by those Articles, the special provisions of Title XXIX CCP must apply. The main difference is that if the seizure takes place during a prosecutorial investigation (preliminary or flagrancy investigation), the seizure cannot be decided by the prosecutor alone but must be authorized by the liberty and custody judge.[47] However, there is no real difference between seizures and special seizure regarding third parties.

---

[43] Art. 56(1) CCP for the flagrant felony and Art. 67 CCP for the flagrant misdemeanour.

[44] See *infra* for the restitution.

[45] Art. 76(4) CCP.

[46] Art. 706-141 CCP. See *infra* for the impact of the penalty of confiscation on third parties.

[47] Art. 706-148(1); 706-150(1); 706-153(1) and 706-158(1) CCP.

3.1.2 Witness Protection

Another category of third parties that can be affected by criminal inquiries is witnesses, that is to say people against whom there is no plausible reason to suspect that they have committed or have attempted to commit an offence and who are in a position to bring useful pieces of evidence to the proceedings. Testifying and providing information during the investigation can sometimes be dangerous for the witness and that is why French law developed witness protection measures.

Indeed, the witness can be authorized by the prosecutor or the investigating judge to declare her registered address to be that of the police station or gendarmerie.[48] Moreover, for the proceedings dealing with a crime or a misdemeanor punishable by at least a 3 years' imprisonment, if the witness' hearing can put her life or health or that of her family members or close relatives in serious danger, the liberty and custody judge, seized of the case in a reasoned application by the prosecutor or the investigating judge, may authorize, in a reasoned decision, that this person's statements will be recorded without her identity appearing in the case file for the proceedings.[49] Only witnesses who had declared their address to be that of the police station or gendarmerie can benefit from the measure.[50] Since their identity cannot be revealed, anonymous witnesses do not sign the record of their hearing. However, they sign another record that is put in a separate file and their identity is written in a classified register.[51] The French Code for criminal procedure is very explicit, stating that under no circumstance will the identity or the address of a witness who has benefited from the provisions of Articles 706-57 or 706-58 be revealed.[52] Disclosure of such information is punishable by 5 years' imprisonment and a fine of €75,000.[53]

Similarly, for the proceedings dealing with a crime or a misdemeanor punishable by at least 3 years' imprisonment, if the witness' hearing can put her life or health or that of her family members or her close relatives in serious danger, the investigating judge or the president of the court seized can decide, on her own motion or on the prosecutor or the parties' motion, that the witness' identity shall not be revealed during the trial or mentioned in any ordinance, judgement or appeal judgments.[54] This decision ordering the witness' confidentiality cannot be appealed[55] and disclosure of such an identity or of any information enabling the identification or location of the witness is punishable by 5 years' imprisonment and a fine of €75,000.[56]

---

[48] Art. 706-57(1) CCP.

[49] Art. 706-58(1) CCP.

[50] Brach Thiel (2020), para. 22.

[51] Art. 706-58(2) CCP.

[52] Art. 706-59 CCP.

[53] *Ibid.*

[54] Art. 706-62-1(1) CCP.

[55] Art. 706-62-1(3) CCP.

[56] Art. 706-62-1(5) CCP.

Lastly, a special protection can be put in place for witnesses where the proceedings deal with crimes against humanity, war crimes or organized crimes.[57] Indeed, for those crimes, if the witness' hearing can put her life or health or that of her family members or her close relatives in serious danger, the president of the judicial tribunal can authorize the use of an assumed identity.[58] It is even possible for her family members and close relatives to use an assumed identity as well.[59] Disclosure of such an identity or of any information enabling the identification or localization of the witness is punishable by 5 years' imprisonment and a fine of €75,000.[60] If the disclosure led to violence against the witness, her spouse, her children or her parents, the penalty goes to 7 years' imprisonment and a €100,000 fine.[61] It goes to 10 years' imprisonment and a €150,000 fine in case the disclosure led to the death of the witness, her spouse, her children or her parents.[62]

Nonetheless, in order to balance witness protection with the rights of the defence of the accused, Article 706-62 CCP states that no conviction can be pronounced on the sole basis of statements recorded under the conditions set out in Articles 706-58 and 706-61. Besides, according to Article 706-60 CCP, the measure of anonymous testimony is not applicable if knowledge of the person's identity is essential to the case for the defence. The person under judicial investigation—and no one else, meaning that the suspect in a prosecutorial investigation doesn't have that power—can challenge the liberty and custody judge's decision to authorise an anonymous testimony before the president of the Investigation Chamber.[63] If the president of the Investigation Chamber deems the challenge justified, the anonymous testimony is nullified. In any case, the president's decision cannot be appealed. The person under judicial investigation or sent to trial can also ask to be confronted with an anonymous witness.[64] In that case, measures are put in place to ensure that the witness' voice is unrecognizable and that she can testify from a distance.[65]

The same kind of protection is offered to offenders cooperating with the authorities. Indeed, Article 706-73-1 CCP states that the president of the judicial tribunal can authorize them to use an assumed identity if it is necessary. This assumed identity is given the same protection as other witnesses. Indeed, the disclosure of the informant's identity or location is punishable by the same penalties: 5 years' imprisonment and a fine of €75,000,[66] 7 years' imprisonment and a €100,000 fine if the disclosure led to violence against the witness, her spouse, her children or her

[57] Art. 706-62-2(1) CCP.

[58] Art. 706-62-2(2) CCP.

[59] Art. 706-62-2(7) CCP.

[60] Art. 706-62-2(4) CCP.

[61] *Ibid.*

[62] Art. 706-62-2(5) CCP.

[63] Art. 706-60(2) CCP.

[64] Art. 706-61(1) CCP.

[65] *Ibid.*

[66] Art. 706-63-1(3) CCP.

parents[67] and 10 years' imprisonment and a €150,000 fine in case the disclosure led to the death of the witness, her spouse, her children or her parents.[68] Here again, family members of the informant can be authorized to use an assumed identity.[69]

A parallel between the protection of witnesses and offenders cooperating with the authorities on the one side and undercover agents on the other can be drawn. Indeed, in case of organized crimes, French law makes it possible for police officers to use an assumed identity in order to infiltrate a criminal organisation.[70] The assumed identity plays the same role as for witness in that it aims at protecting the identity of the police officer. Quite logically, their real identity mustn't be revealed during the proceedings[71] and we can find the same penalties for the disclosure of their identity as for witnesses and informants: 5 years' imprisonment and a fine of €75,000,[72] 7 years' imprisonment and a €100,000 fine if the disclosure led to violence against the witness, her spouse, her children or her parents[73] and 10 years' imprisonment and a €150,000 fine in case the disclosure led to the death of the witness, her spouse, her children or her parents.[74]

However, contrary to other witnesses and offenders cooperating with the authorities, the undercover's family cannot benefit from the possibility to be given an assumed identity.

3.2 *Judicial Investigation*

3.2.1 Third Parties Having Rights on or Over the Property

The same measures can be executed during the judicial investigation. A judicial investigation is compulsory where a felony has been committed but in the absence of special provisions, it is optional for misdemeanours.[75] That kind of investigation is directed by the investigating judge, who takes any investigative step he deems useful for the discovery of the truth.[76] Among those investigative steps, the investigating judge can execute search and seizures himself or authorize police officer by rogatory letter to perform the measures.[77] According to Article 94 CCP, searches are made in

[67] *Ibid.*

[68] *Ibid.*

[69] Art. 706-63-1(5) CCP.

[70] Art. 706-81 CCP.

[71] Art. 706-84(1) CCP.

[72] Art. 706-84(2) CCP.

[73] Art. 706-84(3) CCP.

[74] Art. 706-84(4) CCP.

[75] Art. 79 CCP.

[76] Art. 81(1) CCP.

[77] Art. 81(4) CCP.

all the places where items or electronic data may be found which could be useful for the discovery of the truth. Consequently, the search can happen everywhere and at this stage it might not be possible to know who is going to be involved in the case and who is not. As a result, the search can take place at the home of someone who is going to end up a third party to the proceedings. Article 96 CCP adds that if the search is made in a home other than that of the person under judicial examination, the person in whose home it must be made is invited to attend. Article 97 CCP concludes the provisions regarding search and seizures during the judicial investigation by imposing special rules for documents or electronic data. In that situation, only the investigating judge, or the police officer commissioned by him, can examine such documents before carrying out the seizure. The seizure of any electronic data necessary for the discovery of the truth is carried out either by seizure of the physical medium in which the data is held or by means of a copy of the data made in the presence of those persons who were present at the seizure.[78] Besides, only articles, documents, or electronic data useful for the discovery of the truth or that can be subject to confiscation can be seized with the agreement of the investigating judge.[79]

Special seizures of Title XXIX CCP are also allowed during the judicial investigation, and they are decided by the investigating judge.[80] Apart from that, the conditions are the same as in case of a prosecutorial investigation.[81]

3.2.2 Witness Protection

Witness protection during the judicial investigation is governed by the same rules as during the prosecutorial investigation.

4 Scientific Developments, New Technologies and the Safeguards of Third Parties

The rapid developments that occurred in technologies have led to the use of new investigative measures that can interfere with the fundamental rights of third parties. In French criminal law, three new investigative measures can have such an effect.

First, French law developed the use of international mobile subscriber identity-catcher (IMSI-catcher) as a means of investigation in 2016.[82] It is a tool used to intercept mobile phone traffic and track location data of mobile phone users, but the issue is that an IMSI-catcher doesn't aim at a particular mobile phone. Instead, it

[78] Art. 97(3) CCP.

[79] On the penalty of confiscation see *infra*.

[80] Art. 706-148(1); 706-150(1); 706-153(1) and 706-158(1) CCP.

[81] See *supra*.

[82] Art. 706-95-20 CCP.

intercepts the location data of every mobile phone user in the perimeter.[83] As a result, this investigative measure doesn't only concern formal participants but can also affect third parties. Therefore, French law chose to create strict conditions for its use. Indeed, the IMSI-catcher is only possible in case of organized crimes, for a list of offences provided by Articles 706-73 and 706-73-1 CCP.[84] Besides, the measure can only be authorized by a judge, either by the liberty and custody judge in case of a prosecutorial investigation[85] or by the investigating judge in case of a judicial investigation.[86] Their decision is not subject to an appeal,[87] which seems logical since the point of the IMSI-catcher measure is to be secret. The use of the IMSI-catcher is also submitted to a rather tight timeframe: during the prosecutorial investigation, it can only be used during a month, renewable once.[88] During the judicial investigation, the timeframe is longer, and the IMSI-catcher can be used for 4 months, renewable every 4 months without exceeding 2 years.[89] Lastly, every data collected must be destroyed once the date on which prosecution is barred under the statute of limitations has passed.[90] It is probably the best the law can do to protect rights and data of third parties.

Second, French law permits electronic data capture as an investigative measure. Indeed, Article 706-102-1 CCP makes it possible for the police officer, authorized by the liberty and custody judge[91] or by the investigating judge[92] to put in a place a device to access, save, keep, and transmit electronic data of a person without her consent.[93] This investigative measure is only possible in case of organized crime, for the offences listed by Articles 706-73 and 706-73-1 CC[94] and every data collected must be destroyed once the date on which prosecution is barred under the statute of limitations has passed.[95] The timeframe is the same as for the IMSI-catcher measure: a month, renewable once in case of a prosecutorial investigation[96] and 4 months, renewable every 4 months without exceeding 2 years in case of a judicial investigation.[97] In short, electronic data capture is submitted to the same requirements as the IMSI-catcher measure, probably because it is just as intrusive and threatening for

[83] Peltier (2017), p. 49.
[84] Art. 706-95-11 CCP.
[85] Art. 706-95-12 1° CCP.
[86] Art. 706-95-12 2° CCP.
[87] Art. 706-95-13 CCP.
[88] Art. 706-95-16 1° CCP.
[89] Art. 706-95-16 2° CCP.
[90] Art. 706-95-19 CCP.
[91] In case of a prosecutorial investigation. Art. 706-95-12 (1) CCP.
[92] In case of a judicial investigation. Art. 706-95-12 (2) CCP.
[93] Art. 706-102-1(1) CCP.
[94] Art. 706-95-11 CCP.
[95] Art. 706-95-19 CCP.
[96] Art. 706-95-16 (1) CCP.
[97] Art. 706-95-16 (2) CCP.

third parties' rights. Indeed, since every data can be collected, it can concern a third party who has nothing to do with the offence the investigation is on. This is why every data collected must be destroyed once the date on which prosecution is barred under the statute of limitations has passed.[98]

It must be noted that French law provides police officer with the possibility of remote access and seizure of electronic correspondence without the person's consent.[99] This investigative measure is only possible in case of organized crime and must be authorized by the liberty and custody judge or the investigating judge.[100] However, and contrary to the electronic data capture measure, nothing is provided for the destruction of the data collected by a remote seizure of electronic correspondence.

Lastly, to fight against offences committed on the Internet or by electronic means, French law developed a specific undercover measure to allow police officers to use a pseudonym on the Internet to communicate with people suspected of committing an offence and to collect data and evidence by this means.[101] At first, this investigative measure was only possible in case of organized crimes[102] such as human trafficking, pimping and underage prostitution[103] but since the Act of the 23 March 2019,[104] investigation by means of electronic undercover is possible for every crime and misdemeanour punishable by at least 1 year imprisonment.[105] Contrary to the IMSI-catcher measure, electronic undercover is not always decided by the judge. Indeed, during the prosecutorial investigation, the prosecutor can decide herself, without requesting an authorization by the liberty and custody judge.[106] During the judicial investigation, it is for the investigating judge to make the decision.[107] Electronic undercover can only collect data on suspects[108] so it is a lesser risk for third parties than the IMSI-catcher.

[98] Art. 706-95-19 CCP.

[99] Art. 706-95-1 CCP.

[100] Art. 706-95-1 CCP.

[101] Art. 230-46 CCP.

[102] Art. 706-87-1 CCP as written before 2019.

[103] Art. 706-35-1 CCP as written before 2019.

[104] Act n° 2019-222 of 23 March 2019 of the Program 2018-2022 on the reform of the justice.

[105] Art. 230-46(1) CCP.

[106] Art. 230-46 CCP.

[107] Art. 230-46 CCP.

[108] Art. 230-46 (2) CCP.

5 Pre-trial Measures and the Protection of Fundamental Rights of Third Parties

Among the pre-trial measures that can be taken, it seems that only measures regarding seizures and restitutions deal with the protection of fundamental rights of third parties. Once a property has been seized during the police or the judicial investigation, it can be returned to the owner before the end of the investigations.[109] Indeed, during the police investigation, the prosecutor can decide, on her own motion or upon application, as to the restitution of property the ownership of which is not seriously disputed.[110] The decision belongs to the prosecutor who chooses whether to return the property or not. By exception, the restitution must be denied if the property is likely to cause danger for persons or properties, if the property is the direct or indirect product of the offense or where a specific provision provides for the destruction of properties seized.[111] Generally speaking, if the prosecutor refuses to return the property, the person who asked for the restitution can challenge the decision by petitioning the president of the Investigation Chamber or the Investigation Chamber itself.[112]

Similarly, during the judicial investigation, the investigating judge is competent to decide on the restitution of property that has been seized.[113] Her decision is made by reasoned order either upon the prosecutor's submissions or on her own motion, after hearing the prosecutor's opinion, or upon the application of the accused, the civil party or any other person claiming a right over the property.[114] Here the latter, who is a third party to the proceedings, enjoys the same rights as the private parties regarding restitutions of property. All of them can refer the investigating judge's order to the Investigation Chamber[115] to have the order overturned. This remedy explains why the *Cour de cassation* refused to transfer a priority preliminary ruling on constitutionality to the *Conseil constitutionnel.* Indeed, it was argued that by giving the investigating judge the possibility to refuse the restitution of property when the penalty of confiscation was possible, Article 99 CCP was violating the presumption of innocence, the principles of necessity and proportionality of the penalty, the rights of the defence and the right to an effective remedy.[116] The *Cour de cassation* deemed any transmission to the *Conseil constitutionnel* unnecessary and ruled that the possibility to refuse a restitution was not a penalty and did not infringe the presumption of innocence. Besides, since Article 99 CCP provided

---

[109] For the rules regarding the restitution after a judgment, see *infra* part J.

[110] Art. 41-4(1) CCP.

[111] Art. 41-4(2) CCP.

[112] Art. 41-1(2) CCP.

[113] Art. 99(1) CCP.

[114] Art. 99(2) CCP.

[115] Art. 99(5) CCP.

[116] Crim., 16 July 2010, n° 10-90.083.

remedies against the investigating judge's order, the right to an effective remedy was not being violated.[117] Additionally, the parties and the third party cited by Article 99 CCP can appeal the decision before the *Cour de cassation.*[118]

Once the restitution of property is requested, it is up to the investigating judge to decide whether to grant the restitution. By exception, if the restitution can hinder the discovery of the truth or the safeguard of the rights of the parties, or if the restitution would be dangerous for persons or properties, the investigating judge must refuse to return the property.[119] When the confiscation of the property can be a penalty, the investigating judge may refuse the restitution, meaning that in that situation she can decide whether to return it.[120]

Among the properties that can be returned, special provisions have been introduced in 1999 to deal with live animals seized during investigations. According to Article 99-1 CCP the prosecutor, or the investigating judge in case of a judicial investigation, can decide what to do with the live animals seized. Yet, Article 99-1 CCP is silent regarding their restitution or the remedy against the decision and has been the object of a priority preliminary ruling on constitutionality. It was argued that by not providing any remedy against the decision, Article 99-1 CCP was violating the right to an effective remedy, the right to a fair trial, the adversarial principle, and the right to property. The *Conseil constitutionnel* rejected the arguments and said that the owner of the animal seized could ask for its restitution based on Articles 41-4 and 99 CCP because both those Articles dealt with "property seized" without distinguishing between the properties, so animals could be included. The remedies provided by Article 41-4 and 99 CCP also applied to animals seized, so by reading Article 99-1 CCP together with those two Articles, the *Conseil constitutionnel* concluded that Article 99-1 was not violating the fundamental rights of the owner. Consequently, regarding pre-trial restitutions, the rights of the owner, who can be a third party, are the same regardless of the property seized.

Apart from that, the fundamental rights of third parties are not taken into consideration when the investigating judge or the prosecutor take pre-trial measures. It seems fair since third parties are usually not affected by those measures. For instance, the *Cour de cassation* decided that the third party who is not a civil party, an assisted witness, or an accused, cannot voluntarily intervene before the Investigation Chamber ruling on custody on remand.[121]

---

[117] *Ibid.*

[118] Crim., 16 June 1992, n° 91-86.829. See Eyrignac (2011), para. 44.

[119] Art. 99(4) CCP.

[120] Art. 99(4) CCP.

[121] Crim., 16 June 2010, n° 09-88.638.

6 Third Parties and the Decision to Charge (or to Terminate the Proceedings)

Third parties are never involved in the decision to charge or to terminate the proceedings, nor are their interests taken into consideration.

7 Third Parties in Court Proceedings

7.1 The Right of Third Parties to Be Heard Fairly

Witnesses and experts, who can be included in a broad conception of third parties, are not concerned with the right to be heard fairly. In their case, it is actually a duty to help the court make a decision. Therefore, the right of third parties to be heard fairly only deals with third parties who have rights on or over the property. Indeed, at the end of the trial, the judge can order the confiscation of property. This additional sentence is possible if the offense tried is a felony or a misdemeanour punishable by at least a one-year imprisonment.[122] Being a penalty, confiscation should only affect the person condemned yet, depending on the property confiscated, it can also affect a third party who has rights on or over the property.

Up until December 2021, the third party could not assert her rights and her good faith before the jurisdiction ordering the confiscation and it led to Article 131-21 CC on confiscation being declared unconstitutional.[123] Consequently, the Act n° 2021-1729 of the 22 December 2021 rewrote Article 131-21 CC. The Article now reads that when the confiscation is considered by the court as a penalty, the penalty cannot be pronounced if it has not been made possible, for the owner whose quality is known or who claimed such a quality during the proceedings, to make observations on the confiscation to claim ownership and good faith.[124] In 2022, the *Cour de cassation* applied the new provisions to a case decided by the Court of appeal before the new law came into force. Indeed, the *Cour de cassation* struck the decision of confiscation made by the Court of appeal because the third party had not been able to be heard.[125]

The 2021 Act was completed by the Decree of the 23 December 2021 to detail the procedure to be followed before the Criminal Court[126] and the Assize Court.[127] First, if a confiscation is likely to be pronounced by the court, the public prosecutor must

[122] Art. 131-21(1) CC.

[123] On that point see para. 2.1.

[124] Art. 131-21(12) CC.

[125] Crim., 7 sept. 2022, n° 21-84.322,

[126] Art. D.45-2-1 CCP.

[127] Art. D.45-1-4 CCP.

inform, by any means, the owner whose quality is known or who claimed such a quality during the proceedings, of the trial date, at least 1 month before it starts.[128] This information is due even to the accused's spouse but, by exception, it is not due if the person is already summoned as a witness before the court.[129]

The notice must inform the third party that the confiscation of the property is possible and that she, or her lawyer, can make observations on the matter during the trial, notably to claim her ownership, if necessary, by bringing any supporting document, and her good faith.[130] Those observations can be made orally by the third party or her lawyer, but it can also be made in writing, by giving a document to the court Registry.[131] In that case, the presiding judge is the one reading the observations to the court. If the property has already been seized during the investigations, the third party can ask for its restitution, in which case it deals with her right to intervene in the proceedings.[132]

By exception, the provisions of Articles D.45-1-4 and D.45-2-1 CCP do not apply if the property is dangerous or noxious or if their detention is illegal[133] because in that case, confiscation is mandatory.[134] However, not informing the owner and not letting her make observations before the court is still cause for concern, because it means that the third party is deprived of the possibility to show that the property does not belong to the category of dangerous or noxious properties established by law or regulations or that her detention is not illegal.[135]

In any case, if the confiscation is decided by the court, the third party must be informed of the decision. She will then be able to ask for the restitution of the property by using a special remedy.[136]

7.2 *The Right of Third Parties Not to Be Questioned*

In the right of third parties not to be questioned, third parties must be understood broadly to include witnesses. Indeed, in French criminal procedure, apart from the accused, everyone can be questioned as a witness before a court and no one, except the accused, can refuse to be questioned.[137] This principle is the same during the

[128] Art. D.45-2-1(1) and D.45-1-4(4) CCP.
[129] Art. D.45-2-1(7) and D.45-1-4(7) CCP.
[130] Art. D.45-2-1(2) and D.45-1-4(2) CCP.
[131] Art. D.45.2-1(3) and D.45-1-4(3) CCP.
[132] See para. 7.4.
[133] Art. D.45-2-1(6) and D.45-1-4(7) CCP.
[134] Art. 131-21(7) CC.
[135] Hy (2022), p. 70.
[136] See para. 10.
[137] On the right of the accused to stay silent in French law, see Drevet (2019), p. 94.

judicial investigation, before the Criminal Court[138] and before the Assize Court[139]: any person summoned to be heard as a witness is obliged to appear, to swear an oath, and to make a statement.[140] If the witness refuses to appear before the court, the court can order the witness to be brought by the police.[141] The investigating judge can do the same during the judicial investigation.[142] As a result, a witness who defaults or who refuses either to take the oath or to make his statement may, on the recommendation of the prosecutor, be sentenced by the court up to a €3750 fine.[143] The penalty is even more severe if a person who has publicly declared knowing the authors of a felony, or a misdemeanour refuses to testify and answer questions put to him by the court. In that situation, the sentence is up to 1 year's imprisonment and up to a €15,000 fine.[144] In the same way, if someone who has evidence that a person provisionally detained or sentenced for a felony or misdemeanour is innocent, wilfully abstains from presenting the evidence before the authorities, she can be sentenced up to 3 years' imprisonment and up to a €45,000 fine.[145]

However, French criminal procedure provides two exceptions to the principle of mandatory testimony. First, if the witness is a journalist, she has a right not to be questioned, but that right is rather limited. Indeed, the only thing the journalist can do is refuse to reveal the sources of the information she collected while doing her job. This exception has been introduced in the French Code for criminal procedure in 2010 and applies during the judicial investigation,[146] before the Criminal Court[147] and before the assize court.[148] Apart from that, the journalist must make a statement and answer the questions asked by the investigating judge or the court and the *Cour de cassation* clearly stated that the exemption from testifying granted to journalists does not apply if the information has been collected outside the exercise of the job.[149]

Second, French criminal procedure provides for a larger exception when the witness is bound by professional secrecy. Indeed, Article 226-13 CC forbids the disclosure of information by a person entrusted with such a secret, either because of her position or profession, or because of a temporary function or mission. In that situation, there is a conflict between the obligation to testify imposed by the French

[138] In case the offence is qualified as a misdemeanour.

[139] In case the offence is qualified as a crime.

[140] Art. 109 CCP for the judicial investigation, Art. 437(1) CCP for the Criminal Court and 326 CCP for the Assize Court.

[141] Art. 439 CCP for the Criminal Court, 326(1) CCP for the Assize Court.

[142] Art. 109(3) CCP.

[143] Art. 438 CCP for the Criminal Court and 326(2) CCP for the Assize Court.

[144] Art. 434-12 CC.

[145] Art. 434-11 CC.

[146] Art. 109(2) CCP.

[147] Art. 437(2) CCP.

[148] Art. 326(3) CCP.

[149] Crim., 11 May 1959.

Code for criminal procedure and the professional secrecy imposed by the French criminal Code. To resolve the conflict, French courts make a difference between absolute secret and relative secret.

On the one hand, if the witness is bound by a relative secret, she cannot refuse to be questioned so she must answer questions asked by the court, even if it deals with the matter covered by the secret. For instance, specialized educators cannot refuse to be questioned.[150]

On the other hand, if the witness is bound by an absolute secret, she can refuse to testify on the matter covered by the secret. It is the case where the secret is necessary in the exercise of the profession.[151] For instance, the French *Cour de cassation* has decided that doctors,[152] priests[153] or lawyers in the exercise of the rights of the defence[154] are bound by an absolute secret.[155] However, the *Cour de cassation* also stated that if being bound by a professional secrecy exempts the witness from answering questions regarding the matter covered by the secret, it doesn't exempt the witness from swearing an oath.[156]

The two exceptions to the principle of mandatory testimony deal with the profession or activity exercised by the witness. Consequently, French criminal procedure does not exempt family members from their obligation to make a statement. It means that they too can be sentenced to a fine if they do not appear before the court or if they refuse to be questioned. However, the French Code for criminal procedure does provide a slight exception for family members in that they are exempt from swearing an oath. The exception applies before the Criminal Court[157] and before the Assize Court.[158] The exception also applies to minors under 16 years old, who are exempt from swearing an oath before the Criminal Court[159] and before the Assize Court.[160]

Regarding family members, the members exempted from swearing an oath are not the same before the Criminal Court and before the assize court. Indeed, Article 448 CCP states that before the Criminal Court, are exempt from swearing an oath the father, mother, or any ascendant of the defendant; the son, daughter, or any descendant of the defendant; brother or sister of the defendant; relatives by marriage of the first degree of the defendant; and the husband or wife of the defendant, even if they are divorced. The same list can be found in Article 335 CCP dealing with the

---

[150] Giacopelli and Joseph-Ratineau (2021), para. 24.

[151] *Ibid.*, para. 22.

[152] Crim., 8 April 1998, Dr. pénal 1998, n° 113, obs. Véron.

[153] Crim., 11 May 1959, Bull. crim. n° 253.

[154] Crim., 7 March 1989, Bull. crim. n° 109.

[155] For more examples see Giacopelli and Joseph-Ratineau (2021), para. 22.

[156] Crim., 11 June 1926, *DH* 1926, para. 378.

[157] Art. 448 CCP.

[158] Art. 335 CCP.

[159] Art. 447 CCP.

[160] Art. 335 7° CCP.

procedure before the assize court, but this list adds the civil partner and the common-law spouse of the defendant.

The difference between the two lists is explained by a decision of the French *Conseil constitutionnel*. Indeed, in 2020 the *Conseil constitutionnel* decided that by only mentioning the husband or wife, Article 335 CCP was violating the principle of equality before the law protected by Article 6 of the Declaration of the Rights of Man and of the Citizen of 1789.[161] The judges stated that the point of the dispensation of swearing an oath was to protect the spouse from any moral dilemma she would be exposed to if she had to choose between lying or staying silent and possibly testify against her spouse.[162] The judges then considered that the moral dilemma would exist, regardless of the legal status of the union between the witness and the defendant: the spouse, civil partner or common-law spouse would face the same dilemma.[163] Consequently, it would be unfair to make an exception only for married people. That is why the *Conseil constitutionnel* decided that the part of Article 335 CCP regarding "husband or wife" had to be abrogated. As a result, the legislator intervened by the end of 2020 to include civil partners and common-law spouses in the list of Article 335 CCP.[164] Regrettably, they forgot to add them to the list of Article 448 CCP. Consequently, a civil partner or common-law spouse is exempt from swearing an oath before the Criminal Court but not before the Assize Court.

7.3 The Protection of Non-parties in Court Activities Involving Formal Participants

Witness protection is the same during the trial as it is during the investigations.[165] Indeed, for the proceedings dealing with a crime or a misdemeanour punishable by at least 3 years' imprisonment, if the witness' hearing can put her life or health or that of her family members or her close relatives in serious danger, the investigating judge or the president of the court seized can decide, on her own motion or on the prosecutor or the parties' motion, that the witness' identity shall not be revealed during the trial or mentioned in any ordinance, judgement or appeal judgments.[166] This decision ordering the witness' confidentiality cannot be appealed[167] and disclosure of such an identity or of any information enabling the identification of

[161] Cons. const., 28 February 2020, n° 2019-828/829 QPC.

[162] Cons. const., 28 February 2020, para. 10.

[163] Cons. const., 28 February 2020, para. 11.

[164] Act n°2020-1672 of the 24 of December 2020.

[165] See *supra* 3.

[166] Art. 706-62-1(1) CCP.

[167] Art. 706-62-1(3) CCP.

location of the witness is punishable by 5 years' imprisonment and a fine of €75,000.[168]

However, to make sure that the rights of the defense are not violated, the hearing of the anonymous witness can happen at trial, in which case measures are put in place to ensure that the witness' voice is unrecognizable and that she can testify from a distance.[169]

Offenders cooperating with the authorities are also protected during the trial. Indeed, if she has been given an assumed identity,[170] the court can, on its own motion or on the parties' motion, hear the informant's testimony *in camera* or use the same measures as the one possible for the witness to ensure that the informant's voice is unrecognizable and that she can testify from a distance.[171]

Lastly, undercover agents are also protected during the trial. Indeed, according to Article 706-86 CCP, only the officer coordinating the undercover measure can be a witness during the trial, which means that the undercover agent is not supposed to be heard. Yet, the person put to trial can ask for a confrontation with the undercover agent if she is directly incriminated by the agent.[172] In that case, the same measures as the one possible for the witness to ensure that the informant's voice is unrecognizable and that she can testify from a distance shall be put into place.[173]

7.4 Can Third Parties Take Part in Court Activities?

By principle, only parties can take part in court activities. Yet, exceptions are made for three categories of third parties who can take part in court activities by intervening during the trial. In French criminal procedure, intervention means the right, for a third party, to exceptionally become a party to the trial, either voluntarily or if they are forced to.

First, third parties who have rights on or over the property can voluntarily intervene during the trial. Indeed, before the Criminal Court (misdemeanours),[174] the Court of Appeal,[175] the Assize Court (crimes)[176] and the police court (contraventions),[177] the third party can make a request for the restitution of the property. In

---

[168] Art. 706-62-1(5) CCP.

[169] Art. 706-61 CCP.

[170] See *supra* 3.

[171] Art. 706-63-1 CCP.

[172] Art. 706-86 CCP.

[173] *Ibid.*

[174] Art. 479 CC.

[175] Art. 484 CC.

[176] Art. 373 CC.

[177] Art. 543 CC.

that case, the request is made during the trial[178] and only the official records relating to the seizure of the Articles may be communicated to the third party.[179] It is then up to the court to decide, after hearing all the parties, whether to return the property. Article 373 CCP adds that the Assize Court may refuse restitution where it presents a danger for persons or property and even if no such provision is made for the proceedings before the Criminal Court, there is no reason why the same should not apply before this court since the judge can refuse to return the property.

However, in order for the procedure to be available, the property must have been seized during the investigations. On the contrary, if the property has not been seized but confiscation is contemplated by the court, we go back to the procedure provided for by Articles D.45-2-1 and D.45-1-4.[180]

Second, the legally responsible person, that is to say the person who can be responsible before a civil jurisdiction, can voluntarily intervene during the trial. Indeed, she is concerned with the result of the trial on the accused because if the accused is condemned, the legally responsible person will be the one who will have to compensate the damages caused.[181] Since the legally responsible person can intervene during the trial, she has the right to be represented by a lawyer.[182]

Third, the insurer can intervene during the trial but under stricter conditions. Indeed, the insurer's intervention is only possible in case of involuntary manslaughter or unintentional violence.[183] It means that for every other offence, intervention of the insurer is not possible, and she must stay a third party to the proceedings. Besides, intervention is only permitted for the victim's insurer, the accused and the legally responsible person.[184] Intervention can be voluntary, but it can also be forced, in which case it is not up to the insurer to decide whether she wants to take part in court activities. In both cases, the insurer must be represented by a lawyer.[185] The victim's insurer is always welcome to intervene at the trial but the same cannot be said for the others. Indeed, in order for the accused or legally responsible person's insurer to be able to intervene, the civil action must have been initiated by the victim.[186] Otherwise, the intervention is closed to the insurer who cannot take part in the court activities.

---

[178] See para. 5 for the restitution as a pre-trial measure and para. 10 for the restitution after the end of the trial.

[179] Art. 373(3) for the Assize Court and 479(2) CCP.

[180] See para. 7.1.

[181] Crim. 18 July 1924, see Redon (2022), para. 7.

[182] Art. 415 CCP.

[183] Art. 388-1(1) CCP.

[184] Art. 388-1(1) CCP.

[185] Art. 388-1(2) CCP.

[186] Crim., 12 October 1994, n° 93-85.113, *Bull. crim.* n°330.

8 The Protection of Third Parties in Decision-Making Processes

Strictly speaking, the decision-making process is only concerned with the parties, that is to say the accused and the victim. As a result, the interests of third parties are not taken into consideration when the judges make their decision. Yet, with the new provisions on confiscation and the right for the person having rights on or over the property to be heard by the court, it seems that, at least implicitly, judges will have to keep in mind the effect of a penalty of confiscation on third parties.

9 Third Parties in Appeal Proceedings

In French law, the right to an effective remedy has been consecrated by the *Conseil constitutionnel*, using Article 16 of the Declaration of the Rights of Man and of the Citizen according to which "any society in which the guarantee of rights is not assured, nor the separation of powers determined, has no Constitution".[187] Therefore, every private party has the right to have access to a judge,[188] which, in French criminal law, applies to the accused and the victim.[189] It also means that the parties have the right to appeal decisions. The 2014 decision consecrating the right to an effective remedy dealt not only with parties but also with third parties. Indeed, the case was about Article 41-4(4) CCP, which, at the time of the decision, authorized the prosecutor to destroy the objects seized, if they were no longer useful to the determination of the truth or if they were dangerous or illegally detained. No remedy was offered to the owner who could not appeal against the prosecutor's decision. In fact, no one was even informed of the decision. In the 2014 case, it was then argued that by not providing any remedy, Article 41-4(4) CCP was violating Article 16 of the Declaration of the Rights of Man and of the Citizen.[190] The *Conseil constitutionnel* agreed and ruled that by authorizing the destruction of the object, without informing the owner, the person having rights on or over the object and the accused, nor providing them with a remedy and the possibility to ask for the restitution, Article 41-1(4) CCP was violating the right to an effective remedy.[191] Consequently, Article 41-4(4) CCP was abrogated. By mentioning the owner or the person having rights on or over the object, the decision highlighted the idea that the right to an effective remedy doesn't belong only to the parties but can also belong to third parties.

---

[187] Cons. const., 11 April 2014, n° 2014-390 QPC, para. 3.

[188] Pradel (2019), pp. 381–382.

[189] See para. 1.

[190] Cons. const., 11 April 2014, para. 2.

[191] Cons. const., 11 April 2014, para. 5.

Yet, because, by definition, third parties are not directly concerned with the proceedings, their right to appeal is rather limited. Indeed, most of the time, they can only appeal the part of the decision that deals directly with their interests. For instance, the legally responsible person, that is to say the person who can be responsible before a civil jurisdiction, has the right to appeal a judgment made by the Criminal Court[192] or the Assize Court[193] but only regarding her civil interests. Similarly, the third-party payer can appeal a judgement before the Court of appeal only regarding her interests.[194]

It is a bit different for the insurer because if she is allowed to intervene or is joined as a party to the proceedings,[195] the insurer becomes a party. Therefore, the insurer can logically appeal the decision made by the court.[196] However, if the insurer has not intervened or has not been joined as a party to the proceedings, she cannot appeal the decision made by the court.[197] In that case, the insurer remains a third party. By exception, even as a third party, the insurer can appeal a decision if she has been condemned by the court of first degree.[198]

On the contrary, experts and witnesses do not have the right to appeal judgements.

The situation of the owner remains complicated, even though the French provisions on the subject have just been modified to make sure that their right to property is protected.[199] Nothing in the new provisions gives the owner the right to appeal a decision confiscating the object. Before the introduction of the new law, the French *Cour de cassation* had ruled that the owner of an object that had been confiscated could appeal the decision, even though he was not a party to the proceedings.[200] However, in the case, the owner had not been made aware of the trial, so she had not been able to intervene to have her case heard and that is why the *Cour de cassation* concluded that Article 6 of the European Convention on Human Rights had been violated. Since the new provisions created by the 2021 Act and 2021 decree do provide the owner with the right to intervene during the proceedings, the decision made by the *Cour de cassation* might not last. In that case, the owner would not be able to appeal decisions and their only solution would be the procedure provided by Article 710 CCP.[201]

---

[192] Art. 497(2) CCP.

[193] Art. 380-2(3) CCP.

[194] Crim., 28 November 1989, n° 89-81.771, *Bull.* n° 450.

[195] On that point see para. 7.4.

[196] Art. 388-1(3) CCP.

[197] Crim., 21 May 1986, n° 85-91.970, *Bull.* n° 164.

[198] Crim., 7 October 2003, n° 02-88.383, *Bull.* n° 181.

[199] On that point see para. 7.4.

[200] Crim., 29 November 2000, n° 99-85.366, *Bull* n°356; *RSC* 2001 374, obs. Bouloc; *RSC* 2001 410, obs. Commaret; *RTD com.* 2001. 530, obs. Bouloc; *D.* 2001. 746.

[201] On that point see para. 10.

However, quite recently, the *Cour de cassation* ruled, based on Article 6(1) ECHR, that in case of the execution, by a French court, of a decision of confiscation made by a foreign court, notification to the property's owner must be made by the French court. The owner then has 10 days to appeal the decision.[202]

10 *Res Judicata* and the Effects of Criminal Judgments upon Third Parties

Since the Act of December 2021, the rights of the person having rights on or over the property are more protected. Yet, she can still be deprived of her property at the end of the trial, even though she is not the accused, nor the person condemned. Two different situations can occur, depending on whether or not the sentence of confiscation has been pronounced.

On the one hand, if the confiscation is pronounced as a sentence, the person having rights on or over the property cannot appeal the judgment because she is not a party so, strictly speaking, she is not concerned by the sentence. Before the Decree of December 2021, nothing was provided by the Code for criminal procedure yet, because the person does have a right in or over the property confiscated, the judges decided that some sort of remedy must be offered. The French *Cour de cassation* ruled that the petition made by the owner not condemned to have her property returned was a procedural issue dealing with the execution of sentences, covered by Article 710 CCP.[203] In order for the procedure of Article 710 to be put in motion, the decision pronouncing the confiscation must be final. A decision becomes final once the remedies have been exhausted or once the deadlines to appeal the decision have passed. As a result, the third party who has rights on or over the property must wait for the parties to exercise all the remedies at their disposal (appeal before the Court of appeal and before the *Cour de cassation*) before being able to petition the court who pronounced the confiscation for the restitution of the property. The Decree of December 2021 consecrated this solution into the Code for criminal procedure at Article D.45-2-1*bis*, now Article D.45-2-1 since the Decree of April 2022[204] for the Criminal Court and at Article D.45-1-4 for the Assize Court. The third party who has rights on or over the property must now be informed of the decision of confiscation, by any means.[205]

On the other hand, if no confiscation has been pronounced as a sentence, the person having rights on or over the property remains a third party and has nothing to do with the judgement. Yet in some cases, the property might have been seized

[202] Crim., 5 January 2023, n° 21-87.017.

[203] Crim., 13 April 1999, *Bull.* n° 74; Crim., 7 May 2003, n° 02-80348; Crim., 4 November 2021, n° 21-80.487.

[204] Decree n° 2022-546 of 13 April 2022.

[205] Art. D. 45-2-1(5).

during the investigations so, even though no confiscation has been pronounced, the person may still be deprived of her property. If the court did not decide on the restitution of the property, the person having rights on or over it can ask the prosecutor for such a restitution.[206] In that situation we go back to the procedure of Article 41-4(1) CCP.[207]

References

Ambroise Casterot C (2020) Action civile, Répertoire de droit pénal et de procédure pénale. https://www.dalloz.fr

Brach Thiel D (2020) La protection des témoins. https://www.lexisnexis.com/en-int/products/juris-classeur fasc. 20

Drevet B (2019) Personal participation in criminal proceedings. France. In: Quattrocolo S, Ruggeri S (eds) Personal participation in criminal proceedings, a comparative study of participatory safeguards and in absentia trials in Europe. Springer, Cham, pp 93–121

Eyrignac L (2011) Restitution, aliénation et destruction des objets placés sous main de justice par les juridictions d'instruction. https://www.lexisnexis.com/en-int/products/juris-classeur, 20

Fonteix C (2022) Confiscation: encadrement de l'intervention du tiers propriétaire dans la procédure pénale. https://www.dalloz-actualite.fr

Giacopelli M, Joseph-Ratineau Y (2021) Témoin, Répertoire de droit pénal et de procédure pénale. https://www.dalloz.fr

Hy M (2021) La CJUE renforce la protection des tiers de bonne foi. https://www.lexbase.fr, 35

Hy M (2022) Le statut procédural du tiers propriétaire d'un bien susceptible d'être confisqué. https://www.dalloz-revues.fr/revues/AJ_Penal-33.htm

Peltier V (2017) Les preuves obtenues par IMSI-Catchers et les droits fondamentaux. In: Bonis E (ed) Les écoutes judiciaires en procédure pénale. Les colloques de l'ISCJ. Cujas, Paris, pp 49–58

Pradel J (2019) Procédure pénale, 20th edn. Cujas, Paris

Redon M (2022) Intervention, Répertoire de droit pénal et de procédure pénale. https://www.dalloz.fr

Segonds M (2021) Les droits des tiers. In: Ascensi L, Parizot R, Beauvais P (eds) La confiscation des avoirs criminels, nouveaux enjeux juridiques. Lgdj, Paris, pp 85–109

[206] Art. 41-4(1) CCP.

[207] On that point see para. 5.

Report from Hungary

Zsanett Fantoly and András Lichtenstein

Abstract This chapter discusses third parties in the Hungarian criminal proceedings, focusing on formal participants and specific categories such as financially interested parties, other interested parties, aides, authorized representatives, supporters, and vulnerable persons. The Hungarian criminal justice proceedings, governed by Act XC of 2017 on the Criminal Procedure, involve various participants.

Financially interested parties are those with ownership or legitimate access to properties subject to confiscation or seizure. *Other interested parties*, defined in 58, include individuals or entities whose rights or legal interests are affected by criminal procedure decisions. *Aides, authorized representatives, and supporters* play roles in representing and protecting the rights of defendants, victims, financially interested parties, and other interested parties.

The chapter also addresses *special treatment for vulnerable persons*, primarily *victims and witnesses* in criminal proceedings. Special treatment is based on personal characteristics, health, the nature of the crime, and relationships with other procedure participants. It aims to compensate for disadvantages and ensure the fullest exercise of rights during the criminal procedure.

Furthermore, extraordinary rules also apply specific measures *for persons under 18, victims of sexual offenses, and others.* The paper overall emphasizes the importance of considering the specific needs and vulnerabilities of individuals in the criminal justice system and highlights these characteristics in the Hungarian criminal procedure.

Z. Fantoly (✉) · A. Lichtenstein
Institute of Criminal Law and Criminal Science University of Szeged, Szeged, Hungary
e-mail: fantoly@juris.u-szeged.hu; lichten@juris.u-szeged.hu

S. Ruggeri et al. (eds.), *Third Parties in Criminal Proceedings*, Legal Studies in International, European and Comparative Criminal Law 10,
https://doi.org/10.1007/978-3-031-73970-5_4

1 Introduction. General Features of Domestic Criminal Justice

1.1 Formal Participants in Criminal Proceedings

As of today, the Hungarian criminal justice proceedings are formally governed by Act XC of 2017 on the Criminal Procedure (*2017. évi XC. törvény a büntetőeljárásról—CCP*, hereinafter referred to as: CCP), which entered into force on 1 July 2018. CCP consists of 23 Parts, 111 Chapters and lists the provisions over 878 Sections.

Academia and legislation alike most commonly categorize subjects of criminal procedure into two main categories: *authorities* and *participants*. Part Two of CCP concerns the authorities: the court (Chapter III), the Public Prosecutor's Office (Chapter IV), the investigating authority (Chapter V), and other criminal law enforcement authorities (Chapter VI). As for participants, their legal status is provided for by Part Three of CCP. An exhaustive list of all formal participants is given in Article 37 CCP as follows: in the criminal procedure the defendant, the defence counsel, the victim, the private prosecutor, the supplementary private prosecutor, the private party, the financially interested party, other interested parties, and the legal person affected by the procedure can take part.

1.2 Third Parties to Criminal Proceedings

Since the victim is regarded as a formal participant of the Hungarian criminal procedure, we focus on the introduction of the following third parties for the purposes of this research: the financially interested party, the other interested parties, the aides, the authorized representative, and the supporter. At the end of this chapter, however, we also introduce the special treatment available to vulnerable persons in the Hungarian criminal procedure.

According to Article 57 CCP, a *financially interested party* is a natural or legal person, which is the owner of a property that can be confiscated or seized, has the right to dispose of such properties, or has legitimate access and disposal over electronic data which may be ordered to be permanently inaccessible.[1]

CCP also includes the category of *other interested parties* for those not specifically mentioned above but having an interest other than financial nature as for the outcome of the criminal procedure. According to the legal definition set out in Article 58 CCP other interested parties are natural or legal persons whose rights or legal interests are affected by the decisions made in the criminal procedure, or those, who have certain rights or obligations regarding procedural acts provided for by the

[1] Art. 57(1) CCP.

CCP[2] The act also gives an exemplification of other interested parties, such as *the complainant, the witness, the persons affected by searches, the persons affected by data gathering, the persons involved in expert examinations, reviews or identifications, the aides, the experts and the expert advisors.*[3] Their rights and obligations mainly correspond to those of the financially interested parties.

The defendant, the victim, the financially interested party and the other interested parties are legally entitled to have *an aide* for the representation and protection of their rights and legal interests in the criminal procedure. An aide can be the legal representative or the guardian, an adult relative of the defendant, an official representative of the consul for foreign defendants, victims and witnesses, the spouse or the partner of a person under involuntary mental treatment, an adult caretaker of a minor, an authorized representative, a supporter, an adult designated by the victim and complainant, a lawyer acting on behalf of the witness, an uninterested adult present at searches or designated by the searched person, a trustee on delivery, a protection agent, or a litigation friend.[4] The aide must not be under the age of 18, banned from public matters or under guardianship.[5]

Unless otherwise provided by the CCP, the victim, the financially interested party and the other interested party may proceed through *an authorized representative.* The authorized representative bears the rights of the represented party. An authorized representative can be a lawyer, a law office, a relative, an employee (if the represented is a legal person), a public benefit organization for the victims, or other legally specified persons.[6] A written letter of proxy is required shall be attached to the first brief submitted by the authorized representative.[7] As for the legal status of an authorized representative acting on behalf of the defendant, it is more limited than the above both for the representative as well as regarding the cases. The defendant can only rely on the authorized representation of lawyers or law offices, or an adult relative. The proxy is limited to access to copies of the case file and to the administration of bail or other securities.[8]

As a further third party, *a supporter* is appointed by the public guardianship authority, if the victim, the financially interested party and the other interested party are subject to supported decision-making. The supporter can take part in the criminal procedure.[9] The supporter may be present at each procedural act with the supported person (including closed trials), but his absence is not an obstacle to the procedure. He can discuss with the supported person in order to support his statement but cannot make a statement on his own on behalf of the supported person. As for his presence

---

[2] Art. 58(1) CCP.

[3] Art. 58(2) CCP.

[4] Art. 59(1) CCP.

[5] Art. 59(2) CCP.

[6] Art. 61 CCP.

[7] Art. 62 CCP.

[8] Art. 64 CCP.

[9] Art. 65 CCP.

and the costs thereof, it does not constitute criminal costs and should be advanced and born solely by the supported person.[10]

1.3 Vulnerable Persons and Special Treatment in Criminal Proceedings

Vulnerable persons, primarily victims and witnesses, may qualify for special treatment in the criminal procedure for the enhanced protection of their interests. As per the legal definition,

> The victim or the witness is qualified for special treatment based on their personal characteristics or the nature and circumstances of the criminal offence if they are hindered in understanding and making themselves understood, exercising of the rights and fulfilling obligations, or in their effective participation in criminal procedure.[11]

Exceptionally, certain measures in connection with special treatment can be applied to the defendant, the defence, experts, consultants, financially interested parties, their aides and others as well. By codifying this secondary group of persons, practically anyone who is hindered in exercising his rights or fulfilling his obligations may request certain humane, protective measures. The subjects of this secondary group, however, are not entitled to the full range of special treatment, but a limited extent of measures, based on their legal status in the procedure.

The special treatment can be based on (1) the age of the person concerned; (2) his state of health; (3) the extremely violent nature of the criminal offence committed; and (4) the relationship between the person concerned and other persons subject to the criminal procedure.[12] The aim of this institutional system is to compensate disadvantages resulting from age and other circumstances, or the nature of the committed crime and guarantee the full exercise of rights for the person involved during the whole process of the criminal procedure. The application of certain measures can be implemented if they are effectively justified (*necessity*); and to an extent and in a form that is in accordance with the level of hindrance (*proportionality*). A further requirement is that these measures—according to the main rule—may not result in the infringement of the rights of other participants in the procedure, especially those of the defendant, the defence, and the participation right of the victim. Special treatment can be ordered *ex officio* or upon the motion of the person concerned (or his aide).

Special treatment is granted by statute without a separate ruling in the following three cases: (1) for persons under 18 years of age; (2) for disabled or potentially

[10] Art. 66 CCP.

[11] Art. 81(1) CCP.

[12] Art. 81(2) CCP.

disabled persons; (3) for victims of sexual offences.[13] Some measures of special treatment may be refused by the vulnerable person, but not if the special treatment is statutory obligatory.[14] Furthermore, refusal is also excluded by CCP in certain procedural activities, e.g., sound and video recordings of any procedural activities requiring the participation of victims and witnesses under the age of 18. Special treatment may be reviewed by the court, the public prosecutor's office and the investigating authority without any legal constraint concerning its duration or formal requirements.[15] As a result of the revision, special treatment may be terminated by the acting authority, if its conditions are not fulfilled anymore. During the revision, the authority may neglect certain—formerly applied—measures or decide on introducing new measures. It is also possible that special treatment which was formerly refused is ordered by the authority based on the changes concerning the person himself or his living conditions.

Measures of special treatment can be divided into two main categories: the so-called humane measures facilitating effective due process and exercising rights (1); and witness protection measures (2).

The system of humane measures belonging to special treatment is based on progressiveness. Its first level of individualization contains measures that ensure the exercise of rights and considerate treatment of the concerned person as per Article 85 CCP. Based on these comprehensive provisions, the court, the public prosecutor's office and the investigating authority apply different measures to facilitate the exercise of rights, the fulfillment of obligations and the considerate treatment of persons requiring special treatment—with special regard to the purpose of the procedure. In this respect, the starting point is to ensure that the concerned person should be able to exercise his rights codified in CCP and fulfill his obligations despite the hindrance, which establishes his special treatment. The legislator requires particular attention and utmost caution of the authorities during procedural activities in the case of vulnerable persons eligible for special treatment. Particular attention has to be especially applied when keeping contact with persons requiring special treatment, and utmost carefulness is also required regarding the private life of such persons. Among the use of humane measures, the possibility of making sound and video recording of procedures requiring the presence of the person concerned has an important role, even if taking minutes parallelly may not be neglected. It does not, however, facilitate the work of the investigative authority, since police officers have to make recordings and take the minutes parallelly, which may result in prolonged procedure; and repeated interruptions and questions may distract the victim. Despite all these problems, this procedure is widely used, because although it is only an option for persons under 18 years old, once it is decided it may not be refused. Making sound and video recordings is obligatory in the case of victims of crime

[13] Art. 82 CCP.

[14] Art. 83 CCP.

[15] Art. 84 CCP.

against sexual morality, and sound and video recordings are ordered ex officio in the case of illiterate persons.

As for *protective measures belonging to special treatment,* CCP regulates the use of protective measures, as the second pillar of measures applicable in the case of persons qualified for special treatment according to the principles of progressiveness, proportionality and necessity. The application of relevant measures is bound to certain conditions by the law; these are the protection of the life, physical integrity and personal freedom of the person concerned, and to guarantee that the person concerned can take part in the procedure without being intimidated and manipulated. Protective measures may be applied parallel with humane measures; and in certain cases, they may infringe the procedural rights of other persons (e.g.: the defendant, the defence) participating in the procedure. According to Article 86 CCP (a non-exhaustive list) the protective measures contain the use of telecommunication devices (video conference) and the technical distortion of characteristics suitable for identification. A further protective measure is the limitation of the right of the presence of the defendant and the defence during a given procedural activity; or the right to make motions for questions instead of giving them the opportunity of asking directly. The confrontation of vulnerable persons can also be disregarded for their protection. The most common protective measure is confidential data management, which can even be applied retroactively. The most effective forms of protective measures are the ones of witness protection: providing personal protection, witnesses placed under special protection, or involvement in the Protection Programme.

Regarding *extraordinary rules concerning measures of special treatment,* as already mentioned, special treatment is a statutory obligation without any further ruling in three cases. There are extraordinary rules attached to these cases.

As far as possible, procedural activities requiring the presence of persons under the age of 18 have to be recorded (obligatory if the person is under 14 years of age), furthermore a forensic psychologist may be present at that procedural activity. The use of a child-friendly interrogation room is obligatory for persons under 14 years of age, and the defendant and the defence may not be present at the premises (except for when they proposed the interrogation of the witness under 14). Persons under the age of 18 must not be controlled by lie detection instruments[16]; and their confrontation is only allowed with their consent[17] (in case of witnesses under 14 years old confrontation is excluded). As a general rule, procedural activities requiring the cooperation of persons under the age of 14, may only be conducted if the evidence obtained from it cannot be substituted by anything else. As far as possible, procedural activities shall be conducted by the same person on every occasion during the investigation.[18]

Regarding victims of sexual offences, the general rule is that the procedural activity has to be conducted by the same person and of the same sex on every

[16] Art. 87(2) CCP.
[17] Art. 87(3) CCP.
[18] Art. 88 CCP.

occasion during the investigation. (CCP allows exceptions only if the presence of the same person of the same sex cannot be provided and the procedural activity cannot be neglected.) In the case of sexual crime, the confrontation of the victim may only be ordered or may only take place with the consent of the victim regardless of his/her age. If the victim of sexual crime is under 18 years old, the defendant and the defence may not be present in person at any procedural activities requiring the presence of the victim.[19] (Their presence of the concerned parties may be guaranteed by the use of telecommunication devices.) The limitation to the obligation of the personal presence of the victim also applies at procedures by a designated judge or requested court. (It is however not applicable in cases where the presence of the victim is not obligatory, but the victim wishes to exercise the right of presence.) As a main rule, the procedural activity has to be conducted at premises suitable for this case; and sound and video recordings have to be made by the authorities.

2 Fundamental Rights and Safeguards of Third Parties

2.1 Constitutional Law

Article XXVIII Subsection 1 of the Fundamental Law of Hungary states that everyone shall have the right to have any indictment brought against him or her, or his or her rights and obligations in any court action, adjudicated within a reasonable time in a fair and public trial by an independent and impartial court established by an Act. This latter fundamental right applies not only to the defendant, but everyone, including any third party affected by the criminal procedure. Furthermore, Subsection 7 constitutionally provides the right to a legal remedy, as everyone shall have the right to seek legal remedy against any court, authority or other administrative decision which violates his or her rights or legitimate interests.[20] Involving not only rights, but also legitimate interest, this provision can further be interpreted to apply to non-formal participants in criminal procedure.

Regarding the protection of fundamental rights, CCP provides a general clause for the respect of human dignity, freedom, and security. As a safeguard, the restriction of fundamental rights in criminal procedure is only allowed within the proper legal framework provided by CCP Further to this, a *necessity and proportionality requirement* is also attached, meaning that fundamental rights can only be restricted if, the intended aim cannot be reached by a less severe act or measure.[21]

[19] Art. 89 CCP.

[20] Article XXVIII of the Fundamental Law of Hungary (*Magyarország Alaptörvénye, XXVIII. cikk*).

[21] Art. 2 CCP.

2.2 Domestication of International Law

Further to the most common aspects of international law on the domestic criminal procedure (e.g., acknowledging and providing rules for international criminal offences, international and diplomatic immunity, international arrest warrants, etc.), CCP also provides the possibility of an extraordinary legal remedy against final and binding domestic criminal law judgements in form of a *review (felülvizsgálat)* based on a decision of an international human rights organ (most typically the European Court of Human Rights), if the international forum decides that the domestic criminal procedure or the judgement violated the human rights.[22] However, it must also be noted, that this typically affects the defendant,[23] and the initiation for such review is limited among the third parties to those acting on his behalf (legal representative, spouse, partner, or after the death of the defendant further relatives).[24]

2.3 Implementation of EU Law

Article 878 CCP provides for compliance with EU law and gives an exhaustive list of all 34 EU legal instruments that have been implemented by the CCP In regard to third parties, these most importantly include the following:

- Council Framework Decision 2003/577/JHA of 22 July 2003 on the execution in the European Union of orders freezing property or evidence;
- Council Framework Decision 2005/212/JHA of 24 February 2005 on Confiscation of Crime-Related Proceeds, Instrumentalities and Property;
- Council Framework Decision 2009/299/JHA of 26 February 2009 amending Framework Decisions 2002/584/JHA, 2005/214/JHA, 2006/783/JHA, 2008/909/JHA and 2008/947/JHA, thereby enhancing the procedural rights of persons and fostering the application of the principle of mutual recognition to decisions rendered in the absence of the person concerned at the trial;
- Directive 2010/64/EU of the European Parliament and of the Council of 20 October 2010 on the right to interpretation and translation in criminal proceedings;
- Directive 2012/13/EU of the European Parliament and of the Council of 22 May 2012 on the right to information in criminal proceedings;
- Directive 2012/29/EU of the European Parliament and of the Council of 25 October 2012 establishing minimum standards on the rights, support and

[22] Art. 648(4) CCP.

[23] Lichtenstein (2018), pp. 324–325.

[24] Art. 651(2)(d)-(f) CCP.

protection of victims of crime, and replacing Council Framework Decision 2001/220/JHA;

- Directive (EU) 2016/680 of the European Parliament and of the Council of 27 April 2016 on the protection of natural persons with regard to the processing of personal data by competent authorities for the purposes of the prevention, investigation, detection or prosecution of criminal offences or the execution of criminal penalties, and on the free movement of such data, and repealing Council Framework Decision 2008/977/JHA.

3 Third Parties in Criminal Inquiries

Traditionally, Hungarian criminal procedure used to be divided into two parts: the investigation and the court procedure, without a distinction between preliminary inquiry and prosecution.[25]

With the entry into force of CCP in 2018, the investigation now consists of two phases divided by reasonable suspicion: first, the *exploration (felderítés)*, followed by the *examination (vizsgálat)*.[26] Whereas the exploration mainly bears the characteristics of a general police and law enforcement investigation, the examination is more similar to a prosecutorial inquiry. There is no judicial investigation in Hungarian criminal law, most judicial activities and court tasks are typically limited to the decision about certain coercive measures (e.g., arrest) and approval of certain undercover measures.[27] Provisions regarding the legal status of third parties in criminal inquiries are still not expressly determined by the stages of the procedure, therefore we are hereby dealing with the investigation as a whole.

During the investigation, the *victim* most importantly shall have the right to be present at procedural measures whereby the presence of the suspect is also allowed. This, however, only applies with the statutory restriction that the procedural measure must be related to the criminal offence committed against the victim. His right to access to the case file has the same legal character, since the victim may only gain access to the documents of the investigation in connection with the criminal offence committed against him.[28] Furthermore, the victim has the right to have an aide,[29] express his civil claim during the investigation,[30] and make a victim's personal

[25] Karsai and Szomora (2015), p. 147.

[26] Art. 348(2) CCP.

[27] Art. 464 CCP.

[28] Fantoly and Budaházi (2020), pp. 234–235.

[29] Art. 51(1)(g) CCP.

[30] Art. 51(1)(h) CCP.

impact statement any time during the procedure.[31] The victim can also waive his rights.[32]

As for the *financially interested party*, he can also be present at procedural acts affecting his property,[33] has the right to being informed about coercive measures affecting his property,[34] being informed about his rights and obligations by the public prosecutor and the investigating authority.[35] He shall also have access to the case file with a similar statutory restriction as the victim,[36] and is also entitled to have an aide.[37] For the rights of *other interested* (third) *parties*, the same rule shall apply accordingly.[38]

Regarding legal remedies during the investigation, third parties, such as the victim, the financially interested party and the other interested parties have *the right to file a complaint* against decisions of the public prosecutor's office or the investigating authority.[39]

4 Scientific Developments, New Technologies and the Safeguards of Third Parties

With the entry into force of CCP, the use of new, covert investigation techniques and the procedure thereof has been recodified. CCP has introduced the legal term of *preparatory procedure (előkészítő eljárás)*, which is already a part of the criminal procedure, however, it precedes the main, formal investigation.[40] The aim of the preparatory procedure is to establish whether the suspicion of a criminal offence persists,[41] as the suspicion is a prerequisite of the initiation of a formal investigation. Thus, a preparatory procedure can be carried out, if the data and information available are not sufficient enough for the establishment of the suspicion, but it is reasonably presumed that following the preparatory procedure a decision can be reached on the suspicion.[42] The preparatory procedure can last up to 6, or in some cases up to a maximum of 9 months.[43] During the preparatory procedure, for

[31] Art. 51(3) CCP.

[32] Art. 51(3) CCP.

[33] Art. 57(2)(b) CCP.

[34] Art. 57(2)(c) CCP.

[35] Art. 57(2)(d) CCP.

[36] Art. 57(2)(f) CCP.

[37] Art. 57(2)(g) CCP.

[38] Art. 57(3) CCP.

[39] Art. 369(1) CCP.

[40] Fantoly and Budaházi (2020), p. 224.

[41] Art. 340(1) CCP.

[42] Art. 340(2) CCP.

[43] Art. 344 CCP.

establishing suspicion, the authorities can use *undercover tools*.[44] Undercover tools are now categorized depending on the required approval for their use. *No special (prosecutorial or judicial) approval is needed* for the use of e.g., secretly cooperating persons, secret information gathering and control, or hidden surveillance.[45] *A prosecutorial approval* is needed for monitoring payments, pretend purchases, surveillance with consent, the use of undercover agents and for the use of aliases (including fictitious business names, dummy operations, documents, etc.).[46] The most severe undercover tools, seriously affecting fundamental rights, require *judicial approval*. The following fall into this category: secret monitoring of information systems, secret searches, secret surveillance of places, secret reconnaissance of post, and wiretapping.[47] A procedural safeguard is that after completing the use of judicially approved undercover tools, any technical instruments used, or data planted must be removed immediately without delay.[48] Because of the nature and secrecy of the preparatory procedure, *a wide range of third parties might be exposed to the undercover tools* (e.g. anyone having telephone calls with someone affected by wiretapping). It can also happen, that the preparatory procedure concludes the lack of suspicion, and the procedure is terminated, thus, no formal investigation follows. Bearing these scenarios in mind, a further *procedural safeguard* is attached to judicially approved undercover tools. The person affected by the judicial approval must be informed of the use of undercover tools following the preparatory procedure, if no formal investigation has been launched, or following the termination of the investigation, if the person was not interrogated as a suspect, or was not charged with a criminal offence.[49] It must also be noted however that this safeguard only applies if it does not hurt the interests of further secret information gathering.

5 Pre-trial Measures and the Protection of Fundamental Rights of Third Parties

At the authorization of any coercive pre-trial measures, and during the execution thereof, the fundamental rights must only be limited to the utmost necessary excess and period. A more severe coercive measure can only be authorized if the desired outcome cannot be reached by the means of a lesser measure or other procedural act. All coercive measures must be executed in a gentle manner, with respect to the other, unaffected fundamental rights of the concerned person. Any other persons must only be affected by the coercive measure as it is absolutely necessary. All coercive

[44] Art. 341 CCP.
[45] Art. 215 CCP.
[46] Arts. 216–225 CCP.
[47] Art. 231 CCP.
[48] Art. 233 CCP.
[49] Art. 251(1) CCP.

measures restricting personal freedoms and property shall be executed during the day between 6 am and 10 pm, if possible. It must be made sure that during the execution of a coercive measure no private details or personal data of the concerned come public knowledge outside the criminal procedure. Also, all unnecessary harm and damage shall be avoided when executing such measures.[50]

Pre-trial coercive measures according to CCP fall into either of the two following categories: coercive measures affecting personal freedom and coercive measure affecting property. A coercive measure affecting personal freedom can only be ordered and executed against the defendant and not third parties. It is worth mentioning, however, that the victim has the right to demand to be notified if the defendant has been released or escaped from pre-trial detention,[51] or from preliminary involuntary mental treatment.[52]

For this country report, we limit ourselves to the more relevant coercive measures affecting the property and possible third parties. These are the following: search (of property) and body search. Further coercive measures affecting property include seizure, sequestration, and temporary inaccessibility to electronic data.

A search of property is the search of an apartment, other premises or vehicle in the interest of a resultful outcome of the criminal procedure. A search can be ordered by the court, public prosecutor's office, or the investigating authority, if it is presumed to lead to the apprehension of the perpetrator, the recovery of the traces, the finding of evidence, the finding of objects subject to seizure, or the analysis of IT systems or data storage.[53] As a general rule, the search shall be executed in the presence of the owner, occupant, possessor or user of the property or vehicle. However, their presence can be substituted by the defence counsel, representative or an adult authorized by them. If no such person is present, an independent adult unaffected by the case shall be designated and present. Except for the defendant, any person obstructing the search may be fined.[54]

A body search involves the search of a person's clothing and body with the aim of finding evidence, or other objects subject to seizure. Any object found during a body search can further be examined. A body search can be ordered not only against the defendant, but third parties as well: anybody to be reasonably presumed to possess evidence, or other objects subject to seizure can be searched. For a body search, no court order is required, it can either be ordered by the public prosecutor's office or by the investigating authority.[55] If the aim of the body search is the finding of a certain defined object, the person must first be called to hand it over. If no voluntary handover follows, the body search can be carried on.[56] For the protection of the

[50] Art. 271 CCP.

[51] Art. 51(5)(a) CCP.

[52] Art. 51(5)(d) CCP.

[53] Art. 302 CCP.

[54] Art. 305 CCP.

[55] Art. 306 CCP.

[56] Art. 307(1) CCP.

interests of the person concerned, the procedure must not be carried out in an indecent manner, and body cavities can only be examined by a doctor (other medical staff might be present). For further protection of personal interests, an adult present at the scene designated by the searched person can also be present during the search, given that this does not harm the interests of the procedure. As a general rule (*«the double-gender standard»—kettős nemi szabály*), the body search can only be carried out by a person of the same sex as the searched person, and also only persons of the same sex may be present. Exceptions apply to doctors carrying out body cavity examinations, medical staff present, and to the adult present designated by the searched person: they might be of the opposite sex. A further exception concerns non-delayable cases, where the double-gender standard can be set aside.[57] However, what constitutes a non-delayable case is rather unclear and mostly lies at the authorities' discretion. Still, the violation of the rule is almost unheard of, as it might lead to a breach of evidence law (unlawfully obtained evidence) and thus, result in the corruption of the procedure.

6 Third Parties and the Decision to Charge (or to Terminate the Proceedings)

The Hungarian criminal procedure is still governed by *procedural legality* and the *ex officio principle*, thus in most cases, a mandatory prosecution prevails, and the public prosecutor has a (state) monopoly to decide on prosecution, including the decision to charge or to terminate the procedure. Rules of procedure are in place to ensure fair procedural principles and necessary exceptions are set. Still, faulty prosecutorial decisions may happen. Among those, the most damaging for social justice, the victims themselves, and third parties may be the cases in which contrary to all legal criteria being fulfilled, the decision not to prosecute is made. Therefore, there is an inevitable need for effective means of correcting prosecutorial monopoly and decisions. To have such methods available in the national rules of procedure is also a legal obligation of all EU Member States. The victim's right to a review of a decision not to prosecute is set out in Article 11 of Directive 2012/29/EU. Still, the implementation and the instruments available vary greatly in the national criminal procedures of the member states. In Hungary, the so-called supplementary private prosecution is intended to offer a remedy for such situations.[58] The victim may act as a *supplementary private prosecutor* (*pótmagánvádló*) if the public prosecutor's office or the investigating authority has refused the criminal complaint; terminated the procedure; or the public prosecutor's office revoked the indictment.[59] This allows the victim to act as a substitute to the public prosecutor and provides them

[57] Art. 307(2)–(5) CCP.

[58] Lichtenstein (2021), pp. 73–85.

[59] Art. 787 CCP.

with a limited legal status similar to that of the public prosecutor. Thus, a certain possibility is given to the victim as a third party regarding the decision to charge or terminate the procedure, although its parity and effectiveness are questionable due to the supplementary private prosecutor's relative lack of power and access to investigation tools, legal knowledge and criminal justice infrastructure.

7 Third Parties in Court Proceedings

7.1 The Right of Third Parties to Be Heard Fairly

In court proceedings, third parties in general have the right to produce evidence, make motions and comments.[60] Further to that, the victim has the right to file a so-called *civil law claim* (*polgári jogi igény*) for damages, release of property or financial claim suffered as a direct result of the criminal offence. If doing so, the victim is called a *private party* (*magánfél*).[61] The civil claim can also be launched verbally at the preparatory hearing or at the first trial.[62]

At final pleadings, after the closing arguments of the public prosecutor, the victim, the private party and the financially interested party have the right to make a statement.[63] The victim can state their case similar to a victim's personal statement, and also can express if he wishes the defendant to be found guilty and to be punished.[64] If the victim is also acting as a private party (see above), he can launch further motions regarding the civil law claim. If he is not present at trial, the civil claim must be read out in court from the case file.[65] The financially interested party is also given the opportunity to launch final motions regarding his rights and legal interests. After the statements by third parties, the closing arguments for the defence follow.[66] The last word is given to the accused.[67] As a rule of thumb and a safeguard of fairness, final pleadings, statements and closing arguments cannot be revoked nor interrupted.[68]

---

[60] Art. 51(1)(a), Art. 57(2)(a), Art. 58(3) CCP.

[61] Art. 55 CCP.

[62] Art. 500(3) CCP, Art. 517(2)(b) CCP.

[63] Art. 541(1), 543(1) CCP.

[64] Art. 543(2) CCP.

[65] Art. 543(3) CCP.

[66] Art. 544 CCP.

[67] Art. 545 CCP.

[68] Art. 546 CCP.

7.2 *The Right of Third Parties Not to Be Questioned*

Under Hungarian criminal procedure law, there persists a general obligation for witnesses to provide testimonies.[69] Anyone can be questioned (interrogated) as a witness, who may have information regarding evidence.[70] This obligation is even a protected legal interest under substantive criminal law in Hungary, as the Hungarian Criminal Code (Act C of 2012—hereinafter referred to as: Btk.) entails a specific criminal offence for unlawful refusal to testify: Any witness who in criminal proceedings unlawfully refuses to testify before the court upon being duly advised is guilty of a misdemeanour and shall be punished by confinement.[71]

Yet, as for the right of third parties not to be questioned, CCP sets some exemptions and limits to the obligations of giving evidence: the most significant of which are the obstacles to providing testimony.[72] *In case of absolute obstacles (i.e., prohibitions) of testimony,* the person concerned must not give evidence even if he wants to, because his interrogation is prohibited by law.[73] Any testimony given despite the ban may not be used in evidence. *In case of relative obstacles (exemptions) of testimony*, it depends on the decision of the witness whether to testify or not. The witness may decide not to give a testimony, but if he decides to testify, he has to tell the truth.

As per Article 170 CCP, categories of absolute obstacles or testimonial prohibitions are the following: the defence counsels' secrecy, the religious confidentiality, one's physical or mental state, or the secrecy and confidentiality obligations for classified data.[74] Persons concerned by any of these must not be interrogated as witnesses.

As for relative obstacles, grounds of refusal provide exemptions to the obligation to testify. Testifying may be refused by:

1. the relative of the defendant[75];
2. any person who otherwise would accuse himself or any of his relatives of a criminal offence[76];
3. someone who has a professional confidentiality obligation either as a consequence of his job or public appointment—except for the case of confidentiality

---

[69] Art. 168(2) CCP.

[70] Art. 168(1) CCP.

[71] Btk. 277.

[72] Art. 169(1) CCP.

[73] Art. 170 CCP.

[74] Herke (2018), p. 44.

[75] Art. 171 CCP.

[76] Art. 172(2) CCP. In this case, however, the witness may not refuse to give answers in general, but he may refuse to give answers to those questions by which he would accuse himself or a relative of a criminal offence; but he has the obligation of giving evidence—together with the obligation of telling the truth—in the case of any other questions.

regarding classified data—may refuse to give evidence, if otherwise, he would breach his professional confidentiality obligation[77];
4. media providers and their employees, who—by giving evidence—might reveal the identity of their informants.[78]

Whether the refusal to testify is lawful, is up to the court, public prosecutor's office, or the investigating authority to decide. If the refusal is found lawful, no further questions can be asked to the witness and he cannot be confronted, except if he later decides otherwise and wishes to give a testimony.[79]

7.3 The Protection of Non-parties in Court Activities Involving Formal Participants

A closed handling of personal data can be ordered by the court, public prosecutor's office or investigating authority upon the motion of the victim, financially interested party, other interested parties, or their aids. This data protection order involves their names, birth names, place and date of birth, mother's maiden name, nationality, ID number, address, notification address, residence, and electronic address.[80] In the case of *venerable persons*, closed handling of personal data can also be ordered *ex officio*, without a motion.[81] Confidential data is only accessible to criminal justice authorities within the procedure, and without consent can only be forwarded to the victim support office and the probation services.[82]

When dealing with vulnerable persons, authorities are required to provide special protection concerning personal data making them eligible for special treatment, especially data in connection with health status; furthermore, authorities have to promote that the person concerned may avail himself the help of an assistant during the procedural activities. During the planning and executing procedural activities authorities have to act with special regard to the personal needs of the person involved and they have to abstain from performing activities requiring the personal presence of the concerned person. If the personal presence of the person concerned may not be bypassed during a given procedural activity, the procedure has to be prepared in a way that it can be performed without repetition. A further task of the criminal justice authorities is to ensure that during the procedural activities and at the place of the procedure the person concerned does not needlessly meet other persons participating in the criminal procedure, especially if special treatment is based on the

---

[77] Art. 173 CCP.
[78] Art. 174 CCP.
[79] Art. 175 CCP.
[80] Art. 99(1) CCP.
[81] Art. 99(2) CCP.
[82] Art. 99(7) CCP.

relationship between the person concerned and these persons. Furthermore, authorities have to perform the procedural activities at premises designed or converted for this special purpose, provided the exercise of rights and fulfilment of obligations of the person concerned may not be ensured with other measures. It must be noted that Decree No. 34/2015 (XI. 10.) IM concerning design and control of police premises dedicated to the interrogation of the defendant or witnesses under the age of 14, or victims entitled to special treatment, prescribes similar requirements concerning the design, furnishing and equipment of interrogation premises.

7.4 Can Third Parties Take Part in Court Activities?

As a rule of thumb, trials and public hearings are open to the public and thus anyone can take part in them—except for people under the age of 14, and people under the age of 18, who might be excluded.[83]

The CCP sets out the legal framework for *a closed trial* as well, the main reasons of which are as follows: for moral reasons, for the protection of vulnerable persons and for the protection of classified and other protected data. A closed trial can be ordered *ex officio* by the court, or upon motion of—among others—the victim, financially interested party or other interested parties.[84] Even in case of a closed session, the victim can designate someone present to take part in the closed session.[85]

If the *victim or the witness* are *foreign nationals*, they can move the court to grant to allow the presence of their state's *consular representative* at the court activities.[86]

As for taking part in the *evidentiary procedure*, the victim, the financially interested party, and the expert can ask the defendant questions during his interrogation.[87] The same third parties can also ask the witness questions.[88] Furthermore, the victim and the financially interested party are also allowed to ask the expert questions.[89]

[83] Art. 436(1)–(3) CCP.

[84] Art. 436(4) CCP.

[85] Art. 437(3) CCP.

[86] Art. 427(4) CCP.

[87] Art. 523(4) CCP.

[88] Art. 526(4) CCP.

[89] Art. 529(1) CCP.

8 The Protection of Third Parties in Decision-Making Processes

As for the interests of persons other than formal participants in the judicial decision-making, the *interests of children* are worth mentioning. A peculiarity of the CCP is that it allows for the criminal courts to cease parental custody. Upon the motion of the public prosecutor, the (criminal) court can terminate the parental rights of the accused (in line with the Hungarian Civil Code), if the accused has been found guilty of a deliberate criminal offence against his child. The public prosecutor's motion can be initiated by the child or the other parent.[90] Other than this, no specific formal requirements are set for the protection of non-formal participants of the case. Yet, as we have mentioned, this is explained by the fact that the scope of formal parties in the Hungarian criminal procedure is quite wide, including the other interested party.

9 Third Parties in Appeal Proceedings

Under Hungarian criminal procedure law, the following third parties are entitled to launch an appeal, and thus, granted legal remedies in the appeal proceeding:

- the heir of the defendant, if a civil claim was granted.[91]
- the spouse or partner of the defendant, if the defendant was ordered involuntary mental treatment.[92]
- the private party, if the civil claim was decided upon.[93]
- the financially interested party against rulings concerning him.[94]

The financially interested party most typically can appeal against rulings ordering confiscation, seizure, and sequestration or against ruling ordering the permanent inaccessibility of electronic data.[95] In limited cases, the other interested party can also appeal against rulings concerning and addressed to him.[96]

---

[90] Art. 572 CCP.
[91] Art. 581(d) CCP.
[92] Art. 581(e) CCP.
[93] Art. 581(f) CCP.
[94] Art. 581(g) CCP.
[95] Art. 612 CCP.
[96] Art. 579(3)(b) CCP.

10 *Res Judicata* and the Effects of Criminal Judgments upon Third Parties

The CCP entails detailed provisions in line with the *ne bis in idem principle* as a procedural obstacle against the defendant,[97] but there are no specific implications thereof on natural or legal persons other than defendants in the event of the institution of a new process for the same facts.

As for links between criminal judgments and non-criminal proceedings regarding evidence, upon deciding whether or not the defendant committed a criminal offence, the court, the public prosecutor's office, and the investigating authority is not bound by decisions reached in civil, administrative, disciplinary or any other procedures, nor by the facts ascertained thereof.[98] On the other hand, the final criminal judgment has a binding effect in non-criminal proceedings, as non-criminal justice authorities cannot decide that the convict had not committed the criminal offence.

Furthermore, with special regard to third parties, it is worth mentioning, that even if the victim had not acted as a private party in the criminal procedure (meaning had not launched a civil claim for damages within the criminal process), or his civil claim was deferred to other legal action, he still has the right to claim the enforcement of it in civil procedure.[99] If the criminal case was terminated, the private party shall be notified about his right to claim the enforcement of it in civil procedure.[100]

References

Fantoly Z, Budaházi Á (2020) Introduction to the New Hungarian criminal procedure (Part I.) In: Jogelméleti Szemle 1. http://jesz.ajk.elte.hu/2020_1.pdf

Herke C (2018) Criminal procedure law. Lecture Notes. University of Pécs, Faculty of Law, Pécs. http://www.herke.hu/tan/18cpl.pdf

Karsai K, Szomora Z (2015) Criminal Law in Hungary. Wolters Kluwer, Alphen aan den Rijn

Lichtenstein A (2018) A terhelt emberi jogai és a büntetőeljárás egyes alapelvei. In: Acta Universitatis Szegediensis FORVM Publicationes Discipulorum Iurisprudentiae, I. évf. 1. szám. http://acta.bibl.uszeged.hu/70845/1/forum_discipulorum_2018_305-337.pdf

Lichtenstein A (2021) Az ügyészi vádmonopólium korrektívumai Európa egyes államaiban. In: FORVM: Publicationes Doctorandorum Juridicorum. http://acta.bibl.u-szeged.hu/73161/1/forum_doctorandorum_2021_073-085.pdf

---

[97] Art. 4(3)–(9) CCP.

[98] Art. 7(5) CCP.

[99] Art. 56(6) CCP.

[100] Art. 492(3) CCP.

Third Parties in Italian Criminal Proceedings

Diego Foti and Elisea Malino

Abstract The present study analyses the role of 'third parties' in Italian criminal proceedings. The task is particularly complex because it implies a preliminary definition of parties and non-parties, and also imposes the examination of victim's rights, by considering the victim as a 'potential' party. However, our analysis on the involvement of private persons other than the accused is mainly oriented to outline the safeguards attributed to them by domestic legislation in order to verify if these appear adequate to protect them from the detrimental effect of criminal proceedings.

1 Introduction

1.1 'Subjects' and 'Parties' in Italian Criminal Proceedings

The First Book of the Italian Code of Criminal Procedure (hereafter, CCP) regulates the so-called "*subjects*" of criminal proceedings, who, at first instance, can be defined as individuals and bodies entitled to exercise rights and powers.[1] They are the judge, the public prosecutor, the defendant, the civil plaintiff, the person with civil liability for damages related to the criminal offence, the person with civil obligation for pecuniary penalties, the injured party, and the defender. However, not all "*subjects*" can be considered as formal participants in criminal proceedings:

Diego Foti: Sections 4 and 5
Elisea Malino: Sections 1, 2, 3, 7, 8, 9, 10, and 11

[1] Tonini (2024), p. 66.

D. Foti
Messina University, Messina, Italy
e-mail: d.foti@unime.it

E. Malino (✉)
Law Department, Messina University, Messina, Italy
e-mail: elisea.malino@studenti.unime.it

S. Ruggeri et al. (eds.), *Third Parties in Criminal Proceedings*, Legal Studies in International, European and Comparative Criminal Law 10,
https://doi.org/10.1007/978-3-031-73970-5_5

for example, the judge, who stands out as the first among the subjects listed in this Book, cannot be considered as a party, even if the First Book of the CCP sets the rules for "The Court". On the contrary, the judge should be considered as a non-party, because he must be independent and impartial.

Hence, establishing the concept of 'parties' in criminal proceedings is a truly problematic task, especially because of the absence of a legislative definition.

Over the years, legal scholars have suggested various definitions, which sometimes appear extremely diverse because they reflect various ways of considering the criminal trial and its main issues.[2] According to a rather old interpretation, "party" is every individual related to the criminal offence to which the indictment refers. Following this approach, both the offender and the injured party could be considered as parties, regardless of whether or not they are entitled or not to participate in criminal proceedings. However, although such a broad notion allows the role of 'party' to be extended both to the accused and to the injured party, this definition is problematic, since it does not take into account the approach followed by current procedural law, which establishes a connection between the formal *status* of the parties and the exercise of rights and powers within the criminal proceedings.

The most challenging task is however to identify the distinctive features of the participants in criminal proceedings. In this respect, we could choose between two different options which recall the traditional distinction between formal and substantial parties explained by Professor Carnelutti in 1946. According to the first one, parties are those who are so defined by law; according to the second, parties are those who have specific interests linked to the criminal offence.[3]

However, for the purpose of the present study, we will combine these two definitions and consider as "party" the person who is so defined by the law, which acknowledges rights and powers to specific individuals because of their involvement in the criminal affair.

1.2 Formal Participants in Criminal Proceedings

Even though there is no shared definition of parties in criminal proceedings, nevertheless, there is a certainty: we cannot imagine any party outside the process nor any process without parties. Therefore, before the initiative of the criminal trial, and the preferment of formal charges,[4] we cannot identify parties in a strict sense.[5] Indeed,

---

[2]Dominioni (1985), p. 11.

[3]Carnelutti (1946–1949), pp. 129 ff.

[4]In Italy, the public prosecutor proceeds with criminal prosecution at the end of the preliminary investigation. Preliminary investigation is considered as a pre-trial phase that starts with the registration of the *notitia criminis* in the appropriate register. During this phase, the public prosecutor carries out every necessary activity for that purpose and he also investigates the facts and circumstances in the suspect's favour.

[5]Dominioni (1981), p. 952.

while the CCP permits criminal investigations to be carried out against unknown individuals, the establishment of the criminal process against a non-identified defendant makes no sense.[6]

More specifically, every criminal process requires at least two parties that should be under conditions of equality,[7] *i.e.* the public prosecutor and the defendant. These are the 'necessary' or 'main' parties, because of their close connection with prosecution, stated by the public prosecutor[8] and undergone by the defendant.[9]

Moreover, the individuals actively involved in criminal proceedings may be more than two. This scenario takes place when the injured person brings civil-law action into a criminal trial to obtain the restitution and compensation for the damage related to the alleged criminal offence.[10] In this case, alongside the main parties there are other subjects, called 'eventual' parties since their presence is possible, but not necessary for the institution of the process. They are the civil party (*i.e. parte civile*),[11] the person with civil liability for damages related to the criminal offence (*i.e. responsabile civile*), and the person with civil obligation for pecuniary penalties (*i.e. civilmente obbligato per la pena pecuniaria*).

In particular, other persons with civil liability for damages related to the criminal offence have the duty to pay compensation for the damage caused by the accused. Their involvement in the trial is strictly related to the presence of the civil party,[12] indeed, the so-called *responsabile civile* can be convicted jointly and severally with the accused to the restitution and compensation of damages 'if his liability is recognised' (my translation).[13] He may voluntarily[14] or upon a request[15] join the proceeding at any stage of it,[16] and may be excluded in the same way[17] or *ex*

[6] According to Article 415 CCP, the public prosecutor submits the request to either drop the case or continue investigations to the Judge for Preliminary Investigations but cannot proceed with criminal prosecution.

[7] Article 111(2) Italian Constitution. Actually, on several occasions, the Italian Constitutional Court has recognised the existence of an inequality between the two main parties that can be reduced but not eliminated. Cf. Italian Constitutional Court, judgment no. 286 of 30 July 2003, and Italian Constitutional Court, judgment no. 34 of 26 February 2020. On this point see also Cordero (2012), p. 2012; Lupo (2020), pp. 21 ff.

[8] Art. 112 Italian Constitution.

[9] Art. 60(1)(2) CCP.

[10] Art. 75 CCP.

[11] *Infra* Sect. 1.2.

[12] See Art. 85(4) CCP.

[13] Art. 538(3) CCP (my translation).

[14] Art. 85 CCP.

[15] Art. 83(1) CCP affirms that the request can be presented by the civil party and, in the cases specified by Article 77(4) CCP, also by the public prosecutor. Moreover, according to the Italian Constitutional Court, even the accused is entitled in two specific cases. Cf. Italian Constitutional Court, judgment of 16th April 1998 No. 112; Italian Constitutional Court, judgment no. 159 of 24 June 2022.

[16] Art. 84(1) CCP.

[17] Art. 86 CCP.

officio.[18] The CCP regulates the position of the party civilly liable for the criminal fine (*i.e. civilmente obbligato per la pena pecuniaria*) in a similar way.[19] However, his involvement in the criminal proceedings is related to his powers of authority, supervision, or direction over the accused.[20] Indeed, if the convicted person is insolvent, trial court can convict them also to the payment of the pecuniary penalties inflicted to the accused.[21]

1.3 Victims in Italian Criminal Proceedings

A different discussion should be made in relation to the victims. According to Italian criminal procedural law, they are not formal parties unless they bring a civil-law action into the criminal proceedings (*costituzione di parte civile*).[22]

In other words, victims have a particular status in Italian criminal justice, and even though they are not considered to be formal parties, they may assume this role pursuant to Article 74 CCP. Thus, for this reason, neither may they be considered as third parties.

Moreover, until the last reform of criminal justice there was no legal definition of victims.[23] Indeed, Article 42 of Legislative Decree no. 150 of 10 October 2022 provides for the first time a legal definition by way of establishing that the victim is "the individual who has suffered, as a consequence of a criminal offence, economic or non-economic harm, as well as the family member of the individual whose death was caused by the crime and who suffered a harm as a consequence of the death of that individual".[24]

Despite the auspices of Italian legal scholarship, this legislative innovation did not change the previous procedural framework, since the aforementioned definition was introduced into the Title dedicated to Restorative Justice, and refers only to this particular field.[25] Furthermore, Italian law lacks a uniform status of victims, as it still distinguishes between injured person (*persona offesa*), that is the aggrieved person whose rights are protected by the criminal law provision,[26] and the damaged person

[18] Art. 87 CCP.

[19] Actually, according to Article 89 CCP, he cannot participate voluntarily in the proceedings.

[20] Art. 196 CC-Italy.

[21] Art. 534 CCP.

[22] According to the Italian Constitutional Court, this is "the main and most significant of the faculties granted by law to the person offended by the crime". Cf. Italian Constitutional Court, judgment no. 98 of 3 April 1996, par. 3.

[23] Enabling Law no. 134 of 27 September 2021, Legislative Decrees nos. 150 and 151 of 2022.

[24] See Art. 42(1)(b) of Legislative Decree no. 150 of 10 October 2022.

[25] Along these lines, see also Italian Constitutional Court, judgment no. 203 of 23 September 2021.

[26] According to Article 90(3) CCP "Should the victim die as a consequence of the offence, the rights provided for by law shall be exercised by his next of kin or by a person with whom the victim lived permanently or had a personal relationship".

(*danneggiato*), that is the person who suffered economic and non-economic harm as a consequence of the criminal offence.[27] The range of subjects covered by these two categories does not perfectly overlap and the latter appears broader than the former: we can consider as *danneggiato* someone who is not necessarily a *persona offesa*, but both may and bring a civil-law action within the trial, thus acquiring the formal status of parties in the criminal proceeding (*i.e. parte civile*).[28]

A damaged person can become a civil party by lodging a civil-law action both personally or through a special attorney during the preliminary hearing or, in some cases, at the beginning of the trial hearing.[29] Consequently, if the injured party wishes to participate in a criminal trial, they have to wait until the establishment of these precise phases, which mostly depends on the public prosecutor. Hence, when the authority is inactive, victims cannot become formal parties and the need to ensure their active participation in criminal proceedings is frustrated.[30]

Once a claimant has been formed in the first trial,[31] the injured person acquires the formal *status* of 'eventual private party' (*i.e. parte privata eventuale*) and becomes able to exercise all the rights and powers acknowledged by the law.[32]

However, the role of victims remains weak during the pre-trial investigation in which they are not yet formal parties or whenever they choose not to participate in the criminal trial, and it becomes weaker during the court proceedings.[33] In judicial proceedings, Italian law grants victims only safeguards of the 'first level',[34] rather than participatory rights. To this end, victims shall receive some information from

[27] Art. 74 CCP.

[28] Indeed, according to Italian judges, the civil party may be anyone who has been directly or indirectly damaged by the accused's actions or omissions. Thus, it is possible, but not necessary, that the civil party coincides with the victim of the crime. Cf. Italian Court of Cassation, Division 2, judgment no. 4380 of 13 January 2015, in *CED Cass.*, rv. 262371; ID, Division 2, judgment no. 3129 of 31 May 2018, in *CED Cass.*, rv. 273698.

[29] Art. 79 CCP.

[30] This situation happens very often in Italy. Indeed, the Italian government has been convicted several times by the ECtHR. Cf. ECtHR, *Arnoldi v. Italia*, judgment of 7 December 2017, Appl. No. 35637/04, ECtHR, *Petrella v. Italia*, judgment of 18 May 2021, Appl. No. 24340/07. See also Orlando, in this volume.

[31] According to Article 76(2) CCP, the act of joining the proceeding as a civil party has effect at every stage and instance of it, unless the civil party has been excluded or the civil action revoked (Articles No. 80, 81, 82 CCP). See Italian Court of Cassation, Division No. 5, judgment of 6th April 2018, No. 24637, in *CED Cass.*, rv. 273338; ID., Division 3 judgement of 2nd December 2020, No. 20365, in *CED Cass.*, rv. 281298-01.

[32] Art. 90 CCP.

[33] During the trial, the offended person may submit briefs and request evidence. To this aim, Pennisi (1997), p. 792, affirmed that when the prosecution has been carried out, the injured persons lose most of their procedural safeguards, since they can regain those rights, or even greater rights, by becoming civil parties.

[34] Delvecchio (2016), p. 10.

their first contact with the judicial authority,[35] including that on the prosecutorial request regarding the dismissal of the proceedings.[36]

Moreover, Italian legislation grants the injured person some form of participation in evidence gathering procedures during the preliminary investigation. In particular, for instance, victims must be informed when the competent prosecutor orders the acquisition of expert evidence that cannot be repeated at trial (*accertamento tecnico irripetibile*); in this case, they may appoint their own experts to take part in the process.[37] However, they lack proactive powers as to the activation of a judicial evidence-gathering procedure (*incidente probatorio*), which can only be requested by the defendant and the public prosecutor.[38] The absence of proactive powers can be observed in the field of pre-trial measures, since the aggrieved parties can not even apply for measures that are intended to protect them (*e.g.* removal from the family home). Although victims today have specific rights of information and protection,[39] they cannot appeal against the decision to withdraw or substitute the measure adopted: they can only ask the public prosecutor to do so, and, in case of denial, they are left powerless.[40]

As we can see, defining the victims' role in Italian criminal proceedings is a truly problematic task. Italian lawmakers address this issue by adopting a 'formalistic' approach,[41] as the acknowledgment of participatory rights in favour of the aggrieved parties is strictly dependent on their formal role in the proceeding.

In light of this, victims hold a unique role in Italian criminal proceedings: they are not formal parties, and may not become so either, if they are not entitled to bring a civil-law action before the criminal court or decide not to do so.

1.4 Third Parties to Criminal Proceedings

Although for the purposes of this study we cannot consider victims as third parties or at least as people totally extraneous from the criminal proceedings, this does not mean that there are no 'third parties' in Italian criminal justice. One could consider as 'third parties' all those who, despite not being directly involved in a criminal affair,

---

[35] *Infra* Sect. 2.3. See also Art. 90 *bis* CCP.

[36] Art. 408(3 *bis*) CCP. *Infra* Sect. 2.3.

[37] Art. 360 CCP.

[38] Indeed, according to Article 394 CCP, victims may only require that the public prosecutor request the special evidentiary hearing.

[39] Artt. 90 *ter* CCP and 299 CCP. See Battarino (2013), pp. 13 ff.

[40] Italian Court of Cassation, Joint Division, judgment of 28 September 2022, No. 36754. See also Di Nuzzo (2020), p. 13; Bonini (2018), pp. 349–407; Caraceni (2021), pp. 1783 ff.

[41] Cf. Italian Constitutional Court, judgment of 4 November 2020, No. 249. La Rocca (2020). The Italian judges stressed the need to maintain the categories of *persona offesa* and *danneggiato*, even if this 'formalistic' approach was criticised by the ECtHR in the mentioned decisions *Arnoldi v. Italia* and *Petrella v. Italia*. See note No. 31.

may have an interest in the course of the criminal trial in the light of the public nature of the interests related to the commission of an alleged crime and the judicial ascertainment of the criminal fact.[42] However, this definition appears too wide-ranging as it does not allow us to clearly identify the category of 'third parties'.

Yet, it is of paramount importance to circumscribe this category to properly address the present analysis. On a first level, 'third parties' could be defined as those individuals who are not formal participants, but are involved in criminal proceedings, either thanks to their private or professional knowledge—such as witnesses or experts—or because they are the addressees of measures restricting or affecting their fundamental rights. For instance, the judicial authority may order inspections, searches or seizures against people other than the defendant. All these cases display procedural measures directly addressing 'third parties'. Moreover, procedural measures can have negative effects on people other than the addressees. This scenario frequently takes place during the preliminary investigation, because of the use of technological tools, such as communication intercepts or videorecording that, even if ordered against the accused, inevitably impinge upon all those who enter into contact with them (for example the next of kin).

2 Fundamental Rights and Safeguards of Third Parties

2.1 Constitutional Law

It has been noted that in criminal proceedings, and especially during the investigative stage, the judicial authority adopts measures which may impinge upon the fundamental rights not only of the accused, but also of other people under no suspicion of guilt. It is essential to establish clear limits to these measures to avoid an arbitrary infringement of fundamental rights.

Although the recourse to procedural activities against third parties is very often indispensable for fact-finding purposes, their use should be restricted to the cases in which they appear truly necessary. Otherwise, the legal system would lay the basis for unjustified violations of the rights granted by the Italian Constitution (hereafter IC).

The task of lawmakers is to strike a proper balance between the need for an effective ascertainment of facts and the protection of the individuals who are, directly or indirectly, affected by investigative tools.

The Italian Constitutional Court has accepted this solution, by allowing a restriction even of fundamental rights, since none of them has been acknowledged in 'absolute terms'.[43] Indeed, the Italian Constitution, while enshrining fundamental

[42] Carnelutti (1946–1949), p. 127.

[43] Italian Constitutional Court, judgment no. 85 of 9 May 2013.

rights, at the same time sets the conditions for their limitation.[44] Thus, it is essential to identify the Constitutional rights at risk in order to evaluate the fairness of investigative activities,[45] since a number of relevant measures, which are very often adopted during the pre-trial inquiry (e.g. searches and seizure, inspections, interception of communication, videorecording, etc.) affect fundamental rights such as personal freedom (Article 13 IC), the right of domicile (Article 14 IC), the right to free and private correspondence and communication (Article 15 IC), and the right of property (Article 42 IC).

First, it is important to note that these fundamental rights are inviolable under the Italian Constitution, which, even more significantly, grants the same level of protection to every person, regardless of his/her role in a specific judicial procedure. In other words, the status of a formal party is irrelevant for the activation of the constitutional law protection that consists of two essential safeguards, according to which limitations of fundamental rights must be specifically regulated by law and can only be authorised by a judicial authority by means of an order stating the reason.

The Constitutional Court has confirmed such principles on several occasions, by enhancing the protection of 'third parties' regardless their status as formal parties. For instance, in 1996, the constitutional judges deemed the domestic regulation of coercive taking of DNA samples to be in breach of Article 13 IC, since Article 224 paragraph 2 CCP did not clarify the cases and methods involved, and it thus seemed that the jurisdictional authority could always perform such tests without any restrictions.[46] According to the Court, the coercive taking of DNA samples causes a restriction of personal freedom because it affects the person's physical sphere. But this prejudice is tolerated because it is aimed at satisfying fact-finding needs.

The Court adopted a similar approach in the field of confiscation related to urban planning crimes. Indeed, in 2015 the Constitutional Court confirmed that judges have to ascertain the guilt of the subject affected by confiscation in compliance with the presumption of innocence—both when the addressee of the measure is the accused or a 'third party'. Hence, the standard of proof is the same and the public prosecutor must prove the bad faith of the 'third party'.[47]

On the contrary, some decisions of the Italian Constitutional Court reflect a different approach, and the protection of third parties' fundamental rights seems weak. For example, in 2008, the Court set the foundation for a mitigated protection of the right to domicile, providing a strict interpretation of the notion of 'domicile' and considering videorecording as a particular kind of remote police observation,[48] which does not require any judicial authorisation to be carried out.

Furthermore, according to the constitutional judges, police videorecordings are in breach of Article 14 IC when they capture conduct that cannot be seen from the

[44] Cartabia (2013), p. 9.

[45] Iovene (2014), p. 336.

[46] Italian Constitutional court, judgment no. 238 of 9 July 1996.

[47] Italian Constitutional court, judgment no. 49 of 26 March 2015, par. 5.

[48] Italian Constitutional court, judgment no. 149 of 24 April 2008, par. 2.1.

outside. Therefore, in other cases police can videorecord without any restriction, thus emphasising the risk of jeopardising the right to domicile not only of the accused, but also of third parties. Indeed, very often, third parties, such as those who live with the accused, become subjects of videorecording, even if they are not involved in alleged criminal activity.[49] For these reasons, the decision of the Court appears questionable, since it laid the basis for a massive use of this technological instrument, regardless of its negative impact on the right to domicile. Moreover, while sacrificing the defendant's privacy could be justified by their direct involvement in the criminal proceeding and their personal interest in the fact-finding, the prejudice suffered by third parties appears unjustified.

As we have seen, the Constitution provides for the 'preventive' protection of fundamental rights, but without granting any proactive power to those individuals affected by the investigative measures: the introduction of such specific powers depends on legislators, and often enables only the suspect to exercise them.

However, Articles 2, 3, 24 of Italian Constitution suggest a broad interpretation of the rules that regulates the legal instruments aimed at protecting the fundamental rights of those individuals involved in criminal investigations, thus entitling third parties to use them. Indeed, according to Article 2 IC the Republic recognises and guarantees the inviolable rights of the person, both as individual and in the social groups where human personality is expressed. Thus, someone who suffers a breach of his/her fundamental rights should be entitled to defend those rights, by using the legal instruments provided by the legal system. Moreover, Article 24 IC affirms that anyone may bring cases before a court of law to protect their rights under civil and administrative law and that defence is an inviolable right at every stage and instance of legal proceedings. Combining Articles 2 and 24 IC, we could affirm that those who are affected by an investigative measure should be able to complain before a court, regardless of their formal role in criminal proceedings.

In the light of the proposed interpretation, we could broadly interpret the procedural rules that establish the right to claim for the violation of fundamental freedom perpetrated through investigative measures. Indeed, we could adopt a broader meaning of 'party', that includes so-called 'third parties', which, in this case, can no longer be considered as 'third persons', due to their involvement in the criminal proceeding and their direct need for protection.

Furthermore, Article 3 IC establishes the principle of equality, which imposes the duty to treat the same situations in the same way, and different situations in different ways. Thus, the current system of safeguards, that offers different solutions according to whether the individual is the suspect or a 'third party' could be in breach of Article 3 IC on two different levels. Indeed, despite the damage caused by the implementation of the investigative measure being homogenous, the situations are still treated differently. Moreover, the suspect and the 'third party' have different interests in the criminal proceeding, thus 'third parties' should receive a different protection than those granted to the accused. Indeed, as already observed, while

---

[49] Mazza (2013), p. 10.

suspects could accept a restriction of their rights in order to contribute to fact-finding, and to confirm their innocence, 'third parties' do not have such an interest, meaning that their sacrifice may appear completely unjustified.

Thus, there is a need to ensure that any 'third party' enjoys the same level of protection granted to the accused, if not stronger.[50]

2.2 Domestication of International Law

To properly analyse the role and the protection of 'third parties' in Italian criminal proceedings, one cannot ignore the influence of international law on domestic legislation. On various occasions, national lawmakers have paid attention to third parties' rights to fulfil their international obligations.

Recently, the regulation of searches has been reformed to transpose the principles affirmed by the ECtHR in the case *Brazzi v Italy*.[51] Thus, a new remedy was introduced by Article 252 *bis* CCP: *i.e.*, '*opposizione al decreto di perquisizione emesso dal pubblico ministero*'.

This innovation is of paramount importance to the aim of this study, since an appeal against the search warrant may be submitted by 'the people subjected to the searches', regardless of their formal role in the criminal proceeding.

Italian legislators implicitly addressed the topic of 'third party' to transpose a soft law instrument adopted by the Committee of Ministers of the CoE. Indeed, after the adoption of the *Convention on the Protection of Children against sexual exploitation and sexual abuse*, some new rules were established to grant proper protection for individuals considered 'vulnerable'. The most important regulatory innovations concern hearing and the examination of these individuals:[52] according to Article 5 of law no. 172 of 1 October 2012, judicial authorities shall conduct their hearing and examination by means of protected measures, both when they are heard as victims or witnesses (*i.e.*, 'third parties').[53] Additionally, when the police and the public prosecutor proceed with the ascertainment of violence-related crime, the CCP requires the presence of an expert during the examination of these individuals.[54] However, as we will see *infra*, this kind of protection does not grant proper protection, because of the absence of any legal consequence for the infringement

---

[50] On the negative impact of this solution see Calavita (2022), who addresses the topic with specific regard to searches.

[51] Gialuz (2022); ECtHR, *Brazzi v. Italy*, judgment of 27 September 2018, Appl. No. 57278/11.

[52] *Infra* Sect. 3.2.

[53] Recchione (2013), p. 1.

[54] Art. 351, 362 CCP. Actually, the latter reproduces the provision of Article 498(4) CCP, which affirms that the Court can hear a 'vulnerable' person with the assistance of an expert or a next of kin. See De Martino (2013a, b).

of the regulation: if a judicial authority collects statements by breaching those rules, their content can be still evaluated as proof by the court.[55]

Some years later, the Council of Europe promoted the adoption of another important legal instrument: the *Convention on preventing and combating violence against women and domestic violence*, signed in Istanbul, on 11 May 2011. However, it mainly addresses the topic of victims' protection, and stresses the need to hear and examine young children by means of protective measures. Thus, it is not significant for the purposes of this analysis since it mainly focuses on 'victims' of specific crimes, and, as already said, we do not consider the injured person to be a 'third party'.

On the contrary, the Prüm Convention, signed by the Italian Government in 2009,[56] appears relevant here because it addresses the topic of the forced taking of DNA, which appears able to jeopardise third parties' personal freedom.[57] Italian lawmakers introduced the new Article 224 *bis* CCP[58] to regulate the conduct of investigative measures whose accomplishment causes a limitation of personal freedom. This legal instrument establishes the same safeguards for all those who are subject to these limitations, thus guaranteeing for 'third parties' the same level of protection granted to the 'formal participants'.

2.3 Implementation of EU Law

In recent decades, EU law has played a key role in the field of protection of victims and 'third parties' thanks to the adoption of two legal instruments which address this topic: *Directive 2012/29/EU establishing minimum standards on the rights, support and protection of victims of crime* and *Directive 2014/42/EU on the freezing and confiscation of instrumentalities and proceeds of crime in the European Union.*

In Italy, Legislative Decree no. 212 of 15 December 2015, composed of three articles, partially implemented the Directive 2012/29/EU. Indeed, Italy did not immediately transpose all the innovations suggested by the soft law instruments. For instance, until the recent criminal justice reform, there was no domestic definition of 'victim' nor a uniform and complete discipline of restorative justice, which was introduced for the first time in 2022.[59] In 2015, Italian lawmakers paid attention to the victims' right to information on the assumption that this is necessary in order to lay the basis for their active and informed participation in criminal proceedings. To this purpose, Article no. 1(1)(b) of Legislative Decree no. 212 of 15 December

[55] Cf. Italian Court of Cassation, Division 3, judgment no. 22754 of 20 February 2018, in *CED Cass.*, rv 273308.

[56] Law no. 85 of 30 June 2009.

[57] *Infra* Sect. 4.4.

[58] Art. 24, Law no. 85 of 30 June 2009.

[59] Cf. Title V of Legislative Decree no. 150 of 10 October 2022.

2015 introduced Articles 90 *bis*, 90 *ter*, and 90 *quarter* CCP. Pursuant to Article 90 *bis* CCP, the investigative authorities shall provide the victims with some information from the moment of their very first contact,[60] while Article 90 *ter* CCP transposes Recital no. 32 of Directive 2012/29/UE by introducing the victim's right to be informed in the event of the accused's escape or release. Finally, Article 90 *quarter* CCP provides for a definition of 'vulnerable victims', aimed at establishing those who deserve specific protection. Indeed, pursuant to Articles 190 *bis*, 351(1 *ter*), 362(1 *bis*), 392(1 *bis*), 398, and 498 CCP, the authorities—i.e. the police and the public prosecutor during the preliminary investigation, and the trial thereafter—shall examine vulnerable victims with the assistance of an expert, even if they have reached the age of majority. Furthermore, to comply with EU legislation, Article 190 *bis* CCP states that the number of interviews and any form of contact between the defendant and the alleged victim must be kept to a *minimum*[61] to avoid further harm.[62]

However, despite the potential of Directive 2012/29/EU in the field of victim protection, Italian legislators did not fully grasp this opportunity, and the aggrieved party's status still remains weak, because of the lack of a detailed regulation and the absence of adequate structures to ensure so-called 'service rights'.

Another important legal instrument adopted in the European context is *Directive 2014/42/EU on the freezing and confiscation of instrumentalities and proceeds of crime in the European Union*, which takes into account third parties' rights when they are affected by freezing and confiscation measures.[63] The Italian government implemented Directive 2014/42/EU by means of Legislative Decree no. 202 of 29 October 2016, and Law no. 161 of 17 October 2017. In particular, according to the new provisions, when the confiscation order prejudices third parties' property rights, they have the right to participate in criminal proceedings on the merits of the case.[64] This regulation, aimed at adapting the domestic legal system to EU standards, appears quite important, because it enhances the right of defence and the right to an effective remedy of 'third parties', by enabling them to appeal against a decision on confiscation and freezing,[65] thus promoting the

[60] For example, on the procedures for submitting a report or a complaint; on their rights to be informed of the current stage of the proceedings; on how and under what conditions they are entitled to interpretation and translation.

[61] Art. 19(1) Directive 2012/29/EU.

[62] During their examination aggrieved parties have to recall the criminal event and confront the accused, thus reliving their trauma.

[63] Another fundamental legal instrument adopted by EU legislators is *Regulation (EU) 2018/1805 of the European Parliament and of the Council of 14 November 2018 on the mutual recognition of freezing orders and confiscation orders*.

[64] Art. 12 *sexies* of Decree Law no. 306, of 8 June 1992. Moreover, according to Article 104 *bis*(1 *bis* and 4 *quinquies*) of Implementing Provisions to the CCP, the 'third party' must participate in the trial. The topic will be investigated in *Infra* Sect. 5.

[65] Montagna (2019), p. 15.

alignment of their procedural safeguards with those afforded to 'formal participants'.[66]

3 Third Parties in Criminal Inquiries

3.1 The Main Features of the Italian Preliminary Investigations

The very first stage of an Italian criminal proceeding is the preliminary inquiry (*i.e. indagini preliminari*). It formally starts with the registration of the *notitia criminis* by the public prosecutor,[67] who can proceed *motu proprio* or after having received a complaint from the offended person or a police report.[68]

During this stage, "the public prosecutor and the police, within their respective responsibilities, shall conduct the necessary investigations for the decision on criminal prosecution".[69] Indeed, the main purpose of preliminary investigation is not the collection of evidence, and the knowledge obtained cannot be evaluated by the Court to decide on the guilt of the accused.

The judge (*i.e. Giudice per le indagini preliminari*) cannot interfere with the conduction of the investigations, but acts as a supervisor, whose main tasks are to oversee the correct performance of criminal investigations and to respond to the requests of the parties.[70]

On the contrary, the public prosecutor is in charge of this phase,[71] and conducts the investigation by coordinating police activities. When the police are delegated by the public prosecutor to conduct specific investigative activity, they are considered to be the latter's *longa manus*,[72] thus the officers have to respect the rules envisaged for the public prosecutor's inquiry.[73] Nonetheless, the police can carry out investigations 'on their own initiative', but they have to promptly inform the public prosecutor and respect the latter's general directives.[74] When this happens, Title IV of CCP provides for similar rules to those prescribed for the public prosecutor's own activities. For the purposes of this study, we can jointly analyse all the

[66] Cascini (2022), pp. 157 ff. See also ECJ, judgment of 21 October 2021, C-845/19 and 863/19.

[67] Art. 335 CCP.

[68] Art. 347 CCP.

[69] Art. 326 CCP.

[70] Art. 328 CCP.

[71] Art. 327 CCP, transposing Article 109 IC.

[72] Art. 55(2) CCP.

[73] Hence, when the public prosecutor delegates specific investigative measures to the police, they must assure the respect of the guarantees established by Articles 364, 365, and 373 CCP. Cf. Article 370 CCP.

[74] Art. 348(3) CCP.

investigative acts, by highlighting from time to time the few differences that depend on the competent authority to conduct the activity.

3.2 The Hearing and the Examination of Third Parties

The first steps taken by the investigative authorities are frequently the hearing and the examination of those individuals who can provide statements regarding circumstances that appear relevant to the fact-finding process. As we can imagine, this category is wide-ranging because it includes different people. Indeed, these individuals are very often 'third parties', because they are not directly involved in the criminal offence, and their interviews are regulated by Articles no. 362 and 351 CCP.

Mere questioning is not a dangerous activity in itself, but it can infringe upon several rights of the person being examined (therefore, of 'third parties' as well), as a consequence of several factors, such as the methods of conducting the hearing, the seriousness of the situation that is dealt with, and the individual's particular conditions. It is for this reason that the CCP provides rules aimed at enhancing the individuals' safeguard during their examination.

First of all, according to a general provision, investigative authorities are not allowed to use methods or techniques which may influence the freedom of self-determination.[75] Furthermore, the public prosecutor and the police have to adopt specific measures during the examination of categories of individuals that are particularly vulnerable. As we have already seen, thanks to the influence of international and supranational law, the CCP establishes that the investigative authorities shall be assisted by a family member or a child psychology expert during the examination of a minor. In the case of 'vulnerable victims', the authorities must keep the number of interviews to a minimum, and they must assure that no contact will take place between the defendant and the alleged victim.[76]

Recently, Italian legislators granted these individuals a new safeguard: *i.e.* the right to ask and obtain the record of their statements through video and audio technology.[77] These videorecordings can be reproduced even during the trial, thus diminishing the occasions in which individuals have to recall criminal facts and must be confronted with the accused. In this way, the risk of harm linked to the re-enactment of the events could be reduced.

However, these rules provide ineffective protection, because the realisation of video and audio recording is required only if the technical tools and qualified officers are available. Otherwise, the authorities can record their activities by means of traditional methods.

---

[75] Art. 188 CCP.

[76] Artt. 351(1 *ter*) and 362(1 *bis*) CCP.

[77] Artt. 357(3 *ter*) and 373(2 *quater*) CCP.

3.3 Inspection

Inspection is an investigative activity aimed at finding traces and other material effects of a criminal offence. It consists of a critical and careful observation of places, things, but also persons, regardless of their formal role in the criminal proceeding, hence it is not surprising that it can also involve 'third parties'.

An inspection is ordered by means of a judicial order stating the reason.[78] However the police can proceed on their own when there is the risk that objects, traces, and the crime scene may be altered, lost, or modified,[79] but in no case can they perform bodily inspections.

Even though the inspections infringe upon personal freedom and the inviolability of the home, Italian legislation does not grant a high level of protection to those who undergo it and nor does it assign them with any proactive power. Indeed, the court order cannot be challenged, and no appeal may be submitted.[80]

The CCP simply grants the right to be assisted by the defender[81] or a 'trusted person' during the course of the inspection.[82] The presence of the defender, aimed at ensuring the fairness of the examination carried out by the investigative authorities, represents an important safeguard, but it applies only for suspects, thus compromising the protection of third parties, who may also be involved in inspections.

3.4 Searches

This investigative measure is aimed at searching the *corpus delicti* or anything related to the criminal offence, or at capturing the accused or the escapee for his arrest.[83] There are different types of searches depending on their object: for example, body searches (Article 249 CCP), searches of premises (Article 250 CCP), searches of homes (Article 251 CCP), and those that concern IT systems [Article 247(1 *bis*) CCP].

The searches are authorised by means of a judicial order stating the reason and can be conducted by the public prosecutor personally or by police officers.[84] The

[78] Art. 244 CCP.

[79] Art. 354(2) CCP.

[80] Italian Court of Cassation, Division III, judgment no. 28770 of 15 May 2018, in *CED Cass.*, rv. 273352.

[81] Artt. 356 and 364, 365 CCP.

[82] In particular, the authorities shall conduct the body inspections in presence of a 'trusted person' of the person concerned, if he/she is promptly available and suitable. Cf. Art. 245(1) CCP.

[83] Art. 247(1) CCP.

[84] Art. 247(2)(3) CCP. According to the Italian Court of Cassation the public prosecutor's power to order searches is not in breach of Articles 24 and 111 IC, because the principles enshrined by those provisions refer to the trial and not the preliminary investigations. Cf. Italian Court of Cassation, Division 3, judgment no. 40974 of 15 October 2002, in *CED Cass.*, rv. 222908.

police are allowed to carry out searches on their own, under specific and restricted conditions. Indeed, it not sufficient to have reasonable grounds to believe that a person is hiding an object or evidence related to the offence on his/her body that may be deleted or lost, or that such objects or evidence are in a certain place: it is also necessary that the person has been caught *in flagrance delicto* or that he is escaping. Moreover, a validation procedure is envisaged. To this aim, the police must forward the record of the activities carried out to the public prosecutor without delay and within 48 h. In the following 48 h the public prosecutor shall decide on the confirmation of the searches by means of an order stating the reason.[85]

When they proceed to the search, investigative authorities do not need to previously inform the concerned person, who thus becomes aware of its performance at the time of its accomplishment, when he/she receives a copy of the order authorising the searches.[86]

The CCP affirms the right to assistance of a defence counsel during the conduct of the search, but, as in the case of inspections, only the accused is entitled:[87] the other person (the third parties) may be assisted by a 'trusted person', but only if he/she is promptly available and suitable.[88] Nonetheless, Italian legislation does not prescribe any consequence in the event of violation of the mentioned provision, thus compromising third party protection. This legislative solution is questionable since it does not take into account the rights of third parties, who are often affected by searches. However, this result appears to be reasonable, if one considers that searches may be carried out at the very first stage of preliminary inquiries, when no suspect has yet been identified. If this is the case, every person who undergoes a search can be formally considered as a third party. Lawmakers seemed aware of this circumstance and used a general expression, '*persona che abbia l'attuale disponibilità del luogo*' or '*interessato*', thus confirming the possibility to search premises related to a person other than the suspect.

In 2022,[89] the legislative set-up was amended and a new Article 252 *bis* CCP was introduced to transpose the principles affirmed by the ECtHR in the judgement *Brazzi v. Italy*.[90] This Article introduces the so-called *opposizione al decreto di perquisizione emesso dal pubblico ministero*, a new remedy that allows the suspect, and the concerned person in general (*i.e.* '*persona nei cui confronti è stata disposta la perquisizione*'), to challenge both the public prosecutor's decisions to search and

[85] Art. 352(4) CCP.

[86] The order is written in Italian, but the person concerned may be foreign and not understand Italian. The issue has been addressed by the Italian Court of Cassation, which found that the authorities are not required to translate the order, because the time required for translation is incompatible with the urgency of the searches. This rule also applies in the case of body searches. Cf. Italian Court of Cassation, Division 1, judgment of 23 June 2017, in *CED Cass.*, 270611.

[87] See Artt. 356 and 364, 365 CCP.

[88] Art. 249 CCP.

[89] Legislative Decree no. 150 of 10 October 2022.

[90] ECtHR, *Brazzi v. Italy*, judgment of 27 September 2018, Appl. no. 57278/11.

to validate the searches carried out by the police.[91] For the purpose of this analysis, this instrument appears relevant, since also 'third parties' can avail themselves of it if they are subject to a search order.

Nonetheless, some issues arise from the new Article 252 *bis* CCP.

Firstly, the scope of this remedy is limited because it can be used only if the searches turn out to be fruitless ('*infruttuosa*'). This occurs when the investigative authority finds nothing related to the crime, and no seizure takes place. Consequently, in the event of search and seizure the affected person does not have any chance to challenge the prosecution order or validation. Actually, this legislative option reflects a previous approach whereby a search order could only be challenged together with the seizure, by means of a specific complaint called '*riesame*'.[92]

Secondly, the protection assured to the concerned person appears ineffective, because the law does not explain what happens if the judge finds the search to be unlawful.[93] There could be consequences outside the proceedings themselves.[94] On the one hand, rulings that state the unlawfulness of the search could be used to prove judicial civil liability pursuant to Article 2 of Law no. 177 of 13 April 1988;[95] on the other, they could constitute documental evidence for the ascertainment of the criminal offence punished by Article 609 of the Italian Penal Code ('*perquisizioni o ispezioni arbitrarie*').[96] The proposed solutions cannot be considered suitable for ensuring an effective and adequate safeguard to the person who suffered the search-related harm. The outlined framework seems to provide for compensation that can be obtained only through another proceeding, but this solution is still far from the standard imposed by the ECtHR, which affirmed that 'the possibility to seek disciplinary proceedings [. . .] was not such an [effective] remedy'.[97] Furthermore, the alternatives proposed are expensive and uncertain: for instance, the judicial authorities' liability is rarely established, especially when it refers to investigative measures that are covered by the authority's discretion. Indeed, the CCP does not establish specific and rigorous preconditions for performance of the searches, thus making the judge's evaluation on the legitimacy of the investigative activities difficult and uncertain.

In sum, the remedy introduced by Article 252 *bis* CCP does not seem to significantly improve the protection of the person affected by a search: once again,

---

[91] Art. 352(4 *bis*) CCP.

[92] Italian Court of Cassation, Joint Division, judgment no. 23 of 20 November 1996.

[93] To this end, some legal scholars have proposed introducing the right to compensation for those who undergone (un)justified coercion, in order to remedy their harm and increase the public prosecutor's liability. Cf. Padua (2021), p. 56; Coppola (2022), p. 28.

[94] According to Coppola (2022), p. 27, thanks to the new remedy, the reasoning at the basis of the order could be more precise and detailed, because it should allow the judge to evaluate the legitimacy of the measure.

[95] Cf. Calavita (2022), pp. 13 ff.

[96] Cf. Italian Court of Cassation, Division 4, judgment no. 8031 of 15 December 2016, in *CED Cass.*, rv. 269031.

[97] ECtHR, *Posevini v. Bulgaria*, judgement of 19 January 2017, Appl. no. 63638/14, par. 84.

third parties can only suffer the consequences of an investigative measure, but they are not allowed to contest the investigative authority's decision or to defend their rights.

3.5 Seizures

Seizure is an investigative measure that consists of the public authority taking possession of the results of a search, that are the *corpus delicti* and anything else related to the criminal offence.[98]

Although seizure impinges upon economic rights, Italian lawmakers assured a high level of protection of the interests of the persons involved, regardless of their formal role in the criminal proceeding.

Seizure is ordered by the public prosecutor, who must state the reason, and can be performed by the public prosecutor personally or by the police. The police can actually seize the *corpus delicti* and the objects related to the criminal offence independently, if they find them during the urgent investigation of places, things and persons (Article 354 CCP). In this case, the police must register the activity, and the report must be forwarded, without delay and within 48 h, to the public prosecutor, who, in the following 48 h, must confirm seizure by means of an order stating the reason why the seized objects be returned.[99]

The order authorising or validating the seizure may be discussed in the so-called '*riesame*', which may be proposed by the accused and his/her defender, but also by the 'person whose things were seized and the person entitled to have them returned'.[100] Thus, third parties can directly appeal against the measure that infringes upon their property (or their possessions), and, if they succeed, they reobtain their assets.

3.6 Some Preliminary Observations

The investigative activities analysed in the previous paragraphs represent the main, traditional instruments used by the public prosecutor and the police during the preliminary inquiries. As we have already seen, they may affect the accused's rights, but also the rights of individuals who will not play any formal role in the future criminal proceeding: third parties.

However, Italian legislators do not seem to be interested in them. Indeed, on the whole the CCP does not grant any proactive powers to either the accused or to third

[98] Art. 253 CCP.

[99] Art. 355 CCP.

[100] Art. 355(3) CCP.

parties: it merely provides an *ex ante* protection, by establishing the legal prerequisites of the measures and by requiring the an order from the judicial authority stating the reason, in accordance with the Italian Constitution. Nonetheless, this approach does not appear satisfying, since the provisions are generic and undefined, thus compromising their effectiveness: they grant wide-ranging discretionary powers to public prosecutors (when they have to decide to carry out an investigative measure), but also to judges (when they have to ascertain the legitimacy of the measures ordered by the public prosecutor).

In conclusion, the protection of third parties in pre-trial inquiry appears weak or, in some cases, totally lacking. Third parties' interests are adequately taken into account by Italian lawmakers only on rare occasions, but, even in those cases, the remedies seem inadequate at protecting their interests and fundamental rights. Their protection is entrusted to the public prosecutor, who should strike a proper balance between the need for an effective ascertainment of facts and the protection of the individuals who are, directly or indirectly, affected by investigative tools. This task is very complex, especially if one considers the resources provided by technological and scientific progress, which, on one hand, are able to enhance individuals' protection (such as remote hearings), but, on the other, could negatively affect fundamental rights, by entailing new risks.

4 Scientific Developments, New Technologies and the Safeguards of Third Parties

4.1 Some Brief Preliminary Observations on the Difficult Balance Between the Right to Privacy and Investigative Needs in the Digital Era

By focusing our attention on the specific field of digital investigative tools, we will notice how the use of technological innovation could jeopardise the interests and the fundamental rights of third parties. Particularly, we can note how deeply their rights to privacy can be affected by measures used by investigative authorities during the pre-trial inquiries, with repercussions on the trial phase.

The autonomous nature of the right to privacy has old roots, for it emerged overseas already in nineteenth century. Since the times when the major problems regarded the evolution from a right to be left alone to a positive demand of protection, a lot has happened: today, we must face troubling issues regarding the rights of information and self-determination, as well as *habeas data* (that can be summarised in the right to control the information retained regarding oneself). In the Digital Era or information society, Information and Communication Technologies (ICT) have exponentially enhanced the degree of "intrusiveness" in the private sphere of investigative measures for purposes of crime prevention and repression, such as in the case of wiretapping, room bugging and hacking tools. Several international human rights charters and national Constitutions are still modelled upon the "traditional" systems of the state monitoring of citizens' lives, and imply a physical spatial dimension, which has been deeply challenged by digitalisation. The places where people "express their personality", as stated in Article 2 of Italian Constitution, and where their inviolable rights must be guaranteed, have shifted into "cyberspace", thus creating new challenges for lawmakers to assess a fair balance between investigative needs and the protection of fundamental rights, especially those envisaged under Article 8 ECHR. As has been noted, "privacy *versus* investigation is a naturally unbalanced relationship", and the troubling issues that arise in relation to the new rights of the suspect or accused should not overshadow the other problematic aspects of safeguarding third parties.

4.2 Digital Evidence

Progress in the area of ICT has been above all applied to the field of evidence-gathering procedures. It is no coincidence that nowadays we frequently discuss so-called digital or electronic evidence, which is considered an essential and indispensable tool to investigate both traditional criminal activities and (new) cybercrimes. The relevance of the issue recently led the European Union to adopt Regulation (EU) 2023/1543 for the preservation and circulation of such evidence in the area of freedom, security and justice, in the light of judicial cooperation in criminal matters based on the principle of mutual recognition.[101] In fact, considering the volatile nature of digital forensics, which can easily be altered or deleted, it is of essential importance to ensure a rapid flow of information. This goal cannot be achieved in a legal framework which shows fragmentation among Member States, also because serious challenges are already posed by the fact that the place where relevant electronic evidence is stored, as well as the office of the service provider, may be outside the State in which investigations have been initiated (or even in a third country). The EIO,[102] on the one hand, and the legal assistance models offered by the Convention on Mutual Assistance in Criminal Matters,[103] on the other, appear insufficient to ensure the efficiency and effectiveness of the investigations, so that the new cooperation mechanisms of the European Production Order and the European Preservation Order will be fully implemented soon for the purposes of a

[101] Regulation (EU) 2023/1543 of the European Parliament and of the Council of 12 July 2023 on European Production Orders and European Preservation Orders for electronic evidence in criminal proceedings and for the execution of custodial sentences following criminal proceedings.

[102] Directive 2014/41/EU of the European Parliament and of the Council of 3 April 2014 regarding the European Investigation Order in criminal matters.

[103] Convention established by the Council in accordance with Article 34 of the Treaty on European Union, on Mutual Assistance in Criminal Matters between the Member States of the European Union (OJ C 197, 12.7.2000).

secure transnational circulation of e-evidence in criminal proceedings, independently of the location of the data.

Given its broad scope, this Regulation provides an extensive definition of electronic evidence, thus not reducing the scope of the previously existing definition of electronic evidence, described as

> any data stored or transmitted using a computer that support or refute a theory of how an offence occurred or that address critical elements of the offence such as intent or alibi.[104]

More technically, the Regulation describes e-evidence as "subscriber data, traffic data or content data stored by or on behalf of a service provider, in an electronic form".[105]

Subscriber data is

> any data held by a service provider relating to the subscription to its services, pertaining to: (a) the identity of a subscriber or customer, such as the provided name, date of birth, postal or geographic address, billing and payment data, telephone number, or email address; (b) the type of service and its duration, including technical data and data identifying related technical measures or interfaces used by or provided to the subscriber or customer at the moment of initial registration or activation, and data related to the validation of the use of the service.

Traffic data is

> data related to the provision of a service offered by a service provider which serve to provide context or additional information about such service and are generated or processed by an information system of the service provider, such as the source and destination of a message or another type of interaction, the location of the device, date, time, duration, size, route, format, the protocol used and the type of compression, and other electronic communications metadata and data, other than subscriber data, relating to the commencement and termination of a user access session to a service, such as the date and time of use, the log-in to and log-off from the service.[106]

Finally, content data is "any data in a digital format, such as text, voice, videos, images and sound, other than subscriber data or traffic data".[107]

These concepts appear useful for the purposes of our analysis, since they allow an immediate understanding of the huge variety of the category of electronic evidence: not only IP addresses, personal numbers, and communications within the context of "traditional" social networks (such as Facebook Messenger, WhatsApp, Telegram, etc.), but also "unexpected" ones, for example exchanges of information on online marketplaces, gaming or even gambling platforms. Therefore, digital forensics enable the collection by public authorities of massive amounts of personal data and information with a varying degree of interference with fundamental rights, both of the accused and "third parties". While the former has the right at least to be informed about the production of his/her data on the basis of a European Production

---

[104] Casey (2000), p. 196.

[105] See Art. 3 par. 8 Regulation (EU) 2023/1543.

[106] Art. 3 par. 11 Regulation (EU) 2023/1543.

[107] Art. 3 par. 12 Regulation (EU) 2023/1543.

Order and should have access to an effective legal remedy, the latter (who, for example, may have been randomly involved in the suspect or accused's communications) is not overlooked by the Regulation, which does grant them specific rights, although the principles of necessity, proportionality, confidentiality of communications, protection of privacy and personal data should be granted on substantial and not merely formal grounds.

As for Italy, Italian legislators started to respond to the challenges of digital forensics following the ratification of the Council of Europe Convention on Cybercrime, done at Budapest on 23 November 2001 ("Budapest Convention").[108] Indeed, the transposition of this fundamental international legal instrument provided an important opportunity to amend the Articles of the Italian Code of Criminal Procedure regarding inspections, searches and seizures, and to introduce a new specific provision on the seizure of electronic data.

In particular, the new second paragraph of Article 244 CCP, which regulates the cases and methods of inspections, allows the judicial authority to carry out "digital" inspections, which can be performed by means of descriptive and photographic instruments and any other technical operation in relation to computer or electronic systems, by adopting adequate technical measures to grant the preservation of the original data and prevent their alteration. Concerning searches, the new paragraph 1 *bis* of Article 247 CCP states that if there are reasonable grounds to believe that data, information, software or any other traces relating to the offence are stored in a computer or electronic system, even if it is protected by security measures, a search shall be ordered, adopting adequate technical measures to grant the preservation of the original data and prevent their alteration. Hence, the digital data that is contained in a physical medium, such as the hard disk of a personal computer, is the digital document that can be viewed through an inspection, searched, and seized. All these operations must be conducted by observing the procedural criteria for the validity and integrity of digital evidence. Also, to reduce the harm created by the criminal proceeding, when data is seized from a telecommunications service provider or internet service provider, the judicial authority may establish that a search shall be conducted by copying the information on an appropriate medium and by following technical procedures capable of ensuring the conformity and immutability of the data.[109] This is the only case in which the rights of a third party (the service provider) are directly taken into consideration by the regulations on digital evidence. Here, what can be considered preeminent is the right of the provider to continue its activity, also because any interruption would negatively affect consumers collectively.

Moreover, Law no. 48/2008 explicitly introduced the possibility to seize electronic correspondence pursuant to Article 254 CCP (which should not be confused with the interception of electronic communications that implies a real-time exchange of information). This is considered a special type of seizure that requires the

[108] Law no. 48 of 13 March 2008.

[109] See Art. 254 *bis* CCP.

observance of stricter guarantees because of the particularly high degree of interference with Article 15 of the Italian Constitution and Article 8 ECHR.

All these tools, which are suitable especially in cases of "digital crime scenes", concern a "static" time fore e-evidence,[110] that is offline evidence gathering.[111] A proper protection of individuals' rights calls for a trade-off between the needs of the investigation and the respect of the individual's right to privacy, in all its expressions. Theoretically, the public interest in the repression of crimes offers lawful grounds for restricting individual rights, but this concept does not allow any indiscriminate intrusion into people's private lives. Otherwise, we would see a violation both of the right to private life, in the two aspects of inviolability of the home and correspondence, protected by Article 8 ECHR, Articles 7 and 8 EU Charter of Fundamental Rights, Article 14 and 15 of the Italian Constitution, and of the right to fair trial under Article 6 ECHR, Article 47 EU Charter of Fundamental Rights and 111 of the Italian Constitution.[112] The risks of a breach of such human rights are exponentially exacerbated in the context of the "Infosphere",[113] where in contemporary society people express their personality—in accordance with Article 2 of Italian Constitution—and whose dignity and rights must be respected, regardless of the "immaterial" nature of digital spaces. Consequently, in the digital age the right to privacy (understood in a broad sense)[114] must receive the same level of protection given to "traditional" rights, in the light of the principles of necessity and proportionality and the supremacy of the rule of law,[115] which must establish the circumstances and legitimate grounds for limitations on fundamental rights, and envisage

---

[110]For the problems related to online searches and digital evidence captured in real time, *infra* Sect. 4.3.

[111]Felicioni (2019), p. 1381.

[112]See Quattrocolo (2020), p. 44.

[113]Floridi (2014), p. 24.

[114]Despite the absence in the Italian Constitution of an explicit provision regarding the right to privacy, the Italian Constitutional Court still (correctly) qualifies it as a fundamental right, similarly to the right to the secrecy of correspondence. "This Court believes that the purpose is to ensure the fundamental right to the secrecy of correspondence and any other means of communications, protected by Articles 2 and 15 of the Italian Constitution (*ex plurimis*, Italian constitutional court, judgments no. 366 of 1991, no. 81 of 1993, no. 463 of 1994, no. 372 of 2006), and to the equally fundamental citizens' right to private life in its multiple aspects. An excessive compression of defensive rights, of the right to an effective remedy and the principle of a fair trial may thus not be justified". Cf. Italian Constitutional Court, judgment no. 173 of 22 April 2009.

[115]The ECtHR recently addressed the issue in the following terms "Article 8 par. 2 of the Convention requires the law in question to be 'compatible with the rule of law'. In the context of searches and seizures, the domestic law must provide some protection to the individual against arbitrary interference with Article 8 rights. Thus, the domestic law must be sufficiently clear in its terms to give citizens an adequate indication as to the circumstances and conditions under which public authorities are empowered to resort to any such measures. Moreover, search and seizure represent a serious interference with private life, home and correspondence and must accordingly be based on a 'law' that is particularly precise. It is essential to have clear, detailed rules on the subject", cf. ECtHR, *Saber v. Norway*, judgment of 17 December 2020, Appl. no. 459/18, par. 50. See also ECtHR, *Särgava v. Estonia*, judgment of 16 November 2021, Appl. no. 698/19, par. 87.

judicial authorization case by case, as well as the right to an effective remedy in the event of violations.[116]

In particular, one of the most tangible risks regards digital searches, which have sometimes turned out to be illegitimate "explorative" tools with preventive monitoring purposes for acquiring information on other crimes, instead of a (legitimate) means of examining the *corpus delicti* or traces related to the criminal offence. This happens if, for example, the investigative authorities improperly exercise the power granted to them under Article 248(2) CCP, which allows the examination of documents and correspondence, as well as information, software and data stored in databases for the purposes of seizing the things that can be subject to a search or ascertaining "other circumstances useful for the investigation". Moreover, in the event of refusal to comply with a request for delivery, the judicial authority can proceed by performing an investigative measure. The Italian Court of Cassation strongly criticised the misuse of these faculties for merely explorative intents and without any clear evidentiary purpose linked to a specific and tangible offence.[117] However, a formidable "antidote" to unjustified intrusions into a person's private sphere could be the correct implementation of Article 247(1 *bis*) CCP, which sets out the requirement of reasonable grounds that data, information, software, or any other traces relating to the offence should be stored in a computer or electronic system, and a judicial order must give reasons regarding the existence of such indications. In this way at least an *ex post* examination on the legitimacy of the order is ensured.

However, none of the mentioned provisions regarding electronic evidence takes into consideration the harm which digital forensics might cause to third parties. In fact, the (few) rights attributed to such subjects are those provided in Regulation (EU) 2016/679 and Directive (EU) 2016/680, as well as Directive 2002/58/EC of the European Parliament and the Council regarding the protection of natural persons with regard to the processing of personal data, also in the context of criminal proceedings, and on the free movement of such data. In this regard States are required to provide for personal data to be processed lawfully, fairly and in a secure way, collected for specified, explicit and legitimate purposes in accordance with the principle of proportionality, and to establish time-limits for storage and review.

As for the possibility of digital evidence being seized for evidentiary purposes, it can be obtained by seizing the whole physical electronic system where the data are stored, or by cloning only the relevant data using suitable technical computer forensics procedures. Article 257 CCP allows the accused, "the person from whom objects have been seized" and "the person who would be entitled to their restitution" to submit a request for the re-examination of the prosecution's order regarding the seizure. From this perspective, third parties are also entitled to a judicial review of the decision (such as the holder of a database). Also, restitution of the original seized "documents" may follow the copying of information in accordance with Article 258 CCP. Moreover, according to Article 262 CCP, if the evidentiary purposes of

[116]Felicioni (2019), p. 1404.

[117]See Italian Court of Cassation, judgment no. 19618 of 17 April 2012.

the seizure lapse, the objects shall be returned to the entitled person, even prior to the passing of judgment, and if the objects have been seized from a third party, restitution must not be ordered in favour of others without the third party being fairly heard by the judge. And, in any case, after the final judgment, the seized objects must be returned to the person entitled to them, unless confiscation is ordered. A brief overview of these provisions shows that third parties are taken into consideration from the point of view of the protection of their right to property, to which the right to restitution is linked. However, such rules reflect a "traditional" approach to seizures, since the code of procedural law refers to (material) objects and (material) documents. In the digital era, what is more important for the person entitled to restitution is not the material availability of the seized thing, but the exclusive possession of the acquired information and data. Digital transition, in other words, has led to a sort of shift from the right to property to the right to privacy. This has raised significant issues regarding the application of the mentioned regulation, since the permanence of the interest in restitution is debatable when the physical medium is returned to its owner, while the extracted and copied data remain in possession of the public authorities. However, the ECtHR has stated the need for the safeguards under Article 6 ECHR to be fulfilled also with autonomous regards to the content of the seized data, hence the interest in appealing against the seizure order remains untouched, regardless of the restitution of the material support (for example, a pen drive).[118]

4.3 Wiretapping and Telecommunications Surveillance

After having examined the problems related to "offline" evidence gathering, we will now assess the issues concerning "online" and "live" digital evidence, which belong to the broad area of interceptions of communications and telecommunications. The Italian Code of Criminal Procedure does not provide a legal definition of interceptions, so we will take ours from a famous judgment of the Court of Cassation, according to which it is the real-time

> collection, obtained by means of electronic recording instruments, of the content of an ongoing conversation or a secret communication between two or more people, when the apprehension itself is performed by a subject who hides his presence from the interlocutors.[119]

Wiretapping operations can concern telephone conversations and other forms of telecommunication,[120] face-to-face conversations (so called "environmental interceptions")[121] and digital or electronic communications.[122] Moreover,

[118] See Testaguzza (2019), p. 1459.

[119] Italian Court of Cassation, Joint Division judgment of 28 May 2003, no. 36747, *Torcasio*.

[120] Art. 266 CCP.

[121] Art. 266(2) CCP.

[122] Art. 266 *bis* CCP, introduced by Law no. 547/1993.

communications in specific environments can be tapped by using hacking tools, "trojan horses" and malware, capable of monitoring basically anything that happens both in cyberspace and in the physical space. Therefore, it is easy to understand why this is probably the most intrusive investigative measure with regards to the right to privacy, freedom and secrecy of correspondence and *habeas data*. Not surprisingly, the ECtHR has underlined on many occasions that such interference in individuals' private life is only admissible under Article 8 ECHR "in accordance with the law", if it pursues one or more "legitimate aims" and is "necessary in a democratic society" in order to protect essential public interests, such as crime prevention and repression, and always in the light of the principle of proportionality.[123] The possibility of interference with the private sphere of third parties is very high and, indeed, Italian legislation indirectly protects this: on the one hand, by imposing strict requirements for the judicial authorization of such investigative measures (which became stricter and stricter with the passing of time), and, on the other, by strict limitations on the possibility of disclosing the results of the operations.

More specifically, in Italy wiretapping and similar forms of surveillance are allowed only for very serious offences indicated by the law and, in the event of the surveillance of communication among people in specific places (so-called *intercettazioni ambientali*), they can be performed in places that are considered "homes" only if there are serious grounds to believe that criminal activities are carried out in those exact places. This condition does not apply when the criminal investigations regard particularly serious offences, such as terrorism-related offences or organised crime: in these cases, the interception of communication among people in specific place is "always" allowed.[124] Furthermore, these forms of surveillance may be requested by the public prosecutor and authorised by the judge only if they are deemed to be essential for the continuation of the investigations and there are serious grounds to believe a criminal offence has been committed.[125] When hacking tools are used on an electronic device (such as a smartphone), the order that authorises the surveillance, explaining the reasons, must establish the place and time in relation to which the activation of the recording is allowed (but this rule does not apply when the surveillance of people in specific places is always allowed).

An important provision for the safeguards of the fundamental rights of the individuals whose communications are listened to during wiretapping operations (therefore not necessarily the suspect or accused, but also any "third parties") is that only what is relevant to the needs of the investigation must be noted in the report where the contents of the conversation are written down. Everything else must be left out, and no mention of it must be included in the records, which will contain the expression "the omitted conversation is not useful for the investigations".[126] Moreover, Italian law prohibits entry in the records of verbal expressions that may offend

---

[123] *Ex multis*, ECtHR, *Blaj v. Romania* judgment of 8 April 2014, Appl. no. 36259/04.

[124] See Art. 266(2 *bis*) CCP.

[125] Art. 267 CCP.

[126] Art. 268 CCP.

the person's honour and reputation and any circumstances regarding their private life, unless they are relevant for the investigations. Such procedural rules have recently been introduced[127] by requiring important guarantees for the right to privacy to balance the intrusion into the private sphere and the needs of the investigation. However, third parties who have been accidentally involved in wiretapping operations do not have the right to access the recordings and to participate in the judicial procedure regarding the removal of irrelevant sensible data and the information whose use in trial is prohibited by law. Such rights are granted only to the public prosecutor and the defendant's lawyer. Third parties can only request the judge to order the destruction of the documental recordings, which are not necessary in the criminal proceeding, for the purposes of protecting their privacy, since Article 269 CCP generally mentions any "interested person". In addition, third parties might not know or control at all the results of wiretaps when they are used in criminal proceedings other than those for which they were ordered (this is possible with the limitations imposed by Article 270 CCP).[128] Finally, if the wiretaps have been performed in violation of the mentioned legal provisions, their results cannot be used as evidence, similarly to conversations with lawyers, religious ministers, or healthcare professionals when they concern facts known on account of the latters' function, service or profession.[129] In all these cases, the judge must order the destruction of the recordings of the operations, unless they constitute the *corpus delicti*.

Recently, in the specific field of wiretapping some amendments has been introduced by the so-called *Riforma Nordio*[130] aimed at ensuring protection for third parties unrelated to the proceedings regarding the circulation of intercepted communications. It is therefore prohibited to publish, even partially, the content of any interception, unless such content has been reproduced by the judge in the reasoning of a ruling or used during the trial. Moreover, the dissemination of any interception that is proscribed from being published is prohibited when the request is made by a party other than the parties and their legal counsel. Additionally, the inclusion of expressions in the transcription records of interceptions that could potentially identify individuals other than the parties is prohibited. Furthermore, the public prosecutor is obliged to remove from the logs any expressions that could damage the reputation or reveal sensitive data of individuals other than the parties.

[127] Art. 268 (2)(2 *bis*) was modified by Law Decree no. 161/2019, converted by Law no. 7/2020 and by Law Decree no. 105/2023, converted by Law no. 137/2023.

[128] Indeed, in ECtHR, *Contrada v. Italy (n. 4)*, judgement of 23 May 2024, Appl. No. 2507/19, the Court observed that the Italian legal system does not provide any notification to third parties. Furthermore, third parties lack the possibility of applying to the court to verify the legitimacy and necessity of the measure and to receive, if applicable, an adequate protection. Within this light, the Court concluded that the Italian legal system fails to provide adequate and effective safeguards for individuals subjected to interceptions without being involved in criminal proceedings.

[129] Art. 270 CCP.

[130] D.D.L. n. A.S. 808.

While the CCP poses quite clear guarantees to the rights of the persons affected by wiretapping,[131] despite the deep intrusive nature of such operations, the most serious problems for the protection of the fundamental rights of third parties' (and even more of the accused) arise when the public authorities perform activities that are similar in the scope, nature and extent to wiretapping or surveillance, but are not considered so. For example, the secret recording of conversations carried out by one of the interlocutors is considered by Italian courts as a mere document.[132] Moreover, Article 266 *bis* CCP leaves out some relevant groups with regards to the interception of the flow of communications that happen in electronic or digital systems. In fact, the need for the 'real time' capture of communications between certain subjects prevents some highly intrusive investigative measures, such as online surveillance by means of keylogger software, 'online searches' and the apprehension of existing data from mobile phones from being considered as wiretapping. Only the 'live' secret surveillance of the contents of online chats or mail messages is considered as wiretapping. In other cases, case law tends to apply the rules regarding search and seizures of digital data.[133] In a near future, new challenges will be posed by the spread of AI home assistants, whose hacking can cause a huge intrusion into individuals' private and family life.

4.4 Forensic DNA Profiling: Genetic Fingerprints

It is widely known that every person has a unique DNA, which is present in every single cell of his/her body and carries every kind of genetic information. Nowadays, the analysis of such "genetic fingerprints" by collecting biological samples plays a crucial role in criminal proceedings, above all for personal identification, and has undeniable advantages for the ascertainment of facts. However, the methods used for gathering this particular type of scientific evidence may deeply interfere with a number of fundamental rights (above all the right to privacy and *habeas corpus*), especially if the tests are run by taking biological materials from a living human body. The problem of the intrusion into the individual private sphere becomes even more dramatic if the person being tested does not give his/her consent to the operation that, therefore, may be considered as compulsory medical intervention.[134] Otherwise, if the sample is taken without any coercion ('touch DNA' or low-level

[131] Along these lines, Italian legislators followed the (many) indications provided by the ECtHR in relation to Article 8 ECHR, see *inter alia* ECtHR, GC, *Big Brother Watch and Others v. the United Kingdom*, judgment of 25 May 2021, Appl. Nos. 5810/13, 62322/14, 24960/15; ECtHR, GC, *Roman Zakharov v. Russia*, judgement of 4 December 2015, Appl. no. 47143/06; ECtHR, GC, *Rotaru v. Romania*, judgement of 4 May 2000, Appl. no. 28341/95.

[132] Italian Court of Cassation, Joint Division, Torcasio, cit.

[133] See Torre (2019), p. 1465.

[134] Along these lines, see ECtHR, GC, *Jalloh v. Germany*, judgment of 11 July 2006, Appl. no. 54810/00; ECtHR, *Schmidt v. Germany*, judgment of 5 January 2006, Appl. no. 32352/02.

DNA, that can be obtained by seizing objects with residual organic materials), both the European Court of Human Rights and the Italian Court of Cassation consider this activity as having a minor impact on the rights of the individuals concerned, meaning they may be carried out without respecting any particular defensive guarantee, which must instead be granted in the subsequent phase of expert examination.[135]

The Italian Parliament has introduced some important procedural rules to regulate the field of forensic DNA analysis, by trying to satisfy the difficult task to find a fair balance between the needs of the investigation and the safeguard of the fundamental rights of the person involved.[136] In particular, through Article 224 *bis* CCP, introduced by Law no. 85 of 30 June 2009, Italy adhered to the Prüm Convention of 2005.[137] This regulation concerns the case of expert evidence gathering and allows, under certain conditions, the compulsory performing of "medical checks" and activities that can "affect personal freedom", such as hair sampling or oral swabbing from living persons, to determine the subject's DNA profile.

For the purpose of this study, it is important to note that these activities do not necessarily concern solely the offender. Indeed, if they are deemed essential to the ascertainment of the alleged offence, they can involve everyone: not only the suspect and the victims, but also minors and those who are not formal participants in criminal proceedings.[138] However, the legal safeguards provided for shall apply independently of the status of concerned person as suspect or third party.[139] If the compulsory sampling concerns third parties, they are called upon to appoint a lawyer to be assisted during the operations, otherwise the evidence will be completely invalid.[140]

Concerning the general conditions of lawfulness of the coercive taking of DNA samples, first of all, it is noteworthy that this measure can only be enforced in the event of particularly serious offences explicitly determined by law and by means of a court order stating the reasons. This order must contain certain information, such as a

---

[135] ECtHR, GC, *Saunders v. United Kingdom*, judgment of 17 December 1996, Appl. no. 19187/91; ECtHR, GC, *O'Halloran and Francis v. United Kingdom*, judgment of 29 June 2007, Appl. no. 15809/02; Italian Court of Cassation, Division 2, judgment of 10 January 2012, no. 2087.

[136] The first innovation was brought about through the introduction by the Law Decree no. 144/2005 (converted by Law no. 155/2005) of a new paragraph (2 *bis*) in Article 349 CCP. This provision regards police powers, with the authorization of the Public Prosecutor, to take hair or saliva samples against the suspect's will, for purposes of identification. However, since this rule regards only the suspected person and could not be applied to third parties, it falls beyond the scope of our study.

[137] See Sect. 2.2.

[138] See Art. 72 *bis* Implementing Rules to CCP.

[139] The possibility of forcible collection of third parties' DNA has been openly acknowledged by the ECtHR, for instance, in the case of a relevant witness. See ECtHR, *Caruana v. Malta*, judgment of 15 May 2018, Appl. no. 41079/16, par. 32. The Court considers that recourse to such medical procedures, particularly when minor, is also not a priori prohibited in order to obtain evidence related to the commission of a crime when the subject of the test is not the offender, but a relevant witness, as in the present case. It thus cannot be considered as inherently unlawful. What is of paramount importance is that the measure is in accordance with the relevant Convention requirements".

[140] See Art. 224 *bis*(7) CCP.

list of the specific operations that have to be performed, the reason why they are essential with regards to the ascertainment of the facts related to the offence at hand, and the right to be assisted by a lawyer or a trusted person. A second important guarantee is represented by the general methodological rule that requires full respect for the individual's dignity and decency during performance of any tests (although the precise extent of such provision is naturally submitted to discretional evaluations). Moreover, if various techniques can be used to achieve the same evidentiary results, the least intrusive one must be preferred. Last but not least, there is an absolute prohibition to carry out unlawful measures or activities which can potentially endanger the life, physical integrity or health of the subject or her unborn child, or that are particularly painful according to the medical community. Then, specifically for the offended person, the law provides for his/her right to be notified of the court order concerning such operations, at least 3 days before their execution.[141]

This investigative activity can be carried out on third persons both *ex officio* and following a formal request from participants during trial; in addition, they can be performed during pre-trial inquiry at the public prosecutor's request if authorized by the judge, under the same conditions provided by Article 224 *bis*.[142] In the event of urgency and if there are reasonable grounds to believe that the delayed collection of biological samples may seriously or irreparably endanger the ongoing investigation, the public prosecutor can even proceed without such authorization, issuing an order stating the reasons, and has also the power to order the compulsory appearance of the requested person and his/her forced testing in the event of lack of consent. A counterbalance to this highly intrusive power is represented by the mandatory *ex post* validation by the judge for preliminary investigations, which must be requested by the public prosecutor within 48 h and obtained in the following 48 h, otherwise the gathered evidence is not usable.[143]

As we have seen, these procedural safeguards are strengthened by the provision of invalidity of the act or inadmissibility of the evidence collected. But this might not be enough in the light of the sacrifice that this kind of investigative instrument causes to fundamental freedoms. Indeed, they remain potentially highly intrusive because the objective requirements for their legitimacy have been established under legislation that provides only generic indications. On one hand, the condition of the seriousness of the offence is met for all intentional offences which are punishable with imprisonment for a maximum term exceeding 3 years, and the hypothesis of vehicular homicide or injury; on the other, the essentiality of the evidence for the ascertainment of the facts is a circumstance that can only really be verified *ex post*, while, at the moment of compulsory medical testing, its necessity is mere conjecture. Besides, the addressees of the forced collection of biological materials are not *a priori* defined by the law, so they could literally be anyone. However, the fact that a

[141] Obviously, in any case the judicial order must also be notified to the person to be tested (which may be a "third party"), the accused and his defence counsel.

[142] Art. 359 *bis*(1) CCP.

[143] Art. 359 *bis*(2) CCP.

coercive DNA analysis can affect people who are completely extraneous to the criminal proceeding (third parties) cannot legitimate massive screening practices, as recently clarified by the Italian Court of Cassation.[144] In fact, by interpreting in a restrictive way the requirement of the relevance of the evidence gathering for the ascertainment of the alleged offence, the Court stated the need for a direct connection between the person whose DNA is taken and the criminal offence (for example, it could be someone who directly witnessed the fact at the crime scene).

Finally, as for data retention, Italian law requires the immediate destruction of the biological samples obtained after the execution of the operations described by Article 224 *bis*, unless their storage is deemed essential by the Court and, in any case, they must be destroyed at the latest when the criminal proceeding ends.[145]

4.5 So-called "Atypical" Investigative Activities

The Italian Code of Criminal Procedure, while providing detailed regulations on a number of means of evidence gathering, allows for the collection of further information through means that are not specifically regulated by law, pursuant to Article 189 CCP.[146] The former are defined as "typical" evidentiary activities, while the latter are so-called "atypical" investigative acts, whose results can be acquired by the judge as evidence if they are relevant for the ascertainment of the facts and do not jeopardise the person's moral freedom. Moreover, the admissibility of such proof is subject to the adversarial method between parties on the techniques used for its gathering.

In this way, Italian legislators keep the legal system open to the possible contribution of new technological developments.[147] Of course, this does not imply that under Article 189 CCP, unlawful evidence can be admitted and used in a criminal trial, since the respect for constitutional principles and the fundamental rights protected by supranational law must be ensured in any case. Moreover, Article 188 CCP affirms that evidence gathering shall be carried out without jeopardizing

[144] Italian Court of Cassation, judgment no. 28538 of 17 January.

[145] Art. 72 *quater* Implementing Provisions to CCP. However, the extent of this provision had to be adjusted with the institution of the National DNA Database by law no. 85/2009, which ratified the Prüm Treaty. The conservation of such data does not only pose deep ethical and practical dilemmas with respect to the need to protect the fundamental right to privacy, but the problems are further emphasised by the possibility of their cross-border exchange in a transnational cooperation system on the basis of Council Decision 2008/615/JHA and 2008/616/JHA of 23 June 2008, since we see a sort of rarefaction of the powers of control of the subject whose DNA was taken.

[146] Art. 189 CCP: "If evidence not regulated by law is requested, the court may introduce it if it is deemed suitable to determine the facts and does not compromise the moral freedom of the person. After hearing the parties on the methods for gathering evidence, the court shall order the admission of evidence".

[147] Chiavario (2022), p. 494.

moral freedom and the right to self-determination, thus establishing a limit which cannot be pushed even with the concerned persons' consent.

Article 189 can cover a number of relevant evidentiary activities that may affect third parties' rights and that are carried out through ICTs,[148] such as the video surveillance of non-communicative behaviours by the police during the preliminary investigations (even in private domiciles),[149] or illegal recordings in workplaces. According to the Italian Court of Cassation, also GPS localization and video recording by means of external cameras may be covered by this regulation and, since they are considered as particular forms of police surveillance and stakeouts, fall within the scope of the principle of the autonomy of investigation by the police and can be carried out without judicial authorization.[150] In fact, in these cases, the Court deems applicable the regulation of interceptions (with its safeguards also for third parties), but invokes Article 189,[151] thus excluding everyone who is not a formal party in the criminal proceeding from the process of evaluating the admissibility of evidence. Indeed, since formal parties can participate in the hearing concerning the admission of "atypical" means of evidence gathering, the third parties can only exercise their rights if they hold the status of formal participants in the criminal proceeding (that is they are either a civil plaintiff or the party civilly liable for damages related to the criminal offence or the party civilly liable for the criminal fine). In all other cases, a third party who has been involved by the methods used for evidence gathering has no power regarding its acquisition.

Another case in which the Italian Court of Cassation recalls Article 189 regards the printing of the contents of electronic communications (for example, an email). In fact, in line with common practice, police officers independently do this, without any formal authorisation, thus depriving the person entitled to that information (and whose right to privacy has been compromised) of the possibility to ask for restitution. The Court deems the regulation regarding seizures to be applicable only if the value of the obtained information is strictly linked to their private nature,[152] such as the name of a source or a commercial project, thus connecting once again the right to restitution more to economic values than to the right to privacy.

---

[148] See Spangher (2019), p. 1303.

[149] According to the Italian Court of Cassation, the results of such recordings are usable in trial even without previous authorization by the judicial authorities if they have been carried out with the consent of the owner of the domicile. In the case taken into consideration by the Court the third party directly gave his consent to the video recording in his capacity as offended person. See Italian Court of Cassation, judgment no. 41332 of 7 July 2015.

[150] Italian Court of Cassation, judgment no. 26795 of 28 March 2006. However, many legal scholars suggest a better framing of such activities under the regulation of interceptions pursuant to Articles 266-271 CCP.

[151] See Italian Court of Cassation, Division 4, judgment of 4 June 2013, no. 11419; Italian Court of Cassation, judgment no. 33567 of 12 May 2016.

[152] See Italian Court of Cassation, judgment of 24 February 2015, no. 24617, *Rizzo*; Italian Court of Cassation, judgment of 27 October 2016, no. 25527, *Storari*.

From another perspective, Article 189 provides the legal basis for types of '*new* scientific evidence', by means of modern, rapidly-developing technological tools previously unavailable. These tools are particularly good at providing *apparently* certain information that can deeply affect decision-making processes[153] (such as forensic voice comparison or digital crime scene reconstruction). Hence, the role of expert witnesses—who, as we already said, may be considered for the purposes of this study as 'third parties'[154]—becomes crucial, thanks to their technical and scientific input for the judge's evaluations. Indeed, the scientific nature of the techniques and methods used is essential for the protection of every individual involved in the criminal proceeding, since it grants reliability of the obtained evidentiary results. Both the judge as "gatekeeper"[155] of the expert testimony and the experts themselves must prevent "junk science" from contaminating a criminal trial, in order to ensure the principle of "scientific reasonableness".[156]

4.6 Data Retention

In the light of striking an adequate trade-off between the need to protect the person's right to privacy and investigative needs, Italian regulations on data retention, while requiring that collected or processed personal data cannot be kept longer than is necessary to collect information, requires mobile service providers to store mobile network data for the purposes of crime control.

According to Article 132 of Legislative Decree no. 196 of 30 June 2003 ("Privacy Code")—as recently modified by Article 1(1) (a) of Law Decree no. 132 of 30 September 2021, converted by Law no. 178 of 23 November 2021[157]—telephone

---

[153] See Chiavario (2022), p. 497.

[154] Cf. Sects. 1.4 and 7.5.

[155] The role of the judge as "gatekeeper" of the scientific method was firstly theorised overseas, see Daubert v. Merrell Dow Pharmaceuticals, Inc., 509 U.S. 579 (1993); General Electric v. Joiner, 522 U.S. 136 (1997); Kumho Tire Co. v. Carmichael, 526 U.S. 137 (1999). By now, it is widely recognized also by Italian courts, *ex plurimis* Court of Cassation, judgment no. 43786 of 17 September 2010, Cozzini.

[156] For the progressive development of this principle in Italian Constitutional Court case-law, see judgment of 26th May 1998, no. 185; judgment of 2 April 1999, no. 121; judgment of 10 June 2014, no. 162; judgment of 5 December 2014, no. 274.

[157] The Court of Justice of European Union has stated many times already that Article 15(1) of the Directive 2002/58/EC, in the light of Articles 7, 8, 11 and 52(1) of the Charter of Fundamental Rights of the European Union, "precludes legislative measures which (. . .) provide, as a preventive measure, for the general and indiscriminate retention of traffic and location data". More recently, it further developed individual safeguards, by stating that "Article 15(1) of Directive 2002/58, read in the light of Articles 7, 8 and 11 and Article 52(1) of the Charter, must be interpreted as precluding national legislation that confers upon the public prosecutor's office, whose task is to direct the criminal pre-trial procedure and to bring, where appropriate, the public prosecution in subsequent proceedings, the power to authorise access of a public authority to traffic and location data for the purposes of a criminal investigation" (C-746/18 H.K./Prokuratuur).

traffic data and online navigation data must be retained by the provider, respectively, for 36 months for the purposes of detecting and suppressing criminal offences; while the data concerning non-answered calls must be kept for 30 days. During this time span, data can be acquired from the provider by means of a judicial warrant stating the reasons why they are relevant for the investigations and there are sufficient indications of a serious crime.[158] This warrant may be issued not only if the public prosecutor or the defendant's lawyer requests it, but also on the application of the lawyer of a 'third party'. Moreover, in cases of duly justified urgency, the collection of such data may be directly ordered by the public prosecutor, but this order must be immediately (within 48 h) be communicated to the judge, who is required to validate it within further 48 h—otherwise the data cannot be used at trial.

The provider must not divulge the order received, and the processing of such data shall be carried out by the public authorities in accordance with the indications of the Italian Data Protection Authority (*Garante per la protezione dei dati personali*) to safeguard the concerned persons and in order to ensure the quality and protection of the data (data that, in any case, must be periodically destroyed).

Despite this general rule, the protection of the right to privacy in the context of criminal proceedings is generally weakened because the person cannot exercise his/her rights related to personal data nor present a complaint in every case in which the exercise of such rights could cause a serious prejudice to anti-money-laundering regulations and other particular circumstances, such as the prevention of tax evasion.[159]

Moreover, data retention is allowed for 72 months[160] for the most serious crimes,[161] especially in the field of the fight against terrorism and criminal organisations. This entails a huge breach not only of the accused's rights, but also of those of third parties, that is, of everyone who has communicated with the accused and who has nothing to do with the criminal proceeding. Indeed, every communication between individuals using a telephone or telematic instrument implies some data traffic for the service provider, and the fact that such data is 'external' to the content of the communication should not lead us to underestimate its 'intrusiveness' (such as the possibility of locating someone by tracking the movements of their phone by analysing where calls were made or received, or determining the precise date, time and kind of their communications).

The strong interference with individual rights appears even clearer if we consider that the service provider does not (and could not) know the purposes of the retention, and must store all kinds of personal information for a potentially very long time.[162]

---

[158] In particular, Article 132(3) Code of Privacy refers to crimes for which the law provides for a life sentence or the penalty of imprisonment for a maximum term of at least 3 years, and the aggravated crimes of menace and harassment committed by means of telephone.

[159] Art. 2 *undecies* Code of Privacy.

[160] See Art. 24 of Law no. 167 of 20 November 2017.

[161] We are referring to the criminal offences listed in Articles 51(3 *quater*) and 407(2) (a) CCP.

[162] See Beccari (2019), p. 1599; Marcolini (2019), p. 1579; Ruggieri (2017), p. 2483; Signorato (2022), p. 72.

5 Pre-trial Measures and the Protection of Fundamental Rights of Third Parties

During the pre-trial inquiry, the ordering of pre-trial measures may affect the fundamental rights of others than the formal parties to the criminal proceedings. In particular, measures aimed at securing assets may affect several rights and the freedom of third parties, such as the right to property or freedom to conduct a business, as granted by Article 1 of Protocol no. 1 to the ECHR, Articles 16 and 17 CFREU and Articles 41 and 42 of the Italian Constitution.

The Italian CCP regulates two different forms of seizure: so-called 'precautionary or conservative seizure' (*sequestro conservativo*)[163] and 'preventive seizure' (*sequestro preventivo*).[164] The former is aimed at freezing the properties and economic assets of the person who can be held liable at the conclusion of the criminal proceeding, if there is a *periculum in mora*, that is reasonable grounds to believe that the securities for the payment of a financial penalty, the costs of proceedings and any other sum owed to the Treasury of the State are not available or will be lost. While in this case the only person who can be affected by the pre-trial measure is the accused, if there are reasonable grounds to believe that the securities for civil-law obligations deriving from the offence are unavailable or will be lost, the assets of the person with civil liability for damages of the civil plaintiff may be seized. It is worth noting that the civil party (and thus a formal party) is entitled to request precautionary seizure because of the tight connection with the issue of civil liability. This precautionary seizure is subject to the guarantee of a judicial warrant stating the reasons, that is nevertheless issued without the recognition of the parties' participatory rights. The person affected by the pre-trial measure, however, has the right to request its re-examination, regardless of his formal status.[165] In any case, conservative seizure ceases to have effect if it is revoked by the judge because the party offers adequate guarantees and when the criminal proceeding ends with a sentence of acquittal.[166]

While conservative seizure does not raise relevant issues regarding the safeguards of the fundamental rights of third parties, preventive seizure appears more problematic. This type of seizure may be ordered if the availability of material items related to the criminal offence might aggravate or extend its consequences or facilitate the commission of other crimes.[167] Hence, the authorities may seize any kind of material item which has an instrumental link with the commission of the crime. However, such a generic risk is not sufficient, but there is a need for a concrete and actual danger, as clearly pointed out in the reasoning of the judicial warrant, as underlined

[163] Art. 316 CCP.

[164] Art. 321 CCP.

[165] Art. 318 CCP.

[166] See Artt. 317 and 319 CCP.

[167] Art. 321(1) CCP.

by the Italian Court of Cassation.[168] Moreover, anyone may be affected by this measure and, of course, a third party too, *i.e.* even a person who is completely extraneous to the offence.[169] The extension of the effects of seizure on third parties is explicitly recognized by some *extra-codicem* provision, for example in the field of the fight against organised crime. According to the Italian Constitutional Court, preventive seizure would not even necessitate the existence of a strong suspicion of guilt against an identified suspect (as requested for pre-trial detention and further restrictions on personal freedom), the material commission of a crime being sufficient, since in this matter legislators have wide-ranging discretional powers in their regulatory choices.[170]

Another case of preventive measure is strictly connected to confiscation "by equivalent",[171] according to which any object that may be confiscated may also be seized. This is normally a discretionary power of the judge, even though the law prescribes some mandatory cases of confiscation (for example in the field of crimes of public officials against the public administration). This type of seizure, linked to confiscation, might seriously compromise third-party rights. The Italian Court of Cassation addressed the issue with specific regard to legal entities: preventive seizure aimed at the confiscation by equivalent of the assets of a legal person is possible only for those economic assets that are directly linked to the profits of the commission of the tax offence by the legal entity's offices when such profits are available for the legal entity. Instead, seizure is forbidden when the profits of the offence were not identified by the authorities and when the assets of a person who is not extraneous to the crime can be seized instead.[172]

Preventive seizure is ordinarily issued by means of a court order stating the reason at the Public Prosecutor's request, but in urgent situations the Public Prosecutor may act independently, and the law provides for an *ex post* procedure of validation by the judge, that must be started within 48 h after performance of the seizure. The persons affected by the freezing order may no longer dispose of the seized items, but if a company or firm is seized, the legitimate owner may be appointed as custodian, thus mitigating the interference with his right to property and his freedom to conduct a business.[173]

The effects of preventive seizure may cease because of its withdrawal, which can be requested also by the concerned third party, who has also the power to ask for the re-examination of the decision[174] and to appeal.[175] In any case, the seized objects

---

[168] Italian Court of Cassation, judgment of 18 July 2012, no. 32807.

[169] *Ex multis*, Italian Court of Cassation, Joint Division, judgment of 29 May 2998, no. 25933, *Malgioglio*.

[170] Italian constitutional Court, judgment no. 48/1994.

[171] Art. 321(2) CCP.

[172] Italian Court of Cassation, judgment of 30 January 2014, no. 10561, *Gubert*.

[173] Art. 104 *bis* Implementing Provisions to CCP.

[174] Art. 322 CCP.

[175] Art. 322 *bis* CCP.

must be returned to the legitimate owner in the event of acquittal, unless they need to be confiscated.

6 Third Parties and the Decision to Charge (or to Terminate the Proceedings)

According to the CCP, third parties have no influence on the decision to charge or to terminate the proceedings. However, in the case of offences which can be prosecuted at the request of the aggrieved parties, they could withdraw the formal complaint, and, if the accused accepts the withdrawal, the judge must state that there is no criminal liability.[176]

7 Third Parties in Court Proceedings

7.1 The Main Features of Italian Court Proceedings

The court proceeding represents a crucial stage in Italian criminal justice, which starts only if the public prosecutor makes a criminal charge. It ends with a decision on the criminal and civil liability of the accused (civil liability can be stated only if the offended person brought his/her claim before the criminal court).

The trial phase is aimed at taking evidence requested by formal participants,[177] moreover, the trial court can order the obtaining of additional evidence *ex officio*,[178] in compliance with the principle of the adversarial procedure enshrined by Article 6 ECHR and reaffirmed by Article 111 of the Italian Constitution.

The collection of evidence during the trial appears relevant to the aim of the present study because the core of the hearing is frequently the examination and cross-examination of witnesses, who can be considered as third parties. Indeed, even if they are clearly not formal parties, they are involved in the criminal proceeding due to their knowledge about the circumstances related to the criminal fact. The hearing and examination of the witness is not a dangerous activity in itself, but sometimes the personal conditions of individuals and the criminal offence being prosecuted make it unsafe.

[176] Art. 152 CC-Italy. Moreover, if the accused and the injured person take part in a restorative programme and the report confirms reconciliation and reparation of the damage, in the event of a complaint that can be withdrawn, the proceeding authority shall declare the crime extinguished. (Cf. Article 152(2)(2) CC-Italy).

[177] Art. 190(1) CCP.

[178] Art. 507 CCP.

7.2 The Right of Third Parties to be Heard Fairly

Articles no. 498 and 499 CCP set the rules for witness examination, which is conducted in a public hearing and by means of the adversarial method.

The examination consists of three different stages: direct examination, cross-examination, and re-examination. The first step is necessary and is conducted by the party who requested the witness examination, and the questions have to deal with the circumstances pinpointed in the list required by Article 468 CCP. The second step is cross-examination, an optional phase, conducted by the parties who did not request the examination. During cross-examination, every party can put questions regarding circumstances other than those that emerged during direct examination, but they still have to address those pinpointed in the list provided for by Article 468 CCP.[179] The last step is re-examination, which is conducted by the party who requested examination in the first place, and who may now ask further questions. Moreover, the trial judge can supplement the parties' cross-examination by posing further questions to the witness. The CCP does not properly grant a general right to be heard fairly, but it indirectly addresses this issue. Indeed, it establishes rules aimed at assuring the truthfulness of statements, which incidentally protect the person being examined. To this aim, questions which may jeopardise the sincerity of the answers are never allowed, while leading questions are only prohibited during direct examination.[180]

7.3 The Right of Third Parties Not to be Questioned

Even though the first paragraph of Article 198 CCP requires witnesses to appear in the court and truthfully answer the questions that are addressed to them, Italian legislation admits some exceptions to this general rule.

The first is envisaged under the same Article 198 CCP and refers to all those who play the role of witnesses during the criminal proceeding. Indeed, according to the second paragraph of Article 198 CCP, "the witness shall not be obliged to testify on facts which may reveal his own criminal liability". This rule reflects the principle of *nemo tenetur se ipsum detegere*, recognised by the ECtHR[181] and considered as a feature of the *fair trial* established by Article 6 ECHR. In Italy, the privilege against self-incrimination is granted both on a procedural and a substantial level, as those who render false statements to save themselves or others from the detriment of their freedom cannot be punished for this.[182]

---

[179] Cf. Italian Court of Cassation, Division 6, judgment of 5 December 2018, in *CED Cass.*, rv. 274680; Italian Court of Cassation, Division 4, judgment of 23 March 2005, in *CED Cass.*, rv. 232243.

[180] Article 499 CCP.

[181] ECtHR, *Serves v. France*, judgment of 20 October 1997, Appl. no. 82/1996/671/893.

[182] Art. 384 CCP.

In addition to this general provision, Italian law displays further specific situations that allow a derogation of the general provisions on the 'obligations of witnesses'.

First of all, the next of kin,[183] but also those who are emotionally attached to the accused,[184] cannot be obliged to testify,[185] because of their relationship with the defendant. However, they cannot refuse to answer the questions if they have previously submitted a complaint against the accused: this case, indeed, falls outside the scope of this exception, because a formal complaint is considered as an act which interrupts the family and emotional relationship between the offender and the victim.

Moreover, there are other categories of individuals that may abstain from testifying: for instance, the lawyer and the mediator in the restorative justice program;[186] the ministers of religious faiths whose charters do not conflict with Italian law; licensed private investigators, experts or notaries; doctors and any healthcare professional; persons practicing different functions or professions to whom the law recognises the right to abstain from testifying on account of professional confidentiality.[187] However, the rules regarding these individuals do not overlap with the one established by Article 198 CCP. Indeed, while the next of kin are authorised to refuse to testify, and therefore can refuse to answer all the questions asked, no matter what information is requested of them, the people belonging to the latter category can only abstain from testifying on what they know on account of their function, service or profession. In sum, the scope of the right to refuse testifying varies in these two cases, because the aim pursued by procedural law is different (while Article 198 CCP takes into account the personal, family, emotional relationship existing between the accused and the witness, Article 200 CCP only considers the professional relationship between the accused and the witness).

7.4 The Protection of Non-parties in Court Activities Involving Formal Participants

It has been observed that during the trial witnesses are to be heard according to the rules set out by Articles 488 and 499 CCP. However, this method appears ambiguous: full respect for the adversarial procedure could jeopardise the interests and

[183] The definition of next of kin is provided by Article 307(4) CC-Italy.

[184] Cf. Italian Court of Cassation, Division 1, judgment no. 36608 of 2 September 2016, in *CED Cass.*, rv 267602; Italian Court of Cassation, Division 1, judgment no. 5115 of 21 September 2017, in *CED Cass.*, rv 271599.

[185] Article 199 CCP. The Article established that the judge has to preliminarily inform the next of kin of their right.

[186] Article 52 of Legislative Decree no. 150 of 10 October 2022.

[187] The list is contained in Article 200 CCP.

even fundamental rights of witnesses, because public hearing and cross-examination can be a truly stressful experience, especially for 'vulnerable' people.

Nevertheless, Italian lawmakers are aware of the potential negative effects of the adversarial method and the importance of its contribution to the ascertainment of criminal offences. Therefore, the CCP establishes some rules that depart from the method of direct confrontation, in order to protect individuals who are not formal parties from the risks related to cross-examination.[188]

In particular, the hearing of minors must be carried out by the presiding judge of the court, who should conduct it with the assistance of a guardian, family member or child psychologist.[189] Despite the importance of this provision, which aims to protect the person concerned from the need to relive the trauma experienced, this is not binding and no consequence arises from its violation.[190] Additionally, according to the Italian Court of Cassation, the presiding judge of the court is empowered to order the minor's hearing to be conducted by means of protected measures,[191] regardless of the type of criminal offence in question.[192]

In 1997, the Italian Constitutional Court extended this rule to mentally ill adults, by enabling the president of the trial court to directly question those vulnerable people on the assumption that cross-examination could negatively affect them.[193]

Moreover, when 'vulnerable' victims are heard as witnesses for not playing any formal role in criminal proceedings, they may request to be examined by means of protected measures.

However, the outlined provisions do not ensure a high level of protection for third parties: protective measures are not automatically implemented, because the presiding judge of the court can discretionarily assess the need to dispense with cross-examination.

7.5 *Can Third Parties Take Part in Court Activities?*

Generally, third parties cannot take part in court activities. Indeed, only formal parties are allowed to participate in the trial, exercising their rights and proactive powers.

---

[188] Ruggeri (2017), p. 249.

[189] Article 498(4) CCP.

[190] Cf. Italian Court of Cassation, Division 4, judgment no. 16981 of 12 April 2013, in *CED Cass.*, rv. 254943.

[191] The minor's hearing can be conducted through a glass mirror with an intercom system, or in a 'safe' space, such as his/her home or a social support facility. Cf. Articles 398 and 502 CCP.

[192] See Article 498(4 *ter*) CCP. Cf. Italian Court of Cassation, Division 6, judgment no. 28247 of 13 November 2013, in *CED Cass.*, rv. 257026.

[193] Cf. Italian Constitutional Court, judgment no. 283 of 18-30 July 1997. Some years later, the Court extended the use of the glass mirror with an intercom system to the hearings of mentally ill adults. See Italian Constitutional Court, judgment no. 63 of 29 January 2005.

However, third parties sometimes participate in court activities because of their technical expertise, which may be necessary in order to solve issues related to the criminal offence, which judges are not able to address because of their lack of specific knowledge. This is the case of expert witnesses, and it is worth observing that they are heard in court according to the same rules laid down for the examination of witnesses in general. They may be appointed by the judge (in which case they are referred to as *periti*)[194] or by the formal parties (in this case, *consulenti tecnici di parte*), and their status is partly different. For instance, while the parties are free to appoint an expert witness of their own choosing, the judge has to appoint an expert from among those who are registered with the court.

Since their task is to answer truthfully[195] and impartially[196] the technical questions put by the judge and the parties, we can consider the expert as an 'indispensable third party'. Despite their importance, it is essential to highlight that experts' statements are not binding for the trial judge, who is still considered as *peritus peritorum*, meaning that he is free to assess the expert witness's evidence.

8 The Protection of Third Parties in the Decision-Making Process

Judicial bodies cannot take into consideration, nor are called upon to satisfy, the interests of people other than the formal participants in decision-making. Indeed, judges are allowed to decide on the accused's civil liability only if the offended person institutes a civil-law action within the criminal trial by requesting restitution and compensation for the damage related to criminal offence. Otherwise, the judge can solely investigate and decide on the issues that are strictly related to the criminal responsibility of the accused.

9 Third Parties in Appeal Proceedings

As we have already seen, in a few cases third parties are entitled to challenge judicial orders regarding investigative measures that infringe upon their fundamental rights. Italian procedural law does not grant third parties the right to appeal against the decision on the merits of the case. However, it is not surprising that third parties

[194] Article 221 CCP.

[195] Article 226 CCP. Moreover, 'false expertise' is punished by Article 373 CC-Italy.

[196] To this end, Article 222 CCP clarifies the situations that prevent individuals from participating as an expert.

cannot appeal the decision on the accused's criminal liability, if one considers that neither do formal parties have an absolute right to appeal the judgements.[197]

10 *Res judicata* and the Effects of Criminal Judgements upon Third Parties

The main effect related to a final criminal judgement is *ne bis in idem.*[198] However, the CCP addresses neither this nor other effects of the *res judicata* in relation to third parties.

Notwithstanding the failure of Italian legislation to enact specific rules in this regard, there are cases in which procedural law recognises some effects of *res judicata* also vis-à-vis third parties.

Firstly, it is noteworthy that the final judgement can be relevant as evidence of the facts therein ascertained.[199] When the final judgement can be used as evidence[200] in another criminal proceeding, it produces effects upon individuals (third parties) other than those who took part in the criminal proceeding in which it was issued.[201] However, *res judicata* does not have a binding effect on the judicial authority. Indeed, it must be evaluated in compliance with Articles 187 and 192 CCP.[202] Thus, the facts ascertained by the *res judicata* need to be corroborated by other evidence.

However, we can note the effects of *res judicata* on third parties also on a different level. The issue concerns the effect of *ne bis in idem* on those who did not take part in the criminal proceeding ending with a criminal judgment. The CCP does not specifically address this matter, because Article 649 CCP merely affirms that "the accused who has been dismissed or convicted by a judgment or penalty order that has become final shall not be prosecuted again for the same offence". Hence, the effects of *ne bis in idem* do not presuppose that all the persons involved in

---

[197] For example, the civil party may appeal against the section of the first instance decision concerning the civil action and, for the purposes of civil liability, the judgment of acquittal delivered during the trial. Cf. Article 576 CCP.

[198] Article 649 CCP.

[199] Article 238 *bis* CCP.

[200] Italian courts have clarified in which terms the sentence could be used as evidence. See Italian Court of Cassation, Division 4, judgment no. 12175 of 14 March 2017, in *CED Cass.*, rv. 270384; Italian Court of Cassation, Division 6, judgment no. 6599 of 3 December 2021; Italian Court of Cassation, Division 2, judgment no. 52589 of 6 July 2018, in *CED Cass.*, rv. 275517.

[201] According to the Italian Court of Cassation, a *res judicata* can be used in any criminal proceeding and can be used against someone who did not take part in the proceeding in which it was pronounced. Cf. Italian Court of Cassation, Division 5, judgment of 13 November 2012, in *Cass. pen.*, 2013, pp. 3999 ff.

[202] On this point, see Italian Court of Cassation, Division 6, judgment no. 14096 of 16 January 2007, in *CED Cass.*, rv. 270387.

the criminal offence have taken part in the criminal proceeding. In other words, *res judicata* impedes a new criminal trial, regardless of the participation of the eventual parties, whilst it produces its preclusive effect also on them.

As we can imagine, this represents an important guarantee for the accused. However, at the same time, it can affect those who formally remain 'third parties' in the criminal proceeding, but who have been involved in the criminal offence, for example the victims. Indeed, *ne bis in idem* impedes the establishment of a second proceeding, and, consequently, the chance of access to a criminal court to obtain the 'criminal' protection of third parties' rights.

Both the Italian Court of Cassation and the Italian Constitutional Court have become aware of these negative consequences of *ne bis in idem*, so that they have sought to circumscribe the notion of '*medesimo fatto*' (i.e. the same fact). Italian case-law allows the initiation of a second proceeding, when the accused's conduct affected the rights of persons other than those who were considered in the first proceeding.[203] The solution proposed, aimed at enhancing the protection of victims that remained formally extraneous to the first criminal proceeding, does not seem adequate. Indeed, their protection is strictly related to the interpretation of the concept of "same fact", without considering the effectiveness of their participation in the criminal proceeding. Thus, it does not reflect the standard proposed by the ECtHR, which admits an exception to the principle of *ne bis in idem* if the injured person was not involved in the criminal proceeding.[204]

11 Concluding Remarks

At the end of this analysis, we can note the numerous occasions in which individuals other than the formal participants of criminal proceedings may be involved in procedural activities. Since the very first stage of preliminary inquiries, people other than suspects and victims could be affected by measures able to jeopardise their interests and fundamental rights in the name of the need to ascertain whether and by whom the alleged criminal offence has been committed. However, in these cases, the protection ensured to those individuals does not appear adequate, because it is entirely assigned to the public prosecutor and to the judge, who have to strike a proper balance between fact-finding needs and the protections of the fundamental rights affected by some investigative measures. Indeed, as we already saw, 'third parties' have no proactive powers, because frequently only the suspects are entitled to exercise them. However, this situation is problematic because of the ability of investigative activities to involve, directly or indirectly, a large number of individuals and to affect their fundamental rights.

[203] Italian Constitutional Court, judgment no. 200 of 21 July 2016.

[204] ECtHR, *Sabalić v Croazia*, judgment of 4 January 2021, ric. no. 50231/13. Cf. Di Nuzzo (2021, 2022).

This wide-ranging scope of preliminary inquiries has consequences for the category of 'third parties', which appear broad and indefinite. Moreover, during this initial stage of criminal proceedings, the roles of individuals involved in a criminal act may not yet be clear, and this makes it more difficult to limit the category of 'third parties': if it is not clear who the formal participants are, it is difficult to affirm who are not formal parties, and thus 'third parties'. For this reason, Italian lawmakers should grant the same level of guarantees to those who are affected by investigative measures, allowing a wide interpretation of the current rules regulating specific legal instruments aimed at protecting fundamental rights, and promoting a constitutionally oriented interpretation which assures the same level of protection to all individuals, regardless of their formal role in criminal proceedings.

Differently, after the beginning of a criminal trial, the involvement of 'third parties' is limited to specific occasions, and it is related to their private or professional knowledge. In these cases, 'third parties' could face some risks linked to their vulnerable conditions; thus, the main task of legislators is to provide for specific measures aimed at ensuring a 'safe-space' for their hearing.

In the light of these considerations, we can conclude by resuming the premise of this study about the importance of a proper definition of domestic categories. Indeed, in the Italian legal system, the recognition of powers and rights is strictly dependent on the role played in criminal proceedings, thus the preliminary task is to properly define the concept of 'third parties' in order to create a formal status for those individuals who could be affected by procedural measures.

This is clearly an ambitious aim, which requires time—as the path for the establishment of a victims' status has shown—but, at the same time, which is necessary in order to grant an equal and effective protection of fundamental rights to all individuals.

References

Battarino G (2013) Note sull'attuazione in ambito penale e processuale penale della Convenzione di Istanbul sulla prevenzione e la lotta contro la violenza nei confronti delle donne e la violenza domestica. www.archiviodpc.dirittopenaleuomo.org

Beccari GM (2019) Il trattamento (anche elettronico) dei dati personali per finalità di accertamento dei reati. In: Cadoppi A, Canestrari S et al (eds) Cybercrime. Wolters Kluwer Italia, Milano

Bonini V (2018) Il sistema di protezione della vittima e i suoi riflessi sulla libertà personale. Cedam, Padova

Calavita O (2022) Un mezzo di impugnazione per ogni atto di indagine? Da Gavanozov II un ulteriore stimolo della Corte di giustizia verso l'armonizzazione dei sistemi processuali penali europei. www.lalegislazionepenale.eu

Caraceni L (2021) La vittima nel procedimento de libertate: i precari equilibri di un nuovo protagonismo ancora troppo poco meditato. Revista Brasileira de Direito Processual Penal 7(3):1783–1824

Carnelutti F (1946–1949) Lezioni sul processo penale. Edizioni dell'ateneo, Roma

Cartabia M (2013) I principi di ragionevolezza e proporzionalità nella giurisprudenza costituzionale italiana, Conferenza trilaterale delle Corte costituzionali italiana, portoghese e Spagnola. Palazzo della Consulta, Roma
Cascini N (2022) Confische e tutela dei terzi. In: La Rocca EN (ed) Lo statuto ancora incerto della confisca. Fisionomia, modelli, disciplina. Cedam, Padova, pp 145–161
Casey E (2000) Digital evidence and computer crime: forensic science, computers and the internet. Academic, Orlando
Chiavario M (2022) Diritto processuale penale. Utet, Milano
Coppola R (2022) La tutela delle libertà fondamentali: dalla sentenza della Corte EDU, Brazzi c. Italia, alla Legge 27 settembre 2021, n. 134. Archivio penale (2):1–29
Cordero F (2012) Procedura penale. Giuffrè, Milano
De Martino P (2013a) Legge di ratifica della Convenzione di Lanzarote e tutela dei minori vittime del reato durante le indagini preliminari: brevi considerazioni alla luce della nuova direttiva 2012/29/UE. Un'ulteriore riflessione sulla legge n. 172 del 1° ottobre 2012 anche in relazione alla recente direttiva 2012/29/UE. www.archiviodpc.dirittopenaleuomo.org
De Martino P (2013b) Le innovazioni introdotte nel codice di rito dal decreto-legge sulla violenza di genere, alla luce della Direttiva 2012/29/UE. www.archiviodpc.dirittopenaleuomo.org
Delvecchio F (2016) La nuova fisionomia della vittima del reato dopo l'adeguamento dell'Italia alla direttiva 2012/29/ue. www.archiviodpc.dirittopenaleuomo.org
Di Nuzzo V (2020) Giudizio cautelare e tutela della persona offesa. www.lalegislazionepenale.eu
Di Nuzzo V (2021) "*Ne bis in idem*" e tutela della vittima di reato: la Corte di Strasburgo riconosce la cedevolezza del principio di fronte a gravi violazioni dei diritti delle persone LGBTQ+. Il Foro italiano (10):465–470
Di Nuzzo V (2022) Le trasformazioni di una garanzia: il *ne bis in idem* tra necessaria protezione dell'accusato e nuove istanze di tutela della vittima di reato. Ordine internazionale e diritti umani (1):208–223
Dominioni O (1981) Parti, diritto processuale penale. In: Enciclopedia del diritto, XXXI. Giuffrè, Milano
Dominioni O (1985) Le parti nel processo penale. Profili sistematici e problemi. Giuffrè, Milano
Felicioni P (2019) Le ispezioni e perquisizioni di dati e sistemi in Cybercrime. In: Cadoppi A, Canestrari S et al (eds) Wolters Kluwer Italia, Milano
Floridi L (2014) The fourth revolution: how the infosphere is reshaping human reality. UOP, Oxford
Gialuz M (2022) Per un processo penale più efficiente e giusto. guida alla lettura della riforma Cartabia. Profili processuali. www.sistemapenale.it
Iovene F (2014) Le c.d. perquisizioni online tra nuovi diritti fondamentali ed esigenze di accertamento penale. www.archiviodpc.dirittopenaleuomo.org
La Rocca E (2020) Le due vie per il ristoro economico dell'offeso dal reato che escludono l'equa riparazione per irragionevole durata delle indagini preliminari (Corte cost. n. 249 del 2020). www.diritticomparati.it
Lupo E (2020) Le garanzie di contesto: la parità tra le parti. www.legislazionepenale.eu
Marcolini S (2019) L'istituto della *data retention* dopo la sentenza della corte di giustizia del 2014. In: Cadoppi A, Canestrari S et al (eds) Cybercrime. Wolters Kluwer Italia, Milano
Mazza O (2013) I diritti fondamentali dell'individuo come limite della prova nella fase di ricerca e in sede di assunzione. Diritto penale contemporaneo (3):4–12
Montagna M (2019) Confisca e tutela del terzo estraneo. Archivio penale (2):1–16
Padua G (2021) Opposizione dell'atto perquirente non seguito da sequestro. Processo penale e giustizia (1):49–56
Pennisi A (1997) Persona offesa dal reato. Enciclopedia del diritto, Agg. I.
Quattrocolo S (2020) Artificial intelligence, computational modelling and criminal proceedings. A framework for a European legal discussion. Springer, Cham
Recchione S (2013) Le dichiarazioni del minore dopo la ratifica della Convenzione di Lanzarote. www.archiviodpc.dirittopenaleuomo.org

Ruggeri S (2017) Audi Alteram Partem in criminal proceedings. Towards a participatory understanding of criminal justice in Europe and Latin America. Springer, Cham

Ruggieri F (2017) Data retention e giudice di merito penale. Una discutibile pronuncia. Cassazione penale (6):2483–2488

Signorato S (2022) Diritto alla *privacy* ed esigenze investigative, tra incertezze normative e criticità sistematiche. In: AA.VV. (ed) Studi in onore di Roberto E. Kostoris. Giappichelli, Torino

Spangher G (2019) Le prove informatiche. In: Cadoppi A, Canestrari S et al (eds) Cybercrime. Wolters Kluwer Italia, Milano

Testaguzza A (2019) Il sequestro di dati e sistemi. In: Cadoppi A, Canestrari S et al (eds) Cybercrime. Wolters Kluwer Italia, Milano

Tonini P (2024) Manuale di procedura penale. Giuffrè, Milano

Torre M (2019) L'intercettazione di flussi telematici (art. 266-*bis* c.p.p.). In: Cadoppi A, Canestrari S et al (eds) Cybercrime. Wolters Kluwer Italia, Milano

Report on Portugal

João Gouveia de Caires and Joana Reis Barata

Abstract This chapter relates to the procedural position of third parties in Portugal. Throughout this paper, it will be discussed who are the main characters of the Portuguese criminal procedure and who are the people who may intervene in the proceedings and in what extent. The Portuguese system has some specificities that are not common in other systems, so it will be addressed how certain third parties can really impact in the proceedings.

Besides the intervention of the third parties in the Portuguese criminal proceedings and in what extent they can influence such proceedings, it will also be explained how their rights are safeguarded, the existing measures in relation to them and their global impact in the proceedings.

1 Introduction. General Features of Portuguese Criminal Justice

1.1 Regulatory System

The Portuguese criminal procedure system is based on the Code of Criminal Procedure-Portugal (*Código de Processo Penal*, CCP), approved in 1987[1] and successively amended several times notably during the reform movements of the CCP in 1998, 2007 and 2010–2013.[2]

[1] Approved by Law Decree No. 78/1987 of 17 February 1987.

[2] To an overview of the Portuguese Criminal Procedure see da Silva (2014, 2017, 2024), Antunes (2023), de Albuquerque (2023), Dias and Brandão (2022), Mendes (2023), and Pereira and de Caires (2023).

J. G. de Caires (✉) · J. R. Barata
Faculty of Law, University of Lisbon, Lisbon, Portugal
e-mail: joaogouveiadecaires@fd.ulisboa.pt; joanareisbarata@fd.ulisboa.pt

S. Ruggeri et al. (eds.), *Third Parties in Criminal Proceedings*, Legal Studies in International, European and Comparative Criminal Law 10,
https://doi.org/10.1007/978-3-031-73970-5_6

In addition to the CCP, a number of statutes are also relevant, some of which will be mentioned below in relation to each specific issue. These are characterized by their particular nature, *i.e.* a set of rules intended to regulate unique realities, with their own characteristics, regarding which the general regime of the CCP would be insufficient or inappropriate.[3]

1.2 A Brief Overview of the Procedural Process: Common Form and Special Forms

Portuguese criminal proceedings may be carried out either in the common form (*processo comum*), Articles 262–380 of the CCP, or in one of the three special forms provided for in the CCP: (*i*) summary proceedings (*processo sumário*), (*ii*) abbreviated proceedings (*processo abreviado*), and (*iii*) expedited summary proceedings (*processo sumaríssimo*), provided for in Articles 381–398, all of the CCP. The common form is the subsidiary form, more formal in procedure, with more guarantees and accordingly the most extended form. The special forms, on the other hand, are quicker, with fewer procedural guarantees and are derived from the subsidiary form, except insofar as they are exempt, *e.g.* they do not admit a procedural phase, the pre-trial phase, that is admitted, even if optionally, in the common form. The priority given to the special forms stems from the fact that failure to comply with them generates a nullity, which must be pleaded and is accordingly remediable (Art. 120(2)(*a*) CCP). In general, the special forms are applied to more minor offences where the evidence tends to be less complex.

The special summary proceedings (Arts. 381–391 of the CCP) are characterized by the manifest just cause generated by the arrest of the accused committing the crime (*i.e.* in "*flagrante delito*") for a crime punishable by a maximum custodial sentence of 5 years or in which, not being a crime reserved for the jurisdiction of the collective court or jury (*e.g.* crimes of intentional homicide), the maximum notional penalty exceeds 5 years imprisonment, whereby the Public Prosecutor's Office (PPO) understands that the actual penalty is no more than 5 years. The deadline for the trial to begin is also short: as a general rule, 48 h after the arrest, extendable to 20 days (when necessary, for example, to carry out evidentiary proceedings). Sentence is usually passed orally.

[3]Given the growing importance of perpetrating crimes in the digital environment and the adducing of relevant evidence, the Cybercrime Law, approved by Law No. 109/2009 of 15 September 2009, deserves special mention. Regarding this Law, see Barata JR (2022) O desassossego do Tribunal da Relação de Lisboa quanto à aplicação do regime de apreensão de mensagens de correio eletrónico. In: Prof. Doutor Augusto Silva Dias in Memoriam, Vol. II. AAFDL Editora, Lisboa; Barata JR (2023) "O regime jurídico dos conhecimentos fortuitos em ambiente digital: contributo da plain view doctrine à luz da legislação portuguesa", Novos Desafios da Prova Penal, Volume II, Almedina, Coimbra.

The abbreviated proceedings (Arts. 391-A–391-G of the CCP) is a special successor to the summary form that is characterized by evidentiary proof and is also aimed at small and medium-sized offences (with a maximum custodial sentence of 5 years or in which, if the crime is not reserved to the jurisdiction of the collective court or jury (*e.g.* crimes of intentional homicide), the notional sentence exceeds 5 years and the Public Prosecutor considers that the actual sentence should not exceed 5 years).

Finally, the special expedited summary proceedings (Arts. 392–398 of the CCP) are an alternative to bringing charges in the common form, characterized as an alternative measure to trial. It is necessary for the PPO to conduct this form of prosecution, in a crime punishable by a maximum notional penalty of 5 years imprisonment, where they propose a non-custodial sanction. If the accused person[4] ("*arguido*") agrees (who in this form will know the penalty and can avoid the stigma of a trial), and if the judge considers the penalty to be fair, then the judge will render a conviction. If the accused person does not consent, or if the judge declines the proposed penalty, then the case will proceed to trial.

1.3 The Procedural Stages

In the first instance, the common form consists of an investigation (inquiry), a preliminary judicial phase (optional) and a trial. After that, there may be an appeal phase and, if necessary, an execution phase.

1.3.1 The Inquiry (*Inquérito*)

The investigatory phase, led by the PPO, is the first stage of the investigation and is compulsory once the *notitia criminis* has been acquired. The purposes[5] of the investigatory phase are (i) to ascertain the existence of a crime, (ii) to identify its agents and participants and (iii) to gather evidence in order to decide whether the case should proceed to trial. Although the investigation is led by a prosecutor (Art. 263), and the prosecutor is responsible for the legal acts necessary for the purposes of the investigation (Art. 267 CCP), there are acts which, due to their greater damage to fundamental rights, are the exclusive responsibility of an examining judge, acting as a judge of freedoms or guarantees. Such acts are included in the catalogue of Articles 268 and 269 of the CCP, examples being the application of more serious coercive measures than the mere term of identification and residence (Art. 268(1)(*b*) CCP), or

[4]The Portuguese term "*arguido*" (Arts. 57–59 CCP) was created intentionally to be avoid any negative or pejorative associations. It is also translated as "defendant".

[5]Art. 262(1) CCP.

even the authorization to carry out telephone interceptions (Art. 269(1)(*e*) CCP).[6] In this context, the examining judge acts as a judge of freedoms and as such is competent only at the instigation of the Public Prosecutor. The judge thus respects the direction of the investigation attributed to the Prosecutor, and weighs the conflicting constitutionally protected interests before, according to their discretion, drawing a fair balance between those interests.

The decision to open an investigation rest solely with the PPO and is subject to strict compliance with the law or, alternatively put, the obligation to take criminal action whenever there is news of a crime, particularly a public crime. A distinction is to be drawn between public crimes[7] (*crimes públicos*), (in which the PPO has the power to take criminal action with the *notitia criminis* alone, opening an investigation and pursuing it to completion, independent of the intentions of third parties), and semi-public (*semipúblicos*) and private crimes (*crimes particulares*), in which the preconditions for prosecution must be fulfilled.

In semi-public crimes[8] (*semipúblicos*), the PPO will open an investigation only after a complaint has been lodged by those entitled to do so.[9] The complaint corresponds to the declaration of intention by the one who is entitled (as a rule, the offended party or whoever represents them) that they intend to take criminal action. If there is a complaint, it may be withdrawn, which, provided the accused person raises no objection, extinguishes the criminal proceedings. Such withdrawn can be done until the judgment is handed down at first instance.

Finally, in private crimes (*crimes particulares*), it is necessary not only to file a complaint under the terms already mentioned, but also for the complainant to be constituted as an assistant. Without a request for an assistant, the PPO cannot open an investigation regarding a private crime.[10] While optional with public and semi-public crimes, with private crimes the assistant is mandatory and without one there can be no opening of an investigation into an alleged private crime.

On completion of the investigation into public crimes or semi-public crimes, the PPO must bring charges (Art. 283 CCP) provided it has gathered sufficient evidence that a crime has been committed and that the accused person either committed it or participated in it. Otherwise, charges against the accused person are to be dismissed by the PPO (Art. 277 CCP). Similarly, the case must be dismissed if, in semi-public or private crimes, the complaint is withdrawn and the accused person raises no objection. As diversionary measures, the PPO has the power and duty to promote, as an alternative to prosecution, (*i*) dismissal of the case if the penalty is waived (Art. 280 CCP), (*ii*) provisional stay of proceedings (Arts. 281 and 282), summary proceedings (Arts. 392–398 CCP) or even to refer the case to a criminal mediator (under the Criminal Mediation Law approved by Law No. 21 of 12 June 2007). As will be

[6] See AA. VV. (2021b).

[7] Art. 48 CCP.

[8] Art. 49 CCP and Arts. 113–116 of the Criminal Code (CC).

[9] Art. 113 of the Criminal Code.

[10] Arts. 50, 68 and 246(4) CCP and 113–116 *ex vi* Art. 117 of the CC.

seen below, at the end of the investigation into private crimes, the solution provided for in the law is different.

The decision to prosecute depends on the prosecutor's assessment that there is sufficient evidence that the accused person committed a crime, whereby it is a contentious issue whether this legal criterion is met (see Art. 283(1)(2) CCP). Nevertheless, it is widely understood that this corresponds to a categorical judgment to be made by the PPO and equates to that of a judge who, if required to rule on the matter at that moment, and in view of the existing (uncontradicted) evidence, would have to convict. In any case, the degree of certainty required to bring charges is not the same as that required for a conviction, where the judge has to be convinced that the person committed the crime beyond reasonable doubt.

1.3.2 In Particular—The Idiosyncrasy of the Portuguese System: The End of the Investigation Phase Regarding a Private Crime

In the case of a private crime, on completion of the investigation the PPO may only notify the assistant so as to enable them to bring (private) charges, even in situations where the PPO believes that there is insufficient evidence of a crime on the part of the accused (Art. 285(1)(2) CCP).

The assistant thus has full control over the final decision of the investigation in that it is for the assistant to bring charges (the so-called private charge), which constitutes the principal charge (Art. 285 CCP). If the assistant does not bring charges—despite the PPO having gathered sufficient evidence of the crime, then the PPO is obliged to dismiss the case (Art. 277 CCP); if the assistant does bring charges the case continues, and the PPO may or may not file subordinate chargest to the assistant's (Art. 285(4) CCP). It is therefore up to the assistant to decide on the completion of the private crime investigation.

In the final analysis, in the event of an unfounded charges (where the PPO takes no subsequent action and even states from the outset that it considers there is no evidence of a crime), if the accused person doesn't request a pre-trial in order to avoid an unnecessary trial, then that person could be put on trial solely on the assistant's decision to bring the indictment.

1.3.3 The Preliminary Judicial Phase (*Instrução*) and the Trial Phase (*Julgamento*)

The preliminary judicial phase ("*instrução*"), also called the pre-trial phase or stage (Arts. 286–310 of the CCP), is optional and only exists in the common proceedings. It is optional because it only exists if the accused person or the assistant (in the latter case, only in public or semi-public crimes) ask the examining judge ("*juiz de instrução*") for (judicial) control of the indictment/dismissal in order to decide whether or not to submit the case to trial (Arts. 286 and 287).

This stage is not a repetition of the investigation (this time by a judge), but is merely intended to examine the final decision of the investigation: either to file an indictment or to dismiss the case. The assistant (in public or semi-public crimes) is given the possibility of asking the examining judge to bring the accused person to trial when the Public Prosecutor has filed a case, or alternatively when the Prosecutor has charged but the assistant considers that there is sufficient evidence of a substantial change of facts (*i.e.* the assistant wishes to insert a new fact into the case that leads to an increase in the maximum limits of the applicable sanctions or to the commission of a different crime). The accused person is given the option of avoiding a trial by challenging the decision of the PPO (or of the assistant in private crimes); or even of being subject to a trial, but with more beneficial charges for the accused.

The examining judge directs the pre-trial phase with broad investigative powers, and it is only mandatory to hold a pre-trial debate (a "mini-hearing" of the trial) to allow for adversarial proceedings. At the end of this stage, the examining judge issues a decision to indict or not to indict, depending on whether there is sufficient evidence that the accused person committed a crime or participated in it (Art. 308 CCP).

If an indictment is filed, the case proceeds to trial. Alternatively with a decision not to indict, the case ends. The examining judge's decision (whatever it may be) can be appealed in general terms (Art. 399 CCP), but is unappealable insofar as it indicts the accused person for the same facts that were already included in the prosecution's indictment (Art. 310(1) CCP).

The trial (Arts. 311–380 CCP), as the final stage of first instance proceedings, is subdivided into three stages:[11] (*i*) the initial analysis phase[12] (in which the trial court verifies all procedural assumptions and/or other prior or prejudicial issues and, if necessary, supplements them and notifies the accused person to submit, if so desired, a statement of defence,[13] where the accused will indicate their list of witnesses and may request evidence to be produced),[14] (*ii*) the trial hearing phase,[15] (in which there will be full exercise of the adversarial process and the ideal time to produce evidence), and (*iii*) the sentencing phase,[16] (the court arrives at a decision on the accused person's responsibility, either acquitting or convicting, and in the latter case dealing separately with the questions of guilt and of penalty).

[11] See AA. VV. (2021a).

[12] Arts. 311–320 CCP.

[13] Arts. 311-A and 311-B CCP.

[14] See Mendes (2019).

[15] Arts. 321–364 CCP.

[16] Arts. 365–380 CCP.

1.4 Formal Participants in Criminal Proceedings

A wide range of procedural participants in the Portuguese criminal process are highlighted below.[17]

1.4.1 The Court

The court is the procedural body empowered to "pronounce" the accused person or persons (the decision to "pronounce" is a decision by the criminal investigation court in the pre-trial phase, which can be requested and is therefore optional) and/or to convict the accused persons—Arts. 8 ff. CCP. In addition to criminal jurisdiction, the court may also hear any civil claim for compensation against the accused person. The judicial courts are competent to try criminal cases, without prejudice to the Constitutional Court's competence to review constitutionality.

The courts of first instance are, as a rule, competent to try crimes, and can try singularly, collectively or, when required, by jury (and only in certain crimes or those punishable by more than 8 years imprisonment). By way of exception, the courts of appeal or the Supreme Court of Justice may have jurisdiction to trial a case as first instance courts when it comes to crimes committed in the exercise of the functions of high political office or crimes committed by judges or prosecutors (cases of so-called privileged jurisdiction).

1.4.2 The Accused Person and Their Defence Counsel

The *accused person* ("*arguido*") is the subject of criminal proceedings. Although the CCP contains no definition of an "accused person", such a person may be seen as anyone against whom an investigation is underway, or in respect of whom there is reasonable suspicion of the commission of a crime, or against whom charges are brought or an investigation opened (Arts. 57–59 CCP). The suspect (*person of interest*) or, in general, any person when being questioned, may demand to be declared an accused person (Arts. 59 and 132(2) CCP).

The defence counsel of the accused is the representative or official defender appointed by the State who represents and provides technical assistance to the accused, and is obliged to be present at the most relevant procedural acts (Art. 64 CCP), and able to argue nullities or file an appeal even in the absence of instructions from the accused.

[17] See AA. VV. (2021c).

1.4.3 The Public Prosecutor's Office (PPO)

The PPO directs the inquiry (the investigative phase) representing the State in criminal proceedings. Its actions are governed by the principle of democratic legality in accordance with criteria of strict objectivity, which means that it must accuse (and justify the accusation at trial) if there is sufficient evidence that the accused committed the crime, and, in the opposite situation, must close the case (or ask for acquittal at trial)—Arts 48 ff. CCP.

1.4.4 The Assistant

The assistant is the person to whom the law grants legal standing (as a rule, the offended party) to constitute themselves as such. An assistant has the power to assist the PPO (Arts. 68 and 69 CCP), but in reality they have autonomous powers to act (even contrary to that of the PPO—*e.g.* to challenge decisions by the PPO), even in relation to crimes of a public or semi-public nature (in which it is optional for the assistant to participate).

As for private crimes, the uniqueness of the Portuguese procedural system, as mentioned above, is precisely that it gives the assistant a decisive role in the processing of these crimes. Thus, it is for the assistant to decide whether to bring (private) charges, in which case the case will proceed to the pre-trial or trial stage, or not to press charges with the result that the PPO is obliged to close the case—Arts 69 and 285 CCP.

It should be noted that under the law, the right to act as an assistant is granted, as a rule, to the victim (Art. 68(1)(*a*) CCP) or, when the victim is deceased, this right is passed on to a group of people from the victim's extended family (identified under the terms of Article 68(1)(*c*)).

In certain crimes, for the protection of diffuse or collective interests, any citizen enjoying their civil and political rights may request to be constituted as an assistant under the terms of Article 2(1) of Law No. 81 of 31 August 1995 (the so-called "Popular Action Law").

Lastly, any person may also be an assistant in criminal proceedings relating to crimes against peace and humanity, peddling of influence, nepotism practiced by an official, denial of justice, malfeasance, improper receipt or offer of an advantage, corruption, embezzlement, economic participation in business, abuse of power and fraud in obtaining or misappropriating a subsidy or grant.[18]

---

[18] Art. 68(1)(*e*) CCP.

1.5 Third Parties to Criminal Proceedings

The following third parties may also be identified in the procedural system:

i) The complainant, as the person who has to file a complaint in order for an investigation to be opened in semi-public or private crimes (Arts. 49 and 50 CCP and 113(1) of the Criminal Code—CC);[19] the offended, as the person targeted/protected by the instrumental criminal rule (Art. 113(1) CC); and the victim, as the person who has suffered any damage as a result of the crime, including their family members (Art. 67-A CCP).

On the death of the holder of the right to complain (or their incapacity), the law allows this right to be exercised by any person from a group of people in their extended family (identified under the terms of Art. 113(2) and (4) CC).

ii) The civil parties are those who have suffered civil damage as a result of a crime and who, as a rule, must file a claim for compensation in the respective criminal proceedings (Art. 71 CCP). By filing a civil claim, the injured parties become the true subjects of the civil proceedings, but they will always be mere interveners in the criminal proceedings, since they cannot determine the progress of the proceedings. They will be mere subjects of the civil relationship and "merely" third parties to the criminal proceedings.

iii) Witnesses (including those subject to special protection regimes), experts and consultants participate in the proceedings when requested, with personal protection rights and subject to the duty to cooperate, as set out in the witness protection regime (approved by Law No. 93 14 July 1999, and the respective regulations, approved by Law Decree No. 190 of 22 August 2003); witness evidence (Arts. 128–139 CCP), experts (Arts. 151–163 CCP) and consultants (Art. 155 CCP).[20] Their participation in criminal proceedings is governed by the principle of full co-operation with the court, since they are subject to this duty upon request.

iv) The criminal police agencies

Criminal police agencies assist the judicial authorities at any procedural stage (Articles 55(1) and 1(*c*) and (*d*) of the CCP) under the powers delegated by the competent judicial authority (prosecutors or judges). They have their own powers with regard to precautionary and police measures (*e.g.* identification—Art. 250 CCP—arrest in *flagrante delicto*—Arts. 254–256, etc.).

v) Those subject to procedural measures (*e.g.* wiretapping, image and/or sound capture, emails, searches, etc.), including asset guarantee measures and confiscation of assets/confiscatory measures.

The protection of those who have been made accused persons is implemented through their status as such, who in any case have the right to *ex post* judicial review of the measures they have been subjected to, and may invoke any procedural invalidity or illegality. In the case of more intrusive measures (*e.g.* telephone

[19] Also in private crimes, as already mentioned, the complainant is required to file a complaint—Arts. 50 CCP and 113–116 *ex vi* Art. 117 of the CC.

[20] See AA. VV. (2021d).

tapping, environmental surveillance and image capture, house searches, etc.), the review is also *prior* through the requirement of a (prior) judge's order—see, in particular, the regime contained in Articles 187–189 of the CCP or the provisions of Article 6 of Law No. 5 of 11 January 2002.

There is also protection of the rights of third parties who are not targets/suspects/ accused persons, through the system of preserving the personal data of third parties (for example, the accused person will not need access to the contents of the bank statements of third parties who are not relevant to the incrimination).

Also noteworthy is the protection that is accorded third parties who may be affected by the criminal proceedings. This is particularly the case with seizures of instruments, products or advantages or other objects or things or animals, in which the owners of such things, animals or rights may request the examining judge to modify or revoke the measure.[21]

In addition, if such products or advantages or other objects or things or animals can be forfeited to the State and do not belong to the accused, the judicial authority must order the presence of the third party concerned and hear them before a decision is taken.[22]

vi.) Close people affected (family members of undercover agents; family members of witnesses subject to special protection measures; etc.)

Anyone in need of special protection may apply for special protection measures. They are protected by the witness protection law, which extends to any person in danger.

The witness protection law (Article 1, no. 2 of Law no. 93/99, of 14 July) applies these measures to all "family members of witnesses, persons living with them in conditions similar to those of their spouses and other persons close to them".

The witness protection regime can range from the application of specific security measures that are necessary at any given time (including giving evidence for future reference), to medical and social support and monitoring of the witness, to the reservation of their identity or even giving testimony remotely and using image concealment and/or voice distortion mechanisms.[23]

2 Fundamental Rights and Safeguards of Third Parties

2.1 Constitutional Law

With regard to fundamental rights in criminal proceedings and, in particular, third parties in criminal proceedings, there are several constitutional precepts that are of primary importance. First and foremost, as a structuring principle of the rule of law,

[21] See Art. 178(7)(8) CCP.

[22] See Art. 178(9) CCP.

[23] Cf. in particular the provisions of Arts. 4 and 13–22 of Law 93 of 14 July 1999.

it is worth highlighting the dignity of the human person, set out in Article 1 of the Portuguese Fundamental Law, which is to be respected throughout the proceedings.

There are also other constitutional precepts of a predominantly procedural nature, which are relevant to criminal proceedings. Specifically, the right to a fair and equitable trial is laid down in Article 20(4) of the Portuguese Fundamental Law, which states that “everyone has the right to a decision in a case in which they are involved within a reasonable time and by means of a fair trial”. This principle translates, among other things, into the following safeguards: (effective) access to the law and to justice (in a timely manner); the participation of citizens in the administration of justice; the right to a fair trial.

Also worth mentioning is the right of resistance (Art. 21 of the Portuguese Fundamental Law): the right of resistance (non-cooperation), which is a defensive right, in which the legal system legitimizes a citizen’s right to choose not to comply with an order that offends their rights, freedoms and guarantees or to repel an act of aggression by force, in a defensive context, whenever they cannot resort to a public authority.

In turn, Art. 26(1)(2) of the Portuguese Fundamental Law provides for other personal rights such as “the rights to personal identity, to the development of personality [...] to a good name and reputation, to image, to speech, to the privacy of private and family life and to legal protection against any form of discrimination. “The law also provides “effective guarantees against the abusive obtaining and use, or use contrary to human dignity, of information relating to individuals and families”.

With regard to the application of criminal law, it is worth highlighting the provisions of Article 29(6) of the Portuguese Fundamental Law, which guarantees all citizens the right to a review of their sentence in the event of an unfair conviction.

In the context of Article 32 of the Portuguese Fundamental Law, which refers specifically to guarantees in criminal proceedings, it is worth highlighting paragraphs 8 and 10 relating to the system of prohibition of evidence and the guarantee, in any and all proceedings of a sanctioning nature, of the right to a hearing.

Also of note is the constitutional right to inviolability of the home and correspondence as laid down in Article 34 of the Portuguese Fundamental Law, which states that “all interference by public authorities in correspondence, telecommunications and other means of communication is prohibited, except in cases provided for by law in criminal proceedings”.

Finally, Article 35 of the Portuguese Fundamental Law refers specifically to the protection of personal data. Specifically, the Portuguese Constitution provides that all citizens have the right of access to computerized data concerning themselves, and may demand that it be rectified and updated, and the right, under the terms of the law, to know the purpose for which it is intended. There is a ban on the use of information technology to process data relating to philosophical or political beliefs, party or trade union membership, religious faith, private life and ethnic origin, except with the express consent of the data subject, authorization provided for by law with guarantees of non-discrimination or for the processing of non-individually identifiable statistical data. It is also important to highlight the prohibition of access to third parties' personal data (apart from in exceptional cases provided for by law).

2.1.1 Domestication of International Law

International law is also important in this area, with the European Convention on Human Rights ("ECHR") and the International Covenant on Civil and Political Rights ("ICCPR") being of particular importance, as is the case law of the European Court of the Human Rights ("ECHR"), which influences the interpretation and application of the rules.

In addition, the Council of Europe Convention on Preventing and Combating Violence against Women and Domestic Violence, adopted in Istanbul on 11 May 2011, prompted significant changes to both the CCP and the separate regime provided for in Law 112/2009 of 16 September, and the Convention on Cybercrime, adopted in Budapest on 23 November 2001, influenced the Cybercrime Law, approved by Law No. 109 of 16 September 2009.

2.1.2 Implementation of EU Law

Portugal has adopted and implemented EU law with regard to criminal law and criminal procedure, namely, and by way of example, the EU Directive on victims (see Directive 2012/29/EU of the European Parliament and of the Council of 25 October 2012) which was transposed with the implementation of the victim's statute (Law No. 130 of 7 September 2015), including the amendment to the CCP (see Art. 67-A CCP), the Directive on the protection of whistleblowers (see Directive 2019/1937/EU of the European Parliament and of the Council, of 23 October 2019) transposed by Law No. 93 of 20 October 1991 (which approved the general regime for the protection of whistleblowers), the European Arrest Warrant (EAW; see Framework Decision No. 2002/584/JHA of the Council of 13 June 2002), which led to the approval of the EAW regime by Law No. 654/2003 of 23 August 2003 and the European Investigation Decision (EID) (see Directive 2014/41/EU, of the European Parliament and of the Council of 3 April 2014), transposed by Law No. 88 of 21 August 2017.

3 Third Parties in Criminal Inquiries

3.1 Police and Law Enforcement Investigations

The criminal police must immediately promote precautionary measures, essentially aimed at preserving evidence (Arts. 248 ff. CCP), as well as police measures that prevent crimes from being committed or continuing.

When they learn of a crime, either through their own knowledge or through a report from a third party, they transmit it to the PPO as soon as possible, which cannot exceed 10 days—Art. 248(1) CCP. Also, if a person is arrested, the communication has to be immediately made to the Judge (in case an warrant had been issued) or to the PPO - Art. 259 CCP.

In addition, Police Officers (POs) must also immediately carry out a risk assessment of the victim and promote the protection of particularly vulnerable victims. With regard to domestic violence, there is also an obligation for PO to take special measures to protect victims and carry out a risk assessment.[24]

3.2 *Prosecutorial Inquiry*

3.2.1 Police Officers (Pos)

In general terms, POs assist in the investigation, and their intervention is particularly relevant in the investigation phase.

Specifically, POs carry out various measures to obtain evidence—such as searches, seizures, hearing witnesses, etc.—during the investigation (as a rule such measures are authorized or ordered by the competent judicial authority). In certain cases (particularly in cases of urgency), they may take steps to obtain evidence that are neither authorized nor ordered by the competent judicial authority, provided that the latter validates such steps afterwards.

Also in this regard, POs may carry out the first non-judicial interrogation of a accused person (not in custody), under the terms of Article 272 CCP, and may carry out interrogations subsequent to the first interrogation of a detained accused person, under the terms of Article 144 CCP, provided that the powers of the PPO are delegated to them.

3.2.2 The Complainant/Offended Party/Victim/Assistant

The complainant/offended party/victim/assistant have the rights to information, assistance, protection and active participation in the criminal proceedings, as provided for in the CCP and the Victim's Statute.

In particular, they have the right to collaborate with the competent police or judicial authorities, providing information and evidence that is necessary to determine the truth and decide the case, under the terms of Articles 67-A(4)-(5), 69(1)-(2) CCP. The victim, even if not an assistant, has the right to request to be heard by the examining judge during the pre-trial phase. This request is binding on the judge, who is obliged to hear it—Art. 292(2) CCP.

[24] Special regime provided for in Law No. 112 of 16 September 2009.

3.2.3 Civil Parties/Relatives

The procedural intervention of the injured party is restricted to supporting and proving the claim for civil compensation, with the corresponding rights that the law confers on assistants, under the terms of Article 74(2) CCP.

4 Scientific Developments, New Technologies and the Safeguards of Third Parties

Third party safeguards have accompanied the implementation of each legal regime, albeit only at a later stage, namely when they are detected in practice as affecting the rights of third parties (see, in this regard, the aforementioned seizure regime, under the terms of Article 178(7)-(12) CCP, which now allows the intervention of the holders of "instruments, products or advantages or other objects, things or animals seized" in broader terms, who may ask the judge to revoke or modify the measure).

The Regulation 2016/679/EU of the European Parliament and of the Council of 27 April 2016 on the protection of individuals with regard to the processing of personal data and on the free movement of such data also applies to criminal proceedings, guaranteeing more effective protection of personal data, including access to it and its use for criminal investigation purposes.

There are also safeguards in the system for searching and seizing computer data, emails or other data, as it requires the intervention of a judicial authority to access them (see Arts. 15–17 of the Cybercrime Law, approved by Law No. 109 of 15 September 2009).[25] In the case of e-mails, as they constitute electronic correspondence (regardless of whether or not they have already been read), they require prior authorization from an examining judge.

With regard to telephone tapping, environmental surveillance and image/video capture of those targeted, the CCP establishes the destruction, by order of the examining judge, of technical supports and reports that are "manifestly extraneous to the proceedings", namely when their disclosure could affect the rights, freedoms and guarantees of both the people who may be the target of the tapping and third parties (see Arts 188(7) and 189(6) of Law No. 5 of 11 January 2022).

It should be noted that even when the accused person has access to the case file or when the case becomes public, this does not cover "data relating to the privacy" of third parties (see Art. 86(6) CCP).

With regard to invasive methods not provided for in an express enabling law (*e.g.* GPS; online searches, with or without the use of online monitoring, etc.), their admissibility is debatable, although the majority opinion in doctrine and case law argues that they are inadmissible due to the lack of a prior and express enabling law and with a "certain quality".

[25] See Barata (2022, 2023).

5 Pre-Trial Measures and the Protection of Fundamental Rights of Third Parties

Specific coercive measures may be applied to protect the rights of third parties:

(i) the accused person may continue to be arrested until being brought before a judge if this is essential for the protection of the victim (Art. 385(1)(*c*) CCP);
(ii) the accused may be remanded in custody in order to protect witnesses, victims or other persons relevant to the acquisition of evidence (Art. 204(1)(*b*) CCP);
(iii) patrimonial guarantee measures may be ordered (the preventive seizure provided for in Article 228 CCP), which are designed to preserve the assets of a third party.

6 Third Parties and the Decision to Charge (or to Terminate the Proceedings)

In public and semi-public crimes, the constitution of an assistant is optional. If so constituted, the assistant has the possibility of submitting a subordinate charges (see Art. 284 CCP). This subordinate charges will be either (*i*) for the same facts that the Public Prosecutor charged, (*ii*) for part of them, (*iii*) for other facts that imply a non-substantial change of facts (which means that the introduction of new facts leads neither to an increase in the maximum limits of the applicable sanctions, nor to the accused person being charged with a different crime), or *iv*) for a change in the legal classification, according to the majority opinion in doctrine. In the case of private crimes, the assistant is the one who presents the main charges (private charges)—see Art. 285 CCP—while the PPO may, at its option, present subordinate charges—see Art. 285(4) CCP. It should be noted that, in the case of private crimes, even if the PPO considers that there is insufficient evidence that a crime has been committed and accordingly brings no charges, the proceedings will continue only with the assistant's charges.

In semi-public crimes, the offended party/complainant may terminate the proceedings by withdrawing the complaint before the first instance decision is handed down and provided the accused person raises no objection (see Art. 116(2) CCP). In private crimes, the assistant may terminate the proceedings by dropping the complaint see Art. 116(2) CCP, or simply by not filing private charges see Art. 285 CCP, in which case the Public Prosecutor is obliged to dismiss the case (even if they consider that there is sufficient evidence of a crime).

With regard to any claim for civil compensation, the injured party may, at any time during the proceedings either (i) waive the right to civil compensation and withdraw the claim made, or (ii) request that the object of the compensation payment be converted into a different asset, providing this is permitted by law (see Art. 81 CCP).

7 Third Parties in Court Proceedings

7.1 The Right of Third Parties to be Heard Fairly

The assistant and the injured party have the right to be heard during the proceedings, at their request or that of the accused person, or when the judicial authority deems it appropriate (see Art.145(1) CCP). As with witnesses, the assistant and the injured party are subject to the duty of truthfulness and incur criminal liability for its violation (see Art. 145(2) CCP).

The victim also has the right to be heard, under the terms of Article 67-A of the CCP.

7.2 The Right of Third Parties Not to be Questioned

Portuguese law provides for situations in which a witness may lawfully refuse to testify.

From the outset, a witness is under no obligation to answer questions when they claim that the answers will result in their being held criminally responsible (see Art. 132(1) CCP).

A witness may also validly refuse to testify in cases of special proximity between the witness and the accused person. Specifically, under the terms of Article 134(1) CCP, the following may refuse to testify as witnesses: (*i*) descendants, ascendants, siblings, relatives up to the second degree, adopters, adoptees and the accused person's spouse; or (*ii*) anyone who has been the accused person's spouse or who, being of the other or the same sex, lives with the accused person or has lived with them under conditions similar to those of the spouses, in relation to events that occurred during the marriage or cohabitation.

It may happen that a witness who is related to two (or more) accused persons refuses to testify about one of them and agrees to testify about the others, given that this right of refusal may be exercised by the witness without any restrictions.

If there are multiple co-accused persons, the right of refusal does not apply in relation to facts that are exclusively imputed to a co-accused person with whom the witness is not related (see Art. 134 CCP).

Although Portuguese law makes no express provision to this effect, some legal scholars believe that the witness has the right to refuse to answer questions that may cast doubt on their reputation or the reputation of their family members, as referred to in Article 134 of the CCP, or constitute an intrusion into the privacy of the witness, their family members or relatives, as a derivative of Article 26 of the CRP, so that the witness may lawfully refuse to answer when their answer is not indispensable to the find the truth.

With reference to the criminal liability of legal persons, the member of the body of the legal person or equivalent entity who is not its representative in the proceedings in which it is accused may also refuse to testify (see Art. 134(1)(*c*) CCP).

7.3 The Protection of Non-Parties in Court Activities Involving Formal Participants

There are mechanisms designed to protect third parties, such as statements for future reference ("*declarações para memória futura*"), under the terms of Article 271 CCP. These are intended for cases where a witness is seriously ill or travels abroad, foreseeably preventing them from being heard at trial, as well as in the case of a victim of a crime involving trafficking in human organs, human trafficking or against sexual liberty and self-determination, where the examining judge (at the request of either the PPO, the accused person, the assistant or the civil parties) may proceed to question such a witness during the investigation, so that their testimony can, if necessary, be taken into account at trial.

It should be noted that, under Portuguese law, statements for future reference ("*declarações para memória futura*") must be taken when dealing with a particularly vulnerable witness, and the witness's particular vulnerability may result specifically either from their young or advanced age, their state of health or the fact that they have to testify or make statements against a person from their own family or close social group in which they are subordinate or dependent.

Portuguese law also stipulates that victims of domestic violence must make statements for future reference, even if the victim is not ill or abroad.

There is also an obligation to take statements for future reference in the case of minors who are victims of crimes against sexual liberty and self-determination.

In any case, this mechanism of taking statements for future reference will be exceptional, as it constitutes an exception to the constitutional principle of immediacy.

In addition to this mechanism, the law also provides for the possibility of removing the accused person from the courtroom during the giving of evidence if (a) there is reason to believe that the presence of the accused person would inhibit the declarant from telling the truth; (b) the declarant is under 16 and there is reason to believe that hearing them in the presence of the accused person could cause them serious harm; or (c) an expert is to be heard and there is reason to believe that hearing that expert in the presence of the accused person could seriously harm their physical or mental integrity (see Art. 352(1) CCP).

7.4 Can Third Parties Take Part in Court Activities?

There are various situations in which third parties can actively participate in a trial.

From the outset, witnesses can participate by giving evidence at the trial hearing (see Art. 348 CCP). A witness must first identify themselves and take an oath. Leading or impertinent questions or questions that in any way impair the spontaneity of the witness are prohibited. The witness may be confronted with case files, documents or other relevant elements (such as instruments of the crime or other objects). The witness should be questioned in terms similar to the Anglo-American common law model, i.e. first there is direct questioning of the witness by the person who called the witness (examination in chief) and then so-called cross-examination. The judge may also intervene by asking the witness questions, which is a particular feature of Portuguese law. It should be noted that the witness may only be questioned about the subject matter of the case during the direct examination, and the cross-examination may only deal with the issues that were the subject of the direct examination (and no longer the entire subject matter of the case).

In addition to witnesses, experts or technical consultants may also make statements (see Art. 350 CCP). In this case, it will be the judge who makes the statements, while the other parties (such as the PPO, the defense counsel, and the representatives of the assistants and civil parties) may request that the judge ask questions.

Also, third parties who are the owners of instruments, products or advantages that may be declared forfeited to the state (see Art. 347-A CCP) may make statements and exercise adversarial proceedings, and the same rules apply as for experts and technical consultants.

Naturally, the assistant and the civil parties may also make statements (see respectively Arts. 346 and 347 CCP).

Third parties may also take part in obtaining evidence by recognition (of people or objects) (see Arts. 147 ff. CCP).

8 The Protection of Third Parties in Decision-Making Processes

As mentioned above, the injured party may apply for civil compensation for any damage suffered as a result of the crime committed.

However, even if no claim for civil compensation has been made, Portuguese criminal procedural law provides for the possibility of the court, in the event of a conviction, to arbitrate an amount as compensation for the damage suffered when the particular requirements of protecting the victim so require (see Art. 82-A(1) CCP).

9 Third Parties in Appeal Proceedings

The assistant may appeal against the final decision (see Art. 401(1)(b) CCP).

Civil parties may also appeal against decisions handed down against them (see Art. 401(1)(c) CCP).

Finally, all those who have been ordered to pay any sums, or who are defending a right affected by the decision, may also file an appeal (see Article 401(1)(d) CCP).

The writ of *habeas corpus* may be filed by any "citizen exercising their political rights" (Arts. 220(2) and 222 CCP) as a way of reacting to an illegal arrest or an illegal pre-trial detention. This action is brought before the Supreme Court of Justice as a matter of urgency and is the most common remedy for dealing with the evident illegality of an arrest or pre-trial detention.

An extraordinary appeal for review (i.e. one that can be lodged after the decision has become final and unappealable), for example on the grounds of prohibited evidence that was used to convict the accused person and was only discovered after the decision had become final and unappealable,[26] can be lodged with the Supreme Court of Justice by the convicted person (in condemnatory sentences), or their defender, or even when the convicted person is deceased, their spouse, descendants, adoptees, ascendants, adopters, relatives or affines up to the 4th degree of the collateral line, heirs who show a legitimate interest or anyone who has been expressly entrusted by the convicted person (see Art. 450(2) CCP).

10 *Res Judicata* and the Effects of Criminal Judgments upon Third Parties

There is no express *res judicata* regime in the Portuguese CCP, but the concept is nevertheless applicable. It is in force and imposed in various dimensions, as well as being mentioned on a case-by-case basis in the CCP.

On the one hand, and as distinct from *ne bis in idem* (which prevents the same accused person from being tried and the same investigation or criminal proceedings from being repeated in relation to the same facts), it may be said that there is an effect of closure or preclusion of a certain procedural subject matter when a court decision on it becomes final (in other words, it no longer allows any ordinary appeal). This effect is naturally limited to a particular procedural subject matter and has subjective and temporal limits.

Consequently, and despite being controversial, *res judicata* will only have *inter partes* effects. Third parties who may be affected by a court decision must be part of the process so that they may be covered by *res judicata*. The possibility of third parties, possible owners or holders of things, animals or rights seized or confiscated/

[26] Cf. the provisions of Article 449(1)(a) CCP.

forfeited in favor of the State, taking part in the respective criminal proceedings is therefore relevant.

On the other hand, the CCP expressly takes into account *res judicata* in at least two situations: (*i*) in Article 84 CCP, to express the idea that a criminal decision, even if it is an acquittal, that hears/judges the civil claim constitutes *res judicata* under the terms that civil procedural law attributes the effect of *res judicata* to such a civil judgment; and (*ii*) in Article 219 CCP, to emphasize that the appeal must be heard even if it is an appeal against a measure of coercion (namely pre-trial detention and habeas corpus). This means that the appeal must be assessed even if a writ of *habeas corpus* has been filed in the meantime.

It should also be noted that, without prejudice to the fact that *res judicata* presupposes stability and accordingly the inalterability of the effects of a procedural decision, presupposing the immutability of the assumptions on which the procedural relationship is based, there are still cases in which it is possible for the decision to be altered even after it has become final, through an appeal for review under the terms of Article 449 CCP. In particular, and in relation to the position of third parties to the proceedings and *res judicata*, it should be noted that an appeal for review may be brought if (*i*) another final judgment has proved a crime committed by a judge or juror and related to the exercise of their function in the proceedings, or (*ii*) the facts on which the conviction is based are irreconcilable with those proved in another judgment and the opposition results in serious doubts regarding the fairness of the conviction.

References

AA. VV. (2021a) Comentário Judiciário do Código de Processo Penal – Tomo IV – Artigos 311.° a 398.°, 2.ª ed. Almedina, Coimbra

AA. VV. (2021b) Comentário Judiciário do Código de Processo Penal – Tomo III – Artigos 191.° a 310.°, 2.ª ed. Almedina, Coimbra

AA. VV. (2021c) Comentário Judiciário do Código de Processo Penal – Tomo I – Artigos 1.° a 123.°, 2.ª ed. Almedina, Coimbra

AA. VV. (2021d) Comentário Judiciário do Código de Processo Penal – Tomo II – Artigos 124.° a 190.°, 3.ª ed. Almedina, Coimbra

Antunes MJ (2023) Direito Processual Penal, 5.ª ed. Almedina, Coimbra

Barata JR (2022) O desassossego do Tribunal da Relação de Lisboa quanto à aplicação do regime de apreensão de mensagens de correio eletrónico. In: Prof. Doutor Augusto Silva Dias in Memoriam, Vol. II. AAFDL Editora, Lisboa

Barata JR (2023) "O regime jurídico dos conhecimentos fortuitos em ambiente digital: contributo da plain view doctrine à luz da legislação portuguesa", Novos Desafios da Prova Penal, Volume II, Almedina, Coimbra

da Silva GM (2024) Direito Processual Penal Português - Teoria da Prova - Volume 2 - Tomo 1, Universidade Católica, Lisboa

da Silva GM (2017) Direito Processual Penal Português, 1.° vol. 2.ª ed. Universidade Católica, Lisboa

da Silva GM (2014) Direito Processual Penal Português, Volume III, Universidade Católica, Lisboa de Albuquerque PP (2023) Comentário do Código de Processo Penal à luz da Constituição da República e da Convenção Europeia dos Direitos do Homem. 5.ª ed., 2 Vols. Universidade Católica Editora, Lisboa

Dias JF, Brandão N (2022) Direito Processual Penal - Os sujeitos processuais. Gestlegal, Coimbra

Mendes PS (2019) Prova Penal Teórica e Prática (eds. Paulo de Sousa Mendes and Rui Soares Pereira). Almedina, Coimbra

Mendes PS (2023) Lições de Direito Processual Penal, 10.ª reimp. da ed. de 2013. Almedina, Coimbra

Pereira RS, de Caires JG (2023) Processo Penal. Almedina, Coimbra

Report on Spain

Fernando Gascón Inchausti and Guillermo Schumann Barragán

Abstract This paper aims to study the protection of third parties in Spanish criminal proceedings. In particular, it analyses the status and rights of third parties in criminal investigations, the adoption of pre-trial measures, the criminal trial, the decision-making process, appeals and the execution and effects of criminal judgments. Special attention is given to the recent case law of the Constitutional Court in this area.

1 Introduction. General Features of Spanish Criminal Justice

The Spanish criminal procedure is mainly governed by the Spanish Code of Criminal Procedure (*Ley de Enjuiciamiento Criminal*, CCP hereinafter). It was initially approved in 1882 and has been successively amended. Some relevant features of Spanish criminal procedural law set important differences if compared to other legal systems and are relevant for the purposes of this report.

1.1 Legal Standing to Accuse

It shall first be borne in mind that in the Spanish procedural system there is no monopoly of the State, through the Public Prosecutor's Office, in the exercise of the accusation. On the contrary, the power to accuse is open to any citizen (*acusación*

This chapter has been made possible with the support of the Spanish Ministry of Science and Innovation, in the framework of the project "Eficiencia y acceso a la justicia en tiempos de austeridad» (PID2021-122647NB-I00)".

F. Gascón Inchausti · G. Schumann Barragán (✉)
Complutense University of Madrid, Madrid, Spain
e-mail: fgascon@ucm.es; gschuman@ucm.es

S. Ruggeri et al. (eds.), *Third Parties in Criminal Proceedings*, Legal Studies in International, European and Comparative Criminal Law 10,
https://doi.org/10.1007/978-3-031-73970-5_7

popular) and, especially, to any person who has been offended by the crime (*acusación particular*).[1] This is a very special feature of Spanish criminal proceedings if compared to most systems in the civil law tradition and entails, as a consequence, a blurring in terms of defining the status of parties and third parties: the victim, for instance, may be considered as a party, if she decides to press charges and sustain her accusation; but she will remain a third party if she does not.

1.2 Scope of Criminal Proceedings: Criminal and Civil Liability

A second crucial issue in relation to the legal design of criminal proceedings in Spain regards their scope.

In Spanish criminal proceedings, in addition to criminal liability, the civil action derived from the crime can also be and is usually prosecuted.[2] This has been the system since at least 1882 and it is based on reasons of procedural economy: given that there is an open judicial process, it is reasonable to take advantage of it to try to resolve all the consequences associated with the commission of the crime.

The civil claim ex delicto is defined in Art. 110 of the Spanish Criminal Code as encompassing restitution, reparation of the damage and compensation for material and non-material damages.

In criminal proceedings, however, the Public Prosecutor's Office also has the standing—and usually the duty—to bring a civil action on behalf of the victim, even if the victim herself has joined the proceedings to bring it.[3] The civil claim ex delicto is governed by the principle of party disposition. Therefore, the situation regarding the victim's control over the civil action could be summarised in the following terms:

- The victim, at any time during the criminal proceedings, may, generally, waive the civil action ex delicto. This waiver does not affect the criminal prosecution—except for certain offences against honour—but it usually extinguishes the civil action for both the victim herself and the Public Prosecutor's Offices.[4]
- The victim may also "reserve" the civil action for subsequent civil proceedings. This reservation excludes the civil action from the criminal proceedings, but allows the victim to bring it separately, in a separate civil proceeding.[5] As the

[1] Arts. 101 and 270 CCP.

[2] Arts. 100 and 108 CCP.

[3] Pursuant to Art. 108 CCP, "The civil action must be brought jointly with the criminal action by the Public Prosecutor's Office, whether or not there is a private prosecutor in the process; but if the offended party expressly waives his right to restitution, repair or compensation, the Public Prosecutor's Office will limit itself to requesting the punishment of the accused parties".

[4] Arts. 107 and 108 CCP. According to Art. 112 II CCP, this waiver may be revoked in specific situations.

[5] Art. 112 CCP.

principle of "*le criminel tient le civil en état*" applies in Spain,[6] such civil proceedings can only be brought once the criminal proceedings have been finally terminated.[7] The reservation has the advantage that the civil action receives full and specific attention, rather than being treated among many other issues in the framework of complex proceedings. The counterpart is the need to wait for the completion of the criminal proceedings, as both the law and case law have established certain links between the decisions of the criminal judgement and the development of the civil proceedings.

If the victim does not become a party to the criminal proceedings, the Public Prosecutor's Office shall bring the civil action on behalf of the victim, but it shall do so according to its own criteria. The Public Prosecutor's Office is not entitled to waive the civil action or to negotiate openly about it.

If the victim is a party to the criminal proceedings and brings the civil action, she shall have the burden of determining the amount requested and of making the corresponding allegations and of producing evidence in support of his claim. The victim will concur with the Public Prosecutor's Office in the exercise of both criminal and civil actions. In practice, it is common for the victim to make harsher punitive demands than the prosecution and to request higher compensation than the prosecution. Sometimes the presence of victims in the proceedings is perceived as a kind of "control" over the public prosecution.

The exercise of civil actions in criminal proceedings also contributes to blurring the dividing line between parties and third parties. In terms of standing, the victim may choose to pursue only civil actions and not criminal actions, or vice versa. On the other hand, very often the civil action arising from the crime involves an insurance company, when the crime prosecuted has been committed on the occasion of conduct covered by insurance (e.g. traffic offences or offences against workers' safety).[8] This means that insurance companies will also be parties to the criminal proceedings. Likewise, the State, the autonomous communities (regions) and other public entities, which are civilly liable for offences committed by civil servants, may also become (civil) parties to the criminal proceedings.[9]

1.3 Structure and Development of Proceedings

Spanish criminal proceedings are divided into two main phases, one of investigation and the other of trial in the proper sense.

[6] Art. 114 CCP.

[7] Art. 112 CCP.

[8] Art. 117 of the Spanish Criminal Code.

[9] Art. 121 of the Spanish Criminal Code.

The first phase—the investigation phase or *instrucción*—is conducted under the direction of an examining magistrate (*juez de instrucción*). It is therefore a judge, and not a public prosecutor, who is in charge of leading criminal investigations in Spain.

The second phase of criminal proceedings is the trial phase. A trial will only take place if the investigation has established with sufficient accuracy and evidentiary support the existence of a criminal offence and their apparent authors. The Public Prosecutor or a private person needs to sustain the accusation, in order for the trial phase to be opened. The trial is conducted by a court different to the one in charge of the investigation. Depending on the seriousness of the sanction established in the Criminal Code the trial will be held before a single judge or before a panel of three judges. Single-judge courts are competent to deal with criminal offences punished with imprisonment up to 5 years, with a fine or with other sanctions up to 10 years. Beyond these limits, the case will be in the hands of collegiate courts.[10]

Criminal proceedings are formally opened when an examining magistrate is informed of the apparent existence of a criminal offence. The purposes of proceedings at this stage are to ascertain the relevant facts, to determine the responsible persons, to access the sources of evidence and to adopt provisional and protective measures, both with respect to the criminal action and to the civil action ex delicto. This phase is rather adversarial in nature: the parties may intervene and sustain their claims in relation to the aforementioned issues. The examining magistrate will declare the investigative stage of proceedings concluded once he considers that all necessary investigative measures have been taken and it is concluded that there is evidence of an offence and that the persons to whom the offence can be attributed have been identified.[11]

At this point, the magistrate's investigation is subject to the scrutiny of the parties entitled to prosecute. The Public Prosecutor's Office and the other parties who have decided to intervene as accusers and/or civil actors during the investigation phase must decide whether to ask the investigating judge to formally open the oral trial phase or whether, on the contrary, the proceedings should be dismissed or discontinued. If they want a trial to be opened against all or some of those under investigation, they must request this by directly presenting a written accusation, regulated in Article 781 CCP (with reference to Art. 650 CCP). In this indictment or statement of accusation, they will have to establish the facts of which they are accusing, the requests for conviction that they make to the court and the evidence to be taken at the trial.

If an accusing party has so requested, the examining magistrate will agree to open the oral trial if he considers that there are rational indications of criminality against the accused.[12] At the same time as agreeing to move on to the oral trial phase, the same examining magistrate can also adopt, modify, suspend or revoke precautionary

[10] Art. 14 CCP.

[11] Art. 779.1.4 CCP.

[12] Art. 783.1 CCP.

measures with respect to the civilly liable parties.[13] In practice, it is common to wait until that moment to ask third parties to provide security if the accused has not done so within the time limit set.

Once the oral trial has been opened, the court will communicate all the proceedings to those designated as accused, defendants and responsible third parties in the indictments, so that they may present their statements of defence.[14] Failure to submit a statement of defence does not constitute acquiescence, but rather a presumption that the accused or the civilly liable party opposes what is being sought in respect of them.

Although formally the oral trial phase is already open, the presentation of the statements of defence is carried out before the examining magistrate. Once the pleadings have been received or, where applicable, once the time limit for doing so has expired, all the proceedings will be sent to the court responsible for the trial.

The trial phase is mainly devoted to the taking of the evidence proposed by the parties. At the beginning of the main oral hearing, the parties may still raise procedural issues and produce new evidence. The core of the hearing will be devoted to an adversarial taking of evidence, with the accused, witnesses and experts being examined and cross-examined by the parties. After all evidence has been elicited, the parties will be required to formulate their final submissions in light of the results of the trial.

In its judgment, the court will decide both on the criminal and on the civil liability of the accused parties, considering these final claims and defences formulated by all parties.

Following a relevant reform enacted in 2015, all judgments given by criminal courts in proceedings which started after the reform entered into force may be subject of 'ordinary' appeal proceedings, meaning that both accusing and accused parties may bring an appeal and also that the appeal may be founded on any infringement attributed to the judgment: 'ordinary' appeals may be based on the wrong assessment of evidence by the court, on the infringement of procedural rules and safeguards, or on the infringement of material law. Some judgments given after an ordinary appeal may be subject of a further appeal for cassation before the Spanish Supreme Court. This second appeal shall only be based on legal infringements, either of procedural or material provisions.

Finally, and according to the Spanish constitutional system, if a party deems that a final judgment has been given infringing a fundamental right as enshrined in the Spanish Constitution, she may lodge a specific recourse with the Spanish Constitutional Court, the so-called '*recurso de amparo*'. This '*recurso de amparo*' allows the Constitutional Court to assess whether the decision has infringed a fundamental right and, eventually, to annul it.

[13] Art. 783.2 CCP.

[14] Art. 784.1 CCP.

1.4 Formal Participants in Criminal Proceedings

All that has been described so far explains how, in Spanish criminal proceedings, the list of possible participants is vast.

From the active point of view, the following subjects can be parties:

1. The Public Prosecutor's Office, which will usually hold the status of prosecuting party. However, there are two exceptions to this:
   (a) It is possible for the Public Prosecutor, in a specific case, to request the acquittal of the accused. This is possible if the accusation is brought by another party, since the State does not have a monopoly on the accusation.
   (b) Certain crimes (very few: libel and defamation against private individuals) can only be validly prosecuted by the victim, who is the only one entitled to bring charges: the public prosecutor is not a party to these proceedings.
2. The victim of the offence, when she has decided to bring a criminal and/or civil action.
3. Any Spanish citizen, who is not a victim, but who has decided to bring a public prosecution.

From the passive point of view, in addition to the accused, those who are civilly liable, even if they are not criminally liable, will also be parties to the proceedings if the civil action *ex delicto* is brought against them: it has already been mentioned for insurance companies and the State and other public entities, but this position can also be occupied by any person potentially considered as civilly liable, like the parents of the incompetent person who committed the crime and who were negligent in supervising him/her, for example.[15]

1.5 Third Parties to Criminal Proceedings

The extent to which several categories of persons and legal entities may reach the status of formal parties in the Spanish criminal procedure system must be taken into account when drawing up the catalogue of third parties. For these purposes, third parties are understood to be those subjects who do not formally hold the status of a party, because they do not formulate claims—criminal or civil—nor are claims brought against them—again, criminal or civil—but who have some kind of intervention or leading role in the criminal proceedings, or whose legal position is taken into account by the criminal procedural system.

In a rather instinctive manner, the first third parties coming to our mind are witnesses and expert witnesses, who gain relevance for evidentiary purposes.

[15] Arts. 118 and 120 of the Spanish Criminal Code.

Witnesses may deserve, at least some of them, specific attention when they are interrogated, both during the investigation phase and during trial: this is the case, namely, with vulnerable witnesses, like minors, and with victims that have not decide to bring their own accusation. Both witnesses and expert witnesses may also request measures to protect them, their relatives and their assets, when they are the scope of threatens intended at preventing them to provide evidence against the accused.

However, for the purposes of this study, it will also be important to direct the focus on third parties whose rights, legal interests or even factual situation may be affected by criminal proceedings lead by others and/or against others.

This is the case of the owners of goods and assets that may be frozen and confiscated as a result of criminal proceedings—although it may also be argued that, insofar as the claim for confiscation affects them directly, they should be considered as formal defendant parties to the proceedings.

It is also the case of natural persons employed by legal entities, where an accusation is brought against the legal entity and there is the risk that the court suspends or closes its activity (as a precautionary measure or as a penalty).

In this very same vein, the notion of third parties encompasses the persons that may be affected by an investigative measure, without being accused: this is the case of the owner of a premise where a search is performed; this is also what happens when a wiretap is granted in regard to persons, unconnected to the criminal activity, who talk to the person under investigation and whose privacy may be compromised.

Finally, it is also possible that the personal data of third parties is processed during criminal proceedings. Pursuant to Article 9 of the Organic Law 7/2021, the person in charge of processing the data in criminal proceedings should distinguish the status of the person whose data is treated.[16] These categories include the victims or those who may be affected by the criminal offense, third parties involved in a criminal proceeding, such as witnesses, and persons who may provide information about such offenses, among others. All these persons are entitled to exercise the substantive rights recognized by the law: right of access, right to rectification, right to erasure or right to restriction of processing (Arts. 22 and 23 of Organic Law 7/2021). In addition, they will have the right to compensation for any damages arising from the processing of their data—regardless of whether the processing is carried out by a public or private entity—(Arts. 53 and 54 of Organic Law 7/2021).

[16]Ley Orgánica 7/2021, de 26 de mayo, de protección de datos personales tratados para fines de prevención, detección, investigación y enjuiciamiento de infracciones penales y de ejecución de sanciones penales [https://www.boe.es/buscar/act.php?id=BOE-A-2021-8806&p=20210527&tn=1].

2 Fundamental Rights and Safeguards of Third Parties

2.1 Constitutional Law

The fundamental rights and public liberties are recognized in Articles 14–29 of the Spanish Constitution (CE, hereinafter)[17] and protected by specific safeguards. According to Article 53 CE, these rights

> are binding for all public authorities. [. . .] Any citizen may assert his or her claim to protect the liberties and rights recognized [. . .] through a preferential and summary procedure in the ordinary courts and, when appropriate, by submitting an individual appeal for protection ("recurso de amparo") to the Constitutional Court [. . .].

Article 9 CE also establishes the general subjection of the state and citizens to the Constitution: "[c]itizens and public authorities are bound by the Constitution and all other legal provisions".

Therefore, fundamental rights and public liberties are directly invocable by third parties in criminal inquiries and proceedings. The main fundamental rights and public liberties of third parties at stake in criminal matters could be the right to personal freedom (Art. 17 CE), the freedom of speech (Art. 20 CE), the rights to privacy—including intimacy, home inviolability and secrecy of communications, for instance—(Art. 18 CE) and the right to an effective judicial relief (Art. 24 CE). As mentioned, in addition to the ordinary remedies established by the law—namely by the CCP and by other specific legislation on criminal procedure—the special protection provided by Art. 53 CE means that thirds parties can eventually file an individual appeal for protection before the Constitutional Court for any violation of their rights in criminal proceedings, as was the case in Ruling 30/2022 of the Constitutional Court that will be discussed later on.

2.2 Domestication of International Law

In general terms, it can be said that the Spanish criminal procedure system complies with the standards set by international treaties and European law. The European Convention on Human Rights is also part of the Spanish legal system, and its jurisprudence is taken into account by Spanish courts when applying national laws. The same applies to the International Covenant on Civil and Political Rights and the guarantees set out in its Art. 14. In fact, one of the most recent structural reforms in recent years, undertaken in 2015, generalised the appeal against all criminal judgments, precisely to ensure better compliance with the right of everyone

[17] The English version of the Spanish Constitution is available here: https://www.boe.es/legislacion/documentos/ConstitucionINGLES.pdf.

convicted of a crime to have his conviction and sentence being reviewed by a higher tribunal according to law, enshrined in Art. 14(5) of the Covenant.

2.3 Implementation of EU Law

Within the general framework of implementation of EU law, two main instruments of EU law have a direct relation with third parties in criminal matters: Directive 2012/29/UE establishing minimum standards on the rights, support and protection of victims of crime and Directive 2014/42/UE on the freezing and confiscation of instrumentalities and proceeds of crime in the European Union.[18]

As has been said, the victims should have the consideration of third parties in criminal proceedings when they do not exercise the criminal action—*i.e.*, when they are not formal parties to the proceedings. Directive 2012/29/UE has been transposed in the Spanish national legal order by Law 4/2015 of the Crime Victim Statute—*Estatuto de la Víctima del Delito*.[19] This Law is formed by 35 Articles. and is divided into four titles that deal with the basic rights of the victims (Title I), the participation of the victim in criminal proceedings (Title II), the protection of the victim (Title III) and common provisions related to the victims' assistance offices, cooperation and best practices between administrations, among others (Title IV). The Preamble states that the Law

> not only responds to the minimum requirements set by the European lawmaker with the text finally approved in the aforementioned Directive 2012/29/EU, but also tries to be more ambitious [. . .] is intended to be a general catalog of the procedural and extra-procedural rights of all crime victims [. . .] It is based on a broad concept of a victim, for any crime and whatever the nature of the physical, moral or material damage caused to her. It includes the direct victim, but also indirect victims, such as family members or similar.

On the other side, Directive 2014/42/UE on the freezing and confiscation of instrumentalities and proceeds of crime has been transposed into national legal order through Law 41/2015.[20] The Law introduces in the Spanish Criminal Procedure Act (CCP) a section regulating the intervention in criminal proceedings of third parties that may be affected by the freezing and confiscation of instrumentalities and proceeds of crime [Arts. 803 *ter* a) to 803 *ter* d) CCP] and a "stand-alone" procedure for the freezing and confiscation [Arts. 803 *ter* e) to 803 *ter* u) CCP]. The "stand-alone" confiscation proceedings "allows for the deprivation of the ownership of the

[18]The latter shall be read together with Regulation (EU) 2018/1805 of the European Parliament and of the Council of 14 November 2018 on the mutual recognition of freezing orders and confiscation orders.

[19]Ley 4/2015, de 27 de abril, del Estatuto de la víctima del delito [https://www.boe.es/buscar/act.php?id=BOE-A-2015-4606].

[20]Ley 41/2015, de 5 de octubre, de modificación de la Ley de Enjuiciamiento Criminal para la agilización de la justicia penal y el fortalecimiento de las garantías procesales [https://www.boe.es/buscar/doc.php?id=BOE-A-2015-10726].

assets derived from the crime even though the perpetrator cannot be tried". As the Preamble of the Law establishes, the rights of the third parties who may be affected by the confiscation "are guaranteed not only [with the possibility of intervening in this procedure] but also with the creation of an appeal for annulment [...] if the decision has been made without considering their status as interested parties in the case".

3 Third Parties in Criminal Inquiries

As already explained above, Spanish criminal proceedings are formed by two main phases: the judicial investigation phase—*fase de instrucción*—and the trial phase—*fase de enjuiciamiento*. Both are carried out by a judge or a court. The first one by the examining magistrate/investigation judge—*juez de instrucción*—and the second one by the trial judge or court—*juez o tribunal de enjuiciamiento*.[21] Formally, criminal proceedings start with a judicial decision in which the examining magistrate identifies some facts with criminal appearance—*auto de incoación de las diligencias previas o del sumario*. But, as can be imagined, previously it is possible that some investigation measures—of non-judicial nature—may be carried out by the police or the public prosecutor's office to establish with a sufficient level of detail the *notitia criminis* that must be communicated to the examining magistrate in a criminal report.[22] Therefore, criminal inquires may have a non-judicial and 'pre-procedural' nature—police and prosecutorial inquires—but also, and more normally, a judicial and procedural nature—when they are carried out within the investigation phase of the proceedings.

3.1 Police and Law Enforcement Investigations

We will address first he rights of victims. At this moment the criminal proceedings have not been yet initiated and, therefore, all victims should usually be considered third parties to any law enforcement activity. Article 4 of the Law 4/2015 of the Crime Victim Statute recognizes the so-called right of the victim to understand and be understood "*from the filing of a police report* and during the criminal proceedings". This includes *(i)* the right to a clear, easy and plain language that considers the age or the sensory, intellectual or mental disability of the victim; *(ii)* the right to interpretation in legally recognized sign languages and means of oral communication support for deaf, hard of hearing and deaf-blind people; and *(iii)* the right of the victim to be accompanied by a trusted person from the first contact with the police.

[21] Gascón Inchausti (2024), pp. 132–142 and 223–245.

[22] Gascón Inchausti (2024), pp. 132–138.

Art. 5 recognizes the right to information about available assistance and support measures—whether medical, psychological or of any other kind—the right to file a criminal complaint and the procedure for filing it, the right to provide evidence to the investigating authorities, legal aid, the right to request protective measures, contact details of the authority in charge of handling the procedure, restorative justice services available, among others. The Crime Victim Statute also regulates the rights of the victim to the translation and interpretation if they do not speak or understand Spanish (Art. 9 Law 4/2015) and the right of access to assistance and support services (Art. 10 Law 4/2015). The victims are also recognized the right to file in Spain complaints relating to criminal offenses committed in the territory of other EU Member States (Art. 17 Law 4/2015).

Secondly, we will analyze the *position of third parties—other than victims—during a police investigation*. At this stage it is sometimes difficult to establish whether a person will remain a third party, or he/she will acquire the status of formal party in potential subsequent judicial proceedings.

Police inquiries, previous to a formal judicialized investigation, are limited insofar as only a judge can adopt or authorize investigative measures limiting fundamental rights. Any excessive investigation measure adopted by the police could be controlled through a specific procedure for the protection of the fundamental rights, regulated in Articles 114–122 *quarter* of Law 29/1998 regulating the Administrative Jurisdiction (LJCA).[23]

The time limit for bringing this action against any police activity that allegedly infringed a fundamental right is 10 days (Art. 115 LJCA). In case of *de facto* activity of the police, a 20-day period will run from the date when the administrative activity started. The proceedings commence with a complaint specifying the rights whose protection is sought and describing their infringement. On the same day or in the following, the police shall be required to refer to the tribunal the files together with the reports and data (Art. 116 LJCA). Upon receipt of the file, if so, the court clerk will admit the action (Art. 117 LJCA) and the person will have 8 days to formalize the claim (Art. 118 LJCA). The Prosecutor's Office and the police will have another 8 days to reply to the claim (Art. 119 LJCA). The court will decide on the evidence presented (Art. 120 LJCA) and will give its judgment (Art. 121 LJCA) which could declare that the police activity infringed the fundamental right at stake.

It should be noted that, although in theory this is a way of protection against police activity, it is not used very often in practice. This is probably due to the length and formality of this procedure and, more probably, because the affected person only knows that she has been subject to police investigations once judicial criminal proceedings have already been initiated.

Another ordinary way of protecting individuals during police investigations is the *habeas corpus* proceedings recognized in Art. 17(4) CE and developed in Organic

[23] Ley 29/1998, de 13 de julio, reguladora de la Jurisdicción Contencioso-administrativa [https://www.boe.es/buscar/act.php?id=BOE-A-1998-16718&p=20211012&tn=0].

Law 6/1984.[24] As it is commonly known, the aim of these proceedings is to obtain the immediate delivery of any person illegally arrested to the competent judicial authority—*i.e.*, the court of the place where the person is being held, where there are details about her detention or where the latest news on the person has been known (Art. 2 of the Organic Law 6/1984). In some cases, the *habeas corpus* itself is a way of protecting third parties that do not have any relation with the *notitia criminis* that is being investigated.

3.2 Prosecutorial Inquiry

As mentioned, the investigations before the formal start of criminal proceedings may be carried out by the police or by the Public Prosecutor's Office—who may start an inquiry on its own motion, but also upon receiving a complaint. There are no formal differences between police and prosecutorial inquiries as far as the positions of victims and suspects are concerned. For that reason, what has been discussed above applies accordingly.

3.3 Judicial Investigation

Starting with *the rights of victims*, we shall recall that they shall only be considered as third parties if they do not exercise or intend to exercise the criminal action—*i.e.*, if they choose not to participate formally in the criminal proceedings.

In this phase all the rights enshrined in Law 4/2015 of the Crime Victim Statute, mentioned above, will apply, in a similar way as they do during the police or prosecutorial investigations: the so-called right to understand and be understood, the right to information, the rights to translation and interpretation, or the right of access to assistance and support services (see above). In addition to these, some rights are specifically applicable in the procedural sphere. This is the case, for example, of the right to receive information about the criminal case (Art. 7 Law 4/2015). If the victim has requested it, and irrespective of their formal participation in the process, the victim has the right to know the following judicial decision: *(i)* the decision about the initiation or not of the criminal proceedings; *(ii)* the judgment or any other judicial resolution that ends the proceedings; *(iii)* information related to the imprisonment or subsequent release of the offender, as well of his escape; and *(iv)* any decision of the judicial or penitentiary authority in certain cases. Therefore, the right of information goes beyond the (mere) criminal proceedings and includes also measures related to the enforcement of the judgment itself (Arts. 7 and 13 of Law

[24] Ley Orgánica 6/1984, de 24 de mayo, reguladora del procedimiento de "Habeas Corpus" [https://www.boe.es/buscar/act.php?id=BOE-A-1984-11620].

4/2015). The victim also has the right to an active participation in the criminal proceedings exercising the criminal action (Art. 11 Law 4/2015), the right to be informed of and to lodge an appeal against the dismissal order of the judicial investigation—*auto de sobreseimiento*—or the right to obtain the return of any object that may have been seized during the proceedings (Art. 18 with relation to Arts. 284(4) and 334 CCP). In addition, in judicial investigations the victims have special rights of protection. In particular, the right to the necessary measures to guarantee their life and of their family members, their physical and psychological integrity, freedom, security and sexual freedom (Art. 19 Law 4/2015), the right to avoid contact with the offender during criminal proceedings (Art. 20 Law 4/2015), the right to be heard in the proceedings and to be examined as few times as possible and only when strictly necessary, to be always accompanied with a person of their election—in addition to the lawyer—(Art. 21 Law 4/2015) and the right to the protection of privacy during the investigation (Art. 22 Law 4/2015), among other protective measures specifically regulated for the judicial investigation phase (Art. 25 Law 4/2015). Finally, the Law incorporates certain protection measures for minors and persons with disabilities or needed of special protection (Art. 26 Law 4/2015).

Given that criminal proceedings have already begun, it is easier to identify *third parties—others than victims—during the judicial investigation.* More specifically, we will address the status of individuals *(i)* whose objects or assets have been seized during the police or judicial investigation phase; *(ii)* that are being affected by any judicial investigation measure—*diligencia de investigación*—and, in particular, *(iii)* their possibility of intervening and participating in the proceedings to defend themselves.

During the police or judicial investigations some objects property of third parties related to the crime or crime scene may be seized. These objects could be used as proof in the future trial or may just be necessary for the practice of additional judicial investigation measures. Therefore, these are not cases of freezing and confiscation of instrumentalities and proceeds of crime (Arts. 803 *ter* a to 803 *ter* d CCP), but objects (merely) related to the crime or to its investigation. Pursuant to Art. 334 CCP, any person affected by the confiscation

> may appeal the measure before the Court at any time. This appeal will not require intervention by a lawyer when it is submitted by third parties other than the accused. The appeal will be taken as lodged when the person affected by the measure, or one of their family members, of legal age, have stated their disagreement at the time it is taken.

Other third parties may be also affected by judicial investigation measures. This affectation could be indirect—*e.g.*, the entry in the home of the suspect where third parties also live or the interception of telephone and telematic communications that he is having with thirds parties—or directly—*e.g.*, the entry in the home of the suspect's mother to search for evidence of the crime or the interception of the telephone of a suspect's friend, when it is clear that the suspect is frequently using it. The potential of this "collateral" damages of criminal proceedings is nowadays intensified by the technological investigation measures that can be adopted by the examining magistrate (see below). It is necessary, therefore, to examine to what extent the fundamental rights of third parties can be validly limited or restricted during the judicial investigation and what remedies are available to them to protect their fundamental rights.

We shall recall, from the outset, that any judicial investigation measure that supposes a limitation of any fundamental right—not only of those of the suspect or accused—is subject to specific controls and standards that have been developed in the case law and recently in the law itself. First of all, the investigation measure must be previously authorized by the law and by the court in the specific case. Among other issues, the judge must perform the corresponding proportionality assessment when deciding on the adoption of the investigation measure itself.[25] A recent reform of the CCP in 2015, aimed at regulating technological investigation measures, expressly incorporates these guiding principles, required for their adoption. Pursuant to Art. 588 *bis* a) CCP, the investigation measure

> may be ordered, as long as judicial authorization is issued fully subject to the principles of specialty, adequacy, exceptionality, necessity and proportionality of the measure [. . .] The investigative measures regulated in this chapter will only be considered proportionate when, considering all the circumstances of the case, the sacrifice of the affected rights and interests is not greater than the benefit that their adoption provides for public interest and third parties.

In this regard, the judge must take into consideration the existence of third parties that may be affected by the measure. This affectation is a criterion that the examining magistrate must balance when deciding on the adoption of this kind of measures. Therefore, technically *the affectation of third parties must be balanced in the referred proportionality test.*[26]

We will turn now to the procedural instruments and remedies that the third parties affected by an investigation measure have available to protect their legal sphere and to control the action of the State. The CCP has not created any specific mechanism for this purpose. This legal vacuum, nevertheless, has been solved by the Constitutional Court in a very recent decision (Judgment 30/2022, of 7 March).[27] This ruling is of great importance, insofar as it could be applied by analogy to the other situations that will be examined and in which a judicial measure could directly or indirectly affect third parties (see below).

This judgment has set relevant precedent on the standing of third parties —in the strict sense of the term, encompassing subjects who are not formal parties to the criminal proceedings— to intervene in it and to lodge an appeal against judicial decisions which are contrary to their rights and/or interests, namely where the interest at stake is relating to the exercise of fundamental rights of "substantive" nature—*i.e.*, not just procedural safeguards.

[25] Gascón Inchausti (2024), pp. 159–163.

[26] Bachmaier Winter (2004), pp. 56, 72, 75, 80.

[27] STC 30/2022 de 7 de marzo de 2022 [ECLI:ES:TC:2022:30].

The case is of great interest, as it involved a procedure investigating possible leaks in a highly publicized case. The examining magistrate, among other measures, considered it necessary to proceed to the interception, and downloading, of the telephone device and computer of two journalists, who were also requested to provide any judicial or police document related to the investigation of the case in question. To make the measure effective, they were requested to come to the court and hand over their mobile phones and their unlocking codes. Neither journalist was listed as a suspect in the case. Both tried to appeal the decisions but were denied standing to do so precisely because of their status as third parties.

In the case at hand, the standing of third parties and the right of access to jurisdiction are analyzed from the qualified point of view of the impact that the judicial decision has on fundamental rights (press freedom). As the Constitutional Court affirms, the CCP itself has expressly foreseen the protection of thirds parties and their possibility of directly appealing judicial decisions about property seized during the investigation (Art. 334(1) CCP) and also in the case of freezing and confiscation of instrumentalities and proceeds of crime [Arts. 803 *ter* a) to 803 *ter* d) CCP] (see below). For that reason,

> it must be understood that the reasons that justify the intervention of third parties in the situations described above also apply when recognizing the right of access to jurisdiction when it is justified by the need to defend fundamental rights of substantive content [. . .] It is not possible to deny the legal standing of third parties when contesting the court decisions when they are affected in the exercise of fundamental rights, it is necessary to require the judicial bodies to provide reinforced reasoning that justifies the denial of the right of access to jurisdiction. The reasoning of the appealed decisions also ignores the case law of the ECtHR when interpreting Article 6 ECHR and the *pro actione* principle [. . .] Strasbourg case law has stated that "the effectiveness of the right to effective judicial protection requires that a person enjoys the clear and concrete possibility of challenging an act that constitutes an interference with his rights" [ECHR of 10 January 2017 (ECHR 2017, 1), Aparicio Navarro Revert and García San Miguel y Orueta v. Spain, (para. 34); and 22 June 2006 (ECHR 2006, 44), Díaz Ochoa v. Spain, (para. 41)].

In summary, third parties affected by any judicial investigation measure are granted the possibility of intervening in the proceedings for the protection of their rights. This right to access to justice is subject to the *pro actione* principle that must inspire the interpretation of all procedural rules. This right of access to justice is of special importance when, as has been said, the interests at stake are fundamental rights.

Some issues concerning this "newborn" right of intervention of third parties are still open. For instance, it is not clear if the third party acquires the formal status of a party or not; if she can have access to all the files or just to those related to the measure that affects her. In short, the defence possibilities and procedural rights of these subjects are unclear, due to the lack of legal development. One could say that this possibility of intervention is just a fast-track procedure for the protection of their fundamental rights in the specific criminal proceedings.

4 Scientific Developments, New Technologies and the Safeguards of Third Parties

Technological judicial investigation measures have been introduced in the CCP by Organic Law 13/2015.[28] The Spanish judges may adopt, for investigation purposes, the following measures:

- Interception of telephone and telematic communications [Arts. 588 *ter* a) to 588 *ter* i) CCP].
- Access to data needed to identify users, terminals and connectivity devices [Arts. 588 *ter* k) to 588 *ter* m) CCP].
- Capture and recording of verbal communications using electronic devices [Arts. 588 *quarter* a) to 588 *quarter* m)].
- Use of technical devices for image capture, surveillance and localization [Arts. 588 *quinquies* b) a to 588 *quinquies* c) CCP].
- Search in mass data storage devices [Arts. 588 *sexies* a) to 588 *sexies* c) CCP].
- Remote search of computer equipment [Arts. 588 *septies* a) to 588 *septies* c) CCP].

The preamble of the law recalls how this regulation sets a

> normative proclamation of the principles that the Constitutional Court has defined as determining the validity of the act of interference. Any measure must comply with the principle of specialty [. . .] The technological research measures must also satisfy the principles of adequacy, exceptionality, necessity and proportionality, whose concurrence must be sufficiently justified in the enabling judicial decision, where the judge will determine the nature and extent of the measure in relation to the specific research and the expected results.

According to Article 588 *bis* h) CCP, technological investigation measures "may be ordered even where they affect third parties in the cases and under the conditions regulated in the specific provisions for each of them". Therefore, the CCP expressly accepts and recognizes that these measures will almost certainly affect third parties. This is obvious if we consider that, by nature, almost all technological devices and gadgets are used to have contact with others or to store information related (also) to others.

More specifically, and addressing the interception of telephone and telematic communications, Article 588 *ter* c) CCP states that these measures

> may be [also] ordered for communications emitted from terminals or telematic communication media belonging to a third party provided that (i) there is proof that the individual under investigation uses it to transmit or receive information, or (ii) the owner collaborates with the person under investigation in their illicit purposes or benefits from their activity. Such intervention may also be authorized where the device under investigation is used maliciously by third parties online, without the knowledge of their owner.

[28] Ley Orgánica 13/2015, de 5 de octubre, de modificación de la Ley de Enjuiciamiento Criminal para el fortalecimiento de las garantías procesales y la regulación de las medidas de investigación tecnológica [https://www.boe.es/buscar/doc.php?id=BOE-A-2015-10725].

Thus, either directly or indirectly, third parties may be affected by this technological measure. As already said, this is a circumstance that shall be considered by the court when performing the proportionality assessment required to adopt the measure [Arts. 588 *bis* a) CCP].

Regarding the possible intervention of third parties in the proceedings to challenge a technological investigation measure adopted by the judge, we can refer to what has been said above about the Judgment of the Constitutional Court 30/2022 (*vid. supra*). The impact of these measures on the fundamental rights of third parties—mainly, the right to privacy (Art. 18 CE)—is a constitutional ground that could underpin their intervention in the judicial investigation phase. This is a possibility that derives from the right to effective judicial relief (Art. 24 CE), which is subject to the *pro actione* principle and reinforce by the fundamental rights whose judicial protection is being sought.

From a different perspective, we should also highlight the obligations and duties of collaboration that are imposed on third parties during the investigation. Following Article 588 *ter* e) CCP

> all providers of telecommunications services, of access to a telecommunications network or information society services, and any person who, in any way, contributes to facilitating communications via the telephone or by any other online, logic or virtual communication media or system, are under the obligation to provide the judge, the Public Prosecution Service and members of the Police appointed to carry out the measure, with the assistance and cooperation necessary to facilitate the performance of orders for telecommunications' interception [. . .] Obligated individuals breaching the above duties may be committing the offense of disobedience.

These duties are also laid down in Art. 7(1) of Organic Law 7/2021.[29]

This kind of 'externalization of the criminal investigation' through providers of telecommunications services triggers many problematic issues that are also still open—for instance, about the so-called 'horizontal effectiveness of fundamental rights' (*Drittwirkung*) that are being infringed by these providers or the possibility they have of refusing the collaboration they are asked for.[30]

5 Pre-Trial Measures and the Protection of Fundamental Rights of Third Parties

In general terms, third parties could be also affected by pre-trial measures adopted during the investigation phase. That is the case, for example, in pre-trial measures adopted against a legal person—*e.g.*, a company or an association. In accordance

[29] Ley Orgánica 7/2021, de 26 de mayo, de protección de datos personales tratados para fines de prevención, detección, investigación y enjuiciamiento de infracciones penales y de ejecución de sanciones penales [https://www.boe.es/buscar/act.php?id=BOE-A-2021-8806].

[30] Gascón Inchausti (2019), pp. 193–199.

with Article 37(7) of the Criminal Code (CP), "temporary closure of premises or establishments, suspension of corporate activities and judicial intervention may also be agreed by the investigating judge as a precautionary measure during the investigation of the case". In this case, workers, suppliers, creditors or the company's shareholders themselves could be affected by the adopted measures. There is also the possibility of adopting in any criminal proceedings, as provisional measures, garnishments and attachments of money, property or objects belonging to the suspect. It is conceivable that family members, co-owners of the real estate or object or creditors of the investigated person could also be affected by these measures.

There is no regulation in the CCP addressing the remedies available to these affected third parties. A broad interpretation of the referred Judgment of the Constitutional Court 30/2022 could, nevertheless, justify their intervention in the process in certain cases (see above). Although this judgment was issued in the framework of the protection of fundamental rights of third parties affected by judicial investigative measures, its reasoning could be applied by analogy to justify the intervention of any party affected by any other judicial measure—also pre-trial measures. As it is stated in the ruling, the scope of the constitutional challenge—*recurso de amparo*—was "to rule on the standing of third parties, who are not intervening in a judicial proceeding, to appear in court and appeal against *judicial decisions that are prejudicial to their interests*". As suggested, it is the prejudice itself that justifies the intervention in the proceedings. It should be noted that, although the Constitutional Court declares that the infringement of a (substantive) fundamental right qualifies the importance of the intervention as part of the fundamental right to access to justice (Art. 24 CE), their violation is not the only case in which this interest could be admitted. We cannot rule out the possibility that there are cases in which, although no fundamental rights are at stake, there is a legitimate interest to intervene in the proceedings—*e.g.,* the attachment of immovable property or the closing of the company in which the third party works.

Thirds parties could be also directly affected by those pre-trial measures adopted in the framework of the freezing and confiscation of instrumentalities and proceeds of crime in the criminal proceedings [Arts. 803 *ter* a) to 803 *ter* d) CCP] or at a 'stand-alone' procedure for freezing and confiscation [Arts. 803 *ter* e) to 803 *ter* u) CCP]. As already mentioned, third parties could be affected by the confiscation; and it is precisely this prejudice that allows them to intervene in the proceedings. Following Article 803 *ter* a) CCP,

> [t]he judge or the court will order, ex officio or at the request of a party, the intervention in the criminal proceedings of such persons as may be affected by confiscation [...] [the] person who may be affected by the confiscation may take part in the criminal proceedings once their intervention is ordered, although this intervention will be limited to such aspects that directly affect their assets [Art. 803 ter b) CCP].[31]

[31] On the procedural position of this third party and the critics to the limitations of his defense see Gascón Inchausti (2016), pp. 21–24.

It shall also be recalled that the adoption of pre-trial measures against the assets of the third party is also possible during criminal or "stand-alone" proceedings. Under Article 127 *octies* CP "[i]n order to guarantee the effectiveness of the confiscation, the goods, means, instruments and gains may be apprehended or seized and placed in storage by the judicial authority from the outset of the proceedings". For that reason, the claim for confiscation may include "the application for precautionary measures, justifying the suitability of their adoption to ensure effective confiscation, as appropriate" [Art. 803(1) *ter* h) CCP]. The third party has the burden to invoke all available reasons against that measure in their statement of defence against the claim for confiscation.

6 Third Parties and the Decision to Charge (or to Terminate the Proceedings)

When the investigation phase has been concluded, the examining magistrate must decide on the termination of the proceedings—*sobreseimiento*—or their continuation—*apertura de juicio oral.* Depending on the circumstances, the termination of the proceedings could be final—*sobreseimiento libre*—(Art. 637 CCP) or provisional—*sobreseimiento provisional*—(Art. 641 CCP). The continuation of the proceedings will only be possible if at least one party decides to press charges and exercise the criminal action and the examining magistrate considers that there is sufficient evidentiary support to go to trial.[32]

The judicial decision terminating proceedings can be challenged by any formal party. In addition, and upon implementation of the EU 2012 Directive, the victim may also challenge that decision, even if she was not a formal party to the proceedings. According to Article 12 of the Crime Victim Statute (see above), "[t]he decision of dismissal will be communicated [...] to the direct victims of the crime who had denounced the facts, as well as to the rest of the direct victims whose identity and domicile are known [...] The judicial decision terminating proceedings can be challenged by any formal party". In addition, and upon implementation of the EU 2012 Directive, the victim may also challenge that decision, even if she was not a formal party to the proceedings. Regarding the continuation of the proceedings, it is possible that no party decides to charge and, hence, to exercise the criminal action. In these cases, however, the examining magistrate may still consider that there are sufficient elements to open the trial phase. If so, the judge could propose to summon

> those known to be directly aggrieved or harmed, who were not a party to the proceedings, so that within a maximum of fifteen days they appear to defend their action if they consider this to be appropriate. If they do not do so within the time limit set, the dismissal requested [...] will be ordered [Art. 782.2 a) CCP].

[32] On the so-called "fase intermedia" and the decision to continue or terminate the criminal proceedings in the Spanish legal order see Gascón Inchausti (2024), pp. 223–232.

To sum up, the victim who is not a party to the proceedings has specific procedural rights aimed at avoiding the termination of the proceedings: (1) challenging the examining magistrate's decision not to open the trial phase; (2) being offered the possibility to enter into the proceedings to press charges and request the opening of the trial phase, when no other party decided to charge and request the opening of the trial phase.

7 Third Parties in Court Proceedings

During the trial phase the prosecuting parties and the defense present their statements, make their oral arguments and the relevant evidence is taken.

We have already explained that, under Spanish law, some third parties have a special status that allows them to intervene during criminal investigations. That is the case of the (non-prosecuting) victim of the crime, the third parties affected by judicial investigation measures, or the third parties affected by the freezing and confiscation of instrumentalities and proceeds of crime. Although it is not always clear if their intervention grants them the formal status of parties, they have specific procedural rights to defend themselves.

When proceedings reach the trial phase, these rights may differ in their contents; indeed, different third parties appear, whose legal position may require a specific legal treatment: this is namely the case of witnesses and other subjects involved in the taking of the evidence.

7.1 The Right of Third Parties to Be Heard Fairly

The right to be heard (Art. 24(1) CE) is attributed to the formal parties of the proceedings and to those third parties that, although not having that formal status, may intervene in it. The most important case in this regard is the third party affected by the freezing and confiscation of instrumentalities and proceeds of crime (see above).

When the judge or the court consider that a person may be affected by the confiscation, they will order their intervention in the criminal proceedings [Art. 803 *ter* a) CCP]. Under Article 803 *ter* c) the third party

> may take part in the criminal proceedings once their intervention is ordered, although this intervention will be limited to such aspects as directly affect their assets, rights or legal position and may not be extended to matters relating to the criminal liability of the accused.

That person will be therefore summoned to the court proceedings. This possibility of intervention and this *sui generis status* ensure their right to be fairly heard (Art. 24(1) CE).

7.2 *The Right of Third Parties Not to Be Questioned*

The Law recognizes some exceptions to the general duty to give testimony. In particular, the following persons can refuse to testify: *(i)* family members of the accused in direct ascendant or descendant lines, their spouse or person linked to them by a *de facto* relationship similar to marriage, their brothers and sisters and bloodlines up to the second degree (Art. 416(1) CCP); *(ii)* the lawyer of the accused concerning facts confided in their professional capacity (Art. 416(2) CCP); *(iii)* translators and interpreters of conversations and communications between the person prosecuted or accused and others (Art. 416(3) CCP); *(iv)* the clergy and other religions' ministers on facts that were revealed to them in the exercise of the duties of their ministry (Art. 417(1°) CCP); *(v)* public officials, whether civil or military, where they cannot testify without breaching the secrecy that they are under the obligation to keep (Art. 417(2°) CCP); and *(vi)* the physically or morally disabled (Art. 417(3°) CCP). All these persons have the right to be informed by the court of their exception from the duty to testify.[33]

The exception from the duty to testify finds many justifications and serves for the protection of different fundamental rights. In some cases, protection is ensured to the family member itself because of the moral-legal conflict of interest that arise in his inner self or the ideological and religious freedom of the investigated person.

In addition, any witness—regardless of whether they are entitled to refuse to testify—have the right not to "testify on a question whose answer may, materially or morally and in a direct and significant manner, prejudice either the person or the estate of any of the family members" (Art. 418 CCP).

The issues arises whether the protection of these relationships of confidence and confidentiality, covered by the exception from the duty to testify, could be expanded to other criminal investigation measures: *i.e.*, if it is possible to access by other means to the information that the witness does not have the duty to reveal. That is explained with a very graphical image: "what the mouth does not have to reveal, cannot be torn out by hand either".[34] A proper analysis of this issue requires the determination of the scope of the protection with the exception from the obligation to testify—the information itself or the relationship of the accused and the third party—and the basis of it.[35]

In almost every case, the exceptions from the duty to testify recognized in the CCP aim at protecting the confidence relationship itself: *rectius*, the third party's conflict of interest between complying with her duty to cooperate with the justice and protecting a person with whom she has a relationship of trust—and, therefore, not

---

[33] Bachmaier Winter (2004), pp. 47–50.

[34] Bachmaier Winter (2004), p. 53.

[35] From a comparative perspective it is also of interest to consider how this possibility of the third party to refuse to testify is conceived: as a right—as in Germany, with the *Zeugnisverweigerungsrecht*—or as an exception of a duty to declare—as in Spain.

the information itself.[36] It is also important to distinguish between the *active performance* that is required to testify in court and the *passive position* of the third party that is (merely) subject of a criminal investigation measure—*e.g.*, a search in her home. Therefore, the exception does not usually affect the possibility of adopting other judicial investigation measures: the impact on the legal position of third parties in these cases should be assessed under the criteria of proportionality (see above).[37] There is just a case in which the protection that justifies the exception from the obligation to testify should be (and is) expanded to other criminal measures: the relationship between lawyers and their clients: this privilege—although it admits some exceptions in case of serious crimes—aims at protecting the right of defense itself (Art. 24(1) CE in relationship with Art. 118(4) CCP).[38]

7.3 The Protection of Non-Parties in Court Activities Involving Formal Participants

The Crime Victim Statute recognizes specific rights of protection to the victims of the crimes, minors and vulnerable third parties during court proceedings (Art. 19 Ley 4/2015).

In particular, one or more of the following measures could be adopted for the protection of the victim of the crime: *(i)* measures to avoid visual contact between the victim and the alleged criminal, which could include the taking of evidence with technological devices; *(ii)* measures to ensure that the victim can be heard without being present in the courtroom; *(iii)* measures to prevent questions relating to the victim's private life that have no relevance to the allegedly criminal facts being prosecuted, unless the court exceptionally considers that they should be answered to assess the facts or the credibility of the victim's statement; and *(iv)* the holding of the oral hearing without the presence of the public to protect the intimacy of the victim (Arts. 19, 20, 22 and 25 (2) Ley 4/2015). The objective of all these measures is to avoid the so-called "secondary victimization" (Preamble III and VIII Ley 4/2015).

In addition, when the victim is a minor or a vulnerable party with any physical or mental impairment, the following measures could be adopted during the proceedings: *(i)* the testimony made during the criminal investigation phase will be recorded by audiovisual means and may be reproduced at the trial phase, in order not to take it anew; and *(ii)* the testimony may be received through experts (Arts. 4, 22 and 26 Ley 4/2015).

In that vein, a legal reform in 2021 gave legal nature to the so-called helper advisor—*facilitador*—regulated in Article 7 *bis* of the Code of Civil Procedure (*Ley*

[36] Bachmaier Winter (2004), p. 66.

[37] Bachmaier Winter (2004), pp. 56, 72, 75, 80.

[38] In connection with the confidentiality of the relation lawyer-client in Spain see Villamarín López (2021), pp. 137–172.

de Enjuiciamiento Civil, hereinafter LEC) and established a general duty to take all necessary measures to overcome the hurdles triggered by any disability: although formally established in the LEC, they are also applicable to criminal proceedings due the subsidiary nature of the LEC (Art. 4 LEC).[39] In accordance with the LEC, "[i]n the proceedings where persons with disabilities must participate, the necessary adaptations and adjustments will be made to ensure their participation under equal conditions" (Art. 7(1) *bis* LEC). In particular, to ensure the so-called right to understand and to be understood, the following measures could be adopted: *(i)* all communications with persons with disabilities, whether oral or written, shall be in clear, simple and accessible language; *(ii)* the person with a disability shall be provided with the necessary assistance or support to be understood, including interpretation in legally recognized sign languages and means of oral communication support for deaf people; *(iii)* the participation of an expert will be allowed who, as a helper advisor, will carry out the necessary adaptations and adjustments, so that the person with a disability can understand and be understood; and *(iv)* the person with a disability may be accompanied by a person of his or her choice from the first contact with authorities and officials (Art. 7(2) *bis* LEC).[40]

7.4 Can Third Parties Take Part in Court Activities?

As already explained, both the victim and any other person could take part in court activities becoming a formal party if they choose to exercise the so-called particular or popular accusation. The third parties affected by the confiscation could also take part in court activities under their *sui generis* procedural status.

It should also be added that, as a rule, trials are public (Art. 24(2) CE). Therefore, normally everyone can assist as public, unless the publicity is excluded to protect the intimacy of the victim or due to public order grounds.

8 The Protection of Third Parties in Decision-Making Processes

There are some cases in which parties may be directly or indirectly affected by the final judgment and, therefore, must be considered during the decision-making process. That is the case of the so-analyzed third party affected by the confiscation—who may have intervened or not in the proceedings—and other subjects that,

[39] Ley 1/2000, de 7 de enero, de Enjuiciamiento Civil [https://www.boe.es/buscar/act.php?id=BOE-A-2000-323].

[40] Muyo Bussac (2022a), pp. 73–76. Analysing the helper advisor, see, Muyo Bussac (2022b), pp. 365–379.

although not expressly considered during the investigation, could also be influenced by the final decision. A traditional example of the latter are the employees, creditors or shareholders of the legal person that has been convicted and must endure a monetary penalty or, even worse, a suspension or termination of activities.

The Spanish Criminal Code ("CP") incorporated the criminal liability of legal persons in 2010 (Arts. 31 *bis et seq.* CP).[41] The following penalties may be imposed on legal persons: *(i)* fines; *(ii)* dissolution; *(iii)* suspension of activities for a maximum period of 5 years; *(iv)* closure of premises and establishments for up to 5 years; *(v)* prohibition to carry out in the future the activities through which it has committed, favored or concealed the criminal offense; *(vi)* barring from obtaining public subsidies and aid, to enter into contracts with the public sector and to enjoy tax or Social Security benefits and incentives; *(v)* judicial intervention to safeguard the rights of the employees or creditors for the time deemed necessary (Art. 33(7) CP). All these penalties may affect third persons that have a direct relation with the legal person: the shareholders could see a reduction in the value of the company or the limitation of their rights of participation and the employees could be subject to a geographic mobility procedure to another establishment or, directly, be fired.[42] In addition, these measures could be imposed as a penalty in the judgment or as a preventive measure during the criminal proceedings (Art. 33(7) CP).

In this regard, the protection of the third parties affected by the judgment is something that should be considered by the court. Following Art. 66 *bis* CP, when determining the penalty of the legal person, the court shall consider "their economic and social consequences, and especially the effects on employees".[43] The prosecutor and the judge shall consider these circumstances in their respective procedural roles of accusing/defending and judging. The Law does not contain any provision about the possibility of these thirds-parties intervening in the proceedings. On one hand, it could be argued that, on the basis of the referred STC 30/2022 (see above) these individuals have a legitimate interest in intervening. On the other hand, it could be said that there is not a fundamental right directly affected or such a direct damage that could really justify the intervention. It is probably more reasonable to assume that these persons are suffering an indirect harm, which may not suffice to sustain their intervention in the proceedings; compensation from the possible damages suffered should be requested in subsequent civil proceedings, brought against the legal person or its administrator.[44]

In another vein, it should be recalled that jury courts exist in Spain (Art. 125 CE).[45] However, the individuals who are part of them should not be considered

---

[41] This has been made by the Organic Law 5/2010 [https://www.boe.es/buscar/doc.php?id=BOE-A-2010-9953]. About the criminal liability of legal persons see Gascón Inchausti (2012) and Banacloche Palao et al. (2011).

[42] Gascón Inchausti (2012), pp. 103–106.

[43] Gascón Inchausti (2012), pp. 104–105.

[44] Gascón Inchausti (2012), pp. 105–106.

[45] The jury and the jury proceedings are regulated in Organic Law 5/1995 del Tribunal del Jurado [https://www.boe.es/buscar/act.php?id=BOE-A-1995-12095].

third parties that participate in decision-making processes, but rather as true lay judges—*jueces legos*—who are part of the administration of justice.

9 Third Parties in Appeal Proceedings

The victim of the crime does not have any special right to appeal the judgment if she has not decided to accuse and, therefore, to become a formal party to the proceedings. However, the ruling is not indifferent to other third parties that may have the right to appeal it, such as the persons who have seen some object of their property confiscated. The judgment ordering the confiscation of their property must be served on them. They have the right to appeal it, although they have decided not to actively participate in the proceedings. These third parties could file any challenge available "although such appeal must be restricted to the rulings directly affecting their assets, rights or legal position, and may not extend to matters related to the criminal liability of the accused" [Art. 803 *ter* b) CCP)]. In practice, as happens within the investigation and trial phase, it is difficult to determine the lines of what "directly affects" them and what not and, therefore, to set the limits of their right of defense.

Insofar as the confiscation depends on the illegal source of the objects, the criminal liability of the accused person is something that directly affects the third party that has seen her property seized.

If the third party identified by the court as affected by the confiscation decided not to intervene in the proceedings, she shall be considered in default—as happens in ordinary civil proceedings. Despite this, the judgment shall be served on them and they still can file a challenge against it. In addition, the third party has a special extraordinary remedy for the rescission of the *res judicata* of the final judgment in cases in which the default was due to "involuntary" reasons [Art. 803 *ter* c) CCP in relation to Arts. 496–508 LEC].

10 *Res Judicata* and the Effects of Criminal Judgments upon Third Parties

Res judicata—*cosa juzgada material*—refers to those effects produced by judicial decisions when they become final in proceedings other than the one in which they have been issued. There is a negative dimension—*ne bis in idem*—that excludes a second procedure with the same scope and a positive dimension, by which the ruling of the judgment must be considered by a court hearing a subsequent proceeding with a related scope. These effects are deployed within an objective, personal and temporal scope of application.

Res judicata only operates *inter partes*. This rule requires an "adaptation" in criminal proceedings insofar as is the accused person who delimits the personal scope of *res judicata* and not the prosecuting parties, that may be different in the subsequent proceedings—which would, nevertheless, be affected by the preclusive effect of *res judicata*. The *inter partes* effect is a basic rule based on the rights of defense and on the technical procedural principles in which civil and criminal proceedings are underpinned—at least, in the trial phase. For that reason, a judgment given in criminal proceedings shall not bind third parties.

The connection of the *inter partes* effect of *res judicata* to the right of defense in criminal matters means that it can never be extended to third parties. Consequently, the exceptions to this principle, admitted in civil proceedings—*e.g.*, Art. 222(3) LEC—can never apply in criminal proceedings.[46]

It is also important to bear in mind that *res judicata* describes—or encompasses, if preferred—one of the ranges of *procedural* effects that may arise from a final judgment. Procedural law scholars have traditionally studied the relationship and the distinction between the *inter partes res judicata* effect and the *material* effects of the judgment. Usually, the judgment could be the premise of (civil or criminal) material rules and, therefore, a particular material effect may arise from it. This is what German scholars have called *Tatbestandswirkung*.[47] It is not precluded that this material effect of the criminal judgment could be deployed *vis-à-vis* third parties in other civil, labor or administrative proceedings—*e.g.*. a lawsuit about the civil liability *ex delicto* of the criminal or his insurance company.

In a different vein, the CCP regulates a "stand-alone" procedure for the freezing and confiscation [Arts. 803 *ter* e) to 803 *ter* u) CCP] (see above). This 'modality' may be used by the Public Prosecution Office for convenience or opportunity—*e.g.*, the prosecutor does not want this third party intervening in the 'main' proceedings—or by necessity—the accused person has died or is a fugitive.[48] For the purpose of this report, we must highlight the relationship and effects of *res judicata* between the 'main' criminal proceedings and the 'stand-alone' confiscation proceedings.

There are cases where the confiscation proceedings are initiated against the third party after the criminal conviction of the accused—*i.e.*, a *follow-on* confiscation proceeding. In this case, although the third party is not bound by the *res judicata* effects of the ruling, the latter will deploy its material effect on the follow-on proceedings. The conviction and, with it, the illegal origin of the assets—sustaining the material rule allowing confiscation (Art. 127 *quarter* CP)—*can be proven* with the previous judgment.[49] It must be noted that this is a *material effect* that can be

[46] Gascón Inchausti (2024), pp. 301–305.

[47] Leipold (2018), "§ 322", Rn. 7-16; Gottwald (2020), "§ 322", Rn. 16-23.

[48] Gascón Inchausti (2016), pp. 34–41.

[49] Art. 127 *ter* of the Spanish Criminal Code: "1. The Judge or Court of Law may order the confiscation outlined in the preceding Articles even if no sentence has been handed down, when the unlawful financial position has been demonstrated in adversarial proceedings and in any of the following cases: a) That the subject is deceased or suffers from a chronic illness impeding his trial and that there is a risk that the criminal offences may prescribe; b) He is in a situation of default,

refuted by any other means by the third party: this 'binding' effect is based on the *de facto* nature of the judgment—*i.e.*, as a fact—and not by the procedural effects of *res judicata*. For that reason, normally the reasonable defense of the third party subject to the confiscation proceedings should be focused on the (lack of) knowledge of the illicit origin of the assets.

Conversely, we shall also address the effects of *res judicata* of the 'stand-alone'—and previous—confiscation proceedings on the "main" criminal proceedings. This is a matter regulated by the law. In accordance with Art. 803 *ter* p) CCP,

> [t]he judgment will set out the material effects of res judicata in relation to the persons against whom the action was taken [...] the content of the judgment in the separate confiscation proceedings will not be binding on the later trial of the accused [...] In the later criminal proceedings against the accused, if any, the confiscation of assets ruled on with the effect of res judicata in the separate confiscation proceedings will not be requested to be or be subject to the trial.

The confiscation judgment shall not be binding against the accused of the (future) criminal proceedings. These rules, therefore, confirm and reinforce the *inter partes* positive effect of *res judicata*.

References

Bachmaier Winter L (2004) Intervenciones telefónicas y derechos de terceros en el proceso penal: Revista de Derecho Procesal (No. 1-3)

Banacloche Palao J, Zarzalejos Nieto J, Gómez-Jara Díez C (2011) Responsabilidad penal de las personas jurídicas. Aspectos procesales y sustantivos. La Ley, Madrid

Gascón Inchausti F (2012) Proceso penal y persona jurídica. Marcial Pons, Madrid

Gascón Inchausti F (2016) Las nuevas herramientas procesales para articular la política criminal de decomiso total: la intervención en el proceso penal de terceros afectados por el decomiso y el proceso para el decomiso autónomo de los bienes y productos del delito: Revista General de Derecho Procesal (No. 38)

Gascón Inchausti F (2019) Desafíos para el proceso penal en la era digital: externalización, sumisión pericial e inteligencia artificial. In: Conde Fuentes J, Serrano Hoyo G (dirs) La Justicia digital en España y la Unión Europea. Atelier, Barcelona

Gascón Inchausti F (2024) Derecho procesal penal, 6th edn. Madrid. https://docta.ucm.es/entities/publication/ae6c0422-3be1-43bf-8fe8-ad35b1c1f560

Gottwald P (2020) § 322 ZPO. In: Münchener Kommentar zur Zivilprozessordnung, 6th edn. C.H. Beck, München

Leipold D (2018) § 322 ZPO. In: Stein-Jonas, Kommentar zur Zivilprozessordnung, 3rd edn. Mohr Siebeck, Tübingen

preventing a trial within a reasonable period of time; or c) No sentence is handed down as the individual is exempt from criminal responsibility or said responsibility has been finalized. 2. The confiscation referred to in this Article may only be adopted against individuals who have been formally accused or against defendants for whom there is circumstantial evidence of criminality when the situations outlined in the preceding Section have prevented criminal proceedings from continuing".

Muyo Bussac P (2022a) Sobre el impacto del artículo 7 bis en la práctica de la prueba con discapacidad intelectual en el proceso penal. In: Moreno Flórez, RM (dir) Problemática jurídica de las personas con discapacidad intelectual. Dykinson, Madrid

Muyo Bussac P (2022b) El rol del facilitador en los procesos civiles en los que intervengan personas con discapacidad intelectual. In: Herrero Perezagua JF, López Sánchez J (dirs) Los vulnerables ante el proceso civil. Atelier, Barcelona

Villamarín López ML (2021) Confidencialidad en las comunicaciones con los abogados en España. In: Bachmaier Winter L, Martínez Santos A (dirs) Asistencia letrada, confidencialidad abogado-cliente y proceso penal en la sociedad digital. Marcial Pons, Madrid

Part II
Third Parties in Criminal Justice: The Perspective of International and EU Law

Victims and Third Parties in International Criminal Justice

Ana Beltrán Montoliu

Abstract The role of victims in international criminal proceedings is a controversial issue from a procedural perspective especially in terms of their particular status. For the first time in international criminal justice victims participate in the International Criminal Court's (ICC) proceedings and also have right to reparation. Although victims are not considered «parties» to the criminal proceedings, it is necessary to delimitate the scope of their interventions in the presentation of their views and concerns.

This contribution first focusses of the notion of victims and then critically analyses three different aspects that need to be further studied in order to understand the impact of victim's contribution to development of international recognition of its rights before the ICC. First, the protection of victims in the legal international framework. Second, modalities of participation of victims in the different stages of the proceedings (preliminary examination, investigation, pre-trial, trial and appeal). And third, issues related to reparations, in particular, principles and elements required for an order for reparations, types and modalities, and implementation of reparation. Lastly a special mention will be dedicated to the figure of Amicus Curie to identify the particularities of this figure in the proceedings. Challenges and practical difficulties that appear in the practice of the Court, are addressed in this chapter.

A. B. Montoliu (✉)
Law Department, Universidad Jaume I de Castellón, Castelló de la Plana, Castelló, Spain
e-mail: beltrana@uji.es

S. Ruggeri et al. (eds.), *Third Parties in Criminal Proceedings*, Legal Studies in International, European and Comparative Criminal Law 10,
https://doi.org/10.1007/978-3-031-73970-5_8

1 Introduction

An overview of international criminal justice in relation to the protection of human rights highlights the need to fight forcefully against violence regarding vulnerable victims (children[1] and women[2]), especially in armed conflicts. It is undeniable that national and international war conflicts leave after-effects that are difficult to overcome and affects entire generations.[3] Society and judicial systems at national and international level must make every effort to establish mechanisms to give a voice to the victims in these cases.

In recent decades, in view of manifestations of extreme violence, there has been unanimous condemnation by the international community,[4] although the judicial response has not always provided a rapid[5] or satisfactory solution.[6] Indeed, as Cattin

[1]All children have the right to a life free of violence (Article 19 Convention on the Rights of the Child). This requires the adoption of mechanisms by legal systems to protect them against violations of their rights. It should be noted that in relation to sexual violence, in 38 low- and middle-income countries, close to 17 million adult women report having experienced forced sex in childhood. UNICEF: A familiar face: Violence in the lives of children and adolescents, November 2017, pp. 3–6. Pinheiro (2010), p. 3.

[2]UN Women, Infographic: Violence against women, 06 November 2015, https://www.unwomen.org/en/digital-library/multimedia/2015/11/infographic-violence-against-women, UN Women, Facts and figures: Ending violence against women. Available at https://www.unwomen.org/en/what-we-do/ending-violence-against-women/facts-and-figures.

[3]The effects of sexual violence echo across generations, through trauma, stigma, poverty, poor health and unwanted pregnancy. The children whose existence emanates from that violence have been labelled «bad blood» or «children of the enemy», and alienated from their mother's social group. Their vulnerability may leave them susceptible to recruitment, radicalization and trafficking. SCUN, Report of the Secretary-General on conflict-related sexual violence, (S/2018/250), 23 March 2018, par. 14.

[4]These trends have help to create a veritable social status of victim, one reflecting the magnitude of society's recognition for his/her suffering, Rauschenbach and Scalia (2008), p. 443.

[5]Just to mention two cases: On the one hand, in the Western Balkans, although a reparation scheme is in place in Bosnia and Herzegovina for survivors of conflict-related sexual violence, almost 30 years after the end of conflict, insufficient progress has been made in issuing reparations. Orders to pay compensation are rarely enforced, with perpetrators often insolvent or hiding assets. Witness protection measures for civil proceedings remain inadequate or non-existent, and legal and psychosocial support is limited. Victims who initiated civil proceedings in order to receive compensation from the Republika Srpska are ordered to pay court fees if they lose their cases, which has a chilling effect on the pursuit of justice. On the other, in Nepal, 16 years after the signing of the Comprehensive Peace Agreement, in 2006, accountability for conflict-related sexual violence remains limited and survivors continue to face barriers in gaining access to services, justice and reparations. Despite the appointment in 2020 of commissioners to head the two transitional justice commissions, minimal progress has been made in conducting detailed investigation into the 66,147 complaints of human rights violations. The second national action plan on women and peace and security, which reflects the concerns of survivors of sexual violence, female fighters and children born of wartime rape, is pending endorsement. UNSC (2022), Conflict-related sexual violence Report of the Secretary-General, 29 March 2022 (S/2022/272), par. 63–64.

[6]«On the other hand, the rights of victims, their increasingly obvious presence in the framework of criminal law and criminal proceedings, often become a dead letter, despite the legislative

points out «victims of crime are often left alone, even if there is an effective system justice to bring to adjudication alleged offenders».[7] If we transfer this conception to the international criminal justice system, it is not surprising that the features of an ideal victim of international criminal crime are identified as being: (1) weakness and vulnerability; (2) dependency and (3) grotesqueness[8] if we consider the experience of the international criminal tribunals.

Although it is true that the greatest exponent of the recognition of victims' rights in general is to be found during the 1960–1980s[9] in particular in United States,[10] no justice system has refused to recognize the general principle that the system must accord the victim a right to private redress of wrongs[11] as will be approach *infra*.

Focusing on United Nations contributions,[12] the General Assembly has adopted two resolutions dealing with the rights of victims, that are particularly relevant:

---

advances that have been made in recent decades at European and national levels» Barona Vilar (2018), p. 28.

[7] «Victims are alone because their rights are not fully recognized by the law that is applicable to them, and their life, security and privacy are not always protected before, during and after the trial», Cattin (2022a), p. 2003. See also Gómez Colomer (2015), p. 43 illustrates about the different role of victims in common law and continental systems, being the victim not considered a party in common law systems. See also Planchadell Gargallo (2022), pp. 111–130 for an analysis about the Standing of Victims of Crime in Spain.

[8] As Schwöbel explains, the «ideal» victim is a victimological concept made popular through the work of the renowned Norwegian criminologist Nils Christie. It is a concept introducing value hierarchies in the designation of victimhood, whereby some victims are deemed more readily deserving of the status than others. In detail about the features see Schwöbel-Patel (2018), pp. 710–718. Joris van Wijk (2013), p. 160.

[9] In depth about the tracing the development of victims' rights under international law, see Funk (2015) pp. 19–41. This author analyses the following historical evolution: A. Victim-centric Justice of the 1400s-Customary Law as exemplified by the Code of Leke Dukagjini; B. Centralized State Power in the 1700s and 1800s, the «scientification of Criminal Law, and the decline of Victims' rights under domestic law; C. Twentieth-century resurgence of victims' rights under domestic law; and D. Victims' rights recognized as Part of International Law.

[10] See Fletcher (1995). This author explains clearly the need to protect victims in criminal trial and approaches some of the most controversial and famous trials in the USA History: In 1978, Gay men stream out of the Castro and riot after the unexpected manslaughter verdict in the slaying of Harvey Milk; In 1990, Hasidic Jews march and scream their bitter disappointment after the surprise acquittals in trials for the murders of Meir Kahane and Yankel Rosenbaum; In 1991, Blacks and Hispanics rebel in Los Angeles after the first Rodney King verdict, leaving South-Central L.A. in ruins; Also 1991, Feminists fill the streets to «take back the night» and toughen laws against rape in the Mike Tyson trial. Moreover, highlights how such miscarriages of justice have become endemic. About the History of the Crime Victims' Movement in the United States see https://www.ncjrs.gov/ovc_archives/ncvrw/2005/pg4c.html.

[11] As Funk (2015), p. 20 states: «*The earliest recorded legal systems and religious traditions- from the eighteen-century B.C. Babylonian Code of Hammurabi to the Visigothic Law Codes of the fifth century A.D.- in fact reflect the near universal belief that those wronged must have a right to redress... providing a forum for personal and direct redress has, thus, traditionally formed the very heart of the social contract between the individual and the collective*».

[12] In depth see Bassiouni (2006), pp. 203–279. This author provides a comprehensive analysis about the International Recognition of Victims' Rights from a comparative perspective.

- The 1985 *Declaration on Basic Principles of Justice for Victims of Crimes and Abuse of Power* (Victims Declaration),[13] provides a definition of victim that was considered the starting point in the ICC texts during the Preparatory Committee discussions. It is undeniable that the Victims Declaration although considered soft law in public international law, is the cornerstone of victim issues at the state level.
- The 2006 *Basic Principles and Guidelines on the Right to a Remedy and Reparation for Victims of Gross Violations of International Human Rights Law and Serious Violations of International Humanitarian Law* (Basic Principles).[14]

The system of procedural participation of the victim in the proceedings before the ICC has been a novelty with respect to the international criminal tribunals created previously,[15] since for the first time it allows, albeit as «participants» and not as «parties», their intervention in the procedural proceedings.

In the following sections before focusing to the three main aspects of this contribution, that is: protection, participation and reparation of victims before the ICC, is necessary to define the concept and scope of victims to identify the most controversial issues in practice.

[13] Adopted by General Assembly resolution 40/34 of 29 November 1985. See UNODC, Handbook on Justice for Victims, On the Use and Application of the Declaration of Basic Principles of Justice for Victims of Crime and Abuse of Power, 1999 and UNODC Guide for Policy Makers Victims of Crime and Abuse of Power, on the Implementation of the United Nations Declaration of Basic Principles of Justice for Victims of Crime and Abuse of Power, 1999.

[14] Adopted by the General Assembly resolution 60/147 of 16 December 2005. The Basic Principles recognize that victims should be treated with compassion and respect for their dignity that they should have their right to access to justice and redress mechanisms fully respected, and that national funds for compensation to victims should be encouraged together with the expeditious development of appropriate rights and remedies. Schabas (2007), p. 326.

[15] Victims' involvement in the proceedings before the international criminal tribunals for the former Yugoslavia (UNSC Res 827, 1993) and Ruanda (UNSC 955 (1994) (hereinafter ICTY and ICTR respectively) is limited to the status of witness (arts. 22 and 21 contain the same provision regarding protection of victims and witnesses. Therefore, victims can only testify if one of the parties or the judge so request and, one they are called to do so, their testimony is limited to answering the questions formulated by the parties and judge. Additionally, victims have no right-beyond that of the public- to access the evidence. Ochoa (2013), pp. 208–209. In detail about comparation of different types of victim participation with existing international mechanisms such as the Extraordinary Chambers in the Courts of Cambodia (ECCC), the Special Tribunal for Lebanon (STL), the Kosovo Specialist Chambers & Specialist Prosecutor's Office (KSC) and the International Criminal Court (ICC) see Schafferling and Petrossian (2021), pp. 7–95.

2 Victim and ICC

2.1 Notion

Since the Rome Statute[16] does not contain a definition of victim, we must refer to Rule 85 (Definition of victims) Rules of Procedure and Evidence (RPE) where the following concept is included:

> (a) «Victims» means natural persons who have suffered harm as a result of the commission of any crime within the jurisdiction of the Court;
>
> (b) Victims may include organizations or institutions that have sustained direct harm to any of their property which is dedicated to religion, education, art or science or charitable purposes, and to their historic monuments, hospitals and other places and objects for humanitarian purposes.

Sometimes the concept of «person» is used more generically to refer to victims who, for example, request their participation in the proceedings, or to their family members.[17]

Pursuant to sub-rule a) of Rule 85 RPE, four criteria must be met to obtain the status of victim: the victim must be a natural person, the victim must have suffered harm, the crime from which the harm ensued must fall within the jurisdiction of the Court, and there must be a causal link between the crime and the harm suffered.[18]

This provision has given rise to different interpretations and questions, which are analyzed as follows:

Natural person: The initial jurisprudence of the Court interpreted this criterion in «the ordinary meaning of the term «natural person» as «human being». Therefore a «natural person is any person who is not a legal person».[19] To infer that the «natural persons' requirement does not cause any ambiguity or complexity would be

[16]Core Legal Texts of International Criminal Court, are available at https://www.icc-cpi.int/resource-library/core-legal-texts.

[17]The Office of Public Counsel for Victims-ICC (2020), p. 26.

[18]ICC, *Decision on the Applications for the Participation in the Proceedings of VPRS 1, VPRS 2, VPRS 3, VPRS 4, VPRS 5, VPRS 6, Situation in the Democratic Republic of the Congo* (ICC-01/04-101), PTC I, Judgment of 17 January 2006, para. 79; ICC, *Decision on the Applications for Participation in the Proceedings of a/0001/06, a/0002/06 and a/0003/06 in the case of the Prosecutor v. Thomas Lubanga Dyilo and of the investigation in the Democratic Republic of the Congo, Situation in the Democratic Republic of the Congo*, (ICC-01/04-177), PTC I, Judgment of 31 July 2006, para. 7; ICC, *Decision on the Applications for Participation in the Proceedings of a/0001/06, a/0002/06 and a/0003/06 in the case of the Prosecutor v. Thomas Lubanga Dyilo and of the investigation in the Democratic Republic of the Congo, Prosecutor v. Thomas Lubanga Dyilo*, (ICC-01/04-01/06), PTC I, Judgment of 28 July 2006, para. 7; ICC, *Decision on applications for participation in proceedings a/0004/06 to a/0009/06, a/0016/06, a/0063/06, a/0071/06 to a/0080/06 and a/0105/06, The Prosecutor v. Thomas Lubanga Dyilo*, PTC I, Judgment of 20 October 2006, para 9, among others.

[19]ICC, *Decision on the Applications for the Participation in the Proceedings of VPRS 1, VPRS 2, VPRS 3, VPRS 4, VPRS 5, VPRS 6, Situation in the Democratic Republic of the Congo*, (ICC-01/04-101), PTC I, Judgment of 17 January 2006, para. 80.

impetuous».[20] Two contentious issues are the identification[21] of natural persons and the debatable question of deceased persons. On the identification requirement, jurisprudence has moved from an initial strict approach[22] to a more reasonable stance[23] considering that applications for victims' participation shall contain information and supporting documentation to the extent possible.[24] Another complex issue is related to the dilemma of whether individuals who are no longer alive are encompassed by Rule 85 (a) RPE.[25] Although jurisprudence have consistently proclaimed that deceased persons do not meet the victim criteria,[26] there other decisions sustaining that «victim does not cease to be a victim because of his or her death».[27]

---

[20] Bachvarova (2017), p. 18.

[21] STL, *The Prosecutor v. Salim Jamil Ayyash, Mustafa Amine Badreddine, Hussein Hassan Oneissi & Assad Hassan Sabra,* «Decision on victims' participation in the proceedings», (STL-II-OIIPTIPTJ F0236/201205081R121249-R1212911EN/nc), 8.05.2012, See in para. 33 the list of documents that would suffice as proof of the applicant's identity.

[22] A number of restrict requirements were set regarding to the nature and form of the identification documents, which significantly narrowed the range of the admissible identification material, ICC, *Decision on vitim's applications for participation a/0010/06, a/0064/06 to a/0070/06, a/0081/06 to a/0104/06 and a/0111/06 to a/0127/06, The Prosecutor v Joseph Kony, Vicent Otti, Okot Odhiambo, Dominic Ongwen*, (ICC-02/04-01/05-252), Judgment of 10 August 2007, para. 16: «*The Single Judge takes the view that, in principle, the identity of an applicant should be confirmed by a document (i) issued by a recognised public authority; (ii) stating the name and the date of birth of the holder, and (iii) showing a photograph of the holder*».

[23] To the extent that even in cases of incongruity between application forms and supporting identification documents, the Court has consistently regarded the identities as duly established as long as the applicants would clearly and satisfactorily explain such incoherences. In that sense, among others see: ICC, *Decision on Victim's Participation at the Confirmation of Charges Hearing and in the Related Proceedings, The Prosecutor v. Bosco Ntaganda*, PTC II, (ICC-01/04-02/06-211), Judgment of 15 January 2014, para. 23. ICC, *First Report on Applications to Participate in the Proceedings, The Prosecutor v. Dominic Ongwen*, (ICC-02/04-01/15), Judgment of 16 September 2016, para 33.

[24] ICC, *Decision on victims' participation status, Prosecutor v. Laurent Gbagbo and Charles Blé Goudé*, (ICC-02/11-01/15-379), Judgment of 7 January 2016, paras. 45–46. ICC, *Decision on victims' participation in trial proceedings, The Prosecutor v. Bosco Ntaganda,* (ICC-01/04-02/06-449), Judgment of 6 February 2015, para. 46.

[25] Bachvarova (2017), p. 23.

[26] ICC, *Corrigendum to Decision on the Applications for Participation in the Proceedings of Applicants a/0011/06 to a/0015/06, a/0021/07, a/0023/07 to a/0033/07 and a/0035/07 to a/0038/07 Situation in Darfur, Sudan*, PTC I, (ICC-02/05-111-Corr), paras. 35–36. ICC, *The Prosecutor v. Bosco Ntaganda*, para. 48: «Accordingly, while it is possible to submit an application on behalf of victims, relatives of a deceased person will not be able to participate in these proceedings unless they show that they have suffered harm personally».

[27] ICC, *Fourth Decision on Victims' Participation, The Prosecutor v. Jean-Pierre Bemba Gombo*, PTC III, (ICC-01/05-01/08-320), Judgment of 12 December 2008, paras. 39–52. Deceased persons were recognized as victims: «*In case an application is made on behalf of a deceased person, the Single Judge recognizes this person as a victim of the case provided that (1) the deceased was a natural person, (2) the death of the person appears to have been caused by a crime within the*

Truthfulness of statements: The difficulty that has arisen before the Court is to determine, on the one hand, what parameters must be taken into consideration for a victim to be admitted as a participant and, on the other hand, to establish what assessment must be made. The Court understands that there must be reasonable «grounds to believe» (Art. 55(2) RS) that the described story will be real and will fit within the material, temporal and territorial scope provided for such purposes.[28] In addition, a «consistent» and «coherent» presentation will also be taken into consideration in order to complement the previous criterion.[29]

Concept and content of harms suffered: In the absence of a definition of the term «harm» in the RE and in the RPE, the Court has had to rule on the matter on a case-by-case basis, and the interpretation must be compatible with internationally recognized human rights. It is understood that the harm referred to in Article 85 RPP includes physical, economic and psychological or emotional harm.[30]

Indirect victims: Another issue that has generated decisions in this regard is that of indirect victims, i.e., those who have suffered harm as a consequence of the harm suffered by the direct victims. In this sense, a doctrine has been developed that admits the possibility of participation of indirect victims only to the extent that the relationship between them has been sufficiently demonstrated, and there must be a causal link between the harm that is manifested and the criminal acts that appear in the arrest warrant or in the decision of confirmation of charges. Indirect victims must establish that, as a result of their relationship with the direct victim, the loss, injury, or damage suffered by the latter gives harm to them.[31] Excluded from the category of «indirect victims» however, are those who suffered harm as a result of the (later) conduct of direct victims.[32]

---

jurisdiction of the Court and (3) a written application on behalf of the deceased person has been submitted by his or her successor».

[28] ICC, *Situation in the Democratic Republic of the Congo,* paras. 99–100.

[29] ICC, *Decision on the Prosecution's Application for Leave to Appeal the Decision on Victims' Applications for Participation a/0010/06, a/0064/06 to a/0070/06, a/0081/06 to a/0104/06 and a/0111/06 to a/0127/06, Situation in Uganda*, PTC II, Judgment of 19 December 2007, (ICC-02/04-101), paras. 14–15.

[30] ICC, *Situation in Sudan, Darfur*, para. 30.

[31] As Spiga explains: «*granting the status of indirect victims to those persons who suffered harm as a result of the conduct of child soldiers enlisted in the militias under Lubanga's control would give the Court the unique opportunity to provide redress to two categories of victims in the context of the same trial*». Spiga (2010), p. 196.

[32] ICC, *Redacted version of Decision on indirect victims, Situation in the Democratic Republic of the Congo, The Prosecutor v. Thomas Lubanga Dyilo*, TC I, (ICC-01/04-01/06-1813), Judgment of 8 March 2009, paras. 44–52.

2.2 The Application Process

Pursuant to Rule 89(1) RPP, in order for a person to be considered a victim, he/she must file an application[33] with the Registry of the Court. Such application shall be made by means of a form prepared by the Registry, which must be previously approved by the Presidency of the Court. These standard forms shall, to the extent possible, be made available to victims, groups of victims, or intergovernmental and non-governmental organizations, which may assist in their dissemination, as widely as possible (Regulations 86(1) and 23(2) RegC. The use of standard application forms is not compulsory as long as the applicant provides the information referred to in Regulation 86 (2) of the RegC.[34] Prosecution and the Defence are entitled to reply to any application for participation filed by victims[35] (Rule 89 1 RPE).

The application to participate must refer to a specific procedure, and a new request must be made if victim wishes to participate in another procedure, even in related cases.[36] The content of the form is determined by the provisions of Regulation 86(2) RC and basically refers to the identity of the victim, the account of the facts he/she states, as well as the place and date they were committed, and harm suffered.

In order to expedite the processing of cases in which the number of victims is very high,[37] a «collective approach» is allowed through a joint application and also through a simplified form when the specific circumstances of the case deem it appropriate.[38] Additionally, the A-B-C Approach is in principle an adequate tool to ensure the fairness and expeditiousness of the proceedings, while at the same time

---

[33] Application Form for Individuals and Application Form for Organizations are available at https://www.icc-cpi.int/about/victims.

[34] ICC, *Pubic Redacted Version Decision on the Applications for Participation in the Proceedings of VPRS 1, VPRS2, VPRS 3, VPRS 4, VPRS 5 VPRS 6, Situation in the Demócratic Republic of Congo*, PTC I, (ICC-01/04-101-tEN-Corr), Judgment of 17 January 2006, para. 102.

[35] ICC, *Public Redacted Version Decision on Protective Measures requested by Applicants 01/04-1/do to 01/04-6/dp, Situation in the Democratic Republic of Congo*, PTC I, (ICC-01/04-73), Judgment of 21 July 2005, para. 2.

[36] ICC, *Decision on the Demande de participation de neuf victimes admises dans le procès de M. Thomas Lubanga Dyilo, Prosecutor v. Bosco Ntaganda,* PTC, (ICC-01/04-02/06-75), Judgment of 26 June 2013, para. 17.

[37] Those are victims' figures reflected in the annual report of the ICC on its activities for 2021/22: «*A combined total of approximately 13,000 victims participated in cases before the Court during the reporting period. The Court received more than 2449 new victim application forms, including 468 in the Al Hassan case and 713 in the cases related to the Central African Republic II situation. A total of 195 representation forms were received with regard to the situations in Afghanistan and the Philippines for Article 18 and Article 15 processes, respectively. Altogether, 1110 application forms for reparations were received in the reparation proceedings in the Al Mahdi and Lubanga cases. In addition, the Court received follow-up information for 400 existing applications*» UNGA, Report of the International Criminal Court, Note by the Secretary-General (A/77/305), para. 3.

[38] ICC, *Decision Establishing Principles on the Victims' Application Process, Prosecutor v. Bosco Ntaganda*, PTC II, (ICC-01/04-02/06-67), Judgment of 28 May 2013, paras. 36, 42.

respecting the rights of both the accused and the victims. According to the A-B-C Approach, the Registry examines the applications for participation in light of rule 85 of the Rules and the criteria set by the relevant chamber and classifies the applicants into three categories: (a) applicants who clearly qualify as victims («Group A»); (b) applicants who clearly do not qualify as victims («Group B»); and (c) applicants for whom the Registry could not make a clear determination for any reason («Group C»). While the Registry transmits to the Chamber all applications in unredacted form, it only transmits to the parties the Group C applications with redactions as necessary.[39]

3 Protection

Pursuant to Article 68(1) RE the Court shall take appropriate measures[40] to protect the safety, physical and psychological well-being, dignity and privacy of victims and witnesses. In so doing, the Court shall have regard to all relevant factors, including age, gender and health, and the nature of the crime, in particular, but not limited to, where the crime involves sexual or gender violence or violence against children.[41] The Prosecutor shall take such measures particularly during the investigation and prosecution of such crimes. These measures shall not be prejudicial to or inconsistent with the rights of the accused and a fair and impartial trial.

Protection is a difficult and demanding task for any criminal jurisdiction and particularly so for an international tribunal.[42] Through the definition of this high standard of protection for victims and witnesses, the Rome Statute has set a standard for the progressive development of the law relating to effectively functioning systems of criminal justice, not only international criminal justice.[43]

[39] The A-B-C Approach was first adopted by the Ntaganda Trial Chamber, and subsequently followed in the Al Hassan case (at pre-trial and trial), in the Yekatom and Ngaïssona case (at pre-trial and trial), in the Abd-Al-Rahman case (at pre-trial). ICC, *Judgment on the appeal of Mr Mahamat Said Abdel Kani against the decision of Pre-Trial Chamber II of 16 April 2021 entitled «Decision establishing the principles applicable to victims' applications for participation», Prosecutor v. Mahamat Said Abdel Kani*, (ICC-01/14-01/21 OA2), Judgment of 14 Semptember 2001, paras. 7 and 21. See ICC, Chambers Practice Manual 2021, pp. 30–31.

[40] Appropriate measures shall be interpreted, as entailing those enlisted in Rules 87 (Protective measures), 88 (Special measures) and 112(4) (Recording of questioning in particular case) RPE. Regulations 21 (Broadcasting, release of transcripts and recordings), 41 (Victims and Witnesses Unit), 42 (Application and variation of protective measures) and 101 (Restrictions to access to news and contact) RegC and in Regulations 79 (General provisions) and 100 (Protection and security of victims) of the RegR regarding responsibilities of the Registrar relating to victims and witnesses.

[41] Victims Participation and Reparations Section (VPRS), Victims before the International Criminal Court A guide for the participation of victims in the proceedings of the ICC. Available at https://www.icc-cpi.int/sites/default/files/VPRS_Victim-s_booklet.pdf

[42] Cryer (2019), p. 448.

[43] Cattin (2022a), p. 2011.

It is important to note that special attention is paid to the most vulnerable groups of victims, in particular children, the elderly and victims of gender crimes, when providing for special and/or protective measures.[44]

The object and purpose of this provision is not to attribute to any of the organs of the Court, including the Prosecution, the power to take whichever protective measure the relevant organ may consider necessary to protect a given witness. On the contrary, this provision aims at placing on every organ of the Court the obligation to pay particular attention to the needs of the witnesses in performing their functions and to cooperate, whenever necessary, with those organs of the Court that are competent to adopt specific protective measures such as the relocation of witnesses.[45] This approach means that initiative for adopting protective measures may take place by the Court *proprio motu*[46] but also by other organs of the Court (Prosecutor or Registry).

The principle of proportionality should restrict the rights of the parties only as far as necessary, considering the nature and purpose of the proceedings at stake. Those measures[47] must be adopted on a case-by-case basis if and when the need arises.

---

[44] See in particular: ICC-OTP Policy on the Children, November 2016; ICC-OTP Policy Paper on Sexual and Gender-Based Crimes, 20 June 2014 ICC-OTP Policy of the Crime of Gender Persecution, 7th December 2022. Available at https://www.icc-cpi.int/about/otp/otp-policies

[45] ICC, *Prosecutor v. Germain Katanga and Mathieu Ngudjolo Chui* «Decision on Evidentiary Scope of the Confirmation Hearing, Preventive Relocation and Disclosure under Article 67(2) of the Statute and Rule 77 of the Rules», (ICC-01/04-01/07), 21.04.2008, paras. 26–27.

[46] For example, inviting representatives of organizations to submit observations on current and specific issues related to the protection of victims ICC, PTC I, *Situation in Darfur*, «Decision inviting observations in application of rule 103 of the rules of procedure and evidence», (ICC-02/05-10), 24.7.2006, p. 4, or mandating the non-disclosure of the identity of victim applicants to the Defence, ICC, *Prosecutor v. Katanga and Ngudjolo*, PTC. I, «Decision on the Defence Application for Leave to Appeal the «Decision authorising the filing of observations on the applications for participation in the proceedings a/0327/07 to a/0337/07 and a/0001/08», (ICC-01/04-01/07), 27 February 2008, p. 5 or to the public for security reasons ICC, *Prosecutor v. Katanga and Ngudjolo*, PTC I, «Decision on the Set of Procedural Rights Attached to Procedural Status of Victim at the Pre-Trial Stage of the Case», 13.05. 2008, paras. 21–22.

[47] The protective measures ordered by the Court under Article 68(1) of the ICC Statute include i) the redaction of the applications for participation received from victims under Article 68(3) and transmitted to the parties for a reply under rule 89(1), especially if the suspect or accused may have access to said applications; ii) the redaction of submissions or decisions that are under seal before making them public; or the redaction of evidence before transmitting it to the suspect or accused; iii) the use of *ex parte* filings and *ex parte* hearings; iv) the use of reference numbers assigned by the Victims Participation and Reparations Section to the names of victims and witnesses; v) the prohibition for the parties to directly obtain confidential information on victims and witnesses, without a Chamber deciding whether to allow the parties to disclose confidential information regarding victims and witnesses; vi) the prohibition for the parties to directly contact victims and witnesses and the obligation to do so only through their legal representatives, the VPRS or the VWU if strictly necessary; vii) the non-publication of particular motions or requests, such as those requesting the issuance of warrant of arrests, until otherwise ordered by a Chamber; viii) the holding of hearings in closed session; ix) the provision of assistance to witnesses in the experience of giving oral evidence before the Court so as to prevent them from finding themselves in a disadvantageous position or from being taken by surprise as a result of their ignorance of the

Given the impact of protective measures on fair trial principles, a careful balancing of interest is required.[48] The use of anonymous witnesses (witnesses whose identity is not known to the accused) is a controversial issue:[49] Although anonymous witnesses' statements[50] and summaries thereof are permitted at the pre-trial stage, the better stance is that the identity may be withheld only «prior to the commencement of the trial»,[51] for example during the confirmation of charges hearing.[52]

4 Participation

Victims participation in the proceedings means the introduction of the restorative conception of justice for victims[53] and has produced similar debates at the ICC as in the domestic judicial systems.[54] On the one hand, some scholars and practitioners[55] argue that that this combination has not only created uncertainty and inconsistency in

process of giving oral testimony («witness familiarisation») before the Court; x) the disclosure in advance of the questions or the topics intended to be covered by the parties and participants during their questioning in order to protect traumatised or vulnerable witnesses; xi) the relocation of witnesses included in the Protection Programme of the Court; xii) the denial of provisional release requested by a suspect or accused; and xiii) the modification of the time limits to issue decisions under Article 61, See in depth all selected jurisprudence in Carnero Rojo (2017), pp. 516–517.

[48] Cryer (2019), p. 449.

[49] This practice was allowed once at the ICTY and was criticized and was never repeated. See ICTY, Tadic TC II, Judgment of 10 August 1995 (Judge Stephen dissenting).

[50] As Bachmaier Winter (2019), pp. 307–311, reminds: «the right to cross examinations a fundamental right envisaged in Art. 6(3).d) ECHR». See analysis of the most important jurisprudence in ECHR about this right

[51] As Ruggieri (2018), p. 566 states: «*the accused's right to be confronted with incriminating witnesses lies at the core of the requirement of the parties' involvement in evidence-gathering and the principles of a fair fact-finding, to the point that defendants cannot be convicted on the basis of the statements given by individuals who voluntarily avoided any confrontation with the accused*».

[52] ICC, *Judgment on the Prosecutor's appeal against the decision of Pre-Trial Chamber I entitled «Decision Establishing General Principles Governing Applications to Restrict Disclosure pursuant to Rule 81 (2) and (4) of the Rules of Procedure and Evidence, Prosecutor v. Thomas Lubanga Dyilo*, (ICC-01/04-01/06-568), paras. 34–39.

[53] Musila (2010), *passim.* About legal challenges from the tension between restorative and retributive justice vid.zegl Zago (2014).

[54] While victims activists endorse the Court's new focus on victims, many legal scholars and practitioners have challenged the idea of combining the logics of retributive and restorative justice by maintaining that such a justice experiment can disrupt proper justice making at international criminal justice institutions, Hoyle and Ullrich (2014), 689.

[55] Judge Christine Van den Wyngaert recalls the «countless hours spent on determining the victim status of hundreds ç and in the future perhaps thousands ç of applicants «and purports that the Court's engagement with victims has considerably lengthened its judicial proceedings. On the normative plane, victims' rights to participation threaten to undercut the defendant's right to a fair trial. On this basis, many contend that retributive and restorative justice processes should be separated again. For instance, by conducting trials, on the one hand, and channelling justice for

the Court's judicial interpretations and policy implementation, but threatens to undermine the key norms of international criminal justice: neutrality and impartiality.[56] On the other, other standpoint reminds that «the recognition of victims' rights pay tribute to the centrality of victims «experience by contributing to the justice process and plays a central role in rebuilding societies».[57]

The truth is that learning from past experiences, as well as from the wisdom of partners, victims, intermediaries, civil society, NGOs or States, makes it possible for all elements of the ICC and Rome Statute systems to refine and further improve their approach to victims, and to better realise their responsibilities as duty bearers in relation to victims who have rights under the Rome Statute system.[58]

4.1 General Remarks

The cornerstone on which is based the entire system of procedural participation of victims before the ICC is contemplated in Article 68 (3) RE. In this sense, where the personal interests of the victims are affected, the Court shall permit their views and concerns to be presented and considered at stages of the proceedings determined to be appropriate by the Court. This participation will be possible in a manner which is not prejudicial to or inconsistent with the rights of the accused and a fair and impartial trial.

As mentioned before, these provisions give the victim the status of «participant»[59] but not of «party», which are the Prosecution and the Defense. In this sense, it is true that the intervention of the victims is conditioned not only to the

victims through separate restorative institutions, such as truth and reconciliation commissions, on the other». Van den Wyngaert (2012), p. 478.

[56] *Ibid.*, p. 690.

[57] To the myth «The participation of victims constitutes a burden to the proceedings, creates delays and leads to supplementary costs», FIDH highlights Judge Adrian Fulford experience and opinion, who was the presiding judge of the ICC's first trial, the Lubanga trial, and noted at the outcome of the trial: «*The experience of Trial Chamber 1 has been that the involvement of victims has not greatly added to the length of the case. Their submissions and questioning have been focused, succinct and seemingly relevant to the issues in the case. Whether it is said their role has undermined the fairness of the trial will be revealed in closing submissions, but purely from the point of view of time, they have not significantly extended the proceedings. These are early days, but I am cautiously optimistic that their participation can be accommodated effectively in the individual trials*». FIDH (2014), p. 6.

[58] «Overall, the Court must adapt to the unique aspects of each case and situation. More generally, however, the ICC system must adapt to the insecurity in which most victims live and to the affect it has on them. This means accounting, and where possible compensating, for the huge influence this insecurity has on victims' engagement with the Court». ICC-ASP, Report of the Court on the Revised strategy in relation to victims: Past, present and future (ICC-ASP/11/40), 5 November 2012, paras. 79–80.

[59] About the scope and possibilities of victim's participation before the ICC, identifying most important challenges see, among others, Pena and Carayon (2013), Moffet (2015a, b), Friman

authorization of the Court, but also in many relevant aspects, as we will analyze below. It should be emphasized that victims may not bring criminal actions or challenge admissibility or jurisdiction, nor may they intervene in the examination of witnesses as if they were a party, nor may they file an appeal against the sentence handed down in the proceedings. However, as has been made clear in different decisions, the participation of victims[60] must be meaningful,[61] and cannot remain a mere formality without content or symbolic.[62]

To this end, it has been ensured that victims have the right to free choice of counsel to represent them[63] (Rule 90 RPE), albeit subject to certain limits. Firstly, counsel must meet the requirements of Rule 22(1) RPE. In addition, in the event that there is a large number of victims, the Chamber may request the victims, in order to ensure the effectiveness of the proceedings, to appoint one or more counsel to represent them in a unified manner. Finally, when the interests of justice so require, the Chamber, after consultation with the Registry, may appoint counsel for victims (Regulation 80.1 Regulations of the Court).

Finally, we must indicate that the essential prerequisite to be able to consider a genuine participation is the notification to the victims and their legal representatives of all significant decisions, as provided in Rule 92 RPE. Likewise, jurisprudence holds that the Legal Representative of victims is entitled to be notified, on the same basis as the Prosecutor and the Defense, of:

(i) All requests, submissions, motions, responses and other documents within the meaning of regulation 22 of the Regulations of the Court which are filed as «public» in the record of the case;

(ii) All the public decisions of the Chamber in the present proceedings; and

---

(2009), Wemmers (2009, 2010), Kelly (2012); Glasius (2009), McKay (2008), Pues (2015), McGonigle Leyh (2011).

[60] ASP-ICC (2012) Court's Revised strategy in relation to victims, Annex Rights and Prerogatives of Victims in Proceedings before the ICC, (ICC-ASP/11/38), 5 November 2012, pp. 7–13. For an analysis about the Court's Strategies in Relation to Victims, see Carayon and O'Donohue (2017).

[61] As Sehmi (2018), pp. 579 and 590 states: «the experience in the Kenyatta Case has shown that there are two preconditions for «meaningful» participation of victims. The first is ensuring consistent communication between the Court and victims, and the second is the implementation of a holistic approach to participation with an emphasis on restoring victims'dignity. It is imperative to ensure consistent communication and consultation with victims by codifying best practices. There must be a stronger emphasis on restoring the dignity of participating victims».

[62] ICC, *Decision on the Set of Procedural Rights Attached to Procedural Status of Victim at the Pre-Trial Stage of the Case, Prosecutor v. Germain Katanga and Mathieu Ngudjolo Chui*, PTC I, (ICC-01/04-01/07-474), Judgment of 13 May 2008, para. 49.

[63] About Victims' legal representation before the ICC, see Guerrero Palomares (2014) *passim*. As Spiga highlights: «many procedural rights accruing to victims are exclusively exercised by the victim's legal representatives, in view of the fact that as professional counsel they have both the skills and the ethical boundaries to exercise them in a manner that does not infringe on the accused's farir trial rights. «She also remarks that the widening of victims'participation has also been accompanied by an attempt to consider victims'rights collectively. While victims are in principle free to choose a legal representative, often have been assigned common legal representatives to groups of victims. Spiga (2013), p. 1392.

(iii) Of the confirmation of charges hearing and any postponement thereof, as well as the date of delivery of the decision in accordance with rule 92(5) of the Rules[64]

The access of the victims or their legal representatives to the case files is also contemplated, subject to a restriction with respect to confidential documents and the protection of the national security of a State (Rule 121(10) RPE). Likewise, the record of the proceedings transmitted by the Pre-Trial Chamber may be consulted by the victims or their legal representatives participating in the proceedings (Rule 131(2) RPE).

5 Modalities of Victim Participation in The Proceedings

It is necessary to dedicate, a section to indicate which modalities of victim participation may appear in the different procedural stages of the ICC proceedings.[65] The following is an analysis of the most relevant issues that may affect victims.

5.1 Preliminary Examination Stage

If we take into account that the Court has already emphasized the importance of victims' participation in the proceedings as early as possible,[66] it is logical that the first act of possible intervention of victims before the Court is when the Prosecutor concludes that the information provided does not constitute a reasonable basis for an investigation[67] (Art. 15(6) RE).

[64] ICC, *Decision on Victims' Participation at the Confirmation of Charges Hearing and in the Related Proceedings, The Prosecutor v. William Samoei Ruto and Joshua Arap Sang*, PTC II, (ICC-01/09-01/11-249), Judgment of 8 August 2011, para. 95; ICC, *Decision on Victims' Participation at the Confirmation of Charges Hearing and in the Related Proceedings, The Prosecutor v. Uhuru Muigai Kenyatta,* (ICC-01/09-02/11-267), Judgment of 28 August 2011, para. 112.

[65] As Baumgartner (2008), p. 425 points out victim's participation differs considerably depending on the stage of the proceedings at which it takes place. Flexibility is the main characteristic of the provisions on victim participation.

[66] ICC, *Order to the Victims Participation and Reparations Section Concerning Victims' Representations Pursuant to Article 15(3) of the Statute Situation in the Republic of Cote D'Ivoire*, PTCIII (ICC-02/11-6), Judgment of 6 July 2011.

[67] The very first scenario envisaged by the Statute wherein victims are called upon to play a role is indeed meant to take place prior to a situation, let alone a case, being brought before the Court: such a scenario is the procedure for the authorisation of an investigation *proprio motu* by the Prosecutor. Article 15, paragraph 3, provides that «victims» may make representations to the Pre-Trial Chamber when the Prosecutor concludes that there is a reasonable basis to proceed with an investigation and, accordingly, submits to the Pre-Trial Chamber a request for authorisation of such an investigation in the absence of referral by a State or the Security Council. In this scenario, the «personal interests» of the alleged victim (or victims) may be affected since victims' representations to the Pre-Trial

Therefore, it is foreseen the need to inform victims (Rule 49(1) RPE) and the notification will indicate the possibility of submitting additional information regarding the same situation in the light of new facts and evidence (Rule 49(2) RPE).

In the event that the Prosecutor has requested authorization to open an official investigation, victims may make representations in writing to the Pre-Trial Chamber (Art. 15(3) ER y rule 50(3) RPE). The time limit for victims to make representations shall be 30 days following information given (regulation 50(1) Regulations of the Court) in order to be considered by the Pre-trial Chamber.

In these cases, Prosecutor shall inform victims, known to him or her or to the Victims and Witnesses Unit, or their legal representatives, unless the Prosecutor decides that doing so would pose a danger to the integrity of the investigation or the life or well-being of victims and witnesses (Rule 50 RPE).[68]

5.2 Investigation Stage

The investigation is carried out by the Prosecutor. The priority will be to obtain information about the facts and the circumstances surrounding them, by searching for evidence to decide whether to bring charges against a specific person or persons.

Chamber can provide factual and legal elements for the decision to authorise the investigation into the situation within which the same victims claim to have suffered harm as a result of the commission of crimes within the jurisdiction of the Court. In light of the above, the following two conclusions can be drawn: (i) victims, as well as any other subject, may contact the Court (in particular, the Office of the Prosecutor), prior to and irrespective of whether a situation or a case is pending before it, with a view to triggering the exercise of the prosecutor's proprio motu powers; (ii) in the event that the Prosecutor considers it appropriate to exercise such powers, victims may be involved in the proceedings under Article 15, provided only that they be known to the Court (either the Prosecutor or the Victims and Witnesses Unit). Accordingly, it appears that such victims are likely to play a significant role in the procedure leading to the Pre-Trial Chamber's decision as to whether the Prosecutor should be authorised to exercise his proprio *motu powers*, ICC, *Decision on victims' applications for participation a/0010/06, a/0064/06 to a/0070/06, a/0081/06 to a/0104/06 and a/0111/06 to a/0127/06, Situation in Uganda,* (ICC-02/04-101), Judgment of 10 August 2007, paras. 90–92.

[68]The Chamber is duty bound to ensure that proceedings are carried out in an expeditious manner. Being mindful that victims' representations at this particular stage is a procedure of limited scope, which is merely confined to the Prosecutor's request for authorization of an investigation, the Chamber finds it appropriate to request the Victims Participation and Reparations Section (the «VPRS») to: (1) identify, to the extent possible, the community leaders of the affected groups to act on behalf of those victims who may wish to make representations (collective representation); (2) receive victims' representations (collective and/or individual); (3) conduct an assessment, in accordance with paragraph 8 of this order, whether the conditions set out in rule 85 of the Rules have been met; and (4) summarize victims' representations into one consolidated report with the original representations annexed thereto. ICC, *Order to the Victims Participation and Reparations Section Concerning Victims' Representations Pursuant to Article 15(3) of the Statute, Situation in the Republic of Kenya*, PTC II, (ICC-01/09-4), Judgment of 10 December 2009, para. 9.

In this context, the participation of victims has been a very controversial issue because the possibilities that exist are not clearly delimited.

In accordance with the legal provisions, it is possible for victims to intervene in this stage but limited to the following aspects:

(a) In the review by the Pre-Trial Chamber of the decision of the Prosecutor not to proceed with the investigation or prosecution as provided for in Article 53 RE.
(b) In the incident of securing evidence or protection of victims and witnesses (Art. 56(3) RE). There is also the possibility for the Chambers to request the opinions and observations of the victims on any issue raised, also at this procedural moment (Rule 93 RPE).

5.3 *Pre-Trial Stage*

The pre-trial stage represents a key procedural moment since it is where it will be decided whether or not there is reasonable grounds to open a trial against a person. The two hearings that take place at this stage are the first appearance and the confirmation of charges hearing.

At the first appearance, the Pre-Trial Chamber shall satisfy itself that the person has been informed of the crimes which he or she is alleged to have committed, and of his or her rights under this Statute, including the right to apply for interim release pending trial (Art. 60 ER).

Since the parties are present, it has been asked whether it is possible for the victims to intervene, and the Court has given a negative answer,[69] considering their presence inappropriate for the purpose of this appearance, which is none other than the one just mentioned.

In the confirmation of charges,[70] jurisprudence has precisely delimited victims' intervention by granting them a wide range of possibilities,[71] such as access to decisions, public documents, public evidence and transcripts, the right to receive express notification of this hearing and to present oral or written arguments on issues arising in the course of the hearing itself.

[69] ICC, *Second Decision on the Motion of Legal Representative of Victim Applicants to Participate in Initial Appearance Proceedings and Article 19 Admissibility Proceedings, Prosecutor v. William Samoei Ruto, Henry Kiprono Kosgeyand Joshua Arap Sang*, PTC II, (ICC-01/09-01/11-40), Judgment of 6 April 2011.

[70] Art. 61 RE, Rules 121–130 RPE and regulations 52–53 Regulations of the Court.

[71] ICC, *Decision on the 138 applications for victims' participation in the proceedings Prosecutor v. Callixte Mbarushimana*, PTC I, (ICC-01/04-01/10-351), Judgment of 11 August 2011.

5.4 Trial

Procedural participation of the victims on trial, is where it acquires a greater prominence. The different possibilities of participation will be specified in:

- Be entitled to attend and participate in hearings unless, in the circumstances of the case, the Chamber concerned is of the view that the representative's intervention should be confined to written observations or submissions (Rule 91(2) RPE).
- Observations and applications before the Chambers (rule 91(2) RPP).
- The right to submit evidence.[72] Although it is true that there is no legal provision that empowers the legal representatives of the victims to lead evidence at the trial, the Court has interpreted that in certain circumstances and in accordance with specific parameters, the general clause of participation provided in Art. 68(3) RS allows this possibility. Formal and substantive requirements have been provided for the admission of evidence by the victims' representatives:

On the one hand, the Trial Chamber has correctly identified the procedure and confined limits within which it will exercise its powers to permit victims to tender and examine evidence, being formal requirements: (i) a discrete application, (ii) notice to the parties, (iii) demonstration of personal interests that are affected by the specific proceedings, (iv) compliance with disclosure obligations and protection orders, (v) determination of appropriateness and (vi) consistency with the rights of the accused and a fair trial.[73]

Accordingly, the possibility for the Legal Representatives to call victims who participate in the proceedings to testify in person, is subject to three important limitations: (i) The Chamber may not allow the participation by victims to infringe on the right of the accused to be tried without undue delay, in accordance with Article 67(l)(c) ER; (ii) The Chamber will only allow Victims' Legal Representatives to call witnesses to the extent that this does not in effect transform them into

[72] *«The Trial Chamber considers that the right to introduce evidence during trials before the Court is not limited to the parties, not least because the Court has a general right (that is not dependent on the cooperation or the consent of the parties) to request the presentation of all evidence necessary for the determination of the truth, pursuant to Article 69(3) of the Statute. Rule 91(3) of the Rules enables participating victims to question witnesses with the leave of the Chamber (including experts and the defendant). The Rule does not limit this opportunity to the witnesses called by the parties. It follows that victims participating in the proceedings may be permitted to tender and examine evidence if in the view of the Chamber it will assist it in the determination of the truth, and if in this sense the Court has «requested» the evidence»*. ICC, *Decision on victims' participation, Prosecutor v. Thomas Lubanga Dyilo*, TC I, (ICC-01/04-01/06-1119) Judgment of 21 January 2008, paras. 108–111, 113–114, and 117.

[73] ICC, *Judgment on the appeals of The Prosecutor and The Defence against Trial Chamber I's Decision on Victims' Participation of 18 January 2008, The Prosecutor v. Thomas Lubanga Dyilo*, AP, (ICC-01/04-01/06-1432), Judgment of 11 July 2008, para. 104.

auxiliary prosecutors; (iii) Under no circumstances the Chamber will allow victims to testify anonymously vis-à-vis the Defence.[74]

On the other, substantive requirements are envisaged on the premise that the Trial Chamber must ensure, on a case-by-case basis, that the right of the accused to a fair trial is respected. Therefore, whether a victim will be requested to testify on matters relating to the conduct of the accused will depend on the Trial Chamber's assessment of whether such testimony: (i) affects the victim's personal interests; (ii) is relevant to the issues of the case; (iii) contributes to the determination of the truth;[75] and (iv) whether the testimony would be consistent with the rights of the accused, and in particular the right to have adequate time and facilities to prepare his defence (Art. 67 (1) (b) ER), and a fair and impartial trial.[76]

- Challenge to evidence proposed by the parties. This is a controversial aspect as they do not have the status of a party. However, jurisprudence establishes that the Chamber may consider the victims' requests in the admission or inadmissibility of evidence proposed by the parties.[77]
- Presentation of observations. Victims may participate as witnesses on the specific facts, but it will also be possible for them to intervene to provide their comments provided that a written application[78] has been made, that the right of the accused

[74] ICC, *Directions for the conduct of the proceedings and testimony in accordance with rule 140, Prosecutor v. Germain Katanga and Mathieu Ngudjolo Chui*, PTC II, (ICC-01/04-01/07-1665), Judgment of 20 November 2009, para. 22.c).

[75] The implementation of the ICCs commitment to the victim's search for truth is interwoven with the operationalization of its victim-centred approach. The main mechanism that explicitly safeguards the victim's active contribution to the search for truth is victim participation, supported by the Office of Public Counsel for Victims OPCV) and the Trust Fund for Victims, Stolk (2015), p. 979.

[76] ICC, *Judgment on the Appeal of Mr Katanga Against the Decision of Trial Chamber II of 22 January 2010 Entitled «Decision on the Modalities of Victim Participation at Trial», Prosecutor v. Germain Katanga*, (ICC-01/04-01/07-2288), Judgment of 16 July 2010, para. 114.

[77] ICC, *Judgment on the appeals of The Prosecutor and The Defence against Trial Chamber I's Decision on Victims' Participation of 18 January 2008, Prosecutor v. Thomas Lubanga Dyilo*, AC, (ICC-01/04-01/06-1432), Judgment of 11 July 2008, para. 101.

[78] *«If the Legal Representatives wish to present evidence, their written applications are to explain: i. The nature of the proposed evidence and the manner in which it is to be presented; ii. The estimated time needed for the presentation of the proposed evidence; iii. How the personal interests of the participating victims would be affected by the presentation of the proposed evidence; iv. The relevance of the proposed evidence to the charges; V. How the presentation of the proposed evidence would assist in the Chamber's determination of the truth in this case; vi. Whether a victim who is proposed as a witness has relinquished his or her anonymity; Whether and how the presentation of the proposed evidence would affect the rights of the accused and the fairness of the trial, especially if a victim wishes to testify without relinquishing his or her anonymity; viii. Any disclosure issues that need to be resolved in connection with the presentation of the proposed evidence; ix. Whether the Legal Representatives envisage applying for protective measures, such as redactions and/or in-court protective measures; X. Whether the proposed evidence is to be presented through persons who have been authorized to participate as victims in the trial proceedings, and if so, the application numbers under which those persons are registered»*. ICC, *Order*

to a fair trial before an impartial tribunal is not affected and that the right of the accused to a trial without undue delay is not violated.

- Cross-examination of witnesses, experts and defendants. In principle, questioning by Victims' Legal Representatives should be limited to questions that have as their purpose to clarify or complement previous evidence given by the witness. Nevertheless, Victims' Legal Representatives may be allowed to ask questions of fact that go beyond matters raised during examination-in-chief, subject to the following conditions:[79]

  a) questions may not be duplicative or repetitive to what was already asked by the parties. b) questions must be limited to matters that are in controversy between the parties, unless the Victims' Legal Representative can demonstrate that they are directly relevant to the interests of the victims represented. c) In principle. Victims' Legal Representatives will not be allowed to ask questions pertaining to the credibility and/or accuracy of the witness's testimony, unless the Victims' Legal Representative can demonstrate that the witness gave evidence that goes directly against the interests of the victims represented. d) Unless the Chamber specifically gave authorisation under regulation 56 of the Regulations, Victims' Legal Representatives are not allowed to put questions pertaining to possible reparations for specific individuals or groups of individuals.

- Opening and Closing Statements. The Chamber shall specify the proceedings and manner in which participation of victims is considered appropriate, which may include making opening and closing statements (Rule 89(1) RPE)

5.5 *Appeals Stage*

It is for the Chamber to ensure that the manner in which victims present their views and concerns is not prejudicial to or inconsistent with the rights of the accused and a fair and impartial trial. Accordingly, in ordering the manner of participation of victims to comply with the rights of future suspects or a fair and impartial trial, the Appeals Chamber will limit the victims to presenting their views and concerns respecting their personal interests solely to the issues raised on appeal. Observations to be received by the victims must be specifically relevant to the issues arising in the appeal and to the extent that their personal interests are affected by the proceedings.[80]

---

regarding applications by victims to present their views and concerns or to present evidence Prosecutor v. Jean-Pierre Bemba Gombo, TC III, (ICC-01/05-01/08-1935), Judgment of 21 November 2011, para. 3.

[79] ICC, *Directions for the conduct of the proceedings and testimony in accordance with rule 140, Prosecutor v. Germain Katanga and Mathieu Ngudjolo Chui*, TC II, (ICC 01/04–01/07–1665), Judgment of 20 November 2009, para. 90.

[80] ICC-The Office of Public Counsel for Victims (OPCV), Representing Victims before the International Criminal Court A Manual for legal representatives, fifth ed., p. 189.

Victims are entitled to appeal orders on reparations although it is quite questionable whether they may appeal decisions regarding protective measures.[81]

6 Reparation

Pursuant to Article 75(1) RE:

> The Court shall establish principles relating to reparations[82] to, or in respect of, victims, including restitution, compensation and rehabilitation. On this basis, in its decision the Court may, either upon request or on its own motion in exceptional circumstances, determine the scope and extent of any damage, loss and injury to, or in respect of, victims and will state the principles on which it is acting.

As stated by the Court in its first judgment:

> Reparations fulfil two main purposes that are enshrined in the Statute: they oblige those responsible for serious crimes to repair the harm they caused to the victims and they enable the Chamber to ensure that offenders account for their acts. Furthermore, reparations can be directed at particular individuals, as well as contributing more broadly to the communities that were affected. Reparations in the present case must - to the extent achievable - relieve the suffering caused by these offences; afford justice to the victims by alleviating the consequences of the wrongful acts; deter future violations; and contribute to the effective reintegration of former child soldiers. Reparations can assist in promoting reconciliation between the convicted person, the victims of the crimes and the affected communities.[83]

The right to reparations is a well-established and basic human right that is enshrined in universal and regional human rights treaties,[84] and in other[85] international

[81] Cryer (2019), p. 459.

[82] See Rules 94–99 RPE, regulation 88 Regulations of the Court and regulations 110–111 Regulations of the Registry.

[83] ICC, *Decision establishing the principles and procedures to be applied to reparations, Prosecutor v. Thomas Lubanga Dyilo*, TC I, (ICC-01/04-01/06-2904), Judgment of 7 August 2012, para. 179.

[84] International human rights tribunals have given the victim an active position in the proceedings and have recognized the victim's right to reparation for the damages suffered. However, only recognize the active legitimacy to initiate the procedure the following: European Court of Human Rights (Protocol n. 11) and African Court on Human and Peoples' Rights (Art. 5 Protocol to the African Charter on Human and Peoples' rights on the establishment of an African Court on Human and Peoples' rights. Victim's *Locus standi in juicio* at Inter-American Court of Human Rights is recognized at all stages of the process, particularly at the reparations stage (Art. 25 Rules of Procedure), See in detail Gil Gandía (2020), pp. 30–31.

[85] Initiatives for Redress and international criminal justice in Asia and Europe in Bottigliero (2005), pp. 453–461. This author explains initiatives than have been taking place in the following cases: Victims of «Agent Orange» in Vietnam; Victims of the Marcos regime in the Philippines; Victims of the former Yugoslavia conflict, and Redress for «historical crimes». About the wider legal framework of victim redress, see, among others, McCarthy (2012b), pp. 9–74. For the African Initiatives see Perez-Leon-Acevedo (2019).

instruments.[86] Additionally, significant human reports[87] provided guidance to the ICC in establishing the principles and procedures to be applied to reparations for first time[88] in international criminal justice.[89]

Participation of victims in reparations proceedings becomes a milestone in the road of international criminal justice uniquely establishing a system in which both retributive and restorative justice are combined. In this sense, victim's participation in respect to reparations will be particularly be as follows:

- Right to request for reparations in writing and filed with the Registrar (Rule 94 RPE);[90]

[86] Including the UN Basic Principles; the Declaration of Basic Principles of Justice for Victims of Crime and Abuse of Power; the Guidelines on Justice in Matters involving Child Victims and Witnesses of Crime; the Nairobi Declaration; the Cape Town Principles and Best Practices on the Recruitment of Children into the Armed Forces and on Demobilization and Social Reintegration of Child Soldiers in Africa; and the Paris Principles. In particular about the Remedies for victims of violations of international humanitarian law, see Zegveld (2003).

[87] Study concerning the right to restitution, compensation and rehabilitation for victims of gross violations of human rights and fundamental freedoms. Final report submitted by Mr. Theo van Boven, Special Rapporteur to United Nations Sub-Commission on Prevention of Discrimination and Protection of Minorities, E/CN.4/Sub.2/1993/8, 22 July 1993; The right to restitution, compensation and rehabilitation for victims of gross violations of human rights and fundamental freedoms. Final report of the Special Rapporteur Mr. M. Cherif Bassiouni to the Commission on Human Rights, E/CN.4/2000/62, 18 January 20(X); The rule of law and transitional justice in conflict and post-conflict societies, Report of the United Nations Secretary-General S/2004/616, 23 August 2004; The rule of law and transitional justice in conflict and post-conflict societies. Report of the UN Secretary General, S/2011/634, 12 October 2011, *Ibidem*.

[88] The issue of victim's reparations has also been inadequately addressed by the hybrid tribunals that had been established in East Timor, Sierra Leone and Kosovo and the Extraordinary Chambers in the Courts of Cambodia. See Cryer (2019), Chap. 9. For Cambodia experience, see Elander (2018), *passim* and SaCouto (2012), pp. 336–337. This author explains that the reality of victim participation is that significant limitations remain, mainly for two reasons: First, because victims do not have the opportunity to participate in proceedings unless the harm they experienced is linked to the charges being prosecuted by the court against the accused. And second, the charges against the accused depend on what the prosecution chooses to pursue. See also Zegveld (2010), pp. 86–92 and Henzelin et al. (2006), 318.

[89] At ICTY and ICTR unsuccessful attempts were made to modify the procedure in order to give them restorative powers, Gil Gandía (2020), pp. 21–23. Both tribunals limit reparations to the return of stolen property 'to their rightful owners? Without providing redress for personal injuries of a physical or mental nature. Rule 106 RPE in both tribunals allows a victim or persons claiming through the victim, to bring a legal action in national courts (or other competent body) for compensation, provided that relevant national legislation is available, Bassiouni (2006), p. 242. A study about victim redress and International Criminal Justice in McCarthy (2012a).

[90] Rule 94(1) RPE: «*It shall contain the following particulars: (a) The identity and address of the claimant; (b) A description of the injury, loss or harm; (c) The location and date of the incident and, to the extent possible, the identity of the person or persons the victim believes to be responsible for the injury, loss or harm; (d) Where restitution of assets, property or other tangible items is sought, a description of them; (e) Claims for compensation; (f) Claims for rehabilitation and other forms of remedy; (g) To the extent possible, any relevant supporting documentation, including names and addresses of witnesses*».

- To make submissions prior to the Court's ruling on the principles governing future reparations;[91]
- Before making an order of reparation, the Court may invite and shall take account of representations from or on behalf of the victims (Art. 75(3) RE);
- -Submit their opinions on the reports issued by the experts in the cases of Rule 97(2) RPE;
- Attending the reparation hearing, whether it occurs at the same time as the sentencing[92] or separately (Arts. 75(3) and 76(3) RE, rules 91(4), 94 and 143 RPE). This hearing can be postponed, in exceptional circumstances, by the Trial Chamber, on its own motion or at the request of the legal representatives of the victims participating in the proceedings;
- Appeal against the order for reparations (Art. 82(4) RE, Rule 150 RPE).

In the reparation proceedings,[93] the applicant shall provide sufficient proof of the casual link[94] between the crime and the harm suffered, based on the specific circumstances of the case, including with reference to difficulties encountered by the victims in obtaining evidence in support of their claim. Given the fundamentally different nature of reparations proceedings, the standard need not be the criminal standard of proof[95] «beyond reasonable doubt» and it may generally be appropriate

[91] ICC, *Scheduling order concerning timetable for sentencing and reparations, Prosecutor v. Thomas Lubanga Dyilo*, (ICC-01/04-01/06-2844), Judgment of 14 March 2012, para. 8: «*In particular these should address, inter alia: i) whether reparations should be awarded on a collective or an individual basis (see Rule 97(1) of the Rules); ii) depending on whether there should be individual or collective reparations (or both), to whom are they to be directed; how harm is to be assessed; and the criteria to be applied to the awards; iii) whether it is possible or appropriate to make a reparations order against the convicted person pursuant to Article 75(2) of the Statute; iv) whether it would be appropriate to make an order for an award for reparations through the Trust Fund for Victims pursuant to Article 75(2) of the Statute; and v) whether the parties or participants seek to call expert evidence pursuant to Rule 97 of the Rules*».

[92] Victim participation during sentencing may rise concerns about defense rights, in particular in respect of fair sentencing proceedings, the principle of proportional punishment, and avoidance of improper or unfair sentencing disparities. Pérez-León-Acevedo (2019), pp. 433–435: «*In their written submissions in Lubanga, Katanga, Bemba and Al-Mahdi, the victims' lawyers invoked a variety of arguments including: the extent of damage to victims and their families as a sentencing factor; the need to examine gravity qualitatively and quantitatively; views on types of penalties, namely, imprisonment, confiscation and fines (Article 77 and Rule 146); aggravating circumstances such as abuse of power/official capacity, defenceless victims and crimes committed with particular cruelty and discrimination; the need for severe and exemplary sentencing or sentencing beyond the maximum threshold; international and domestic sentencing practices; absence of mitigating circumstances, including irrelevance of the offender's young age, no statement of deep and genuine remorse and lack of the offender's apologies or intention to redress; etc*».

[93] Martínez Ventura (2014), pp. 350–369 identifies different stages.

[94] In depth about the casual link between the crime and harm suffered particularly in reparation stage at Lubanga, vid. Aponte Cardona (2014), pp. 431–456.

[95] García Falconí (2014), pp. 377–388. Explains three standards: proof beyond reasonable doubt; clear and convincing evidence and finally preponderance of evidence, the one chosen by the ICC in reparations proceedings.

to require proof on the «balance of probabilities».[96] In these sense, various factors specific to the case should be considered, including the difficulty victims may face in obtaining evidence in support of their claim due to the destruction or unavailability of evidence.[97]

As for child victims,[98] the age-related harm experienced as well as their needs must be considered and the Court should be guided by the principle of the «best interest of the child» as enshrined in the Convention on the Rights of the Child as well as other guidelines in other international instruments.[99]

Regarding the modalities of reparation, we can refer to the first decision of the ICC in the *Lubanga Case* in this regard,[100] which provides further definition of the concepts of restitution, compensation and rehabilitation:

Restitution should, as far as possible, restore the victim to his or her circumstances before the crime was committed, but this will often be unachievable for victims of the crimes of enlisting and conscripting children under the age of 15 and using them to participate actively in the hostilities. Restitution is directed at the restoration of an individual's life, including a return to his or her family, home and previous employment; providing continuing education; and returning lost or stolen property. Restitution may be apposite for legal bodies such as schools or other institutions.[101]

---

[96] ICC, *Decision Establishing the Principles and Procedures to be Applied to Reparations, Prosecutor v. Thomas Lubanga Dyilo,* (ICC-01/04-01/06-2904), Judgment of 7 August 2012, para. 101. ICC, *Judgment on the appeals against the «Decision establishing the principles and procedures to be applied to reparations» of 7 August 2012 with AMENDED order for reparations (Annex A) and public annexes 1 and 2, Annex A, Prosecutor v. Thomas Lubanga Dyilo,* (ICC-01/04-01/06-3129), Judgment of 3 March 2015, para. 22).

[97] *Ididem*, para. 252.

[98] ICC-OTP, Policy on Children, 2016, paras. 106–107: «*The Office supports a child-sensitive approach to reparations, taking into account the differentiated effects and the harms caused to boys and girls by the crimes for which an individual was convicted, as well as their right to reintegration into their communities. The Office also supports consultation with the victims, including children, in order to determine the most effective, appropriate and gender-sensitive forms of reparation within a particular community. This approach is intended to promote reparations that are transformative in nature and that contribute to the best interests of children. The Office will, in framing any submissions, bear in mind that individual reparations awards, including non-monetary awards such as apologies, may enhance a child's sense of justice.127 At the same time, collective reparations, such as commemorations or the (re)construction of schools or health care facilities, may promote community reconciliation and provide the greatest benefit to groups of victims*».

[99] ICC, *Judgment on the appeals against the «Decision establishing the principles and procedures to be applied to reparations» of 7 August 2012 with AMENDED order for reparations (Annex A) and public annexes 1 and 2, Annex A, Prosecutor v. Thomas Lubanga Dyilo*, (ICC-01/04-01/06-3129), Judgment of 3 March 2015, paras. 23–24).

[100] See in analysis about the Thomas Lubanga Dyilo Case, the first judgement of the ICC, Ambos et al. (2014), *passim*. Catani (2012).

[101] ICC, *Decision establishing the principles and procedures to be applied to reparations, Prosecutor v. Thomas Lubanga Dyilo*, TC I, (ICC-01/04-01/06-2904), Judgment of 7 August 2012, paras. 223–225.

Compensation should be considered when (i) the economic harm is sufficiently quantifiable; (ii) an award of this kind would be appropriate and proportionate (bearing in mind the gravity of the crime and the circumstances of the case); and (iii) the available funds mean this result is feasible. Consistent with internationally recognised human rights law, compensation requires a broad application, to encompass all forms of damage, loss and injury, including material, physical and psychological harm.[102]

Rehabilitation:[103] The right of victims to is to be implemented by the Court on the basis of the principles relating to non-discrimination, and this shall include a gender-inclusive approach that encompasses males and females of all ages. Rehabilitation shall include the provision of medical services and healthcare (particularly in order to treat HIV and Aids); psychological, psychiatric and social assistance to support those suffering from grief and trauma; and any relevant legal and social services.[104]

If the convicted person does not have any means to afford reparations («indigent»), the Trust Fund for Victims may be requested to compliment the order for reparations so that the victims may receive some form of redress.

In accordance with Article 79 RE

> A Trust Fund[105] shall be established by decision of the Assembly of States Parties for the benefit of victims of crimes within the jurisdiction of the Court, and of the families of such victims. The Court may order money and other property collected through fines or forfeiture to be transferred, by order of the Court, to the Trust Fund. The Trust Fund shall be managed according to criteria to be determined by the Assembly of States Parties (see also Rule 98 RPE).

[102] *«Although some forms of damage are essentially unquantifiable in financial terms, compensation is a form of economic relief that is aimed at addressing, in a proportionate and appropriate manner, the harm that has been inflicted. Examples include: a. Physical harm, including causing an individual to lose the capacity to bear children; b. Moral and non-material damage resulting in physical, mental and emotional suffering. c. Material damage, including lost earnings and the opportunity to work; loss of, or damage to, property; unpaid wages or salaries; other forms of interference with an individual's ability to work; and the loss of savings. d. Lost opportunities, including those relating to employment, education and social benefits; loss of status; and interference with an individual's legal rights (although the Court must ensure it does not perpetuate traditional or existing discriminatory practices, for instance on the basis of gender, in attempting to address these issues) e. Costs of legal or other relevant experts, medical services, psychological and social assistance, including, where relevant, help for boys and girls with HIV and Aids». Ibidem*, paras. 226–231.

[103] Participation in the proceedings ex Art. 68 (3) may, in and of itself, constitute a form of rehabilitation for those victims who, as right-bearers, freely determine to exercise their right to access to justice. Therefore, rehabilitation cannot be limited to forms of reparations imposed on the convicted persons, but must be also conducted with society at large, in order to help victims to promptly recover from trauma. Cattin (2022b), p. 2247.

[104] *Ibidem*, paras. 232–236.

[105] The Trust Fund for Victims, https://www.trustfundforvictims.org/

The Trust Fund for Victims' (TFV) mission[106] is to respond to the harm resulting from such crimes by ensuring the rights of the victims and their families through the provision of reparations and assistance and by providing a voice for the victims.[107] The Rome Statute uniquely establishes a system in which both retributive and restorative justices are combined. Reparation orders will be directed to individual or collective[108] victims depending on the case[109] and it is also possible to provide a symbolic[110] compensation award as in Katanga Case where the Trial Chamber ordered awards for reparations to 297 identified victims, comprised of an individual

---

[106]In 2022, the Trust Fund is engaged on five cases at the reparations phase (Lubanga, Katanga (at the final stage), Al Mahdi, Ntaganda, and Ongwen) at an implementation value of over €5 million and has 20 ongoing assistance projects at a value of more than €3 million for the ongoing contractual year. In 2023, the resources required for implementing reparation programmes will need to increase in order to enable the TFV to continue implementation in Lubanga/Ntaganda (former child soldiers) and Al Mahdi and procure a partner for implementing the reparations for the group of victims of attacks in the case of Ntaganda. The TFV operates assistance programmes in the Central African Republic (CAR), Côte d'Ivoire (CIV), the Democratic Republic of Congo (DRC), Mali and Uganda, with new assistance programmes in Georgia, Kenya and Mali at the contracting stage. The TFV aims to maintain the investment value of the assistance programmes, which will only be possible if the revenue from voluntary contributions to the Trust Fund increases considerably already as of the second half of 2022 onwards. See ICC-ASP, Report of the Board of Directors of the Trust Fund for Victims to the Assembly of States Parties on the activities of the Trust Fund for the period 1 July 2021 to 30 June 2022, (ICC-ASP/21/14), 23.08.2022, para. 5.

[107]By mid-2022, the Trust Fund had: (a) mostly implemented court-ordered collective reparations awards in the Katanga case, pending completion of the award modalities for housing and psychological support; (b) officially launched the implementation of collective reparations awards in the Al Mahdi case, while having assessed the eligibility of and administered individual reparations awards to over 880 victims; (c) begun to provide collective service-based reparations to the beneficiaries in the Lubanga case, having reached over 550 victims to date; and (d) started to provide reparations to priority victims in urgent need in the Ntaganda case, and submitted the draft implementation plan for providing collective reparations with individual components to all victims in the Ntaganda case. The Trust Fund also submitted observations on reparations in the Ongwen case. UNGA, Report of the International Criminal Court, Note by the Secretary-General, (A/77/305), 19.8.2022. para. 97.

[108]In Keller's opinion collective awards seem better-suited to achieving restorative justice than indivual awards. First, restorative justice is tied to the society as a whole; collective reparations might facilitate social healing more effectively than individual awards. Second, collective awards might draw more heavily on victim input. The process of developing community priorities based on victim's needs can be part of the healing process. Collective awards might also benefit the broader society and promote reconciliation between victims and other groups», Keller (2007), p. 212.

[109]Thus, for example, in the situation of the Republic of Mali, in the case against Ahmad Al Faqi Al Mahdi, Trial Chamber VIII issued an order for reparations establishing Mr. Al Mahdi's liability in the amount of Al Mahdi at €2.7 million for the following reparations: individual reparations for financial losses and for moral damages to victims with a close connection to the destroyed mausoleums, collective reparations through the reconstruction of the protected buildings, and collective reparations for the community of Timbuktu, ICC, *Reparations Order, Situation in Mali, Prosecutor v. Ahmad Al Faqi Al Mahdi*, (ICC-01/12-01/15-236), Judgment of 17 August 2017, para. 60.

[110]Simbolic reparation emphasizes Galain Palermo (2014), p. 428, «will be the antidote to situations of injustice that may be caused by criminal selectivity that does not depend on reasons of abstract justice».

symbolic compensation award of $250 to each victim and four collective awards to all identified victims in the form of housing assistance, education assistance, income generating activities, and psychological rehabilitation.[111]

7 Special Reference to *Amicus Curiae*

The figure of the *amicus curiae*[112] is provided for in the ICC as well as in its predecessors.[113] The purpose of this figure is to make submissions on any matter requested by a Chamber.[114] The *Milosevic case*[115] was very interesting in the delimitation of the functions attributed to *amicus curiae*. Slobodan Milosevic informed the Chamber in writing[116] and indicated during his initial appearance at the Kosovo trial, that he intended to defend himself and did not want to be represented by legal counsel.[117] In addition, the Chamber found that the defendant

[111] ICC, *Public Ordonnance de réparation en vertu de l'Article 75 du Statut Accompagnée d'une annexe publique (annexe I) et d'une annexe confidentielle ex parte réservée au Représentant légal commun des victimes, au Bureau du conseil public pour les victimes et à l'équipe de la défense de Germain Katanga (annexe II), Prosecutor v. Germanin Katanga*, (ICC-01/04-01/), Judgment of 24 March 2017. And ICC, «*Draft implementation plan relevant to Trial Chamber II's order for reparations of 24 March 2017 (ICC-01/04-01/07-3728) Confidential Annex 1: Detailed Overview of beneficiary categories, proposed awards within each category, and estimated values and budget costs thereto Public Annex 2: Defence correspondence regarding Mr Katanga's potential participation Confidential, ex parte available to the Registry only Annex 3: Table of harm categorizations on an individual basis of all 297 victims Confidential, ex parte available to OPCV Legal Representative only Annex 4: Table of harm categorization of victims represented Confidential, ex parte available to the Legal Representative only Annex 5: Table of harm categorization of victims represented, Prosecutor v. Germain Katanga*, (ICC-01/04-01/07-375), 25.7.2017.

[112] For a in depth analysis of *amicus curiae* before International Courts and Tribunals, see Wiik (2016), *passim*.

[113] Rule 103 RPE Amicus curiae and other forms of submission: «*At any stage of the proceedings, a Chamber may, if it considers it desirable for the proper determination of the case, invite or grant leave to a State, organization or person to submit, in writing or orally, any observation on any issue that the Chamber deems appropriate. 2. The Prosecutor and the defence shall have the opportunity to respond to the observations submitted under sub-rule 1. 3. A written observation submitted under sub-rule 1 shall be filed with the Registrar, who shall provide copies to the Prosecutor and the defence. The Chamber shall determine what time limits shall apply to the filing of such observations*».

[114] See Rule 74 ICTY and ICTR, see Williams and Woola (2006).

[115] See, among others, in general Ambos (2005),, pp. 3–7; Damaska (2005), pp. 3–8; Gaparayi (2004), pp. 737–766; Steinitz (2005), pp. 103–123.

[116] A person choosing to represent himself or herself shall so notify the Registrar in writing at the first opportunity. Rule 21(4) RPE ICC, and Rule 44 (G) ICTY and rule 45 (F) ICTR.

[117] ICTY, *Milosevic* Written Note by the Accused, (IT-02-54), 3.7.2001, Registry pp. 3371–72; Initial Appearance, 3.7. 2001, Transcript pp. 1–2.

had demonstrated that he possessed the diligence necessary to defend himself,[118] rejecting the Prosecutor's proposal that he should additionally assign defense counsel to the defendant.[119] However, to ensure that the defendant received a fair trial and that the rest of the defendant's rights were fully respected, the chamber ordered the Registrar to appoint three *amici curiae* for the proper functioning of the proceedings.[120]

But throughout the Milosevic trial there was an evolution and development of the work to be performed by the amicus curiae, especially with regard to their intervention[121] when necessary to guarantee the right to a fair trial,[122] considering that while «the essential function of an amicus curiae is to be a friend of the court, not of the accused,[123] and that an *amicus curiae* is not a party to the proceedings and is not legally qualified to act as counsel for the accused»[124] it should be noted that where there is a recognized «identity of interests between the accused and the amici with respect to a particular matter and this does not create an inequitable situation for the prosecution, and is necessary in the interests of justice», the *amicus curiae* may assume certain functions that would belong only to the parties.[125]

In respect to the ICC, according to the constant jurisprudence, *amicus curiae* submissions may be admitted by a Chamber if it is desirable for the proper determination of the case and if the observations relate to an issue that the Chamber deems appropriate. This determination is made by the Chamber on a case-by-case basis and aims at having the opportunity to get experts' information on relevant issues of legal

---

[118] As he had deliberately waived his right to be assisted by a lawyer, he was under a duty to show diligence himself, ECHR, Case of *Melin v. France* (Application no. 12914/87), 22–6.1993, para. 25.

[119] ICTY, *Prosecutor v. Miloševic*, Status Conference (IT-99-37-PT), Transcript, 30 August 2001, p 18.

[120] ICTY, *Prosecutor v. Milosevic* «Order Inviting Designation of Amicus Curiae» (IT-02-54), 30.9.2001. ICTY, Judicial Supplement 26, *Prosecutor v. Milosevic* (IT-99-37-PT), «Order Inviting Designation of Amicus Curiae», 31.9.2001, Trial Chamber III (Judges May (Presiding) Robison and Fassi Fihri). The Trial Chamber stressed that the role of the Amici Curiae would not be to represent the Accused but to assist the court by: (1) making any submissions properly open to the accused by way of preliminary or other pre-trial Motion1; (2) making any submissions or objections to evidence properly open to the accused during the trial proceedings and cross-examining witnesses as appropriate; (3) drawing to the attention of the Trial Chamber any exculpatory or mitigating evidence; and (4) acting in any other way which designated Counsel considers appropriate in order to secure a fair trial».

[121] *Prosecutor v. Milosevic*, 2.9.2004, Transcript, p. 32387.

[122] ICTY, *Prosecutor v. Milosevic*, «Decision on Appeal by Amici Curiae», 20.1.2004, para. 4.

[123] ICTY, *Prosecutor v. Milosevic* «Amici Curiae Submissions in Response to the Trial Chamber's «Further Order to Future Conduct of the Trial Concerning Assignment of Defence Counsel», 6.9.2004, A*mici Curiae* 13 August 2004, para. 18 (iii)(a).

[124] ICTY, *Prosecutor v. Milosevic*, Decision on the Interlocutory Appeal by the Amici Curiae against the Trial Chamber Order Concerning the Presentation and Preparation of the Defence Case, Separate Opinion Judge Shahabuddeen, (IT-02-54-AR73.6), Ap. Ch., 20.1.2004, paras. 1, 2 and 11.

[125] Ibidem, para. 5.

interest for the proceedings.[126] Particular interesting are contributions of *amicus curiae* in reparations stage[127] because assist chambers to determining the most affected victims and specific types and extent of harms suffered.

8 Final Remark

The participation of victims in the criminal proceedings before the ICC consists primarily on the possible presentation and consideration of their opinions and observations. This intervention is conditioned to the acquisition of the status of victim, provided that the victim is a natural person who has suffered harm caused by a crime under the jurisdiction of the Court and that there is a causal link between the crime and the harm suffered. In this context, a system of participation in the different procedural phases has been articulated to delimit the extent and limits of this action, which, since it does not have the status of «party» in the strict sense, raises many questions in practice. It is in the reparation phase that the victims have been given maximum protagonism, establishing different modalities of restitution, compensation and rehabilitation. Taking into account these considerations, it is difficult to qualify this «participation» as a third party in the proceedings, because victims' contributions to the process before the ICC is a unique and *sui generis* status, not suitable to any other experience at national or international level.

References

Ambos K (2005) El proceso contra Slobodan Milosevic: Un balance provisional. Revista Penal 15: 3–7

Ambos K, Malarino E, Steiner C (eds) (2014) Análisis de la primera sentencia de la Corte Penal Internacional: El Caso Lubanga. EDPAL, Konrad Adenauer Stiftung

Aponte Cardona A (2014) El nexo de causalidad en sede de reparación en el caso Thomas Lubanga. In: Ambos K, Malarino E, Steiner C (eds) Análisis de la primera sentencia de la Corte Penal Internacional: El Caso Lubanga. EDPAL, Konrad Adenauer Stiftung, pp 431–456

Bachmaier Winter L (2019) Principio de inmediación y confrontación paralelismos, diferencias y tendencias en la prueba testifical. In: Ambos K, Malarino E (eds) Fundamentos de derecho probatorio en materia penal. Tirant lo Blanch, Valencia, pp 279–331

---

[126] ICC, *«Decision on the Request submitted pursuant to rule 103(1) of the Rules of Procedure and Evidence»*, *Situation in the Democratic Republic of the Congo,* (ICC-01/04-373), 17.8.2007. paras. 3–4.

[127] See, for example, ICC, *The Prosecutor v Dominic Ongwen*, *«Submissions of amicus curiae observations»*, (ICC-02/04-01/15-1925), 30.11.2021, p. 5: *«submission will assist Trial Chamber IX in determining the most affected victims and the specific types and extent of harms suffered, types and modalities of reparations most appropriate to address individual and collective harm suffered by the victims of the crimes for which Mr. Ongwen was convicted and concrete estimates as to repair the harms suffered by the victims».*

Bachvarova T (2017) The standing of victims in the procedural design of the International Criminal Court. Brill Nijhoff, Leiden

Barona Vilar (2018) Encuentros restaurativos, tránsito de la guerra a la paz: ¿instrumento paliativo o reconstructivo? Estudios de Derecho 75(165):19–43

Bassiouni MC (2006) International Recognition of Victims' Rights. Hum Rights Law Rev 6(2): 203–279

Baumgartner E (2008) Aspects of victim participation in the proceedings of the International Criminal Court. Int Rev Red Cross 90(870):409–440

Bottigliero I (2005) Redres and International Criminal Justice in Asia and Europe. Asia Eur J 3: 453–461

Carayon G, O'Donohue J (2017) The International Criminal Court's Strategies in Relation to Victims. J Int Crim Justice 15:567–591

Carnero Rojo E (2017) Article 68 Protection of the victims and their participation in the proceedings. In: Klamberg M (ed) Commentary on the law of the International Criminal Court. Torkel Opsahk Academic EPublisher, Brussels, pp 514–531

Catani L (2012) Victims at the International Criminal Court, some lessons learned from the *Lubanga* case. J Int Crim Justice 10:905–922

Cattin D (2022a) Article 68. Protection of victims and witnesses and their participation in the proceedings. In: Ambos K (ed) Rome Statute of the International Criminal Court Article-by-Article Commentary, 4th edn. Beck Hart Nomos, pp 2001–2036

Cattin D (2022b) Article 75 reparations to victims. In: Ambos K (ed) Rome Statute of the International Criminal Court article-by-article commentary, 4th edn. Beck Hart Nomos, pp 2036–2262

Cryer R (2019) Victims in the international criminal process. In: Cryer R, Robinson D, Vasiliev S (eds) An introduction to International Criminal Law and Procedure, 4th edn. Cambridge University Press, pp 445–465

Damaska M (2005) Milosevic's right to defence: assignment of counsel and perceptions of fairness. J Int Crim Justice 3:3–8

Elander M (2018) Figuring victims in International Criminal Justice: the case of the Khmer Rouge Tribunal. Routledge, New York

FIDH (2014) Five myths about victim participation in ICC proceedings. https://www.fidh.org/IMG/pdf/cpi649a.pdf

Fletcher GP (1995) With justice for some. In: Victim's Rights in Criminal Trials. Addison-Wesley Publishing Company

Friman H (2009) The International Criminal Court and participation of victims: a third party to the proceedings? Leiden J Int Law 22:485–500

Funk TM (2015) Victims' rights and advocacy at the International Criminal Court, 2nd edn. Oxford University Press, New York

Galain Palermo (2014) Modalidades de reparación y adecuación al tipo de víctima. In: Ambos K, Malarino E, Steiner C (eds) Análisis de la primera sentencia de la Corte Penal Internacional: El Caso Lubanga. EDPAL, Konrad Adenauer Stiftung, pp 389–430

Gaparayi I (2004) The Milosevic trial at the halfway stage: judgement on the motion for acquittal. Leiden J Int Law 17:737–766

García Falconí RJ (2014) Los estándares probatorios utilizados por la Corte Penal Internacional al fijar las reparaciones en el caso Prosecutor v. Thomas Lubanga Dyilo. In: Ambos K, Malarino E, Steiner C (eds) Análisis de la primera sentencia de la Corte Penal Internacional: El Caso Lubanga. EDPAL, Konrad Adenauer Stiftung, pp 377–388

Gil Gandía C (2020) La reparación de las víctimas de crímenes internacionales y la Corte Penal Internacional. Tirant lo Blanch, Valencia

Glasius M (2009) What is global justice and who decides? Civil society and victim responses to the International Criminal Courts's first investigations. Hum Rights Q 31:496–520

Gómez Colomer JL (2015) Estatuto Jurídico de la Víctima. La posición jurídica de la víctima del delito ante la Justicia Penal. In: Un análisis basado en el Derecho Comparado y en la Ley

4/2015, de 27 de abril, del Estatuto de la Víctima del Delito en España, 2nd edn. Tirant lo Blanch, Valencia
Guerrero Palomares (2014) La defensa procesal de las víctimas ante la Corte Penal Internacional. Thomson Aranzadi, Navarra
Henzelin M, Heiskanen V, Mettraux G (2006) Reparations to Victims before the International Criminal Court: Lessons from International Mass Claims Processes. Crim Law Forum 17:317–344
Hoyle C, Ullrich L (2014) New Court, New Justice? The evolution of justice for victims at Domestic Courts and at the International Criminal Court. J Int Crim Justice 12:681–703
Keller LM (2007) Seeking justice at the International Criminal Court: victims' reparations. Thomas Jefferson Law Rev 29:189–217
Kelly S (2012) The role of victims in the International Criminal Court: challenges and opportunities. New Eng J Int Comp Law 18:243
Martínez Ventura (2014) Análisis del caso Lubanga, El procedimiento de reparaciones. In: Ambos K, Malarino E, Steiner C (eds) Análisis de la primera sentencia de la Corte Penal Internacional: El Caso Lubanga. EDPAL, Konrad Adenauer Stiftung, pp 343–375
McCarthy C (2012a) Victim redress and International Criminal Justice competing paradigms or compatible forms of justice? J Int Crim Justice 10:351–372
McCarthy C (2012b) Reparations and victim support in the International Criminal Court. Cambridge University Press, Cambridge
McGonigle Leyh B (2011) Procedural justice? Victim participation in international criminal proceedings. Intersentia
McKay F (2008) Victim participation in proceedings before the International Criminal Court. Hum Rights Brief 15(3):Article 1
Moffet L (2015a) Meaningful and effective? Considering victims' interests through participation at the International Criminal Court. Crim Law Forum 26:255–289
Moffet L (2015b) Elaborating justice for victims at the International Criminal Court, beyond Rhetoric and The Hague. J Int Crim Justice 13:281–311
Musila GM (2010) Rethinking International Criminal Law: restorative justice and the rights of victims in the International Criminal Court. LAP Lambert Academic Publishing
Ochoa JC (2013) The rights of victims in criminal justice proceedings for serious human rights violations. Martinus Nijhoff Publishers, ProQuest Ebook Central. https://ebookcentral.proquest.com/lib/univjau1/detail.action?docID=1124339
Pena M, Carayon G (2013) Is the ICC making the most of victim participation? Int J Transit Justice 7:518–535
Pérez-León-Acevedo JP (2019) Assessing victim participation during sentencing at the International Criminal Court. J Int Crim Justice 17:431–451
Perez-Leon-Acevedo JP (2019) Victims and reparations in International Criminal Justice: African initiatives. Nordic J Int Law 88(4):525–557
Pinheiro PS (2010) UNVAC world report on violence against children, p 3
Planchadell Gargallo A (2022) La víctima. In: Gómez Colomer JL, Barona Vilar S (eds) Proceso penal: Derecho procesal III. Tirant lo Blanch, Valencia, pp 119–136
Pues A (2015) A victim's right to a fair trial at the International Criminal Court? Reflections on Article 68 (3). J Int Crim Justice 13:951–972
Rauschenbach M, Scalia D (2008) Victims and international criminal justice: a vexed question? Int Rev Red Cross 90(870):441–459
Ruggieri S (2018) Equality of arms, impartiality of the judiciary and the role of the parties in the pre-trial inquiry: the perspective of Italian criminal justice. Revista Brasileira de Direito Processual Penal 4(2):559–603
SaCouto (2012) Victim participation at the International Criminal Court and the Extraordinary Chambers in the Court of Cambodia: a feminist project? Mich J Gend Law 18:297–359
Schabas W (2007) An introduction to the International Criminal Court, 3rd edn. Cambridge University Press

Schafferling C, Petrossian G (2021) Victims before the International Criminal Court, definition, participation, reparation. Springer
Schwöbel-Patel C (2018) The «ideal» victim of International Criminal Law. EJIL 29(3):703–724
Sehmi A (2018) «Now that we have no voice, what will happen to us?» Experiences of victim participation in the Kenyatta Case. J Int Crim Justice 16:571–591
Spiga V (2010) Indirect victims' participation in the Lubanga Trial. J Int Crim Justice 8:183–198
Spiga V (2013) No redress without justice, victims and International Criminal Law. J Int Crim Justice 10:1377–1394
Steinitz M (2005) The Milosevic trial live! An iconical analysis of International Law's Claim of Legitimate Authority. J Int Crim Justice 3:103–123
Stolk S (2015) The victim, the International Criminal Court and the search for truth on the interdependence and incompatibility of truths about mass atrocity. J Int Crim Justice 13:973–994
The Office of Public Counsel for Victims-ICC (2020) Representing victims before the International Criminal Court. A manual for legal representatives. 5th revised ed., p 26
Van den Wyngaert C (2012) Victims before International Criminal Courts: some views and concerns of an ICC trial judge. Case West Reserve J Int Law 44(1):476–496
Van Wijk J (2013) Who is the «little old lady» of international crimes? Nils Christie's concept of the ideal victim reinterpreted. Int Rev Victimol 19(2):159–179
Wemmers J (2009) Victims and the International Criminal Court (ICC): evaluating the success of the ICC with respect to victims. Int Rev Victimol 16:211–227
Wemmers J (2010) Victims' rights and the International Criminal Court: perceptions within the court regarding the victims' right to participate. Leiden J Int Law 23:629–643
Wiik A (2016) Amicus Curiae before International Courts and Tribunals. Nomos, Baden-Baden
Williams S, Woola H (2006) The role of the Amicus Curiae before International Criminal Tribunals and International Criminal Court. Int Crim Law Rev 6(2):151–189
Zago G (2014) The role of victims at the International Criminal Court: legal challenges from the tension between restorative and retributive justice. Dirit Penale Contemp:1–17
Zegveld L (2003) Remedies for victims of violations of international humanitarian law. IRRC 85(851):497–526
Zegveld L (2010) Victims's reparations claims and International Criminal Courts, incompatible values? J Int Crim Justice 8:79–111

Third Parties in Criminal Proceedings in the Jurisprudence of the Inter-American Court of Human Rights (IACtHR)

Frederico Valdez Pereira and Luís Felipe Schneider Kircher

Abstract The present study deals, in a broad perspective, with the issue of third parties in criminal proceedings, taking as a reference the precedents of the Inter-American Court of Human Rights that refer to third parties acting or interfering in criminal proceedings. The aim is, in particular, to present the Court's jurisprudential construction of the application of rights, focused on other characters in the criminal process than just the defendants, especially the victim and their families, witnesses, justice bodies and their assistants. To this end, initially, a brief explanation is presented about the functioning of the Inter-American Court and its peculiarities in relation to criminal proceedings. Then, starting from the observation of the relevance that the Inter-American Court gives to the protection of victims and their families in the criminal field, the study seeks to analyze the main themes involving third parties from the court's interpretative perspective. Finally, it is noteworthy that within each of the themes of analysis, the subjects that are covered by them are also mentioned.

1 Introduction

The multilevel protection of fundamental rights, implemented by the international affirmation of human rights, and, mostly, by the influx of the regional Courts of law,[1] gave rise to an important change of perspective in the understanding of the criminal justice system. The set of procedural guarantees and directives consolidated by the international system for the protection of human rights started to require that studies of the criminal procedure in general and of specific institutions and procedural

[1]Regarding the multi-level protection of rights, including integration of national and international plans: Tega (2011), p. 193. Broadly, see: Cardone (2011), pp. 335–422.

F. V. Pereira (✉)
University of Pavia, Pavia, Italy

L. F. S. Kircher
USP, Sao Paulo, SP, Brazil

S. Ruggeri et al. (eds.), *Third Parties in Criminal Proceedings*, Legal Studies in International, European and Comparative Criminal Law 10,
https://doi.org/10.1007/978-3-031-73970-5_9

categories be conducted considering the influences of conventional jurisprudence regarding criminal prosecution.

The constant action of the supranational courts of law evaluates, in detail, the effective implementation of the conventional postulates that condition the legitimacy of the state action in the exercise of the function of solving crimes. Certainly, it is not the objective of supranational human rights courts to investigate criminal acts or criminal responsibilities, which means that the Inter-American Court of Human Rights (IACtHR), object of this study, does not exercise criminal jurisdiction. However, the detailed analysis conducted by the Court on the observance of conventional criminal justice standards based on national criminal procedures makes it essential to know these lines of force centered on Inter-American jurisprudence.

In this context, this research focuses on the theme of third parties in criminal proceedings, having as a reference the precedents of the Inter-American Court of Human Rights that refer to third parties acting or interfering in criminal procedures. The Inter-American Court is the institutional interpreter of the American Convention on Human Rights; therefore, it is the jurisdictional body that guides the normative meaning of the conventional text. The States Parties are bound not only to cases judged by the Inter-American Court to which they have been a party, but they shall also observe the other precedents of the regional court, as true interpretative canons of national law. Thus, it can be said that there is an international obligation to interpret and apply the national legal system in a manner consistent with supranational law, which means to give normative value for the Inter-American exegesis.

Furthermore, with regard to criminal proceedings, the Court provides an expansive perspective of the application of rights, which is based on a sophisticated jurisprudential construction and focused on other characters and not only on the defendants themselves. These characters, in a broad sense, are the third parties in the criminal procedure, mainly the victims and their family members, the witnesses, the justice organs, and their assistants. Therefore, an analysis of the rights and guarantees predicted in the American Convention on Human Rights that are more directly related to these other actors in the criminal procedure is made. The main focus relies on the conformation given to these rights by the Inter-American Court which, with this, improves a conventional model of due process.[2]

The knowledge of the Court's interpretation of the rights and guarantees provided for in the American Convention on Human Rights is essential to know how these rights should operate in concrete reality (*in action*). This is because the formal prediction of an extensive list of rights (*in the books*) is meaningless if there is no real-world effectiveness.[3]

[2]The Court, for a long time, has defined standards that shall be complied with in order to have a due process, as in: IACtHR, *Loayza Tamayo v. Perú*, judgment of 17 September 1997, para. 62.

[3]Among the various judgments of the Inter-American Court, see: IACtHR, *Castillo Páez v. Perú*, judgment of 3 November 1997, para. 86; IACtHR, *Blake v. Guatemala*, judgment of 24 January, para 102; IACtHR, *Ximenes Lopes v. Brasil*, judgment of 4 July 2006, para. 192.

It is important to make an initial clarification about the methodological option adopted in this study. Instead of dividing the text into items related to each of the distinct subjects, that is, to each of the categories of third parties in criminal proceedings, it was preferred to separate the topics according to the major themes in which they are inserted. The preference for structuring the text based on themes, and not on subjects, results from the fact that many of them are concurrently applied to more than one subject (victims and family members, for example). Therefore, there would be unnecessary repetition in the text if a more traditional approach were used (making a separation by the kinds of third parties in the proceedings).

Also, as an introductory clarification, it is worth mentioning that the concept of third parties in criminal proceedings has a clear variation from system to system, and even at the national level. The very notion of victims, properly speaking, would not fit into a strict notion of «third parties». For this reason, it can even be admitted that the present investigation slightly expands what would be a specific approach to the topic.

It is understood, however, that in a broad sense, the topic of victims and family members in criminal prosecution deserves to be approached in an investigation into the evolution of Inter-American jurisprudence on the topic of the protection of third parties in criminal proceedings. This would already be justified by the observation of the relevance that the Inter-American Court confers upon the protection of victims and their families in the criminal area.

Thus, after a brief explanation of the functioning of the Inter-American Court and its peculiarities in relation to criminal proceedings, the main issues involving third parties are analyzed from the court's interpretative perspective. The subjects covered by each of the themes are also mentioned.

2 The Inter-American Court and the General Aspects of Criminal Procedure

The American Convention on Human Rights (ACHR), also known as the Pact of San José, signed in 1969, is the treaty or multilateral convention governing the protection of human rights at the American regional level, capable of creating obligations at the international level. The ACHR only entered into force internationally on July 18, 1978, after 11 ratifications. To date, it has been ratified by 25 of the 35 member states of the Organization of American States (OAS). The main bodies of the ACHR to effectively protect and monitor rights are the Inter-American Commission on Human Rights (IACHR) and the Inter-American Court of Human Rights (IACtHR).

The Inter-American Commission on Human Rights was originally an organ of the OAS, created in 1959 to promote and protect human rights. It also became an organ of the ACHR, regulated in Chap. VII, with functions established in Article 41, including making recommendations, conducting on-site inspections, and requesting information from States Parties. The right to petition by individuals or groups of persons is exercised before the IACHR, which is entitled to submit cases to the Inter-American Court, when the proposals or recommendations of the defendant State are not complied with.[4]

The Inter-American Court[5] is the jurisdictional body of the ACHR with advisory and litigation competence in relation to allegations of violation of the rights provided for in the Convention, having litigious action only in relation to States that have recognized their international jurisdiction. This way, its decisions are both mandatory and binding on the State Party, with *res judicata* authority. In addition, its final decisions bear the peculiar authority of a matter judged, revealing the official and binding exegesis rendered by the Court regarding the content and scope of the rights and guarantees instigated by the inter-American system.[6] According to the Inter-American Court, all national law, including the Constitution and constitutional interpretation, shall consider the ACHR, as interpreted by inter-American judges.[7]

States shall make their domestic legal order compatible with the directives of the «block of conventionality», which includes the decisions of the Court. According to the Inter-American Court, the American system for the protection of rights makes the domestic actions of the signatory countries of the ACHR submit to conventionality control before the Court.[8] It is a duty to comply with national legislation and all domestic emanations that may affect guaranteed rights.

Thus, conventionality control acts on abstract norms and on acts and procedures carried out at the national level, including criminal procedures for the determination of responsibilities. Suffice it to say that the Inter-American Court has been considered essentially an international Court in criminal matters, with more than 80% of its cases referring to criminal justice.[9] Regarding criminal proceedings, the San José court examines whether the administrative and judicial procedures actually carried out complied with conventional directives, considering the process in its entirety. It does not act as a criminal court, as it does not analyze criminal culpability, but rather the State's internal role in conducting the procedure.

The right to due criminal process, as stated, although not expressed in the ACHR, is constantly indicated by the Inter-American Court, based on the broad reading given to Article 8 of the ACHR, which results in a true expansion of the directives regarding procedural justice. The Court's judgments are directly binding on the parties of the dispute, and indirectly on all the States Parties, as this is an «interpreted

---

[4]Ramos (2020), pp. 437–438.

[5]Statute approved by resolution AG/RES. 448 (IX-O/79), adopted by the OAS General Assembly at its Ninth Regular Session, held in La Paz, Bolivia, October 1979.

[6]In this sense, Ramos (2002), p. 241.

[7]Carducci and Mazzuoli (2014), pp. 82 ff., 126 ff.

[8]IACtHR, *Almonacid Arellano and others v. Chile*, judgment of 26 September 2006, para. 124; Benavente Chorres (2012); Piovesan (2013), pp. 115–145; Giacomolli (2016), p. 29 ff.

[9]Ferrer Mac-Gregor (2014), p. 29; García Pino (2016), p. 112.

conventional norm».[10] The peculiarities of the source jurisprudence[11] and the requirement of interpretation in accordance with conventional law, which bind all organs of the national criminal justice administration, reinforce the importance of knowing, in more detail, the evolution of the jurisprudence of the Inter-American Court when studying the matter of third parties and victims in criminal proceedings.

3 Effectiveness of the Criminal System as a Guarantee for Victims and Their Family Members

The safeguarding of fundamental rights in the criminal justice system entails an influence in two directions, which are not exactly harmonious. On the one hand, it sets limits to the performance of criminal prosecution, which should observe individual defense rights and guarantees. They would be, therefore, «*impositions of guardianship in criminal procedure*», conditioning the course of the procedure to the observance of these individual guarantees. On the other hand, fundamental rights are understood as an indispensable object of penal protection, which, under the strictly procedural aspect,[12] generate «*impositions of guardianship by criminal procedure*», through the criminal system.[13]

It is on this second aspect, of the defense of fundamental rights by the criminal justice system, that the inter-American judicial area establishes the obligation of States parties to have an efficient criminal prosecution mechanism to elucidate violations of fundamental rights and prosecute and sanction those responsible for the offenses. The supranational affirmation of the state's duty to promote the investigation and criminal proceedings in an effective and serious manner, capable of elucidating the crimes, entails the recognition of procedural rights for victims and their families.

The process of reception, or rediscovery of the victim in criminal justice, which to a greater or lesser extent, has been observed throughout the West since the 1980s,[14] has the San José Court judgments as its most fruitful catalyst in the inter-American legal space. It is important to highlight that the concern of these judgments is not only related to the consequences of the penal solution on the claim for civil damages. The effective performance of criminal prosecution is conceived by inter-American jurisprudence also as an instrument of justice; therefore, it is related to the interest of the victims and their families in effective criminal protection.

[10] Ferrer Mac-Gregor (2013), pp. 633 ff. and 639 ff.

[11] Sagüés (2010), p. 125, which explains that the court adds something to the initial formal content of the treaties, even if these have not been changed.

[12] On the material aspect of penal protection, Andrade (2019), *passim*.

[13] Fischer and Pereira (2023), *passim*.

[14] Gialuz (2016), p. 19.

The fundamental basis for recognizing this right for victims, based on the existence of an effective criminal investigation and procedure, suitable for elucidating the facts and punishing the aggressors, are the legal goods protected by the inter-American system.[15] The Court states that the requirement to investigate a violation of a substantive right «can be a means to protect, secure and guarantee this right»,[16] insisting that anyone who considers themselves a victim of violations can access justice so that «this duty of the State be fulfilled, for their benefit and of society as a whole».[17] The necessary criminal response to the most serious attacks on legal goods depends on the quality of the criminal mechanism for investigating the offenses.

Important reasons are also mentioned, such as the demand for effective, and not merely symbolic state action,[18] and the deterrent importance of the criminal justice system, in order to avoid a context of impunity, which would encourage the repetition of aggressions.[19] There are also few argumentative references, indirectly related to the criminal defense of victims and family members, such as the fact that the absence of a serious and complete investigation would translate into a form of assistance from the public authorities to the aggressor, to which is added the possibility of international accountability of the State.[20]

Since the first contentious judgments, the Inter-American Court has established that the obligation imposed on States Parties to respect recognized rights and guarantee their full exercise entails an equally generic duty to organize all state

[15] The broad clause of Article 1 of the ACHR, which imposes on States the duty to respect the rights affirmed in the Convention, is the general foundation of the requirements for the protection of victims through criminal proceedings, cf., e.g., IACtHR, *Velásquez Rodríguez v. Honduras*, judgment of 29 July 1988, para. 166. This provision is normally complemented by the clause for the protection of the specific violated right, cf. IACtHR, *Baldeón García v. Peru (Fondo, Reparaciones y Costas)*, judgement of 6 April 2006, série C, No. 147, paras. 77 ff. On many occasions, the Inter-American Court has used Articles 2, 8 and 25 as a foundation for the victims' right to criminal justice, cf., for example., IACtHR, *Garibaldi v. Brasil*, judgment of 23 September 2009, para. 120; IACtHR, *Bámaca Velásquez v. Guatemala*, judgment of 25 November 2000, paras. 189 ff.

[16] IACtHR, *Villaseñor Velarde and others v. Guatemala*, judgment of 28 January 2019, para. 110; IACtHR, *Perozo and others v. Venezuela*, judgment of 28 January 2009, para. 298. There were situations in which the Court recognized that the serious and effective investigation of threats could have contributed to preventing the continuation of the threats and the concrete violation of rights, cf. IACtHR, *Vélez Restrepo y familiares v. Colombia*, judgment of 3 September 2012, paras. 187, 192.

[17] IACtHR, *Villaseñor Velarde and others*, para. 110; IACtHR, *Case of Caracazo v. Venezuela*, judgment of 29 August 2002, para 115.

[18] The Inter-American Court, in general, makes use of the following notion: "this duty (to investigate) must be assumed by the State as a legal duty of its own, and not as a simple formality condemned in advance to be fruitless", cf. IACtHR, *Escher and others v. Brasil*, judgment of 6 July 2009, para. 195.

[19] In these terms, e.g., IACtHR, *Loayza Tamayo v. Perù*, judgment of 27 November 1998, para. 170; IACtHR, *Case de la "Panel Blanca" (Paniagua Morales and others) v. Guatemala*, judgment of 8 August 1998, para. 173.

[20] IACtHR, *Gómez Virula and others v. Guatemala*, judgment of 21 November 2019, para. 65; IACtHR, *Kawas Fernández v. Honduras*, judgment of 03 April 2009, para. 78.

structures so as to ensure the full exercise of human rights. Based on this understanding, in the *Velásquez Rodríguez* case, the notion that the States should not only prevent attacks on rights, but also investigate and sanction any violation of conventional rights, was introduced. They should also aim to reestablish the violated right and repair the resulting damages.[21]

4 The Reception of the Victims and Their Relatives in The Criminal Legal System: From International Legal Duty to Subjective Right in Criminal Procedures

The original perspective of the Court of San José was eminently focused on the legal duties assigned to States Parties, especially regarding the fulfillment of these international duties. The reference provisions in the analysis were Articles 1(1) and 2 of the ACHR.

The Inter-American Court has always recognized the legal duty of national public authorities to seriously investigate violations of rights, so as to identify those responsible for them, applying the respective sanctions and guaranteeing the victims adequate reparation.[22] It was clarified that this is a legal duty of its own, which should be enforced *ex officio* and cannot depend upon the actions of the victims or their family members,[23] as it is shown in detail below.

The approach of the Inter-American Court to assess compliance with the international obligations of States Parties has continued to evolve in supranational jurisprudence over the years, always referring to the opening Articles of the Convention, which list the generic duties of the signatory countries.[24] What needs to be emphasized is that there was a considerable complement in the basis of the inter-American judgments, especially when it comes to the recognition of the rights and interests of victims and their families in the criminal justice system.

The Court began to examine the actions of the States regarding criminal prosecution based on Articles 8 and 25 of the American Convention, which provide, respectively, judicial guarantees and the right of access to justice, analyzed, in this perspective, by the interests of victims and family members. In other words, the judges of San José went on to assert that States Parties are obliged to provide

[21] IACtHR, *Case Velásquez Rodríguez v. Honduras*, para. 166.

[22] IACtHR, *Case Velásquez Rodríguez v. Honduras*, para. 174.

[23] IACtHR, *Mendoza and others v. Argentina*, judgment of 15 May 2013, para. 235; IACtHR, *Case del Penal Miguel Castro Castro v. Perú*, judgment of 25 November 2006, para. 400; IACtHR, *Godínez Cruz v. Honduras*, judgment of 20 January 1989, para. 188.

[24] Cf. among many, IACtHR, *García Prieto and other v. El Salvador*, judgment of 20 November 2007, paras. 98–9; IACtHR, *Rodríguez Vera and others (Desaparecidos del Palacio de Justicia) v. Colombia*, judgment of 14 November 2014, para. 459;

effective judicial remedies to victims of human rights violations, making it clear that this apparatus shall comply with the rules of due process.[25]

State activity carried out in national criminal proceedings shall comply with the rights and guarantees of victims and their families recognized in Articles 8(1) and 25 of the American Convention.[26] The judges of San José also point out that the obligation to investigate and the corresponding right of victims and family members also derives from national legislation that provides for the state's duty to investigate *ex officio* certain unlawful conduct.[27] This examination of conventional compliance to which internal procedures are submitted is promoted by the Inter-American Court mainly from two basic perspectives: respect for the principle of reasonable duration of proceedings and the effectiveness of the processes.[28]

5 The Guarantee of the Reasonable Duration of Proceedings (Article 8.1 of the ACHR): Beyond the Individual Perspective of Defense

The American Convention on Human Rights included the express provision of a guarantee of «reasonable duration of proceedings» [Art. 8(1) ACHR]. This prescription appears in the list of judicial guarantees addressed to all the people in a generic way, in a broader sense, with no specific implementation in the normative-textual prism.

It is known that the issue of the slowness of justice is not new and has a significant impact on the legitimacy of the authority of the Judiciary in a democratic society, appearing as one of the most serious problems in the criminal system.[29] Therefore, an effort to effectively implement this human right is necessary and it is imperative to know its conceptual and structural bases.

[25] IACtHR, *Las Palmeras v. Colombia*, judgment of 6 December 2001, para. 60; IACtHR, *Baldeón García v. Perú*, para. 143; IACtHR, *Ximenes Lopes v. Brasil*, judgment of 4 July 2006, para. 175; IACtHR, *Goiburú and others v. Paraguay*, judgment of 22 September 2006, para. 110.

[26] It is common for the jurisprudence of the Inter-American Court to support the affirmation of the duty of States Parties to guarantee effective judicial remedies to victims of violations of rights, combining Articles 25, 8(1) and 1(1) ACHR, cf., for ex., IACtHR, *Guzmán Albarracín and others v. Ecuador*, judgment of 24 June 2020, para. 176; IACtHR, *Suárez Peralta v. Ecuador*, judgment of 21 May 2013, para. 92; IACtHR, *Case del Penal Miguel Castro Castro v. Perú*, para. 381.

[27] IACtHR, *Guzmán Albarracín and others v. Ecuador*, para. 178; IACtHR, *García Prieto and other v. El Salvador*, para. 104.

[28] These are the words of the Inter-American Court in the case *19 Comerciantes v. Colombia*, judgment of 5 July 2014, para. 180: "*Con respecto a los procesos penales de la jurisdicción ordinaria, el Tribunal analizará la alegada violación a los artículos 8.1 y 25 desde dos perspectivas: el respeto al principio del plazo razonable y la efectividad de los procesos*".

[29] Pastor (2002), pp. 49–52.

In a first approximation, it can be seen, by the indication of the Inter-American Court itself, that this guarantee of reasonable term is closely linked with the right to the possibility of access to justice and with the requirement of a judicially efficient and adequate response on the part of the States.[30] The definitive response of the Judiciary, especially in the area of criminal proceedings, loses much of its usefulness and interest if it comes long after the occurrence of the fact or the activation of the jurisdiction.

Furthermore, the Court clearly points out that the guarantee of a reasonable duration of the process falls within the scope of the judicial process (properly said or *stricto sensu*) and, also, in the area of the investigation. Thus, all criminal prosecution (*lato sensu*) should respect reasonableness in terms of temporal duration.[31]

It is worth considering that the time of the criminal procedure and investigation is impacted by several factors, ranging from the structure of administrative and jurisdictional bodies and institutions that act before the administration of justice to the appeal rules in each country. Therefore, it is essential to know what a proceeding without undue or unjustified delays means, so that it is possible to analyze *in concreto* the respect or not to the guarantee under analysis.

That is the reason why it is essential to analyze the interpretation given to this guarantee by the Court of San José in the development of its doctrine on the content and scope of the guarantee clause of the «reasonable duration» in the context of criminal proceedings. In this framework, it can be seen that there is, as stated, a dual perspective of application.[32] On the one hand, the guarantee is directed to the accused in general (the defendants and the investigated subjects) and, on the other, to the victims of crimes (violations of human rights) and their family members.

Regarding the first aspect, the Inter-American Court demonstrates a strong concern for the duration of the process in relation to the accused in general. In particular, this concern is more considerable in relation to prisoners, which is a result of the ACHR itself, which contains a specific provision stating that the detained person shall be taken personally before a judge «without delay» [Article 7(5) of the ACHR].

In this regard, the Court reiterates in several judgments the need to avoid excessive preventive detentions in temporal terms (since they are precautionary and non-punitive measures) and, also, the mandatory existence of a quick and expeditious judicial remedy so that the situation of possible violation of rights is lightly scrutinized (by someone holding jurisdictional functions). It is, in the words

[30] IACtHR, *Gutiérrez Hernández and others v. Guatemala*, judgment of 24 August 2017, para. 147.

[31] Exemplifyingly: IACtHR, *Ortiz Hernández and others v. Venezuela*, judgment of 22 August 2017, paras. 143 and 145.

[32] Aspect also pointed out by Pastor (2002), p. 53.

of the Court, a prerequisite for guaranteeing the right to liberty and physical integrity of the detained person.[33]

These are measures aimed at alleviating or preventing the arbitrariness and illegality of arrests decreed by the State. As it seems evident, these are safeguards aimed at the incarcerated individual from a singular perspective, resulting from the aggravated situation of vulnerability of illegally detained individuals[34] and which serves to enable the guarantee of their most elementary individual rights.

More than that, there is concern about the reasonable duration of the proceeding and investigation in relation to the investigated/accused subjects, given the need to have a jurisdictional response. This is because, as it is well known, the very existence of criminal proceedings or a criminal investigation already affects the *dignitatis status* of the human person.[35]

With regard to the second aspect, the central object of this research, the Court considers that the unreasonable delay in the process or in the investigation may constitute a flagrant denial of justice, in addition to a violation of the victims' and their families' right of access to justice.[36] It is an impairment to the purpose of protecting essential legal goods when this is recognized by national law as socially relevant.

The Court considers the lack of an expeditious response in cases of serious human violations to human rights (e.g., torture) as a real impairment of the victim's right to due judicial protection. And this right includes not only the victim's access to the criminal proceeding as such, but also the right to obtain a definitive ruling through effective legal mechanisms.[37]

Complementarily, the Court states that the right of access to justice does not end with the formal processing of the internal proceeding, but it shall also ensure, within a reasonable term, the right of the alleged victim or their family members to know the (historical) truth about what happened and to know that those responsible for the violation can be prosecuted and punished.[38]

In this regard, the judgments of the Inter-American Court even state that breaching the guarantee of investigation within a reasonable duration can have severe consequences for third parties, such as family disintegration, insecurity, frustration, anguish, and impotence. This understanding is often reiterated particularly in cases involving enforced disappearances.[39]

---

[33] IACtHR, *Tibi v. Ecuador*, judgment of 07 September 2004, paras. 118–120; IACtHR, *Acosta Calderón v. Ecuador*, judgment of 24 May 2005, paras. 75–76.

[34] IACtHR, *Tibi v. Ecuador*, para. 147.

[35] In this sense: IACtHR, *Tarazona Arrieta and others v. Perú*, judgment of 15 October 2014, paras. 98–100.

[36] IACtHR, *Veliz Franco and others v. Guatemala*, judgment of 19 May 2014, para. 219.

[37] IACtHR, *Bayarri v. Argentina*, judgment of 30 October 2008, para. 117.

[38] IACtHR, *las Hermanas Serrano Cruz v. El Salvador*, judgment of 01 March 2003, para. 66.

[39] IACtHR, *las Hermanas Serrano Cruz v. El Salvador*, para. 112.

Furthermore, in order to carry out a concrete analysis of the observance of the reasonable duration of criminal prosecution, whether in the context of the investigation or the proceeding, the Court traditionally took into account the following elements: *a)* the complexity of the matter, *b)* the procedural activity of the interested party, and *c)* the conduct of judicial authorities.[40] Therefore, it is necessary to analyze how each of these criteria are interpreted and operated in the jurisprudential practice of the Court.

Regarding the complexity of the matter, the Court considers several aspects in this assessment, including the evidential difficulty, the plurality of procedural disciplines, the number of victims, the time lapse since the violation, the appeal provision in national legislation, and the context in which the violation itself occurred.[41] Likewise, if the case involves technical aspects of the investigation, this can be considered in terms of complexity (for example, an investigation conducted within the scope of the air forces and the army[42] or that involves medical aspects and depends on expert evidence).[43]

In 2014, the Court, following the guidelines previously indicated by the European Court of Human Rights, stated, in a more objective and concise way, that the complexity of the case should be examined considering three criteria: *1)* the large number of defendants; *2)* the complex political and social context; and *3)* the difficulties in obtaining evidence.[44] As a result, in later cases, the Inter-American Court returned to the previously mentioned traditional and more detailed list as a reference.[45]

With regard to the procedural activity of the parties, the reasonableness of the interventions carried out by the intervening subjects in the proceeding is evaluated. More specifically, it shall be analyzed the extent to which the behavior of the parties had an impact on the extension of the development of the case, whether by action or omission, and what the justification for this is.[46]

In this regard, the Inter-American Court makes it clear that the State cannot justify its investigative inaction on the grounds that the actions of the victims or of their family members were insufficient. The basic idea supported by the Court is that it is up to the State bodies to direct the investigation and promote it *ex officio* in accordance with the strategies or lines determined by them to clarify the facts. In

---

[40] Exemplifyingly: IACtHR, *Genie Lacayo v. Nicaragua*, judgment of 29 January 1997, para. 77; IACtHR, *Suárez Rosero v. Ecuador*, judgment of 12 November 1997, para. 72; IACtHR, *Case Ximenes Lopes v. Brasil*, para. 196; IACtHR, *Escué Zapata v. Colombia*, judgment of 04 July 2007, para. 102; IACtHR, *Case de la "Masacre de Mapiripán" v. Colombia*, judgment of 15 September 2005, para. 217.

[41] IACtHR, *Furlan y familiares v. Argentina*, judgment of 31 August 2012, para. 156.

[42] IACtHR, *Masacre de Santo Domingo v. Colombia*, judgment of 30 November 2012, para. 165.

[43] IACtHR, *Suárez Peralta v. Ecuador*, judgment of 21 May 2013, para. 100.

[44] IACtHR, *Argüelles and others v. Argentina*, judgment of 20 November 2014, para. 190.

[45] For example: IACtHR, *Yarce and others v. Colombia*, judgment of 22 November 2006, para. 289; IACtHR, *Wong Ho Wing v. Perú*, judgment of 30 June 2015, para. 210.

[46] IACtHR, *Cantos v. Argentina*, judgment of 28 November 2002, para. 57.

any case, the investigation shall be initiated *ex officio*. It is not the responsibility of the victims or their families to take on such investigative initiatives and impulses.[47]

In fact, the Court points out that during the investigation procedure and the judicial proceeding, victims of human rights violations, or their families, as it is to be seen in detail, shall have ample opportunity to participate and be heard. They shall be able to assist in the search for clarification of the facts and punishment of those responsible, as well as in the search for fair compensation. However, the imposition of an effective search for the broad investigation of the facts corresponds to the State, and it does not depend on the procedural initiative of the victims or their family members, nor even on their evidential contributions.[48]

Regarding this point, the Inter-American Court stresses that the judicial conduction of criminal proceedings by the judge shall be oriented to avoid undue delays and suspensions. Both the effectiveness of jurisdictional protection and the due judicial protection of human rights depend on a proceeding with adequate processing, under penalty of generating impunity.[49]

With regard to the third element of this analysis, the conduct of judicial authorities, the assessment is similar to the above mentioned, but aimed especially at the judging or investigating body. It shall be verified whether the action of the judicial authority or the investigative authority was diligent and swift, or if it suffered from any undue inaction, that is, some inactivity without reasonable explanation (such as in cases of delay in requesting a diligence or to drive the proceeding or investigation).[50]

From 2008 onwards,[51] the Court incorporates one more requirement to conduct the analysis of the reasonableness of the duration of the proceeding. Inter-American judges began to consider the impact of the duration of the procedure on the legal status of the person involved. Among other elements, the subject matter of controversy (criminal or non-criminal) is considered. Therefore, if the passage of time has a relevant impact on the individual's legal situation (detained or released[52] defendant, for example), it will be necessary for the procedure to be carried out more promptly so that the case can be resolved in less time.

[47] IACtHR, *Veliz Franco and others v. Guatemala*, judgment of 19 May 2014, para. 221.

[48] IACtHR, *Masacre de Mapiripán v. Colombia*, para. 219; IACtHR, *Masacres de Ituango v. Colombia*, judgment of 01 July 2006, para. 296.

[49] IACtHR, *Bayarri v. Argentina*, judgment of 30 October 2008, para. 116.

[50] IACtHR, *las Hermanas Serrano Cruz v. El Salvador*, para. 71; IACtHR, *Gonzales Lluy and others v. Ecuador*, judgment of 01 September 2015, paras. 307–308.

[51] IACtHR, *Valle Jaramillo and others v. Colombia*, judgment of 27 November 2008, para. 155. Later, several others, such as: IACtHR, *Case Anzualdo Castro v. Perú*, judgment of 22 September 2009, para. 156. Judge Sérgio Ramirez had already mentioned this criterion previously in his votes, as in: IACtHR, *López Álvarez v. Honduras*, judgment of 01 February 2006, para. 36 (reasoned vote).

[52] Addressing the individual perspective of imprisoned defendants: IACtHR, *Argüelles and others v. Argentina*, judgment of 20 November 2014, para. 196.

There are also practical applications of this requirement. The examples taken from the jurisprudence of the Inter-American Court are varied in relation to victims. One can illustratively mention the case in which the criminal judgment may condition the civil reparation claimed by the victim's family members[53] or by the victims of serious human rights violations themselves (such as those in slavery conditions).[54] Still, it is pointed out that an excessive delay in the investigation of a homicide (14 years, for example) brings serious harm to the victim's family members who are in a state of vulnerability and have their right to the truth subtracted from them.[55]

Based on the establishment of these criteria for analyzing the «reasonableness of the term» of a proceeding or investigation, the Court makes it clear that the verification shall be carried out in light of the circumstances of the specific case.[56] It is important to note that, in this assessment of procedural terms, State justifications related to financial or technical deficiencies[57] or even to the implicit complexity of the facts shall not be deemed important.[58]

Furthermore, it is important to note that the analysis of the reasonableness of the deadline for processing the criminal prosecution shall be carried out taking into account the entire course of the procedure (until its final decision).[59] Thus, the examination shall be done globally, that is, scrutinizing the total duration of the case in the internal jurisdiction of the State.[60]

The Court considers that a prolonged delay is, in principle, in itself, a violation of judicial guarantees. There are concrete examples of elapsed time, in which the Court has ruled that 10 years of a criminal proceeding,[61] as well as an investigation that lasts for 15[62] or 17 years,[63] is unreasonable.

Another important consideration in the Court's assessment of the guarantee of reasonable duration is that the State is responsible for explaining and proving the reasons why it took longer than reasonable to reach the final judgment in the particular case, always taking into account the criteria indicated by the Court,

---

[53] IACtHR, *Ximenes Lopes v. Brasil*, paras. 203–204; IACtHR, *Gonzales Lluy and others v. Ecuador*, judgment of 01 September 2015, paras. 310–311.

[54] IACtHR, *Case Trabajadores de la Hacienda Brasil Verde v. Brasil*, judgment of 20 October 2016, para. 381.

[55] IACtHR, *Kawas Fernández v. Honduras*, judgment of 03 April 2009, paras. 115–116.

[56] Among others: IACtHR, *Masacre de Mapiripán v. Colombia*, para. 218; IACtHR, *Case de la Masacre de Pueblo Bello v. Colombia*, judgment of 31 january 2006, para. 171.

[57] IACtHR, *Masacre de Mapiripán v. Colombia*, para. 221.

[58] IACtHR, *Masacres de Ituango v. Colombia*, judgment of 01 July 2006, para. 294. In this case, the State argued, unsuccessfully, that the delay in investigations was due to the complexity of an implicit "Macrocrime" scenario.

[59] IACtHR, *Ticona Estrada and others v. Bolivia*, judgment of 27 November 2008, para. 79.

[60] IACtHR, *Genie Lacayo v. Nicaragua*, judgment of 29 January 1997, para. 64.

[61] IACtHR, *Bayarri v. Argentina*, judgment of 30 October 2008, para. 106.

[62] IACtHR, *Anzualdo Castro v. Perú*, judgment of 22 September 2009, para. 156.

[63] IACtHR, *Radilla Pacheco v. México*, judgment of 23 November 2009, para. 245.

which are summarized above.[64] There are several situations in which the Court considered that there was a delay in the procedural process without a reasoned explanation and, therefore, it considered that Article 8(1) of the American Convention had been violated.[65]

Inter-American jurisprudence also clarifies that it is the obligation of States Parties, at the legislative level, to regulate expedited procedures that enable the celerity of the judicial response, avoiding unreasonable delays in the definitive conclusion of criminal proceedings in the domestic sphere.[66] Thus, the internal normative design shall be provided to allow the fulfillment of the guarantee of the reasonable duration of the proceeding.

Therefore, it is clear that the Court has a central concern for ensuring a reasonable duration, which is present in most of its decisions. As seen above, this is an individual *prima facie* right, but it also has strong application in relation to third parties in criminal proceedings, especially from the perspective of the victim and their families.

6 State Duty to Investigate, Prosecute and, if Applicable, Punish (Effectiveness)

Regarding the effectiveness of the criminal justice system in the specific case, the Court of San José examines the national criminal procedures carried out by the public authorities in order to elucidate the facts and identify those responsible for them. In a broad sense, the Inter-American Court checks whether an effective remedy has been offered to ensure the rights of access to justice, knowledge of the truth of the facts and reparation for victims and their families.[67]

The consideration that the formal existence of internal resources is not enough is important for this reasoning. Although it is an obligation of means, and not of result, the criminal investigation shall be effective. Procedures «shall be capable of producing results or responses to violations» of fundamental rights.[68] The lack of state response is already a determining factor to assess the disrespect to the imposition

[64] IACtHR, *Hilaire, Constantine y Benjamin and others v. Trinidad y Tobago (Fondo, Reparaciones y Costas)*, judgment of 21 June 2002, serie C, No. 94, para. 145; IACtHR, *Anzualdo Castro v. Perú*, para. 156; IACtHR, *Favela Nova Brasília v. Brasil*, judgment of 16 February 2017, para. 218.

[65] IACtHR, *Bayarri v. Argentina*, judgment of 30 Octobre 2008, para. 107; IACtHR, *las Hermanas Serrano Cruz v. El Salvador*, para. 69–71; IACtHR, *Hilaire, Constantine y Benjamin and others v. Trinidad y Tobago*, para. 145.

[66] IACtHR, *Reverón Trujillo v. Venezuela*, judgment of 30 June 2009, para. 74.

[67] IACtHR, *Baldeón García v. Perú*, para. 139; IACtHR, *Masacres de Ituango v. Colombia*, judgment of 01 July 2006, para. 321.

[68] IACtHR, *Baldeón García v. Perú*, para. 144.

extracted from Articles 8(1) and 25(1) of the ACHR, concerning the effectiveness of the criminal investigation.[69]

This analysis is also driven by the subjective aspect of the rights of victims and their families. The supranational courts started to recognize a subjective right for the act violating rights to be effectively investigated by the State authorities, for a proceeding to be initiated against those responsible for the crimes, for the sanctions provided for in the legislation to be imposed and for the damage caused to be repaired.[70]

The state's duty to investigate, prosecute and, if applicable, punish crimes has as a counter-face, or necessary complement, the right of victims and family members to effectiveness in the administration of criminal justice. In numerous judgments, the Inter-American Court has stated that the victims and their family have the right to know what happened and who was responsible for the unlawful acts.[71] The affirmation of a right to the effectiveness of criminal justice, a right held by victims and relatives of serious crimes, is very explicit in the judgments. As a corollary of the right to effective criminal investigation, the State shall effectively conduct criminal proceedings.[72]

The greatest importance of this finding, in the expanded consideration that is being made to third parties in criminal proceedings, is that it allows us to identify the incorporation of the interests of victims and their families in the criminal process.[73] In other words, victims and family members are guaranteed the right to due process.[74]

It is emphasized that there is a recognition, in numerous judgments of the Inter-American Court, that the criminal procedure owes something to victims and family members, and not only in the civil reparatory aspect, assisting or shortening the search for compensation for damages resulting from the crime. Fair civil compensation for injuries is an element that is highlighted in the Court's appreciation,[75] but

[69] IACtHR, *García Prieto and other v. El Salvador*, judgment of 20 November 2007, para. 115; IACtHR, *Heliodoro Portugal v. Panamá*, judgment of 12 August 2008, para. 157. The affirmation of the principle of "effective judicial protection" in the criminal area is, for example, in: IACtHR, *Luna López v. Honduras*, para. 170; IACtHR, *Poblete Vilches and others v. Chile*, judgment of 08 March 2018, para. 184.

[70] IACtHR, *García Prieto and other v. El Salvador*, judgment of 20 Novembre 2007, para. 103; IACtHR, *Case del Penal Miguel Castro Castro v. Perú*, para. 393

[71] IACtHR, *García Prieto and other v. El Salvador*, para. 102.

[72] IACtHR, *Escué Zapata v. Colombia*, judgment of 04 July 2007, para. 166.

[73] According to Gozaíni (2019), p. 98, the recognition of victims is important because it is a way of acknowledging the value of people as individuals, victims, and holders of rights.

[74] IACtHR, *V.R.P., V.P.C. and others v. Nicaragua*, judgment of 08 March 2018, para. 218; IACtHR, *González Medina y familiares v. República Dominicana*, judgment of 27 February 2012, para. 207.

[75] IACtHR, *Suárez Peralta v. Ecuador*, para. 105; IACtHR, *García Lucero and others v. Chile*, judgment of 28 August 2013, para. 183.

the idea of reparation is expanded to encompass reparation for the performance of criminal justice.

The penal mechanism shall be organized to conduct a thorough, impartial, and effective investigation. Impositions of effectiveness and diligence in the criminal investigation that also extend to the judicial phase[76] until the final conclusion of the criminal proceedings.[77] In this respect, it is a strictly State commitment to criminal justice, which conditions the legitimacy of criminal proceedings and grants victims and family members a right to effective criminal justice.

The right of victims and family members to know the truth of what happened[78] is included in the prolific affirmation in the Inter-American Court judgments of the right to the effectiveness of the criminal investigation, which depends on the proper clarification of the facts and on the identification and sanction of those responsible for them. There are countless judgments that include in the legal argument the importance of the «efficient determination of the truth»,[79] or that the serious, impartial, and effective investigation shall be oriented to the determination of the truth.[80] In addition to being an obligation of States derived from the guarantees of justice, the right to the truth also constitutes a form of reparation in cases of violations of fundamental rights.[81]

[76] IACtHR, *Case V.R.P., V.P.C. and others v. Nicaragua*, para. 281; IACtHR, *Suárez Peralta v. Ecuador*, para. 93; IACtHR, *Gutiérrez y familia v. Argentina*, judgment of 25 November 2013, para. 99; IACtHR, *García Prieto and other v. El Salvador*, para. 103;

[77] According to the Inter-American Court, it is an imposition that goes to the criminal execution phase: "*La obligación de investigar abarca la investigación, identificación, procesamiento, juicio y, en su caso, la sanción de los responsables. Aún cuando es una obligación de medio, ello no significa que no abarque el cumplimiento de la eventual sentencia, en los términos en que sea decretada*"; IACtHR, *Caso Rodríguez Vera and others (Desaparecidos del Palacio de Justicia) v. Colombia*, para. 460.

[78] On the search for truth in the Court's approach, see Ferrer Mac-Gregor (2016), pp. 151–190.

[79] IACtHR, *Case Suárez Peralta v. Ecuador*, para. 93; IACtHR, *Case del Penal Miguel Castro v. Perú*, para. 383; IACtHR, *Case Ximenes Lopes v. Brasil*, para. 171.

[80] IACtHR, *Vélez Restrepo y familiares v. Colombia*, para. 247. In general, the Court considers that the "right to know the truth" is subsumed in the broader right of victims and their families to clarify the facts and responsibilities (arts. 8 and 25 of the ACHR), cf. IACtHR, *Uzcátegui and others v. Venezuela*, judgment of 09 March 2012, para. 240.

[81] IACtHR, *Cases Velásquez Rodríguez v. Honduras*, para.181; IACtHR, *Kawas Fernández v. Honduras*, para. 190. See CIDH, *Derecho a la verdade em América*. OEA/Ser.L/V/II.152 Doc. 2, de 13/8/2014, p. 57 ff.

7 Standards of Investigation in Criminal Procedure

In addition to this elaboration of generic meaning,[82] there is an imposition of standards of action in criminal procedures. Not only does the Inter-American Court affirm the right of victims and their families to an effective criminal process, in compliance with the judicial guarantees of Art. 8 (1), but it also indicates criteria and parameters for criminal investigation that shall be observed in practice. A basic requirement is that as soon as the authorities become aware of the harmful event, they shall officially initiate a serious, impartial, and effective investigation.[83]

Subsequently, the San José Court assesses whether the entire criminal procedure has complied with the essential steps to investigate and resolve the case.[84] The key idea is that state agents shall conduct all the necessary inquiries and investigations to seek the desired result.[85] As expressly mentioned, for example, in the *Carvajal Carvajal* case, it is not the Court's responsibility to replace domestic jurisdiction by defining specific modalities of investigation and prosecution. Its function is to verify whether domestic criminal process procedures have violated the international obligations of States or not.[86]

In several judgments, the Inter-American Court assesses the effectiveness and completeness of the criminal investigation, analyzing the measures taken and those omitted. The following considerations should be mentioned: the technical examinations on the victim's body (the *Vargas Areco* case);[87] whether photographic records were taken at the scene of the events, whether weapons were collected and inspected, and the state of conservation of the evidence (the *Uzcátegui* case);[88] the non-exploitation of important evidential elements (the *Gudiel Álvarez* case);[89]

---

[82] The Inter-American Court even makes explicit its demand for a broad, complete, and effective criminal investigation, referring to the duty of exhaustiveness in the investigation, IACtHR, *Osorio Rivera y familiares v. Perú*, judgment of 26 November 2013, paras. 199 e 211; IACtHR, *García Prieto and other v. El Salvador*, para.153.

[83] IACtHR, *Case García Prieto and other v. El Salvador*, para. 101; IACtHR, *Case del Penal Miguel Castro Castro v. Perú*, para. 378.

[84] IACtHR, *Suárez Peralta v. Ecuador*, para. 96.

[85] IACtHR, *Caso V.R.P., V.P.C. and others v. Nicaragua*, para. 151; IACtHR, *Carvajal Carvajal and others v. Colombia*, judgment of 13 March 2018, para. 102. Regarding the desired outcome in the criminal proceedings, the Court explains: "*debe estar orientado hacia una finalidad específica, la determinación de la verdad y la investigación, persecución, captura, enjuiciamiento, y en su caso, la sanción de los responsables de los hechos*", cf. IACtHR, *Kawas Fernández v. Honduras*, judgment of 03 April 2009, para. 101.

[86] IACtHR, *Carvajal Carvajal and others v. Colombia*, para. 118; IACtHR, *Díaz Loreto and others v. Venezuela*, judgment of 19 november 2019, para. 103.

[87] IACtHR, *Vargas Areco v. Paraguay*, judgment of 26 September 2006, paras. 87 ff.

[88] IACtHR, *Uzcátegui and others v. Venezuela*, paras. 218 ff.

[89] IACtHR, *Gudiel Álvarez and others ("Diario Militar") v. Guatemala*, judgment of 20 November 2012, para. 256.

omission or delays in taking statements (the *Suárez Peralta* case);[90] lack of conservation of the crime scene (the *Luna López* case);[91] absence of confrontation and provisional arrest of the investigated subject (the *Poblete Vilches* case);[92] omissions in the collection of traces of genetic material for DNA examination (the *López Soto* case);[93] lack of immediate collection of relevant evidence (the *Azul Rojas Marín* case).[94]

Especially when it comes to serious violations of human rights, the Inter-American Court observes compliance with investigative standards established in international norms and jurisprudence.[95] The determination of a violent death shall observe rules similar to those contained in the Minnesota Protocol of the United Nations.[96] A list of specific standards is also indicated in the investigation of other serious crimes such as torture, ill-treatment, and sexual violence.[97] It is also necessary, among other specifications,[98] to thoroughly investigate the crime scene, conduct forensic examinations using the appropriate methods for forensic investigations,[99] and preserve the chain of custody of all forensic evidence.[100]

When dealing with the specific reparations in actual cases, the decisions reaffirm the obligation of the States to carry out all the necessary investigations to identify, take to trial, and punish those responsible for the violations. In the *López Soto* case, for example, it was determined that the State should effectively promote criminal the resolution of the pending proceedings at the domestic level, and, if applicable, sanction those responsible for the crime.[101] Proper compliance with this measure of reparation requires compliance with the standards established by Inter-American

---

[90] IACtHR, *Suárez Peralta v. Ecuador*, judgment of 21 May 2013, para. 96.

[91] IACtHR, *Luna López v. Honduras*, paras. 159 and ff.

[92] Poblete IACtHR, *Vilches and others v. Chile*, para. 190; also IACtHR, *Case Véliz Franco and others v. Guatemala*, para. 202.

[93] IACtHR, *López Soto and others v. Venezuela*, judgment of 26 September 2018, para. 214.

[94] IACtHR, *Azul Rojas Marín and other v. Perú*, judgment of 12 March 2020, para. 195.

[95] IACtHR, *Masacres de El Mozote y lugares aledaños v. El Salvador*, judgment of 25 October 2012, para. 247.

[96] United Nations Manual on the Effective Prevention and Investigation of Extrajudicial, Arbitrary and Summary Executions. Among many, only IACtHR, *Uzcátegui and others v. Venezuela*, judgment of 03 Septembre 2012, para. 217; IACtHR, *Ximenes Lopes v. Brasil*, para. 179.

[97] IACtHR, *Azul Rojas Marín and other v. Perú*, paras. 180, 182.

[98] The doctrine even mentions that it is possible to extract a true "investigation manual" from the jurisprudence of the Inter-American Court on the issue of effectiveness of the criminal investigation, Brenes Vargas (2012), p. 252.

[99] IACtHR, *Véliz Franco and others v. Guatemala*, judgment of 19 May 2014, para. 191.

[100] IACtHR, *Defensor de Derechos Humanos and others v. Guatemala*, judgment of 28 August 2014, para. 207.

[101] IACtHR, *Case López Soto and others v. Venezuela*, para. 278. Among others, see IACtHR, *Mota Abarullo and others v. Venezuela*, judgment of 18 November 2014, para. 141; IACtHR, *Case de los Empleados de la Fábrica de Fuegos de Santo Antônio de Jesus y sus familiares v. Brasil*, judgment of 17 July 2020, para. 267.

jurisprudence.[102] The investigations shall be comprehensive and detailed, sufficient to «determine, judge and, if applicable, sanction those responsible».[103]

In a close correlation with this conception of the Inter-American Court is the duty of States to avoid and combat impunity for human rights violations,[104] an essential step to avoid the repetition of aggressions[105] and to bring justice to the specific case.[106] The Court itself defined impunity as the «failure to investigate, prosecute, capture and convict those responsible for crimes involving violations of the rights protected by the American Convention».[107]

Impunity, in this case, led the Inter-American Court, on some occasions, to consider the victims' family members as victims of human rights violations. The decisions state that the lack of response from the state authorities, which did not clarify the fact or prosecute those responsible for it, affects the integrity of the victim's family, given the frustration of the desire to obtain justice.[108]

It is interesting to draw attention to the final decision of the Inter-American Court in which it was stated that investigations of a different nature do not complete or replace the State's obligation to establish the truth and investigate crimes in judicial proceedings. Fulfillment of the State's duty to promote diligent and effective investigations of crimes shall be conducted in the criminal sphere.[109] The basic conception is summed up in the idea that the action of national States in criminal justice shall observe rationality and proportionality in order to avoid both the "leniency characteristic of impunity, as well as the excess and abuse in the application of penalties".[110]

8 Victims in Particularly Vulnerable Conditions

The recognition and criminal protection of victims, which are guaranteed by the Inter-American Court, receive some reinforcement specifications when it comes to individuals considered by the national or supranational order as vulnerable, such as

[102] IACtHR, *Valenzuela Ávila v. Guatemala*, judgment of 11 October 2019, para. 233.

[103] IACtHR, *Azul Rojas Marín and other v. Perú*, para. 229.

[104] IACtHR, *Baldeón García v. Perú*, para. 165; IACtHR, *Case Véliz Franco y Otros v. Guatemala*, para. 183

[105] IACtHR, *Vargas Areco v. Paraguay*, para. 81.

[106] IACtHR, *Case del Penal Miguel Castro Castro v. Perú*, para. 405.

[107] IACtHR, *Olivares Muñoz and others v. Venezuela*, judgment of 10 November 2020, para. 131.

[108] IACtHR, *Mota Abarullo and others v. Venezuela*, judgment of 18 November 2020, para. 130; IACtHR, *Luna López v. Honduras*, judgment of 10 October, para. 212.

[109] IACtHR, *Defensor de Derechos Humanos and others v. Guatemala*, para. 202.

[110] IACtHR, *Rodríguez Vera and others*, para. 459.

women, children, and mentally incapable people,[111] as well as indigenous peoples.[112] In this elaboration, the seriousness of the aggression is also taken into account.

8.1 Women

The Court combines the general normative basis of Articles 1(1), 8 and 25 with the specific treaty for the protection of the right, such as the Convention of Belém do Pará,[113] which deals with violence against women and reinforces the requirement to investigate and sanction violence against women. This duty of criminal investigation has additional scope in situations where there is a general context of violence against women, and also when it comes to gender-based violence.[114]

As a result, state authorities shall investigate possible gender-based discriminatory connotations in the act of violence. The Inter-American Court demands that the prosecution should try to clarify other acts that affect personal integrity, such as torture and sexual violence. For the Court, the criminal investigation shall include a gender perspective and be conducted by trained officials.[115] Consequently, judicial ineffectiveness in investigating and punishing these cases and failure to comply with the parameters indicated are, in themselves, a form of discrimination against women in their right to access justice.[116]

8.2 Victims of Sexual Violence

When it comes to investigations for sexual violence, regardless of whether the victims are men or women, the San José Court refers to specific standards both for preserving the dignity and integrity of the victims and for guaranteeing the effectiveness of the criminal investigation.[117] The Inter-American Court reinforces the intention to prevent the criminal investigation from being affected by gender

[111] IACtHR, *Ximenes Lopes v. Brasil*, paras. 137 ff., 147; IACtHR, *Furlán y familiares v. Argentina*, judgment of 31 August 2012, paras. 137, 268, judged that it dealt with civil matters, but with general indications.

[112] IACtHR, *Tiu Tojín v. Guatemala*, judgment of 26 November 2008, para. 96.

[113] Inter-American Convention to Prevent, Punish and Eradicate Violence against Women, 9 June 1994.

[114] IACtHR, *Véliz Franco y Otros v. Guatemala*, para.186.

[115] IACtHR, *Velásquez Paiz and others v. Guatemala*, judgment of 19 November 2015, para. 145; IACtHR, *Véliz Franco y Otros v. Guatemala*, para. 188.

[116] IACtHR, *Véliz Franco y Otros v. Guatemala*, para. 208.

[117] IACtHR, *Azul Rojas Marín and other v. Perú*, paras. 178 ff., 194; IACtHR, *Fernández Ortega and others v. México*, judgment of 30 August 2010, para. 194.

stereotypes or discrimination,[118] which have disastrous effects on the effectiveness of the investigation and imply disregard for the dignity of the victims.[119]

8.3 LGBTI People

In situations involving LGBTI victims of violence, the Inter-American Court determined the adoption of a protocol for the investigation and administration of justice, which shall guide all criminal prosecutions.[120] In addition to qualifying the investigation of facts, the purpose is to preserve the dignity of victims and prevent revictimization in the course of criminal proceedings. The directive also includes witnesses, who shall be able to report crimes of this kind with a guarantee of privacy and secrecy.[121]

8.4 Children and Adolescents

Particular measures are also indicated by the courts of San José when the victim is a child or a teenager, especially in the event of possible sexual assault. The Court refers to the governing principles of supranational law for the protection of children to affirm the duty of increased diligence in the examination of the facts in the context of investigation and criminal proceedings. Failure to comply with this imposition, in the specific case, is a cause of damage to the right of access to justice of the deceased victim's family.[122]

In addition to these impositions of reinforced effectiveness in the investigation, judgment and sanction of facts that affect minors, the Inter-American Court adds another group of measures that shall be observed in criminal proceedings involving children and adolescents. These are the so-called special protection measures before and during the course of criminal investigations and prosecutions,[123] many of which deal specifically with the legal position of the vulnerable victim in the criminal

---

[118]IACtHR, *Velásquez Paiz and others v. Guatemala*, para. 180 ff. In sexual offences, evidence relating to the victim's sexual history is not admissible; cf. IACtHR, *Véliz Franco and others v. Guatemala*, paras. 204 e ff.; IACtHR, *Espinoza Gonzáles v. Perú*, judgment of 20 November 2014, para 278–9.

[119]IACtHR, *López Soto and others v. Venezuela*, para. 236 ff.; IACtHR, *Guzmán Albarracín and others*, paras. 189–191.

[120]IACtHR, *Azul Rojas Marín*, paras. 241–4.

[121]IACtHR, *Azul Rojas Marín*, para. 244.

[122]IACtHR, *Guzmán Albarracín*, paras. 186, 201.

[123]The Court also refers to measures subsequent to the criminal process, which allow the minor's recovery, rehabilitation and social reintegration, measures that should be extended to the victims' relatives; cf. IACtHR, *V.R.P., V.P.C. and others v. Nicaragua*, para. 170.

procedure. Although the content has been indicated in previous judgments,[124] the further specification of these measures came in the judgment of the case *V.R.P., V.P.C. and others.*[125]

States shall guarantee the participation of children and adolescents who are victims of crimes in criminal proceedings, not only when necessary for the investigation and proof of facts, but, especially, as subjects of rights. Therefore, information on the rite, legal and health assistance, as well as other protective measures shall be ensured. It shall also be ensured that they actively participate, with legal assistance from a specialized lawyer, and may act as a procedural party, carrying out procedural acts to defend the rights of children, which shall be free and ensured by the State.[126]

Furthermore, there is a special concern with the non-revictimization in criminal proceedings, with indication of some measures, such as: participating in person only when strictly necessary, avoiding the presence and interaction with possible aggressors, and providing multidisciplinary monitoring and protection throughout the procedure.[127] The effective guarantee of the right to be heard also requires that the proceeding takes place in a non-intimidating context, that is, non-hostile. Also, the official who receives the report shall be properly trained and may be a specialized psychologist or a professional from a similar area. The Court highlighted the special practices of taking the testimonies of children and adolescents in the countries of the Inter-American space, using closed television circuits.[128]

Thus, the investigation and criminal prosecution of crimes involving child and adolescent victims shall observe the duties of increased diligence, special protection and non-revictimization. Failure to comply with these standards of action can lead to recognition by the supranational Court of the violation of the right to access justice without discrimination, as well as the conversion of the State into a second offender, due to the commission of institutional violence through revictimization.[129]

8.5 Indigenous Peoples and Migrants

With regard to other specific victims, the Court adds that, in order to guarantee access to justice for indigenous victims, it is necessary to ensure that they understand and make themselves understood in the course of the investigation procedures, with interpreters and other effective means. In addition, their access to the centers for the

[124] IACtHR, *Rosendo Cantú and other v. México*, judgment of 31 August 2010, para. 201, situation of vulnerability reinforced by being indigenous.

[125] IACtHR, *V.R.P., V.P.C. and others v. Nicaragua*, paras. 155 ff.

[126] IACtHR, *V.R.P., V.P.C. and others v. Nicaragua*, paras. 159 ff.

[127] IACtHR, *V.R.P., V.P.C. and others v. Nicaragua*, para. 163–5.

[128] IACtHR, *V.R.P., V.P.C. and others v. Nicaragua*, paras. 168, 183.

[129] IACtHR, *V.R.P., V.P.C. and others v. Nicaragua*, paras. 295–299, 345.

administration of justice shall be facilitated, including the payment of amounts to ensure that victims can act in the criminal procedure.[130] With regard to migrants, the Court has broadly established the right to due process and all the guarantees related thereto.[131]

8.6 *Context and Motivation of Offenses*

Another concern of the Court that appears in cases involving private victims, but also in other situations, is the need to investigate the motive for the crime, its context, and the structure in which it was committed. The investigation shall endeavor to clarify whether there are discriminatory reasons for the practice of violence,[132] including the aforementioned gender perspective in the criminal investigation.[133]

In an indication with a broad sense, several judgments refer to the importance of the criminal investigation considering the context that enabled the crime, understanding the operational structure, intellectual executors, or potential beneficiaries.[134] At the base is the understanding that an investigation of facts will only be effective and complete if it adopts a comprehensive vision, which takes into account the context and motivation for committing the crimes.[135]

9 Victim Participation: The Need for the Feasibility of Formal and Effective Participation

In line with what has been referred to, the specific theme of the victim's internal participation throughout the criminal prosecution has gained prominence, notably with regard to what their rights are and the role they play.[136] At this point, the guidelines of the Inter-American Court are important to delimit, in terms of a due

[130] IACtHR, *Fernández Ortega and others v. México*, para. 200; IACtHR, *Tiu Tojín v. Guatemala*, para. 100.

[131] Inter-American Court. Condición jurídica y derechos de los migrantes indocumentados. Advisory Opinion OC-18/03, 17 September 2003, para. 124; IACtHR, *Nadege Dorzema and others v. República Dominicana*, judgment of 14 October 2012, para. 165.

[132] IACtHR, *Azul Rojas Marín*, para. 196.

[133] IACtHR, *Velásquez Paiz and others v. Guatemala*, paras. 145–6.

[134] IACtHR, *García y familiares v. Guatemala*, judgment of 29 November 2012, para. 150; IACtHR, *Uzcátegui and others v. Venezuela*, para. 222.

[135] IACtHR, *Isaza Uribe and others v. Colombia*, judgment of 20 November 2018, para. 153; IACtHR, *Rodríguez Vera and others*, para. 500.

[136] As point out, for example: Langer (2008), p. 4.

(fair) criminal procedures,[137] what the dynamics of involvement of this important character in the process and investigation.

It is known that the recognition of the victim's intrinsic dignity cannot be ensured without guaranteeing the protection of their interests and rights. And one of the main points here is precisely the direct interest that victims and family members have in the solution of the criminal case, an interest resulting from the aggression suffered and the search for the realization of criminal justice.

Thus, the first point highlighted by the Inter-American Court is that victims of human rights violations (and/or their families) shall have ample opportunity to be heard and to act in the respective proceedings. It is a possibility of action related precisely to the search for clarification of the facts, and for the punishment of those responsible or them. In addition to, evidently, the search for due civil reparation.[138]

More specifically, in accordance with the guarantees recognized in Articles 8(1) and 25(1) of the American Convention, the Court established that States have an obligation to guarantee, at all stages of their respective proceedings, that the victims be able to plead, receive information, provide evidence, formulate allegations and, in short, assert their rights. In the words of the judges of San José, victims shall have ample opportunity to be heard and act in the respective processes, so that they can formulate claims, complaints, receive information, and present evidence, as well as that these claims be analyzed in a way by the authorities prior to the legal definition of the case.[139] Such participation shall have as its purpose the access to justice, knowledge of the truth about the facts and the granting of just reparation.[140]

It is important to clarify the understanding of Inter-American jurisprudence in the sense that the right to the truth is subsumed in the right of the victims or their family members to obtain clarification of the facts from the competent State bodies and the arbitration of the corresponding responsibilities, through an investigation and serious, effective, and timely judgment.[141]

States have the obligation to adapt their national legislation to the provisions of the Convention, including constitutional provisions and all legal directives of a secondary or regulatory nature. In this way, the internal normative apparatus may be able to implement, in practice, the norms for the protection of victims' rights.[142]

[137] On due (fair) criminal proceedings by supranational courts, see: Pereira (2020), p. 31 ff.

[138] Among several cases: IACtHR, *los "Niños de la Calle" (Villagrán Morales and others) v. Guatemala*, judgment of 19 November 1999, para. 227; IACtHR, *las Hermanas Serrano Cruz v. El Salvador*, judgment of 01 March 2005, para. 129; IACtHR, *Garibaldi v. Brasil*, judgment of 23 Setember 2009, para. 116.

[139] Cf., more recently, IACtHR, *Roche Azaña and others v. Nicaragua*, judgment of 03 June 2020, para. 84. See also: IACtHR, *Radilla Pacheco v. México*, judgment of 23 November 2009, para. 247; IACtHR, *González Medina y familiares v. República Dominicana*, para. 251.

[140] IACtHR, *Radilla Pacheco v. México*, judgment of 23 November 2009, para. 247.

[141] IACtHR, *Rodríguez Vera and others (Desaparecidos del Palacio de Justicia) v. Colombia*, judgment of 14 November 2014, para. 509.

[142] IACtHR, *Radilla Pacheco v. México*, para. 247.

In this regard, the Inter-American Court has established an understanding that it is the obligation of States Parties to create a legislative framework that guarantees the participation of victims and/or their families in the investigation phase, whether presided over by the police, the Attorney's office, or any other organ. Domestic regulation shall allow the aforementioned participation of victims and family members in the course of criminal proceedings to be formal and effective.[143]

In the scope of the investigation, the Court considers it essential that the police and investigative bodies in general offer effective mechanisms for denunciation that are accessible and that these are disseminated for the knowledge of society. It is an obligation of the State to receive allegations of human rights violations.[144]

Furthermore, it is very clear that the rule is that victims have access to the content of investigations and the respective proceedings.[145] The admissible exception is only when the victim's access could compromise the investigative effectiveness of some specific ongoing investigation.[146]

However, it should be considered, as mentioned, that the existence of all these broad powers of action and participation obviously does not bring the burden of promoting the criminal procedure to the victim. In other words, the State cannot exempt itself from its obligation to promote the investigation and procedural instruction based on the possibility of initiative of the victims or their families.[147] The Inter-American Court expresses that the victims and/or family members are not primarily responsible for ensuring the effectiveness and speed of the procedural impetus, conditions that are necessary for an adequate criminal response within a reasonable time.[148]

In the same perspective, the understanding of the judges of San José is that the possibility for the victim to appeal decisions in the course of the procedure does not remove the functional duty of the body responsible for the accusation to act actively in the appeal sphere. Thus, even if the victim and his/her family members may present a particular accusation, even if it is supporting or complementary, this does not replace the accuser's role in his/her duty to act.[149]

From all this panorama presented, it is clear that the Inter-American Court has given a relevant emphasis to the victim's participation in the criminal procedure. And this is materialized not only by the widely recognized right of victims and/or family members to receive information on the main acts and stages of criminal prosecution, but also by the possibilities recognized for victims and relatives to exercise purposeful action in the course of the procedure, consisting in the presentation of allegations and evidentiary material.

---

[143] IACtHR, *Favela Nova Brasília v. Brasil*, judgment of 16 February 2017, para. 329.

[144] IACtHR, *Azul Rojas Marín and other v. Perú*, judgment of 12 March 2020, para. 176.

[145] IACtHR, *González Medina y familiares v. República Dominicana*, para. 253.

[146] IACtHR, *Radilla Pacheco v. México*, para. 252.

[147] IACtHR, *Ximenes Lopes v. Brasil*, judgment of 04 July 2006, para.198.

[148] IACtHR, *Vargas Areco v. Paraguay*, para. 155.

[149] IACtHR, *Suárez Peralta v. Ecuador*, judgment of 21 May 2013, para. 117.

10 Right to Safety and Protection of the Parties Involved in the Procedure

Another recurring theme in the jurisprudence of the Inter-American Court is the protection of those involved in criminal proceedings. There is a concern to ensure the safety of all parties acting in the course of criminal prosecution, in order to prevent people from suffering aggression or threats or fearing to participate when they wish and/or are necessary.[150]

The Inter-American Court considers that, in order to guarantee due process, the State shall provide all the necessary means to protect operators of justice in general, investigators, witnesses and families of victims of persecution and threats aimed at hindering the progress of the investigation or of the procedure. The basic idea is that these behaviors can hinder the clarification of the facts. This is because, if these people are frightened, there is a real risk that they will not fulfill their purposes.[151]

More than that, these procedural actors can, due to their performance, suffer serious violations of their rights. This is visible, especially regarding the right of movement and residence, direct privacy and family life, protection of the family and, in some cases, the very right of minor children to live with their close family.[152]

In addition, the Inter-American Court considers that threats perpetrated against judges, witnesses, victims' families, and other operators can affect the effectiveness of the criminal procedure. For this reason, the State has the positive obligation to adopt sufficient protection and investigation measures in the face of acts of intimidation and threats to the subjects involved in the proceeding.[153]

The Inter-American Court explained the idea that, faced with a context of intimidation and threats to important witnesses to the reconstruction of the facts, an isolated and decontextualized view cannot be taken. Threats shall be considered in the context of obstacles to the investigation of the criminal case. Otherwise, such events can become a means of perpetuating impunity, avoiding the full clarification of criminal events.[154]

It is clear in the grounds of the judgments that the Inter-American Court links the right to security and protection of all potential interveners in the criminal procedure with the value of the effectiveness of the criminal investigation. It is a necessary, although it is not sufficient, condition to obtain a correct decision and potentially enabling knowledge of the truth about the facts.

---

[150] The Court also addresses in several cases the State's duty to provide security in social terms, so that human rights violations are avoided (prevention perspective), such as: IACtHR, *Pacheco León and others v. Honduras*, judgment of 15 November 2017, para. 170.

[151] Among others: IACtHR, *Myrna Mack Chang v. Guatemala*, judgment of 25 November 2003, paras. 198–199; IACtHR, *Case de la Masacre de La Rochela v. Colombia*, judgment of 11 May 2017, para. 171.

[152] IACtHR, *Carvajal Carvajal and others v. Colombia*, judgment of 13 March 2018, para. 188.

[153] IACtHR, *Masacre de La Rochela v. Colombia*, judgment of 11 May 2005, para. 165.

[154] IACtHR, *Masacre de Las Dos Erres v. Guatemala*, judgment of 24 November 2009, para. 145.

11 Faceless Witness Considerations of a Special Duty of Protection

In the same sense as explained above, the sub-topic of witness protection is also an issue worthy of attention by the Inter-American Court, given the epistemic importance generally attributed to this source of evidence in criminal proceedings. In this regard, the issue arises of the possibility of using «faceless witnesses»[155] in criminal proceedings, as a means of guaranteeing the rights to life, integrity, freedom, and personal safety of those who testify.

This form of protection involves not revealing the identity, to the defendants and their defenses, of the witness listed by the prosecution, so that the witness tends to be free from possible retaliatory measures. The central problem in the use of protected witnesses, with reservation of identity, concerns the exercise of the right of defense, more specifically the right of the accused subjects to confront the oral evidence. Witness protection systems denote limitations on the defense's ability to challenge possible situations of enmity, prejudice, and reliability of the person of the declarant, as well as other aspects that would allow arguing that the testimony itself is false or inaccurate.[156]

For this reason, in order to guarantee compatibility between the witness's right to safety and the defendant's right to defense, the Inter-American Court considered that the existence of compensatory measures is necessary. Although the Inter-American Court does not consider the use of witnesses with private identities incompatible with the defense guarantees, it does impose some conditions. In particular, it is required that the judicial authority responsible for the case knows the identity of the witness and is able to observe their behavior during the interrogation, in order to form their own impression about the reliability of the declarant and his/her testimony. The defense shall also be assured of ample opportunity to directly question the witness (with the exception of issues related to their identity and location) at any stage of the process so that they can verify their behavior and, eventually, raise doubts about the credibility or reliability of their statements.[157]

Sharing the understanding of the European Court of Human Rights, the Inter-American Court also states that, even when sufficient compensatory measures have been adopted, the conviction cannot be based solely, or in a decisive degree, on the statements of witnesses with reserved identity. It means to say that for the formation of a condemnatory judgment, it is necessary the existence of other types of evidence that corroborate the statements of the faceless witness.[158]

---

[155] The paradigmatic case is: IACtHR, *Pollo Rivera and others v. Perú*, judgment of 21 October 2016, para. 205.

[156] IACtHR, *Pollo Rivera and others v. Perú*, para. 205.

[157] IACtHR, *Pollo Rivera and others v. Perú*, para. 205; IACtHR, *Norín Catrimán and others (Dirigentes, Miembros y Activista del Pueblo Indígena Mapuche) v. Chile*, judgment of 29 May 2014, para. 246.

[158] IACtHR, *Pollo Rivera and others v. Perú*, para. 205; IACtHR, *Case Norín Catrimán*, para. 247.

12 Criminal Procedure and the General Public: Advertising, Media, and Public Opinion

Finally, another relevant topic is the one that concerns the relationship between criminal proceedings and public opinion, for which the Inter-American Court brings in its jurisprudence some fundamental indications. As a sort of complement to States obligations to investigate, prosecute, and punish those responsible for human rights violations, and also to reinforce the value given to the truth, the Court affirms that the results of domestic criminal proceedings shall be made widely available to the public, allowing society in general to know the truth about the facts.[159] The Court clarified that the final criminal court decisions, of final judgment of the criminal process, whether of an acquittal or condemnatory nature, shall be disclosed in order to enable the community in general, and the surroundings in which the victim is inserted, know the facts examined and, if applicable, those responsible for the commission of the crimes.[160]

On the subject of the relationship between the criminal procedure and the general public, and the duty to provide information, the Court bases itself on Article 8(5) of the Convention to affirm that publicity is the general rule, being an essential element of the democratic criminal system. In addition to ensuring that the accused can have immediacy with the judge and the evidence, it is necessary to facilitate public access to procedural acts.[161] Transparency in the administration of criminal justice fosters confidence in the exercise of judicial activity, and contributes to the control of impartiality,[162] in addition to being a defendant's right.[163]

The need to restrict the publicity of criminal proceedings shall be demonstrated by the State, on grounds that indicate the importance of «preserving the interests of justice». Thus, to depart from the general rule, the agents involved in the criminal prosecution shall prove the necessity and proportionality in limiting the guarantee of publicity.[164] The limitation also occurs in legal proceedings that deal with issues related to children and adolescents, cases in which the broad rule of public access to procedural acts can be restricted to meet the best interests of the minor.[165] Thus, in consideration to the principle of presumption of innocence, the Inter-American jurisprudence referred to the impossibility for the State to informally condemn a

---

[159] IACtHR, *Servellón García and others v. Honduras*, judgment of 21 September 2006, para. 196; IACtHR, *Case Baldeón García v. Perú*, para. 199.

[160] IACtHR, *Escué Zapata v. Colombia*, judgment of 05 May 2008, para. 15.

[161] IACtHR, *Pollo Rivera and others v. Perú*, para 178; IACtHR, *Case Cantoral Benavides v. Perú*; para 147; IACtHR, *Castillo Petruzzi and others v. Perú*, judgment of 30 May 1999, para. 172.

[162] IACtHR, *J. v. Perú*, para. 217; IACtHR, *Palamara Iribarne v. Chile*, judgment of 22 November 2005, para. 168.

[163] IACtHR, *Caso García Asto y Ramírez Rojas v. Perú*, judgment of 25 November 2005, para. 149.

[164] IACtHR, *J. v. Perú*, para. 220; IACtHR, *Case Cantoral Benavides v. Perú*, para. 148.

[165] Inter-American Court. Condición jurídica y derechos humanos del niño. Advisory Opinion OC-17/02 28 August 2002, para. 134.

person, or to issue a judgment to society of a fact with an investigation still in progress. State agents cannot advance public opinion until there is a final judgment in the criminal case. Public statements, press conferences or information in general in which a public official assigns a person criminal responsibility for the offense under investigation constitute violations of the guarantee of the presumption of innocence,[166] and may also constitute an offense to the honor and dignity not only of the accused subject, as well as their family members.[167]

The Inter-American Court expressly refers to the jurisprudence of the European Court of Human Rights to point out that the presumption of innocence can be violated not only by criminal justice agents. Other public authorities may disregard the guarantee by statements about a criminal case before the person has been tried and definitively convicted.

In the case of *J. v. Perú*, it has been stated by the Court of San José that members of the prosecution can assert in the criminal procedure the culpability of the accused subject. However, statements to the press attributing individual responsibilities, without restrictions or reservations, are excessive, induce public opinion and can influence the competent judicial authority.[168]

The Court makes a distinction. It recognizes that it is legitimate, and even a duty, for state authorities to speak out on matters of public interest. However, care shall be taken so that they do not become violations of rights. The Inter-American judges point out that there is a clear difference between statements by public officials who merely suspect that an individual may be responsible for a certain crime, and those in which criminal responsibility is clearly established, despite the absence of a definitive conviction.[169]

Using the same considerations as indicated in the preceding paragraph, in the *Acosta and others* case, the Inter-American Court considered statements made to the press by the investigating judge to be offensive, since the judge went too far in referring to the spouse of the murder victim, suggesting that she had covered up the offense. Public statements about ongoing criminal proceedings violated the rights to the presumption of innocence, integrity, and honor of the victim's family member in addition to the guarantee of impartiality.[170]

[166] IACtHR, *J. v. Perú*, judgment of 27 November 2013, paras. 235 ff.; IACtHR, *Lori Berenson Mejía v. Perú*, judgment of 25 November 2004, para. 158; IACtHR, *Cantoral Benavides v. Perú*, judgment of 18 August 2000, para. 119.

[167] IACtHR, *Case del Penal Miguel Castro Castro v. Perú*, para. 358–9.

[168] IACtHR, *J. v. Perú*, para. 244.

[169] IACtHR, *Pollo Rivera and others v. Perú*, para. 177; IACtHR, *J. v. Perú*, para. 247.

[170] IACtHR, *Acosta and others v. Nicaragua*, judgment of 25 March 2017, paras. 189–191; 204.

13 Conclusion

From all the foregoing, it can be clearly seen that the IACHR advances in the issue of third parties in criminal proceedings to establish a minimum standard of guarantees regarding these subjects. This occurs from a reading that goes beyond the perspective of defending the individual rights of the accused subject in the criminal proceedings.

In other words, there is an interpretive perspective of various rights and guarantees with a focus on agents other than the defendant, especially in relation to the victim and their families. The aim is guarantee to the victim of serious human rights violations that there is an efficient criminal prosecution mechanism, which makes it possible to clarify the facts related to these violations (the truth about what happened), as well as enable the prosecution and sanction of those responsible for the aggressions.

Based on the analysis of national criminal proceedings conducted by public authorities, the Court emphasizes that an effective remedy shall be offered to ensure the rights of access to justice, knowledge of the truth of the facts, and reparation for victims and their families. The supranational courts have come to recognize a true subjective right that the act that violates rights needs to be effectively investigated by the State authorities and, if applicable, the person responsible for it to be prosecuted and shall be punished.

There is also the imposition of compliance with standards of action in criminal proceedings, since the Inter-American Court indicates minimum criteria and parameters for criminal investigation that shall be observed, with a view to ensuring the effectiveness of the prosecution. At this point, an assessment is made of whether the criminal procedure complied with the essential steps to investigate and resolve the case and whether the victim's vulnerabilities considered or not.

Moreover, specifically, the efficiency of the prosecution requires respect for the reasonable duration of the process and investigation, which shall take place without undue delays, which is scrutinized based on verification criteria established in the inter-American jurisprudence. Added to this, the victim shall have broad possibilities of participation, formally and concretely, whether by being heard or presenting allegations and evidence; and there is, equally, an emphasis on the need for procedural publicity in order to foster trust in the exercise of judicial activity. At the same time, the Court also pays attention to the need to guarantee the security of all those involved in the criminal procedure, so that procedural actors are not afraid to participate whenever they wish and/or when necessary. Nevertheless, in the case of faceless witnesses, there is a search for a balance so that the right of defense is not excessively harmed, requiring further corroborating evidence.

In conclusion, it can be said that the Inter-American Court has repeatedly stated that States Parties are obliged, observing due process rules, to provide effective judicial remedies to victims of human rights violations. In other words, the criminal justice system shall work respecting the guarantees of the accused, but also with systemic effectiveness, preserving the interests and rights of the victim and other interveners.

References

Andrade CGC (2019) Mandados Implícitos de Criminalização: a tutela penal dos direitos humanos na Constituição e na Convenção Americana. Lumen Juris, Rio de Janeiro

Benavente Chorres H (2012) La Investigación Judicial y el Control de Convencionalidad en el Proceso Penal. Bosch, Barcelona

Brenes Vargas R (2012) Crónica de jurisprudencia de la Corte Interamericana de Derechos Humanos. Rev Int Droit Penal 1(83):233–266

Cardone A (2011) Diritti fondamentali (tutela multilivello dei). In: Enciclopedia del diritto, annali IV. Giuffrè, Milano, pp 335–422

Carducci M, Mazzuoli VO (2014) Teoria tridimensional das integrações supranacionais: uma análise comparativa dos sistemas e modelos de integração da Europa e América Latina. Forense, Rio de Janeiro

Ferrer Mac-Gregor E (2013) Eficacia de la sentencia interamericana y la cosa juzgada internacional: vinculación directa hacia las partes (res judicata) e indirecta hacia los estados parte de la convención americana (res interpretata) (sobre el cumplimiento del caso gelman vs. uruguay). Estudios Constitucionales 11(2):617–669

Ferrer Mac-Gregor E (2014) Las siete principales líneas jurisprudenciales de la Corte Interamericana de Derechos Humanos aplicable a la justicia penal. Revista IIDH 59:29–118

Ferrer Mac-Gregor E (2016) El derecho a la verdad en el derecho internacional de los derechos humanos (Y su eventual desarrollo como derecho autónomo en la jurisprudencia interamericana). In: Santolaya Machetti P, Wences I (eds) La América de los derechos. Centro de Estudios Politicos y Constitucionales, Madrid, pp 151–190

Fischer D, Pereira FV (2023) As Obrigações Processuais Penais Positivas, 4th edn. Livraria do Advogado, Porto Alegre

García Pino G (2016) La vanguardia de la Corte IDH. Decisiones sobre amnistía e impunidad, sobre desapariciones forzadas y sobre acceso a la información pública. In: Santolaya Machetti P, Wences I (eds) La América de los derechos. Centro de Estudios Politicos y Constitucionales, Madrid, pp 109–132

Giacomolli NJ (2016) O Devido Processo Penal: bordagem conforme a Constituição Federal e o Pacto de São José da Costa Rica, 3rd edn. Atlas, São Paulo

Gialuz M (2016) La protezione della vittima tra corte edu e corte di giustizia. In: Luparia L (ed) Lo statuto europeo delle vittime di reato. Modelli di tutela tra diritto dell'Unione e buone pratiche nazionali. Cedam, Padova, pp 19–29

Gozaíni OA (2019) El Debido Processo: estándares de la Corte Interamericana de Derechos Humanos. Rubinzal-Culzoni, Santa Fe

Langer M (2008) Revolución en el proceso penal latinoamericano: difusión de ideas legales desde la periferia. Revista de Derecho Procesal Penal II:4–60

Pastor DR (2002) El Plazo Razonable en el Proceso del Estado de Derecho: una investigación acerca de la excesiva duración del Proceso Penal y sus posibles soluciones. AdHoc, Buenos Aires

Pereira FV (2020) Fundamentos do Justo Processo Penal Convencional – as garantias processuais e o valor instrumental do devido processo. D'Plácido, Belo Horizonte

Piovesan F (2013) Controle de convencionalidade direitos humanos e diálogo entre jurisdições. In: Marinoni LG, Mazzuoli VO (eds) Controle de convencionalidade: um panorama latino-americano. Gazeta Jurídica, Brasília, pp 115–145

Ramos AC (2002) Processo Internacional de Direitos Humanos, 2nd edn. Saraiva, São Paulo

Ramos AC (2020) Curso de Direitos Humanos, 7th edn. Saraiva, São Paulo
Sagüés NP (2010) Obligaciones internacionales y control de convencionalidad. Estudios Constitucionales 8(1):117–136
Tega D (2011) L'ordinamento costituzionale italiano e il "sistema" CEDU: accordi e disaccordi. In: Manes V, Zagrebelsky V (eds) La convenzione europea dei diritti dell'uomo nell'ordinamento penale italiano. Giuffrè, Milano, pp 193–239

The Acknowledgment of a Statute of Procedural Guarantees of Third Parties in Criminal Proceedings in ECHR Law: The Contribution of the European Court of Human Rights

Claudio Orlando

Abstract This study deals with the protection of third parties in criminal proceedings within the perspective of ECHR law. Having provided a notion of third parties within the scope of ECHR law, the analysis will focus on the contribution of the European Court of Human Rights to the recognition of a statute of procedural guarantees for individuals involved in various ways in criminal proceedings.

1 ECHR Notion of Formal Parties, Substantial Parties, and Third Parties in Criminal Proceedings. Introductory Remarks

This study deals with the protection of 'third parties' in criminal proceedings in ECHR law, with specific regard to the contribution of the European Court of Human Rights (hereafter, ECtHR) to the acknowledgment of a statute of procedural guarantees for individuals who are involved in various ways in criminal proceedings without being suspects, defendants or formal/substantial participants.

To tackle this problem suitably, it is of paramount importance to clarify first the meaning of 'third parties' in criminal proceedings for the purpose of this study.[1] Traditionally, the European Convention of Human Rights has focused on the protection of the rights of the accused. This is especially true if we consider that Article 6 ECHR—which, as is well known, establishes the right to a fair trial—

[1] It must be stressed that this study does not deal with third-party intervention in proceedings before the ECtHR. Therefore, this analysis will not cover third-party intervention under Article 36(2) ECHR.

C. Orlando (✉)
Law Department, University of Messina, Messina, Italy
e-mail: corlando@unime.it

S. Ruggeri et al. (eds.), *Third Parties in Criminal Proceedings*, Legal Studies in International, European and Comparative Criminal Law 10,
https://doi.org/10.1007/978-3-031-73970-5_10

applies to a person subject to a 'criminal charge'.[2] The ECtHR has constantly highlighted that a 'criminal charge' exists from the moment that "an individual has been substantially affected by actions taken by the authorities as a result of a suspicion against him".[3] The Court, indeed, adopted an autonomous interpretation of the notion of 'criminal charge' that looks at the impact of criminal investigations on the fundamental rights of a person against whom evidence of guilt has been collected. Thus, the application of Article 6 ECHR does not necessarily require an indictment and does not entail the need for the accused to have been brought to court due to a formal charge. Even a person arrested or questioned on the basis of a suspicion of guilt may be regarded as being charged with a criminal offence and, therefore, claim the protection of Article 6 ECHR.[4]

The approach adopted by the Court to clarify the concept of 'criminal charge' is of the utmost importance for identifying the categories of people this study will deal with. The notion of 'third party' presents challenging issues in relation to criminal proceedings. Indeed, it should be firstly assessed whether a third person could be considered a party or should be regarded, conversely, as an informal participant. Upon closer examination, it seems apparent that the traditional distinction between formal and informal participants is inadequate to identify the very notion of 'third parties' within the scope of ECHR law. Furthermore, contracting parties follow different approaches in developing these categories. For instance, in some jurisdictions, such as Italy, victims are not allowed to take on the role of formal participants unless they lodge a civil-law action after the court proceeding has been formally instituted. This renders the concept of 'third parties' suitable only for injured persons until they file a formal compensation suit.[5] In contrast, some countries, such as Spain, allow victims to initiate a criminal-law action or to act as joint prosecutors in

[2] It is worth noting that, since its earliest case law, the ECtHR stressed that the concept of 'criminal charge' has to be understood within the scope of the Convention, regardless of the definition provided by the contracting parties. See ECtHR, *König v. Germany*, judgment of 28 June 1978, Appl. No. 6236/73, para. 88; ECtHR, *Neumeister v. Austria*, judgment of 27 June 1968, Appl. No. 1936/36, para. 28. More recently see ECtHR, *Blokhin v. Russia*, judgment of 23 March 2016, Appl. No. 47152/06, para. 179.

[3] ECtHR, *Simeonovi v. Bulgaria*, judgment of 12 May 2017, Appl. No. 21980/04, para. 110; ECtHR, *Ibrahim and Others v. The United Kingdom*, judgment of 13 September 2016, Appl. Nos. 50541/08, 50571/08, 50573/08 and 40351/09, para. 249; ECtHR, *McFarlane v. Ireland*, judgment of 10 September 2010, Appl. No. 31333/06, para. 143; ECtHR, *Eckle v. Germany*, judgment of 15 July 1982, Appl. No. 8130/78, para. 73; ECtHR, *Deweer v. Belgium*, judgment of 27 February 1980, Appl. No. 6903/75, paras. 42–46.

[4] Cf. ECtHR, *Heaney and McGuinness v. Ireland*, judgment of 21 December 2000, Appl. No. 34720/97, para. 42: "While the present applicants had not yet been formally charged on 24 October 1990 when the section 52 requests were made, the Court considers that they were, at that stage, 'substantially affected' and therefore 'charged'"; ECtHR, *Stirmanov v. Russia*, judgment of 29 January 2019, Appl. No. 31816/08, para. 39. See also ECtHR, *Brusco v. France*, judgment of 14 October 2010, Appl. No. 1466/07, paras. 47–50; ECtHR, *Aleksandr Zaichenko v. Russia*, judgment of 18 February 2010, Appl. No. 39660/02, paras. 41–43; ECtHR, *Kalēja v. Latvia*, judgment of 5 October 2017, Appl. No. 22059/08, paras. 36–41.

[5] See Foti and Malino, in this volume.

criminal proceedings, thus making the concept of 'third parties' unsuitable for them.[6]

In light of this, a formalistic approach is unfitting for providing a comprehensive definition that can fulfil the specific aims of this study. It seems, therefore, more appropriate to adopt an autonomous approach that looks at the impact of criminal proceedings on third parties. This solution seems to be confirmed by the formulation of Article 34 ECHR, which allows the victim of a violation of the rights established in the Convention by one of the High Contracting Parties to lodge an application to the ECtHR. The notion of 'victim' has itself been interpreted autonomously, since it encompasses all those individuals whose rights have been substantially infringed—or even potentially threatened—at a national level.[7] This impact does not solely concern the person against whom procedural acts are addressed, but also all those individuals who passively undergo the effects of several acts, provided that no suspicion of guilt has fallen upon them. Moreover, these effects may impact on third parties in a direct or indirect manner, depending on whether procedural acts are targeted against third parties or indirectly concern them. As we will see, indirect interference with third parties can occur in cases of covert investigative measures, such as communication intercepts, and in court activities, such as cross-examination of undercover agents.

In the light of this, the notion of 'third parties' seems to encompass a wide range of people: *i.e.*, all those individuals that undergo the effects of investigative activities without being charged with a criminal offence, the owners of goods and assets that may be timely frozen, seized, and confiscated against whom no evidence of guilt has been gathered, witnesses, and those persons who may provide information about a criminal offence at the investigative stage.

The role posing the most challenging issues is certainly that of the person who suffered the consequences of the crime (*i.e.* the victim). Victims hold a *sui generis* position in criminal proceedings, as their participation, procedural rights, and powers may vary depending on how their role is interpreted in national systems. Therefore, the greater the extent to which victims are permitted to take part in criminal proceedings as formal parties or substantial parties, the less they can be considered as third parties. Within this light, for the sake of this study victims may be regarded as third parties only when their knowledge is needed for fact-finding.

Even more problematic is the classification of next-of-kin and relatives of victims. They surely can be considered as third parties when they undergo the effects of investigative and court activities (e.g. when they are requested to provide information about a criminal offence at the investigative stage or when they indirectly undergo the effects of the taking of witness evidence at trial). However, we will see that there are cases (e.g. those involving the death of the victim) in which their

---

[6] Cf. Gascón Inchausti and Schumann Barragán, in this volume.

[7] See ECtHR, *Roman Zakharov v. Russia*, judgment of 4 December 2015, Appl. No. 47143/06, paras. 173–178, in which the Court recognised the applicant's victim status by the mere existence in Russia of rules permitting secret surveillance measures.

role is equivalent to that of injured parties, thus making the concept of 'third parties' unsuitable for them.

Therefore, for the sake of clarity, we shall distinguish between formal parties (*i.e.* all those persons who are entitled by law to formally participate in criminal proceedings), substantial parties (*i.e.* all those individuals who, although not holding 'formal party' status, have a substantial interest in the recognition of rights and powers that are necessary for assuming such a role in criminal proceedings), and third parties to criminal proceedings.

Against this background, in the last years the ECtHR has followed an autonomous approach to establish a set of procedural guarantees for those individuals who undergo the effects of procedural acts without being suspects, defendants or formal/substantial participants. This interpretation makes it possible to combine the perspective of ECHR law with the categories developed by each contracting party. Therefore, to tackle these issues properly, there is a need for a comprehensive approach aimed at providing an overview of the standard of protection granted by ECtHR case-law to victims and third parties in criminal proceedings.

2 The Protection of Victims in ECtHR Case-Law

Over recent decades, the Strasbourg Court has consistently recognised the necessity of protecting the rights of victims in criminal proceedings.[8] This approach has given rise to a significant case-law that deals with the protection of victims in a twofold manner: on one hand, the ECtHR has acknowledged the extension of the rights granted under Article 6 ECHR to victims taking part in criminal proceedings by adopting a broader interpretation of the concept of civil rights and obligations; on the other hand, the Court has amplified the protection of victims by enacting substantial and procedural obligations of States—mainly under Articles 2, 3, 4 and 8 ECHR—which require national authorities both to not interfere with their rights and to take the necessary measures for protecting those rights.[9]

[8] As we saw in the previous paragraph, for a long period of time only the accused was entitled to claim protection under Article 6 ECHR. This strict understanding entailed the inadmissibility *ratione personae* of applications lodged by victims of criminal offences under Article 6 ECHR. Within this framework, the ECtHR had constantly ruled out the possibility of extending fair trial rights to victims participating in criminal proceedings. In general terms, the protection of victims had depended on the possibility to lodge a civil-law action in civil proceedings. Cf. ECtHR, *Asociación de victimas del terrorismo v. Spain*, decision of 29 March 2001, Appl. No. 54102/00. See also Trechsel (2005), p. 37 ff.

[9] See Chiavario (2001), p. 939 ff.; Romanelli (2023), p. 98 ff.; Malino (2022), p. 3 ff.; Grisonich (2021); Montagna (2019), p. 1 ff.; Montagna (2016), p. 351 ff.; Valentini (2019), p. 3 ff.; Mezykowska (2011), p. 288 ff.

2.1 The Protection of Victims under Article 6(1) ECHR

As to the applicability of Article 6 ECHR to victims, the ECtHR has highlighted that the European Convention does not grant the victim the right to demand the prosecution and conviction of the accused.[10] In general terms, victims are allowed to claim the protection of Article 6 ECHR when their participation in criminal proceedings is related to the determination of their civil rights and obligations. In light of this, it was long discussed whether the victim is to be granted the fair trial guarantees laid down by Article 6 for a person charged with a criminal offence.

In order to address this problem, we should start with the solution adopted in the case *Helmers v. Sweden*. In this decision, the ECtHR outlined that, even though Article 6 does not recognise the right of the victim "to institute a criminal prosecution himself",[11] whether domestic law grants an individual the right to have a determination of his or her civil rights and obligations in criminal proceedings, the guarantees set forth by Article 6(1) will apply. If the victim claims the protection of Article 6 under these circumstances, the ECtHR has to verify whether the criminal proceeding has been conducted fairly, publicly, within a reasonable time, and before an independent and impartial body. This ruling implied a significant extension of several safeguards to victims taking part in criminal proceedings: *i.e.*, the right to a public hearing, the right to be heard in person, the right to information, support and assistance, and the right to trial within a reasonable time.[12] Such a solution testifies the need to grant victims an adequate protection and a proper place in criminal proceedings.[13]

However, it is worth noting that these safeguards apply only to individuals who have been able to take part in criminal proceedings. Yet, the ECHR lays down no provision which expressly recognises the right of victims to participate in criminal proceedings. Moreover, victims' participation may be regulated differently by each contracting party. Thus, there is a need to understand whether Article 6 applies to victims only if they are entitled under national law to formally participate in criminal proceedings and to bring a claim for compensation. Within this perspective, the cases *Moreira de Azevedo v. Portugal* and *Perez v. France* are all the more poignant. In *Moreira*, the ECtHR recognised that the guarantees enshrined in Article 6 apply to a person having the status of '*assistente*' (*i.e.*, a party assisting the public prosecutor) even if he or she had never claimed compensation for the damaged suffered by the

[10] ECtHR, *Asociacion de victimas del terrorismo v. Spain*.

[11] ECtHR, *Helmers v. Sweden*, judgment of 29 October 1991, Appl. No. 11826/85, para 29.

[12] Chiavario (2001), p. 939 ff.

[13] See *inter alia* ECtHR, *Perez v. France*, judgment of 12 February 2004, para. 72, in which the Court emphasised "the need to safeguard victims' rights and their proper place in criminal proceedings. Simply because the requirements inherent in the concept of a 'fair trial' are not necessarily the same in disputes about civil rights and obligations as they are in cases involving criminal trials, as evidenced by the fact that for civil disputes there are no detailed provisions similar to those in Article 6 §§ 2 and 3 does not mean that the Court can ignore the plight of victims and downgrade their rights".

offence, outlining that this intervention in criminal proceedings is equivalent to the submission of such a claim. In *Perez*, the Court stressed that Article 6 may be applicable even if the victim participates in criminal proceedings as a civil party without filing a formal compensation suit.[14] The Court, therefore, adopted an autonomous approach to understand the concept of '*contestations sur [l]es droits et obligations de caractère civil*' by acknowledging the applicability of Article 6 even in the absence of a formal compensation suit "if the outcome of proceedings is decisive for the 'civil right' in question".[15] In the view of the Court, by acquiring such a status "victims demonstrate the importance they attach not only to the criminal conviction of the offender but also to securing financial reparation for the damage sustained".[16]

Nevertheless, it should be noted that under this case-law the protection of victims in criminal proceedings is strictly linked to their formal participation. Therefore, it is of the utmost importance to verify whether nowadays victims are entitled to protection only when they become a formal party to criminal proceedings. In dealing with this problematic issue, the ECtHR has considered the standard of protection granted by domestic legislation to injured persons, by examining whether they could take part in national proceedings as a civil party and whether and under which circumstances they are entitled to exercise their civil rights and submit complaints at all stages of the proceeding.[17] Within this framework, the solution adopted in the case *Arnoldi v. Italy* is extremely relevant.[18] As a general rule, in Italy the victim may be entitled to lodge a civil-law action after the court proceeding has been formally instituted (*i.e.*, at the beginning of the intermediate phase).[19] From this moment the injured person becomes a formal party to criminal proceedings. However, in this case, the applicant could not exercise her civil rights since prosecution had been barred due to the statute of limitations during the investigative stage. For this reason, the applicant complained that there was a violation of Article 6 ECHR due to the excessive length of the proceeding. The Government argued that the application of Mrs. Arnoldi was inadmissible *ratione personae* since she did not join the criminal proceeding as a civil party.[20] Nevertheless, the ECtHR recognised that the applicability of Article 6 ECHR does not require the applicant to become a formal party to the domestic proceeding, thus implying the acknowledgment to victims of the right to proceedings of a reasonable length, starting at the investigative phase. The Court, indeed, stressed that "*l'applicabilité de l'article 6 § 1 ne saurait dépendre de la*

[14] ECtHR, *Perez v. France*, para. 64; ECtHR, *Helmers v. Sweden*, para. 29.

[15] ECtHR, *Perez v. France*, para. 65; ECtHR, *Maini v. France*, judgment of 26 October 1999, Appl. No. 31801/96, paras. 28–29; ECtHR, *Calvelli and Ciglio*, judgment of 17 January 2002, Appl. No. 32967/96, para. 62.

[16] *Ibid.*

[17] ECtHR, *Sottani v Italy*, judgment of 24 February 2005, Appl. No. 26775/02.

[18] See ECtHR, *Arnoldi v. Italy*, judgment of 7 December 2017, Appl. No. 35637/04.

[19] Cf. Foti and Malino, in this volume.

[20] See ECtHR, *Arnoldi v. Italy*, para. 23.

reconnaissance du statut formel de 'partie' de la part du droit national".[21] In order to ascertain whether Article 6 ECHR is applicable the Court must verify: (i) whether the applicant intended to claim protection of his or her civil rights by exercising any rights and powers expressly afforded to him or her by law;[22] (ii) whether the outcome of the investigative stage is decisive for the civil right in question.[23] Such an evaluation must be carried out regardless of the injured person's formal status in national proceedings.[24] This implies that under ECtHR case-law the standard of protection granted by Article 6 ECHR to an injured person who was not able to take part in court proceedings is the same as that of a civil party, provided that these two conditions are fulfilled. The most relevant conclusion of this case-law, for the purpose of this study, is that the ECtHR considers injured persons as substantial parties to criminal proceedings.[25]

The solution adopted in *Arnoldi* also strengthened the acknowledgment to victims of the right of access to court, which entails the right of everyone to have their claims brought before a court or tribunal. Indeed, in *Petrella v. Italy* and *Fabbri and Others v. San Marino*—to name just a few—the Court found a violation of the right of access to court, since prosecution was barred at the investigative stage without there being a determination on the applicants' complaints as a result of the inactivity of domestic judicial authorities, despite the possibility for the applicants to bring separate civil proceedings subsequently.[26] In such circumstances, it may be unreasonable to demand the victim to file a separate civil action. This is because such an action could require the gathering of new evidence, which the applicant would have the burden to produce before a civil court. Additionally, establishing civil liability may be extremely difficult given the passage of time. This implies that if victims call for protection of their civil rights through criminal proceedings, they cannot be forced to bring a separate action before a civil court.

---

[21] *Ibid.*, para. 28.

[22] See ECtHR, *Gorou v. Greece (no. 2)*, judgment of 20 March 2009, Appl. No. 12686/03, para. 24; ECtHR, *Perez v. France*, cit., para. 70: "To fall within the scope of the Convention such right must be indissociable from the victim's exercise of a right to bring civil proceedings in domestic law, even if only to secure symbolic reparation or to protect a civil right such as the right to a good reputation". ECtHR, *Sottani v Italy*; ECtHR, *Patrono, Cascini and Stefanelli v. Italy*, judgment of 20 April 2006, Appl. No. 10180/04, paras. 31–33.

[23] See ECtHR, *Arnoldi v. Italy*, cit., para. 30.

[24] ECtHR, *Fabbri and Others v. San Marino*, judgment of 6 March 2023, Appl. No. 6319/21, para. 37.

[25] Cf. Malino (2022), p. 5; see ECtHR, *Arnoldi v. Italy*, cit., para. 40: "*Par conséquent, la Cour estime qu'en droit italien la position de la partie lésée qui, en attendant de pouvoir se constituer partie civile, a exercé au moins l'un de ces droits et facultés dans la procédure pénale, ne diffère pas en substance, pour ce qui est de l'applicabilité de l'article 6, de celle de la partie civile. Au vu de ce qui précède, la Cour considère que l'issue des investigations préliminaires est déterminante pour le droit de caractère civil en cause*".

[26] See ECtHR, *Fabbri and Others v. San Marino*; ECtHR, *Petrella v. Italy*, judgment of 18 March 2021, Appl. No. 24340/07. Cf. Grisonich (2021); Cassibba (2021), p. 1141 ff.; Malino (2022), p. 4; Marandola (2021); Aloisi (2021).

The analysis carried out hitherto demonstrates that the ECtHR is gradually shaping the ECHR system in such a way as to construct a statute of guarantees of victims in criminal proceedings. This is a natural reflection of the approach adopted by the Court to grant a set of procedural safeguards to substantial participants who call for protection of their rights and interests in criminal proceedings.

2.2 The Protection of Victims and their Relatives Through Effective Investigation

The previous section highlighted that the ECtHR has limited the safeguarding of victims' rights under Article 6(1) ECHR to situations where they request protection for their civil claims in criminal proceedings. However, it should be noted that in recent years the Court has expanded the protection of victims by imposing substantial and procedural obligations on States, mainly under Articles 2, 3, 4, and 8 of the ECHR.[27] These obligations require national authorities to protect these individuals from the beginning of the investigative stage.[28]

Within this framework, the ECtHR has acknowledged the duty of investigative authorities to institute and conduct an 'effective investigation', which means "instituting and conducting an investigation capable of leading to the establishment of the facts and of identifying and—if appropriate—punishing those responsible".[29] The requirement to conduct an effective investigation has had a significant impact on the extent of victims' rights in criminal proceedings, thus entailing that their involvement in criminal inquiries is indispensable for the fulfilment of this obligation. In any case, it must be stressed that this obligation is triggered only in the event

[27] For instance, "Article 2 contains two fundamental elements: the general obligation to protect by law the right of life, and the prohibition of intentional deprivation of life". Cf. ECtHR, *Boso v. Italy*, decision of 5 September 2002, Appl. No. 50490/99, para. 1. Moreover, "Article 2 contains a procedural obligation to carry out an effective investigation into alleged breaches of its substantive limb". ECtHR, *Armani Da Silva v. The United Kingdom*, judgment of 30 March 2016, Appl. 5878/08, para. 229.

[28] Montagna (2019), p. 1 ff.; Montagna (2016), p. 351 ff.; Valentini (2019), p. 3 ff.; Gialuz (2016), p. 28 ff.

[29] ECtHR, *Zoletic and Others v. Azerbaijan*, judgment of 7 October 2021, Appl. No. 20116/12, para. 187; ECtHR, *A.P. v. Moldova*, judgment 26 October 2021, Appl. No. 41086/12, para. 30: «*Pour ce qui est plus précisément de l'obligation procédurale de mener une enquête effective, elle rappelle que, lorsqu'une personne allègue de manière défendable avoir été victime d'actes contraires à l'article 3 de la Convention, les autorités nationales doivent mener une enquête officielle effective propre à permettre l'établissement des faits ainsi que l'identification et la punition, le cas échéant, des personnes responsables*»; ECtHR, *Opuz v. Turkey*, judgment 9 June 2009, Appl. No. 33401/02, para. 150: "The Court reiterates that the positive obligations laid down in the first sentence of Article 2 of the Convention also require by implication that an efficient and independent judicial system should be set in place by which the cause of a murder can be established and the guilty parties punished".

of a violation of a core right of the victim, such as the right to life, the prohibition of torture, slavery and forced labour and the right to respect for private and family life. Clearly, it is an "obligation of means rather than of results".[30] Therefore, it does not entail a duty for the judge to convict the accused or a right for the victim to prosecute and secure the conviction of the perpetrators of the offence.

Nevertheless, the acknowledgment of such an obligation implies a significant expansion of victims' rights in criminal proceedings and especially during the investigative stage. Victims, indeed, should be involved in prosecutorial inquiries to the extent necessary to safeguard their interests. This implies that those who have suffered the consequences of the crime must receive regular information on the advancement and outcome of the investigation, including that on the prosecutorial request regarding the dismissal of the proceeding.[31] They should also be granted access to both investigation and court records, including statements of those who provided information about the criminal offence.[32] Additionally, they should be entitled to secure legal representation, participate in evidentiary procedures, submit evidence, and be fairly heard at the early stage of criminal inquiries.[33]

The recognition of such rights and powers supports the argument that, within the framework of ECHR law, victims assume the role of substantial parties during the investigative phase, in any case, until they join the proceedings as civil parties or as formal parties in those systems that enable them to initiate a criminal-law action or to act as joint prosecutors in criminal proceedings.

---

[30] ECtHR, *Zoletic and Others v. Azerbaijan*, para. 188: "The procedural obligation is a requirement of means and not of results. There is no absolute right to obtain the prosecution or conviction of any particular person where there were no culpable failures in seeking to hold perpetrators of criminal offences accountable. Thus, the fact that an investigation ends without concrete, or with only limited, results is not indicative of any failings as such. Moreover, the procedural obligation must not be interpreted in such a way as to impose an impossible or disproportionate burden on the authorities. Nevertheless, the authorities must take whatever reasonable steps they can to collect evidence and elucidate the circumstances of the case. In particular, the investigation's conclusions must be based on thorough, objective and impartial analysis of all relevant elements". See also ECtHR, *Carter v. Russia*, judgment of 21 September 2021, Appl. No. 20914/07, para. 138; ECtHR, *De Giorgi v. Italy*, judgment of 16 June 2022, Appl. No. 23735/19, paras. 87–88; ECtHR, *Penati v. Italy*, judgment of 11 May 2021, Appl. No. 44166/15. Cf. Parlato (2018), p. 108 ff.; Gialuz (2019), p. 95 ff.

[31] ECtHR, *Güleç v. Turkey*, judgment of 27 July 1998, Appl. No. 21593/93, para. 82; ECtHR, *Oğur v. Turkey*, judgment of 20 May 1999, Appl. No. 21594/93, para. 92. Cf Mezykowska (2011), p. 304.

[32] *Ibid.*

[33] ECtHR, *Talpis v. Italy*, judgment of 2 March 2017, Appl. No. 41237/14, para. 114. In this case the ECtHR found a violation of Article 2 and Article 3 ECHR since the investigative authorities failed to comply with their obligation to protect the applicant during the investigative stage. Indeed, the alleged victim was questioned for the first time by the police 7 months after she had lodged her complaint. "Such a delay could only serve to deprive the applicant of the immediate protection required by the situation. Admittedly, as submitted by the Government, during the period in question the applicant was not subjected to further physical acts of violence by A.T. However, the ECtHR cannot disregard the fact that the applicant, who was being harassed by telephone, was living in fear while staying at the shelter". See Casiraghi (2017), p. 378 ff.; Conti (2017); Romanelli (2023), p. 101; Di Nuzzo and Malino (in press).

An issue that raises challenging difficulties is the role that must be assigned to next-of-kin and relatives during the investigative stage. They surely can be considered third parties when they undergo the effects of investigative activities (*e.g.* when they are requested to provide information about the criminal offence) or even when they are indirectly concerned by a pre-trial measure adopted against the accused (*e.g.* when the accused is compelled to leave the family home). However, there are cases in which their role is equivalent to that of injured persons: *e.g.* in cases regarding the loss of life of the victim. In these situations, the ECtHR has constantly highlighted that next-of-kin and relatives should necessarily be involved in the investigation. Indeed, for criminal inquiries concerning a person's death to be considered efficient under Article 2, the next-of-kin of the victim must be granted all the rights and powers expressly afforded to victims, including the right to be informed about the ongoing investigation and to play an active role in evidentiary procedures.[34] Moreover, it is worth noting that the ECtHR attaches significant importance to their participation in criminal investigations, thus acknowledging that Article 2 ECHR could be triggered if next-of-kin and relatives of the victim are hindered from participating.[35]

In the light of this, the concept of 'third parties' seems to be inappropriate for them. Conversely, they should be regarded as substantial parties during the investigative phase until they join the criminal proceeding as a civil party to claim compensation for the damage suffered from serious crimes or as a formal party in those systems that allow private prosecution. Therefore, next-of-kin and relatives represent a hybrid figure since their role in criminal proceedings may change depending on the different degrees of participation that ECtHR case-law grants them.

3 The Standard of Protection Granted to Witnesses in the Taking of Oral Evidence in ECtHR Case-Law

The autonomous approach adopted by the ECtHR to emphasise the protection needs of victims and third parties in criminal proceedings suggests broadening the spectrum of this study by examining the adverse effects that evidence gathering procedures in court activities may have on third parties' rights. In this section, consideration will firstly be given to the standard of protection granted by ECHR law to witnesses in the collection of oral evidence.

Firstly, it should be highlighted that the term 'witness' has been autonomously interpreted by the ECtHR, irrespective of the legal classifications provided for by

[34] ECtHR, *Talpis v. Italy*.

[35] ECtHR, *Slimani v. France*, judgment of 27 July 2004, Appl. No. 57671/00, para. 49.

contracting parties under national law.[36] For instance, this term encompasses evidence given by a person during an identification parade or face-to-face confrontation with a suspect;[37] evidence given by a co-accused,[38] expert witnesses[39] and police officers;[40] evidence provided by victims, and their relatives,[41] notwithstanding the extent to which they are treated as substantial parties, as seen.

Although Article 6 does not expressly require the consideration of witnesses' protection needs, it is noteworthy that their life, liberty, or security and that of their family members may be jeopardised as a result of the gathering of testimonial evidence, so that rights expressly afforded by Article 8 ECHR would be at stake.[42] Consequently, the principles governing a fair trial require a careful balance of the interests of the defence against those of witnesses called upon to testify.[43] Contracting States, indeed, should organise their criminal proceedings in such a way that those interests are not unjustifiably impaired.[44]

This is a challenging issue to address since: on the one hand, for the accused to be convicted, Article 6(3)(d) requires evidence to be produced in his presence at a public hearing with a view to adversarial argument and, in any case, the accused should be given an adequate and proper opportunity to challenge witnesses against him, either when the statements were made or at a later stage of the proceedings;[45] on

---

[36] ECtHR, *Damir Sibgatullin v. Russia*, judgment of 28 May 2015, Appl. No. 1413/05, para. 45; ECtHR, *S.N. v. Sweden*, judgment of 2 July 2002, Appl. No., 34,209/96, para. 45.

[37] ECtHR, *Vanfuli v. Russia*, judgment of 3 November 2011, Appl. No. 24885/05, para. 110.

[38] ECtHR, *Trofimov v. Russia*, judgment of 4 December 2008, Appl. No. 1111/02, para. 37; ECtHR, *Oddone and Pecci v. San Marino*, judgment of 17 October 2019, Appl. Nos. 26,581/17 and 31,024/17, paras. 94–95.

[39] ECtHR, *Doorson v. The Netherlands*, paras. 81–82.

[40] ECtHR, *Ürek and Ürek v. Turkey*, judgment of 30 July 2019, Appl. No. 74845/12, para. 50. Article 6(3)(d) may also be applied to documentary evidence, including reports prepared by an arresting officer. Cf. ECtHR, *Mirilashvili v. Russia*, judgment of 11 December 2008, Appl. No. 6293/04, paras. 158–159; ECtHR, *Chap Ltd v. Armenia*, judgment of 4 May 2017, Appl. No. 15485/09, para. 48; ECtHR, *Butkevich v. Russia*, judgment of 13 February 2018, Appl. No. 5865/07, paras. 98–99.

[41] ECtHR, *Doorson v. The Netherlands*, judgment of 26 March 1993, Appl. No. 20524/92, para. 70; ECtHR, *Van Mechelen and Others v. The Netherlands*, judgment of 23 April 1997, Appl. Nos. 21363/93 21364/93 21427/93 22056/93, para. 53; ECtHR, *Vladimir Romanov v. Russia*, judgment of 24 July 2008, Appl. No. 41461/02, para. 97; ECtHR, *Stoichov v. Bulgaria*, judgment of 24 March 2005, Appl. No. 9808/02, para. 55.

[42] ECtHR, *Doorson v. The Netherlands*, para. 70; ECtHR, *Van Mechelen and Others v. The Netherlands*, para. 53. Cf. Romanelli (2023), p. 103; Lonati (2008), p. 227 ff.; Chiavario (2001), p. 940.

[43] *Ibid.*

[44] *Ibid.*

[45] ECtHR, *Al-Khawaja and Tahery v. The United Kingdom*, judgment of 15 December 2011, Appl. Nos. 26766/05, 22228/06, para. 118; ECtHR, *Hümmer v. Germany*, judgment of 19 July 2012, Appl. No. 26171/07, para. 38; ECtHR, *Lucà v. Italy*, judgment of 27 February 2001, Appl. No. 33354/96, para. 39; ECtHR, judgment of 31 October 2001, *Solakov v. The Former Yugoslav Republic of Macedonia*, Appl. No. 47023/99, para. 57.

the other hand, it is of paramount importance to protect witnesses from the potential adverse effects of cross-examination.[46]

This necessity becomes even more compelling when we consider the specific protection needs of particular categories of witnesses, such as anonymous witnesses, victims, family members and, in general, individuals in vulnerable situations. Indeed, undergoing a criminal trial may impact their physical and mental well-being, especially when subjected to cross-examination. Moreover, cross-examination in open court can not only increase the risks for special categories of third parties (minors, undercover agents etc.) but also for non-participants who indirectly undergo the effects of the taking of witness evidence (mainly, family members or acquaintances).

For instance, in the case of anonymous witnesses, anonymity becomes necessary when witnesses fear for their life and the safety of their family members.[47] However, ECtHR case-law shows that witnesses often experience a general fear of testifying, rather than a fear directly stemming from threats made by the defendant or their representatives. In numerous cases, this fear has been linked to the notoriety of defendants or their associates.[48] Furthermore, relevant issues arise when witnesses who claim anonymity are police officers. The Court has acknowledged that, as long as the defence rights are upheld, it can be deemed legitimate for police authorities to seek the maintenance of the anonymity of agents engaged in undercover activities in order to ensure their safety and that of their families, as well as to maintain the agents' usefulness for future operations without them being compromised.[49]

When it comes to vulnerable witnesses, the necessity of establishing a set of procedural guarantees is all the more crucial, as being subjected to cross-examination could potentially trigger psychological traumas or situations of 'secondary victimisation', intimidation, and retaliation.[50] When they are called upon to testify, they are required to report criminal facts and confront the accused, thereby reliving their trauma. Consequently, judicial authorities must undertake necessary means to minimise this risk and prevent additional harm by employing protective measures and providing sufficient safeguards in the taking of witness evidence.[51]

Within this framework, the acknowledgement of a statute of procedural guarantees of witnesses in criminal proceedings may clash with the right of the accused to be granted an adequate and proper opportunity to challenge and question

---

[46] Paulesu (2022), p. 1070.

[47] ECtHR, *Doorson v. The Netherlands*, para. 70

[48] ECtHR, *Al-Khawaja and Tahery v. The United Kingdom*, para. 124; ECtHR, *Balta and Demir v. Turkey*, judgment of 23 June 2015, Appl. No. 48628/12, para. 44.

[49] ECtHR, *Van Mechelen and Others v. The Netherlands*, paras. 56–57; ECtHR, *Bátěk and Others v. the Czech Republic*, judgment of 12 January 2017, Appl. No. 54146/09, para. 46; ECtHR, *Van Wesenbeeck v. Belgium*, judgment of 23 May 2017, Appl. No. 67496/10 and 52,936/12, paras. 100–101.

[50] Paulesu (2022), p. 1073 ff.; Mazza (2017), p. 130 ff.; Presutti (2017), p. 378 ff.; Cesari (2015), p. 296 ff.; Ubertis (2009), p. 4066.

[51] See Di Nuzzo and Malino (in press).

prosecutorial witnesses. Therefore, it is relevant to understand whether the need to strike a balance between the protection of witnesses and confrontation rights meets the requirements set out by Article 6(3)(d) ECHR. In its earlier case law, the ECtHR, in order to verify whether proceedings were conducted fairly, applied the 'sole or decisive rule'. This rule—which was developed to balance out a strict understanding of the right to confrontation and the use of untested evidence in national proceedings[52]—entailed that, if the accused had no chance to challenge evidence at any stage of the domestic proceedings, he or she cannot be convicted solely or mainly on the basis of such evidence.[53] In the case *P.S. v. Germany*, the accused had been found guilty of sexual assault against an 8-year-old girl in the domestic proceeding.[54] The conviction was mainly based on the hearsay statements provided by the victim's mother, who recounted what her daughter had told her, and the police officer who had questioned the child immediately after the incident.[55] Moreover, the trial judge had ruled out the need to examine the victim to avoid further psychological traumas. In the light of this, the ECtHR found a violation of Article 6(3)(d) ECHR, since the defence had had no opportunity of challenging the reliability of the decisive evidence.[56] Consequently, the ECtHR attributed greater value to the right of the accused to confront witnesses against him or than to the right of the victim to avoid further psychological distress resulting from cross-examination.

However, in recent years the approach of the ECtHR in the field of the right to confrontation has significantly changed. In the landmark decisions *Al-Khawaja and Tahery v. The United Kingdom* and *Schatschaschwili v. Germany*, the ECtHR ruled out that 'the sole or decisive rule' could be inflexible, highlighting that, where a conviction is based solely or decisively on untested evidence, the Court must scrutinise whether domestic authorities provided for sufficient counterbalancing factors aimed at compensating for the lack of confrontation.[57] It is important to

[52] Ruggeri (2017a), p. 329.

[53] See ECtHR, *Lucà v. Italy*, para. 40: "where a conviction is based solely or to a decisive degree on depositions that have been made by a person whom the accused has had no opportunity to examine or to have examined, whether during the investigation or at the trial, the rights of the defence are restricted to an extent that is incompatible with the guarantees provided by Article 6". Cf. Ruggeri (2017a), p. 329; Ruggeri (2017b), p. 4 ff.; Quattrocolo (2020), p. 82; Ubertis (2017), p. 392 ff.; Cesari (2003), p. 1451 ff.

[54] ECtHR, *P.S. v. Germany*, judgment of 20 December 2001, Appl. No. 33900/96.

[55] *Ibid.*

[56] *Ibid.*

[57] See ECtHR, *Al-Khawaja and Tahery v. The United Kingdom*, para. 147: "The Court therefore concludes that, where a hearsay statement is the sole or decisive evidence against a defendant, its admission as evidence will not automatically result in a breach of Article 6 § 1. At the same time, where a conviction is based solely or decisively on the evidence of absent witnesses, the Court must subject the proceedings to the most searching scrutiny. [...] The question in each case is whether there are sufficient counterbalancing factors in place, including measures that permit a fair and proper assessment of the reliability of that evidence to take place. This would permit a conviction to be based on such evidence only if it is sufficiently reliable given its importance in the case". Cf. Spencer (2014), p. 48 ff.; Kostoris (2020), p. 1676 ff.; Casiraghi (2019), p. 1363 ff.

stress that these principles apply not only to cases regarding absent witnesses but also to situations in which the defence faced excessive difficulties in exercising the right to confrontation due to the admission of evidence.[58] This may concern the admission as evidence of statements made by anonymous witnesses,[59] "traditional" witnesses, including the co-accused, who refused to testify at trial or to confront the defence,[60] and witnesses whose examination has been carried out through special examination techniques, like videoconferencing.[61] Moreover, these principles gain particular relevance in cases involving victims and, in general, individuals in vulnerable situations. In assessing the overall fairness of criminal proceedings, the rights of these subjects must always be taken into account. Indeed, the ECtHR stressed that Article 6(3)(d) ECHR cannot be interpreted as requiring in all cases that questions be put directly by the accused or his or her defence counsel through cross-examination or by other means, since direct confrontation between the accused and the alleged victim could trigger further traumatic situations.[62] In any case, it must be stressed that this approach does not entail that measures aimed at safeguarding witnesses—particularly, the non-attendance of a witness at trial, the video recording of a witness interview,[63] and the possibility of examining the witness indirectly through written questions at trial or at the pre-trial stage[64]—

[58] ECtHR, *Schatschaschwili v. Germany*, judgment of 15 December 2015, Appl. No. 9154/10, para. 116: "Given that the Court's concern is to ascertain whether the proceedings as a whole were fair, it must review the existence of sufficient counterbalancing factors not only in cases in which the evidence given by an absent witness was the sole or decisive basis for the applicant's conviction but also in those cases where, following its assessment of the domestic courts' evaluation of the weight of the evidence, it finds it unclear whether the evidence in question was the sole or decisive basis but is nevertheless satisfied that it carried significant weight and that its admission may have handicapped the defence".

[59] ECtHR, *Al-Khawaja and Tahery v. The United Kingdom*, para. 127; ECtHR, *Scholer v. Germany*, judgment of 18 December 2014, Appl. No. 14212/10, para. 51; ECtHR, *Balta and Demir v. Turkey*, paras. 36–41; ECtHR, *Asani v. the former Yugoslav Republic of Macedonia*, judgment of 1 February 2018, Appl. No. 27962/10, paras. 36–37; ECtHR, *Süleyman v. Turkey*, judgment of 17 November 2020, Appl. No. 59453/10.

[60] ECtHR, *Craxi v. Italy*, judgment of 5 December 2002, para. 88; ECtHR, *Vidgen v. The Netherlands*, judgment of 10 July 2012, Appl. No. 29353/06, para. 42; ECtHR, *Cabral v. The Netherlands*, judgment of 28 August 2018, Appl. No. 37617/10, para. 33; ECtHR, *Breijer v. The Netherlands*, judgment of 3 July 2018, Appl. No. 41596, paras. 32–33.

[61] ECtHR, *Papadakis v. The Former Yugoslav Republic of Macedonia*, judgment of 26 February 2013, Appl. No. 50254/07, para. 89; ECtHR, *Zhukovskiy v. Ukraine*, judgment of 3 March 2011, Appl. No. 31240/03, para. 45. See Daniele (2012), p. 133; Falcone (2023), p. 1 ff.; Bachmaier Winter (2013a), p. 137; Bolognari (2022), p. 159.

[62] ECtHR, *R.B. v. Estonia*, judgment of 22 June 2021, Appl. No. 22597/16; ECtHR, *S.N. v. Sweden*, para. 52; ECtHR, *Y. v. Slovenia* judgment of 28 May 2015, Appl. No. 41107/10, para. 106.

[63] ECtHR, *Gani v. Spain*, judgment of 9 September 2013, Appl. No. 61800/08; ECtHR, *A. L. c. Finland*, judgment of 27 April 2009, Appl. No. 23220/04, para. 41; ECtHR, *D. v. Finland*, judgment of 7 July 2009, Appl. No. 30542/04, para. 50; Gialuz (2015), p. 22 ff.

[64] ECtHR, *Paić v. Croatia*, judgment of 29 March 2016, Appl. No. 47082/12, para. 47; ECtHR, *Scholer v. Germany*, para. 60; ECtHR, *Yevgeniy Ivanov v. Russia*, judgment of 25 April 2013, Appl.

apply automatically. Since such measures do not grant the defence the same opportunities as cross-examination, their application must be subjected to the most careful scrutiny by domestic authorities.

The analysis carried out so far has revealed the significant effort of the Court to reconstruct the right to confrontation with a comprehensive approach aimed at considering all interests at stake and especially the fundamental rights of witnesses that undergo the effects of the taking of oral evidence. Particular attention has been drawn to specific categories of witnesses whose protection needs are magnified by risks directly stemming from cross-examination. It is noteworthy that the need to mitigate the risks of repercussions on fundamental rights of individuals who undergo the effects of court activities has led the ECtHR to redefine the scope of the right to confrontation, thus acknowledging protection concerns that have been neglected for too long.

4 The Impact of Covert Investigative Measures on Third Parties' Fundamental Rights and the Procedural Safeguards Developed by the ECtHR

As we have seen, procedural acts and, more broadly, criminal proceedings may have an impact on the fundamental rights of a wider range of individuals other than suspects, defendants, or formal/substantial participants. Whereas the taking of testimonial evidence could have a strong impact on witnesses and, especially, on individuals in vulnerable situations, interference with fundamental rights represents the ordinary outcome of specific investigative activities aimed at detecting serious forms of crimes by the gathering of enormous amounts of data and information on individuals who do not necessarily have to be involved in criminal investigations.[65]

In almost every country, an increasing number of investigative measures, such as wiretapping and online searches, may be addressed against third parties. This becomes even more worrisome if such means of investigation are employed by investigative authorities in a hidden form through the recourse to digital instruments, thus enhancing the risk of creating troubling scenarios of mass surveillance.[66]

Within this framework, the ECtHR has developed extensive case-law aimed at minimising the risk of interference with third parties' fundamental rights by recognising minimum safeguards with a view to preventing abuses of power by law enforcement officers and by identifying the limits within which the use of intrusive investigative measures may be justified.

No. 27100/03, para. 49; ECtHR, *Vronchenko v. Estonia*, judgment of 18 July 2013, Appl. No. 59632/09, para. 65.

[65] Cf. Kusak (2016), p. 132.

[66] See Bachmaier Winter (2021), p. 317 ff.

In the case *Iordachi and Others v. Moldova*, the Court found a violation of Article 8 ECHR, since national law did not provide a specific definition of the categories of people liable to have their communications tapped, only generally referring to "suspects, defendants, or other persons involved in a criminal offence".[67] Indeed, "no explanation has been given as to who exactly falls within the category of other persons involved in a criminal offence".[68]

This solution, which was later confirmed in several judgments regarding cases of bulk surveillance, offers significant methodological guidance for revising the approaches adopted by some legal systems in both domestic and transnational cases.[69] Nevertheless, some countries still lack adequate indications about who falls into the category of people who may have their communications intercepted, thus permitting the use of intrusive means of investigation against individuals regardless of whether they are effectively involved in a criminal offence.

A clear example of this problematic issue was outlined by the Court in the case *Roman Zacharov v. Russia*. In this case, the ECtHR highlighted that, even though "interception measures in respect of a person who was not suspected of any offence but could possess information about such an offence might be justified under Article 8 of the Convention", neither Russian law nor domestic case-law clarify how the term "a person who may have information about a criminal offence or relevant to the criminal case" needs to be interpreted in practice.[70]

Furthermore, in *Amann v. Switzerland*, the ECtHR stressed that particular attention must always be paid towards any real or potential violation of the privacy of individuals against whom no suspicion of guilt has been addressed and whose conversations are tapped fortuitously (*e.g.* individuals targeted by specific calls or random users of the tapped device).[71] For instance, the Federal Criminal Procedure Act of Switzerland at Section 66(1 *bis*)—which was in force at the time this judgment was delivered—specified that "where the conditions justifying the monitoring of the accused or suspect are satisfied, third parties may also be monitored if specific facts give rise to the presumption that they are receiving or imparting information intended for the accused or suspect or sent by him". However, the Court emphasised that national law does not consider the 'persons monitored fortuitously' as 'necessary participants' in a telephone conversation recorded by investigative authorities.[72] Furthermore, it does not specify the precautions and

---

[67] ECtHR, *Iordachi and Others v. Moldova*, judgment of 10 February 2009, Appl. No. 25198/02, para. 44. See widely Kusak (2016), p. 132.

[68] ECtHR, *Iordachi and Others v. Moldova*, para. 44.

[69] ECtHR, *Roman Zakharov v. Russia*, judgment of 4 December 2015, Appl. No. 47143/06, para. 245; ECtHR, *Amann v. Switzerland*, judgment of 16 February 2000, Appl. No. 27798/95, para. 76; ECtHR, *Kennedy v. the United Kingdom*, judgment of 18 May 2010, Appl. No. 26839/05, para. 167.

[70] ECtHR, *Roman Zakharov v. Russia*, para. 245.

[71] ECtHR, *Amann v. Switzerland*, para. 61.

[72] *Ibid.*, para. 76.

safeguards that should be taken with regard to these categories of people to prevent potential abuses.[73]

In the light of this, the ECtHR developed the following minimum guarantees that national legal systems should provide in order to ensure proper protection of the fundamental rights of these individuals:

> the nature of the offences which may give rise to an interception order; a definition of the categories of people liable to have their telephones tapped; a limit on the duration of telephone tapping; the procedure to be followed for examining, using and storing the data obtained; the precautions to be taken when communicating the data to other parties; and the circumstances in which recordings may or must be erased or the tapes destroyed.[74]

Moreover, in a domain where abuse is potentially straightforward in individual cases and could yield detrimental consequences for democratic society, it is generally advisable to entrust supervisory control to a judge who has to assess whether the investigative measure is necessary and proportionate to the aim pursued.[75] Judicial oversight turns out to be a fundamental safeguard against abuses of power. However, the ECtHR does not consider such a control as a 'necessary requirement', thus also accepting the supervision of an independent body which should be informed of both the purpose of the interception and the bearers or communication routes likely to be tapped.[76] These are all essential elements that allow an assessment of the necessity and proportionality of the investigative activity.[77] The Court emphasised the need for each stage of the interception process to be subjected to oversight by either a judicial or an independent authority and that this control must be strict enough to avoid unlawful interference with third parties' fundamental rights.[78]

In addition, national law systems should provide effective remedies for anyone who suspects that their communications have been intercepted by law enforcement officers in order to ensure proper compliance with the European Convention and to challenge the lawfulness of the investigative activity.[79] The effectiveness of

---

[73] *Ibid.*

[74] ECtHR, *Weber and Saravia v. Germany*, decision of 29 June 2006, Appl. No. 54934/00, para. 95. See also ECtHR, *Huvig v. France*, judgment of 24 April 1990, Appl. No. 11105/84, para. 34; ECtHR, *Amann v. Switzerland*, para. 76; ECtHR, *Prado Bugallo v. Spain*, judgment of 18 February 2003, Appl. No. 58496/00, para. 30.

[75] ECtHR, *Klass and Others v. Germany*, judgment of 6 September 1978, Appl. No. 5029/71, para. 56; ECtHR, *Kennedy v. the United Kingdom*, para. 167; Kusak (2016), p. 133.

[76] ECtHR, *Big Brother Watch and Others v. the United Kingdom*, judgment of 25 May 2021, Appl. Nos. 58,170/13, 62,322/14, and 24,960/15, para. 352; ECtHR, *Centrum för rättvisa v. Sweden*, judgment of 25 May 2021, Appl. No. 35252/08, paras. 265–266; cf. Turanjanin (2023), p. 128. ECtHR, *Trabajo Rueda v. Spain*, judgment of 30 May 2017, Appl. No. 32600/12. Cf. Bachmaier Winter (2021), p. 317 ff.; Bachmaier Winter (2013b), p. 94 ff.; Bachmaier Winter (2004), p. 41 ff.; Bernardini and Sanvitale (2023), p. 94.

[77] *Ibid.*

[78] ECtHR, *Roman, Zakharov v. Russia*, para. 232; ECtHR, *Klass and Others v. Germany*, para. 49–50; ECtHR, *Weber and Saravia v. Germany*, para. 106.

[79] ECtHR, *Big Brother Watch and Others v. the United Kingdom*, para. 357; ECtHR, *Roman ECtHR, Zakharov v. Russia*, para. 234; ECtHR, *Kennedy v. the United Kingdom*, para. 167.

remedies is closely tied to the "notification" of intrusive activities.[80] This requirement has been considered a crucial factor in assessing the effectiveness of remedies and the presence of adequate safeguards against abuses of power.[81] Unfortunately, several countries still lack sufficient safeguards in this regard.[82] Indeed, individuals may have limited opportunities to apply to the court if they are not informed about measures taken without their knowledge.[83] Nonetheless, in recent years, the ECtHR ruled out that 'notification' is a necessary requirement for determining the effectiveness of legal remedies and acknowledged that remedies that do not depend on prior notification may even offer better guarantees.[84] In particular, the Court outlined that the activities envisaged may not necessitate a bespoke individual notification system, provided that remedies are granted on a general basis to the entire population.[85] It is imperative that domestic remedies without any prior notification system permit every person whose communications are being or have been intercepted to apply to the courts.[86]

Within this framework, it is worth mentioning the approach adopted by the Court of Justice of the European Union (hereafter, CJEU). In *Digital Rights Ireland and Others,* the CJEU highlighted that "the absence of notification is likely to generate in

[80] Cf. Di Nuzzo (2022), p. 142; Nicolicchia (2020), p. 156 ff.

[81] ECtHR, *Association for European Integration and Human Rights and Ekimdzhiev v. Bulgaria*, judgment of 28 June 2006, Appl. No. 62540/00, para. 58; cf. Turanjanin (2023), p. 128.

[82] See ECtHR, *Contrada v. Italy (n. 4)*, judgement of 23 May 2024, Appl. No. 2507/19. The Court observed that the Italian legal system does not provide any notification to third parties (who, therefore, might never know that they have been subjected to interceptions and are unable to contest their legitimacy). Furthermore, third parties lack the possibility of applying to the court to verify the legitimacy and necessity of the measure and to receive, if applicable, an adequate protection. Within this light, the Court concluded that the Italian legal system fails to provide adequate and effective safeguards for individuals subjected to interceptions without being involved in criminal proceedings. See Foti and Malino, in this volume.

[83] ECtHR, *Roman, Zakharov v. Russia*, para. 234; ECtHR, *Klass and Others v. Germany*, para. 57; ECtHR, *Weber and Saravia v. Germany*, para. 135.

[84] ECtHR, *Big Brother Watch and Others v. the United Kingdom*, para. 358: "Regardless of whether material was acquired through targeted or bulk interception, the existence of a national security exception could deprive a notification requirement of any real practical effect. The likelihood of a notification requirement having little or no practical effect will be more acute in the bulk interception context, since such surveillance may be used for the purposes of foreign intelligence gathering and will, for the most part, target the communications of persons outside the State's territorial jurisdiction. Therefore, even if the identity of a target is known, the authorities may not be aware of his or her location". See De Hert and Malgieri (2020), p. 26 ff.; Neroni Rezende (2022), p. 84; Di Nuzzo (2022), p. 142.

[85] Cf. Neroni Rezende (2022), p. 89.

[86] ECtHR, *Big Brother Watch and Others v. the United Kingdom*, para. 357; ECtHR, *Roman, Zakharov v. Russia*, para. 234; ECtHR, *Kennedy v. the United Kingdom*, para. 167. More recently see ECtHR, *Contrada v. Italy (n. 4)*.

the minds of the persons concerned the feeling that their private lives are the subject of constant surveillance".[87]

One might say that it is the very absence of knowledge that ensures the effectiveness of investigation. However, this does not seem enough to exclude notification, especially if no suspicion of guilt has been addressed to all those persons tapped by chance, and notification is no longer liable to jeopardise the investigative activities. Therefore, in cases where the intrusiveness of investigative measures involves individuals against whom no evidence of guilt has been gathered, it seems more appropriate to establish a dual system of remedies: one independent of prior notification, which allows anyone who suspects that their communications are being or have been intercepted to apply to the courts; another that relies on notification for individuals tapped by chance.[88]

5 The Protection of Third Parties whose Assets and Goods Have Been Tainted in ECtHR Case-Law

The analysis carried out hitherto has shown that, in recent years, the ECtHR has identified violations of the European Convention on Human Rights primarily linked to the adverse effects of procedural acts. We have seen that procedural acts have the potential to encroach upon the fundamental rights of a progressively broader spectrum of individuals—extending beyond just suspects, defendants, and formal participants—which encompasses all those persons who may experience both direct and indirect consequences of criminal prosecution. This paragraph focuses on those individuals whose goods and assets may be timely frozen or seized for purposes of confiscation or confiscated even in the absence of any suspicion of guilt against them.

Providing a comprehensive overview of the standard of protection granted to these persons by ECtHR case-law is a challenging task. This is due to the fact that the "ECtHR has a casuistic approach that makes it difficult to identify a solid framework to assess the legitimacy of confiscation regimes".[89] Indeed, as Judge Paulo Pinto de Albuquerque highlighted in his partly concurring and partly dissenting opinion in *Varvara v. Italy*:

Under the *nomen juris* of confiscation, the States have introduced *ante delictum* criminal prevention measures, criminal sanctions (accessory or even principal criminal penalties), security measures in the broad sense, administrative measures adopted within or outside criminal proceedings, and civil measures *in rem*.

[87] CJEU, *Digital Rights Ireland and Others*, judgement of 8 April 2014, Joined Cases C-293/12 and C-594/12, para. 34. See Falcone in this volume.

[88] ECtHR, *Big Brother Watch and Others v. the United Kingdom*, para. 337; ECtHR, *Roman, Zakharov v. Russia*, para. 234; See Di Nuzzo (2022), p. 142; Neroni Rezende (2022), p. 89.

[89] Cf. Simonato and Fernandez-Bertier (2019), p. 15; Simonato (2017), p. 366; Boucht (2017).

Confronted with this enormous range of responses available to the State, the Court has not yet developed any consistent case-law based on principled reasoning.[90]

Nevertheless, it is worth mentioning that in recent years the European Union has played an important role in developing a common understanding of confiscation regimes between member states. Indeed, Directive 2014/42/EU provided a specific concept for extended confiscation, non-conviction based confiscation, and third party confiscation.[91] In particular, Article 6 of the Directive enables third party confiscation where the "proceeds or other property the value of which corresponds to proceeds" are directly or indirectly either transferred by the suspect or the accused to third parties, or acquired by third parties from the suspect or the accused. In any case third party confiscation is allowed only if "third parties knew or ought to have known that the purpose of the transfer or acquisition was to avoid confiscation, on the basis of concrete facts and circumstances".[92] Consequently, *bona fide* third parties should be excluded from confiscation regimes and should be provided with effective remedies if their goods and assets are unlawfully tainted.

Within this framework, ECtHR case-law has long addressed this problematic issue, seeking to identify the limits within which it is possible to justify the adverse effects of confiscation systems on third parties in criminal proceedings, and to establish a set of procedural guarantees aimed at protecting third parties' rights from such interference.[93]

ECtHR case-law regarding the protection of third parties whose goods and assets have been affected by freezing, seizure, or confiscation orders has developed mainly under Article 1 of Protocol no. 1 to the ECHR and Article 6(1) ECHR.[94] This is quite understandable, given that third parties are by definition not involved in criminal

---

[90] ECtHR, *Varvara v. Italy*, judgment of 29 October 2013, Appl. No. 17475/09.

[91] Directive 2014/42/EU of the European Parliament and of the Council of 3 April 2014 on the freezing and confiscation of instrumentalities and proceeds of crime in the European Union. See on this theme Falcone in this volume.

[92] However, it must be stressed that despite the efforts of the European Union to establish common rules regarding confiscation models, several difficulties arise since the differences between these models are not entirely clear. Legal scholarship, indeed, has outlined that, even though extended and third party confiscation has been interpreted by EU law as 'post-conviction' models of confiscation, they can be considered to some extent as confiscation without previous conviction. For instance, those individuals whose goods and assets are confiscated without being suspects or defendants are, by definition, not involved in criminal proceedings. See Simonato and Fernandez-Bertier (2019), p. 11.

[93] Boucht (2019), p. 526: "when implementing confiscation schemes, which may have considerable adverse effects on the individuals subjected to them, it is crucial that also the rights of these individuals are safeguarded in an effective manner".

[94] It must be stressed that in several cases the ECtHR considered that it was not necessary to assess whether there has been a violation of Article 6(1) ECHR if the Court found a violation of Article 1, Protocol 1, ECHR. See ECtHR, *Microintelect Ood v. Bulgaria*, judgment of 4 March 2014, Appl. no. 34129/03, para. 54; ECtHR, *Bowler International Unit v. France*, judgment of 23 July 2009, Appl. No. 1946/09, para. 61. Conversely, The Court found a violation of Article 6(1) ECHR where third parties (e.g. heirs) were deprived of their property as a result of the misconduct of the *de cuius*. Cf. ECtHR, *Lagardère v. France*, judgment of 12 April 2012, Appl. No. 18851/07.

proceedings and that these kinds of measures mainly impinge upon their property rights.[95]

In particular, Article 1 of Protocol no. 1 to the ECHR mandates that "no one shall be deprived of his possessions except in the public interest and subject to the conditions provided for by law and by the general principles of international law". In light of this, a preliminary assessment on the existence of a legal basis that justifies the interference with third parties' property rights is necessary.[96] In particular, to ensure adequate protection against arbitrariness the ECtHR requires that the legal basis is at once foreseeable and accessible.[97] Moreover, the Court demands that any interference with third parties' fundamental rights must be proportionate to the aim being pursued.[98] A fair balance must be struck between the demands of the general interest of the community and the requirements of protecting the fundamental rights of individuals.[99] Once these conditions are fulfilled, ECtHR has to verify whether third parties who suffered the consequences of confiscation regimes have been granted the right to a fair and public hearing and an effective remedy to challenge the lawfulness of such interference.[100]

In *Microintelect Ood v. Bulgaria*, the Court stressed that "although the second paragraph of Article 1 of Protocol No. 1 contains no explicit procedural requirements, it has been construed to require that persons affected by a measure interfering with their possessions be afforded a reasonable opportunity of putting their case to the responsible authorities for the purpose of effectively challenging those measures".[101]

---

[95] See Finocchiaro (2022), p. 424 ff.

[96] ECtHR, *Vistiņš and Perepjolkins v. Latvia*, judgment of 25 October 2012, Appl. No. 71243/01, para. 95; ECtHR, *Béláné Nagy v. Hungary*, judgment of 13 December 2016, Appl. No. 53080/13, para. 112.

[97] ECtHR, *Lekić v. Slovenia*, judgment of 11 December 2018, Appl. No. 36480/07, para. 95; ECtHR, *Centro Europa 7 S.r.l. and Di Stefano v. Italy*, judgment of 7 June 2016, Appl. No. 38433/09, para. 187.

[98] ECtHR, *G.I.E.M. S.r.l. and Others v. Italy*, Judgment of 28 June 2018, Appl. Nos. 1828/06, 34,163/07, and 19,029/11; ECtHR, *Korshunova v. Russia*, judgment of 6 September 2022, Appl. No. 46147/19; ECtHR, *Sud Fondi srl and Others v. Italy*, judgment of 20 January 2009, Appl. No. 75909/01; ECtHR, *Agosi v. The United Kingdom*, judgment 24 October 1986, Appl. No. 9118/80.

[99] ECtHR, *Gogitidze and Others v. Georgia*, judgment of 12 May 2015, Appl. No. 36862/05, para. 97; ECtHR, *The former King of Greece and Others v. Greece*, judgment of 23 November 2000, Appl. No. 25701/94, paras. 79 and 82; See also Finocchiaro (2022), p. 419 ff.

[100] ECtHR, *Gogitidze and Others v. Georgia*, para. 109; ECtHR, *Veits v. Estonia*, judgment of 15 January 2015, Appl. No. 12951/11, para. 70; ECtHR, *Jokela v. Finland*, judgment of 21 May 2002, Appl. No. 28856/95, para. 45; ECtHR, *Webb v. The United Kingdom*, judgment of 10 February 2004, Appl. No. 56054/00; ECtHR, *Grayson and Barnham v. The United Kingdom*, judgment of 23 September 2008, Appl. Nos. 19,955/05 and 15,085/06. Cf. Simonato and Fernandez-Bertier (2019), p. 28.

[101] ECtHR, *Microintelect Ood v. Bulgaria*, para. 44; ECtHR, *Bowler International Unit v. France*, para. 41; ECtHR, *Denisova and Moiseyeva v. Russia*, judgment of 1 April 2010, Appl. No. 16903/03, para. 59.

In *Gogitidze and Others v. Georgia*, the Court outlined that third parties (*i.e.* in this case family members and other close relatives who were assumed to handle the unlawfully obtained property on behalf of defendants, or who lacked the status of *bona fide*) need to be afforded "a reasonable opportunity of putting their arguments before domestic courts", either by submitting written questions or by taking part in court activities.[102]

Consequently, the ECtHR expressly recognises the right of third parties whose assets and goods have been tainted to have adequate protection in criminal proceedings.[103] This is because the peaceful enjoyment of one's possessions is a fundamental aspect of a democratic society.

6 Concluding Remarks

The results of this study show that providing a comprehensive overview of the standard of protection afforded by ECHR law to third parties in criminal proceedings is a complex issue. This is mainly due to the difficulties that arise in determining the meaning of the concept of 'third parties' within the scope of ECHR law.

We have seen that a formalistic approach proves inadequate in identifying the very notion of 'third parties', especially since the ECtHR aims to fulfil the challenging task of reconciling the perspective of ECHR law with the specific characteristics of the different national law systems of each contracting party.

In this light, after overcoming any distinction based on a formalistic approach, it seemed more appropriate to define the concept of 'third parties' by considering both the adverse effects that procedural acts may have on individuals who are involved in various ways in investigative and court activities, and the different degrees of participation that the ECtHR case-law and domestic legislations have granted them. The more such individuals are enabled to take part in criminal proceedings as substantial parties or as formal parties, the less they may be regarded as third parties to criminal proceedings.

Bearing in mind these criteria, we have tried to provide a distinction between third parties, substantial parties, and formal parties to criminal proceedings from a human rights perspective. This has led us to conclude that within the scope of ECHR law:

(a) the concept of 'third parties' encompasses not solely those individuals against whom procedural acts are addressed, but also all those people who directly or indirectly undergo the effects of criminal proceedings, provided that they are under no suspicion of guilt;
(b) the notion of 'substantial parties' refers to all those individuals who, although not holding a 'formal party' status, have a substantial interest in the recognition

[102] ECtHR, *Gogitidze and Others v. Georgia*, para. 109; Simonato (2017), p. 376; Simonato and Fernandez-Bertier (2019), p. 25.

[103] ECtHR, *Gogitidze and Others v. Georgia*, para. 109.

of rights and powers that are necessary for assuming such a role in criminal proceedings;

(c) the concept of 'formal parties' refers to those persons who are entitled by law to formally participate in criminal proceedings.

While this distinction helps to clarify the specific aims of this study, we have seen that some individuals may hold a unique role in criminal proceedings, depending on the degree of the participatory rights and powers expressly afforded to them. This is the case of victims and their relatives. On one hand, they may be regarded as third parties when they undergo the effects of investigative and court activities: *i.e.* when they are requested to provide information about the criminal offence at the investigative stage; when they are called upon to testify at trial; when they indirectly undergo the adverse effects of cross-examination (e.g. the adverse effects on family members resulting from the cross-examination of undercover agents). On the other hand, they can take part in criminal proceedings as substantial parties or as formal parties when they are called upon to play an active role during the investigative stage and in court activities to safeguard their interests.

This demonstrates that reaching a common understanding on the concept of 'third parties' and the standard of protection that needs to be provided to those individuals is a challenging issue to address. However, in our opinion, it must be stressed that analysing these topics from the perspective of ECHR law may represent a turning point in dealing with these difficult tasks, since it makes it possible to combine the perspective of international human rights law with the different approach adopted by each contracting party.

References

Aloisi M (2021) Prescrizione del reato e inerzia del pubblico ministero: nuove prospettive e limiti dei diritti della vittima nelle indagini preliminari. Processo penale e giustizia 5:1241–1248

Bachmaier Winter L (2004) Intervenciones teléfonicas y derechos de terceros en el proceso penal. La necesidad de una regulación legal del secreto profesional y de otras relaciones de confiancia. Revista de Derecho Procesal 1-3:41–82

Bachmaier Winter L (2013a) Transnational criminal proceedings, witness evidence and confrontation: lessons from the ECtHR's case-law. Utrecht Law Rev 9(4):127–146

Bachmaier Winter L (2013b) The role of proportionality principle in cross-border investigations involving fundamental rights. In: Ruggeri S (ed) Transnational inquiries and the protection of fundamental rights in criminal proceedings. A study in memory of Vittorio Grevi and Giovanni Tranchina. Springer, Heidelberg, pp 85–110

Bachmaier Winter L (2021) Proportionality, mass surveillance and criminal investigation: the Strasbourg Court facing Big Brother. In: Billis E, Knust N, Rui JP (eds) The principle of proportionality in crime control and criminal justice. Hart Publishing, Oxford, pp 317–335

Bernardini L, Sanvitale F (2023) Searches and seizures of electronic devices in european criminal proceedings: a new pattern for independent review? Revista Ítalo-Española de Derecho Procesal 1:73–119

Bolognari M (2022) La videoconferenza transnazionale nell'ordine europeo di indagine penale. Rivista di diritto processuale 77(2):513–524

Boucht J (2017) The limits of asset confiscation. On the legitimacy of extended appropriation of criminal proceeds. Hart Publishing, Oxford

Boucht J (2019) Asset confiscation in Europe – past, present, and future challenges. J Financ Crime 26(2):526–548

Casiraghi R (2017) La Corte di Strasburgo condanna l'Italia per la mancata tutela delle vittime di violenza domestica e di genere. Diritto penale contemporaneo 3:378–382

Casiraghi R (2019) I nuovi approdi "europei" del diritto al confronto. Cassaz Penal 3:1363–1376

Cassibba F (2021) Durata irragionevole delle indagini preliminari e archiviazione. Riv Ital Dirit Proced Penal 64(3):1141–1144

Cesari C (2003) Prova irripetibile e contraddittorio nella Convenzione europea dei diritti dell'uomo. Riv Ital Dirit Proced Penal 46(4):1447–1469

Cesari C (2015) "La campana di vetro": protezione della personalità e rispetto del contraddittorio nell'esame dibattimentale del teste minorenne. In: Buzzelli S, Caraceni L, Siracusano F, Coppetta MG, Patanè V, Mazza O, Cesari C (eds) Il minorenne fonte di prova del processo penale. Giuffrè, Milano, pp 263–324

Chiavario M (2001) Il «diritto al processo» delle vittime dei reati e la corte europea dei diritti dell'uomo. Rivista di diritto processuale 4:938–947

Conti R (2017) Violenze in danno di soggetti vulnerabili, tra obblighi (secondari) di protezione e divieto di discriminazione di genere. Questione Giustizia

Daniele M (2012) La formazione digitale delle prove dichiarative. Giappichelli, Torino

De Hert P, Malgieri G (2020) Article 8 ECHR compliant and foreseeable surveillance: the ECtHR's expanded legality requirement copied by the CJEU. A discussion of European surveillance case law. Brussels Priv Hub Work Pap 6(1):1–40

Di Nuzzo V (2022) Search and seizure of digital evidence: human rights concerns and new safeguards. In: Bachmaier Winter L, Ruggeri S (eds) Investigating and preventing crime in the digital era. New safeguards, new rights. Springer, Cham, pp 119–150

Di Nuzzo V, Malino E (in press) The victim's role in cross-border situations in European and international law a multilevel perspective. Galileu Revista de Direito e Economia. (forthcoming)

Falcone A (2023) La videoconferenza nel procedimento penale italiano: riflessioni a margine della recente riforma Cartabia in materia di partecipazione a distanza. La legislazione penale:1–47

Finocchiaro S (2022) Art. 1 Prot. Add. Protezione della proprietà. In: Ubertis G, Viganò F (eds) Corte di Strasburgo e giustizia penale. Giappichelli, Torino, pp 413–438

Gialuz M (2016) La protezione della vittima tra Corte edu e Corte di Giustizia. In: Donati L (ed) Lo statuto europeo delle vittime di reato. Modelli di tutela tra diritto dell'Unione e buone pratiche nazionali. Cedam, Padova, pp 19–30

Gialuz M (2019) Il diritto alla giurisdizione dell'imputato e della vittima tra spinte europee e carenze dell'ordinamento italiano. Riv Ital Dirit Proced Penal 62(1):75–100

Grisonich E (2021) Il dirompente incidere delle garanzie processuali della vittima nella giurisprudenza di Strasburgo: il caso Petrella c. Italia, tra ragionevole durata del procedimento, diritto di accesso al giudice e rimedio effettivo. Sistema penale

Kostoris RE (2020) Per una "grammatica" minima del giudizio di equità processuale. Rivista italiana di diritto e procedura 63(4):1675–1698

Kusak M (2016) Mutual admissibility of evicence in criminal matters in the EU. A study of telephone tapping and house search. Maklu-Publishers, Antwerpen

Lonati S (2008) Il diritto dell'accusato a "interrogare o fare interrogare" le fonti di prova a carico (studio sul contraddittorio nella Convenzione europea dei diritti dell'uomo e nel sistema processuale penale italiano). Giappichelli, Torino

Malino E (2022) Tutela della vittima e completezza delle indagini preliminari tra giurisprudenza edu e prospettive di riforma della giustizia penale italiana. La legislazione penale:1–23

Marandola A (2021) Persona offesa e durata irragionevole delle indagini tra Corte costituzionale e corte edu. Penale, Diritto e procedura

Mazza O (2017) Il contraddittorio attutito di fronte ai testimoni vulnerabili. In: Negri D, Orlandi R (eds) Le erosioni silenziose del contraddittorio. Giappichelli, Torino, pp 119–130

Mezykowska A (2011) Does the victim of a crime have the right to a fair trial? Remarks on the protection of crime victims in the light of the guarantees in the European Convention on Human Rights. Pol Yearb Int Law 31:283–315
Montagna M (2016) Necessità e completezza delle indagini. In: Gaito A (ed) I principi europei del processo penale. Dike Giuridica, Roma, pp 299–324
Montagna M (2019) Obblighi convenzionali, tutela della vittima e completezza delle indagini. Archivio penale 3:1–18
Neroni Rezende I (2022) Facial recognition for preventive purposes: the human rights implications of detecting emotions in public spaces. In: Bachmaier Winter L, Ruggeri S (eds) Investigating and preventing crime in the digital era. New safeguards, new rights. Springer, Cham, pp 67–100
Nicolicchia F (2020) I controlli occulti e continuativi come categoria probatoria. Una sistematizzazione dei nuovi mezzi di ricerca della prova tra fonti europee e ordinamenti nazionali. Cedam, Padova
Parlato L (2018) Effettività delle indagini ed "equità processuale". In: Chinnici D, Gaito A (eds) Regole europee e processo penale. Cedam, Padova, pp 105–143
Paulesu PP (2022) An overview on the "crisis" of testimonial evidence as a judicial decision making tool, between ECHR and Italian Criminal Proceeding: protected witnesses, media interference, principle of immediacy and right to cross-examination. Revista Brasileira de Direito Processual Penal 8(3):1066–1092
Presutti A (2017) Le audizioni protette. In: Bargis M, Belluta H (eds) Vittime di reato e sistema penale. Giappichelli, Torino, pp 375–400
Romanelli B (2023) La persona offesa vulnerabile nel procedimento penale italiano. Cedam, Padova
Ruggeri S (2017a) Audi alteram partem in criminal proceedings. Towards a participatory understanding of criminal justice in Europe and Latin America. Springer, Cham
Ruggeri S (2017b) Le contestazioni nell'esame testimoniale. Un'analisi critica della disciplina italiana in prospettiva interdisciplinare e nell'ottica del diritto comparato. La legislazione penale:1–30
Quattrocolo S (2020) Artificial intelligence, computational modelling and criminal proceedings. A framework for a European legal discussion. Springer, Cham
Simonato M, Fernandez-Bertier M (2019) Confiscation and fundamental rights: the quest for a consistent European approach. In: Bernardi A (ed) Improving confiscation procedures in the European Union. Jovene editore, Napoli, pp 3–30
Simonato M (2017) Confiscation and fundamental rights across criminal and non-criminal domains. ERA Forum 18:365–379
Spencer JR (2014) Hearsay evidence in criminal proceedings. Hart Publishing, Oxford
Trechsel S (2005) Human rights in criminal proceedings. Oxford University Press, Oxford
Turanjanin V (2023) When does bulk interception of communications violate the right to privacy? The limits of the state's power and the European Court of Human Rights Approach. Int Cybersecur Law Rev 4:115–136
Ubertis G (2009) La prova dichiarativa debole: problemi e prospettive in materia di assunzione della testimonianza della vittima vulnerabile alla luce della giurisprudenza sovranazionale. Cassaz Penal 10:4058–4067
Ubertis G (2017) Equità e proporzionalità versus legalità processuale: eterogenesi dei fini. Archivio penale 2:389–393
Valentini C (2019) La completezza delle indagini, tra obbligo costituzionale e (costanti) elusioni della prassi. Archivio penale 3:1–23

The Protection of Third Parties and Victims in Criminal Proceedings in the Area of Freedom, Security, and Justice: Developments in EU Law

Antonella Falcone

Abstract This study focuses on the protection of third parties and victims in criminal proceedings from the perspective of European Union law. Having outlined the notions of 'third parties' and 'victims' in light of the current European Union legal framework, the analysis also investigates whether and to what extent the third-party categories provided for by EU legal instruments can be broadened in order to grant protection to those who are affected variously by criminal (trans)national proceedings.

1 Introduction. Outline of the Study

This study deals with the protection of third parties and victims in criminal proceedings from the perspective of European Union law (hereafter, EU law). In order to comprehensively analyse this subject, we should first try to outline the notions of 'third parties' and 'victims' in light of the current European Union legal framework, as well as draw a clear line between these two categories of individuals.

However, before addressing these preliminary issues, it might be useful to explain once again the significance of the topic under discussion and why it deserves attention both from scholars and criminal justice policymakers across Europe and, above all, at the EU level.

It is worth recalling that in recent years we have witnessed important developments in the field of criminal justice that have raised several questions regarding the structural and ideological basis of continental criminal procedural systems, traditionally understood as two-party contests between the State and the accused.[1] It is sufficient to note that these changes have highlighted the necessity to recognise,

[1] Along these lines, see introductory chapter, in this volume.

A. Falcone (✉)
Present Address: Law Department, University of Messina, Messina, Italy
e-mail: antonella.falcone@unime.it

S. Ruggeri et al. (eds.), *Third Parties in Criminal Proceedings*, Legal Studies in International, European and Comparative Criminal Law 10,
https://doi.org/10.1007/978-3-031-73970-5_11

nationally and internationally, the interests of individuals other than the suspects and defendants, such as the victims and their family members or the witnesses, and, in general, of all those involved in criminal proceedings. An important role in seeking such a recognition has been certainly played by the caselaw of the European Court of Human Rights (hereafter, ECtHR) which has granted protection to those who claim a breach of a right enshrined in the European Convention of Human Rights (hereafter, ECHR), especially by way of extending the guarantees provided for by Article 6.[2]

Additionally, over the years the Court has also found violations of the ECHR that are mostly attributable to the 'afflictive' nature of modern criminal proceedings as being able to interfere with the fundamental rights of an ever-wider category of people that goes far beyond that of suspects, defendants, and offenders, and consists of individuals who may be directly or indirectly involved in criminal proceedings. A case in point may be those whose goods and assets, without there being any formal accusation against them, may be searched or frozen, seized, and confiscated or, more generally, of people who may provide information about a criminal offence, especially at the investigative stage.[3]

These and other interferences are particularly apparent in the case of recourse to Information Technology (hereafter, IT), which has extended the range of targets of investigative measures—as in the case of wiretapping—or of criminal procedural measures. Even more worrying is the current massive use of new investigative tools (*e.g.*, drones, digital searches, etc. . .) that has led to a critical scenario where criminal proceedings indistinctively pose risks to everybody's daily life and freedoms.

Such problems, moreover, are intensified in cross-border cases, where coercive measures of investigation are often required in international cooperation procedures.

These introductory remarks have shown that several individuals other than suspects, accused, and offenders may seek recognition of their private interests and require them to be incorporated in criminal procedural law as part of the overall public interest that has traditionally governed the administration of criminal justice across Europe.

Finally, individuals who are not formally suspected or accused may now be "trapped" in increasingly afflictive criminal proceedings. Thus, the limitless violation of private rights and freedoms as enshrined in the Nice Charter calls for an appropriate discussion about the need for enacting both domestic and EU legislative solutions aiming (1) to clarify, whenever possible, the hierarchy of the potentially

---

[2] Cf. Orlando, in this volume.

[3] "The human impulse to share creates an important opportunity for criminal investigators. When wrongdoers share with others, they often expose evidence of their crimes. A corrupt businessman might disclose records to his accountant. A mob boss might tell his brother about an assault. A drug dealer might reveal his plans to a confidential informant. In all these cases, someone other than the criminal or the police—some third party—comes to possess evidence of crime. Investigators often want to collect evidence from these third parties, as they are more likely to cooperate and less likely to tip off the suspect that an investigation is afoot". Kerr Orin (2009), p. 562 f.

competing rights and interests of each person involved[4] and (2) to circumscribe the above-mentioned interference on the basis of the principles of necessity and proportionality.

2 Semantic Difficulties Inherent in the Very Concepts of Third Parties and Victims under EU Law

The above-mentioned purposes cannot be appropriately achieved without providing a preliminary definition of 'third parties' and 'victims' in light of the specific aims of this study. However, designating the very concept of these two categories is more complex than it might appear to be at first sight.

At the European level, the role of third parties in criminal proceedings has received scant consideration over the years, while in recent decades much more attention has been paid to assessing and protecting the position of victims who have long been "forgotten persons" in many criminal justice systems.[5] We need merely consider the 2001/220/JHA Framework Decision and Directive 2012/29/EU, which aimed at the establishment of a Union *Magna Carta* for victims by attributing to them a set of fundamental rights, starting with the right to take part in criminal proceedings and safeguarding them against the risk of so-called secondary victimisation.

Despite the particular focus on the aggrieved parties, the category of third parties is not entirely unknown in EU policymaking. Thus, several legal instruments make explicit mention of third parties, even though they neither provide for a uniform and descriptive meaning nor clearly distinguish them from the victims of crimes. For instance, on some occasions, EU lawmakers use the term to indicate persons other than witnesses, victims, experts, the accused, and defendants;[6] on others, they identify those parties—other than the prosecuted—who are entitled to claim the protection of a specific right that they assume to be infringed during the criminal proceedings.[7] Conversely, according to the European Public Prosecutor's Office (hereafter, EPPO) Regulation 2017/1939/EU, "third parties" are surprisingly "suspects", but also "the victims, and other interested persons whose rights may be adversely affected by procedural acts" adopted before the formulation of the indictment (Recital 87 EPPO Regulation).

---

[4]For example, as a rule, remote access to a computer or cyber-infiltration are measures that are only allowed to investigate serious crimes, as these measures entail a severe encroachment on various subjects' right to privacy.

[5]Del Río Ayala Alejandra (2015), p. 1 ff.

[6]See Art. 10(3)(c), of the Directive on European Investigation Order, hereafter EIO.

[7]See right to property as stated in Article 29 of the Framework Decision on the European Arrest Warrant, hereafter EAW, or in Article 6 of the Directive on the freezing and confiscation of instrumentalities and proceeds of crime in the European Union.

It is principally due to the patchwork approach of EU legislation that drawing up a general definition of "third parties" becomes very difficult, as the meaning of this concept mainly depends on the scope of the legal instrument mentioning them. Indeed, this *modus operandi* adjusts the notion of third parties to the goals pursued by EU lawmakers, as in the case of legal intervention on transnational justice or in the event of implementing enhanced cooperation or approximation of laws and harmonisation of national rules with a standard prescribed by EU law. Additionally, as we will see, it is not irrelevant that some provisions provide for a definition of third parties in relation to the investigative phase or, conversely, to the whole criminal proceedings.

Against this unclear legal background, we should also ask ourselves whether the Union's lawmakers consider a third person as a formal party or, conversely, an informal one.[8] EU law does not include specific indications regarding this aspect. More precisely, we should remind ourselves that in order to facilitate "mutual recognition of judgments and judicial decisions and police and judicial cooperation in criminal matters having a cross-border dimension", the EU may, "by means of directives adopted in accordance with the ordinary legislative procedure, establish minimum rules", regarding "any other specific aspects of criminal procedure". However, it seems difficult that Union institutions aim to define the formal or informal nature of parties in criminal procedural law.

On closer inspection, one should note that, at the EU level, the recourse to the traditional distinction between formal or informal participations proves to be inadequate to find the exact nature of these individuals, and it may make it difficult to distinguish them from the victims.[9] Indeed, from the viewpoint of national procedural law, third parties are usually understood to be those subjects who do not formally hold the status of a party, because neither can they formulate claims nor are criminal or civil claims brought against them.[10] This definition is intimately connected with the position victims ought to play in criminal justice. Additionally, it is particularly challenging to define this issue since some countries, such as Italy, do not allow victims to assume the role of formal participants in criminal proceedings unless they can seek compensation by way of a civil claim for damages. In this light, they can certainly be seen as 'third parties'. On the contrary, some jurisdictions (for example, the Spanish and German ones) enable the victims to bring a criminal-law action or to assume the role of joint claimants in criminal trials, thus rendering the concept of 'third parties' unsuitable for them.

Besides, the absence of a shared definition of victim in the European legal scenario contributes to this blurry situation.[11] The lack of a uniform understanding

---

[8]Pursuant to Article 82 TFUE, however, the harmonization should protect individuals regardless their formal or informal status.

[9]On this topic, cf. Foschini (1965), p. 1 ff; Dominioni (1985), p. 3 ff.

[10]On this issue, see, in this volume, Gascón Inchausti, Guillermo Schumann Barragán, para. 1.2.

[11]Article 1 of Framework Decision 2001/220/JHA, for instance, defined the victims as natural persons who have suffered "harm, including physical or mental injury, mental suffering or material

of victims across Europe justifies the recourse to an EU legislative technique that in general terms overlooks the distinction between their formal or informal participation in criminal proceedings, but focuses on the need for the suitable protection of the rights of these harmed and vulnerable persons, such as the right to be actively involved in the proceedings, the right to be heard during the proceedings in order to introduce evidence, and the right to information, as a fundamental requirement to allow their effective contribution to criminal proceedings.[12]

These introductory observations have highlighted the problematic nature of this topic. Nevertheless, since the term 'third party' is used interchangeably, we should first try to sketch the different notions of third parties as tailored to the goals pursued by those EU legal instruments that deal with them, and to investigate whether and to what extent they effectively protect this category of persons. The accomplishment of these tasks lays the premises for analysing whether victims ought to be seen as third parties or not according to EU law.

Finally, to tackle all these issues suitably, the best method to adopt is based on a comprehensive approach aimed at providing an overview of the principal rules and caselaw that are currently available in the EU legal scenario.

---

damage caused directly by acts or omissions that constitute a violation of the criminal law of a Member State" and attributes to them several rights that may be exercised during criminal proceedings. Article 2(1) of Directive 2012/29/EU, conversely, broadened the scope of the meaning of 'victim', who is currently seen as "a natural person who has suffered harm, including physical, mental or emotional ones, or economic loss, which was directly caused by a criminal offence", as well as "a family member of a person whose death was directly caused by a criminal offence and who has suffered harm because of that person's death". Furthermore, for the sake of completeness, we recall that according to Article 1 of the UN Declaration of Basic Principles of Justice for Victims of Crime and Abuse of Power "victims mean persons who, individually or collectively, have suffered harm, including physical or mental injury, emotional suffering, economic loss or substantial impairment of their fundamental rights, through acts or omissions that are in violation of criminal law operative within Member States, including those laws proscribing criminal abuse of power". On this topic, see Malino and Di Nuzzo (2023), p. 1 ff.

[12] Such an approach is confirmed by Recital 20 Directive 2012/29/EU, according to which "The role of victims in the criminal justice system and whether they can participate actively in criminal proceedings vary across Member States, depending on the national system, and is determined by one or more of the following criteria: whether the national system provides for a legal status as a party to criminal proceedings; whether the victim is under a legal requirement or is requested to participate actively in criminal proceedings, for example as a witness; and/or whether the victim has a legal entitlement under national law to participate actively in criminal proceedings and is seeking to do so, where the national system does not provide that victims have the legal status of a party to the criminal proceedings. Member States should determine which of those criteria apply to determine the scope of rights set out in this Directive where there are references to the role of the victim in the relevant criminal justice system". As we will try to show, this legislative approach based on the human-rights perspective proves to be useful in establishing a general category of third party.

3 The Notions of Third Party According to the Current EU Legal Instruments

The starting point of our study is represented by those legal instruments based on the mutual recognition principle that deal with the role and the functions of third parties expressly.

First, we will focus on the EIO Directive, which has been enacted to govern the evidence gathered and carried out in another EU Country.

Second, we will look at the EAW FD, which simplifies the cross-border judicial surrender procedure in the European Union for prosecution or executing a custodial sentence or detention order.

Third, we will examine together Directive 2014/42/EU on the freezing and confiscation of instrumentalities and proceeds of crime in the European Union and Regulation 2018/1805/EU on freezing orders and confiscation.[13]

Before addressing the main issues surrounding the identification of third parties within these instruments, we should first of all highlight that, while the EIO Directive, the EAW FD and the Directive 2014/42/EU apply specifically to

[13]The following analysis does not include the Regulation 2023/1543/EU of 12 July 2023 on European Production Orders and European Preservation Orders for electronic evidence in criminal proceedings and for the execution of custodial sentences following criminal proceedings, that will enter into force from August 2026. For the sake of completeness, however, we recall that the Regulation aims to expedite the process for law enforcement and judicial authorities to access electronic evidence that are crucial for investigating and prosecuting criminals. This initiative includes both a Regulation and a Directive, designed to: (i) create a European Production Order that will allow a judicial authority in one Member State to obtain electronic evidence (such as emails, text or messages in apps, as well as information to identify a perpetrator as a first step) directly from a service provider or its legal representative in another Member State; (ii) create a European Preservation Order: this will allow a judicial authority in one Member State to request that a service provider or its legal representative in another Member State preserves specific data in view of a subsequent request to produce this data via mutual legal assistance, a European Investigation Order or a European Production Order; (iii) create a decentralised IT system through which all communication between authorities and service providers can take place in a secure and reliable way, ensuring authentication of all participants. As far we are concerned, the new rules ensure protection of fundamental rights, prominently safeguarding the right to the protection of personal data, including those of third parties (Art. 5), even if the Regulation does not provide an exact definition of this category of people. However, Article 1 states that the Regulation "applies without prejudice to fundamental principles, in particular the freedom of expression and information, including the freedom and pluralism of the media, respect for private and family life, the protection of personal data, as well as the right to effective judicial protection". In this light, the Regulation seems to identify individuals who may embody the concept of third party, such as the family members. In any case, individuals, whose data is sought, including third parties, will enjoy several safeguards and have access to legal recourse [Art. 18(1)]. Moreover, "the right to effective remedies should be exercised before a court in the issuing State in accordance with its national law and should include the possibility of challenging the legality of the measure, including its necessity and proportionality, without prejudice to the guarantees of fundamental rights in the enforcing State, or other additional remedies in accordance with national law" (Recital 80). On this topic, see the recent volume of de Hoyos Sancho (2024).

transnational criminal proceedings,[14] the Regulation on freezing and confiscation has a broad scope of application, since it covers offences that should not be limited to particularly serious transnational crime.

Lastly, we will turn to EPPO, a supranational prosecutorial body that investigates and prosecutes economic crimes against the financial interests of the EU within the framework of enhanced judicial cooperation.

3.1 The Concept of Third Party According to the EIO Directive

As has been noted above, Article 10(2)(c) EIO Directive considers the hearing of a third party in the territory of the executing State, as well as that of a witness, expert, victim, suspected or accused person, as being included in the evidence which always must be available under the law of the executing State. Even though Directive 2014/41/EU does not provide an accurate definition, at first sight, it seems that a 'third party' is any person, other than a witness, expert, victim, suspected or accused person, who renders or has already rendered statements abroad. Therefore, the term 'third party' seems to comprise all those who can provide relevant information for the investigation, as in the case of an out-of-court testimony made to the police or public prosecutor by people who may be called upon to testify at latest at the trial stage as witnesses or victims.[15] In addition, just as oral evidence gathered abroad—which under the EIO Directive is a non-coercive investigative measure—must always be available under the law of the executing State, any order of the issuing authorities seeking to obtain a hearing cannot be refused due to the absence of the dual criminality requirement, thus resulting in a strict application of the logic of mutual recognition.[16]

In this light, some problematic issues may arise with regard to the conditions in which the requested out-of-court statements are rendered overseas by third parties. In particular, we refer to those extremely delicate situations in which a person's status may change from someone with knowledge of the facts of an investigation to suspect. As is well known, this change requires the protection of a person's right to remain silent and not to self-incriminate. Moreover, it is undisputed that where the

[14] Directive 42/2014/EU, for instance, aims to adopt minimum rules that approximate the Member States' freezing and confiscation systems, thus facilitating mutual trust and effective cross-border cooperation, with a special view to fighting organised crime (Recitals 1 and 2).

[15] See, for instance, the case of informed persons pursuant to Art. 351 of the Italian Code of Criminal Procedure (CCP-Italy).

[16] Cf. Mangiaracina (2018), p. 119 f.; Caianiello (2015), p. 5.

person concerned was previously interviewed as a "witness", the investigative authorities shall not use her/his past statements against her/him in any way.[17]

Nevertheless, what may happen is that both the issuing and executing countries, or at least one of them, disregard these relevant rights, thus entailing concrete risks for the defence rights of the individuals involved. This worrisome scenario is magnified by the absence, at present, of EU rules on the collection, use, and admissibility of evidence ensuring the protection of fundamental rights, which are delegated to the national criminal procedural systems of the Member States.

By contrast, it is worth observing that EU lawmakers tend to be more concerned with the suspects and witnesses' position during a videoconference since the latter, respectively, "shall be informed in advance of the hearing of the procedural rights which would accrue to them, including the right not to testify, under the law of the executing State and the issuing State", and "may claim the right not to testify which would accrue to them under the law of either the executing or the issuing State and shall be informed about this right in advance of the hearing" [Article 24(5)(e)].[18]

In this light, we should then wonder whether such provisions should also be extended to persons who may provide information about the investigative facts, namely third parties according to Article 10. In this regard, we can clearly see that such norms are neither referred to in Article 10(2)(c) nor apply to the third-party category explicitly. Therefore, does this conclusion imply that they cannot be heard by videoconferencing? Or, worse, if heard by video-link connections, are the guarantees at issue not valid for them?

Moreover, in order protect these individuals, one should emphasise the provisions provided for by Recital 18 and Article 1 EIO Directive, according to which the Directive shall not have the effect of modifying the obligation to respect the fundamental rights and legal principles as enshrined in Article 6 of the TEU,[19] including the defence rights and the presumption of innocence of persons subject to criminal proceedings as also protected by the Charter of fundamental rights of the European Union (hereafter, the Charter) and in the ECHR.[20] Therefore, if one of the

[17] It should be borne in mind that the ECtHR has shown no hesitation in considering both those who render out-of-court statements and courtroom declarants as witnesses. See on this topic Maffei (2012), p. 29 ff.

[18] "With a view to the proportionate use of an EAW, the issuing authority should consider whether an EIO would be an effective and proportionate means of pursuing criminal proceedings. The issuing authority should consider, in particular, whether issuing an EIO for the hearing of a suspected or accused person by videoconference could serve as an effective alternative" (Recital 26 EIO Directive).

[19] Along the same lines, see also Article 11(1)(f), recalled by Article 10(1), according to which "there are substantial grounds to believe that the execution of the investigative measure indicated in the EIO would be incompatible with the executing State's obligations in accordance with Article 6 TEU and the Charter".

[20] In a case regarding the protection of the right to silence during administrative proceedings, the Luxembourg court has stated that, in accordance with the Article 52(3) of the Charter, read in conjunction with the Explanations annexed to it, Article 47(2) of the Charter corresponds to Article 6(1) ECHR, while Article 48 of the Charter corresponds to Article 6(2) and (3) ECHR. Therefore,

aforementioned rights (Art. 47 and Art. 48 of the Charter) is infringed, the party being harmed can bring the case to the European Union Court of Justice (hereafter, CJEU). However, such an explanation tends to overlook the fact that the intervention of the Court takes place after the violation of rights has already occurred.

3.2 The Seizure and Handing Over of Property Belonging to Third Parties According to EAW Framework Decision

A different notion of 'third party' can be drawn from those EU instruments concerning the seizure, freezing, and confiscation of goods. As often happens in national criminal proceedings, people suspected of a crime, or defendants in criminal proceedings are not the only persons who may have their assets seized and restrained pending investigation and proceedings, or find their ownership of assets in jeopardy because of confiscation or detention/forfeiture. Spouses, relatives, friends, business associates, lawyers, and so on, may find that the investigative authorities seek to attribute, or the court determines, that ownership of an asset belongs to a suspect or defendant even when it is not registered in their names, or they may have only partial interests in it (this is commonly referred to as *in rem* confiscation).

What is even more worrying is the interference with the third parties' rights to property whenever criminal proceedings are in course in two or more Member States. All this leads us to consider the role of these people during the freezing, seizure and confiscation of assets and proceeds of crime within the framework of international judicial cooperation.

The 1959 European Convention on Mutual Assistance in Criminal Matters not only lacks a specific set of rules, but also allows the requested State to refuse to hand over goods which are deemed to be necessary for the carrying out of criminal proceedings in the territory of the requesting State (Article 6). Against this background, Article 29 of the EAW Framework Decision, for the first time, dealt with both the seizure and handing over of property, "that may be required by the issuing authority as evidence, or because it has been acquired by the requested person as a result of the offence". Additionally, the EAW FD presupposes that seizure may be

the Court of Justice has underlined that it must take into account the corresponding rights protected by Article 6 ECHR, as interpreted by the ECtHR, which constitutes the minimum threshold of protection guaranteed for the right to remain silent and the privilege against self-incrimination. See CJEU, 2 February 2021, *DB v. Commissione Nazionale per le Società e la Borsa (Consob)*. According to consistent case-law of the ECtHR, the right to remain silent applies from the point at which the suspect is questioned by the police. See ECtHR, 8 *February* 1996, *John Murray v. United Kingdom,* para. 45. In addition, a person "charged with a criminal offence" for the purposes of Article 6 has the right to be notified of his or her privilege against self-incrimination. In this sense, see ECtHR, 2016, *Ibrahim and Others v. the United Kingdom*, para. 272.

requested whenever the arrest warrant is aimed at executing a decision of imprisonment issued as a result of either a preservative measure or a final conviction.[21]

It is interesting to note that this provision combines the extradition of property and mutual legal assistance in evidence-gathering matters,[22] whereas other European Union legal instruments appropriately distinguish between these two cases.[23] For the sake of this study, it is of the utmost importance to stress that the surrender of property is barred to safeguard the property rights of both the executing State and third parties. Therefore, "where such rights exist, the issuing Member State shall return the property without charge to the executing Member State as soon as the criminal proceedings have been terminated" [Art. 29(4)].

Despite the European lawmakers' interest in the property rights of third parties in the surrender proceedings, various questions, however, arise. These mainly relate to the excessive leeway of the national law when defining significant aspects of ownership rights and their object (*e.g.* things, pecuniary benefits, funds, bank accounts, web profiles, etc...). For instance, does Article 29 also refer to mere possession? Furthermore, who defines what should be handed over and according to which criteria? To guarantee the rights of third parties, should the handing over of property be temporary as in the case of freezing? To avoid the seizure and the handing over of property, how can third parties prove their rights?[24]

There is little doubt that the lack of precise indications about these relevant aspects makes the identification of both third parties and their rights a challenging task, which leads to an uncertain situation that, in turn, jeopardises their protection. Moreover, national law can also fail to provide for adequate remedies aiming to both demonstrate the *bona fides* of a third party and to obtain the recovery of the assets seized. The notion of *bona fides* itself appears unclear, and national judicial authorities have thus been called upon to find an accurate interpretation of this term in the jurisprudential argumentation of both the ECtHR and CJEU.[18]

As assets may start losing value from the moment they are seized until the final return of property decision, one should also highlight that the management of detained assets is also an aspect forgotten by the EAW FD.

Therefore, due to this blurry backdrop, over the years Member States have introduced special arrangements for handing over property when executing an EAW, thus implementing the FD in different ways.[25] This patchwork approach has posed risks to the safeguarding of the parties involved. Indeed, the satisfactory protection of fundamental rights largely depends on the attitudes adopted by Member States during the implementation of Directives and Framework Decisions. At

[21] In the former case, it is apparent that the handing over of property operates as non-conviction-based confiscation.

[22] Gleß and Schaffner (2009), p. 300, who refers to "two instruments in one box".

[23] Furthermore, under Article 29(2), the executing Country is not obliged to execute the handing over that, however, is allowed if the requested person is dead or a fugitive.

[24] See para. 3.3

[25] See Gleß and Schaffner (2009), p. 304 ff.

any rate, we hope that some of the highlighted gaps have been filled by way of employing subsequent EU law, whose aims, as we will see, have not only been that of harmonising but also approximating national rules on confiscation and asset recovery with a concrete view to the protection of third parties.

3.3 The Protection of Third Parties in Confiscation and Asset Recovery under EU Law

As already noted, over the years the European Union has been strongly committed to developing common rules in the field of freezing, confiscation, and asset recovery in order to ensure that crime does not pay. Indeed, one of the strategies that have made the greatest impact in the fight against organised and terrorist crime, at both national and international levels, is the attack on assets of illicit origin or otherwise used to finance such criminal activities.

To these ends, "the EU has been particularly active in the field of substantive approximation of confiscation regimes, and for creating a procedural infrastructure that intends to enhance horizontal cooperation between the EU member states, for example by facilitating mutual recognition of freezing and confiscation orders".[26]

After the entry into force of the Lisbon Treaty, Directive 2014/42/EU on the freezing and confiscation of instrumentalities and proceeds of crime in the European Union was finally enacted (and partially replaced the existing acts[27]), aiming to harmonise national law in relation to all forms of confiscation (direct, equivalent, extended, and third-party).[28] More recently, Regulation 2018/1805/EU on the mutual recognition of freezing orders and confiscation orders replaced the FD 2003/577/JHA on the execution in the European Union of orders freezing property or evidence and the FD 2006/783/JHA on the application of the principle of mutual recognition of confiscation orders. The idea behind both Directive 2014/42 and Regulation 2018/1805 is that a Member State shall recognise and execute in its territory a freezing and a confiscation order issued by a judicial authority of another Member State in the framework of criminal proceedings without further formalities

---

[26] Boucht (2019), p. 527.

[27] As to the instruments introduced under the so-called 'third pillar' of the Union, it is worth mentioning the Joint Action 98/699/JHA on money laundering, identification, tracing, freezing, seizing and confiscation of instruments and the proceeds from crime, and FD 2001/500/JHA on money laundering, identification, tracing, freezing, seizing and confiscation of instrumentalities and the proceeds of crime. Furthermore, FD 2005/212/JHA on the confiscation of crime-related proceeds, instruments, and property, sets out detailed rules on extended confiscation and made the first attempt to harmonise third-party confiscation (Art. 3).

[28] Directive 2014/42/EU also allowed for non-conviction-based confiscation only in cases of escape and sickness when, however, proceedings *in personam* have already started and those proceedings could have resulted in a criminal conviction against the suspect or defendant if they would have been able to stand trial.

being required. In particular, to simplify the freezing and confiscation process in the EU, Regulation 2018/1805/EU covers all types of freezing and confiscation orders delivered following proceedings in relation to a criminal offence and irrespective of a final conviction. The shift from Framework Decisions and Directives to the Regulation greatly increased the power of these EU provisions to penetrate domestic legal systems. Indeed, the previous approach posed significant risks of the abstract measures failing to achieve a concrete result.

Along with the enhancement of these legal instruments, EU institutions have undertaken initiatives to avoid the infringement of the property rights not only of the defendant but also of other persons—namely third parties—involved in various ways in the criminal proceedings, especially in those linked to organised crime. Hence, when implementing confiscation schemes, "which may have considerable adverse effects on the individuals subjected to them, it is crucial that also the rights of these individuals are safeguarded in an effective manner".[29]

In this regard, the Regulation on freezing and confiscation understands "affected persons" as "natural persons or legal persons", including "the person against whom a freezing order or confiscation order was issued or the person who owns the property that is covered by that order, as well as any third parties whose rights in relation to that property are directly prejudiced by that order, including *bona fide* third parties" (Recital 15).[30] This notion seems to be consistent with the rationale of the last generation of confiscation rules, i.e. extended and non-conviction-based (NCB) confiscation. In NCB confiscation, for instance, the term third party may simply refer to anyone who holds the tainted property.

As regards third-party criminal confiscation, it may be relevant where criminal proceeds have been transferred, directly or indirectly, to third parties to avoid confiscation (Art. 6 of 2014 Directive that refers to the reasonable-person-test[31]). This is exactly what the European Union Court found in the recent case *DR* and *TS*, in which it pointed out that "confiscation from a third party presupposes establishing that a suspected or accused person has transferred proceeds to a third party or that a third party has acquired such proceeds and that a third party knew that the purpose of the transfer or acquisition was to avoid confiscation". On this occasion, the CJEU also stated that "national legislation must allow third parties to appear as a party in the confiscation proceedings".[32] Indeed, the Bulgarian Court of Appeal of Varna not only referred to the Union Court of Justice questions regarding the extent of the confiscation provided for by Directive 42/2014/EU, but also about the scope of the

[29] Boucht (2019), p. 526.

[30] Similarly, see also Recital 24 Directive 2014/42/EU.

[31] According to the Explanatory Memorandum of the Directive 2014/42 Proposal, "the third-party confiscation must be based on concrete facts and circumstances to prevent arbitrary decisions. Moreover, third-party confiscation should be possible only following an assessment, based on specific facts, that the confiscation of property of the convicted, suspected or accused person is unlikely to succeed, or in situations where unique objects must be restored to their rightful owner". See https://eur-lex.europa.eu/LexUriServ/LexUriServ.do?uri=COM:2012:0085:FIN:EN:PDF.

[32] CJEU, 21 October 2021, *DR and TS*, C-845/19 and C-863/19.

right to an effective remedy by third parties if they should claim that they are the owners of property subject to confiscation.[33]

This was not the first time the Court had dealt with this topic. Indeed, in its judgment of 14 January 2021, the CJEU had already clarified EU Member States' duties regarding confiscation of crime-related proceeds, instrumentalities, and property.[34] The case addressed the rights of third parties acting in good faith in confiscation proceedings in Bulgaria. The Court of Appeal of Plovdiv first asked the CJEU whether its national legislation, which allows for the confiscation of the means of transport used to commit the offence even if it belongs to a third person acting without ill faith, is aligned with Article 17 of the Charter. Second, having regard to Article 47 Charter, the referring Court called into question the compatibility of the Bulgarian provisions that prevent the owner of the means of transport, who is not the offender, from bringing the case to the national courts.

This decision of the CJEU deserves attention, since the Luxembourg judges specified that the "right to property does not constitute an absolute prerogative but may be subject to limitations", on condition, however, that the latter "correspond to objectives of public interest pursued by the European Union and do not constitute, in relation to the aim pursued, a disproportionate and intolerable interference, impairing the very substance of the right so guaranteed". Therefore, the Court found that the confiscation of property is contrary to EU law because of the third party's good faith.

Finally, the most troublesome issues for the third party's rights stem from the criminal investigation. Indeed, the investigative phase, regardless of the identification of an offender, purports to find and track criminal assets, both with a view to their subsequent confiscation and for the investigation of an offence. These assets may constitute evidence which can be used in criminal proceedings, especially when related to financial offences (such as money laundering, corruption, or fraud)".[35]

[33] In this specific case, two Bulgarian citizens were sentenced to imprisonment and a fine in Bulgaria for unauthorised possession of highly dangerous narcotics with the intent to distribute them. During a search of their respective homes, conducted in the context of pre-trial proceedings, a sum of money had been discovered and seized.

[34] CJEU, 14 January 2021, C-399/19, *OM* that dealt with the interpretation of Framework Decision 2005/212/JHA. Also, the ECtHR focused on the Bulgarian confiscation law and condemned Bulgaria for violation of Article 1, Protocol 1, ECHR because the applicant, a "third party" whose property was affected, could not intervene in the proceedings against the alleged offender. Moreover, as there was no chance for a judicial review of the decision, the Court found that national law did not provide adequate safeguards against unjustified interferences with property rights. ECtHR, 4 March 2004, *Microintelect Odd v. Bulgaria*, no. 34129/03. See Simonato (2017), p. 376 ff.

[35] For the sake of completeness, we recall that the Framework Decision 2003/577/JHA, on the execution in the European Union of freezing assets or evidence orders was replaced, regarding the seizure of evidence, by Directive 2014/41/EU, which introduced the EIO. The EIO, however, does not apply to seizure for confiscation purposes, which therefore remains governed by Framework Decision 2003/577/JHA that, as already noted, pursuant to Article 39 was replaced by the Regulation 2018/1805. In turn, the Directive 2014/41 deals with "provisional measures only with a view to gathering evidence" (Recital 34 EIO Directive).

Besides, the distinction between the two objectives of these activities is not always apparent, and may also change in the course of the proceedings.[36] For this reason, the assessment of whether the frozen or confiscated item is to be used as evidence and is then to be the object of an EIO is left to the issuing authority. However, the fact that the EIO Directive does not consider explicitly the protection of third parties affected by a European order implies that such an instrument may be issued to obtain an investigative measure with a view to subsequent third-party confiscation. Hence, this may result in disregarding more guaranteeing provisions to those provided for by Directive 2014/42.[37]

It emerges from the analysis carried out so far that the freezing and confiscation risk affects the rights of those who are not formally suspected or accused of having committed any crimes, namely third parties who are not subject to criminal prosecution. To legitimise such a restriction, European law provides guarantees meant to protect fundamental rights (Art. 8 Directive and Art. 33 Regulation), among which we should recall, for example, the right to a fair trial, service of the judgment setting forth the seizure and confiscation setting forth the grounds for seizure and confiscation measures, the possibility of filing an appeal before a higher court, the summons, the right to be heard and to confrontation, as well as to introduce evidence before the handing down of a final judgment.

4 The Definitions of Third Parties under the EPPO Regulation

Turning now to the EPPO, it is worth observing that the term "third parties" is recurrent in the 2017 Regulation, where it appears for the first time in Recital 87, which, as has been anticipated, defines these persons as "the suspects, the victims, and other interested persons whose rights may be adversely affected by procedural acts" adopted prior to indictment. Notably, the identification of these subjects is strictly linked to the effects that may come from those acts undertaken by the EPPO during its investigations as being closely related to the prosecution of crimes (Recital 87).[38] These acts encompass a wide range of investigative instruments the EPPO has at its disposal and that the Member States shall ensure at the

[36] For this reason, scholars have wondered whether the requirements of the provisions on confiscation must already exist at the time when the prevention restraint of unavailability takes effect. Cf. Belfiore (2019), p. 260.

[37] However, it is worth noting that according to the EIO Directive "It is crucial to maintain a smooth relationship between the various instruments applicable in this field" (Recital 34).

[38] The notion of procedural acts can be also traced from Recital 89, which in delimiting the area of review that can be exercised over the EPPO's administrative decisions, explicitly excludes form this control EPPO decisions "adopted in the exercise of its functions of conducting investigations, prosecuting cases or bringing cases to trial".

request or by order of the European Delegated Prosecutors (hereafter, EDPs).[39] In other words, according to the Preamble of the Regulation, all those activities of the EPPO that take place before indictment may potentially cause negative effects on suspects, victims and other individuals involved, thus requiring strong protection of their position and, above all, of their procedural rights, such as the right to an effective remedy. Indeed, procedural acts that produce legal effects *vis-à-vis* third parties as well as failures to adopt such acts shall undergo judicial review, at the latest at the trial stage, by the competent national courts in compliance with the requirements and procedures laid down by national law (Art. 42 EPPO Regulation).[40]

In this light, it appears that suspects, victims, and other persons affected by investigations are to be understood as part of a wide category, namely as third parties, in relation to the EPPO's investigative power and the national courts, whenever the latter are called upon to carry out judicial review. This understanding seems to enact a sort of 'triangulation', where any decision of the European Prosecutor should take into account not only the public interests embedded in the prosecution of PIF crimes but also those of the suspect, victim, and any other affected parties in respect of which the national court plays the role of guarantor. In addition, among the procedural acts subject to judicial supervision we find those regarding the "choice of the Member State whose courts will be competent to hear the prosecution" (Art. 42).[41]

However, this scenario would operate perfectly if the protection ensured by the EPPO Regulation did not prove to be inconsistent because of Recital 30 of the EPPO Regulation:

Where the national law of a Member State provides for the internal review of certain acts within the structure of the national prosecutor's office, the review of such decisions taken by the European Delegated Prosecutor should fall under the

---

[39] Pursuant to Article 30(1) of the EPPO Regulation, these can be summarised as follows: "a) search any premises, land, etc... and "take any conservatory measures necessary to preserve their integrity or to avoid the loss or contamination of evidence; b) obtain the production of any relevant object or document and of c) stored computer data, encrypted or decrypted, including banking account data and traffic data; d) freeze instrumentalities or proceeds of crime, including assets, that are expected to be subject to confiscation by the trial court, where there is reason to believe that the owner, possessor or controller of those instrumentalities or proceeds will seek to frustrate the judgment ordering confiscation; e) intercept electronic communications to and from the suspect or accused person, over any electronic communication means that the suspect or accused person is using; f) track and trace an object by technical means, including controlled deliveries of goods".

[40] This provision echoes the expression of Article 263(1) TFEU (on this see below, para. 7); it, therefore, appears to constitute an autonomous concept of EU law, which must be interpreted uniformly throughout the European Union.

[41] As argued by Ruggeri (2018), p. 214, "There are no indications as to the criteria that should govern this judicial review and the way in which the interested parties can properly challenge the Permanent Chamber's decisions. The fact that this judicial review shall be carried out 'in accordance with the requirements and procedures laid down by national law' does not seem to ensure effective protection of the individuals concerned".

supervision powers of the supervising European Prosecutor in accordance with the internal rules of procedure of the EPPO. In such cases, Member States should not be obliged to provide for review by national courts, without prejudice to Article 19 TEU and Article 47 of the Charter of Fundamental Rights of the European Union ('the Charter').

This solution, on one hand, appears well suited to tackling the problem of the coexistence of different legal systems; on the other, it raises several concerns regarding the effective protection of third parties, intended as 'judicial protection' or 'judicial review', expression of both a general principle of the EU law—stemming from the European Constitutions—and a right enshrined in Art. 19(1) TEU and Art. 47 of the Charter.[42]

These observations pose the premises for a closer consideration of the protection of "suspect, victims and other interested persons". Postponing to the following paragraphs the analysis of the victims' safeguarding as provided for by the 2017 Regulation, we should now focus on suspects and other affected parties.

Starting with suspects, it is worth noting that Article 5(1) of the Regulation specifies that the EPPO's investigations should be carried out in full compliance with the fundamental rights of these people and that the EPPO shall be bound by the principles of the rule of law and proportionality in all its activities (2). Additionally, Article 41 of the 2017 Regulation refers to the 'Charter', under the title "Scope of the rights of the suspects and accused persons", with explicit mention of the right to a fair trial and the right to defence.[43]

Despite this, only a few provisions are specifically dedicated to procedural rights within the EPPO's investigative action, so that uniform guarantees for the defence are limited to the minimum standards required by EU Directives for strengthening the procedural rights of suspects or accused persons in criminal proceedings. This is undoubtedly a delicate subject, since the protection of the rights of the suspect is mostly left to the national legislation of the Member State where the EDP performs the investigations. The lack of clear safeguards and rules governing restrictions to the EPPO's investigative activities constitutes a step backwards in the development of a coherent criminal justice system. The risk is that of expanding and enhancing the investigative powers of EPPO without balancing them with a set of rules protecting fundamental rights.[44] The legal framework established by the 2017 Regulation and

---

[42] On this topic, Ružičková (2022), p. 84 ff.

[43] We should also consider the fundamental rights enshrined in the European Directives transposed by the Member States on the interpretation and translation, information and discovery of investigative acts, the right of access to a lawyer and to communicate with third parties in the event of detention, the right to silence and the presumption of innocence, as well as on free legal aid [Art. 41(2)]. On this topic, see Illuminati (2018), p. 184 ff.

[44] By contrast, the inquiries of the EPPO ought to comply with the rights of suspects as protected by the Charter (Art. 41); the right to presumption of innocence (Art. 48); the right to effective remedy and fair trial (Art. 47); the *non bis in idem* principle (Art. 50); the principle of legality and proportionality of criminal offence and sentence (Article 49); the right to life (Art. 2), the right to human dignity (Art. 1), the prohibition of torture and degrading treatment (Art. 4), the right to bodily integrity (Art. 3), and the right to privacy and family (Art. 7).

relating to the distribution of the competence between supranational and domestic judicial bodies runs the risk of leading to a situation of uncertainty regarding the identification of the regulatory, procedural, and substantive model that underpins the handling of the cases.

What now follows is the potential infringement of "other interested persons'" rights, which may be affected by the EPPO's procedural acts. To this purpose, when we look at the above-mentioned Art. 41, we find that a set of procedural rights, such as the right to interpretation and translation, the right to information and access to the case materials, and the right of access to a lawyer, enshrined in paragraph 2, surprisingly are not extended to the "other persons". It is true that EU lawmakers did not forget the concerned category, since paragraph 3, albeit generically, clarified that the procedural rights (including the possibility to present evidence, to request the appointment of experts or expert examination and hearing of witnesses) must be available also for other persons involved in the proceedings of the EPPO, however, on condition that these rights are foreseen by the applicable national law.

A further relevant aspect to focus on is the array of possible measures and acts that are at the disposal of the EPPO regarding other interested persons. From the viewpoint of the purpose of this study, indeed, carrying out an analysis on this subject is the best solution. When dealing with such measures, we precisely refer to searches, preventive measures aimed at ensuring the authenticity or avoiding the contamination of evidence, the production of objects, documents, and data (banking, computer, and traffic data), the freezing of crime-related assets (such as instrumentalities or proceeds) also for subsequent confiscation, wiretapping, and tracing.[45]

It has already been observed that all these instruments have become increasingly intrusive *vis-à-vis* individuals involved in criminal proceedings. In general terms, it is important to note that the EDP may only order the measures where "there are reasonable grounds to believe that the specific measure might provide information or evidence useful to investigation, and where there is no less intrusive measure available which could achieve the same objective" [Art. 30(4)]. Moreover, pursuant to Article 30(5), such investigative "measures shall be available 'at least' in cases where the offence subject to investigation is punishable by a maximum penalty of at least 4 years of imprisonment". These provisions show a certain interest in the EPPO Regulation in providing safeguards for the suspects and other persons, and they are applicable to all investigations carried out by the EPPO in every Member State, even if national law does not require them.

Alongside these general provisions, specific attention can be seen in the field of wiretapping activities, which can only be authorised when the person subject to the proceedings is known, thus restricting the scope of this investigative instrument, whereas outside the scope of competences of the EPPO it is mostly applied in

[45] One might note that data production, interception and tracking measures, including controlled deliveries of goods, may be subject to further conditions and restrictions provided by national law pursuant to Article 30(2), but only with regard to interception and tracking, Member States may limit the adoption of these investigative tools to a closed number of serious criminal offences and notify the list to the EPPO.

practice as a tool to identify the perpetrator. It can be argued, however, that this limitation is also beneficial for third parties when these are understood as "other interested persons".

Similar considerations can be made regarding the preventive seizure for confiscation of assets subject to the offences falling within the scope of competence of the EPPO. This should only be adopted in cases where the danger of dissipation of the assets earmarked for confiscation may derive from conduct attributable to the person who exercises or materially possesses them. Once again, this provision may be potentially excluded from the seizure of all those third parties extraneous to the crime under investigation.

Even more worrisome are those aspects relating to cross-border investigations. As a rule, recourse to legal instruments of mutual recognition or cross-border cooperation (EIO, EAW) should not replace the specific rules on cross-border investigations under the 2017 Regulation (Recital 73). All the investigative measures undertaken by the EPPO pursuant to Article 30 and Article 31 of the Regulation are free to circulate throughout Member States along the lines of mutual recognition. Indeed, Article 37 EPPO Regulation, states that "evidence presented by the prosecutors of the EPPO or the defendant to a court shall not be denied admission merely on the grounds that the evidence was gathered in another Member State or in accordance with the law of another Member State". Furthermore, "such evidence is presumed to meet any relevant evidentiary requirement under the national law of the State where the court is located".

Therefore, the most serious failure of the EPPO Regulation is the absence of common or at least harmonised rules on the gathering of evidence during investigations, as well as the lack of common, specific and detailed safeguards protecting defence rights in that phase.

In this light, one might note that if the situation is already problematic for suspects, it will be even worse for other parties.

5 The Protection of Victims within the EU Legal Framework

As the principal topic of this paper is to distinguish a third party from a victim, we should now deal with the category of aggrieved persons, by firstly examining those legal instruments that mention them at the EU level and, above all, provide them with proper protection at both national and transnational levels.

In this respect, it is worth noting that in recent years the protection of victims of crimes and their next of kin has become nationally and internationally all the more relevant. For a long time, however, domestic law has endeavoured to protect victims' rights by considering the harmed person from a criminological perspective, that is, as someone who has suffered damage resulting from a criminal offence, and who because of this demands support and help.[46]

5.1 *The* Magna Carta *of Victims of Crimes in the EU Legal Environment*

At the EU level, several provisions in the EU Fundamental Rights Charter "provide 'foundations' for the rights of victims".[47] Among them, we recall the rights enshrined in Chap. 1 on the dignity of the human person, as well as Articles 6, 7 and 8 regarding, respectively, the right to liberty and security, respect for private and family life and the protection of personal data, and Article 24 relating to the protection of the child. Those judicial rights enshrined in Article 47 of the Charter are also relevant since they acknowledge for everyone, including victims of crimes, the "right to an effective remedy and a fair trial", thus ensuring their access to a judge, a fair trial within a reasonable time, the legal assistance and legal aid.

According to the Treaty on the Functioning of the European Union (hereafter, TFEU), the rights of victims of crime are among the areas in which the European Parliament and the Council may establish minimum standards through Directives.

In particular, Directive 2012/29/EU paid specific attention to the issues related to victims and next of kin's protection and identified types of crimes, most of which may be transnational (such as violent crimes, terrorism, human trafficking), and categories of victims (children or subjects understood as vulnerable after individual assessment), which imply the enactment of specific safeguards by Member States when dealing with them.[48]

This paper is not a call for a debate about victims. Hence, it falls beyond the scope of this research to analyse in detail each of the rights granted by this Directive. However, with a view to providing a general overview of the current *Magna Carta* of victims within the European Union, we cannot fail to consider them in general terms. This is of the utmost importance for highlighting the most significant shortcomings of the current EU law in this field and for proposing future legal provisions that may contribute to the widest effective protections of this category of persons.

For this purpose, we should remember that the 2012 Directive emphasises victims' right to participate in criminal proceedings without any further prejudice or harm. To this end, protective measures must be implemented by national procedural law and, among those designated as examples by European law, we recall the

[46] Lupária Donati and Della Torre (2021), p. 312 ff.

[47] Mazzucato (2019), p. 23.

[48] Directive 2012/29/EU of the European Parliament and of the Council of 25 October 2012 establishing minimum standards on the rights, support, and protection of victims of crime, and replacing Council Framework Decision 2001/220/JHA, [2001] OJ L 315/57.

video recording of interviews and separate venues so they can avoid visual contact with the alleged offenders.

Against this backdrop, already in 2011, Directive 2011/99/EU was enacted to introduce a remarkable measure, *i.e.*, the European protection order (hereafter, Directive EPO) aimed at broadening safeguards for victims in all the Member States and ensure them the right to freedom and free movement across the Union. In practice, such national protection measures entail a ban on entering certain places or defined areas, place limitations on contact, or require the observance of a minimum distance from the protected person.[49] Although useful, this Directive has so far received scant consideration due to "the lack of information on the existing cooperation mechanisms between Member States, the lack of efficient coordination and cooperation among Member States, and the lack of financial resources and/or necessary means to guarantee effective cross-border criminal proceedings".[50]

Furthermore, since victims have increasingly requested to make their voices heard in criminal proceedings, to this end EU lawmakers have acknowledged the victim's right to information, support, and assistance, and, above all, the right to be heard.

In light of this, the very first safeguard that the domestic authorities must grant victims is the possibility of understanding the content of the communication received. Indeed, the Directive on Victims' Rights does not only allow the injured party to use their mother tongue but also to request the translation of the documents considered fundamental, *i.e.* those enabling victims to actively participate in criminal proceedings.[51]

Ensuring the participation of victims in criminal proceedings means addressing the problem of the lack of legal knowledge of the victim and his or her relatives. What may happen is that the aggrieved parties, albeit adequately informed by the national authorities, are unable to effectively exercise their procedural rights on their own and may moreover lack the financial resources to face all the legal expenses.

Needless to say, the right to be heard lies at the core of the guarantee of participation. Nonetheless, the 2012 Directive stresses that the victims' involvement in criminal proceedings depends on several variables, such as the various solutions provided by national legislation regarding their formal status.

From this perspective, one should underline that the victim can provide information that constitutes the main evidence in the trial; this explains why the injured party is often called upon to cooperate with the authorities. In line with this, Article 20, which establishes the "right to protection of victims during criminal investigations", points out that interviews must be carried out without "unjustified delay after the complaint regarding a criminal offence has been made to the competent

[49] In sum, these measures are mostly applied to protect women in cases of intimate partner or domestic violence, harassment, stalking, or sexual assault.

[50] See *Commission Staff Working Document Evaluation of Directive 2012/29/EU*, p. 19, https://eur-lex.europa.eu/legal-content/FR/TXT/?uri=SWD:2022:179:FIN.

[51] On this topic, see Ruggeri (2017), p. 385 ff.

authority". Furthermore, pursuant to Articles 19(1) and 20(19)(b), national authorities must keep to a minimum the number of hearings and the contact between the defendant and the alleged victim, even though the achievement of these purposes could negatively impact the guarantees of a fair trial.

This observation poses the premises for considering the need for balance between the protection of victims and the accused's rights, thus contributing to an extensive meaning of the rights enshrined by Article 6 ECHR and at the same time promoting overall fairness that includes all the individuals involved in criminal proceedings.[52]

Finally, in most domestic jurisdictions the participation of victims in criminal proceedings has led to nothing more than economic compensation for the injured person. In this regard, European law has recognised the significance of the victims' right to compensation, by allowing for a specific form of reparation for the harmed person when replacement or recovery is not possible. In particular, Article 16 of the 2012 Directive enshrines the right to obtain a decision on compensation within a reasonable time during criminal proceedings. In addition, it asks for Member States to promote measures encouraging perpetrators to provide adequate compensation to aggrieved persons.

5.2 *The Protection of Victims in Transnational Proceedings*

Remarkably, Directive 2012/29/EU specifies in general terms that Member States must ensure the victim's protection regardless of their citizenship or nationality.[53] This provision leads us to consider the position of victims when it comes to cross-border crimes and transnational proceedings.

Despite this significant recognition, little progress has been made in this field, hence it can be preliminary stated that EU procedure "still considers transnational proceedings almost exclusively from the point of view of the issuing, transfer and executing of cooperation requests", thus failing to take into account not only the role of defendants but that of victims. Furthermore, more worrying is the existence of several legal sources in the European scenario, which, on one hand, have contributed to the strengthening of victim protection, on the other, have built a fragmented setting that emphasises the differences existing between the legal systems involved in the judicial cooperation. For instance, it has been stressed that the victims often must face "difficulties in communicating in another language, explaining what

[52] The CJEU has stressed this concept. See CJEU, 16 June 2005, *Pupino*, C-105/03. The *Grande Chambre* stated that "the Framework Decision must thus be interpreted in such a way that fundamental rights, including in particular the right to a fair trial as set out in Article 6 of the Convention and interpreted by the European Court of Human Rights, are respected" (para. 59).

[53] Furthermore, Recital 51 addresses the case in which the victim has left the territory of the Member State where the criminal offence was committed, and states that the Member State should provide protection "for what is directly related to any criminal proceedings it is conducting regarding the criminal offence concerned, such as special protection measures during court proceedings".

happened when reporting the facts in a foreign State. This can result in probable and excessive delays, compromise the interests of the aggrieved party, and lead to secondary victimisation".[54] Such difficulties are magnified in cross-border cases since the victims may not be aware of the legal system in the trial State.

As to evidence-gathering procedures, the EIO Directive, for instance, does not appropriately consider the victim's position in either the issuing or the execution phase. This explains why it has been argued that victims' rights are not suitably safeguarded in the EIO procedure.[55]

Article 17 of Directive 2012/29/UE suggests the use of videoconferencing and telephone conferencing to hear victims who reside in a State other than that where the criminal offence was committed. As is well-known, video and audio link-ups have great potential in the field of victims' participation and right to be heard safely, and may prove extremely useful in transnational proceedings, allowing the subjects involved to participate even when they are not physically present in the trial State. However, even if EU law has encouraged the recourse to videoconference when gathering evidence abroad, an EIO can be issued for the hearing of witnesses, experts, suspects and accused but the victim's position in either the issuing or in the execution phase is taken into account by the Directive only when the victim is formally considered as a witness.

A further delicate aspect to deal with is the concrete need for identifying which State is responsible for assisting the victims when multiple States are involved. It was precisely in this regard that the 2012 Directive provided that:

> If the victim has left the territory of the Member State where the criminal offence was committed, that Member State should no longer be obliged to provide assistance, support and protection except for what is directly related to any criminal proceedings it is conducting regarding the criminal offence concerned, such as special protection measures during court proceedings. The Member State of the victim's residence should provide assistance, support and protection required for the victim's need to recover (Recital 51).

A positive feature to consider is the right to compensation in the event of transnational proceedings. To this end, specific measures were introduced by the so-called 'Compensation Directive', with the purpose of ensuring that "where a violent intentional crime has been committed in a Member State other than the Member State where the applicant for compensation is habitually resident, the applicant shall have the right to apply to an authority or any other body in the latter Member State" (Article 1 Directive 2004/80/EC of 29 April 2004).

5.3 *Victim Protection under the EPPO Regulation*

The last issue to deal with relates to the victims' protection within EPPO.

---

[54] Malino and Di Nuzzo (2023).

[55] Kusak (2011), p. 233 available at https://repozytorium.amu.edu.pl/bitstream/10593/12125/1/Projekt_10.pdf.

First, pursuant to the 2017 Regulation, EU institutions are seen as primary victims of PIF crimes (Recital 107).

Second, the Regulation refers to 'other victims' as third parties who may have been discovered because of other crimes that are intrinsically linked to an EPPO inquiry or who may have been found to be affected by crimes where the Union is the primary victim. To both ensure that their rights are not hampered and provide them with appropriate protections in terms, for instance, of victims' rights to challenge EPPO actions,[56] some information rights are set out in the Regulation. Overall, they aim at enabling aggrieved persons to participate in the EPPO procedures appropriately. For example, when the EPPO chooses to initiate an investigation, it is called upon to notify the authority that reported the criminal conduct, "as well as [...] crime victims and, if provided by national law, [...] other persons who reported the criminal conduct".[57]

Third, the EPPO's Prosecutors are required to be considerate of such victims.[58] For instance, where an EPPO deems a dismissal or alternative procedural form to be the best route, the Regulation imposes active consideration of the interests of these victims during such decision-making.[59] Indeed, EDPs may drop cases for legal reasons but also on (European) public interest grounds; they may further decide to recur to alternative procedural forms and make deals with suspects across Europe. Thus, during these activities, EPPO authorities shall attach importance to the victims' roles and interests (such as claims for compensation), especially when case-disposal mechanisms covering victim-offender mediation occur outside the traditional full proceedings.

In contrast to earlier positive findings, however, the system also has several serious drawbacks. If the EPPO decides not to initiate an investigation, no specific provision is provided for by Article 26(2), hence, in principle, neither victims nor persons who reported the criminal conduct would be informed. Likewise, for the exercise of the right of evocation, Article 27 makes no provision. Even more serious concerns arise in the event of reallocation of the case during the pre-trial inquiry: after all the investigations have been carried out in State A, the prosecution should be initiated in State B, but the Regulation does not give defendants and victims, in particular—who undergo the consequences of this decision—any opportunity for making themselves heard. All these observations pose the premises for future

[56] Judicial review of pre-trial decisions as regulated in Recital 87 or making claims against perpetrators (preamble 107) and rights to compensation (Article 38). Pursuant to Recital 107, the protection of victims may also "include taking precautionary measures, in particular to prevent any continuous wrongdoing or to protect the Union from reputational damage, or to allow them to intervene as a civil party in the proceedings in accordance with national law".

[57] Articles 24, 34(3) and 103 EPPO Regulation.

[58] Articles 25(3)(b) EPPO Regulation.

[59] The right to be considered in relation to case dismissal or alternative procedural forms is provided for by Articles 39 and 40(1), respectively.

examination about how victims of crimes would exercise their rights in investigations and proceedings conducted by the EPPO.

Moreover, the situation described under Article 39(4), pursuant to which victims will be notified of the decision to dismiss a case, "where appropriate under national law", proves inconsistent with Article 6 (1)(a) of Directive 2012/29/UE, which requires Member States to ensure that victims are notified "of any decision not to proceed with or to end an investigation or not to prosecute the offender". Nonetheless, scholars have argued that "mandatory notification to victims might jeopardise the outcome of the investigation that may be initiated by national authorities following a decision of the EPPO not to initiate an investigation, affecting national rules on secrecy of proceedings and disclosure".[60]

In general terms, the EPPO Regulation cannot be depicted as a piece of legislation particularly concerned with the victims' rights.

This is reasonable if we assume the unique viewpoint of the Union lawmaker whose main goal, through the enactment of this supranational institutional body, is fighting against financial offences affecting the 'core' of the economic EU integration process.

However, the goals pursued should not only be the recovery of EU funds but also the consideration of the interests and needs of manifold victims affected by PIF crimes across Europe, as they, for instance, could be interested in knowing how funds might otherwise have been used for. Not to mention the specific loss to citizens, "whether it be infrastructure projects not funded or farmers deprived of their livelihood".[61]

6 Preliminary Conclusions and Observations

Having defined what is meant by "third parties" according to the EU legal instruments that make explicit mention of them, we will now move on to express some preliminary conclusions and observations.

The first and very general consideration is that, in spite of the highlighted shortcomings, it can be affirmed that the provisions under consideration are generally concerned with the protection of procedural rights.

Second, the analysis carried out above demonstrated that, apart from the definition provided by the EPPO Regulation, third parties and victims are to be understood as two different categories of individuals according to EU law. In a nutshell, third parties may be individuals other than witnesses, suspects accused and experts, who

---

[60] Pérez Enciso (2017), p. 279.

[61] Wade (2021), available at https://journals.sagepub.com/doi/epub/10.1177/1023263X211006516. The scholar argues that it "requires careful consideration of the rights and interests of all actors engaged in the criminal justice process, including victims", and she also points out that, in relation to the EPPO "this much is surely true: the symbolism of the creation of this Office might at least have been used to highlight the nature of victimization differently".

may participate in a transnational hearing as long as they can provide useful information for the investigation. They may also be owners of assets subject to freezing, seizure, or confiscation, acting without *bona fides*.

Third, what we have found is that the EPPO Regulation distinguishes between a 'broad' notion of the category and a 'narrow' one, although the latter, as discussed above, includes an ever-wider range of people affected by the EPPO's procedural acts. We should also observe that under the 2017 Regulation rules the distinction between third parties (other persons affected by PPO criminal investigation) and first parties (suspects, and victims) is unclear.

Moreover, while the research conducted hitherto has confirmed that EU law-makers provide for different notions of third parties in order to be consistent with the rationales underpinning such instruments, we should now think of a broader category of third parties other than those already designated by each EU legal instrument.

Hence, to suitably carry out such an analysis, we need to accept a preliminary definition of 'third party', who is to be understood as any person against whom no evidence that proves her/his suspicion of guilt has been collected. In broader terms, 'third party' may generally refer to all those individuals who may assume a role—not necessarily a formal one—in criminal trials, or have an interest in intervening in the proceedings, or whose legal position is affected by procedural activities. In other words, everyone who suffers as a result of the criminal proceedings and for this reason requires strong protection. Once again, the viewpoint adopted by the EPPO Regulation appears to be the most useful for our purposes here, since it is the first legislative instrument to officially take into account a variety of individuals who may experience the consequences of criminal proceedings in different ways.

On closer inspection, the given definition resembles that provided for by Article 263 TFEU, which states that:

> the Court of Justice of the European Union shall review the legality of legislative acts, of acts of the Council, of the Commission and of the European Central Bank, other than recommendations and opinions, and of acts of the European Parliament and of the European Council intended to produce legal effects vis-à-vis third parties. It shall also review the legality of acts of bodies, offices or agencies of the Union intended to produce legal effects *vis-à-vis* third parties.

According to the caselaw of the Court of Justice, an act is intended to produce legal effects and is, therefore, challengeable on pain of inadmissibility, when "it is intended to produce binding legal effects", which in turn must be "capable of affecting the interests of the applicant".[62]

[62] From this, it follows that Member States are not obliged to envisage the judicial review of procedural acts that are not intended to produce legal effects *vis-à-vis* third parties. CJEU, 11 November 981, *IBM/Commissione*, C- 60/81.

7 Third Parties as a Wide Category Including Individuals Affected by Criminal Proceedings in Various Ways

Having previously discussed how to identify a "third party", this section of this article aims to establish who these individuals are, at the same time pointing out a few of the most problematic aspects regarding the protection of this wide-ranging category.

As has been clarified, a privileged perspective for carrying out this research is clearly represented by the recourse to those preventive measures *in rem*, which aim to protect the criminal trial's purposes by way of restricting patrimonial rights or interests pertaining to third parties. Indeed, seizure, whether for conservation or preventive purposes, also with a view to future confiscation, targets assets over which individuals, unrelated to criminal proceedings, hold some rights. Although we have already discussed this topic, what should be highlighted here is that not only may the rights strictly related to the property be hampered (e.g., the right of ownership or other rights *in rem*) but also rights of a different nature. This is particularly the case when companies or productive assets are seized, thus jeopardising free private economic initiative, the cornerstone of EU integration, as well as the right of those who make use of goods to carry out their work. As it emerges here, the concept of the third party widens to the point of encompassing the whole community or, worse, the entire society. The scope becomes ever wider if one considers the transnational dimension of crimes in Europe, thus impinging upon an undetermined number of EU citizens' rights.

Setting aside traditional searches and seizures, another interesting field to consider from the perspective of this analysis, which shows the increasing tendency to affect the rights of other persons involved in criminal investigations, is represented by the widespread use of digital technologies, as being increasingly able to provide law enforcement agents with efficient tools to trace, detect, prevent, and investigate criminal activities. In the current scenario, electronic communications and activities leave an abundance of digital footprints that can be easily gathered, analysed, and archived.

These technological tools, for example, have led to the increasing use of digital search and seizures as well as cyber interceptions using trojan horses, spyware, and further malware. These aim to intercept communications made through a computer or telematic technologies, such as Chat or Voice Over Internet Protocol (VoIP) connections and created through widespread applications.

In the given examples, relevant questions arise. First, it is difficult to identify and circumscribe the range of people involved in the targeted communication. Second, it is not always conceivable for the judicial authority to select in advance those digital data which are specifically related to both the ongoing investigation and the formal suspect or accused. In this regard, one should think about the risk to the right of defence whenever information between lawyers and their clients is intercepted or seized and only later is found to be relevant for the sake of the defence strategy. It is also important to note that the Budapest Convention on cybercrimes demands the contracting countries to consider the impact of computer-related investigative activities on "the rights, responsibilities and legitimate interests of third parties" [Article 15(3)]. However, as legal scholarship has argued, this "provision sounded like a declaration of principle, as it did not explain how contracting States concretely ought to protect the interests of third parties, thus leaving an excessively wide discretionary power to national lawmakers".[63]

Similar issues concern the continuous monitoring of people's activities and lives, which has given rise to an increasing number of cases in which third parties, specifically service providers, collect criminal evidence by GPS and cell phone location techniques. Not only live movements but also a chronology of location crowdsourced data is nowadays almost always stored by third-party providers such as map apps (*e.g.* Google Maps). Even though such GPS evidence (of the location of the suspect and/or of victims) and track points could "hold major evidentiary value for a case both in terms of *alibis* and in terms of conviction",[64] it may be difficult for judicial authorities to limit data regarding people who are completely unrelated to the proceedings.

In all these situations, therefore, carrying out digital inquiries imposes a restrictive approach, that is, close scrutiny on the part of the investigative authorities, who can only resort to them when other less intrusive measures are unavailable or inadequate.[65]

If one looks more closely, this lays the premises for a general consideration of the respect of digital privacy across the EU,[66] to which EU legislators have attached importance over the years. Alongside the right to private and family life under Article 7 CFR, Article 8 guarantees that everyone is entitled to the protection of personal data concerning them. Specific guarantees are also included in Article 8(2).[67]

---

[63] Di Nuzzo (2022), p. 123 f.

[64] Militello (2022), p. 30 ff. Allowing for aerial surveillance through drones, or satellites as well as flying thermoscanners to look for drugs also poses unique challenges.

[65] Articles 14 and 15 of the Budapest Convention on cybercrime, for instance, expressly refers to the guarantees acknowledged by international fundamental rights Charters, namely the ECHR and the ICCPR, which include within the framework of the proportionality principle the existence of grounds justifying the use of computer-related investigations, the supervision by judicial or other independent authorities, the establishment of a maximum duration for remote surveillance, and procedures to preserve the data's integrity in compliance with the rule of law.

[66] According to Picotti (2000), p. 20, digital privacy can be defined as an "interest in the enjoyment and exclusive control of both certain data and information, and of the related IT and telematic means and processing procedures; that while always taking the form of the right to exclude unauthorised third parties from the corresponding access and use, it is wholly or partially regardless of the traditional limits and assumptions of the civil concepts of ownership and possession, or of the conditions that underpin the legal significance of secrecy or personal confidentiality in general". On this topic, Foti (2022), p. 151.

[67] We should firstly recall the principle of fairness and purpose specification and, second, the existence of a legitimate basis either in law or by consent of the data subject. The third guarantee concerns access to and correction of the data. According to Article 8(3) Charter, compliance with

The Court of Justice has also focused on the importance of such a right over the years. In a German case regarding mass data retention, for instance, the Court confirmed that EU law precludes the general indiscriminate retention of traffic and location data, except in the case of a severe threat to national security. Indeed, in order to fight the most serious crimes, the Member States may, in accordance with the principle of proportionality, provide for the targeted or expedited retention of such data and the general and indiscriminate retention of IP addresses.[68] From this finding it follows that third parties' private life and secrecy shall be limited to the minimum level also under the occurrence of a threat to national security. A truly worrisome shortcoming stemming from indiscriminate data retention, indeed, is that of drawing a profile of the persons whose data are based on their everyday habits, permanent or temporary places of residence, daily or other movements, activities, social and environment relationships. These issues are coupled with both the lack of a uniform data retention Framework in criminal matters since Directive 2006/24/EC (Data Retention Directive) was invalided by the Court of Justice, and the finite scope of the national data retention legal frameworks.[69]

These problems are further exacerbated in the cases of procedural measures *vis-à-vis* people who are not only formally extraneous to criminal proceedings but also are often unaware of an ongoing criminal law action in another State. Indeed, the development of modern technologies allows for bulk interception of cross-border cyber communications, commonly referred to as "digital surveillance", which poses unique challenges to European citizens' (digital) privacy and security.

In this respect, some of the most troublesome issues stem from the EIO, the use of which enables different categories of electronic information to be accessed, collected, and exchanged through direct cooperation among judicial authorities across borders.

---

these obligations must be amenable to control by an independent authority. For the sake of completeness, we should also recall Directive 2006/24/EC of the European Parliament and of the Council of 15 March 2006 on the retention of data generated or processed in connection with the provision of publicly available electronic communications services or of public communications networks and amending Directive 2002/58/EC. Lastly, it was only in 2008 that a Framework Decision was adopted to regulate the processing of personal data in the field of police and judicial cooperation; while the General Data Protection Regulation (GDPR) and the Law Enforcement Directive (LED), both applicable from 24 May 2018, represent the latest generation of data protection law.

[68] CJEU, 20 September 2022, *SpaceNet and Telekom Deutschland*, joined cases C-793/19 C-794/19. Along these lines, see, *inter alia*, judgments of 5 April 2022, *Commissioner of An Garda Síochána and Others*, C-140/20 and of 6 October 2020, *La Quadrature du Net and Others*, C-511/18, C-512/18 and C-520/18. It is noteworthy that exceptions to the general rule demand the adoption of 'counterbalancing factors', for example when the threat is shown "to be genuine and present or foreseeable"; or the indiscriminate and general retention must be subject "to effective review, either by a court or by an independent administrative body, and can be given only for a period that is limited in time to what is strictly necessary, but which may be extended if that threat persists". See https://curia.europa.eu/jcms/upload/docs/application/pdf/2022-09/cp220156en.pdf.

[69] CJEU, 8 April 2014, *Digital Rights Ireland and Seitlinger and Others*, joined cases C-293/12 and C-594/12.

However, on some occasions, the Court of Justice has underestimated the tremendous intrusive capacity of certain digital investigative acts. In the case *A and a.* regarding the judicial review of the issuance of the EIO, probably having in mind more traditional investigative activities, such as personal searches or searches in private places, the EU judges stated that the issuing authority, which requests data exchange, could also be a public prosecutor who depends on the executive power.[70] In such a context, it is apparent that the search for evidence can be just as harmful as the temporary deprivation of liberty, thus requiring an independent judicial authority.

8 Concluding Remarks

As anticipated in the introduction, the main purposes of this study were both to determine the meaning of the concept of "third party" within the framework of EU law and to detect whether and to what extent EU policymaking has achieved a proper protection of this category.

However, by overcoming any distinction between formal and informal participation in criminal proceedings and starting with the legal instruments that make explicit mention of third parties, we have found several definitions of this category, which embodies a multitude of concepts, mainly related to the goals pursued by these legal instruments.

Bearing this in mind, we then tried to draw a distinction between victims and third parties. In this regard, EU legislative instruments, apart from in the EPPO Regulation, distinguish victims from third parties explicitly (the EIO Directive represents the most notable example). On closer inspection, the positions of these two categories of individuals seem to be conceptually different. Indeed, whereas victims have always struggled to obtain recognition of their rights within the criminal proceedings, being directly affected by the criminal offence, third parties are normally people who undergo the effects of criminal proceedings as the result of, for instance, a criminal investigation.

Despite the different notions of third parties within the Union's legal scenario, by embracing a broader perspective, we examined whether a more general category of third party could be conceivable. To this end, we adopted a 'bright line rule' that led us to consider all individuals whose rights may be affected in various ways by criminal proceedings. We not only referred to those rights relating to the safeguarding of privacy, secrecy, personal and family private life, or property rights,

[70]CJEU, 8 December 2020, *A. e a.*, C-584/19. Nevertheless, in another judgment the Court prohibited a public prosecutor from issuing an EIO to obtain traffic data if the adoption of such an investigative measure would be within the competence of a court in a similar domestic case. It also denied the executing authorities the possibility to authorise the execution of an EIO, for the purpose of obtaining traffic data, where such an authorisation would have been required by the law of the issuing State in a similar domestic case. CJEU, 16 December 2021, *HP*, C-724/19.

but also to the right to a fair trial, including in particular the right to information, the right of defence and to legal remedy, and the right to be heard. The analysis of such rights has also highlighted the need for in-depth discussion about the trade-off between the protection of fundamental rights and security. Besides, the adoption of this method has been inspired by the legislative technique of the EPPO Regulation.

Finally, notwithstanding the interest of EU lawmakers in the third-party category, this study has revealed that several questions concerning the position of third parties remain to be answered, and that more work needs to be done in this problematic field of research, especially from the viewpoint of their protection. With this regard, the most sensitive problems relate to the excessive recourse to IT tools which are used in an uncontrolled manner, thus encroaching on the fundamental rights of parties involved in the criminal proceedings, albeit not formally related to them. The indiscriminate use of modern technologies has given rise to a blurry situation where it is not always easy to trace a clear line between the prevention and prosecution of crime activities.[71]

In this light, it must, once again, be pointed out that the challenge lies in striking a balance between the efficient investigation. and prosecution of crime and the respect for individuals' human rights. The achievement of this goal is even more necessary in cases of investigative measures involving people not formally related to the criminal proceedings, in which the competent authority is called upon to scrutinise whether and under which criteria the intrusion within the rights of persons (*e.g.*, right to privacy, secrecy of communications, and so on) other than suspects and defendants is legitimate and truly necessary, and, above all, to establish the duration of such interference.[72]

References

Bachmaier Winter L (2022) Criminal investigation, technological development, and digital tools: where are we heading? In: Bachmaier Winter L, Ruggeri S (eds) Investigating and preventing crime in the digital era. Springer, Cham, pp 3–17

Belfiore R (2019) Il sequestro preventivo. Tra esigenze impeditive e strumentalità alla confisca. Giappichelli, Torino

Boucht J (2019) Asset confiscation in Europe – past, present, and future challenges. J Financ Crime 26(2):526–548

Caianiello M (2015) La nuova direttiva UE sull'ordine europeo di indagine penale tra mutuo riconoscimento e ammissione reciproca delle prove. Processo penale e giustizia 3:1–11

De Hoyos Sancho M (2024) La nueva regulación en la Unión Europea sobre obtención transfronteriza de información electrónica en procesos penales. Aranzadi, Pamplona

Del Río Ayala Alejandra C (2015) El rol de la víctima en el acceso a la justicia. Papeles del Centro de Investigaciones, Facultad de Ciencias Jurídicas y Sociales, UNL 5(16):140–161

[71] Bachmaier Winter (2022), p. 1 ff.

[72] Di Nuzzo (2022), p. 127.

Di Nuzzo V (2022) Search and seizure of digital evidence: human rights concerns and new safeguards. In: Bachmaier Winter L, Ruggeri S (eds) Investigating and preventing crime in the digital era. Springer, Cham, pp 119–149
Dominioni O (1985) Le parti nel processo penale. Profili sistematici e problemi. Giuffrè, Milano
Foschini G (1965) La visione processuale del diritto. Foro Italiano 88(1):1–6
Foti D (2022) Digital privacy and cyber-interception of communications. In: Bachmaier Winter L, Ruggeri S (eds) Investigating and preventing crime in the digital era. Springer, Cham, pp 151–166
Gleß S, Schaffner D (2009) The Handing over of Property according to Art. 29 of the European Arrest Warrant Framework Decision: legal Scope, Implementation and Alternative Regimes for Handing over Property in the EU Member States. In: Keijzer N, van Sliedregt E (eds) The European Arrest Warrant in practice. Springer, Den Haag, pp 297–315
Illuminati G (2018) Protection of fundamental rights of the suspect or accused in transnational proceedings under the EPPO. In: Bachmaier Winter L (ed) The European Public Prosecutor's Office. The challenges ahead. Springer, Cham, pp 179–199
Kerr Orin S (2009) The case for the third-party doctrine. Mich Law Rev 107(4):562–602
Kusak M (2011) Crime's victim and the procedure of executing the freezing order and the European investigation order, pp 231–238 available at https://repozytorium.amu.edu.pl/server/api/core/bitstreams/bbf7cd34-d29f-4e1f-8b80-95eb26a6fb30/content
Lupária Donati L, Della Torre J (2021) Victims of crime in the area of freedom, security and justice. In: Iglesias Sánchez S, González Pascual M (eds) Fundamental rights in the EU area of freedom, security and justice. Cambridge University Press, Cambridge, pp 328–329
Maffei S (2012) The right to confrontation in Europe. Absent, anonymous and vulnerable witnesses. Europa Law Pub, Amsterdam, pp 1–280
Malino E, Di Nuzzo V (2023) The victim's role in cross-border situations in European and international law: a multilevel perspective. Galileu (forthcoming)
Mangiaracina A (2018) L'acquisizione "europea" della prova cambia volto: l'Italia attua la direttiva relativa all'ordine europeo di indagine penale. Dir Pen Proc 2:158–180
Mazzucato C (2019) "Direttiva Vittime" e giustizia riparativa: problemi, sfide, prospettive. In: Ceretti A (ed) La giustizia riparativa nelle politiche educative del Comune di Milano, atti del convegno svoltosi a Milano il 16 maggio 2018, pp 197–225
Militello E (2022) Geolocation in crime detection and prevention. In: Bachmaier Winter L, Ruggeri S (eds) Investigating and preventing crime in the digital era. Springer, Cham, pp 19–42
Pérez Enciso P (2017) Exchange and processing of information between the European Public Prosecutor's Office and National Authorities. The case management system. In: Bachmaier Winter L (ed) The European Public Prosecutor's Office. The challenges ahead. Springer, Cham, pp 253–279
Picotti L (2000) (voce) Reati informatici. Enc Giur Treccani Agg VIII:1–36
Ruggeri S (2017) *Audi Alteram Partem* in criminal proceedings. Towards a participatory understanding of criminal justice in Europe and Latin America. Springer, Cham, pp 1–724
Ruggeri S (2018) Criminal investigations, interference with fundamental rights and fair trial safeguards in the proceedings of the European Public Prosecutor's Office. A human rights law perspective. In: Bachmaier Winter L (ed) The European Public Prosecutor's Office. The challenges ahead. Springer, Cham, pp 201–233
Ružičková V (2022) Effective judicial protection and the regulation implementing enhanced cooperation on the establishment of the European Public Prosecutor's Office. Slovak Yearb Eur Union Law 2:83–92
Simonato M (2017) Confiscation and fundamental rights across criminal and non-criminal domains. ERA Forum 18:365–379
Wade ML (2021) The EPPO and the pitfalls of actuarial justice. Maastricht J Eur Comp Law 28(2): 265–280

Part III
Comparative Frameworks

Third Parties and Their Formal and Substantial Participation in Criminal Justice: A Comparative-Law Analysis of Domestic Jurisdictions

Viviana Di Nuzzo and Antonella Falcone

Abstract This chapter deals with the legal comparison of six selected legal systems (Portugal, Spain, France, Italy, Hungary and Brazil), with the aim of examining whether domestic legislation and case law have taken into adequate consideration the protection of third parties' rights in the context of criminal proceedings. The comparative analysis appears to be extremely useful in depicting possible infringements of third parties' fundamental rights in criminal investigations and procedural activities and in identifying the necessary safeguards aimed at defending their interests. So far, the legal debate on third parties' involvement in criminal proceedings has been marginal, and few domestic jurisdictions have dealt with this issue. Instead, the consideration of third parties' role in criminal proceedings has not been systematically addressed, since the need to prevent, investigate, prosecute, and ascertain criminal offences has been given higher priority than private subjects' interests, which, as a result, have been sacrificed. This study examines the structure of the criminal justice systems in the six chosen legal systems by comparing them at all stages of proceedings covered by the domestic reports. Specific attention is paid to the classification of formal parties and the role left to substantive parties, as well as investigative and other pre-trial measures affecting third parties' liberties and freedom. Furthermore, the chapter discusses and compares the legal remedies available under national law for third parties during each procedural phase and evaluates the effectiveness of their safeguards.

Viviana Di Nuzzo: Sections 1, 2, 3, 3.1, 3.2, 5, 6, 7, and 12
Antonella Falcone: Sections 4, 4.1, 4.2, 4.3, 8, 9, 9.1, 9.2, 9.3, 9.4, 10, 11, and 13

V. Di Nuzzo · A. Falcone (✉)
Law Department, Messina University, Messina, Italy
e-mail: viviana.dinuzzo@unime.it; antonella.falcone@unime.it

S. Ruggeri et al. (eds.), *Third Parties in Criminal Proceedings*, Legal Studies in International, European and Comparative Criminal Law 10,
https://doi.org/10.1007/978-3-031-73970-5_12

1 Introduction

This study deals with the role and protection of third parties in criminal proceedings. This difficult topic has so far been given proper attention in legal debate at neither a domestic nor supranational and international level. Due to the difficulty in even identifying who third parties are and to provide a complete and coherent system of their safeguards, this study aims at comparing the legal systems of six domestic jurisdictions (Portugal, Spain, France, Italy, Hungary and Brazil) in which the structure of criminal proceedings entails the involvement of subjects different from the ones who hold the status of formal participants. This matter is of the utmost relevance in order to make criminal justice truly respectful of human rights, not only of the accused, but also, and above all, of those persons accidentally involved in criminal proceedings and who appear not to be linked to the crime. This study aims to update and improve the principles of criminal justice, with a particular focus on the concepts of fair trial and equality of arms. It is suggested that these concepts should be applied more broadly than in the past, not only to formal participants in criminal proceedings but also to other subjects involved in procedural activities.

The most interesting aspect is that every domestic legal system considered for the purpose of this study has dealt with the protection afforded to third parties but none of them has done so systematically and coherently. In each of these legal systems we can find some rules or case-law without a proper definition of third parties. This is the reason why, before starting our comparative study, we have to provide a provisional meaning of this notion, in order to lay the grounds for an effective analysis of the selected legislation.

For the scope of this chapter, we can consider third parties as non-formal participants who are involved in criminal proceedings for different reasons. Their lack of formal participatory status is due to the absence of a clear definition or specific rules regarding their status in domestic law. In the light of the nature of their participation, we can identify three main types of third parties: *(a)* subjects of the criminal proceedings other than formal participants;[1] *(b)* persons whose fundamental rights are limited by pre-trial measures and procedural activities;[2] *(c)* persons whose knowledge and contribution are essential to the fact-finding process (witnesses and experts).[3]

---

[1] In a strict sense, this concept relates to specific natural or legal persons other than formal participants in criminal process, who are granted some procedural powers which are equivalent or similar to those of formal participants (access to the materials of the case, *ius postulandi*, etc.).

[2] Adopting a human rights perspective, *i.e.* a viewpoint oriented towards the degree of intrusiveness of procedural measures in the sphere of fundamental rights, we may broaden the notion of 'third parties' by extending it to people that, even though criminal investigations are not addressed against them, may be indirectly affected by procedural activities (*e.g.* the family members of undercover agents or people under a special protection programme).

[3] The need to protect witnesses or vulnerable victims can determine some risks for the defendant's rights, since they may be heard by means of special measures in order to avoid any further prejudice to their safety while avoiding their contact with the accused.

We can already anticipate that the most problematic role is that granted to victims of crime, since every state sets out rules providing a level of participation and judicial instruments that may determine an increase or a reduction of their safeguards. Indeed, some legal systems allow victims to accuse the suspect criminally and formally, while in others they can only bring a civil claim within criminal proceedings. Even in the EU legal scenario, where Directive 2012/29/EU strongly contributed to the enhancement of a shared standard for victim protection, multiple Member States still present significant differences in terms of the range of possibilities available to the injured person to actively participate as a formal party in the criminal proceeding.[4]

For the scope of this study, individuals who have suffered the consequences of a crime are considered as borderline figures,[5] since they may be considered either as formal participants or third parties, depending on the safeguards and legal remedies granted to them. In this perspective, a comparative law approach may be helpful in order to analyse the legal classification of subjects other than the formal participants in criminal proceedings and evaluate which guarantees may be effective for their protection.

2 Aim, Methods and Structure of the Comparative Analysis

As legal systems evolve to meet contemporary challenges posed by the globalisation of criminal activities, third parties' rights are constantly at risk due to the invasive nature of certain procedural activities. In the absence of detailed legislation and specific studies regarding this issue, comparative research in criminal procedural law can contribute to the development of legal protection by promoting human rights and facilitating cross-border cooperation.

This chapter aims to provide a comparative analysis of the selected legal systems, while examining legal principles, rules, and practices across six different jurisdictions. The reasons for selecting the reporting countries were as follows. Firstly, this study focuses on five civil-law jurisdictions belonging to the EU, due to the need to analyse how and to what extent supranational law has influenced the way national legislators have implemented European Union provisions. Secondly, the study also examines Brazilian legislation, as an example of extra-EU jurisdiction, which has experienced the influence of Spanish and Portuguese law. Thirdly, the national legislation under discussion provides notable examples of differences in the role of the judiciary in the investigative stage, which is a core aspect for addressing the topic

---

[4] Cf. Falcone, in this volume, para. 5.1.

[5] See Malino, Foti, in this volume, para. 1.3, who describe the victim as a '*sui generis*' subject, since they can become a formal participant in Italian criminal proceedings only when they claim for civil damages. Similarly, see both Falcone and Orlando, in this volume, who underline the hybrid role of victims within the EU and ECHR legal systems.

dealt with in this study. For instance, while France, Hungary, Portugal and Spain have an investigating judge who leads the investigation, in conjunction with the Public Prosecutor's Office, Italy and Brazil present the peculiar figure of judge who authorises investigative activities requested by the public prosecutor. This different approach may help us to assess which mechanisms can be adapted to provide effective protection of third parties during criminal inquiries and how the presence of a judicial authority may supervise the interest of these subjects during a particularly intrusive phase of the criminal proceedings.

This comparative approach will allow us to identify similarities, differences, and best practices regarding the protection of third parties and their involvement in criminal justice systems. The task is truly challenging because the scope of the comparison encompasses different stages of the criminal proceedings, from investigation to trial, decision-making process, and subsequent effects. This comprehensive method is necessary in order to detect which procedural activities may require the contribution of subjects other than the accused, the reasons for and limitations of such involvement, and also the protection afforded to them.

Against this backdrop, the study of different approaches to the problem of third-party safeguards in the different stages of criminal proceedings may help verify whether and to what extent national laws align with the evolution of social rules (such as digital privacy) and with the requirements and obligations stemming from international and supranational legal instruments.

In the light of this, we must recognise that the need for specific rules on the protection and involvement of third parties in procedural activities arises, above all, from the evident broadening of the reach of criminal investigations, which nowadays makes the number of potentially affected persons indeterminable. In this sense, the activities carried out by competent authorities to prevent and detect criminal offences is a task that inevitably impacts on individuals other than the formal parties.

Furthermore, examining the arrangements made by different legal systems which have attempted to balance the rights of the accused with the interests of non-parties sheds light on areas where improvements can be made in order to avoid undue involvement of such persons in procedural activities or to provide adequate legal remedies to safeguard their interests. In the light of this, comparative insights concerning these issues may influence reforms aimed at strengthening due process, preventing unjustified restrictions on fundamental rights, and improving the overall fairness of criminal proceedings.

3 Parties Within the Domestic Criminal Justice Systems

The domestic criminal justice systems examined in this study mainly present a similar structure, since in all of them public prosecutors, alongside a judge with investigative competence, are empowered to investigate and prosecute criminal offences. This is the reason why we can undoubtedly exclude this subject from the list of third parties. Of course, suspects and defendants cannot be considered as a third party. As we said above, the concept of third parties should be formulated in relation to the formal participants, and traditionally the prosecution and the defence have held the leading role in criminal proceedings.

However, we can observe that some legal systems grant the person who has suffered the effects of a criminal offence the power to bring charges privately (Portugal and Spain) or in conjunction with the Public Prosecutor's Office (Brazil, Spain, Portugal and France).

This setup entails a different classification of formal participants in criminal proceedings, because the injured person may be considered as a party, having a role not limited to the possibility of merely submitting a claim for civil compensation, if this is allowed. In this sense, Spain represents an interesting model, since the power to bring charges is available not only to any person offended by a crime (*acusación particular*)[6] but also to any citizen (*acusación popular*).[7] However, "sometimes the presence of victims in the proceedings is perceived as a kind of 'control' over the public prosecution".[8]

At the same time, Portuguese law entitles some subjects (generally the '*ofendido*') to become an assistant to the public prosecutor, who may aid the prosecution or even perform certain procedural activities on their own.[9]

In the case of private crimes, assistants can, therefore, exercise their control over the final decision of the inquiry, since establishing the legal classification of the facts and bringing charges (the so-called 'private accusation') lie in their hands.[10] In other words, in the case of a private offence the Public Prosecutor's Office, at the end of the investigation, can only notify the assistant that they may bring (private) charges, even in situations where the public prosecutor believes there is insufficient evidence against the accused. Portuguese legislation also grants all citizens (forms of) popular participation in criminal prosecution aimed at protecting widespread or collective interests.[11]

These preliminary remarks clearly show the difficult task of giving a common definition of who is party to the proceedings and who is not, a difficulty that increases due to the fact that the jurisdictions examined for the purpose of this study set different rules to pinpoint participants and non-participants in their criminal proceedings, thus also granting different levels of protection.

---

[6] See Art. 270 CCP-Spain: "*Todos los ciudadanos españoles, hayan sido o no ofendidos por el delito, pueden querellarse, ejercitando la acción popular establecida en el artículo 101 de esta Ley. También pueden querellarse los extranjeros por los delitos cometidos contra sus personas o bienes o las personas o bienes de sus representados*".

[7] See Art. 101 CCP-Spain: "*La acción penal es pública. Todos los ciudadanos españoles podrán ejercitarla con arreglo a las prescripciones de la Ley*".

[8] See Gascón Inchausti, Schumann Barragán, in this volume, para. 1.2. Indeed, the victim will often concur with the Public Prosecutor's Office in the exercise of both criminal and civil law actions and demand harsher punitive damages and higher compensation than the prosecution.

[9] See Gouveia de Caires, Reis Barata, in this volume, para. 1.4.4.

[10] See Art. 285 CCP-Portugal.

[11] See Art. 2(1) of Law 31 August 1995, No. 81 ('*Lei da Ação Popular*').

In the light of this, it is of the utmost relevance to start our analysis by identifying who are formal participants in all of the six domestic jurisdictions. This is, indeed, a necessary step to extrapolate the notion of third parties and give it the proper meaning, in order to include all those individuals that 'take part' in procedural activities, both during pretrial and court stages, and, afterwards, to verify whether or not they are granted adequate safeguards.

3.1 Formal Participants in Criminal Proceedings

The comparative analysis of the selected legal systems has shown a general tendency to assign the status of formal participants, first of all, to public prosecutors, since they generally are in charge of the investigative phase and decide whether the case must be dismissed or brought to trial before a criminal judge. Indeed, the investigative initiatives taken by the Public Prosecutor's Office can lead to a hypothesis regarding the commission of a crime by a specific person, namely the accused, who is in a sense the counterpart of the investigating authority, and to the subsequent activation of certain safeguards related to this role.

The Public Prosecutor's Office does not always stand out as the only party empowered to start a prosecution. Outside Europe, Brazilian law lists different participants for each type of action:[12] for example, in private criminal-law actions the victim is the active party,[13] while in a writ of *habeas corpus* anyone can be the petitioner and the public prosecutor is only entitled to make a statement and give their opinion. Moreover, the Constitution of the Federal Republic of Brazil allows private criminal prosecution for some offences whenever the *Ministério Público* does not initiate a public prosecution within the statutory time limits.[14] This can happen only if there are 'identified victims', who are allowed by Article 268 of the CCP-Brazil to act as formal parties and are granted some strong procedural powers, such as the right to request means of evidence, question witnesses, present their arguments and appeal against acquittal.[15]

At the same time, also Spanish and Portuguese legislation, as noted above, entitle the victim to bring a criminal and/or civil action against the accused person,[16] while

[12] According to Brazilian legal scholars, "parties are the persons who participate in the adversary hearing before the State Judge". See Dinamarco et al. (2020), p. 362.

[13] As emerged from the Brazilian Report, the victim's successors also can be parties actively in this type of prosecutions. See Gomes de Vasconcellos, Brenner Lucchesi, in this volume, para. 1.1.

[14] See also Art. 5(LIX) of the Brazilian Constitution.

[15] While in this case the victim is a private prosecutor, there is also the hypothesis for them to act as an assistant to the Public Prosecutor and, in this circumstance, they are not considered as parties nor as witnesses for the prosecution, since the injured persons are not an uninterested party in the way that a witness should be. See Gomes de Vasconcellos, Brenner Lucchesi, in this volume, para. 1.2.

[16] "In the case of private crimes (slander and insults), the prosecution is exercised by the victim by means of the so-called *acusación privada*". See Pastrana (2015), p. 129.

giving them the role of a formal accuser. But the injured party has no subjective right to have the State inflict a defined punishment, nor can they influence the severity of this punishment, as underlined by the EU Court of Justice.[17]

Interestingly, we can find a similar provision in the Hungarian code of criminal procedure, which grants the injured person the possibility of bringing a supplementary private prosecution.[18]

A comparative analysis allows us to observe two prevailing models that differ from each other mainly in terms of whether victims may initiate criminal proceedings. Alongside the prevalence in many European States of the model based on the monopoly of the Public Prosecutor's Office, some legal systems, both inside and outside the EU, empower the aggrieved party by elevating their status to that of a potential alternative or subsidiary prosecutor.[19]

But even those countries that have not adopted this participatory model have at some point dealt with the possibility of introducing forms of private prosecutions.[20] For example, in Italy in the past some leading legal scholars argued for the introduction of a complementary or a subsidiary form of private prosecution, while never proposing prosecutions initiated exclusively by victims.[21] Their ideas have re-emerged in recent years. Similarly, the Italian Constitutional Court stated that Article 112 of the Italian Constitution, which stands out among other constitutions for enshrining at the primary-law level the principle of mandatory public prosecution, does not preclude the attribution of the power to prosecute to other subjects.[22] This means that Italian legislators may introduce and regulate forms of private

---

[17] CJEU, *Kuts*, judgment of 9 September 2008, C-404/07. See Rafaraci (2015), p. 218.

[18] See Art. 37 CCP-Hungary.

[19] Notwithstanding the requirements on the scope of criminal law and the level of the penalties prescribed, the European Court of Human Rights (hereafter, ECtHR) has consistently held that Article 6(1) ECHR does not guarantee a right for the individual to require the institution of a criminal prosecution against an alleged perpetrator of an offence or to be able to institute one themselves. See ECtHR, *Helmers v. Sweden*, judgment of 29 October 1991, Appl. No. 11826/85, para. 29; *Perez v. France* (GC), judgment of 12 February 2004, Appl. No. 47287/99, para. 70; *Atanasova v. Bulgaria*, judgment of 2 October 2008, Appl. No. 72001/01, para. 35.

[20] In the past, victims were the main accusers, but with the building of modern States the power to prosecute became public, and injured parties were relegated to the role of witnesses. See Schünemann (2013), p. 119, according to whom the idea to introduce the victim as the opponent of the accused, who finds themselves in a position already lower than the prosecution, may seem truly 'bizarre'. The author clearly expresses some doubts about the possibility of considering the victim as a formal party in criminal proceedings. Instead, he shows a preference for the civil law action in criminal proceedings and promotes the creation of an 'intermediary space' between civil law and criminal law: criminal policies should adopt the concept of a penalty to remedy damage from the former, while the latter is the place where the protection is enacted.

[21] Lucchini (1873), p. 313; Carrara (1875), p. 13 ff.

[22] Italian Constitutional Court, judgment No. 154 of 13 December 1963, underlined that national legislation did not entail the possibility of any other subject substituting the Public Prosecutor in his main task. Even more specifically, the Italian Constitutional Court, judgment No. 84 of 26 July, explained that Article 112 of the Italian Constitution does not allow subjects other than the Public Prosecutor to exclusively prosecute a criminal offence.

prosecution, but cannot limit in any case the public prosecutor's power to issue an indictment. However, Italian law, at least so far, has not provided victims with any prosecutorial power,[23] instead considering them as witnesses and as a mere addressee of information rights and forms of protection.

The legal debate in Italy on the victim's power to personally prosecute represents a clear example of the influence of criminal policy on the role of the injured party. The more victims are allowed to take part in criminal proceedings, also, and above all, with some really effective legal remedies to protect their interests, the less they can be considered as third parties. Victims, indeed, are involved in criminal proceedings but occupy a borderline position. Both the legal instruments that national legislation provides for them and the way the injured persons choose to act in criminal proceedings can enlarge or restrict the number of formal parties. Likewise, bringing a civil action in criminal proceedings contributes to expanding the number of participants and also *res judicanda*, since those who are civilly liable will also be considered as parties, and the criminal judge must examine the civil matter, in order to determine whether there has been civil damage. This is also the case of the French law, where, similarly to Italy, the aggrieved person can become a civil party and, therefore, gains the status of a formal participant who asks for reparation or financial compensation.[24]

Comparative research clearly shows the difficulty for domestic jurisdictions to find a proper trade-off between the criminal policy-making regarding the status of victims in criminal proceedings and the need to balance it with defence rights, which cannot be compromised by strengthening the injured party's role.

3.2 Third Parties to Criminal Proceedings

We have already seen that, for the purpose of this study, third parties are understood to be those persons who do not hold the status of formal participants, because they are not allowed to file any claim concerning the main object of the ongoing criminal trial, and the *res judicanda* does not involve them directly. However, criminal investigations and trials increasingly require the intervention of such subjects and,

[23] According to the Italian Constitutional Court, the institution of a civil law action in criminal proceedings constitutes the main and most significant of the faculties granted by law to the person injured by the offence. Cf. Italian Constitutional Court, judgment No. 98 of 3 April 1996, para. 3. Nonetheless, the ECtHR found the Italian authorities responsible for having prejudiced the victim's right to exercise their powers, since the beginning of the judicial stage depends on the choices taken by the Italian Public Prosecutor. Hence, when the authority does not commit the accused for trial, the injured person cannot become a formal party and the need to ensure their active participation in criminal proceedings is frustrated. Cf. ECtHR, *Arnoldi v. Italia*, judgment of 7 December 2017, Appl. No. 35637/04; *Petrella v. Italia*, judgment of 18 May 2021, Appl. No. 24340/07.

[24] In the last few years, the injured person has become the "*nouvelle étoile de la scène pénale*". Along these lines, see Tulkens (2002), p. 41.

above all, can also affect their rights or interests negatively. In this regard, we can identify some new categories, as emerged also in all the national reports, such as the owners of goods and assets seized or confiscated, the persons who undergo investigative measures such as searches or interceptions of communications, witnesses and experts, and, more generally, the individuals whose data are processed during the criminal proceedings. In some cases, the need to safeguard their rights results in limiting the most invasive measures or in procedural powers to challenge the activity performed against them. In other cases, domestic legislation is still lacking specific provisions which ensure an adequate level of protection to the individuals concerned, above all when intrusive technologies are deployed to gather a massive amount of relevant information in a short span of time and the number of individuals affected by such means cannot be determined *a priori*.

The results of the comparison demonstrate that the difficulty to define who third parties are strictly relates to the recognition of formal participants in criminal proceedings and hugely complicates the task for national lawmakers to provide a coherent set of rules. Indeed, none of the six legal systems analysed has so far provided a general legal definition of 'third party', but all of them reach a point in which they must deal with this topic. This does not mean however that no specific provisions are addressed to third parties.

For example, if we consider the 2017 Hungarian CCP, Chapter X includes rules concerning 'parties with pecuniary interest and other interested parties' and specifically lists some subjects who have a direct or indirect interest in the criminal proceeding and its termination. In particular, the interested parties described in Article 58 include: *(a)* persons reporting a crime, *(b)* witnesses, *(c)* persons affected by search or subject to a body search, *(d)* persons affected by data collection activities, *(e)* persons affected by expert examination, inspection, or presentation for recognition, *(f)* aides, *(g)* experts and consultants. All the interested parties are legally entitled to have an aide in order to represent and protect their rights and interests in criminal proceedings.[25] Another participant in Hungarian criminal procedure taken into account is the 'supporter',[26] who can be involved in criminal trials by way of supporting the victim, the financial interested party or other interested parties. This is a unique figure, as our research did not find similar subjects in the other countries analysed.

The Hungarian list of 'interested parties', while being fairly extensive, does not provide a general definition of third parties nor include all the possible categories, thus leaving subjects other than those listed in Article 58 without specific protection.

---

[25] An aide can be a legal representative or guardian, an adult relative of the defendant, an official representative of the consul for foreign defendants, victims and witnesses, the spouse or the partner of a person under involuntary mental treatment, an adult caretaker of a minor, an authorised representative, a supporter, an adult designated by the victim and complainant, a lawyer acting on behalf of the witness, an uninterested adult present at searches or designated by the searched person, a trustee on delivery, a protection agent, or a litigation friend.

[26] Art. 65 ff. CCP-Hungary.

At the same time, the other jurisdictions also fail to provide an exhaustive legal definition of third parties or a general set of rules to protect their rights, but they do grant some procedural safeguards to certain individuals in the light of a specific interest or status. For example, Brazilian law, while giving victims a different position based on their role as a private prosecutor or as an assistant to the public prosecution, recognises both protection from secondary victimisation and harassment and some procedural powers, such as the right to be heard, the authorisation to request means of evidence (when they assist the public prosecution), the possibility to claim for moral and material compensation and to challenge the decision even if the *Ministério Público* does not file an appeal. Notably, Brazil views injured parties in a partially different way from the other countries, since its legislation deems victims to be parties only when they prosecute on their own, while they cannot hold the same status when they lack this possibility.[27] We can thus argue that under Brazilian regulations, victims can be considered as third parties to a limited extent.

As mentioned above, apart from Brazilian law, the other jurisdictions examined have displayed a general tendency to identify who third parties are on the basis of the level of impact produced mostly by means of investigation, pretrial measures and the processing of personal data within criminal proceedings. With regard to the latter point, for example, Article 9 of Spanish *Ley Orgánica* 7/2021 delivers some categories of '*interesados*' when it comes to data processing and includes '*terceros involucrados en una infracción penal*'. According to Spanish law, these individuals are entitled to exercise the right of access, the right to the erasure or restriction of processing and the right to compensation for any damages caused by data processing.[28]

We can already argue that, among the legal systems analysed in this comparative study, Spain stands out as perhaps one of the most advanced ones in protecting third parties, particularly in the use of pre-trial measures involving intrusive technologies. Meanwhile, the other domestic legislations considered in this analysis still appear to be lagging far behind in providing adequate safeguards for third parties affected by such measures. And this phenomenon may be exacerbated by the increasing use of Information and Communication Technology (hereafter, ICT) tools. It is therefore useful to carry out a comparative analysis to classify the most common categories of third parties in criminal proceedings. This is a necessary first step towards improving their protection.

---

[27] See Gomes de Vasconcellos, Brenner Lucchesi, in this volume, para. 1.2.

[28] See Arts. 22 and 23 of the Spanish Organic Law 7/2021.

4 The Fundamental Rights and Safeguards of Third Parties

The complex nature of this topic calls for a comparative analysis on the constitutional protection afforded to third parties. In addition, this study looks at both international and EU law, which provide a range of rights, freedoms and procedural safeguards to persons who are not formal participants in criminal proceedings.

Against this background, we aim to summarise the main aspects that have emerged from the investigation conducted so far and discuss the principal findings of the national reports in these specific areas of research. Our main purpose is to highlight differences and similarities in the protection of third parties in the reviewed criminal proceedings, particularly considering constitutional, international, and supranational perspectives. Indeed, by examining how different jurisdictions consider third parties at these levels, this study seeks to ultimately identify common solutions to strengthen the position of these subjects in criminal proceedings. This involves a preliminary analysis comparing specific parts of each country's report, as well as the overall context.

4.1 Constitutional Law

The study conducted thus far has shown that a preliminary question, which emerged in all criminal justice systems examined, regards the constitutional recognition of rights and safeguards for third parties. Upon closer inspection, this methodological approach is the most appropriate way to address a sensitive topic like the one dealt with in this study. Indeed, the accounts analysed have demonstrated that constitutional law plays a crucial role in protecting third parties who, although traditionally ignored by criminal procedural law and scholars, require special attention.

Furthermore, our investigation revealed that there are both significant similarities and differences in the protection of the rights and freedoms of third parties across constitutional laws, thus calling for an in-depth analysis. For instance, a common aspect that emerged from our research is the constitutional acknowledgment of inviolable freedoms and rights of individuals, regardless of their formal or informal status in criminal proceedings. In all cases examined, it was reported that the protection of fundamental rights and public liberties of third parties, which are at the core of criminal justice, includes the right to personal freedom, the right to privacy—encompassing intimacy, home inviolability, and secrecy of communications—the right to legal representation, and the right to effective judicial remedies, just to give a few examples.

Notably, the Brazilian report emphasised the principle of human dignity which presupposes an inherent and distinctive quality in every individual.[29] In particular, it grants the right to equal treatment and consideration from both the state and society.

[29] Art. 1(III) of the Brazilian Constitution.

In this light, third parties are entitled to seek the safeguarding of their human dignity to which fundamental rights and freedoms are certainly linked. The Hungarian report echoes this finding, since its constitution includes a general clause for the respect of human dignity, freedom, and security. Furthermore, the Portuguese Fundamental Law also attaches great importance to this value, by stressing the need for respecting the dignity of the person throughout criminal proceedings.[30] Furthermore, it is important to consider the constitutional principles, particularly those of a procedural nature, relevant to third parties in criminal proceedings. For instance, Article 20(4) of the Portuguese Fundamental Law enshrines the right of all individuals to a fair and impartial trial, including access to justice and participation in the administration of justice.

Despite these important acknowledgments, constitutions lack detailed provisions of how to effectively ensure the protection of individuals, including those who are not formal participants in criminal proceedings. All this is exemplified in the works undertaken by the contributors in this comparative investigation. They also highlighted the strategic role played by constitutional case-law in enhancing the protection of a broader range of individuals involved in criminal proceedings that goes beyond that of formal parties. Indeed, based on constitutional provisions safeguarding fundamental rights and liberties, constitutional judges have broadened the degree of protection to include individuals who are not implicated in criminal proceedings. This expansion of protection is illustrated by the study conducted by Fernando Gascón Inchausti and Guillermo Schumann Barragán.[31] In Spain, fundamental rights and public liberties can be directly invoked by third parties in criminal inquiries and proceedings. As mentioned earlier, this interpretation resulted from the Spanish Constitutional Court's ruling 30/2022 on the impact of investigative measures on third parties. We need merely recall that this decision enables any third party to file an individual appeal before the *Tribunal Constitucional* for any violation of their 'substantive rights' stemming from procedural activities.[32] These two scholars firmly believe that this judgment carries significant weight, as its implications could potentially extend by analogy to other scenarios where judicial measures, including pre-trial ones, may affect third parties directly or indirectly.[33] Indeed, there may be situations where there is a legitimate interest of third parties to lodge a *recurso de amparo* in the event of a violation of 'substantive rights'. For instance, this could happen in the case of measures affecting immovable property or the closure of the company where the third party is employed. Indeed, as stated in the report, pre-trial measures taken in the context of freezing and confiscating

[30] Art. 1 of Portuguese Fundamental Law.

[31] See Gascón Inchausti, Schumann Barragán, in this volume, para. 2.1.

[32] Spanish Constitutional Court, judgment No. 30 of 7 March 2022.

[33] As stated by the *Tribunal Constitucional*, "it is not possible to deny the legal standing of third parties when contesting the court's decisions, when they are affected in the exercise of fundamental rights; it is necessary to require the judicial bodies to provide reinforced reasoning that justifies the denial of the right of access to jurisdiction". See Gascón Inchausti, Schumann Barragán, in this volume, para 3.3.

instrumentalities and proceeds of crime in criminal proceedings could also have a direct impact on third parties.

Similarly, the Italian Constitutional Court has considered third parties to be formal participants in the criminal proceedings on several occasions. For instance, in a case concerning the taking of DNA samples, the Constitutional Court ruled that those national provisions allowing for coercive gathering of genetic materials violated Article 13 of the Italian Constitution (IC) on personal freedom. Despite this, Elisea Malino and Diego Foti have reported some inconsistencies within the trend of constitutional case-law.[34]

In the current analysis, it is also interesting to note that, following the Italian Constitutional Court's assumption, courts must establish the guilt of individuals subject to confiscation in accordance with the principle of the presumption of innocence.[35] This principle applies whether the measure is addressed to the accused or to a third party. Consequently, the burden of proof should remain consistent, and the responsibility for proving the *mala fide* intentions of the third party rests with the public prosecutor. In this light, this decision is relevant as it establishes a strict relationship between the infringement of a general principle of utmost importance and its effects on the procedural safeguards of a third party.

On closer inspection, the solution provided for by the Italian Constitutional Court resembles that found in France, where the *Conseil Constitutionnel* dealt with the confiscation of property and the rights of third parties in at least three considerable decisions. In this regard, the 2021 rulings compelled the French Parliament to pass measures for more effective protection of the rights of this category of subjects.[36] Even more remarkably, these decisions granted third parties the right to participate in the criminal proceedings and to be heard as a crucial part of the right to legal remedy and, above all, of the right to be presumed innocent until proven guilty.

Outside Europe, Vinicius Gomes de Vasconcellos and Brenner Lucchesi reported that in Brazil third parties in criminal proceedings have the right to review any decisions that impinge upon their privacy, liberty, or property. Significantly, this involves rulings or pre-trial measures that freeze or seize their assets or violate their constitutional rights.[37]

In conclusion, it is worth emphasising that a common trend in the analysed reports on the implementation of EU law is the effort to maintain a balance between legal ascertainment and the safeguarding of fundamental rights. Along these lines, Zsanett Fantoly, András Lichtenstein, as well Elisea Malino and Diego Foti, have respectively argued that limitations on fundamental rights in criminal proceedings are only acceptable within the established legal framework.[38] In their reports, they

---

[34] See Malino, Foti, in this volume, para. 4.4

[35] Italian Constitutional Court, judgment No. 49 of 26 March 2015, para. 5.

[36] See Drevet, in this volume, para. 2.1.

[37] See Gomes de Vasconcellos, Brenner Lucchesi, in this volume, para. 2.1.

[38] See Fantoly, András Lichtenstein, in this volume, para. 2.3 and Malino, Foti, in this volume, para. 2.2.

also highlight the importance of the requirements of necessity and proportionality. Additionally, they stress that violations of fundamental rights are permissible only when essential and when the intended objective cannot be achieved through a less restrictive measure or activity. These considerations are especially important when the fundamental rights of third parties are at risk of being violated during legal proceedings. At the same time, this highlights the need for limiting the interference with third parties' sphere of rights and freedoms and supervising any intervention which may impinge upon their rights.

4.2 Domestication of International Law

This section discusses the need to incorporate international instruments into national legislation, so that the rights and obligations acknowledged in such treaties, including those related to the protection of third parties in criminal proceedings, can be applied and enforced domestically.

When addressing the domestication of international law, most of the reporters in this study have noted that their national jurisdictions are bound by major international agreements both on human and fundamental rights. For example, the Spanish system adheres to the standards set by international treaties, including the European Convention on Human Rights. As a result, the caselaw of the ECtHR must be considered a source of law by Spanish national courts. Furthermore, domestic case law incorporates the guarantees outlined in Article 14 of the International Covenant on Civil and Political Rights, ensuring their application at a national level. In 2015, a reform extended the scope of the right to appeal against all criminal decisions to better respect the right of any person convicted of a crime to have their decision reviewed by a higher court. However, it is unclear from the reporting description whether this remedy includes third parties or not. Moreover, for the sake of this study, it is important to recognise the category of third parties in the international legal instruments to which the countries surveyed are parties. However, there is limited information on how these countries have incorporated international protection for these individuals. The scant consideration of this aspect is certainly problematic, and possibly explained by the prevalent and deeply rooted national perspective that views criminal proceedings as two-party contests between the State and the accused. This also explains why national jurisdictions are often hesitant to extend protection to those outside of the criminal proceedings, even if it means breaching treaty obligations. For instance, even though France is a party to the Council of Europe Convention on Laundering, Search, Seizure and Confiscation of the Proceeds from Crime, which calls for the rights of third parties to be taken into account, French law has historically failed to provide adequate protection for this category. This represents a clear breach of the Convention, which states that a request for cooperation and recognition of a judicial decision taken in the requesting State may be refused if third parties have not had sufficient opportunity to have their rights safeguarded. This inconsistency is also evident in relation to the UN

Convention against Transnational Organised Crime, which asserts that confiscation should not undermine the rights of *bona fide* third parties. Once again, French legislation has failed to protect this category of people for years.

It is worth observing that the Brazilian report differs in some respects from the others and provides noteworthy elements that deserve our attention. In Brazil, in addition to constitutional rights and guarantees, the American Convention on Human Rights recognises safeguards for all parties, including defendants (Arts. 7 and 8). The procedural rights in this country include the right to a trial within a reasonable time,[39] access to public records,[40] reparation in the event of judicial error,[41] and judicial protection.[42] These rights are incorporated into Brazilian law with a supra-legal status, meaning they are below the Constitution but above ordinary laws, and therefore prevail over any legal text that conflicts with the protection afforded to parties. At any rate, as emerged from the reported description, it is generally accepted that these rights are intended to be granted to third parties.

Turning once more to Europe, Italy provides a considerable example of how international law has pushed Italian lawmakers to enact measures aimed at protecting third parties. Indeed, the country has recently reformed its law on searches to align it with the principles laid down by the ECtHR in the well-known case *Brazzi v. Italy*.[43] This has resulted in the introduction of a new remedy against the decision of the public prosecutor to carry out a search. Moreover, Italian legislators implicitly addressed the issue of protecting a third party by adopting the Convention on the Protection of Children against Sexual Exploitation and Sexual Abuse, a soft law instrument of the Committee of Ministers of the Council of Europe. This Convention established new rules to protect vulnerable individuals, particularly witnesses who require special measures. Additionally, the Prüm Convention is relevant to our investigation as it deals with the issue of coercive DNA sample taking, which may also violate the personal liberty of third parties. Italy enacted a new Article 224-*bis* into the Italian CCP on the execution of investigative measures affecting personal freedom, granting third parties the same level of protection as formal ones, thus ensuring objectivity and the balanced treatment of all parties involved.

Another significant finding that has emerged from this research is that the Hungarian legal system provides for an extraordinary legal remedy against final and binding domestic criminal judgments. In particular, this consists of a review of the decision of an international human rights body, such as the European Court of Human Rights, whenever the international court determines that the domestic criminal procedure or judgment violated human rights. Under Hungarian law, indeed, the defendant may request such a review, which is limited to those who represent the defendant's interests, such as legal representatives, spouses, and, in the

[39] Art. 8(1) ACHR.

[40] Art. 8(5) ACHR.

[41] Art.10 ACHR.

[42] Article 25(1) ACHR.

[43] ECtHR, *Brazzi v. Italy*, judgment of 27 September 2018, Appl. No. 57278/11.

event of the defendant's death, relatives. It is important to note that although these individuals are classified as third parties, they are ultimately treated as formal parties in this context, as they assume the position of the convicted person. Certainly, this is an example of how the status of a third party can evolve during criminal proceedings, depending on the powers granted to them by the law, and it also confirms the difficulty of providing a comprehensive and preliminary definition of this category that may cover all the steps of the criminal proceedings.

4.3 Implementation of EU Law

In order to suitably discuss the results that have arisen from the reports on the implementation of EU law, it is necessary to focus our attention on those relating to Spain, Italy, Portugal, Hungary, and France, excluding Brazil, as it is not an EU Member State.

The reports have revealed a crucial aspect of EU law regarding freezing, seizure, and confiscation procedures, where the impact of EU law is significant. Indeed, the research data show that third parties, including spouses, relatives, friends, business associates, and even lawyers, are frequently faced with violations of their rights, particularly property rights, during asset freezing and confiscation when individuals are suspected or accused of a crime. The effects of such measures thus extend far beyond suspects or accused persons. We need merely recall that investigating and judicial authorities or the court may rule on the ownership of an asset, linking it to a suspect or defendant, even if it is not officially registered in their name. Moreover, the infringement of property rights becomes even more alarming when criminal proceedings involve two or more EU Member States. As a result, the EU institutions have taken steps to consider the interests of individuals affected by the freezing, seizing, and confiscation of assets and proceeds of crime in the context of international judicial cooperation. Directive 2014/42/EU has played an essential role in addressing this issue at the EU level. Indeed, this legislative instrument ensures that informal parties are afforded the same protection as formal ones. Besides, this comparative study demonstrates that some countries, such as France and Italy, have implemented additional measures to provide greater protection to third parties with rights to confiscated property in response to the EU Directive. For instance, in 2018, the French *Cour de Cassation* ruled that the rights of *bona fide* third parties must always be taken into consideration, even if the confiscated property is linked to the crime, based on Article 6(2) of the Directive. The Court's decision aligned Article 131-21 of the CCP with the EU instrument, extending protection to third parties with rights in or over confiscated property. Furthermore, the Italian, Spanish, and Hungarian Parliaments incorporated the 2014 EU Directive, enabling third parties to participate in confiscation proceedings where their property rights have been violated.

Significantly, all the reports analysed in this volume highlight a widespread focus on the victims who, although not being strictly categorised as third parties, may be treated as such in some jurisdictions. Once again, these data show both the need to be explicit about what exactly is meant by the word 'victim' and whether or not this individual may be considered as a third party. Indeed, as previously stated, the persons who suffer the consequences of a crime are in a somewhat ambiguous position, as they can be classified either as formal participants or third parties, depending on the safeguards and instruments provided to them.[44] In this context, it is worth recalling that, at the EU level, Directive 2012/29/EU has contributed significantly to standardising the status of victims of crimes across European jurisdictions. We have already stated that this Directive grants them various rights, including fundamental ones such as participation in criminal proceedings and timely information regarding such rights, as well as information about the accused's escape or release, to name but a few. However, despite the potential of this EU legal instrument to protect victims, the position of the aggrieved party is still fragile due to the lack of comprehensive national provisions and insufficient resources tackling so-called 'service rights', which include support services and protection from secondary and repeat victimisation.[45]

Finally, among European countries, Hungary has provided a comprehensive overview of the implementation of EU legal instruments relating to third parties. Apart from addressing issues concerning freezing, confiscation, and victims' rights, this country extends significant procedural guarantees and rights to other third parties. These are all enshrined in the directives associated with the well-known 'Stockholm Programme', covering areas such as the right to interpretation, translation, and information in criminal proceedings, among others. Furthermore, the Hungarian report also considered Directive 2016/680/EU, which deals with the protection of natural persons regarding the processing of personal data by competent authorities for criminal purposes, thus also including third parties.[46] Even more importantly, João Gouveia de Caires and Joana Reis Barata have shed light on Portugal's implementation of the Directive on the protection of individuals reporting breaches of EU Law.[47] As might be expected, this achievement suggests that protection of those reporting violations of Union law may be extended to persons who are extraneous in subsequent criminal proceedings that may arise from the reported violations.

Although the Brazilian report may not be directly relevant to this section, it is worth considering its focus on the role of third parties in international cooperation. Indeed, the report provides an interesting description of the potential interference

---

[44] For example, injured persons are considered as third parties unless they initiate criminal actions (see Portugal, France, and Spain), or act as joint claimants, or bring civil claims for damages (cf. Italy), or pursue supplementary private prosecutions (along these lines, see Hungary, Portugal, Brazil).

[45] See, in particular, Malino, Foti, in this volume, para. 2.3.

[46] See Fantoly, Lichtenstein, in this volume, para. 2.4.

[47] See Gouveia de Caires, Reis Barata, in this volume, para. 2.1.2, who mention Directive 2019/1937/EU.

that these parties may face in cases of judicial or police cooperation, as well as a useful classification of this category of subjects at the international cooperation level.

Broadly speaking, legal cooperation involves two main participants: *(a)* States and, at times, international intergovernmental organisations responsible for cooperation which are immediately and directly involved in the cooperation procedures; *(b)* individuals who may be indirectly affected by aid or assistance measures. Moreover, the effects of these procedures may be positive or negative, depending on whether the requested measure is granted or denied. In particular, the category of indirectly affected subjects also extends to third parties, such as offshore corporations, located outside the owners' domicile country and established as *de facto* partnerships. Therefore, in criminal prosecution, offshore corporations are often viewed as foreign entities involved in illicit activities, such as money laundering, corruption, drug trafficking, and tax fraud. In this light, international cooperation can be used by authorities to request the freezing of assets held in foreign bank accounts by defendants or third parties, including legal entities, to secure the seizure of funds derived from criminal activities. However, it is important to note that in cases of national investigations into money laundering offences, Brazilian Law No. 9613/1998 explicitly protects the rights of third parties in good faith from the effects of protective pre-trial measures, as outlined in Article 8(1) of the Anti-Money Laundering Act.

5 Third Parties in Criminal Inquiries

The involvement of third parties in criminal investigations aims to enhance the breadth and depth of information available to law enforcement authorities, ultimately contributing to a more comprehensive understanding of the case. It is important to note that the extent and nature of such involvement can vary depending on the specific legal jurisdiction and the nature of the criminal investigation. This stage, indeed, represents a crucial stage in criminal proceedings, especially in the light of this study, since it is at this very moment that third parties may experience the most worrying infringements of their rights and interests, mainly due to the need to collect items of evidence. Public prosecutors, assisted by police officers, can also be competent for investigating criminal offences and identifying suspects, and collecting evidence to decide whether to file charges. Moreover, they represent the state in court. Depending on the national system, judicial authorities are responsible for authorising some procedural acts or overseeing the lawfulness of the inquiry.

It is of the utmost relevance to underline that during the investigative phase there are still no parties, as this term typically refers to the different individuals or groups involved in the judicial proceedings that can follow the investigation, particularly during the trial phase. In this sense, it can be difficult to establish whether a person will assume a specific role in subsequent phases or will remain a third party.

We can also observe that at this stage the public prosecutor (as well as the investigating judge) has a dominant role in the building of the case and in the decision on whether to bring charges or to dismiss them. Generally, in this phase, judges can only supervise the fairness of the procedure and authorise the most intrusive measures, such as search warrants, interception of communications or any pretrial measures affecting personal freedom. In the light of this, we can argue that the judge's role is mostly to guarantee respect of the rules. However, under Spanish law, an investigative judge (*juez de instrucción*) often takes an active role in overseeing the investigative phase of certain serious criminal cases, especially those involving complex or lengthy investigations.[48] The investigative judge has powers to gather evidence, question witnesses, and make decisions regarding the direction of the investigation. When an investigative judge is involved, preliminary hearings may be conducted to examine evidence and determine whether there is sufficient justification to proceed with formal charges.

In this regard, judicial supervision is not merely a formality, but rather a robust safeguard for all the parties involved, particularly the accused and the victim, as well as third parties, against any potential abuse.

Regarding specifically the victim, in all the legal systems considered for the purpose of the study this subject has the power to report the *notitia criminis* to law enforcement authorities.[49] From this moment on, they are allowed to receive information, support and protection. Concerning this aspect, the European framework set out by Directive 2012/29/EU contributed to harmonising Member States' legislation on this matter. As already stressed, this legal instrument highlights the relevance of specific protection in order to enable victims to participate in criminal proceedings without suffering any further harm.[50] Among the protective measures listed as examples by European law, the video recording of interviews and separate premises have the specific purpose of avoiding contacts between victims and their family members with the alleged offender.[51]

In addition, Chapter 4 of the Directive on victims' rights provides for specific indications regarding the victims' right to be protected from any harm, while emphasising the need to undertake special measures available for some categories of people considered to be particularly vulnerable.[52]

---

[48] See Gascón Inchausti, Schumann Barragán, in this volume, para 3.3.

[49] This is not the only way to initiate criminal proceedings, as some offences can be investigated *ex officio*, without a formal complaint by private individuals.

[50] However, fewer than half of the Member States comply with this provision, since they systematically lack specific measures aimed at protecting family members. In a few Member States, these relevant measures are not available to all victims, or the existing measures do not consider protection against the risks of emotional or psychological harm. See *Report from the Commission to the European Parliament and the Council on the implementation of Directive 2012/29/EU*, p. 7.

[51] Only few Member States fulfil this requirement with practical, non-legislative measures. Cf. *Report from the Commission to the European Parliament and the Council on the implementation of Directive 2012/29/EU*, p. 8.

[52] Cf. Arts. 22 ("Individual assessment of victims to identify specific protection needs"), 23 ("Right to protection of victims with specific protection needs during criminal proceedings") and 24 ("Right to protection of child victims during criminal proceedings. See Illuminati (2015), p. 70 ff.

Therefore, all the EU States examined in this study have dealt with these aspects of victim protection, reinforcing measures to safeguard the injured parties and allow them to be heard fairly during this stage.

In Brazil, also victims have the right to file a complaint and assist the police in their investigation by means of requests for specific actions and measures.[53] They can also conduct a private investigation and share the results with police officers, who may use such evidence at their own discretion. Similarly, Hungarian legislation grants victims the right to be present at procedural measures where the presence of the suspect is also allowed. Moreover, they can access the case file and the documents of the investigation relating to the criminal offence committed against them.

However, while victims have been seeking a role in criminal proceedings for decades, some individuals prefer to remain uninvolved, particularly during the investigative phase when fundamental rights are often restricted.

First of all, third parties may undergo inspections and searches of premises or, nowadays, even IT systems. These investigative measures are generally conducted without prior warning and may affect directly or indirectly people other than the suspect (for example, the relatives of the accused who live with them or the owner of a place frequently used by the accused). In all the legal systems considered for the purpose of this study, the legal protection of third parties in such situations is often unclear and substantially ineffective.

In these cases, Italian legislation gives third parties the possibility to be assisted by a person whom they trust, only if this person is immediately available.[54] But there is no consequence if this provision is not fulfilled and third parties remain without any proper protection in such a situation. It was not until 2022 that a reform of the criminal justice system introduced a legal instrument to challenge the lawfulness of the search when no item has been seized,[55] under pressure to avoid further breaches of Article 8 ECHR, since the Italian government had already been found responsible for undue interference in private life.[56] The Italian report, however, critically underlined the ineffectiveness of this remedy, since the code does not explain what happens when the judge finds the unlawfulness of the search carried out without any subsequent seizure of assets.[57] Furthermore, the Italian CCP does not strictly specify the circumstances under which a search can be performed, thus making it difficult and uncertain for the court to evaluate the legitimacy of such investigative activity.

Similarly, the Spanish report explained that, as has been noted, challenging the lawfulness of police activities interfering with fundamental rights is not a common

[53] Art. 14 CCP-Brazil.

[54] Art. 249 CCP-Italy.

[55] See Art. 252-*bis* CCP-Italy. Cf. Malino, Foti, in this volume, para. 3.4.

[56] ECtHR, *Brazzi v. Italy*, judgment of 27 September 2018, Appl. No. 57278/11.

[57] To this aim, some legal scholars suggest introducing the right to compensation for those who undergo investigative measures, in order to remedy their suffering and to encourage responsible conduct on the part of the public prosecutor.

practice, due to the complexity and formalities of this procedure. Moreover, the procedure has an administrative nature, and the affected persons usually discover that they have been subject to police investigations only after judicial criminal proceedings have already been initiated.[58]

As far as concerns French legislation, the individuals affected by searches or house visits are called upon to provide express written consent, but this condition is requested only for minor offences, punished with less than 5 years of imprisonment.[59] For serious crimes, the measures can be performed without any consent; however, judicial authorisation is required under Article 76–1 of the French CCP and must specify the nature of the offences in respect of which some piece of evidence is sought, the factual evidence underlying the belief that they have been committed, and the address of premises where the operations take place.

Our comparative analysis has shown that the protection of third parties is typically stronger when a search results in the seizure of goods or assets, because in such cases the affected person can challenge the seizure in order to regain the ownership of the item. To this end, all jurisdictions surveyed provided some legal remedies to challenge the effects of seizure.

Italy and Brazil have similar options for interested parties seeking the return of seized property on the basis of '*bona fide*' and non-involvement of third parties in criminal activities. On such grounds, they are allowed to challenge judicial authorisation in order to protect their property rights. The difference is that, while in Brazil, third parties can file a *bona fide* third-party interplea or an outside interplea,[60] in Italy they can appeal against the judicial order or ask for the matter to be re-examined (the review procedure is called '*riesame*') by a judge other than the one who issued the measure.

The possibility for third parties to appeal against a seizure is also recognised under Spanish legislation (Art. 334 CCP-Spain) even without legal assistance, while Hungarian law gives the financially interested party and other interested people the right to be informed about the operations and to be present when such activity is performed, to access files and records of the operations,[61] and to lodge a formal complaint.[62]

It should also be noted that the effectiveness of these legal remedies is closely linked to the content of the judicial authorisation of the seizure: the more specific the reasoning of the judicial order, the easier it is for the parties to challenge the basis of the measure. Consequently, Spanish legislation requires the judge to evaluate the

---

[58] See Gascón Inchausti, Schumann Barragán, in this volume, para 3.1.

[59] Art. 76 CCP-France.

[60] According to the Brazilian report, some courts allow the possibility to make an appeal, but domestic legislation does not include this case in the list of the reasons that justify the appeal of a judicial order. See Gomes de Vasconcellos, Brenner Lucchesi, in this volume, para. 5.

[61] Art. 57 CCP-Hungary.

[62] See Gascón Inchausti, Schumann Barragán, in this volume, para. 3.3.

proportionality of all those investigative measures that affect persons other than the accused.

As we will see below, this proportionality test required by Spanish law also applies to interceptions of communications addressed to the devices owned or used by third parties on the basis of some kind of relationship with the crime or the accused whereas,[63] in other countries examined, such as Italy, this investigative means can be deployed by the inquiring authorities only in cases of serious evidence showing that a crime (falling within a list of offences for which the law authorises the interception of communications) has been committed, without the need to specify the link between the criminal offence or the suspect and the person concerned.

In order to complete the analysis of criminal inquiries involving third parties, this study has also looked at the contribution that they can make by rendering oral evidence. Indeed, although undoubtedly, such persons can be useful for the gathering of relevant information on the case under investigation, we must underline that some safeguards are necessary for the protection of the persons being heard.

Outside the EU legal area, in Brazil witnesses have the right to access investigative records and, in the case of vulnerable subjects, they are granted a 'damage free deposition', during which questions are asked by professionals under the judge's oversight.

Similarly, European countries, over the last few years, have amended their own legislation to safeguard vulnerable victims and children when they need to be examined without causing any further harm. To this end, Portuguese police officers must promptly conduct a risk assessment to determine if victims require special protective measures to prevent further victimisation. It is noteworthy that, according to Article 292(2) CCP-Portugal, the victim has the right to request to be heard by the examining judge during the pre-trial phase. This request is binding for the judge, who must hear the victims if they so desire, allowing them to give their contribution to the case.

Following a protective approach, French law provides strong safeguards for witnesses whose lives or families are in danger, allowing them to be heard without their identity being recorded in the case file.[64] In the most serious cases, such as war or organised crimes, witnesses as well as their family members can use an assumed identity. This last measure can be adopted also in the case of police officers who infiltrated criminal organisations during undercover operations.

Furthermore, Hungarian lawmakers adopted special treatment for vulnerable persons, based on age, psychophysical conditions and nature of the investigated crime, aimed at enhancing the protection of their interests.[65] The most commonly

---

[63] *Ibidem*, para. 4.

[64] Anyone who reveals the protected witnesses' identity shall be punished with 5 years' imprisonment and a fine of € 75,000. These sanctions may be aggravated in the case of violence against witnesses or their family members, or of their death as a result of such violence.

[65] As stated by Article 81 CCP-Hungary, "the victim or the witness qualifies for special treatment based on their personal characteristics or the nature and circumstances of the criminal offence if they are hindered in understanding and making themselves understood, exercising their rights and

used measure is video recording the interviews, while police officers are required to take minutes of the statements rendered. In terms of safeguards, protective measures may interfere with the procedural rights of other parties, especially the defence: for example, the presence of the accused may be restricted during procedural activities involving vulnerable persons.

Likewise, Italian legislators recently amended procedural law to allow vulnerable persons to be recorded by audio and video. Furthermore, the Italian CCP requires that these individuals must be heard in the presence of a professional and without any contact with the accused.[66]

Along with pursuing protective needs, all these measures aim at securing oral evidence in the investigative stage. Indeed, the comparative analysis conducted so far shows that the legal systems under review consider third parties as holders of evidentiary information that needs to be secured. The examination of the legislation of all the six jurisdictions shows a manifest approach towards the protection of witnesses (and also victims) during interviews, while other categories of third parties involved in investigative activities are not granted with adequate safeguards.

This trend is based on a traditional approach, according to which individuals who are not formal participants in criminal proceedings may be involved to provide their knowledge in order to help establish what occurred.

In any case, this study has shown that, apart from the testimony, which is the least invasive way to involve subjects other than formal participants, there are other procedural measures that can affect third parties in multiple ways, above all through the use of ICT technologies, which can widen the scope of individuals affected.

6 Scientific Developments, New Technologies and the Safeguards of Third Parties

The rapid developments occurring in science and technology have led to the use of ever changing investigative measures that may interfere with the fundamental rights of an increasing number of individuals other than formal participants in criminal proceedings. ICT tools may have not only a significant impact on the private lives of the individuals subjected to a criminal investigation, but also on persons unrelated to the investigative activities.

---

fulfilling obligations, or in their effective participation in criminal proceedings". The aim of this institutional system is to compensate for disadvantages resulting from age and other circumstances, or the nature of the committed crime, and to guarantee the full exercise of rights for the person involved throughout criminal proceedings.

[66] See Malino, Foti, in this volume, para. 3.2.

The growing reliance on science and technology for investigation requires the development of new categories and procedural safeguards that respond to the challenges posed by the digital transformation of criminal inquiries.[67]

Outside Europe, the Brazilian Constitution already protects the confidentiality of correspondence and data, as well as phone communications, except when a judicial order is required to authorise the access to private information for purposes of criminal inquiries or evidence gathering.[68] More recently, Constitutional Amendment Act No. 115 of 2022 enacted into the Brazilian Constitution a fundamental provision that recognises the right to the protection of personal data, including digital data.[69] Nonetheless, the national report highlights that the Brazilian CCP has no specific provisions regarding the gathering of digital evidence. In the absence of such a regulation, solutions have been acquired by recourse to case law. In particular, the Superior Court of Justice has ruled that *Google* can disclose static data about all users who have crossed a specific area of Rio de Janeiro, but cannot reveal the content of their communications.

As already noted,[70] in several jurisdictions the protection of a new generation of fundamental rights, including digital privacy, is still based on an extensive interpretation of the pre-existing constitutional rules, which have become extremely relevant due to the invasive potential of criminal investigations. In Europe, only a few countries have already amended their own legislation to include a set of safeguards granted to persons involved in investigative activities that are performed using new technologies. For example, since 2015 the Spanish CCP has listed the measures that the judge may adopt, namely interception of telephone and telematic communications, access to data, use of electronic devices to capture and record verbal communications, surveillance and geolocation, searches in mass data storage, and remote searching of computer systems. According to Article 588-*bis*(*h*) CCP-Spain, technological investigative measures "may be ordered even where they affect third parties in the cases and under the conditions regulated in the specific provisions for each of them". Therefore, Spanish law expressly recognises and accepts the concrete possibility that such measures may affect third parties, as technological devices are primarily used to connect people and store data related not only to the owner but also to other individuals. Furthermore, Spanish legislation outlines the specific circumstances in which third parties may be subject to such measures. These include: *(i)* when there is evidence that the individual under investigation is using a third party's electronic device to transmit or receive information; *(ii)* when the owner is collaborating with the person under investigation in their illicit activities or benefiting from their actions; *(iii)* when the device under investigation is being

[67] See Leacock (2008), p. 225. In the opinion of this author, legal reforms regarding the electronic world should take into consideration the extent to which new technologies, especially search and seizure systems, can be used for the effective investigation and prosecution of cyber conduct.

[68] Art. 5(XII) of the Brazilian Constitution.

[69] Art. 5(LXXII) of the Brazilian Constitution.

[70] See para. 4.1.

maliciously used online by third parties, without the knowledge of the owner.[71] As mentioned above, the Spanish Constitutional Court held that the violation of third parties' substantive rights entails granting them access to a court and allowing their intervention in the procedure to safeguard their interests. The domestic report, indeed, summarises as follows: "the impact of these measures on the fundamental rights of third parties – mainly, the right to privacy (Art. 18 of the Spanish Constitution) – is a constitutional tenet that could underpin their intervention in the judicial investigation phase".[72] Furthermore, Spanish legislation requires a judicial authorisation specifying the reasons for the deployment of invasive measures in order to ensure the protection of all parties involved, including third parties.

As far as concerns French jurisdiction, the intervention of a judge (either the 'liberty and custody judge' in the case of a prosecutorial investigation, or the investigating judge in the case of a judicial investigation) is demanded by law to carry out invasive technological measures, such as international mobile subscriber identity-catcher (IMSI-catcher)[73] or electronic data capture, since they make it possible to collect a huge amount of data and information concerning plenty of users. Both measures are of limited duration, but can be extended for a maximum of 2 years. After that period of time, which is significantly long, all the collected data must be destroyed once prosecution is barred under the statute of limitations. The deletion of data, instead, is not envisaged in the case of remote access and seizure of electronic correspondence without the addressed person's consent.

However, the level of protection afforded to third parties targeted by the interception of communications or other technological means of investigation varies across the European Union. For example, Hungarian legislation, despite the enactment of the 2017 CCP, which regulated some technological tools for investigative purposes, demands judicial supervision only for some measures (secret monitoring of information systems, secret searches, secret surveillance of places, secret interception of post, and wiretapping),[74] while others can be carried out by police officers with the public prosecutor's approval (monitoring payments, pretend purchases, surveillance with consent, the use of undercover agents and the use of aliases)[75] or even without any kind of preventive authorisation (hidden surveillance).[76] As a result, investigative activities involving judicial supervision are those that provide the most adequate safeguards for third parties, who are also granted the right to be informed once the preparatory procedure has been completed, unless disclosure could be prejudicial to further investigation.

---

[71] See Art. 588-*ter*(*c*) CCP-Spain (translation by the authors).

[72] See Drevet, in this volume, para. 4.

[73] This investigative tool intercepts the location data of every mobile phone user within the perimeter. See Peltier (2017), p. 49.

[74] Art. 231 CCP-Hungary. See Fantoly, Lichtenstein, in this volume, para. 4.

[75] Art. 216 ff. CCP-Hungary.

[76] Art. 215 CCP-Hungary.

The problem of the disclosure of evidentiary information concerning third parties has recently been dealt with also in Portuguese legislation. Here, the examining judge has the power to order the destruction of material media containing data manifestly extraneous to the proceedings, above all when they affect third parties' rights.[77] Nor can the accused access or receive information related to third parties, nor can such information be publicly disclosed. Under Portuguese legislation, the judicial authorisation is required to search personal computers or other electronic devices or to access private correspondence, such as e-mails, regardless of whether they are read or not.

The need to strike a proper balance between the protection of privacy, especially for subjects not involved in the ongoing criminal investigation, and the evidence-gathering procedure has also been emphasised in the Report on Italy, where the influence of international and supranational legal instruments has led to various amendments to the Code of Criminal Procedure in order to provide a legal basis for some investigative measures which are particularly invasive for all the persons concerned. This report, which delivers an analytical description of some investigative activities based on the use of scientific and technological tools, highlights the extent to which they interfere with fundamental rights and also the risk of a violation of Article 8 ECHR if the addressee of the measure is not granted certain specific safeguards.[78] However, in Italy there are no provisions that properly tackle the issue of protecting third parties in the case of criminal investigations using technological and electronic tools.[79] Similarly to the other countries analysed, Italy only safeguards the interest of third parties to ask and obtain the restitution of seized devices. However, Elisea Malino and Diego Foti emphasise that the legal remedies granted to third parties in the event of seizure are intended to protect their property rights. Nevertheless, in the case of the seizure of electronic data, the main interest is not linked to property rights, but to the exclusive possession of such information and the control of its dissemination.[80]

[77] This provision was introduced only in 2022 with Law No. 5 of 11 January 2022.

[78] This risk is exacerbated in the case of a digital search, "which sometimes has turned out to be an illegitimate 'explorative' tool with preventive monitoring purposes for acquiring new *notitiae criminis*". See Malino, Foti, in this volume, para 4.1. The authors note that the Italian Court of Cassation expressed strong disapproval of the distorted use of these instruments solely for exploratory purposes, in the absence of any clear evidentiary relevance to a specific and concrete offence. See Italian Court of Cassation, judgment No. 19618 of 17 April 2012.

[79] The only specific case where the interest of a third party is taken into account concerns the search of computer systems belonging to telecommunications service providers. According to Italian law, in such a situation the judicial authority should determine that a search should be carried out by copying information onto a suitable medium and employing technical procedures to guarantee data consistency. In this context, the interest safeguarded is the provider's right to continue their activities, as any interruption could have a negative impact on the collective interests of consumers.

[80] As underlined by the Italian report, the digital transition has led to a kind of shift from the right to property to the right to privacy. Even the permanence of the interest in restitution is questionable if the physical medium is returned to its owner, while the extracted and copied data remain in the hands of the public authorities. See Malino, Foti, in this volume, para. 4.2.

The Italian report also addresses the use of investigative tools to collect communication streams. These instruments, among which spywares and malwares stand out, are capable of seriously undermining the right to privacy, freedom and secrecy of correspondence and *habeas data*. When it comes to such means of investigation, there is a significant danger of encroaching upon the privacy of third parties.[81]

As we have already seen in the reports on other countries, the order issued or validated by the competent judge must take into account the necessity of the interception for the ongoing investigation and, as a general rule, specify the places and times in which the recording is allowed. Similarly to Portuguese legislation, Italian law prohibits the transcription of recordings containing information that is not useful for the investigation or that may offend the person's reputation. Furthermore, third parties have the option to request a judicial order to destroy documentary recordings that are deemed unnecessary for the criminal proceeding, citing the protection of their privacy.[82] However, third parties may remain unaware of, or have no control over, the outcome of communication interceptions when they are used in criminal proceedings different from those for which they were initially authorised.[83]

According to Italian law, the rules provided for interceptions of communications also apply in the event of remote electronic surveillance, when the software installed in the target device collects messages, chats and e-mails, which are considered as 'communications', while the collection of the contents stored in the electronic device is subject to the rules on search and seizure.

While the digitalisation of criminal proceedings impinges upon the protection of users' data and information, the scientific developments deployed in the context of criminal investigations can affect the personal freedom and physical integrity of the persons concerned, who may also be third parties. As underlined in the Report on Italy, the practice of collecting genetic information, such as DNA samples, can address individuals who are not directly involved in a criminal investigation.[84]

---

[81] The Italian regulations indirectly safeguard them by imposing strict criteria for judicial authorisation of these investigative measures and by limiting the disclosure of operational results. For a specific analysis of the conditions under which interceptions can be authorised in Italy, see Malino, Foti, in this volume, para. 4.3.

[82] See Art. 269 CCP-Italy.

[83] In Italy, if wiretapping is carried out in violation of regulations, the information thus gathered cannot be used as evidence; similarly, nor can conversations with lawyers, clergymen or healthcare professionals concerning facts known by virtue of their function, service, or profession. In such cases, the judge has a duty to order the destruction of any investigative recordings, unless they constitute a *corpus delicti*. See Malino, Foti, in this volume, para. 4.3.

[84] See Art. 224-*bis* of the CCP-Italy, introduced by Law No. 85 of 30 June 2009, and Art. 72-*bis* of the Implementing Rules to CCP-Italy. The challenge of intruding into an individual's private sphere intensifies when the person undergoing the test has not provided consent. In such cases, the operation can be viewed as a coercive medical intervention in violation of Article 13 of the Italian Constitution, as underlined above. Cf. ECtHR (GC), *Jalloh v. Germany*, judgment of 11 July 2006, Appl. No. 54810/00; ECtHR, *Detlef-Harro Schmidt v. Germany*, judgment of 5 January 2006, Appl. No. 32352/02. On the contrary, when samples are collected without coercion, both the

As underlined by the Italian report, these activities may affect a broader range of individuals other than the suspect, including not only victims but also minors and those who are not formally involved in the criminal proceeding. Nevertheless, these legal safeguards apply regardless of a person's status as a suspect or third party.[85]

In addition to all of this, the Italian report clarifies that Article 189 CCP can encompass various significant evidence-gathering activities conducted by means of ICTs that may impact the rights of third parties.[86] Examples include video-surveillance by the police, even within private premises, capturing non-communicative behaviours during preliminary investigations, or unauthorised recordings in workplace settings.[87] Since only formal parties are entitled by Italian regulation to participate in the hearing on the admission of such 'atypical' (this is the word used by Article 189 of the Italian CCP) means of evidence, a third party, who has no formal role in the criminal proceedings but suffered the effects of the investigative measure, does not have any power regarding its performance or evaluation.

Finally, the Italian report analytically, and above all critically, describes the national data retention system. Indeed, in accordance with the provisions of the so-called 'Privacy Code', telephone traffic data and online navigation data must be retained by service providers for the purpose of preventing and detecting criminal offences.[88]

ECtHR and the Italian Court of Cassation consider this activity to have a minimal impact on fundamental rights. Cf. ECtHR (GC), *Saunders v. United Kingdom*, judgment of 17 December 1996, Appl. No. 19187/91; ECtHR (GC), *O'Halloran and Francis v. United Kingdom*, judgment of 29 June 2007, Appls. Nos. 15809/02 and 25624/02; Italian Court of Cassation, judgment No. 2087 of 10 January 2012.

[85] In cases where compulsory sampling involves third parties, they are required to appoint legal representation for assistance during the procedures; otherwise, the evidence may be rendered completely invalid [Art. 224-*bis*(7) CCP-Italy]. As recently clarified by the Italian Court of Cassation, the fact that a forced DNA analysis may affect persons who are not involved in the criminal proceedings (third parties) cannot justify massive screening practices. Italian Court of Cassation, judgment No. 28538 of 17 January 2019. In this case, the Court underlined the need for the existence of a direct relationship between the tested person and the crime to be ascertained.

[86] See Malino, Foti, in this volume, para. 4.5.

[87] According to the Italian Court of Cassation, the results of such recordings are usable in trial even without prior authorization by the judicial authorities if they have been carried out with the consent of the owner of the domicile. In the case taken into consideration by the Court the third party directly gave his consent to the video recording in his capacity as the offended person. See Italian Court of Cassation, judgment No. 41332 of 7 July 2015.

[88] In the light of the Italian rules, users may be seriously prejudiced not only if they are suspected of having committed a crime, but also if they are third parties to the criminal proceedings. Indeed, a judicial warrant (or even an order issued by the Public Prosecutor's Office in cases of duly justified urgency, which must be validated by the competent judge within 48 h) can authorise the collection of such data if they are considered relevant for investigative purposes and there are sufficient indications of a serious crime. In addition to this, we also should observe that service providers must retain these data for a significant period of time, which can be up to 72 months for the most serious crimes, with detrimental effects for the protection of the users' privacy. See Malino, Foti, in this volume, para. 4.6.

As emerged from the domestic reports under examination, the recourse to scientific and technological tools during the investigative stage, while undoubtedly useful for the gathering of evidence, is truly harmful for third parties, who are generally unaware that their data and information are being processed in the context of criminal proceedings. Research has shown that judicial control or validation within a short span of time is an indispensable safeguard in order to limit infringements upon third parties' freedom and liberties. Especially in the case of investigative tools based on scientific or technological developments, the judicial authority should establish (at least when this is possible) which persons will be targeted by such investigative methods, excluding those persons against whom there are no suspicions.

Therefore, we can argue that the most adequate protection for third parties' rights is afforded by those jurisdictions that specifically require prior judicial scrutiny of the lawfulness of the measure. Such a guarantee is of the utmost relevance, since the independent authority has the duty to issue an order which explains the reasons why the chosen means of evidence gathering is indispensable and why the persons concerned should be involved.

In addition, as pointed out by most reports, third parties are left with limited legal remedies once the measure has been enforced. Indeed, as happens in the case of interception of communications or remote searches, the persons who have suffered restrictions of their rights generally remain unaware of the measure adopted. Even in those legal systems where third parties can initiate judicial or administrative procedures aimed at protecting their interests, the lack of information or the complexity of the procedure makes the protection inadequate and ineffective. Whether third parties have been informed or not of the collection of their data or the taking of their genetic material, all the national legal systems analysed impose the destruction of information regarding them. The destruction of collected data and information for investigative purposes is often viewed as a measure to rectify privacy breaches and protect individual rights. However, it is essential to recognise that the mere erasure of data does not fully address the consequences of violating fundamental rights. The infringement has already occurred and the data have been processed in the context of criminal proceedings. Deletion may prevent further misuse, but it cannot undo the initial harm caused by the violation that occurred during evidence gathering, as this is when a person loses exclusive control over information regarding them. While data destruction is a necessary step in the aftermath of privacy breaches, it should be complemented by efforts to address the systemic issues that lead to such violations. This is the reason why a prior judicial review (or even the scrutiny of an independent administrative authority) seems crucial in order to prevent investigative activities from unduly interfering in the private sphere of persons extraneous to the criminal proceedings.

7 Pre-Trial Measures and the Protection of Fundamental Rights of Third Parties

In criminal investigations, the enforcement of pre-trial measures has the potential to impact on the fundamental rights of individuals beyond the parties formally involved in the criminal proceedings. In particular, procedural tools aimed at securing assets may have adverse effects on several rights, freedoms and interests of third parties.

In general, the justification for freezing the assets or goods of third parties is their illicit origin or the need to prevent other crimes from being committed or other serious consequences if the property or availability of such items poses a concrete threat to public security. Along these lines, the Italian Constitutional Court has ruled that a preventive seizure does not even require the existence of a reasonable suspicion of guilt directed at a specifically identified suspect, and even property in the possession of third parties may be seized.[89] As observed by the national report, Italian law also allows the seizure of items that may be confiscated. Both of these cases may prejudice the property rights of third parties. However, the rules on such pre-trial measures provide some procedural safeguards in order to protect their interests. Preventive seizure is ordinarily authorised by a judicial order following the public prosecutor's request. Nevertheless, in urgent situations, the Public Prosecutor's Office may autonomously order seizure, subjected to subsequent validation (within 48 h of the seizure) by the competent judge. Consequently, individuals affected by the order lose control over the seized items. It is interesting to note that, in cases where a company or a firm is seized, the legitimate owner may also be appointed as a custodian, thereby mitigating the measure's impact on their property rights and business freedom.[90] Indeed, pre-trial measures, especially when targeting legal entities, can also severely impinge upon workers or creditors' rights.

In Spain, also, the investigating judge is competent to order pretrial measures, such as the temporary closure of premises or the suspension of corporate activities, which could potentially affect stakeholders and shareholders.[91] Additionally, provisional measures, such as garnishments and attachments of money or properties, could also target the suspect's family members, co-owners of real estate, bank accounts or other assets, or creditors related to or associated with the individual under investigation. Even though the aforementioned decision No. 30/2022 of the Spanish Constitutional Court was rendered within the context of safeguarding the fundamental rights of third parties affected by investigative activities, its reasoning might be extended by analogy to promote the intervention of any party affected by various judicial measures, including pre-trial measures.[92] As stated in this judgment, the purpose of *recurso de amparo* was to recognise the right of third parties, not

[89] Italian Constitutional Court, judgment No. 48 of 17 February 1994.

[90] Art. 104-*bis* Implementing Provisions to the CCP-Italy.

[91] Art. 37(7) CCP-Spain.

[92] See Spanish Constitutional Court, judgment No. 30 of 7 March 2022.

actively involved in a criminal proceeding, to access courts and appeal against judicial decisions affecting their interests.

Furthermore, in Spain third parties can be directly affected by pre-trial measures related to the freezing and confiscation of assets in criminal proceedings. In accordance with Article 803-*ter*(a) CCP-Spain, the judge or the court may, on its own initiative or at the request of one of the parties, order the intervention of the persons targeted by a confiscation order. In this way, third parties are allowed to participate in the proceedings regarding the confiscation, focusing on aspects directly impacting on their interests and presenting all available arguments against such measures in their defence statement.[93]

Within the European Union, France also provides for the issuing of pre-trial measures, such as seizures, affecting third parties' rights. In France, if property is seized during a police or judicial investigation, the owner can obtain its restitution before the investigation is completed. The public prosecutor holds the authority to decide on restitution, considering factors such as disputed ownership and potential danger posed by the item. If the prosecutor declines to return the seized item, the concerned person can challenge the refusal by petitioning the president of the Investigation Chamber or the Investigation Chamber itself. As underlined by the national report, even during the judicial investigation, a person claiming a right over the property "enjoys the same rights as the private parties regarding restitution". According to the *Cour de Cassation*, the choice to refuse restitution cannot be considered a penalty and does not violate the presumption of innocence.[94] Moreover, France guarantees the right to an effective remedy, as Article 99 of the CCP provides for an appeal against the order of the investigating judge. Furthermore, not only formal participants but also third parties can challenge the decision before the *Cour de Cassation*. Both French legislation and case law have shown particular attention to third parties' right in pre-trial measures, even recognising them the right to petition for seized animals.[95] However, the *Cour de Cassation* ruled that a third party, who does not hold the status of defendant, civil party, or assisted witness cannot voluntarily intervene in proceedings before the Investigation Chamber rendering a decision on pre-trial detention. It is worth observing that no domestic report has mentioned the procedural power of third parties to request the pre-trial detention of the defendant, as the issues related to limitations of personal freedom are generally dealt with by the Public Prosecutor's Office and the accused's defence counsel.

Similarly to the other European countries examined in this research, Hungary's legislation includes some invasive pre-trial measures potentially detrimental to third parties' rights: alongside the search of premises or body search, the Hungarian report mentions seizure, sequestration, and temporary inaccessibility to electronic data. On the contrary, it is worth observing that Portuguese law provides specific measures, such as property guarantees, which can be applied to protect third parties' rights.

---

[93] Art. 803-*ter*(b) CCP-Spain.

[94] French Court of Cassation, No. 10-90.083, judgment of 16 July 2010.

[95] Art. 99-1 CCP-France.

Outside the European framework, Brazilian legislation includes some *medidas assecuratórias* and *medidas cautelares patrimoniais*. Among them, seizure is an *in-rem* measure directed primarily at the assets of the accused, but may also be extended to assets belonging to third parties, when there are compelling indications of their criminal origin.[96] Even though such assets have been transferred to third parties, they may still be seized if they are found to have been derived from criminal activity. In situations in which the seizure affects the property of a third party, the Brazilian CCP provides for two legal remedies to challenge such measure: a third party interplea based on their '*bona fide*' (*embargos do terceiro de boa-fé*)[97] and an outside third party interplea (*embargos de terceiro estranho ao processo*).[98] The first type applies when the purchaser claims innocence and unawareness regarding the criminal origin of the acquired asset. Article 131(II) of the Brazilian CCP allows the seizure to be lifted if the third party provides a guarantee, but this possibility is limited to third parties who have obtained the attached property fairly and in good faith. On the other hand, the second type of interplea is based on the allegation that the seized property was not obtained through criminal gains and that the owner is unrelated to the crime. Third parties, such as the defendant's spouse, who have in some way been affected by the seizure order, may use this type of interplea. These concerned subjects may also challenge the decision rendered on their interpleas before an appeal court.[99]

Regarding these pre-trial measures, comparative analysis has shown that domestic legislations pay particular attention to the protection of property rights of third parties concerned by seizures. Furthermore, the conditions on which these safeguards are based seem quite similar among the different legal systems examined, and mostly depend on the good faith of the owner and the lack of connection with the offence.

The analysis of these procedural activities has demonstrated that it is possible to afford, at least at a later stage, adequate and specific protection for third parties' rights and interests, whenever acts carried out in the context of a criminal proceeding have adverse effects on persons other than the accused or the other formal participants.

---

[96] Art. 125 CCP-Brazil.

[97] Arts. 130(I) and 130(II) CCP-Brazil.

[98] Art. 129 CCP-Brazil.

[99] Art. 593(II) CCP-Brazil. It has been discussed whether an order of seizure can be challenged directly through appeal, but the authors of the report exclude this option, as Article 593 does not include specifically this case in the list of hypotheses that can justify the application of such a remedy.

8 Third Parties and the Decision on Whether or Not to Charge

As is well known, the main purpose of the decision to charge or terminate criminal proceedings is to determine whether the suspicion of a crime can be substantiated in order to bring an indictment before a court. It is therefore crucial to present and secure evidence of the accused person's guilt, as well as any elements that may rule out their culpability. If the main goal of this decision is to assess whether the charges brought by the public prosecutor constitute a reliable basis for the subsequent trial, the contribution of persons other than the suspect is also important. Indeed, the latter may provide useful information that will help the Public Prosecutor's Office to take a correct decision on the termination of the case, thus considering the interests of parties other than the accused. In short, the success of the entire criminal trial depends on the fact that pre-trial inquiry has been conducted properly; not to mention the positive effects that may be produced, in terms of human and economic resources management, by an involvement of different persons in this peculiar stage, as they may introduce from very early on arguments supporting the termination of the proceedings.

Nevertheless, the contribution of third parties is generally underestimated at this stage. This is confirmed by our comparative study, which shows that in particular that those who may report on the criminal conduct, as well as experts, owners of confiscated assets, persons indirectly affected by wiretapping, or other interested subjects whose rights may be in any way adversely affected by procedural acts, are not adequately considered during this crucial step of the criminal proceedings. Again, a possible explanation for this might be that these persons, despite their diverse interests and functions, are generally regarded as unrelated to the criminal proceedings. This explains why, in France, they have no word in the decision to charge or terminate the proceedings and their interests are not taken into account. Similarly, under the Italian CCP, a third party has no power to influence the public prosecutor's decision to prefer charges or request discontinuance of the trial. In Spain, in general, only a formal party can challenge a judicial decision on the criminal proceedings, including that related to charge or dismissal. Besides, these results are comparable to those reported in Portugal, where, as previously specified, only the *assistente*, who is considered a (formal) civil party, can bring a secondary accusation or terminate the proceedings by withdrawing a formal request to prosecute or exclusively prosecute, in the case of semi-public offences. Furthermore, as already seen, in the case of private offences, this party can withdraw the complaint or decide not to initiate a private prosecution.

Nonetheless, upon in-depth analysis, third parties are not completely excluded from the decision to charge or terminate the proceedings. This is particularly true if we adopt a broad definition of third party to include the victim who, although lacking formal status, is directly affected by the criminal offence, thus requiring active participation in the proceedings.

We can take a few examples to illustrate this point. In Spain, thanks to the implementation of Directive 2012/29/EU, victims have procedural rights intended to prevent the termination of the case. As has been previously reported, these include the possibilities (*i*) to challenge the examining magistrate's decision not to initiate the trial phase and (*ii*) to participate in the proceedings by filing charges and requesting the institution of the trial, especially when no other party has chosen to do so. In Italy—where private prosecution no longer exists—in the case of offences prosecuted upon request of the injured person, the individual may retract the accusation. If the accused agrees to this withdrawal, the judge is then required to declare the extinction of any criminal liability.

At any rate, these considerations on the aggrieved parties lead to the observation that discussions are particularly rich when dealing with this category of persons, as shown by the reports on several occasions. This is due to the adoption of provisions that focus on the strengthening of victims' rights, such as the right to initiate a prosecution if directly harmed by the crime. For this reason, according to Barbara Drevet, they must be classified as formal parties.[100] In Hungary, where the Public Prosecutor's Office has a monopoly on prosecution, victims do not only have some influence on the decision to press charges or drop the case but can also act as complementary private prosecutors *(pótmagánvádló)* if the public party rejects the complaint or concludes the proceedings. However, Hungarian law does not fully define the exact nature of these subjects, as it does not precisely identify their formal or informal status nor depict them expressly as 'substantive parties'.

From the viewpoint of victim's rights, one of the most interesting results emerges from the Brazilian report, which revealed the existence of a constitutional provision that allows this subject to prosecute on behalf of any inactive public prosecutor, even for crimes that require unconditional public action.[101] It is noteworthy that, despite these clear powers, the injured person is regarded as a third party who supervises and represents the public interest in the prosecution of crimes.[102] This finding may be explained by the failure of the Brazilian law to provide for forms of popular prosecution. Moreover, it should be recalled that, in the case of less serious offences, the victim has considerable power in the decision to initiate criminal proceedings. As mentioned above, whenever criminal proceedings depend on a victim's complaint, the injured party must authorise the prosecution. Notwithstanding this, the Brazilian report has specified that even in this case, the prosecutor remains formally responsible for both the decision to charge and the overall management of the proceedings, whereas the victim plays the role of a third party.[103]

---

[100] See Drevet, in this volume, para. 1.1.

[101] Art. 5(LIX) of the Brazilian Constitution. We recall that in the Brazilian criminal procedure system, typically, the public prosecutor (*MP*) presents and directs a criminal charge without requiring authorisation or a request from the victim. Moreover, the two main classifications of criminal action are: 1) public initiative criminal action; 2) private initiative criminal action.

[102] The so-called 'private criminal action' which is subsidiary to the public action.

[103] See Gomes de Vasconcellos, Brenner Lucchesi, in this volume, para. 6.

Finally, the Brazilian report leads us to further explore the link between the victim's reaction to the prosecutor's dismissal of the case and the possible judicial review of this decision, which affects their interests. As reported by Gomes de Vasconcellos and Brenner Lucchesi, in contrast to the situation prior to 2019, public prosecutors are no longer obliged to request the judge to dismiss the case; they can do so themselves, although they can review this decision internally at the request of the victim or automatically. This seems to be a real challenge from the point of view of the victim's right to be heard. However, it could be pointed out that even when procedural law provides for judicial oversight, as happens in Italy, it may not be very effective and may end up being merely formal. There are probably two reasons for this. Firstly, victims have limited and inadequate access to request the evidence gathered by the investigating authorities. Secondly, judicial supervision is often based solely on the information provided by the Public Prosecutor's Office, which also has considerable discretion in the selection of files (see, in this sense, the Italian system). This situation is certainly problematic, particularly from the perspective of the principle of equality of arms.

9 Third Parties in Court Proceedings

As has been previously clarified, national jurisdictions take into consideration certain categories of third parties, enabling them to intervene in criminal investigations. These particular categories include victims without prosecutorial powers, third parties affected by investigation and pre-trial measures or those affected by the freezing and confiscation of the instrumentalities and proceeds of crime. Although it is not always clear whether their intervention presupposes the status of a formal party, they have specific procedural rights to defend their interests. However, as criminal proceedings progress to the trial stage, these rights may change. Moreover, different third parties emerge whose legal standing may require different legal treatment. This is particularly true in the event of witnesses and other persons involved in the gathering of evidence. With this in mind, we will delve into the comparative analysis of the right of these parties to be heard fairly and not to be questioned. An additional aspect to be considered is the potential impact of court activities on third parties and the measures taken by judicial authorities to provide them with adequate protection. Furthermore, given that third parties may have an interest in participating in court activities, it is important to summarise the main findings of this study in this particular area of analysis.

9.1 The Right of Third Parties to Be Heard Fairly

Starting with the right of third parties to a fair hearing, some preliminary considerations are worth making. Indeed, if we try to compare how the right to a fair hearing of third parties is treated in the legal systems under review, we may find certain common denominators. Firstly, it should be noted that all the national reports use a broad concept of third party, thus including in their analysis witnesses and experts, who do not hold a formal status. Secondly, they pay particular attention to third parties claiming ownership of the property as a result of freezing or confiscation procedures. Thirdly, as we will see from the following examples, these persons are treated differently depending on their role in the judicial process. The former (witnesses and experts) are usually required to cooperate with the court, while the latter (third parties claiming ownership) are usually offered the right to be heard. Even more interesting is the position of the victim, who may be considered either as a witness or as a third party entitled to take an active part in the proceedings and to demand a fair hearing.

France represents a significant example in this regard. As the French report explains, witnesses and experts, who are classified as third parties, are not entitled to a fair hearing, and are obliged to cooperate with the court; victims, conversely, hold the status of formal parties, for whom a right to a fair hearing is fully envisaged. Moreover, the right to a fair hearing for third parties applies specifically to those who have rights to or over the property. Significantly, at the end of the trial, the judge may order the confiscation of property as an additional measure if the offence prosecuted is a felony or a misdemeanour punishable by imprisonment for a minimum of 1 year. Consequently, although confiscation is usually directed against the convicted person, it can also affect the interests of third parties in or over the confiscated property. As mentioned above, until December 2021, third parties had faced difficulties in having their rights acknowledged and good faith demonstrated before the court ordering confiscation, which led to Article 131-21 of the French CCP being declared unconstitutional. Subsequently, Law No. 1729 of 22 December 2021 amended Article 131-21 of the Criminal Code (CC). The revised provision stipulates that when confiscation is considered a punishment, it cannot be imposed without giving the owner, whose identity will be revealed during the proceedings, the opportunity to make observations on this procedure, such as the affirmation of ownership and good faith. This is also in line with the ECJ case law, which requires Member States to grant third parties claiming ownership of the property the right to a fair trial and an effective remedy, including the right to a fair hearing and to present their case adequately.[104] However, the French CCP provides for some exceptions. The provisions of Articles D. 45-2-1 and D. 45-1-4 CCP-France do not apply if the property is considered dangerous or harmful, or if its detention is illegal, which in such cases leads to compulsory confiscation. These data should be interpreted carefully. Indeed, as Barbara Drevet has critically argued, the decision not to inform the owners and to allow them to make representations before the court raise several concerns, as it

[104] See, among others, CJUE, *Criminal proceedings against DR and TS*, judgment of 21 October 2021, C-845/19 and C-863/19.

implies that third parties are deprived of the opportunity to prove that their property is not dangerous or harmful, or that its detention is not illegal.[105]

In Spain, the right to be heard extends both to formal parties and third parties without a formal status.[106] Once again, an illustrative case is any subject extraneous to the criminal proceedings who undergoes the freezing and confiscation of instrumentalities and proceeds of crime. When the court identifies individuals targeted by confiscation, it is then called upon to involve them in the criminal proceedings.[107] Pursuant to Article 803-*ter*(c) CCP-Spain, indeed, third parties "may participate in the criminal proceedings as soon as their intervention is ordered, focusing on aspects directly affecting their assets, rights, or legal position and not extending to matters relating to criminal liability". These observations suggest the possibility of intervening in order to guarantee the right to a fair trial.[108]

Significantly, the Portuguese report confirms the importance of the right to be heard fairly. This legal system grants the *assistente*—any injured person who can bring a civil law action and is thus recognised as a formal party to the proceedings—the right to be heard during the proceedings, at their request or that of the defendant, or when the court deems it appropriate. Like witnesses, the assistant and the injured person are also subject to the duty of truthfulness and may be held criminally liable for its violation, in accordance with Article 145(2) CCP-Portugal. Furthermore, with regard to the problematic position of the victim, this person is granted the right to be heard in accordance with Article 67-A of the Portuguese CCP.

As for Hungary, it should be noted that third parties may submit evidence, requests and comments. In particular, during the final arguments, after the prosecutor's closing statement, the victim (as well as the private party and the party with a financial interest) has the right to render a statement and also to ask for the punishment of the accused.

As far as Italy is concerned, the CCP-Italy does not explicitly grant third parties the right to a fair hearing, even though the Code itself lays down rules aimed at ensuring the truthfulness of witnesses and victims' statements, thus protecting third parties who are incidentally heard. To this end, it is forbidden to ask questions that may jeopardise the sincerity of the answers, and leading questions may not be used in direct examination.

Against this background, it is worth observing that the Brazilian report displays a different scenario, as it approaches the issue of the right to a fair hearing from the perspective of the right to personal participation in the proceedings. We have already remembered that, in criminal proceedings, especially those initiated by the state, the victim can assist the prosecution. This participation requires the permission of the judge and is facilitated by legal representation through a lawyer. If the victim is dead, any spouse, parent, child, or sibling may act on their behalf as an assistant, with the

[105] See Drevet, in this volume, para. 7.1.

[106] Art. 24(1) of the Spanish Constitution.

[107] Art. 803-*ter*(a) CCP-Spain.

[108] Art. 24(1) of the Spanish Constitution.

right to present evidence, question witnesses, take part in the oral discussion and also challenge the prosecution's motions.

What is also striking from the perspective of this study is that any interested party can join the discussion before the Federal Supreme Court by becoming an *amicus curiae*. This allows a third party to be heard in order to contribute to the resolution of the criminal case, by submitting memorials and rendering oral statements. To participate, the *amicus curiae*'s contribution must be relevant to the issue at hand, regardless of the judge's approval. While initially more common in the field of constitutional review, this figure has since been extended to other proceedings, such as those relating to the collective writ of *habeas corpus*.

Furthermore, a current issue in the Brazilian criminal proceedings that deserves to be examined in this study is the participation of additional perpetrators who have not been officially charged. This situation can result from the benefits of cooperation agreements or from procedural separation. In this scenario, although the perpetrators are linked to the offence, they are not treated as co-defendants in the same proceedings, but as third parties. If they are part of a plea bargain, their role as co-defendants must be disclosed to the parties involved.

9.2 The Right of Third Parties Not to Be Questioned

In order to suitably deal with the right of third parties not to be questioned, national reporters adopted a similar approach. They first described the compulsory testimony and then identified the most significant exception to it. However, to do so, they first interpreted the term 'third parties' broadly, encompassing a wide category of witnesses, among which they also included victims, experts, and undercover agents. The comparative analysis of the selected legal systems has shown a distinction between two main categories of grounds for refusing to testify: absolute obstacles or testimonial prohibitions, and relative obstacles or different treatment.

This differentiation clearly emerges from the Hungarian and Portuguese reports, which set out some exemptions and limits to the obligations of giving evidence, the most significant of which are the impediments to providing testimony. In the same way, Elisea Malino and Diego Foti have highlighted a general duty to testify, along with a few exceptions.[109] Under Article 198 CCP-Italy, indeed, witnesses cannot be compelled to render statements on facts that may reveal their own criminal liability. In addition, individuals who have a close relationship with the accused, such as their next of kin or those emotionally attached, cannot be compelled to testify. Moreover, there are other categories of individuals who may choose not to testify, but only regarding matters within their knowledge by virtue of their function, service, or profession. These include restorative justice programme lawyers and mediators, religious ministers, private investigators, experts or notaries, doctors, and all other

[109] See Malino, Foti, in this volume, para. 7.3.

healthcare professionals, as well as individuals who have the right to decline to testify due to professional secrecy.

Similarly, Spain recognises exceptions to the general obligation to testify. Certain persons may refuse to render statements, including family members of the accused, lawyers, translators, clergymen, journalists, public officials bound by secrecy, and persons who are physically or mentally disabled.

In France, witnesses other than the accused are obliged to appear before the court and give testimony. The accused is the only person who can refuse to be questioned. However, there are two fundamental exceptions to the principle of compulsory testimony. Firstly, if the witnesses are journalists, they may not be questioned, and if questioned, they may refuse to reveal the sources of information gathered in the exercise of their professional duties. Secondly, the CCP-France provides for a further exception if the witness is bound by professional secrecy (for example, doctors, priests, or lawyers when exercising their rights of defence). Unlike previous findings, French law does not exempt family members, including spouses, life partners, or cohabitants, from the obligation to testify, even if they are exempt from taking the oath.

Within this framework, a question of paramount importance is whether the exception to the duty to testify, which protects confidential relationships, can be applied to other categories of evidence. Specifically, can relevant information be disclosed through means other than testimony? National jurisdictions, except for the Spanish one, have not fully addressed this issue yet. At any rate, to conduct a thorough analysis of this aspect, it is necessary to identify the scope of the exception to the obligation to testify. This includes determining whether the exemption applies to the information itself or to the relationship between the defendant and the third party, as well as understanding the underlying rationale.

In general, the duty to testify is often given priority for the purpose of protecting fundamental rights. Exceptions to this rule may arise in specific cases, such as when a third party's duty to cooperate with justice conflicts with their obligation to protect someone with whom they have a relationship of trust. Fernando Gascón Inchausti and Guillermo Schumann Barragán have highlighted that legal protection usually does not cover the contents of the information sought.[110] Therefore, it is essential to distinguish between the active role required to testify in court and the passive position of a third party who is only the subject of a criminal investigation measure, such as a house search. Consequently, exceptions should not normally affect the adoption of other judicial investigation measures. The impact on the legal position of third parties in these cases should be assessed based on proportionality criteria. However, we may argue that there is only one situation in which the protection justifying an exemption from the obligation to testify encounters no limitations, that is attorney-client privilege, which, while allowing some exceptions in the case of serious crimes, as in Spain or Italy, is designed to safeguard the right of defence.

---

[110] See Gascón Inchausti, Schumann Barragán, in this volume, para. 7.2.

9.3 *The Protection of Non-Parties in Court Activities Involving Formal Participants*

Moving on now to consider another relevant aspect related to the protection of non-parties in court proceedings, we aim to focus on the position of non-parties in court activities involving formal participants. Despite the relevance of the topic under discussion, however, very little was found, and what emerged can be summed up as follows. Based on the national reports, we can identify at least two categories of implications that may affect all third parties. These consequences depend on whether they relate to the individual engaged in the procedural activity (such as in the case of vulnerable or minor witnesses) or other persons (such as family members of the individual under scrutiny, for example, an undercover agent) who occupy a unique position.

The former category has been the most extensively described. For instance, when dealing with victims of crimes, vulnerable individuals, and minors, authorities must ensure special protection. It has been observed that the competent authorities must be cautious when handling personal data of vulnerable persons and provide them with special treatment, particularly regarding information related to their health status, as demonstrated in some of the reports under consideration (Hungary, Italy, Spain, Portugal, and France). Among these measures, it is important to ensure that the aggrieved person can provide statements without being physically present in the courtroom. Certainly, we may argue that this implies the need for an appropriate trade-off between the right of the accused to question witnesses at trial and the protection of vulnerable subjects. Irrelevant questions about the victim's private life should also be avoided unless the court deems it necessary to assess the facts or the credibility of the statement. The oral hearing should be conducted without public presence to safeguard, *inter alia*, the privacy of the injured party. In addition, competent authorities should aid the person involved during procedural activities. Furthermore, to ensure the right to understand and be understood, specific measures must be taken, such as using clear and accessible language in all communications with people with disabilities, providing necessary assistance and support, including sign language interpretation and oral communication help for deaf people, allowing both the participation of an expert as an assistive consultant to facilitate necessary adaptations and people with disabilities to be accompanied by a person of their choice from their very first contact with the authorities.

Concerning the offenders cooperating with the authorities and undercover agents, significant data has been found in the French report. If the informant has a hidden identity, the court can, at its own discretion or upon request, hold their testimony privately or use measures similar to those foreseen for a witness in order to protect the identity and allow remote testimony. Undercover agents are protected during the trial pursuant to Article 706–86 of the CCP-France. Typically, only the coordinating officer of the undercover operation can be a witness, while undercover agents do not testify. However, if an undercover agent directly accuses a person, a direct confrontation may be requested. In such cases, measures similar to those enacted for a witness are necessary to maintain anonymity and enable remote testimony.

9.4 Can Third Parties Take Part in Court Activities?

The findings reviewed indicate that only formal parties are ordinarily allowed to participate in judicial activities. For instance, victims can participate as formal parties in court proceedings as long as domestic law provides them with the possibility to indict or file a civil-law action. However, some exceptions are made for specific categories of third parties who may participate in court activities. For instance, the Portuguese report notes that a third party may also act as a witness. In France, third parties can exceptionally become a party to the trial, either voluntarily or on request. Third parties who have rights over the property, which has been seized during proceedings can intervene during the trial. Before the criminal court, the court of appeal, the assize court, and the police court (in case of contraventions), a third party can bring a claim for the restitution of the property. Additionally, a person held legally can intervene during the trial. The trial outcome concerns them because they will have to compensate for the damage caused if the accused is convicted. Moreover, in cases of involuntary manslaughter or unintentional violence, the insurer of the accused may intervene under strict conditions. This intervention may be compulsory or voluntary, but the insurer does not have the authority to decide whether to participate in the judicial activities. The insurer of the victim, meanwhile, is always allowed to take part in the trial, but this is not the case for other individuals. For instance, the intervention of person held legally responsible intervention presupposes the victim's civil action. Otherwise, they will not be permitted to take part in the proceedings.

As pointed out by Elisea Malino and Diego Foti,[111] as well as by João Gouveia de Caires and Joana Reis Barata,[112] in both the Italian and Portuguese justice systems, experts may be involved in court activities due to their technical knowledge, which is essential in resolving issues associated with the offence. Experts are subject to the same rules as regular witnesses, and they can be appointed either by the judge or at the request of the formal parties. At any rate, it is undeniable that they play a crucial role in answering technical questions truthfully and impartially, thus making them indispensable third parties. Despite their importance, it is worth stressing that, in Italy, the trial judge is not bound by their statements. Consequently, the judge, still considered as *judex peritus peritorum*, is free to assess the evidence provided by the experts.

Finally, it should be noted that trials are generally open to the public, unless the protection of the victim's privacy or considerations of public order justify an

[111] See Malino, Foti, in this volume, para. 7.5.

[112] See Gouveia de Caires, Reis Barata, in this volume, para. 7.4.

exception to this rule. Even if the term 'third parties' in this study does not include general categories of individuals, society as a whole may exercise its right to supervise the administration of justice. For this reason, it can be considered a third party.

10 The Protection of Third Parties in Decision-Making Processes

Having focused so far on third parties in judicial proceedings, we will now move on to consider whether judicial bodies can take into account (or are even called upon to satisfy) the interests of persons other than formal participants in the decision-making process. In other words, this task leads us to address the range of negative effects that a procedural decision of conviction or acquittal may have on the third parties. This section sets out the premises for an overall consideration of the limits of the decision's scope (*res judicanda*), which will be also further discussed from a *res judicata* perspective.

As a rule, judicial bodies are neither obliged to consider nor required to address the interests of individuals other than formal participants in decision-making processes. National reports suggest that penalties, except for confiscation, should only apply to the convicted person and cannot be transferred to third parties. However, the consequences of criminal judgments may not be solely of a criminal nature but may also extend to other areas, especially to relevant issues from a civil-law perspective. However, courts can only rule on the civil liability of the accused if the injured party has not filed a civil claim for restitution and compensation for damages resulting from the offence. Otherwise, the court's decision is restricted to matters directly related to the criminal liability of the accused. However, there is an exception to this, contrary to previous findings. In particular, in Portugal, if there is no claim for civil compensation, the court may award a sum of money as reparation for the damage suffered by the victim in the event of a conviction. This is clearly intended to protect the victim.[113] A similar solution is adopted in Brazil, where the sentencing judge can set a minimum amount of pecuniary reparation for the victim, provided that this has been requested by the prosecution, including the public prosecutor, and has been debated during the trial.

Moreover, the jurisdictions examined provide mechanisms aimed at safeguarding civil interests of third parties involved in decision-making whenever the ruling may affect them. It is important to note that Hungarian law in particular attaches attention to the vulnerable position of children involved in legal proceedings. The Hungarian CCP, indeed, provides an exceptional provision that allows criminal courts to revoke parental custody. If the accused is found guilty of a criminal offence against their child, the court, following the public prosecutor's request, has the authority to

[113] Art. 82-A(1) CCP-Portugal.

terminate their parental rights in accordance with the Hungarian Civil Code. Likewise, in Brazil, a conviction for intentional crimes punished with imprisonment committed against a son, daughter, or other descendant, or against a ward may result in the loss of custody. This can be declared through an order of "incapacity to exercise family power, guardianship or curatorship".[114]

In France, the decision-making process is narrowly focused solely on the parties involved, namely the public prosecutor, the accused, and the victim. As a result, the protection of third parties is not considered during the decision-making process. However, recent provisions on confiscation and the right of owners to present their case in court suggest that judges will have to implicitly consider the impact of such a measure on third parties.

The Brazilian report also provides notable evidence in this particular area. Generally, a conviction only requires compensation for damages and does not impose restrictions on the convicted person's property. This is enshrined in the Brazilian Constitution. However, there may be restrictions on the property of a third party. Article 91(II)(b) CCP-Hungary establishes the confiscation of the proceeds of crime, while expressly reserving the right of the injured party or third party in good faith. Therefore, if it is proven that the acquisition was made in good faith because the third party was unaware or could not have known that the property acquired was derived from criminal activity, the acquirer is entitled to reparation for the loss suffered. In contrast, if a third party acted in bad faith and was aware of the criminal origin of the property, forfeiture by collusion will apply. Nevertheless, a recent reform introduced so-called 'extended confiscation', which applies after a conviction for offences with a maximum sentence of more than 6 years and leads to the confiscation of assets that correspond to the difference between the value of the convicted person's assets and the value compatible with their lawful income.[115] Extended confiscation is therefore essentially based on the legal presumption that property in excess is part of the convicted person's income criminally acquired. In this case, the burden of proof is on the convicted person. Under the Criminal Code, the definition of "convicted person's property" is extended to include other assets belonging to third parties. This encompasses goods that the convicted party "has domain over and the direct or indirect benefit of, on the date of the offence or subsequently received"[116] and assets "transferred to third parties free of charge or upon negligible consideration, from the beginning of the criminal activity".[117] To safeguard property from confiscation, it is important to establish its lawful origin. However, it is noteworthy that this approach should be used with caution, as it may be argued that it reverses the burden of proof.

The Brazilian report highlights another notable concern relating to the evidentiary assessment of the victim's testimonies, especially in sexual crimes. Thus, the

[114] Art. 9(II) of the Brazilian Constitution.

[115] Art. 91-A CP-Brazil.

[116] Art. 91-A(1)(I) CP-Brazil.

[117] Art. 91-A(1)(II) CP-Brazil.

enhanced protection afforded to victims means that, during the decision-making process, their statements are often considered highly reliable, even to the extent of leading to a conviction based solely on their testimony. This is a complex and contentious issue, as it involves balancing the interests of injured subjects with the presumption of innocence and the standard of proof required to convict.

11 Third Parties in Appeal Proceedings

The national situations reported in this book have demonstrated how important it is for a legal system to envisage the right to appeal to those whose fundamental and procedural rights could be violated. Despite this, we have seen that only in a few cases do third parties have the right to challenge judicial orders related to investigative measures that infringe their rights. Significantly, in Portugal the writ of *habeas corpus* can be filed by any "citizen enjoying political rights"[118] as a way of reacting to an unlawful arrest or unlawful pre-trial detention. This action is brought before the Supreme Court of Justice as an urgent matter and represents another remedy for challenging the illegality of an arrest or pre-trial detention.

Let us now consider the third party's right to appeal against decisions on the merits of the case, with particular regard to those concerning criminal liability. To this end, however, we might stress that designating the very concept of criminal liability is more complex than it might appear to be. What resulted from the national accounts is that, in general terms, the jurisdictions under analysis do not afford third parties the right to appeal against decisions, due to their indirect involvement in the proceedings. As a rule, third parties can only appeal against decisions directly impacting their interests.

As pointed out by Elisea Malino and Diego Foti, it is not surprising that third parties cannot appeal against decisions on the accused's criminal liability, since even formal parties may not be entitled to challenge such decisions, or may only have rights limited to specific aspects, such as those relating to civil-law damages. With regard to the victims of crime, for instance, it is undisputed that they are not granted with any special right to appeal if they decide not to bring a civil action and formally join the proceedings. Similarly, in Portugal, civil parties may appeal against decisions enacted against their civil-law interests.[119] In Brazil, the possibility of the victim and the prosecutor's assistant to take part in appeal proceedings is also limited, since "the assistant may brief the appeals filed by the public prosecutor or by himself, when it is restricted to cases of appeal against an acquittal or dismissal, if the MP does not appeal".[120] In other words, their right to challenge the ruling is subsidiary and subject to certain restrictions.

[118] Arts. 220(2) and 222 CCP-Portugal.

[119] See Art. 401(1)(c) CCP-Portugal.

[120] Art. 271 CCP-Brazil.

A special category of third parties, such as owners whose property has been confiscated, have the right to appeal against specific aspects of the criminal decision that may be linked to criminal liability in some way. This is the case in Spain, where such persons must be notified of the freezing of their goods, and are allowed to appeal even if they do not actively participate in the proceedings. Such persons may lodge an appeal, but only on matters that directly affect their property, rights, or legal situation, and not on matters relating to the criminal liability of the accused.[121] In short, defining what directly affects them and determining the limits of their defence may be a difficult task, which explains why Spanish legislation makes recourse to a legal fiction. Since confiscation depends on the illegal origin of the objects, the criminal liability of the accused directly affects the third party who has undergone the seizure of their property. Therefore, if the court identifies a third party who is affected by confiscation but does not participate in the proceedings, that party is considered to be in default. Despite this, they are notified of the final decision, and thus retain the right to file an appeal. Moreover, this third party has an extraordinary remedy against the final judgment's *res judicata* in cases where default is caused by "involuntary" reasons.[122]

Moreover, it is interesting that under Portuguese law, not only those who have been ordered to pay any sums may appeal but also those who are defending a right affected by the court's ruling.[123]

In France, it is also significant that the right to an effective remedy, enshrined in Article 16 of the Declaration of the Rights of Man and Citizens, allows for access to a judge for all individuals, including the accused and the victim in criminal law. These persons are formal participants in the appeal proceedings, and as already seen, the notable 2014 ruling of the *Conseil constitutionnel* extended the right to an effective remedy also to third parties. As has also been observed by Barbara Drevet, the persons held legally responsible can appeal against a criminal or assize court judgment regarding their civil interests.[124] Moreover, a third-party ordered to pay damages can appeal against a decision before the Court of Appeal solely on issues that concern their interests. An insurer can challenge a court decision, if they are parties to the proceedings; otherwise, as a third party, they cannot appeal unless condemned by the court of first instance. However, in France, the situation of third-party owners is even more complex, despite recent legislative adjustments to protect their property rights. Indeed, the current provisions do not explicitly grant them the right to appeal against a decision to confiscate their assets. The *Cour de Cassation* has previously ruled in favour of owners, but only when they were unaware of the proceedings. Therefore, the introduction of new rules affording these subjects the

---

[121] See Art. 803-*ter*(b) CCP-Spain.

[122] See Art. 803-*ter*(c) CCP-Spain in relation to Arts. 496–508 CCP-Spain. See para. 12 of this Chapter.

[123] See Art. 401(1)(d) CCP-Portugal.

[124] See Drevet, in this volume, para. 9.

right to intervene during the proceedings may have an impact also on the right to appeal.

Finally, we have to analyse the issue of third parties in appeal proceedings by addressing it from the perspective of extraordinary remedies. Specifically, the Brazilian report mentions the possibility of lodging an appeal with the Supreme Court of Justice after the decision has become final. For instance, this may occur if inadmissible evidence is used to convict the accused, or if evidence that could have led to an acquittal is only discovered after the decision has become final and unchallengeable. It is worth noting that the right to such a review is not limited to the convicted person or their defence counsel, but extends to "spouse, descendants, adoptees, ascendants, adopters, relatives or relatives up to the fourth degree of consanguinity or affinity, heirs who can show a legitimate interest, or anyone who has been expressly entrusted with the task if the convicted person is deceased".[125] The same rights have been affirmed in Hungarian caselaw.

Remarkably, based on the so-called "extensive effect" of appeals,[126] in Brazil, co-defendants who have not appealed against the decision can benefit from a favourable decision taken on behalf of those who did. In other words, if the reasons that justify the appeal can be shared with other defendants, the ruling then applies to them. In this light, they are seen as third parties with respect to the trial. However, if the appeal is based on reasons exclusively linked to the appellant, the benefits will not extend to other subjects.

12 *Res Judicata* and the Effects of Criminal Judgments Upon Third Parties

Traditionally, *res judicata* is a phenomenon that produces effects mainly on the defendant, on the civilly liable party and on the injured party, while other individuals, who remained extraneous to the judicial proceedings, are not considered by the final decision. This legal concept has always served to prevent the perpetual re-examination of criminal cases and ensure the stability of legal decisions. Once a final decision has been issued, the accused is generally protected from facing subsequent charges for the same criminal act or conduct. This aspect of *res judicata* is designed to shield individuals from the burdens of being repeatedly prosecuted for the same alleged offence, promoting legal certainty and protecting against potential abuse by the State.

This comparative study has shown that the final decision of criminal proceedings can have a binding effect on a civil claim for damages filed by the victim who did not participate as a civil party. For this reason, Hungarian legislation requires the victim to be informed of the conclusion of criminal proceedings, in order to allow them to

[125] Art. 450(2) CCP-Brazil.

[126] Art. 580 CCP-Brazil.

file a civil claim for damages. The final decision in the criminal proceeding thus also has a binding effect on proceedings of a different nature.

Brazilian regulations on this matter provide an interesting model, according to which an acquittal can, in some cases, prevent the filing of a civil action.[127] This is particularly the case when the acquittal is based on a clear acknowledgement that no crime has been committed, or that the accused did not commit or was not involved in it. However, a civil claim can be filed whenever the decision recognises the existence of a criminal act, but rules that the author is not liable for criminal punishment, since said act was performed out of necessity, in self-defence, in strict compliance with a legal duty or in the regular exercise of the law.[128] Additionally, acquittal may also produce positive effects for co-defendants and persons who participated in the commission of the offence but did not take part in the criminal proceedings. In the latter case, we can affirm that third parties can also benefit from the *res judicata* stemming from an acquittal. The Italian report reached a similar conclusion, as it noted that "*res judicata* impedes the holding of a new criminal trial, regardless of the participation of any parties, whilst it produces its preclusive effect also for them".[129] What seems particularly remarkable in Italian case law is the admissibility of a second criminal proceeding against the same person when the final judgment issued in the first trial affected the fundamental rights of individuals who were not party to it.[130] Italian legislation allows a final judgment to be used as evidence in a separate criminal case. In this case, the decision will impinge upon individuals beyond those involved in the original criminal proceeding

In addition, the possibility of enforcement against the person civilly liable for the consequences of the criminal conviction has been discussed in Hungary.[131] Legal scholarship, indeed, criticises the admissibility of this hypothesis, as it would violate the adversarial principle, pointing out that third parties can only be considered civilly liable at the end of a civil trial.[132]

As mentioned above, also in Portugal, mainly as a result of domestic case law, *res judicata* applies exclusively to the parties who have been involved in criminal proceedings. Indeed, the effects of a final decision are not binding for third parties not involved in criminal proceedings. For this reason, it is crucial for third parties, such as potential owners or possessors of items or properties seized or confiscated, to participate in criminal trials. Moreover, if the criminal court has examined the civil claim and issued a decision on the matter, this ruling has the effects of *res judicata* in accordance with Portuguese procedural civil law.[133]

[127] See Gomes de Vasconcellos, Brenner Lucchesi, in this volume, para. 10.

[128] Art. 65 CCP-Brazil.

[129] See Malino, Foti, in this volume, para. 10.

[130] Italian Constitutional Court, judgment No. 200 of 21 July 2016.

[131] See Fantoly, Lichtenstein, in this volume, para. 10.

[132] Grinover (1978), p. 51.

[133] See Gouveia de Caires, Reis Barata, in this volume, para. 10.

The limits of the effects of *res judicata* are strictly linked to the actual formal participants in the criminal proceedings. In this sense, the Spanish report also emphasised that decisions issued at the end of criminal proceedings cannot bind third parties.[134] This report has clearly explained that the binding effects of a ruling only apply to formal parties, as they have had the chance to exercise their right to defence and to benefit from the principles governing fair trial.

However, also in Spain, criminal judgments may produce effects against third parties in other civil, labour or administrative proceedings. Indeed, the judgment may have *de facto* effects, which may be detrimental to third parties, as happens in the event of confiscation following the conviction of the accused.[135] In this case, third parties targeted by the confiscation should prove their good faith regarding the origin of the assets.

As also emerges in French law, the criminal punishment of confiscation can affect third parties' property rights. The Report on France observes that if confiscation is ordered, the person with rights over the property cannot appeal against the judgment directly.[136] However, the French *Cour de Cassation* recognised the need for a remedy and held that the procedural remedy provided for in Article 710 of the French CCP could be appealed to by third parties, in order to obtain the restitution of their goods, once the decision had become final. According to the 2021 Decree,[137] third parties having rights on or over the property must be informed of the decision regarding confiscation. Moreover, the owner of an item seized during the proceeding but not confiscated at the end of it can ask the Public Prosecutor's Office for its return.

In sum, as far as the effects of a *res judicata vis-à-vis* third parties are concerned, the comparative analysis of the chosen countries has revealed several similarities. As noted above, the effects of a final decision are generally *inter partes*, meaning that only the formal parties to the criminal proceedings can be affected by it, and that detrimental consequences cannot impinge upon third parties' rights. It is not surprising that the most common exception is constituted by confiscation ordered as a penalty, since it directly targets illicit goods, regardless of the owner.

It is clear that nobody can undergo the negative effects stemming from a decision taken without their participation or contribution and, above all, without being able to defend themselves and their interests.

[134] See Gascón Inchausti, Schumann Barragán, in this volume, para. 10.

[135] According to Article 127-*ter* of the Spanish CCP, the judge or court of law may order confiscation "when the unlawful financial position has been demonstrated in adversarial proceedings".

[136] See Drevet, in this volume, para. 10.

[137] Act No. 2021-1729 of 22 December 2021. On the contrary, the owner of an item seized during the proceeding but not confiscated can ask the Public Prosecutor's Office for its restitution.

13 Concluding Remarks

In the current scenario, the reach of criminal proceedings involves subjects other than the suspect, whose contribution may be necessary or, at least, useful for the ascertainment of facts. Furthermore, procedural activities may target directly and indirectly third parties. In the light of this, the present study was designed to determine the effects of criminal proceedings on third parties. Bearing this in mind, this chapter has compared the main findings of national reports chosen for the purposes of this volume. In addition, by understanding similarities and differences in the definition and protection of third parties across six jurisdictions, we have attempted to provide a description of the complex role played by these individuals and their safeguards in criminal proceedings. This task has implied comparing specific elements of each country's report alongside with the overall contextual framework. The comparative analysis has taken into consideration the classification of formal parties provided by all domestic reports, as the notion of third parties is inextricably linked with the subjects formally entitled to participate in criminal proceedings. Furthermore, this study has contributed to the understanding of the concept of substantive parties; they deserve adequate attention, since their interests may be affected by the procedural activities. An illustrative example of this are the victims of crime, who do not formally join the proceedings (even if they are allowed to do so) but still experience the effects of a criminal court's decision.

This study has also sought to develop guidelines aimed at strengthening the protection of third parties. This may be achieved by analysing the different stages of criminal proceedings and verifying how each national system has tackled this issue.

This study has shown how difficult it is to establish what we mean by a third party. As noted previously, each national jurisdiction has addressed the issue related to the classification of these individuals incidentally, but none of them has done so systematically, comprehensively, or coherently. The lack of attention given to this subject, or perhaps a lack of awareness among academics of the third party's status, is likely the reason for this. In addition, research into the factors involved in this issue has historically addressed the accused and the accuser, after a long period of focusing solely on the public prosecution. By contrast, recent years have seen significant advances in the field of criminal justice, prompting numerous inquiries into the structural and ideological underpinnings of criminal justice systems. These developments have underscored the need to recognise, both nationally and internationally, the interests of parties far beyond suspects and defendants,[138] thus reversing the traditional view of the proceedings as a two-party contest between the state and the accused.

In this light, this study has reinforced the idea that there is no category or general definition of these parties in the jurisdictions under examination. Instead, national reports have showed that several studies have looked at specific persons, which we

[138] See para. 4 ff.

have tentatively categorised for the purposes of this investigation,[139] in order to encompass subjects other than formal participants who are in some way affected by, or simply involved in, procedural activities. These include witnesses, who may certainly be regarded as extraneous to the proceedings, while at the same time deserving protection in certain vulnerable situations. We have also observed that victims and close relatives, who may be involved in different ways during the proceedings, require special attention from legislators. This is true whether their involvement is at the trial stage or at an earlier phase.

Furthermore, even if it is clear that the effects of a final decision are generally *inter partes*, there are situations where the decision has effects on third parties who may therefore exercise specific powers, as in the case of an *ad hoc* judicial review. Another example of what is meant by third parties is undercover agents and persons under protection programmes. In other words, there does not seem to be a single category of third parties, but several ones. The number of third parties also depends on the fact that criminal proceedings comprise various stages. As criminal proceedings progress to the trial phase, the rights and interests at issue may change, and there may be the involvement of parties unrelated to the proceedings, whose legal status may require specific legal treatment and consideration.

In particular, criminal investigations may interfere with third parties' interests. This phenomenon is apparent in the use of ICT tools, which widen the scope of targets for investigative measures, such as in the case of the interception of communications and other criminal procedural measures. As we have seen, even more worrying is the widespread use of new means of investigation (such as geolocation and digital searches), creating a precarious situation in which criminal proceedings indiscriminately threaten the daily lives and freedoms of everyone. In this field, however, the findings are not encouraging, since, with the exception of Spain, the jurisdictions examined do not provide adequate solutions to safeguard third parties' freedom and liberties. Spain, in fact, represents a model, as it pays particular attention to this category of individuals by restricting the recourse to these intrusive measures as well as affording them powers to challenge the encroachment of their fundamental rights.

In contrast, a significant finding of this study is that owners of confiscated and frozen assets, even in the absence of a formal accusation, can provide a paradigm of how a third party should be treated. Upon closer examination, all the jurisdictions examined in this study provide a clear understanding of the subjects targeted by the freezing of goods. Furthermore, these individuals are granted almost identical rights and guarantees in all the legal systems studied. Confiscation's relevance to property rights has been a significant factor in legal debates throughout history. Nevertheless, today, it is important to acknowledge that property rights extend beyond assets and goods to include personal data, which can be copied and stored by authorities even after electronic devices are returned to their owners. In summary, even when users

[139] See para. 1.

regain possession of their devices, they have no control over the personal data that are still retained.

To conclude, the analysis undertaken here has attempted to deepen the understanding of the interests of this category of individuals and, above all, of their need for more adequate protection. However, the study has shown the lack of an all-encompassing, single definition for this category. Thus, several questions still remain to be answered and considerably more work will need to be done to determine the hierarchy of the potentially competing rights and interests of all the persons involved in criminal proceedings other than formal participants and to restrict and circumscribe the interference with third parties' rights on the basis of the principles of necessity and proportionality. These criteria seem to be the most adequate to grant third parties safeguards, since they form the basis on which the competent authorities are called upon to assess and prevent the risk of encroachment of their rights.

References

Carrara F (1875) Azione penale. Rivista Penale 3:5–20

Dinamarco CR, Badaró GH, Lopes BV (2020) Teoria Geral do Processo, 32nd edn. Malheiros, São Paulo

Grinover AP (1978) Eficácia e autoridade da sentença penal. In: Revista dos Tribunais, São Paulo, pp 1–67

Illuminati G (2015) The victim as a witness. In: Lupária Donati L (ed) Victims and criminal justice. European standards and national good practices. Wolters Kluwer, Assago, pp 65–80

Leacock C (2008) Search and seizure of digital evidence in criminal proceedings. Digital Evidence and Electronic Signature Law Review 5:221–225

Lucchini L (1873) Il carcere preventivo ed il meccanismo istruttorio che vi si riferisce nel processo penale. Studio di legislazioni comparate antiche e moderne seguito da uno schema-progetto di legge, 2nd edn. Ferdinando Ongenia, Venezia, pp 1–373

Pastrana AT (2015) Victim's right to participate in the process and Acusación particular in Spain. In: Lupária L (ed) Victims and criminal justice. European standards and national good practice. Wolters Kluwers, Assago, pp 127–136

Peltier V (2017) Les preuves obtenues par IMSI-Catchers et les droits fondamentaux. In: Bonis E (ed) Les écoutes judiciaires en procédure pénale – 2 – Les colloques de l'ISCJ, pp 49–58

Rafaraci T (2015) New perspectives for the protection of the victims in the EU. In: Ruggeri S (ed) Human Rights in European Criminal Law. New developments in European Legislation and Case Law after the Lisbon Treaty. Springer, Heidelberg, pp 215–225

Schünemann B (2013) A posição da vítima no sistema da justiça penal: um modelo em três colunas. In: Schüneman B, Greco L (eds) Estudos de direito penal, direito processual penal e filosofia do direito. Marcial Pons, São Paulo, pp 112–123

Tulkens F (2002) Victimes et droits de l'homme dans la jurisprudence de la Cour Européenne des droits de l'homme. Archives de Politique Criminelle 24:41–59

The Protection of Third Parties in Criminal Proceedings: A Constitutional Law Perspective

Erika La Fauci

Abstract This study proposes a comparative constitutional analysis on the safeguard of third parties' fundamental rights in criminal proceedings. Specifically, the essay focuses on the regulations that have been adopted by the countries whose legal systems have been commented on in this book, stressing their merits and limitations and the way such provisions could be modified in order to protect these subjects' rights. Moreover, the study theorises a possible balance between investigative needs and the safeguard of third parties' fundamental rights.

1 The Controversial Notion of Third Party

The notion of 'third party' is difficult to define. This is firstly because it has often been conceived merely as a support in contraposition to the main parties in criminal proceedings: prosecutor and defendant. Consequently, it seems that most studies have focused more on attempting to define who third parties *are not* than on questioning who they truly *are.*

Secondly, the syntagma itself of 'third party' itself cannot help but be controversial. Indeed, if one of the grammatical meanings of the word 'third' is "the person [. . .] less directly involved in a matter than the main people [. . .] that are involved",[1] it is contradictory to describe those who are not formally parties to a criminal trial as third *parties.*

This is a logical issue. On the one hand, if someone is a third person—*i.e.,* he is somebody who is external to something—he cannot in any way be a part of that something. On the other, if a person is directly involved in a condition, he could

[1] See the definition of "third", in *Cambridge Dictionary* (online version), available at https://dictionary.cambridge.org/dictionary/english/third-party.

E. La Fauci (✉)
Law Department, University of Messina, Messina, Italy
e-mail: erilafauci@unime.it

S. Ruggeri et al. (eds.), *Third Parties in Criminal Proceedings*, Legal Studies in International, European and Comparative Criminal Law 10,
https://doi.org/10.1007/978-3-031-73970-5_13

never be external to that condition and, by consequence, will never be able to be a third in relation to it.

For these reasons, the expression ‘third party’ does not seem to be the most appropriate to describe the status of those who are not directly involved in a criminal proceeding but who can, nonetheless, be influenced by certain decisions or measures that could be taken during it. In spite of this, it is necessary to establish the identity of these subjects in order to understand their potential role in criminal processes and to assess how their rights could be safeguarded.

Indeed, if we try to compare how third parties are conceived in some legal systems, we may find certain common denominators. For example, both the French[2] and the Spanish[3] reports in this volume show that the condition of these parties is essentially characterized by the harm they suffer as a result of investigative needs rather than the active role that they actually play in proceedings. In fact, the French study defines third parties as “those people who undergo procedural measures, that is, all those persons against whom procedural measures can be addressed without being formal participants”.[4] Similarly, the Spanish report considers this status as referring to those “individuals whose objects or assets have been seized during the police or judicial investigation phase; that are being affected by any judicial investigation measure” and who have “the possibility of intervening and participating in the proceedings to defend themselves”.[5]

Thus, the more third parties’ rights are violated during an investigation, the more a law deems (or should deem) it necessary to attribute appropriate powers to those subjects in order to allow them to see their rights safeguarded and balanced in relation to investigative needs. In this regard, one of the most important powers that should be conferred on third parties is the possibility of being aware of the adoption of a restrictive measure concerning them. Consequently, they should also be able to challenge a judicial decision that unfairly caused a breach of their rights[6] and they should have proper procedural powers and guarantees.

These issues will be analysed in the following sections. Nonetheless, some other preliminary considerations are still worth making.

Firstly, it must be clarified that the concept of third party cannot help but be a relational one. In fact, from a subjective point of view it is impossible to conceive a ‘third’ without a ‘second’ and a ‘first’ person being referred to. Consequently, it is crucial to understand who the second and the first are and the role they play in a specific criminal trial, in order to properly comprehend who third parties truly are.

---

[2] See Drevet, para 2.

[3] Gascón Inchausti and Schuman Barragán, in this volume, para. 3.

[4] Drevet, in this volume.

[5] Gascón Inchausti and Schuman Barragán, in this volume, para. 3.

[6] For example, Art. 334 LECrim (*Ley de Enjuiciamiento Criminal)*, acknowledges the right for any person who may be affected by a confiscation order to “appeal the measure before the Court at any time”.

Secondly, the relational essence of the notion of third party can also be considered from an objective point of view. In fact, if we examine the non-involvement of such a subject from an ongoing process that does not directly deal with him but that influences his legal position and the safeguard of his fundamental rights, the thirdness that characterizes his identity may be easily understood. Thus, the relation a third party has with the main parties to criminal proceedings and the trial itself determines his status.

2 The Influence of New Technologies on Criminal Proceedings and on Third Parties' Rights from a Comparative Constitutional Perspective

New technologies (NT) influence almost every aspect of the contemporary society. For these reasons, digital data have become a "valuable resource"[7] in several fields: economic, social and processual. Particularly, the arrival of NT has influenced both how crimes are committed and how they are investigated and prevented.[8]

However, since these new tools naturally have a 'centrifugal' tendency to affect people's daily life in different ways, it is always necessary to analyse the role they may play in trials and how they may affect parties' rights.

Indeed, new technologies offer undisputed advantages. For example, communication interception are more incisive and effective than they used to be thanks to *trojans* and IMSI catchers, and nowadays investigations are possible that would have been unthinkable in the past. We could never have imagined, for example, that communications would be transmitted by those who unintentionally helped an investigation occur because of the devices they own.[9]

Thus, while it seems to be impossible to conceive a modern society without the help and the support of new technologies, it is necessary to understand how they can be used (and how they may be useful) without violating the fundamental rights of those who could be damaged by their improper use. For these reasons, there are fundamental prerogatives that should—as far as possible—be ensured: the right to privacy, the right to data protection, the right to the secrecy of correspondence and the right of defence.

Starting with the former, this is clearly one of the rights most sacrificed due to investigative needs. A criminal investigation of any kind is bound to be naturally invasive of the privacy of those involved. However, what truly matters is the aim of the investigation and respect for the principle of proportionality in the adoption of any investigative measures. Not surprisingly, Article 588 bis a) of the Spanish

[7] Camon (2021), p. 1.

[8] Di Nuzzo (2022), p. 120. For further studies regarding the relationship between technologies and criminal law see *ex multis* Savona (2010), Nissan (2012), Hagan (2013), Montasari et al. (2021).

[9] Caprioli (2017), p. 494.

Criminal Code (so called *LECrim*) rules that an investigative measure must be considered "proportionate when, considering all the circumstances of the case, the sacrifice of the affected rights and interests is not greater than the benefit that their adoption provides for public interest and third parties".[10]Thus, only the existence of a benefit can justify an intrusion of somebody's privacy by the police.

Indeed, from the perspective of comparative constitutional law, the way a legal system manages the use of new technologies in criminal proceedings and the way it allows investigators to interfere with the right to privacy seems to reflect the nature of a legal system: in other words, how democratic or not it is. For example, the Brazilian case that involved the criminal courts and Google over the murder of Marielle Franco and Anderson Gomes[11] is a prime example of the complex balance a State is called upon to achieve between public and private interests in such circumstances.

Specifically, the lawsuit was related to a terrorist attack in Rio De Janeiro, in which a city councilwoman and her driver were assassinated.[12] The Brazilian police asked Google to provide the localization data of all the "*Google accounts*" and "*Device IDs*" of those who found themselves near the crime scene in the 15 min prior to the assassination, and who had searched on the net for specific terms.[13] The dispute arose because of Google's refusal to give the authorities the documents requested, objecting that such a request would have led to a violation of the right to its users' privacy, since it was too generic and disproportionate. Nonetheless, both the Fourth Section of the Rio De Janeiro Criminal Tribunal[14] and the Federal Supreme Court[15] rejected Google's complaints, deeming that the data capture ordered by the police was due to the seriousness of the crime at issue.

Several scholars have strongly criticized this ruling,[16] arguing that the balance on which it was based was not fair or proportionate. Thus, the Brazilian authorities justified the capture of data of those who were near the crime scene because they deemed the existence of a public interest and the need to fight criminality to be superior to the right to privacy. However, notwithstanding the seriousness of the crime at issue, it seems to be questionable that a legal system could admit such an infringement of a fundamental right due to the general existence of a public interest. Indeed, in order to consider data capture as a reasonable measure, it should be

---

[10] For a comment on the article see Gascón Inchausti and Schuman Barrágan, in this volume, para. 3.

[11] Superior Tribunal de Justiça, 3ª Seção, judgement No. 1568445 of 24 June 2020. The lawsuit has been commented *ex multis* by Monteiro Sarkis (2022); Souza (2020).

[12] It occured on 14 March 2018.

[13] Such as "Marielle Franco", "vereadora Marielle", "agenda Marielle", "agenda vereadora Marielle", "Casa das Pretas", "Rua dos Inválidos 122", "Rua dos Inválidos". In this regard cf. Monteiro Sarkis (2022), p. 126.

[14] Rio de Janeiro Criminal Tribunal, judgment of the 5 February 2019.

[15] Brazilian Supreme Court, judgment of the 8 February 2021, No. 175162.

[16] *Ex multis*, Gascón Inchausti and Schuman Barrágan, in this volume; Monteiro Sarkis (2022); Souza (2020).

comprehensively demonstrated by the judiciary authority, which should precisely indicate the causes that justify the sacrifice of a right so important as the right to privacy.

Otherwise, the existence of a general public interest could legitimize a wide variety of investigative measures, which could be adopted in heterogeneous circumstances, ignoring the rights of the people involved in an inquiry.[17] After all, it should be difficult to legitimize the acquisition of the localization data for those who, by chance, found themselves in the wrong place at the wrong time[18] and, for this reason, found their privacy indiscriminately violated. It would perhaps have been fairer and more justifiable if such a measure had been adopted only in relation to those who were already considered suspects.

In this way, there would not have been an indistinct capture of personal data but, on the contrary, it would have regarded only those who were suspected of being really connected with a criminal act.

2.1 The Necessary Balance Between Investigative Efficiency and the Right to Privacy

Indeed, the Brazilian case above clearly shows how difficult and crucial it is to establish the limits of the use of new technologies on a criminal proceeding in order to avoid it being disrespectful of the right to privacy of main and third parties. It is evident that the doubtless advantages brought by new technological tools are bound to be—at the same time—considerably dangerous if they are not precisely regulated by law. In fact, the inherent capacity of new technologies to track devices even at great distances could allow investigators to reach people who might not be connected in any way with an ongoing criminal proceeding. Moreover, these subjects (*i.e.,* third parties) could potentially never learn about the capture of their personal data by the authorities.

For these reasons, for example, the Italian Constitutional Court has constantly underlined the importance of the respect by prosecutors and police for the rules which safeguard the right to privacy of persons under investigation. Thus, the Court stated that the breach of such a right would determine an infringement of human dignity and personality within social groups[19] (Art. 2 Const.). Indeed, there is an unavoidable and essential link between privacy and dignity, which limits the use of communication interception in order to prevent its excessive intrusiveness into people's private lives. Hence, the Court has clarified that

[17] Monteiro Sarkis (2022), p. 136.

[18] *Ibid.*

[19] Italian Constitutional Court, judgment of 26 February 1993, No. 8, para. 2.

> the court must strive for a balancing of the two protected constitutional interests in order to prevent the right to confidentiality of telephone communications from being disproportionately sacrificed by the need to ensure an effective suppression of criminal offences.[20]

Consequently, the need to ensure investigative efficiency cannot always prevail on the right to privacy (as happened in the abovementioned Brazilian caselaw related to the murder of Marielle Franco and Anderson Gomes).

Therefore, Italian law prohibits the courts from taking as evidence any information that has been obtained without respecting the right to privacy and the *audi et alteram partem*'s principle.[21] Unsurprisingly, the Italian Court of Cassation has deemed unlawful a recording made by a person appointed by the police to do so, because of his personal relationship with an investigated person.[22]

Indeed, it is evident that in this case there was a clear breach of the guarantees provided by the Italian legal system to the parties of a criminal proceeding, since such an activity would allow the authorities to take advantage of the unsolicited statements of person under investigation, ignoring the use that would be made of obtained data. Thus, if the State expresses concerns that an investigation could violate parties' fundamental rights, it should be even more concerned about the indiscriminate use by police of third parties' data merely because of investigative needs.

However, Italian law does not provide for specific rules on third party's rights, since the code of criminal procedure does not define them and does not specifically envisage them. Thus, these parties—except in the case of searches[23]—have no chance to challenge measures which could be adopted by police, and which could violate their fundamental rights.[24]

Along these lines, the Spanish Constitutional Court has deemed the impossibility for a third party to take legal action against a measure which has been detrimental to his fundamental rights as unlawful.[25] Specifically, the Constitutional Court ruled on a lawsuit which involved two journalists whose computers and mobile devices had been intercepted by police even though these people had never been involved in an

---

[20] Italian Constitutional Court, judgment of 1 June 1998, No. 229, para. 2.

[21] The legitimacy of this obligation has constantly been confirmed by the Italian Constitutional Court. See *ex plurimis* Italian Constitutional Court, judgment of the 4 April 1973, No. 34; Italian Constitutional Court, judgment of the 2 April 1976, No. 98; Italian Constitutional Court, judgement of the 3 June 1987, No. 223; Italian Constitutional Court, judgement of 23 July 1991, No. 366; Italian Constitutional Court, judgement of 26 February 1993, No. 81. See also Italian Court of Cassation, judgment of the 28 March 2006, No. 26795.

[22] Italian Court of Cassation, judgment of 24 September 2003, No. 36747, para. 5b. On this subject cf. also Scalfati (2019).

[23] Art. 352 (4 *bis*), Code of Criminal Procedure provides for the right of opposition which can be exercised by a third party who should be searched by police.

[24] As it has been pointed out by ECtHR, *Contrada vs. Italy*, judgment of the 23 May 2024, Appl. No. 2507/19, para. 95.

[25] Italian Constitutional Court, judgment of the 7 March 2022, No. 30.

inquiry.[26] The journalists were however prevented from challenging the abovementioned measures because the court ruled that their status as third parties did not enable them to exercise any right to appeal.[27] Nonetheless, the journalists decided to contest this decision before the Spanish Constitutional Court.

The *Tribunal Constitucional* firstly clarified that the choice made by police to intercept data contained in the personal computers and mobiles of the claimants was not legitimate since the prosecutor did not consider that this information could reveal some particularly details news about the private lives people.[28] Moreover, by referring to a previous judgment of the same Constitutional Court, the judges believed that it was necessary to establish a series of guarantees against the risks to public rights and freedoms (in particular personal privacy) due to the improper use of computers and new information technologies.[29] For these reasons, the *Tribunal Constitucional* held that it was not possible to admit that a democratic legal system could acknowledge the existence of fundamental rights without allowing their owners to learn about the adoption of a measure and to challenge the latter if it violated their rights. Thus, the Spanish Court deemed that the Court before which recourse had been lodged should have considered the high risk to essential aspects of private life that the judicial authorities should have assessed when analysing the legal standing to appeal.[30] Consequently, the *Tribunal Constitucional* underlined that when the police intend to use technological tools during an investigation, they must assess more strictly the necessity of employing those means rather than others that are less invasive of the privacy of third parties.

Hence, the Spanish constitutional judges stated that the guarantees that must be safeguarded in these circumstances are the following: the existence of a reasonable balance between investigative needs and the safeguard of fundamental rights of those being investigated; judicial oversight of the measure adopted by a prosecutor; adequate reasoning of the measure that the investigator intends to adopt; the recognition of the right to appeal to the people who undergo such measures.[31]

Indeed, the latter guarantee clearly expresses the need of safeguarding the "pro actione *principle*" that allows parties to take part in proceedings and to challenge a measure that could have violated their fundamental rights. Thus, the reasoning of the abovementioned judgment is based on the idea that there should never be

---

[26] For a detailed description of the case, see Gascón Inchausti and Schuman Barrágan, in this volume, p. 15 ff.

[27] Provincial Court of Balearic Islands, First section, ordinance of the 20 May 2019. No. 12; Provincial Court of Balearic Islands, First section, ordinance of the 21 May 2019, No. 12; Tribunal for Preliminary Investigations of Palma of Mallorca, ordinance of 6 February 2019, No. 12; Tribunal for Preliminary Investigations of Palma of Mallorca, ordinance of the 25 January 2019, No. 12.

[28] Italian Constitutional Court, judgment of the 7 March 2022, No. 30, para. 4.

[29] Constitutional Court, judgment of the 7 November 2011, No. 173, para. 3.

[30] Para. 5.

[31] *Ibid.*

interference by the police in the private sphere of a person without recognizing their right to appeal a provision if such an interference could affect their fundamental interests.

2.2 *The Judicial Safeguard of Third Parties' Fundamental Rights*

The experiences set forth above underline how important it is for a legal system to envisage the right to appeal for those whose fundamental rights could be violated by the adoption of investigative measures. Nonetheless, the importance of procedural and judicial guarantees is not only relevant in relation to the recognition of the possibility to challenge such measures. In fact, it is also necessary that a judge authorizes and controls the lawfulness of a choice made by investigative bodies to intercept third party communications by using technological tools.[32]

In this regard, French law seems to attach great attention to the safeguard of those who could be intercepted even if they could be not directly involved in a criminal proceeding. Specifically, it requires prior authorization from a judge in order to use the so called "IMIS-catcher" *(i.e.,* international mobile subscriber identity-catcher).[33] In fact, since the latter was approved as a means of investigation in 2016,[34] French legislation has provided for prior judiciary authorization in order to allow investigative bodies to use such a tool for investigations.

This measure could naturally involve individuals who are not in any way implicated in a criminal proceeding. Nonetheless, in a trade-off between investigative needs and the protection of privacy, this legal system considers the abovementioned solution to be the most reasonable and balanced. Moreover, art. 706-95-19 CCP rules that the data that have been obtained in such an investigation must be destroyed once prosecution can no longer be taken forward in that criminal proceeding.[35] Thus, although it is not possible for those who have been subjected to such a measure to appeal against the measure adopted by the judge who authorized the use of the "IMIS-catcher" by police,[36] the balance achieved by the French legislator can be assessed positively, since it seems able to prevent the misuse of personal data. After all, the mandatory destruction of acquired data (as will be discussed in the next section) seems to be one of the best ways to achieve a proper

---

[32] As it has been pointed out by ECtHR, *Contrada vs. Italy*, judgment of 23 May 2024, Appl. No. 2507/19, para. 88.

[33] For a more detailed analysis of such a regulation see Drevet, in this volume.

[34] Art. 706-95-12 1° *Code de procedure pénale* (hereafter, CCP).

[35] A similar regulation has been provided for the electronic data capture (art. 706-102-1 CCP). For a comparison between the two legislations, see Drevet, para. 4.

[36] Such a provision cannot but be justified since the aim of this investigation is to keep the addressee in the dark about its existence. See Drevet, para. 4.

trade-off between the indiscriminate use of new technologies by police for investigative needs and the impossibility for agents to take advantage of these means.

Indeed, if the recognition of judicial safeguards for third parties whose fundamental rights could be violated in the course of a criminal trial they are not involved in is so important, it is evident that establishing when they are informed about any communication interception activity targeting them is equally crucial.[37] Indeed, if these people were told about such an investigation when it was too late for them to appeal or when their data had already been captured and used by agents, this knowledge would clearly be useless. Thus, the awareness of third parties about communication interception that concerns them should always be functional to their possibility of exercising their right of defence.[38]

However, the Hungarian Code of Criminal Procedure states that a person concerned specified in a authorisation from a judge shall be informed about the fact of the use of covert means subject to authorisation from of a judge only after the completion of a preparatory proceeding, if no investigation is launched or after the completion of an investigation, if the person concerned is neither questioned as a suspect nor indicted.[39] Nonetheless, it is hard to agree with the choice of informing the intercepted person only when an investigation has ended or when it did not even start due to insufficient evidence.[40]

Of course, it is not possible to preventively inform a person that they will be subject to communication interception (since it would thus become useless). However, it is difficult to accept that a person may learn about it only when data regarding him taken by investigators have already been used in a criminal proceeding (since the investigation is over) or when an inquiry has not yet begun. Moreover, such information could never be conveyed to the wiretapped person if doing so could

> jeopardise the success of another criminal proceeding or any secret information gathering carried put under the Act on the prosecution service, the Act on the police, the Act on the National Tax and Customs Administration, or the Act on national security services.[41]

Thus, it could happen that even sensitive information could have been acquired by the police and that the person whom the data refers to never learns about its use.

Actually, as has been previously remarked, the moment a person learns about the existence of communication interception is as important as knowledge of the existence of communication interception itself. Indeed, when a person learns that hidden means of investigation are being employed, and cannot do anything to

[37] Cf. Di Nuzzo (2022), p. 142. The importance of granting proper information to the people involved in an interception has been affirmed by the European Court of Human Rights especially in ECtHR, *Big Brother Watch v. United Kingdom*, judgment of 13 September 2018, Appl. No. 58170/13, para. 310.

[38] Cf. ECtHR, *Contrada vs. Italy*, judgment of 23 May 2024, Appl. No. 2507/19, para. 93.

[39] Section 251, I c., Be.

[40] For a more detailed analysis of the Hungarian regulation of third parties' rights see Fantoly and Lichtenstein, in this volume.

[41] *Ibidem.*

safeguard his rights, he will not have any benefit from this information and his privacy will already have been violated. Thus, third parties should learn about the existence of communication interception when they are still in a position to appeal against the measure that authorised investigative bodies to take advantage of it and, consequently, are still able to contest such a provision in order to safeguard their right to privacy.[42]

3 How Can Investigative Needs and Third Parties' Rights Be Fairly Balanced?

The national legal systems analysed in this Book represent a milestone in trying to outline the complex and controversial status of third parties in criminal proceedings. Hence, as has been underlined, their condition seems to be changeable and vulnerable. In fact, these subjects' status deeply depends on how the inquiry develops, on the type of crime a body is investigating, and on their relationship with the other parties involved. Moreover, third parties are highly vulnerable since, unlike the other people directly involved in the same criminal proceeding, their fundamental rights risk being sacrificed for investigative needs without them being able to contest the measures by which a judge allowed such an invasive investigation.[43]

For these reasons, it is of crucial importance to consider how the law may achieve the fairest balance between investigative needs and safeguarding third-party rights. In other words, the "problem is not to establish what science and technology can today achieve, or has already achieved, but which arrangements are compatible with human rights standards set out at either international or domestic law".[44] In order to answer these questions, we should bear in mind several factors.

First of all, we should properly consider the role currently played by new technologies and how they by now influence the daily lives of the majority of people all over the world. We may presume that investigative bodies' frequent recourse to NT investigative tools arises from their conviction that they need to adapt their inquiries to the dynamics and relationships of modern society. After all, these are precisely the dynamics and relationships that agents should detect and analyse in their investigations and which they unavoidably deal with.

Thus, considering the enormous impact technology increasingly has on our daily lives, it would be almost impossible to imagine an inquiry not based on the use of such a tool. This is the reason why technology represents both a problem and an

---

[42] In this sense see ECtHR, *Szabó et Vissy v. Hungary*, judgement of 12 January 2016, Appl. No. 37138/14, para. 98; *Roman Zakharov vs Russia* (GC), judgement of 4 December 2015, App. No. 47143/06, para. 312; ECtHR, *Contrada vs. Italy*, judgment of 23 May 2024, Appl. No. 2507/19, para. 93.

[43] As the ones that could occur when an investigative body decides to use new technologies tools.

[44] Ruggeri (2022), p. 224.

opportunity for criminal justice.[45] Thus, on one hand the possibilities offered using new technologies can undoubtedly make an investigation easier and more efficient. However, on the other hand (as has been underlined) an indiscriminate, unregulated use of technology by the police risks violating the fundamental rights of those who may be only indirectly involved in a criminal proceeding. Of course, this is the case of third parties.

Indeed, the latter could be subjected to the same intrusive investigations as the other parties, but without ever being directly accused or subject to investigation. Therefore, the rights of such people would not be safeguarded as well as those of the main parties to the proceeding. For these reasons it is so important for a country to limit and regulate the cases in which agents can use NT tools for communication interception or other types of hidden investigations. In fact, a detailed regulation of such circumstances could allow the police to investigate efficiently without being disrespectfully invasive of people's privacy. Moreover, specific provision for those cases in which an agent could use new technologies should be accompanied by a recognition of third parties' right to defence. Indeed, as has been pointed out, the possibility for these subjects to appeal to the courts in the event of an infringement of their fundamental rights by the police allows a fair balance between investigative needs and respect for third-party privacy to be achieved. This would allow a measure potentially restrictive of third parties' rights to be checked by a separate, neutral judicial authority.

Thus, the crucial point of the use of new technologies by agents does not seem to consist of their general utilization of technological tools during an investigation but, on the contrary, of the utilization that they decide to make of those means and of the use of the data they have collected using such tools. Indeed, as has been stressed, since such instruments are inevitably pervasive and may rapidly obtain sensitive information concerning almost anybody, their use in criminal proceedings should be regulated. Thus, if during an investigation an agent obtained personal data having been reasonably and previously authorized by a judicial authority, there would not presumably be an infringement of any third party's rights.

On the contrary, in this case, if the subject whose rights could have been violated during an investigation cannot appeal against the measure that authorised the capture of his data by police, the use of such information would be illegitimate, having been captured without any adversarial procedure.

Moreover, a further relevant breach of such a prerogative would probably occur if an investigative body obtained the personal data of a third party without any previous supervision from the judicial authority that authorized the adoption of that measure. Consequently, if the person involved was not aware of the adoption of such a measure and had not the chance of challenging it, the use of this evidence should be considered unlawful.

For these reasons, the existence of a previous judiciary authorization for the adoption of such measures and the recognition of procedural and judiciary powers

---

[45] Bronzo (2017), p. 329.

to the third parties who should be involved in such proceedings, could represent a reasonable perspective. On one hand, the latter would make it possible to avoid forbidding police the use of new technologies in any circumstance that could concern third parties and, on the other hand, it would ensure proper guarantees of those people's rights in criminal proceedings. Moreover, it is believed that the law should also provide for the destruction of all the information obtained by agents and subsequently discarded by them as useless by the agents. Indeed, such a solution could ensure the respect of the right to privacy and the right to the protection of personal data of those who became involved in an investigation, even if they were not part of that proceeding.

This is therefore the balance that could be achieved in order to tackle and try to overcome the problem of the use of new technologies by police. After all, such a solution seems to be deeply respectful of the principle of legality, necessity and proportionality that the ECtHR has considered as the guideline when dealing with such circumstances.[46]

Ultimately, there is no doubt that "digitalisation has also caused an unprecedented increase of the 'transnationalisation' of the criminal proceedings as well as a 'delocalisation' of evidence".[47] Thus, this cannot but require a "new legal approach to overcome the traditional national views of investigative measures".[48] Hence, if the crimes being investigated have changed, investigative methods must also change to keep up with them, if they are to be efficient and successful. After all, how could it ever be possible to search for something if the means used for its research will never find it because of its different characteristics? It is evident that an innovation in criminal procedure must occur.

As has been pointed out,[49] technological progress involves the way we conceive of traditional legal categories and, maybe, the very way certain fundamental rights are intended.

This is the reason why it is impossible to reflect on these issues without duly considering the type of offence an inquiry is focused on. Indeed, the balance between investigative needs and the safeguarding of parties' rights (and, especially, those of third parties) is bound to change if an investigation concerns terrorist rather than common crimes, for example. Actually, it is believed that the former requires a different, more pervasive and articulated investigative approach than the one an agent would adopt for 'normal' crimes. Consequently, as the kind of crime changes, an inquiry should also change. Thus, this circumstance would justify the need perceived by agents to use new technologies more often in order to investigate.

---

[46] As has been stated by ECtHR, *Big Brother Watch v. United Kingdom,* judgment of 13 September 2018, Appl. No. 58170/13.

[47] Bachmaier Winter and Ruggeri (2022), p. 10.

[48] *Ibid.*

[49] Kostoris (2011), p. 179. See also Bronzo (2017).

However, such a circumstance could never justify a disproportionate use of technological tools by investigative bodies only because of the necessity of investigating a terrorism offence. In fact, as has been previously mentioned,[50] in the case of the murder of Marielle Franco and Anderson Gomes there was an unreasonable balance between the safeguarding of the privacy of those who were near the crime scene and investigative needs.

Indeed, the seriousness of an offence should never allow the excessive sacrifice of fundamental rights, which are as important as investigative requirements. Thus, if the terrorist nature of a crime could justify a more detailed, intrusive investigation, the privacy of those who could be indirectly involved in a criminal proceeding should also be protected as well. If it were not so, it would mean that whenever a terrorist crime occurred, the rights of those in any way involved should be restricted because of the existence of a superior, public interest. However, it is evident that such a circumstance would undoubtedly be unlawful. In other words, terrorism could never justify a lack of guarantees of fundamental rights and, definitively, of respect for the principles of legality, proportionality and necessity.

This is the reason why it is important to always achieve a balance between investigative needs and third-party rights, not letting any of them prevail over the other.

4 Conclusions

In the light of the abovementioned considerations, we need to draw some conclusions.

First of all, it must be underlined that nowadays, even though it might appear to be risky and hard to regulate, it is difficult to imagine a criminal investigation without the support of new technologies. Indeed, as discussed here, the influence that NT have on our contemporary society inevitably requires a frequent and unavoidable resort to these new tools by investigative bodies. If this were not so, it would be extremely difficult to investigate crime efficiently and effectively.

Secondly, since we should take for granted that criminal procedure can no longer continue without taking advantage of new technological tools, we should consider what the most reasonable and fairest regulation of their use may be in such proceedings. Indeed, as has been previously stressed, the essential guarantees for third parties would firstly consist of the recognition of their right to challenge a measure that they deem to have infringed their rights. Nonetheless, the judge appealed to should be different from the one who authorized an agent to adopt such a measure. This way, the impartiality of the judicial authority could be better safeguarded.

Thirdly, it is important both to establish when third parties should learn about the existence of an investigation that involves them, which may have involved the

---

[50] Above, para. 2.

acquisition of their sensitive data, and to ensure their right to challenge the measure that authorized this type of investigation. In fact, if they find out about its adoption at a point when they are unable to contest the abovementioned provision, their right to appeal becomes useless and meaningless.

Fourthly, in the case of third-party data acquired by investigative bodies, it is crucial both the way agents obtain these data and the use they make of such information in criminal proceedings. This is the reason why it is deemed essential to envisage the immediate destruction of those data captured without prior authorization from a judiciary authority, especially when the owners of such information have not been given the opportunity to be informed of or to challenge the measure that allowed their acquisition. Indeed, in this circumstance, the right to privacy and the right to the protection of personal data would be unreasonably violated.[51]

Finally, the abovementioned conditions and requirements related to the cases when the use of new technological tools by investigative bodies could involve third parties may be a way to strike a reasonable balance between investigative needs and the safeguard of third-party rights. Thus, considering the need to regulate situations of this nature, allowing judicial authorities to resort to new technologies and, at the same time, providing limits for the use of such new tools could be a way to let criminal procedure adapt to the changes in contemporary society.

After all, progress is inevitable but should always be monitored and supported to ensure its benefits are not fewer and worse than its disadvantages.[52] However, the use of new technology (when carefully regulated by legal systems) seems so far to have shown above all advantages. Moreover, deployment of technological means undoubtedly represents a precious means to improve efficiency and the effectiveness of criminal investigations. Thus, if in the future such a balance between benefits and disadvantages changes, legal systems will also have to change. Nonetheless, until that moment comes, there should be a common effort to let technology and criminal procedure peacefully coexist. After all, the best is yet to come.

References

Bachmaier Winter L, Ruggeri S (2022) Investigating and preventing crime in the digital era. New safeguards, new rights. Springer, Cham

Bronzo P (2017) L'impiego del *trojan horse* informatico nelle indagini penali. Rivista italiana per le scienze giuridiche 8:329–356

Camon A (2021) The project devices and digital evidence in Europe. In: Caianiello M, Camon A (eds) Digital forensic evidence. Towards common European standards in antifraud administrative and criminal investigations. Cedam, Milano

[51] As it has been pointed by out by ECtHR, *Contrada v. Italy*, para. 93.

[52] The scientific debate on the worrisome development of artificial intelligence in contemporary society demonstrates how hard it is to manage progress and its effects. See *ex plurimis* Müller (2016); Osoba and Welser (2017); Russell (2020); Taplin (2022).

Caprioli F (2017) Il"captatore informatico" come strumento di ricerca della prova in Italia. Rev Bras Direito Proc Pen 3(2):483–510
Di Nuzzo V (2022) Search and seizure of digital evidence: human rights concerns and new safeguards. In: Bachmaier Winter L, Ruggeri S (eds) Investigating and preventing crime in the digital era. New safeguards, new rights. Springer, Cham, pp 119–149
Hagan FE (2013) Research methods in criminal justice and criminology. Pearson Education, London
Kostoris RE (2011) Ricerca e formazione della prova elettronica: qualche considerazione introduttiva. In: Ruggieri F, Picotti L (eds) Nuove tendenze della giustizia penale di fronte alla criminalità informatica. Giappichelli, Torino, pp 179–182
Montasari R, Jahankhani H, Hill R, Parkinson S (2021) Digital forensic investigation of internet of things (IoT) devices. Springer, Berlin
Monteiro Sarkis J (2022) Dados telemáticos no caso "Marielle Franco e Anderson Gomes": violações à privacidade em tempos de vigilância. In: Moreira V, Machado J, De Marcelino Gomes C, Gomes C, Ribeiro Nunes CA, Soares LR (eds) Anais de Artigos Completos, vol 5, VI. CIDH, Campinas, Coimbra
Müller VC (2016) Fundamental issues of Artificial intelligence. Springer, Oxford
Nissan E (2012) Computer applications for handling legal evidence, police investigation and case argumentation. Springer, Berlin
Osoba OA, Welser W (2017) An intelligence in our image: the risks and bias and errors in artificial intelligence. Rand, Santa Monica
Ruggeri S (2022) The Digital Transition in Criminal Trials: New Premises, New Risks, New Challenges. In: Bachmaier Winter L, Ruggeri S (eds) Investigating and preventing crime in the digital era. New safeguards, new rights. Springer, Cham, pp 213–225
Russell SJ (2020) Human compatible: Artificial Intelligence and the problem of control. Viking, London
Savona U (2010) Crime and technology. New frontiers for regulation, law enforcement and research. Springer, Berlin
Scalfati A (2019) Le indagini atipiche. Giappichelli, Torino
Souza CA (2020) Caso Marielle Franco – Tensão entre o segredo de justiçia e a libertade de imprensa (proposta de distensionamento entre os princípios constitucionais). Cuestiones constitucionales 43:481–513
Taplin R (2022) Artificial Intelligence, intellectual property, cyber risks and robotics: a new digital age. Routledge, London-New York

Part IV
Reconstruction and New Challenges

A Phenomenology of Thirdness in Law: Preliminary Remarks

Guglielmo Ciaccio and Angela Condello

Abstract This brief philosophical remarks on the figure of the third party within the legal realm aim to describe a phenomenology of thirdness. Various dimensions of human experience show a relevant connection with thirdness: in language, thirdness is the space that transcends words; in politics, as in law, it is the constitutive element of relationships and a fundamental portion of the rule of law; in ethics, finally, the concept of responsibility also, if not above all, rests on the category of thirdness.

These dimensions show a possible common underlying sense of the concept of thirdness. Without delving into one dimension of human experience in particular, the paper briefly shows some emerging properties of thirdness. Thirdness seems to be a fertile possibility to overcome binarism in relationships.

1 Introduction

As the authors of the only legal-philosophical contribution in a volume mainly addressed to scholars engaged with criminal justice, we are aware of the complexity of the task we accepted, for which we want to thank the editors of this Book—both for the occasion to reflect on the figures of the third and on the ontology of third parties in the legal realm and for a continuous and prolific dialogue between legal philosophy and the general theory of criminal procedure.

Our task, to be precise, is the following one: we aim to build a connection between the perspective on thirdness described in this volume, i.e., the perspective mainly related to the juridical contextualization of third parties in procedure from a comparative point of view, and a brief phenomenology of thirdness in law, namely

G. Ciaccio
University of Pisa, Pisa, Italy
e-mail: guglielmo.ciaccio@phd.unipi.it

A. Condello (✉)
University of Messina, Messina, Italy
e-mail: acondello@unime.it

S. Ruggeri et al. (eds.), *Third Parties in Criminal Proceedings*, Legal Studies in International, European and Comparative Criminal Law 10,
https://doi.org/10.1007/978-3-031-73970-5_14

by considering various forms and aspects of thirdness as they emerge within the realm of legal experience.

As a matter of fact, in ordinary language, when we mention the term 'third' we think of different interpretations, both figurative and more concrete: indeed, our mind goes to referents such as the third parties in a trial, or the institutions mediating among conflicting subjects (*e.g.*, the court or the State understood as a thirds), or even to the very conceptualization of the law as a discourse representing other discourses, as well as to the dimension of alterity and transcendence in which all human relations are rooted, both inside and outside the legal regulation (thirdness as an ethical problem linked to intersubjective responsibility *à la* Levinas). It is specifically on this last perspective that we shall try to shed light, with the purpose of finding a way to categorize third parties within an ever-changing world. Because of this complex semantic field, our brief remarks here are aimed at valuing what we phrased a phenomenology of thirdness and not just one of the aspects just mentioned: they shall stem from, in other terms, a broader space of thirdness intersecting the legal and the political realm, as well as the ethical and the logical-linguistic dimension of legal operations. But then, again, we are going to focus mainly on how philosophy can help us defining the very concept of 'third party': what kind of object does such expression refer to, in criminal procedure and more broadly in the legal realm? The core of our text is hence focused on the possibility/impossibility to depict an ontology of thirdness and of third parties: in a world continuously changing, in which the forms of information and communication and interaction are out of a subject's control, it is becoming harder and harder to define a priori what a third party actually is, and we shall see how philosophy actually confirms that thirdness, i.e., the core property of third parties, can only be grasped contextually and pragmatically.

2 Three Levels of Thirdness

Since these are merely preliminary remarks that should help framing the problem of thirdness from a theoretical point of view, we do not intend to go in depth in the singular perspectives (this would be not only inappropriate, but even impossible in such a brief series of remarks).

2.1 Signs, Language

Against this background, we must immediately observe that thirdness is displayed under various forms. At the general level of the connection between words and the world, following Peirce, we can say that thirdness mediates among our system of categories—it usually plays the function of a representation (i.e., what Peirce names 'interpretant') between signs and objects. In other words, at the foundational level of semiotics, on which all our discourses are built, thirdness is a space that transcends the words and the things in the world and correlates these two dimensions. As pointed out by Bobbio, philosophy of law is a metalanguage, a discourse on other language(s)—law, first of all—that have their own semantic rules. Hence, we can say that thirdness concerns legal practices starting from their very basic logical-linguistic structure.

2.2 *Politics, Law*

Following a relevant legal philosophical tradition, what led humanity to have a political and legal organization was the need for a figure aimed at mediating among disagreements. In the *Leviathan*, Hobbes claims that, when conflicts emerge, natural law (that for Hobbes is a rule of reason) obliges the counterparties to "*submit their Right to the judgement of an Arbitrator*".[1]

Such rule is rooted in the idea that nobody can be one's own judge. Not so much for the fact that one can defend a certain position for one's own advantage, but, rather, for the necessity, if one admits that one is one's own judge, to recognize an equal right to the other party as well, essentially making the dispute unresolved—and unsolvable.

It follows that the third party must not have any reason for being partial, with respect to the cause and, above all, that the third must judge fairly, giving to each of the parties what by reason belongs to them. It is by virtue of this that disputes can be decided outside the spectrum of war.[2]

Within the contractualistic horizon, it is perhaps with Locke that impartiality (thirdness in its political meaning) acquires full relevance. It is on it, in fact, that the entire structure of civil society is built, and it is through it that the goodness of absolute monarchy as a form of government is disregarded. If it is true that "it is unreasonable for men to be judges in their own cases", and that to face such situation they create civil governments, "the proper remedy for the inconveniencies of the state of nature", in which men are their own judges, it is impossible not to question the goodness of a government in which "one man, commanding a multitude, has the liberty to be judge in his own case, and may do to all his subjects whatever he pleases, without the least liberty to anyone to question or control those who execute his pleasure".[3] In other words, it is on impartiality that the rule of law is built.

---

[1] Hobbes (1651) I, XV. Analogously, Hobbes (1642) III, 20.

[2] Hobbes writes: "For without that [the Equity], the Controversies of men cannot be determined but by Warre. He therefore that is partiall in judgment, doth what in him lies, to deterre men from the use of Judges, and Arbitrators; and consequently, (against the fundamentall Lawe of Nature) is the cause of Warre". Hobbes (1651) I, XV.

[3] Locke (1688) II, p. 13.

We have seen, briefly, how the need to resolve conflicts, thus preventing their destructive potential, has led to the constitution of thirdness in politics. The very idea of political organization, on closer inspection, seems to manifest itself fully only if it is framed within a triadic scheme of relations. In this sense, in fact, to think of itself as a unit, a dual entity needs the signification that can only be attributed to it by a third party, which therefore constitutes a fundamental component of the relationship: this is the idea of the intrinsic tripolar nature of political (both national and international) institutions developed in Portinaro's work on the political category of the third.[4]

2.3 *Ethics, or Thirdness-Otherness*

Alongside the political-institutional possibility of the thirdness, there is another relevant connotation of such expression: the category of third parties, i.e. all those subjects who are not actually parties within a legal dispute. These subjects are not merely subjects external to the legal relationship, that are to be defined only by their position "outside" such relationship. They are not, therefore, merely subsidiary subjects. The idea is that these subjects are fundamental to the construction of the legal relationship, precisely because of their being "outside" the dual relationship.

As Sartre would have it, "*il faut remarquer que la relation s'est découverte par la médiation d'un tiers*",[5] wich implies that "*les relations réciproques et ternaires sont le fondement de tous les rapports entre les hommes, quelque forme qu'ils puissant prendre ultérieurement*".[6] In other terms, thirdness is a condition of possibility for human relations: such perspective on our theme could be named "ethical", following the work of Lévinas, as it brings the focus on the importance of considering the others as figures of our world, both when we perceive them, and we they are invisible.

This point of view builds an idea of thirdness as a transcendental dimension in which we are all included, those who have a relationship and those who don't, those who are in conflict and those who coexist peacefully.

With Lévinas, the relationship between human beings began to be phrased in ethical and no longer merely in ontological terms. The original experience of responsibility does not derive from a subjective power, but from the engagement with otherness, i.e., with face-to-face relations: "*la notion du visage [...] nous conduit vers une notion de sens antérieur à ma Sinngebung et, ainsi, indépendante de mon initiative et de mon pouvoir. Elle signifie l'antériorité philosophique de*

[4]On this, see in particular Portinaro (1986).

[5]Sartre (1985), p. 218.

[6]*Id.*, p. 223.

l'étant sur l'être, une extériorité qui n'en appelle pasa u pouvoir ni à la possession".[7]

3 Polysemy of a Concept

The three levels of thirdness that we have described are intertwined with each other and they are all relevant from the legal perspective.

In the legal realm, thirdness reveals itself, at least in principle, to be structurally tripolar. At a theoretical level, there are three poles of the legal activity: the norm, the recipient of the norm and the third called upon to resolve conflicts (judge, court, and the dynamics involved in procedure). Moreover, in the realm of procedure the structure is also triadic: there are always two or more parts and then potential third parties—hence, he third dimension can be that of conflict resolution as well as that of the subjects potentially involved in a conflict that might suffer from the consequences of a certain relation: let us say that procedure (both criminal and civil) performs the features of both we have termed the "political" and the "ethical" thirdness.

In a philosophical sense, the *triality of the logos*—the subject who speaks by addressing others within the third space of the discourse—is accompanied by the *thirdness of the nomos*, that is to say, in terms of a rule that does not come from one side and is not imposed on another, but which instead is fulfilled in the "mutual recognition among speaking subjects, which is unconditional and universal and which, as such, forms the core of human law, a law distinct from the laws of things, animals and machines".[8]These forms of thirdness are additional to that of legal judgment, which is such only if it is said, performed, and pronounced by an impartial and disinterested third subject.

This does not mean, however, that the third in the legal realm is necessarily neutral. It becomes, therefore, essential to distinguish between *neutrality* and *impartiality*, where one seems to correspond to the position of those who abstain, while the other seems to be characterized by the need to choose, to judge, to take responsibility of a certain position.[9] As Sergio Cotta clearly states, impartiality is the "condition that structures judgment, without whom there can be no judgment".[10] The impartiality and disinterestedness of the judge are relevant in a deeply philosophical sense, determining, (1) on the one hand, the principle that it is the act that is judged and not the essence of the person—that is, the principle that every human being is a person and, as such, is responsible only for her actions—and, (2) on the other hand, the protection of the equality of all the addressees of the law.

---

[7]Lévinas (1971), p. 44.

[8]Romano (2006), p. 14–15. Our translation.

[9]See Trujillo (2003).

[10]Cotta (1984) p. 430. Our translation.

It is clear, therefore, that if it is possible—although it is far from being peaceful—to think of the State in terms of a neutral third space, the judge, otherwise, can only constitute an impartial thirdness. In both civil and criminal procedures, the trial is constructed as a triangular relationship between the two parties and the judge or between the defendant—or, rather, the defense counsel—, the prosecution and the judge. Such thirdness of the judge must be both personal, namely, there must be no private interest in the outcome of the case,[11] and institutional, namely, it must be devoid of any public or institutional interest.[12]

However, in the contemporary, there is no doubt that all court actions aimed at judging must be impartial and disinterested. Since national sovereignty has been increasingly constrained by supranational pressures, whether euro-communitarian or international, jurisprudence has ceased to be—if it ever was, apart from theorizations—a mere arbitration between private disputes, expressing itself in terms of a third space or dimension that cannot be said to be intrinsically disinterested, but which, on the contrary, tends to promote and preserve certain interests, as it has been clearly argued and demonstrated by Habermas.[13]

And yet, with the loss of the requirement of disinterestedness, there is a risk that a fundamental prerequisite for qualifying a certain judgment as juridical will be lost. On closer inspection, a contrast arises. Either we admit that disinterest is not a constitutive prerequisite of legal impartiality, disconnecting the idea that impartiality and disinterest go hand in hand, or we must question the scope of this impartiality and the idea that talking about thirdness in law means, in the end, discussing the effectiveness of systemic operations. The risk, as Romano points out, is that "a third-function, a de-subjectivized place of the pursuit of the simplification of complexity - necessary for the success of systems"[14] is thus generated. The disinterested impartiality protecting all relationality gives way to the efficiency of the function, to the strength of the success of a result that is only contingent, factual, computable. The purpose, the cause or reason, is replaced by the end, and the third is reduced to being the mechanism functioning behind an organization.[15] And yet, the judge

[11] As Ferrajoli points out, to guarantee this indifference towards the interests at stake, it is necessary for the parties to have the power to refuse to be judged by a certain judge. This is due, above all, to the fact that the judge "must be trusted by the individual and by the subjects judged by him, so that they do not have (and nor can they fear to be in front of) an enemy or in any case an impartial judge". Ferrajoli (1990), p. 595. Our translation.

[12] Ferrajoli also emphasizes the need for the judge to be devoid of an "accusatory interest, and therefore not to simultaneously exercise the functions of accusation as it happens in the inquisitorial rite and, albeit ambiguously, in the mixed rite". Only following such rule, he states furthermore, can "the process maintain its 'cognitive' attitude [...] and it does not degenerate into an 'offensive trial' where the judge becomes the enemy of the offender". *Ibid*. Our translation.

[13] Habermas (1996), especially chapters 4–6.

[14] Romano (2006), p. 27. Our translation.

[15] Against this functional fundamentalism, Romano reaffirms the "artistic" dimension of legal reason, in that the legal judgment "addresses the dysfunctional fullness of the being-subject and not a fragment of it desubjectivized and made functional to the physiology of the market", awakening the ego in its entirety and indivisibility. *Id.*, p. 55. Our translation.

(as third) is the interpreter and guardian of objectivity, both because it calls the legislator to respect the law, and because it distinguishes between those who observe and those who transgress the norm. It is through the action of the courts that the rule of law is consolidated.

Given this overall picture, it becomes important to question the balance between the neutrality of the State and the impartiality of the judge, as well as the correct configuration of their impartiality within the broader frame of the semantic field of thirdness that we have imagined in these preliminary remarks. If none of the powers of the state were neutral, what could its neutrality consist of? And to what extent can the judging organisms be "interested" third parties? Is the impartiality of the judge "affirmed in the direction of the dispute, or of the litigants, or of the subject-matter of the dispute, or of the interests of one rather than the interests of the other, in the direction of the institutional interest or of the public interest"?[16] Finally, how could we reconcile impartiality with fairness, a concept that, given the increasing inequalities in our contemporary societies, will become more and more relevant?

We mentioned at the beginning the polysemy of the expressions 'thirdness' and 'third party' within legal language. While we have thus far focused on the constitutive significance of thirdness in its being a necessary dimension for the construction of the legal institutional world, as well as of legal procedure, it is in relation to this that another form of thirdness is configured, i.e. that form concerning all those who are not parties within the judgement. The issue, already foundational, is gaining relevance increasingly in an era characterized by the universalization of connections between human beings, in the specific sense of the worldwide extension of the effects—due to the diffused uses of new digital technologies—that an action can potentially have and, by consequence, of the enlargement of the group of recipients of the potential consequences of such relationships. The argument could be developed in the following terms: on the one hand, everyone is, at least potentially, a third party vis-à-vis those who take part in a trial; on the other hand, this potentiality—which is not only theoretical, but also practical—determines the need to question how to identify this third party, both with regard to the attribution of responsibility and the identification of legitimate claims.

As far as we are concerned, we will leave the discussion and analysis of the multiple possibilities of concrete identification of third parties to the reflections of those who are properly involved in legal procedure scholarship. Here, instead, we will try to sketch a very brief theoretical framing of the theme, suggesting a link based on the constitutive dimensions of third parties.

It has been mentioned that, for Sartre, thirdness is a condition of existence of human relations. It is endowed with synthetic power. What does this mean? That the unity of duality comes not from itself, but from outside, from the third. Sartre writes: "*le tiers découvre à elle-même la réciprocité qui se referme sur soi en le niant pour le viser de nouveau par sa propre insuffisance*".[17] It means that the reciprocity of the

---

[16] Avitabile (1998), p. 126. Our translation.

[17] Sartre (1985), p. 228.

dual relationship could not exist without that thirdness which, precisely in order to discover itself as reciprocity, it must deny. This reciprocity experienced by referring to the third, and which finds its very foundation in the ternary relationship, constitutes the "*lien fondamental entre les hommes*".[18] This foundational capacity of thirdness, therefore, is open. It means, in other words, that this "third party" does not define the third parties that realize the reciprocity. Indeed, the problem of identifying the third party tends to be unsolvable because, within the social context, there are both indefinite possibilities of being 'third' and an equally indefinite possibility of reciprocity.[19] This complication has its own clear origin: "*la pluralité, c'est-à-dire la multeplicité des organismes agissants*".[20] Can this radical indeterminacy be resolved? On a pragmatic level, Sartre argues, the relationship between individuals can be determined, but only after "*l'ensemble des circostances matérielles sur la base desquelles ce rapport s'établit*"[21] are defined. Therefore, Sartre seems to be suggesting that a "third" can only be defined contextually and according to a specific situation, and that theoretically it is hard, if not impossible, to define what thirdness—in other words, the nature and essence of what is "third" in relation to a certain situation—means, involves, or entails. Philosophy seems to be suggesting, to put it bluntly, that it is wrong to define the metaphysical characteristics of thirdness in advance and that these can instead be grasped only within certain contexts and circumstances.

In this sense, the opposition between the inner tension towards reciprocity and the loneliness of the exteriority of living beings is resolved in a relationship that combines the inner with the outer, reciprocity with loneliness, transforming this opposition into some sort of *sérialité*. As this is dictated by material conditions, it cannot but be, by definition, mutable. If we consider a multitude of people waiting for the bus, they become a group, they determine themselves in their relations of reciprocity and thirdness, by the fact that they are all there waiting for the bus and have, consequently, an interest that puts them in common.[22]

It seems, therefore, impossible to conclusively identify third parties—except within material, and therefore inevitably changeable and contestable, situations. The issue, then, becomes, from a legal point of view, inevitably linked to the question of liability. And, in this sense, the problem becomes specifically that of

[18] *Ibid.*

[19] Quite explicitly: "*d'autant que des individus peuvent se constituer comme tiers en tant que groupes et qu'il peut y avoir des réciprocités de réciprocités et des réciprocités de groupes; enfin, le même individuo u le même groupe peut être engagé dans une action réciproque et, en même temps, se définir comme tiers*". *Id.*, p. 231.

[20] *Ibid.*

[21] *Id.*, p. 363.

[22] "*Ces hommes séparés forment un groupe en tant qu'ils sont tous supportés par un même trottoir qui les protège contre les autos qui traversent la place, en tant qu'ils sont groupés autour de la même station, etc. Et surtout ces individus forment un groupement en ce qu'ils ont un intérêt commun, c'est-à-dire en tant que, sépares comme individus organiques, une structure de leur être pratico-inerte leu rest commune et les unit de l'extérieur*": *Id.*, p. 366.

reciprocity and its constitution. In the multi-level interconnected contemporary world, it becomes very difficult to identify the various multitudes to which a person belongs—and which therefore do not imply recognizable ties—and the various groups, or, to phrase it differently, all the contexts in which relationships of reciprocity and thirdness are identifiable.

The problem, on closer inspection, is far from being marginal. The possibilities of being a third party, we have seen, are basically incalculable. And such impossibility to foresee all the declinations, inevitably, is also reflected in the legal dimension. Suffice it to think of the relevant discussion on intergenerational responsibilities: in a dispute over possible damage done to the environment, are human beings who have not yet been born a third party, or not?[23] Then, the theoretical issue lies precisely in the very possibility of imagining responsibility, both moral and legal, outside of a symmetrical reciprocal relationship. Perhaps a chance could be to move towards the responsibility coming from one's "right to be", as Lévinas would phrase it. After all, "*mon «au monde» ou ma «place au soleil», mon chez-moi, n'ont-ils pas été usurpation des lieux qui sont à l'autre homme déjà par moi opprimé ou affamé?*".[24]

Phenomenologically, it is in the primacy of otherness that we find a fertile possibility for overcoming binarism in relationships. An *Other* that is not just a generic *You* but is above all *every subject* insofar as it is third with respect to a certain relationship, but with respect to which, as we have said, it constitutes the essential element. Hence, we can say that otherness is both necessary and impossible to define once for all. It is paradoxical, in this sense.

The third, with its extraordinary polysemy, invites to go beyond the legal obligation based exclusively on the rationality of interests and the correlation of rights. Hence it reminds us that if we do not want to stick to a merely descriptive identification of third parties according to a scheme designed inevitably to represent duality—right/duty, party/counterparty—it is necessary to try to reason in terms that allow such dualities to open up, in order to imagine thirdness both in its complexity and completeness.

Then, the third party becomes some sort of bridge that binds law to morality, shedding light to the evolution from a responsibility consequent to the expression of subjective power to an inevitable responsibility, constituted by the bond and which is always directed towards third parties, that is, towards everyone because everyone is a third party with respect to a relationship of reciprocity. In other words, as Lévinas would have it, towards that third party who calls me and affects me even if it does not look at me.

[23]The studies by Ferdinando Menga on the subject are groundbreaking: Menga (2016), Menga (2021a); Menga (2021b). Tiziana Andina's also deals with such issues: Andina (2020).

[24]Lévinas (1991), p. 148.

References

Andina T (2020) Transgenerazionalità. Una filosofia per le generazioni future. Carocci, Roma
Avitabile L (1998) Forme del terzo nel diritto. Interpretazione e testi di Kojève, Sartre, Luhmann. Giappichelli, Torino
Cotta S (1984) L'istituzione giudiziaria tra diritto e politica. Rivista di diritto civile XXX
Ferrajoli L (1990) Diritto e ragione. Teoria del garantismo penale. Laterza, Roma-Bari
Habermas J (1996) Between facts and norms. Contributions to a discourse theory of law and democracy. Translated by Rehg W. The MIT Press, Cambridge
Hobbes T (1642) De Cive
Hobbes T (1651) Leviathan
Lévinas E (1971) Totalité et infini. Essai sur l'extériorité. Kluwer Academic
Lévinas E (1991) Entre nous. Essais sur le penser-à-l'autre. Éditions Grasset & Fasquelle, Paris
Locke J (1688) Two treaties of government. In Id., Works (1823), ed. 1963, vol. 5, Scientia Verlag, Aalen
Menga F (2016) Lo scandalo del futuro. Per una giustizia intergenerazionale. Edizioni di Storia e Letteratura, Roma
Menga F (2021a) L'emergenza del futuro. I destini del pianeta e le responsabilità del presente. Donzelli, Roma
Menga F (2021b) Etica intergenerazionale. Morcelliana, Brescia
Portinaro PP (1986) Il terzo. Una figura del politico. Franco Angeli, Milano
Romano B (2006) Sulla trasformazione della terzietà giuridica. Sette domande al giurista e al filosofo. Giappichelli, Torino
Sartre JP (1985) Critique de la raison dialectique, Tome I. Théorie des ensambles pratiques. Librairie Gallimard, Paris
Trujillo I (2003) Imparzialità. Giappichelli, Torino

Third Parties in Criminal Justice: An Everlasting Mystery in a Constantly Developing Legal World?

Stefano Ruggeri

Abstract The evolution of criminal justice, in both national and transnational domain, reveals the multiple roles of an ever-wider range of individuals other than formal participants in criminal proceedings. Criminal inquiries in particular are increasingly characterised by the use of measures addressed against third parties, even more, new digital tools of investigation with enormous potential of interfering with an enormous and often unpredictable number of people. By means of a complex, wider-ranging approach and comparative-law method, this book has dealt with the new roles and protection of third parties. This study cuts across the results achieved by providing a reflection on the procedural thirdness in the light of a comparison between the status of third parties, the role of formal participants and the judicial impartiality. By calling into questions the traditional perspective based upon the idea of extraneousness and disinterestedness, our research proposes a substantial approach to the condition of thirdness, founded on a broader understanding of human participation in the complex experience of the criminal process.

1 Third Parties and the Increasing Complexity of Criminal Justice

The completion of our research allows us now to cut across the results achieved. The difficult aims of this study have led us to choose three main levels of investigation, that is, the perspective of national law concerning six criminal justice systems, the viewpoint of two international human rights courts (namely, the ECtHR and the IACtHR), and the legal frameworks drawn by international criminal law and EU law, viewed along the jurisprudences of the ICC and the CJEU, respectively. To properly combine these levels, several legal competences and disciplines were

S. Ruggeri (✉)
Law Department, University of Messina, Messina, Italy
e-mail: steruggeri@unime.it

S. Ruggeri et al. (eds.), *Third Parties in Criminal Proceedings*, Legal Studies in International, European and Comparative Criminal Law 10,
https://doi.org/10.1007/978-3-031-73970-5_15

needed, from procedural criminal law to constitutional and EU law, substantive criminal law, international law, and ultimately comparative law.

Within this demanding scenario, we could certainly not expect to find a uniform meaning and a coherent system of protection of 'third parties', which fit all the challenges posed by different jurisdictions and legal contexts. If it is more doubtful that an unequivocal notion of 'third parties' exists at all in the general theory of law, and especially in the general theory of procedural law, we must accept that an inevitable degree of relativism is inherent in the concept of procedural thirdness in the field of criminal justice. Several relevant factors may seem to support this outcome, and especially cultural factors reveal relevant developments which are taking place in almost all legal orders, due their transformations and mutual interaction, and the growing level of complexity that criminal justice systems are more and more gaining in the current society.

If criminal justice is perhaps the most reliable yardstick to measure how civilised a certain society is,[1] the shift towards a participatory criminal justice, promoted especially by international human rights jurisprudences and mostly by the caselaw of the ECtHR,[2] requires a fresh examination on some key questions, precisely in the light of a wide-ranging view of criminal trials today. Thus, who can today be considered entitled to be involved in the criminal process? Who should be deemed as a party and who is not? Who can undergo—and mostly, on which grounds and under which conditions—the effects of procedural activities without being a party?

A reflection on such issues has become indispensable especially in the field of criminal investigation, in which no formal participants still exist, and an increasing set of ever newer measures, no matter whether expressly covered by law,[3] touch upon fundamental rights and freedoms of individuals other than suspects, at different levels and in jurisdictions with different tradition and approach. This outcome is surely magnified by the deployment of ever more advanced technological means of investigation with the potential of interfering with an unforeseeable number of people.[4] Moreover, the fact that technological means are more and more used for purposes of criminal control turns out to further blur the division line between prevention and criminal investigation.[5]

A study on the role and safeguards of third parties in criminal proceedings, therefore, provides a privileged viewpoint on the deep changes that criminal trials have undergone in the last decades. It seems no exaggeration to affirm that analysing

---

[1]This assumption, which was recently recalled by Oliviero Mazza [see Mazza 2020], had already been held by different scholars in various times. Cf. already Lucchini (1899), p. 7, and Cordero (1966), p. 17.

[2]Balsamo and Lo Piparo (2008), p. 334 ff.

[3]For an overview of some among the new technological measures of investigation without (specific) legal basis cf. *inter alia* Scalfati (2019).

[4]Such deep transformation can be observed particularly in digital communication intercepts and online searches. See respectively Foti (2022), p. 151 ff., and Di Nuzzo (2022), p. 119 ff; Bachmaier Winter (2021), p. 317 ff.

[5]On this topic, among others, see the recent contributions of Neroni Rezende (2022), p. 67 ff., and Orlando (2022), p. 101 ff.

the legal category of the procedural thirdness enables us to focus the very role of the criminal process today, and particularly the degree of complexity that criminal justice has achieved until now and will presumably achieve in a near future.

2 Participation and Non-Partial (and Impartial) Thirdness: An Inevitable Dichotomy?

To start with, we should take into consideration that the problem of third parties in criminal justice is a portion of a much more general and complex problem that concerns the relevance of thirdness in law. Following a traditional approach, thirdness, far from being a stand-alone category, is a part of a dialectical relationship between two essential concepts, *i.e.*, those of thirdness and participation. That procedural law is mainly focused on the participants, and especially on those who hold the status of formal parties to judicial proceedings, has long led legal scholarship to understand this relationship in terms of a dichotomy.

At first glance, this approach appears to best fit the field of criminal justice, from at least two main perspectives. The first one directly relates to third parties, understood as all those individuals who, without holding the status of formal participants in criminal inquiries or court proceedings, are either involved in procedural activities or are (often severely) affected by procedural measures. To be sure, this view does not exclude the existence of some common points that bring both concepts of thirdness and participation closer to each other. On the one hand, unlike in other procedural experiences, in criminal justice formal parties may not necessarily be defined so for holding prosecutorial powers or being able to lodge claims. On the other, even formal participants can be involved in criminal proceedings against their will and can be seriously jeopardised by procedural acts and means of investigation, as happens to defendants who do certainly not decide to be subjected to a criminal enquiry nor to be brought to court. Yet it is precisely their formal status that enables formal participants to play a proactive role and exercise those rights and safeguards which are legally acknowledged to them, whereas third persons generally lack the right to actively intervene in the proceedings, and to accede procedural tools and safeguards—or this possibility is weak and fragmentary, as clearly shown by the comparative-law analysis of the jurisdictions selected in this study.

Furthermore, a second and not less relevant perspective may seem to confirm the exactness of the traditional way of approaching the relationship between formal and third parties in terms of an irreducible alternative. This perspective does not relate to the safeguards due to third parties but focuses on the fundamental role of the judge who, for historical and today also institutional grounds, is a constitutive component of every model of judicial process, and especially of every criminal process, as the most powerful tool of administrating justice in terms of a law-founded experience of *dike*.[6] It is not a coincidence that in the old Greek culture, precisely the involvement of a third person or body, understood as a non-party and therefore an impartial subject, ensured the evolution from the old revenge-based *bia* to a new social and legal order in which adjudicating by means of a trial turned out to be the main factor of creating law.[7] Moreover, even today, the activation of any judicial process presupposes the institution of an impartial body, which as such sets an indispensable condition for the existence of a truly fair trial and mainly of a final decision aimed at producing the effects of *ne bis in idem*.[8]

It is in the light of the impartiality of judicial authorities, and of decision-makers in general,[9] that the judge is often conceived of as a third person. Remarkably, Salvatore Satta, reflecting on the mystery of the judicial process by focusing on the experience of revolutionary trial, envisaged the core essence of any trial in the requirement that judgment be rendered by an impartial third person.[10] It is also worth noting that today the guarantee of judicial thirdness is enshrined in some constitutional charters (*e.g.*, in the Italian Constitution).[11]

One might wonder why such different meanings of the procedural thirdness exist, and above all, *how* they can co-exist. Manifestly, there are enormous differences between the role of judges and that of third parties—so enormous, indeed, that we could argue that we are dealing with two quite opposites notions of procedural thirdness. The thirdness of judges—and especially of the criminal judges—aims to preserve their neutrality and reflects a disinterestedness that is a necessary condition for decision-making. By contrast, this condition does not fit the situation of third

[6]On this second perspective, oriented towards the procedural thirdness of judges, see Ciaccio and Condello, in this volume.

[7]For an in-depth reflection on this transformation starting with Aeschylus' Oresteia cf. Lo Giudice (2023), p. 61 ff.

[8]Remarkably, international human rights caselaw tends to relativise the effects of this fundamental safeguard in cases of rulings issued by a judicial body that lacks independence and impartiality. See IACtHR, 24 October 2012, *Nadege Dorzema and others v. Dominican Republic*, § 195.

[9]This requirement, indeed, does not solely regard judges bu. also other bodies empowered to decision-making, such as the juries in common law countries.

[10]Satta (1949), p. 284 ff.

[11]Moreover, the evolution of criminal justice shows that impartiality (together with independence) provides a strong protective shield against revenge not only in decision-making processes but must also in the investigative phase. Indeed, this essential requirement must characterise, albeit with some relevant adjustments, the legal action of public prosecutors as well, by requiring a proper and exhaustive investigation of the alleged offence with a view to verifying whether there is a need to institute a criminal trial against a person accused of a crime. Remarkably, in countries based upon the principle of mandatory prosecution, this has traditionally been considered linked to the fundamental requirements of *par condicio* and independency of the judiciary. It is precisely this viewpoint that shows that both the procedural context and that of the overall legal order in which each trial is carried out determine the pre-condition of a true equality of arms. Thus, where the judicial authority lacks thirdness from both such perspectives, *par condicio*, far from being a pillar of a fair trial, turns out to be a merely proclaimed principle. In the European scenario, furthermore, a huge debate has recently emerged on the developments occurred in supranational caselaw on the independence of public prosecutors in the field of judicial cooperation. See Falcone (2021).

persons who are neither neutral nor disinterested in relation to the ongoing procedure.

We shall see that this assumption calls for in-depth reflection on the notion of 'procedural participation', while opening a very useful perspective that will enable us to better understand the essence of procedural thirdness as well. Yet it is apparent that at least one point of convergence brings these two meanings of procedural thirdness closer to each other. On close examination, the neutral position of the judges should not only be defined in relation to the formal parties to judicial proceedings, but also to a wider range of persons, which encompasses all those who can undergo the effects of procedural acts and measures, not to mention also those forces and factual powers that can have a strong impact on some judicial processes.[12]

This conclusion could revolutionise the traditional understanding of our problem and of the judicial impartiality, at the same time. From this it follows, indeed, that the thirdness of judicial bodies and that of third parties are closely connected to each other, to the extent that the one can be properly defined only in the light of the other, and *vice versa*.

While this *trait d'union* may seem to call into question the traditional way of approaching the procedural thirdness in general, a closer look at this category from a different viewpoint reveals that it fits neither the standing of the third judge nor that of the third party in the field of criminal justice.

The traditional justification of the judicial thirdness, indeed, lies in the experience of strongly contentious trials, which are typical of civil proceedings, whose basic structure is characterised by one plaintiff (*primus*) and one defendant (*secundus*).[13] This structure, however, is manifestly not adequate for criminal trials. Especially in those criminal justice systems that allow the institution of civil-law actions within criminal proceedings, but also in those jurisdictions in which forms of private prosecution are permitted, it is apparent that the judicial thirdness is a too reductive way of describing the judge's complex role today and his duty to ensure a constant balancing among the (often) conflicting interests regarding not only *primus* and *secundus* but furthermore, at least, all those who are formal parties to judicial proceedings. Yet even this conclusion is clearly misleading, since there is an ever wider number of people whose freedoms can be impinged upon and whose interests need be balanced in almost all criminal justice systems, which confirms the need to redefine the notion of judicial impartiality in the light of the strict link that, as we noted, exists between the judicial thirdness and the standing of third parties.

Furthermore, these considerations also suggest adopting a critical approach to the traditional understanding of third parties as such in criminal justice. It is clear that their standing can no longer be defined in relation to the sole formal parties, who

---

[12] See again Satta (1949), p. 286.

[13] This does not rule out the existence of various forms of involvement or intervention of third parties in civil trials with contentious structure, which often also entail the assumption of the role of parties to the judicial proceedings.

might be more than the public prosecutor and the accused, thus encompassing further participants such as the damaged parties, the victims, eventual private prosecutors, and so on. But a close examination shows that individuals other than formal participants cannot be deemed to be third parties even in strongly dualistic criminal trials and with regard to either *primus* or *secundus*. In particular, it seems extremely difficult to accept a relationship between third parties and public prosecutors who, regardless of their standing in domestic jurisdictions, can never be equated to private individuals. In other words, *e.g.* a witness or a family member of the victim could be treated as a *tertius* in relation to the defendant but will never be a *tertius* in a rigorous sense and in relation to the public prosecutor, who holds a different role and function from those of any other private parties involved in criminal proceedings.

Moreover, the standing of a third party may fit even less the dynamics of criminal investigations, even though this category is more and more used in relation to new investigative measures. Thus, especially when a pre-trial inquiry is instituted and carried out against unknown suspects, it is apparent that any other individual involved in the ongoing inquiry cannot be seen as a third person in a strict sense, nor can there be any relational link between them and law enforcement bodies, or the competent prosecutor or any judge intervening the procedure.

Based on such arguments, we can therefore affirm that this category is not appropriate to the needs of criminal justice and the peculiar features of the criminal process, which render it a unique legal phenomenon. The criminal trial, indeed, can be compared to no other procedural experience, and even in its most elementary structure, it is so far away from contentious dualistic trials that a true thirdness appears to be a conventional and somewhat misleading notion. Maintaining a perspective founded on a dichotomy between parties and non-parties, *i.e.*, third parties and impartial bodies respectively, can therefore produce more confusion than clarity in approaching the complexity of today's criminal proceedings and the developments that we are witnessing in most criminal justice systems.

3 From Extraneousness to Substantial Involvement: Thirdness and Participation as a Continuum

These conclusions suggest us to choose an alternative perspective to deal with our topic. It has been observed that reflecting on the procedural thirdness in the light of the ongoing evolution of criminal justice shows that thirdness and participation share more elements than those which distinguish them, and somehow even converge towards a set of common problems.

The most difficult one, as has been noted, is the lack of a clear division line between of the categories of formal and third parties. At first glance, it is a simple task to identify those who are parties to a criminal trial, while the notion of procedural thirdness is far from being clear and well-defined. Only judges can be identified clearly, even though we saw that the relevance and rationale of the judicial thirdness need be reconstructed in relation to a wider range of people other than that of formal participants. On the contrary, the traditional concept of third parties, understood in negative terms, can potentially be extended without limits, encompassing several and very heterogeneous categories of individuals. But it is clear that the procedural thirdness would turn out to be a somewhat useless category without any clear features. Thus, including all those who are *not* parties to the proceedings, says almost nothing that helps delimit these individuals, since everybody other than formal participants might be a third party.

It is interesting to note, moreover, that not only the category of third parties but also that of formal parties is not as self-evident as it might seem to be. This is evident in those jurisdictions in which popular prosecution is permitted (*e.g.* Spain): this model is particularly relevant for the purposes of this research, showing that any citizen is potentially a third party but may become a formal party, depending on their decision.[14] But a similar outcome can materialise in those criminal justice systems in which victims are entitled to institute criminal proceedings, for the number of the aggrieved parties is not always predictable in advance. Furthermore, there is little doubt that the "exercise of civil actions in criminal proceedings also contributes to blurring the dividing line between parties and third parties", for civil-law actions often involve in criminal proceedings a number of legal entities encompassing insurance companies, state and regional authorities, and so on, as rightly pointed out by Fernando Gascón and Guillermo Schumann.[15] It is worth observing, moreover, that even those countries which do not allow for forms of private prosecution, such as Italy, acknowledge an increasing number of safeguards to the injured person who, regardless of the possibility of lodging a civil-law claim, therefore gains a substantial role of a party.[16]

In more general terms, and independently from the characteristics of each criminal justice system, the need to promptly identify the aggrieved parties holds enormous practical relevance, since the failure to involve them in criminal proceedings may severely impact on the outcome of the criminal trial and the force of *res iudicata*. The evolution not only of ECtHR caselaw,[17] but also of domestic

[14] Cf. Gascón Inchausti and Schumann Barragán, in this volume, para. 1.4. Similarly, in Portugal, any citizen may request to be constituted as an assistant under the Popular Action Law, with a view to the protection of diffuse or collective interests. See Gouveia de Caires, Reis Barata, in this volume, para. 1.4.4.

[15] *Ibid.*, para. 1.2.

[16] As a consequence, legislative terminology has progressively been adapted to these developments, so that Italian code of criminal procedure today contains some reference to the injured party (*parte offesa*).

[17] ECtHR, *Sabalić v. Croazia*, judgment of 14 January 2021, Appl. No. 50231/13, on which cf. Di Nuzzo (2021), p. 465 ff. For an in-depth examination of this topic see recently Malino (2021), p. 81 ff.

constitutional jurisprudence,[18] clearly shows that in criminal matters the *auctoritas rei iudicatae* largely depends on the subjective limits of the effects of criminal judgements, which limits should today however be redefined from the viewpoint of the victims as well. Remarkably, this does not only concern the binding effects of criminal judgments in civil trials instituted with a view to compensation for damages caused by the offence, but furthermore the ban on new proceedings against the same person on the same *res iudicanda*. Thus, the fact that the aggrieved parties have not been granted a fair opportunity to be involved in the criminal trial can weaken the guarantee of *ne bis in idem*.

It is also noteworthy that the European Court of Justice, by dealing with the transnational *ne bis in idem*, has also acknowledged the importance of giving the victim a fair opportunity for being heard already during the investigative phase, as a pre-condition for pre-trial orders to gain the effects of final decisions in cross-border situations. A remarkable case was adjudicated in *Kossowksi*,[19] in which the Court significantly extended this argument to victims and witnesses. This reasoning is of the utmost systematic importance, insofar as it blurs the traditional division line between formal and third parties, demonstrating that the overall fairness of a criminal trial can also largely depend on how effectively victims and even witnesses, who have traditionally been deemed to be extraneous to criminal proceedings, have been involved in criminal proceedings.

Moreover, we might surprisingly find out that the extraneousness to the ongoing trial—which, as noted, has traditionally been considered the typical feature of the procedural thirdness and the essential point of convergence of its two main notions, respectively in terms of judicial neutrality and equal distance from the parties, and disinterestedness of third parties in relation to *res iudicanda*—could also regard formal participants, and even the main parties to criminal proceedings. Comparative law may even show that in some countries, the procedural thirdness could be characterised by a relationship between the judicial authorities, the formal parties, and further private individuals in quite opposite terms than those that we have described hitherto. For instance, the fact that in Spain certain crimes can only be prosecuted by the victim leads to the result that the public prosecutor, being unable to assume the role of a party to the proceedings,[20] should be treated as a third party. Paradoxically, even the accused may turn out to be extraneous to their own trial, an outcome that can materialise in different situations: *e.g.*, a police arrest of the alleged perpetrator might result in being unlawful and could not be judicially validated, with the consequence that the arrested person must immediately be released and treated as a third person. Moreover, it is apparent that, whenever the defendant, after having been formally accused, is acquitted for not having taken part in the criminal *affair*, he

[18] An emblematic case was the Eternit case, dealt with by the Italian Constitutional Court in the judgment No. 200 of 2016 that declared Article 649 of the code of criminal procedure, *i.e.*, the provision regarding the *ne bis in idem*, unconstitutional.

[19] CJEU, Grand Chamber, *Kossowski*, judgment of 29 June 2016, C-486/14.

[20] Gascón Inchausti and Schumann Barragán, in this volume, para. 1.4.

inevitably becomes extraneous to *res iudicanda*.[21] Furthermore, other formal parties, or those who are entitled to assume such status, can also turn out to be extraneous to questions regarding *res iudicanda* that are strictly concerned with their interests: *e.g.*, where domestic law enables public prosecutors to bring a civil-law action on behalf of the damaged party, who chooses not to lodge it, the latter inevitably gains the status of a third party in his own case.

On the contrary, it would be difficult to imagine that formal participants may become extraneous to the ongoing procedure for the simple fact that they decide not to intervene in a specific stage, or not to lodge a legal remedy and give rise to a further instance of the proceedings. Manifestly, the accused remain such—and most importantly, must still be granted fundamental safeguards, starting with the presumption of innocence—even if they do not appeal the judgment challenged by the public prosecutor's office or a private prosecutor, if any. Moreover, where domestic law permits them to take part in the appeal proceedings activated by another co-defendant and allows for some decisions to produce certain beneficial effects also in their favour, this means that no *res iudicata* has materialised in relation to them, notwithstanding their decision not to challenge these decisions, but they still maintain the status of parties to criminal proceedings. A similar outcome can be observed in relation to other formal participants: *e.g.*, Italian caselaw has acknowledged the possibility of the court of appeal to rule on the civil-law claim in spite of the failure by the damaged party to challenge the decision against which the public prosecutor's office has lodged an appeal, which demonstrates that the damaged party remains a formal participant in a higher instance as well.

A somehow different discussion should be made in relation to the judicial thirdness, starting with reconsidering, however, the standing of judges as non-partial bodies, which is also not so clear as it seems to be. That judges are—and must be—extraneous to the case under their examination, as noted, is a quite obvious pre-condition of decision-making. This does not however mean that judges can always maintain the necessary neutrality which enable them to ensure proper trade-offs among all the conflicting interests at stake. As is well-known, a number of relevant factors can impinge on the judicial neutrality and inevitably affect their impartiality. Alongside exogenous factors, among which a significant role is undoubtedly played by the enormous potential of mass and social media to orient and often even manipulate the public opinion with regard to alleged offences that are

[21] In some countries, this result enables the competent authorities to question such defendants pursuant to the ordinary rules on witnesses testimony. Italian law, for example, provides for a hybrid regulation regarding witnesses with legal assistance (*testimonianza assistita*), which in certain situations may also concern co-accused tried in separate proceedings. It is interesting to note, however, that in the case described in the text, following a landmark ruling of the Constitutional Court (judgment No. 381 of 2006), the co-accused acquitted for being extraneous to the case at stake no longer need be assisted by a lawyer, with the result that this situation bring them closer to the regime laid down for normal witnesses.

still under investigation,[22] some endogenous factors can also have a strong impact on the judicial impartiality.

In particular, the acknowledgment of excessive powers of *ex officio* intervention by judicial authorities in evidence-gathering procedures can alter the standing of judges as impartial bodies. Moreover, this outcome can also be due to the exercise of other judicial powers, particularly of the power to change the legal classification of the alleged offence as resulting from the indictment, as has emerged from the European caselaw dealing with the repercussions on the right to effective defence of the *iura novit curia* principle,[23] as happened in the landmark *Drassich* case.[24] Even limiting the possibility of legal re-classification of facts to the sole cases regarding the so-called 'apparent concurrence' (*Scheinkonkurrenz*), it is clear that the judicial interference with the prosecutorial competence to formulate and amend the indictment inevitably entails the bringing forward of the adjudication process, which does not appear to be compatible with an impartial decision-making.

But what is to be understood by formulations such as 'non-partial' or 'impartial'? We saw that the traditional idea of extraneousness may turn out to be a rather misleading concept that gives rise to more confusion than clarity, not only because even formal participants may result in being extraneous to their own case, but also, and more significantly, because several categories of individuals who are usually deemed as third parties (witnesses, owners of goods etc.) may not be deemed to be truly extraneous to *res iudicanda*. Thus, even third parties, whenever their rights and freedoms have been affected by procedural measures adopted on the basis of *fumus delicti*, are all the more interested in participating in criminal proceedings, or at least in taking part in those specific procedures regarding their interests (*e.g.*, a procedure aimed at a judicial review of search or seizure of assets, a procedure concerning the selection of the information obtained through digital communication intercepts, and so on). That the range of these individuals is not always predictable—and procedural measures with massive intrusive effects are more and more carried out in criminal inquiries against several unforeseeable people—magnifies, as noted, the difficulty of identifying the exact limits of the category of third parties. Nevertheless, there is no doubt that these third parties are fully entitled to be involved in (and therefore to be treated as parties to) criminal proceedings from a substantial viewpoint. The main

---

[22] The impact of mass and social media on the tasks of the judiciary can be observed already in the pre-trial phases. Thus, even in those jurisdictions in which the competence for carrying our criminal inquiries does not lie with investigative magistrates or judges but with public prosecutors and the judicial police, while special judges act as guarantors for the safeguarding of fundamental rights (the so-called *jueces de garantías* in Spanish-speaking countries), there is a risk that trials by media may strongly influence the tasks of both the prosecutorial and the judicial authorities in the pre-trial inquiries.

[23] For in-depth analysis of the European jurisprudence and an interesting reconstruction of this problem see Quattrocolo (2011).

[24] ECtHR, *Drassich v. Italy*, judgment of 11 December 2007, Appl. No. 25575/04. As to EU caselaw, see more recently CJEU, *BK*, judgment of 9 November 2022, C-175/22.

challenge is precisely to find a way of enhancing their participatory rights, while preserving their condition (and the corresponding safeguards) of third parties.

Therefore, a human rights perspective, based upon the interference with (or the risk of restriction on) individual rights, may seem to provide the best methodological criterion to define whether individuals other than formal participants need to be treated as parties to criminal trials, or at least to specific interim procedures within criminal proceedings. Furthermore, a substantial parameter appears to be the best way of approaching also the role of victims in criminal proceedings, regardless of their different status in European jurisdictions. We saw that various countries enable the aggrieved parties to institute a criminal trial, or to act as concurrent or accessory prosecutors. However, even in those jurisdictions that walked a different road, it would be somewhat paradoxical, viewed from a human rights perspective, if precisely the aggrieved parties were to be considered extraneous to a trial aimed at ascertaining the criminal liability for a conduct that allegedly caused them harm or endangered their rights and legal goods, only because domestic law does not grant them the role of formal parties. It is worth observing that in the field of international criminal justice, the role of victims and especially the relationships among them, formal participants, and third parties have evolved considerably according to different jurisdictions. As Ana Beltrán clearly put it,

> procedural participation of the victim in the proceedings before the ICC has been a novelty with respect to the international criminal tribunals created previously, since for the first time it allows, albeit as 'participants' and not as 'parties', their intervention in the procedural proceedings.[25]

In the light of this, it might be argued that in the field of criminal justice, the two notions of procedural thirdness and procedural participation, far from being antithetical legal concepts, reveal different parts of a common phenomenon. Following the approach adopted decades ago by Francesco Carnelutti, we might distinguish between a formal and a substantial (or material) involvement in judicial proceedings. This distinction proves very useful, notwithstanding it would surely be impossible to transpose to criminal trials the idea of a dispute or litigation (*lite*), on which Prof. Carnelutti founded his entire construction of the civil process and that led him to draw a division line between third parties who can become substantial participants in a dispute (*e.g.* by means of a joint intervention in the court proceedings) and those who are formal parties to the judicial trial for being able to institute them through a civil-law action.[26] Thus, while individuals other than those who hold the power (or the right) to lodge a criminal-law action can also formally participate in criminal proceedings, the great (and constantly increasing) number of persons who are not entitled to be formal participants encompasses people who, either for having been affected by the alleged offence (the victim) or for undergoing restrictions on their fundamental rights through intrusive measures based on a *fumus delicti* (third parties), deserve to be considered as substantial parties too.

[25] Beltrán Montoliu, in this volume, para. 1.

[26] Carnelutti (1936), p. 393 ff.

A unified approach, therefore, shows the clear convergence of thirdness and participation towards a common conceptual line and requires us to view them as different components of a continuum. But most interestingly, this perspective also allows us to look at the judicial impartiality with different eyes. Certainly, the judge's independence from any influence by other state powers must be preserved at all costs, which is the precondition of a true thirdness. The judicial impartiality, however, works on a different level. That judges must have no interest in the case subjected to their examination, for not being affected or damaged by the alleged offence nor having allegedly committed it, justifies, as noted, their thirdness in relation to *res iudicanda* and the main parties. Yet it does not entail that fact-finders remain uninvolved in the proceedings during the entire decision-making process. Adjudication, far from being the ultimate goal of the criminal process, cuts across the overall procedure and all the steps of the judicial activity, in which judges must always maintain their non-partiality by not sharing the claims and views of individual parties. Even in those criminal justice systems that are strongly characterised by the concentration of prosecutorial powers in the hands of independent public prosecutors, there must remain a clear division line between prosecutorial and decision-making powers, so that judge must never hold the tasks of prosecutorial bodies.

This does not mean that the judicial thirdness rules out any substantial involvement in a criminal trial, even though this assumption must be interpreted correctly. Far from maintaining a passive role and a distance from everything and everybody, by finding facts and law during the all process, the judge—unlike any party—must make all the necessary efforts to embrace all the individual partialities. It is noteworthy that, according to the second of the three maxims elaborated by Immanuel Kant in relation to the *sensus communis* in his *Critique of Judgment*, adjudication does not only imply thinking for oneself but furthermore, and above all, think from the standpoint of everyone else. From the perspective of the legal (and mostly of the judicial) judgment, it follows that the judge, by means of "a broadened way of thinking",

> overrides the private subjective conditions of his judgment, into which [. . .] others are locked [. . .], and reflects on his own judgment from a *universal standpoint* (which he can determine only by transferring himself to the standpoint of others).[27]

This way of thinking must be maintained untouched until the time in which the power of *ius dicere* will be exercised. Yet in this extraordinary moment, in which the judge will not act as an individual but as the voice of the entire legal order, he will also consume his own impartiality and being called upon to decide in *one* direction, he will also share *one* among the existing partialities and thus inevitably become a party. This is demonstrated by the fact that judges can never rule again on the same matter they have adjudicated, a fundamental rule existing in almost all procedural

[27] Kant (1987), paras. 294 ff. For in-depth analysis of Kant's approach and its implications on the legal judgment see Lo Giudice (2023), p. 141 ff.

experiences, which confirms that the judicial impartiality, differently from the *communis opinio*, is far removed from a non-partiality.

The need to maintain distance from individual parties, therefore, requires the judge to encompass the standpoint of everybody by adopting a broad perspective. This standing has often been confused with a position *super partes*, *i.e.*, above all parties, whereas it consists in the quite super-human task of encompassing all the possible partialities by remaining on the same footing. There is little doubt that this is also a form of participation, understood in the etymological sense of the word. Yet this broad involvement in the case, which is far away from a condition of extraneous to the case, also has an inevitable time-limit that is marked by the moment in which the decision-making process is completed and *res iudicanda* is adjudicated. In this very moment, the judge, who has until then been 'des-interested', or to say in more rigorous terms, engaged in understanding and embracing the interests of all parties, shares one partiality, and by doing so, loses any further possibility of thinking in that broad way on the same subject matter.

The problem arises when a judicial body is not only empowered to prefer charges but also to gather evidence and rule on the accusation *inaudita altera parte*. Such a situation, which unfortunately still existed in a recent past and can still be observed in some procedural experiences, highlights a pathological mixture of roles, which entails the consequence that the judge, by exercising the functions of a prosecutor, becomes a partial body before and during the decision-making process.[28]

4 Towards an Overall Fair Trial in the Light of Procedural Thirdness

4.1 Relativising the Participation in Criminal Proceedings by Means of a De-Formalised Approach

The adoption of a substantial approach, based upon a human rights perspective, has therefore led us to overcome the rigid distinction between a non-participatory thirdness and a formal participation in criminal proceedings, founded on the traditional dichotomy between extraneousness and intraneousness to *res iudicanda*. The convergence of third and formal parties towards the common perspective of their involvement in criminal proceedings now requires us to redefine the very concept of procedural participation depending on various factors, which include, along with the roles of parties and the types of the proceedings, the individual and state-related interests that can be brought about in criminal trials and need to be managed and often balanced with each other.

In the light of this, one might wonder whether it is meaningful to maintain a unified approach, based on a formal division between those who are parties to the

[28] Cordero (1966), p. 589.

overall criminal procedure and those who are not. A close examination of the dynamics of criminal trials and the increasing number of interim and pre-trial procedures (mainly, the remand proceedings and further procedures regarding coercive measures) has shown that even the number of formal participants can largely vary during the criminal process according to several situations (acquittal of some defendants, separation of the proceedings, or *vice versa*, the re-unification of different procedures, and so on). Is has also be observed that individuals who were initially extraneous to the criminal trial are allowed to joint it (*e.g.* by way of instituting a civil-law action), and above all, that an increasing number of persons, despite being still defined as third or non-parties, can be touched upon by procedural acts and intrusive means of investigation.

It is precisely this phenomenon that suggests us to rethink the very concept of individual involvement by considering as participants—and providing with the necessary participatory safeguards—also all those individuals who are concerned with some interim procedures (arrest proceedings, remand proceedings, procedures on communication intercepts, etc.). In other words, nothing obliges us to use the categories of formal and informal parties in relation to the entire criminal trial. By contrast, the dynamics of criminal proceedings and the peculiarities of interim procedures, together with the different degree of involvement of several persons in such procedures, justifies broadening the idea of participation to those who are involved in those procedures which are specifically concerned with their interests. This approach, which looks at the effectiveness of involvement in criminal proceedings more than at the formal role of individuals, highlights the potentials of a broad and flexible notion of 'participation' that now enables us to deal with some problematic issues.

4.2 The Victim's Right to Access to Justice

The dialectical relationship between participation and the right to access to justice gains different features depending on the role of the individuals concerned. A specific perspective deserves consideration in this regard, from the viewpoint of our study, namely the victim's right to access to justice, especially within those legal systems and in those circumstances which, as has been noted, do not allow them to assume the role of formal participants. Such situations hold particular relevance within ECHR law, in the light of the jurisprudence of the ECtHR, which more and more tends to consider the injured person as a party to criminal proceedings from a substantial viewpoint. Thus, the case-law elaborated since *Arnoldi v. Italy* and further developed by subsequent jurisprudence—albeit still mainly linked to the perspective of enabling the aggrieved parties to take part in the criminal process with a view to exercising their civil rights—has strengthened the protection of victims by extending to them the safeguards that Article 6 ECHR grants the damaged party, starting with the right to a reasonable length of the proceedings, whenever their claim for justice has been frustrated by the prosecution being time-barred due to the excessive duration of the criminal inquiry.[29] According to Strasbourg case-law, the acknowledgment of fair trial rights, including the right to be heard personally, does therefore not depend on the existence of a formal role in criminal proceedings, with the result that these must be granted to both the person who has gained the status of a formal damaged party and to those who, although being entitled, were hindered to do so by the (in)activity of the investigative bodies, and thus deserve to be treated as substantial participants.

Notwithstanding its merits, a substantial approach to participatory rights encounters inevitable limits, which can put at risk their proper protection. In particular, in those jurisdictions in which the institution of criminal proceedings remains in the hands of the competent public prosecutor, the victim's claim for justice will remain unheard if the aggrieved party neither holds the right to start prosecution nor can request the intervention of a judge. In such cases, the possibility of lodging a complaint before the ECtHR, as well as the mechanisms established by domestic law to comply with a European judgment that found a breach of one or more safeguards enshrined by the Convention, including a retrial, will not be able to change this outcome, insofar as there is still no opportunity for the injured person to determine the institution of the criminal process. Yet, according to constant Strasbourg caselaw, the European Convention does not provide any binding indications in this regard, as it does not acknowledge the defendant's "right to demand the prosecution and the conviction of the accused".[30]

4.3 The Problem of the Accused's Personal (and Effective) Involvement in Criminal Proceedings

A de-formalised approach, moreover, can be useful to deal with the formal parties, or those who can assume such role, who, as noted, may also happen to assume a third position in criminal proceedings. This approach, indeed, characterises the evolution of the European caselaw regarding some essential safeguards of the accused, *e.g.* the privilege against self-incrimination, which must not only be given to the person against whom no formal accusation has yet been raised, but also to the individual who is not even formally under investigation and nevertheless runs the risk of being subjected to a criminal investigation (in particular, during police questioning), as well as to the person subjected to certain administrative-law inquiries.

Remarkably, a discussion on the procedural thirdness allows us to re-examine from a different perspective some core questions regarding the accused's involvement in criminal trials, which relate to their personal participation in judicial hearings and in other procedural activities. This problematic topic has been examined with comparative-law method and interdisciplinary approach in a study that has

[29] See extensively Orlando, in this volume, para. 2.1.

[30] *Ibid.*

been published in this Book Series,[31] and which has highlighted the different relevance of the defendant's personal contribution in the criminal process depending on general features of every criminal justice system. Within this framework, the way of displaying this contribution in terms of an individual right or a duty aimed at ensuring a proper fact-finding gains particular importance from the perspective of this study.

Comparative law shows that a few jurisdictions require the accused to be present at trial, as a rule. Most criminal justice systems hold a somewhat neutral standing in relation to the accused's presence at trial and in court proceedings in general, which justifies the compromise-like approach adopted by EU institutions in Directive 2016/343/UE. In other words, defendants are allowed to take part personally in criminal process instituted against them, but they are generally not required to do so, since the criminal process can follow its course, and the accused who have been tried *in absentia* can therefore be adjudicated and even convicted.

This approach has been considerably smoothed by the evolution of European caselaw. Since the landmark decision *Colozza v. Italy*,[32] the European Court has progressively defined the requirements justifying the carrying out of criminal proceedings in default, by acknowledging the general right of defendants to be granted a fair opportunity for taking part personally in their own trial, along with (and without excluding) the right to be assisted by a lawyer. Significantly, the complementary role of personal and legal assistance was confirmed by the fact that even in those cases in which the European judges recognised the obligation of the accused with legal knowledge to participate in criminal proceedings, while providing for the possibility of certain sanctions to avoid "unjustified absences",[33] they expressly ruled out that such sanctions could imply depriving the accused of legal assistance, and in particular of the right to appoint a lawyer of their own choosing.[34]

The most interesting aspect of this problem, from the viewpoint of this study, regards how the way of conceiving the role of accused in criminal proceedings has evolved thanks to European caselaw. Far from being a mere object of fact-finding in the hands of the authorities holding the state's prosecutorial power, defendants have also ceased to be the absent holder of rights in a trial that could start and proceed without them, and ceased to be a third party in their own trial!

The most relevant implication of the acknowledgment by European caselaw of the defendant's right to personally participate in criminal proceedings is that, regardless of the approach adopted by European jurisdictions, the domestic

[31] Quattrocolo and Ruggeri (2019).

[32] ECtHR, *Colozza v. Italy*, judgment of 12 February 1985, Appl. No. 9024/80.

[33] ECtHR, *Poitrimol v. France*, judgment of 23 November 1993, Appl. No. 14032/88, para. 35.

[34] To be sure, the Court has never provided clear indications as to the nature of such sanctions, by limiting itself to laying down what could *not* be used to sanction the accused. Along with legal assistance, European caselaw Court also ruled out national law adopting drastic measures to obtain the defendant's presence by coercive means, *e.g.* by requiring that defendants should undergo pre-trial imprisonment to challenge a conviction issued against them. In this sense cf. ECtHR, *Poitrimol v. France*, para. 38. On this topic see Negri (2014), p. 149 ff.

authorities must set all the necessary conditions which enable the accused to exercise their right to make their own contribution to fact-finding. Such conditions must preferably occur in advance, in order to reduce to the minimum extent the risk that a criminal trial is instituted and conducted against a person who was not properly informed of the charges preferred, and who was not put in a position to choose whether to take part in court proceedings. But when this is impossible, the relevance of this fundamental right in the framework of a participatory understanding of criminal justice—and the corresponding obligation of the competent authorities—is such that the accused must be granted a new trial. Significantly, this result must be ensured even after conviction has become final, and if a domestic remedy does not exist, the strong convergence of European jurisprudence and EU legislation has led to the acknowledgment of the need to adopt *ad hoc* mechanisms aimed at granting defendants unlawfully tried *in absentia* the right to a retrial.

Despite the merits of European caselaw and EU legislative intervention, there is still certain reluctance by several jurisdictions to avoid the carrying out of criminal trials against absent defendants. Doubtless, there is still a cultural barrier in this approach, which may explain why the accused are still often deprived of, or at least are not granted, the necessary conditions to take part personally in their proceedings instituted against them. That defendants are often excluded from the possibility of making their personal contribution to the procedure, therefore, still renders defendants substantially extraneous to their own trial. Of course, this outcome, which is due to various factors, can be neither justified nor compensated for by guaranteeing the assistance of a lawyer, as happened in the transnational case *Melloni v. Ministerio Fiscal*, despite the relevance attached by the European Court of Justice to the fact that the applicant had been represented in court by two lawyers.[35]

Moreover, a substantial condition of extraneousness of the accused from their own proceedings can also be observed in fields other than that of *in absentia* procedures. This outcome frequently occurs in cases of alternative proceedings, depending on the approach followed by each jurisdiction and especially domestic caselaw. For instance, while Spain attaches considerable importance to the personal participation of defendants not only in bargaining procedures (*conformidades*) but also in the new procedure based upon penalty order (*procedimiento por aceptación*

---

[35] CJEU, Grand Chamber, *Melloni v. Ministerio Fiscal*, judgment of 26 February 2013, C-399/11. Indeed, the fact that notice of the proceedings was sent to the two lawyers of Mr. Melloni was clearly not enough to ensure his awareness of the proceedings, as it did not put him in a position to decide whether to attend the court hearing in person. Moreover, there was no clear evidence that he decided not to participate in the court proceedings. To be sure, even the appointment of a lawyer of one's own confidence does not in itself demonstrate the accused's waiver of his right to take part personally in criminal proceedings. In this case, however, the lawyers who defended Mr. Melloni on appeal no longer represented him, since he had withdrawn their mandate. This in turn cast doubts as to the fulfilment of the requirements set forth by the 2009 EU legislation, invoked by the Luxembourg judges. Thus, this legal instrument, although not requiring the proof of the unequivocal waiver of personal participation, conditioned the accused's surrender on the fact that he was truly defended by a counsel who, no matter whether appointed by the state or by himself, was mandated to do so.

de decreto), Italy is still far from enabling the accused to be personally involved in some crucial decisions to be issued in the context of alternative proceedings. Under Italian law, indeed, defendants are radically excluded from the possibility of making any contribution to the decision on the issuing on a penalty order (*procedimento per decreto penale*), the conviction being issued *inaudito reo* by the competent judge, while their involvement in the bargaining procedures (*patteggiamento*) is an eventuality that in the practice is somewhat infrequent.

Moreover, comparative law shows a persistent outdatedness in reaching standards of effective participation of the defendant even in cases in which he might be present at trial. Notwithstanding multiple legislative reforms of criminal justice, Italy provides a clear example in this respect too. Thus, following a solution adopted by the Joint Sections of the Court of Cassation in relation to the abbreviated proceedings[36] and subsequently extended by the same Court to the bargaining procedures,[37] the failure of the defendant who is present at trial to oppose the request of such alternative procedures, lodged by his defence lawyer without a special power. It is manifestly an unfortunate approach, which turns out to entail relevant implications on the problems concerned with the procedural thirdness. Italian law, indeed, does not require any competent authority (i.e., neither the judge nor the public prosecutor) to inform the accused, who might not have any legal knowledge and might even not speak the trial language, about the consequences of the decision either to consent or to oppose the institution of an alternative procedure. Nothing therefore ensures that the accused are fully aware of the request lodged by their lawyer, and that they effectively agreed with such request, which can severely impinge upon a number of individual rights (personal freedom, property, etc.). From this it follows that under Italian law, defendants often paradoxically remain excluded from (or are often not properly granted the necessary safeguards to face) some core decisions regarding their most precious rights.

The proposed perspective, therefore, enables us to look with critical eyes at the right to personal participation of the accused who, in spite of its formal role, often still plays a marginal role in a criminal trial, and is sometimes excluded from core decisions that may affect his own position.

4.4 Equality of Arms, Third Parties, and the Need for Wide-Ranging Balances in Criminal Proceedings

The adoption of a substantial approach to the relationship between formal and third parties, and the re-definition of the scope of 'participation' in criminal proceedings, should now lead us to further broaden the viewpoint beyond the perspective of

[36] Court of Cassation, Joint Sections, 31 January 2008, n. 9977, *Morini*, in *C.E.D.* No. 238680.

[37] Court of Cassation, 16 February 2011, n. 8492.

individual persons, by examining the reach today of the principle of equality of arms, which lies at the core of every model of a truly fair trial.

Without a doubt, the analysis of ECHR law provides a privileged viewpoint to address this problematic topic. As is well-known, it was precisely by adopting a wide-ranging notion of procedural fairness that the ECtHR has developed, through an extensive caselaw, an innovative approach to the fair trial rights enshrined by the European Convention, which, as far as criminal justice is concerned, were laid down in 1950 with the main goal of enhancing the accused's standing *vis-à-vis* the state's prosecutorial power. The purpose of this caselaw, however, was not to extend the defendant's safeguards to other parties,[38] and even to third persons, such as witnesses, but to include them into a broader framework of values in which the accused's guarantees, far from having an absolute relevance, encounter clear limits in the need not to endanger the core rights of other individuals involved in procedural activities.

This approach gains special importance in the light of the perspective followed in our research. This does not however entail that the defendant's rights must be sacrificed in order to satisfy the protection needs of substantial parties; it means recognising the accused's right to an overall fair trial, that is, their right to a criminal trial which must fit the requirements of fairness in relation to all the persons concerned with their own needs and claim for justice in each concrete case. This is precisely the profound sense of balancing rights and safeguards, which requires a constant search for trade-offs among conflicting interests.

One of the fields in which this perspective has taken root is that of evidence law, especially because of the enshrinement by the ECHR of the right to confrontation and its fundamental role in the framework of any dialectical model of criminal trial. The very notion of 'confrontation' entails (at least) a bilateral legal relationship, which has progressively led the European Court, as we shall see, not only to de-formalise the concept of 'accused' by including suspects and the person investigated in another country, but also, and above all, to broaden the concept of 'witness' by encompassing several categories of individuals, such as co-defendants, victims, expert witnesses, and so on.[39]

It was precisely such a broad understanding of 'accuser' that enabled the Strasbourg Court to mitigate the strong accused-centred perspective of the ECHR's model of a fair trial by compensating for the lack of specific safeguards regarding individuals other than defendants, who are called upon to render oral evidence in criminal proceedings from the first steps of the investigative phase. Thus, dealing with confrontation rights has provided European caselaw with an extraordinary opportunity to enhance the protective shield of the right to a fair trial, by way of including

---

[38] Yet, as has been noted, some guarantees, such as the right to the reasonable length of the proceedings, also applies to the damaged party and even to the injured party who claims for the institution of a criminal trial with a view to lodging a civil-law action.

[39] For in-depth analysis of the European caselaw on the right to confrontation from the perspective of this study cf. Orlando, in this volume, para. 3.

into the judicial balancing the need to protect an increasing number of persons from the adverse effects especially of cross-examination in open court. This approach, therefore, confirms that even the right to confrontation, notwithstanding its enormous importance, cannot be interpreted in absolute terms, but is a part of the complex trade-offs regarding the overall fairness of criminal proceedings.

From this it follows that *par condicio* can no longer be related to the sole formal parties but must be understood with a broader viewpoint, which encompasses a wide range of further individuals who, although not having the status of formal participants, are more and more involved in criminal inquiries and court proceedings. As has been noted, this does not entail a hierarchy of values, in the sense that the interests and protection needs of third persons must prevail over those of the accused, or *vice versa*. It means that even a fundamental right, such as the right to confrontation, must be ensured in a way that does not imply undue restrictions on other human rights acknowledged by ECHR law, and might in specific circumstances be delimited in order not to endanger core values such as those of life, liberty, and physical integrity of other persons who, precisely due the high rank of such rights, deserve to be considered as substantial parties.

Interestingly, such balances may lead to relativise the stand of the confrontation rights to protect persons who due to their profession and functions cannot be deemed as third *private* parties (*e.g.*, police officers). But the reach of the protection shield elaborated by the ECtHR is even broader, as it covers a variety of combinations, which aim at avoiding that the full exercise of the right to confrontation in an oral hearing may have indirect effects *vis-à-vis* third persons related to 'witnesses' with public functions (*e.g.*, family members of undercover agents), as well as individuals who can be included into a wide category of aggrieved parties (*e.g.*, the next of kin of the injured person). It is worth observing that the need to enlarge the subjective scope of the principle of equality of arms has gained increasing relevance in some domestic jurisdictions, such as Italy, which by enacting a constitutional model of fair trial has coupled the confrontation right in criminal proceedings with the guarantee of a judicial body before which the accused must be granted the opportunity of examining or having examined any person who renders evidence against them.[40]

The significant evolution of European caselaw after the landmark decision *Al-Khawaja and Tahery v. The United Kingdom* marked a point of no return in the approach of the Strasbourg Court, not only in the treatment of the right of confrontation but also, and more generally, in the balancing of the fundamental rights and interests of formal and third parties, in the light of a new distribution of competences between the Court and domestic judicial bodies.[41] Thus, the solutions set out by this judgment in relation to absent witnesses, and which were further developed by the

[40] Art. 111(3) of the Italian Constitution.

[41] ECtHR, Grand Chamber, *Al-Khawaja and Tahery v. United Kingdom*, judgment of 15 December 2011, Appl. No. 26766/05 and 22228/06.

Grand Chamber in *Schatschaschwili v. Germany*,[42] enabled the European judges to overcome the 'Pillars of Hercules' constituted by the sole and decisive evidence rule. In this way, Strasbourg caselaw enhanced the participatory rights of individuals who, not being able to be present at trial, could hardly be considered even as substantial participants, on condition, however, that the domestic authorities provided for adequate counterbalancing factors to compensate for the lack of confrontation. This acknowledgment proves particularly relevant in situations such as that in which the victim has died before the institution of the criminal trial, insofar as it satisfies the right to be heard of persons who, no matter their role established by domestic law, could not make their voice heard in court and could therefore not be examined by the accused.

Another remarkable development of European jurisprudence was the extension of the doctrine elaborated in *Al-Khawaja and Tahery* to further categories of individuals, who are not impeded from rendering evidence at trial, but may refuse to do so, or consent to be examined through special examination techniques, like videoconferencing. This led the Court to broaden the scope of the balancing between the defendant's right to confrontation and the rights of third parties, while giving rise to new challenges for the achievement of an overall fair evidentiary procedure. Doubtless, there are situations in which face-to-face confrontation in open court does not only help achieve a reliable ascertainment of facts but can also negatively impinge on fundamental rights of specific categories of 'witnesses': *e.g.*, in cases of vulnerable victims, minors and undercover agents, direct confrontation with the accused in an oral hearing would entail the risk of traumatisation. Yet, as Claudio Orlando has rightly held,

> this approach does not entail that measures aimed at safeguarding witnesses – particularly, the non-attendance of a witness at trial, the video recording of a witness interview, the possibility of examining the witness indirectly through written questions at trial or at the pre-trial stage – apply automatically. Since such measures do not grant the defence the same opportunities as cross-examination, their application must be subjected to the most careful scrutiny by domestic authorities.[43]

There is little doubt, furthermore, that the most complex challenges arise in the field of covert investigations with far-reaching scope, such as digital communication intercepts, online searches, digital seizure, and so on. Because of their capability of gathering a huge amount of data and information regarding individuals who are often unrelated to the alleged offence, and the person under investigation, such tools raise several difficult questions which are still far from achieving satisfactory solutions. The main factor that differentiates them from any other investigative measure, and which is surely due to the ceaseless and increasing impact of the digital evolution on the investigative techniques, is that covert investigative measures may not only be addressed against third parties but also, and regardless of the

[42] ECtHR, Grand Chamber, *Schatschaschwili v. Germany*, judgment of 15 December 2015, Appl. No. 9154/10.

[43] Orlando, in this volume, para. 3.

fact that their addressee is a suspect or a third person, can affect an unpredictable number of people without their identity being known and foreseeable at the time the investigation started.

Here also, the European Court reveals a clear awareness of the problems concerned with the use of covert digital tools of investigation.[44] On one hand, the evolution of Strasbourg caselaw from *Iordachi and Others* to *Roman Zacharov* reveals a constant argumentation which extended to digital communication intercepts the approach started years before in respect of interception measures in the analogical era in *Kruslin v. France*,[45] by way of requiring specific indications by domestic law or practice of the categories of person who can be intercepted. On the other, in the 2000 *Amann* case the European Court was already called upon to face the problem of the effects on interception activities on people fortuitously tapped, and even though it denied their role as 'necessary participants' in the phone conversations being tapped, it laid down a set of safeguards that the domestic authorities must comply with to avoid abuses. It is worth observing that—whereas such safeguards include, *inter alia*, the precautions to be taken when communicating the data to other parties, as well as the conditions on which recordings may or must be erased or the tapes destroyed—two of the main guarantees aimed at preventing uncontrolled interference with the right to privacy and digital communication, i.e. the guarantees of a judicial oversight and of a prior notification, were considerably smoothed by recent European caselaw, which replaced the former with the control by an independent body, while excluding the latter from being a necessary requirement with a view to the effectiveness of legal remedies.

This approach is more than questionable from a methodological viewpoint. Instead of weakening the safeguards due third persons whose conversations or data have been fortuitously gathered through covert means of investigation, the Court should have engaged in requiring domestic authorities to rigorously justify the adoption of measures which result in a bulk surveillance, and which should be subjected to a test of strict necessity and call for constant check by a judicial authority.

4.5 The Challenges of Transnational Criminal Justice

Certainly, cross-border situations enhance the need for a de-formalised approach to this problematic topic. This clearly results from the examination of the procedural safeguards concerned with the roles of the individuals involved in criminal proceedings. Since such roles are strictly linked to a specific jurisdiction, it is apparent that springing from one jurisdiction to another, those who are parties in state A may not have any participatory role in state B. Following the approach adopted in this

[44] *Ibid.*, para. 4.

[45] ECtHR, *Kruslin v. France*, judgment of 24 April 1990, Appl. No. 11801/85.

study, one could have the impression that the division line between formal and substantial participants, is by definition blurred in the context of transnational criminal proceedings.

It was precisely the need to compensate for the implications of such outcome in terms of lowering the standards of human rights protection that led the former EComHR to adopt, in the 1973 case *X., Y. and Z. v. Austria*, a very innovative approach to the right to confrontation by dealing with the problem of testimonial evidence being obtained by means of letters rogatory.[46] This approach enabled extending to the addressee of incriminating statements the main safeguards of the accused, starting with the right to confrontation, notwithstanding no criminal process had been not initiated against him and consequently he did not hold the formal status of 'accused' in the jurisdiction in which evidence ought to be collected. Years later, the Strasbourg Court further developed this understanding in the judgment *A. M. v. Italy*. In spite of the lack of instruments based on combined methods in force in Italy at that time, the European judges found in this ruling a breach of the Convention due the failure of Italy to ensure to the accused a fair opportunity of confrontation. This result was not only due to fact that the letters rogatory had been issued without the applicant's knowledge, but furthermore because the Italian public prosecutor had expressly requested the US authorities not to allow the attendance of both defendant and his lawyer at the examination of key witnesses abroad.[47]

Another important development, moreover, may seem to demonstrate the attempt to reduce the distance between formal participants and third parties, while consequently improving the safeguards of the main parties, mainly of the accused, in the field of transnational criminal justice. This development concerned the methods of evidence-gathering, and particularly the ways of ensuring both the effectiveness of the right to confrontation and the dialectical structure of the criminal process. An early attempt to shorten such distance was made by the former European Commission in *P.V. v. Federal Republic of Germany*, which stressed that the guarantee of confrontation can be complied with in different forms than cross-examination.[48] This simple assumption led to European case-law developing an approach based on the possibility of forwarding written questions to the competent court for examining witnesses on commission, an approach that was maintained by the Court for two decades. It was only in more recent years, and thanks to the evolution of science and the availability of modern technologies, that the Strasbourg Court started testing the overall fairness of the criminal trial in the light of the ability of domestic authorities to "offer more interactive type of questioning of witnesses abroad, like a video link".[49] The duty of diligence on the part of the defence that characterised its jurisprudence until then was abandoned in *Damir Sibgatullin v. Russia*, when the European judges focused on the obligation of the contracting states to provide

---

[46] EComHR, *X., Y. and Z. v. Austria*, decision of 5 February 1973, Appl. No. 5049/71.

[47] ECtHR, *A.M. v. Italy*, judgment of 14 December 1999, Appl. 37019/97.

[48] EComHR, *P.V. v. Federal Republic of Germany*, decision of 13 July 1987, Appl. No. 11853/85.

[49] ECtHR, *Zhukovskiy v. Ukraine*, judgment of 3 March 2011, Appl. No. 31240/03, para. 45.

alternative forms of obtaining testimonial evidence abroad, particularly through modern means of audio-visual communication.[50] The enhancement of the right to confrontation in turn brought the accuser closer to the accused in the context of proceedings that, because of their transborder nature and the difficulties concerned with territorial distance, tend to separate them.

While ECHR caselaw therefore reveals the clear intention to fill the gap between formal and substantial participation in transnational procedures by extending the accused's safeguards to those who do not hold such status in the jurisdiction in which evidence is to be collected, the evolution of EU law does not provide us with uniform indications as to the relationship between formal and third parties in the field of transnational criminal justice. Most interestingly, the evolution of EU legislation reveals a variety of different versions of third parties, which at first sight could seem to impede a consistent understanding of this categories. Thus, whereas the EIO Directive treats the procedural thirdness in relation to different individuals not only from the defendants, but also from the victim and further persons who are typically considered as third parties, such as witnesses, the EPPO Regulation instead proposes a very broad category of thirdness that encompasses even suspects and victims. Certainly, as Antonella Falcone held,[51] such different conceptions reflect (and are therefore aimed to satisfy) the different purposes pursued by the EU instruments of judicial cooperation, which justify a relativistic approach from the perspective of European transnational criminal justice. On close examination, one could however observe some common points towards which the main EU legal tools may seem to converge.

The main point of convergence is that EU law does not take into consideration any third party but only those individuals who are involved in, or can be touched upon by, procedural activities. This approach is also confirmed by the EIO Directive, in which the inclusion of the hearing of third parties, along with other categories of individuals, into a list of measures that appears to be characterised by their non-coercive nature should be interpreted *cum grano salis*. Indeed, the absence of interference with fundamental rights and freedoms, as happens with search and seizure, or communication intercepts, does not entail that the taking oral evidence cannot impinge on fundamental rights. Several fundamental rights can be endangered by the way in which not only a suspect is questioned, but also witnesses and third parties are heard, and this highlights the need for enhanced protection in transnational cases, in terms of informational safeguards, defence rights, and so on.

From a human rights perspective, cross-border procedures certainly set additional challenges to those existing in domestic situations, and while EU law has long favoured recourse to modern technologies, this approach, which has recently been confirmed by Regulation 2023/1543 on European Production Orders and European Preservation Orders for electronic evidence in criminal proceedings and for the execution of custodial sentences following criminal proceedings, requires further

[50] ECtHR, *Damir Sibgatullin v. Russia*, judgment of 24 April 2012, Appl. No. 1413/05, para. 56.
[51] See Falcone, in this volume, para. 2.

guarantees than those provided in purely domestic situations. The need for enhanced protection in transnational evidence-gathering procedures was already evident in the EIO Directive, however. Pursuant to this legislative instrument, in particular, suspects and defendants must "be informed in advance of the hearing of the procedural rights which would accrue to them, including the right not to testify at all", under the law of *both* the executing State and the issuing State, while witnesses must be granted a more limited, but not less relevant safeguard, namely they "may claim the right not to testify which would accrue to them under the law of either the executing or the issuing State and shall be informed about this right in advance of the hearing" [Article 24(5)(e)].

Of course, the need to strengthen the protection of third parties increases when investigative measures and tools of judicial cooperation are at stake which entail restrictions on core rights and freedoms. It is worth observing that EU lawmakers have somehow tightened the scope of third persons who can undergo especially patrimonial measures. This clearly results from Directive 2014/42/EU, which, by dealing with third parties in its Article 6, requires member states to undertake the "necessary measures to enable the confiscation of proceeds, or other property the value of which corresponds to proceeds", but only if the instrumentalities or proceeds of crime,

> directly or indirectly, were transferred by a suspected or accused person to third parties, or which were acquired by third parties from a suspected or accused person, at least if those third parties knew or ought to have known that the purpose of the transfer or acquisition was to avoid confiscation, on the basis of concrete facts and circumstances.

This approach reveals the clear intention of EU institutions to circumscribe the category of third parties whose patrimony can be frozen or confiscated by highlighting a strict link to the alleged offence, which is demonstrated by the practice of suspects or accused "transferring property to a knowing third party with a view to avoiding confiscation". The concept of 'knowing third party' is certainly in line with the general understanding of third parties proposed in this study as founded on their involvement in (or their connection with) criminal proceedings.

This explains the attention attached by EU lawmakers to the requirement that the rights of *bona fide* third parties be not jeopardised, which in turn shows another important element to reconstruct the way of approaching third parties by EU law, that is, the focus on the entitlement of certain categories of third persons to claim the protection of those rights they assume to be infringed by procedural activities and investigative measures in particular. The 2002 Framework Decision on the EAW had already walked a similar road by treating the issue of the rights of third parties regarding the seizure and handing over of property in the context of such surrender procedures. Unfortunately, this legislative instrument, as well as more recent EU legislation, failed to specify several relevant aspects, starting with the definition of the categories of rights comprised in this provision, the applicable law according to which protection can be claimed, and so on. Without a doubt, all these aspects necessitate of proper clarification considering the vulnerable condition of the persons involved especially in criminal procedures having a transnational dimension, and therefore also third parties. The achievement of a higher degree of precision is a clear commitment of supranational lawmakers, who are called upon to strengthen the protection of the individuals implicated in cross-border situations, beyond their formal status.

This perspective allows us to better understand the approach adopted by the EPPO Regulation, which puts on equal footing defendants, victims, and third parties from the viewpoint of the adverse effects of procedural activities addressed against them. It might be argued that under this legal instrument suspects, victims, and other persons affected by investigations should be seen "as part of a wide category, namely as third parties, in relation to the EPPO's investigative power and the national courts carrying out judicial review".[52] Such conclusion may seem to be somehow misleading in the light of the approach followed in this study, due to the clear heterogeneity of functions and roles relating to those individuals and a supranational prosecutorial body. Nevertheless, one should acknowledge that the EPPO's investigative action must always consider not only the "public interests embedded in the prosecution of PIF crimes but also those of the suspect, victim, and any other affected parties in respect of which the national court plays the role of guarantor".[53] From this viewpoint, therefore, the condition of thirdness appears to concern the interests at stake more than their holders, and the bodies and persons involved.

5 Towards a Relativistic Approach to the Procedural Thirdness. Concluding Remarks

The evolution of European law, and especially the perspective adopted by European caselaw, proves extremely useful to reconstruct the role and protection of third parties in criminal proceedings. A comparison of the jurisprudences of the ECtHR and the CJEU, indeed, provides us with a viewpoint that in both areas of domestic and transnational criminal justice looks at the specific interests in investigative and judicial procedures. This approach, enhancing the substantial way of approaching the procedural thirdness, leads us to relativise its scope of application depending on types on proceedings. The CJEU clearly followed this approach in *DR* and *TS*, in which it expressly held that "national legislation must allow third parties to appear as *a party in the confiscation proceedings*".[54]

This conclusion provides a relevant methodological indication to deal with the procedural thirdness. We saw that, far from being a condition of extraneousness, it highlights the existence of specific, albeit different, interests in a legal—and especially in a procedural—relationship, which justifies broadening the concept of

---

[52] See Falcone, in this volume, para. 4.

[53] *Ibid.*

[54] CJEU, *DR and TS*, judgment of 21 October 2021, C-845/19 and C-863/19. See Falcone, in this volume, para. 3.3.

'participation' from a substantial viewpoint. Unfortunately, domestic jurisdictions are still far from achieving satisfactory standards of protection of third parties, and even though they are more and more severely touched upon by investigative measures, they are often denied essential participatory safeguards, and the existing guarantees are not proportional to the magnitude of the restrictions on freedom. This outcome shows the widespread reluctance to consider (and treat) them as effective participants in criminal proceedings, or at least in those specific procedures regarding their sphere of interests and rights.

The caselaw of the ECtHR also has on various occasions demonstrated the outdatedness of the domestic legislation of European countries, and the recent judgment *Contrada v. Italy (No. 4)* provides an enlightening example.[55] In this case, the European Court found a breach of Article 8 ECHR on the ground that Italian law does not grant the person whose communications have been intercepted the status of a party in criminal proceedings, unless he already holds it for other reasons, and consequently does not ensure adequate and effective safeguards against abuses. Most interestingly, the Strasbourg judges focused on some qualitative requirements, which Italian legislation unfortunately still lacks, and which should instead characterise all procedures regarding communication intercepts, that is, the need to ensure that third parties are duly notified of the delivery of the documentation regarding an interception that captured their conversation, can obtain a judicial oversight of the lawfulness, proportionality, and necessity of such intrusive measure, and eventually can request the erasure of irrelevant communications and reparation for the unlawful interception. It is apparent that the informational requirement could pose delicate problems in relation to third parties whose communications have been fortuitously gathered during an interception ordered against other individuals, no matter whether suspects or third parties.[56] But there is no valid ground for ruling out the possibility for a person affected by a communication intercept to access a judicial control, which is still the most powerful means of reducing the risk of abuses. Furthermore, the acknowledgment of these rights to third parties as well, and the provision of the need for the judicial authority to issue a reasoned decision in any case, might also prevent in advance an excessive use of interception tools, and to limit especially the recourse to spyware due to their widespread intrusiveness, as has been noted, in respect of an unpredictable number of people.

The Court of Justice also has pointed out the relevance of a perspective oriented to the intrusiveness of legal acts and their capability of affecting the interests of the applicants regardless of their role and status. This perspective—which today finds a clear legal basis in Article 263 TFEU, insofar as it links the guarantee of judicial review to the ability of acts of bodies and agencies of the Union to "produce legal effects *vis-à-vis* third parties"[57]—confirms the exactness of a reconstruction of the procedural thirdness in the light of the right to be involved in the proceedings

[55] ECtHR, *Contrada v. Italy (n. 4)*, judgment of 23 May 2024, Appl. No. 2507/19.

[56] In this sense Foti (2024).

[57] See Falcone, in this volume, para. 4.

regarding the procedural acts and measures endangering their interests and individual freedoms.

This approach, moreover, raises further questions which are still far from being solved. Alongside the viewpoint based upon the negative effects *vis-à-vis* third parties, the procedural thirdness needs to be considered from different perspectives too, which stand out at the conclusion of our research. What about those who can be advantaged by the effects of legal acts within a procedure in which they do not hold any role of formal parties. That the interests of such individuals can be enhanced does not rule out that they may undergo negative consequences by the failure to provide certain safeguards, *e.g.* family members of a person injured by alleged offences, such as domestic violence, stalking and violence against children. Here it is apparent that there is no need for subsequent remedies to measures or procedural acts affecting third persons; on the contrary, they claim for a legal response which is able to protect in advance their most precious interests, such as physical integrity and even life, by means of a set of legal actions, *e.g.* by issuing of pre-trial measures specifically aimed at reducing the risk of further illicit conducts (for instance, removal from family home) and providing the aggrieved parties and family members of constant information about the development of such measures.

It is apparent that the difficult challenges set by the evolution of criminal justice require a comprehensive intervention by lawmakers and caselaw, which can however not be limited to providing procedural safeguards to (or strengthening the existing guarantees of) those who have already suffered from restrictions on their rights and freedoms. Thus, there is also a need for preventive law intervention to enhance the participatory safeguards of those who could receive the beneficial effects of procedural acts addressed against formal participants or could not gain the status of parties to criminal proceedings, although being entitled to do so.[58] Doubtless, a wide-ranging, deformalized and flexible approach is the best way of satisfying the multiple needs regarding the increasing roles and the new forms of involvement of third parties in criminal trials.

References

Bachmaier Winter L (2021) Proportionality, mass surveillance and criminal investigation: The Strasbourg Court facing Big Brother. In: Billis E, Knust N, Rui JP (eds) The principle of proportionality in crime control and criminal justice. Hart Publising, Oxford, pp 317–335

Balsamo A, Lo Piparo A (2008) Principio del contraddittorio, utilizzabilità delle dichiarazioni predibattimentali e nozione di testimone tra giurisprudenza europea e criticità del sistema italiano. In: Balsamo A, Kostoris RE (eds) Giurisprudenza europea e processo penale italiano. Giappichelli, Torino, pp 333–372

Carnelutti F (1936) Sistema di diritto processuale civile, vol I. Cedam, Padova

[58] Italian law, for example, protects the damaged person who was not enabled to lodge a civil-law action in a criminal trial by avoiding that the final criminal judgment can produce legal effects in civil proceedings.

Cordero F (1966) Procedura penale. Giuffrè, Milano
Di Nuzzo V (2021) «Ne bis in idem» e tutela della vittima di reato: la Corte di Strasburgo riconosce la cedevolezza del principio di fronte a gravi violazioni dei diritti delle persone LGBTQ+: Foro Italiano, 465 ff
Di Nuzzo V (2022) Search and seizure of digital evidence: human rights concerns and new safeguards. In: Bachmaier Winter Lorena, Ruggeri S (eds) Investigating and preventing crime in the digital era. Springer, Cham, pp. 119–149
Falcone A (2021) Indipendenza del pubblico ministero e cooperazione internazionale in materia penale nello scenario giuridico europeo: https://rivista.eurojus.it/indipendenza-del-pubblico-ministero-e-cooperazione-internazionale-in-materia-penale-nello-scenario-giuridico-europeo/
Foti D (2022) Digital privacy and cyber-interception of communications. In: Bachmaier Winter L, Ruggeri S (eds) Investigating and preventing crime in the digital era. Springer, Cham, pp 151–166
Foti D (2024) La disciplina italiana delle intercettazioni viola l'art. 8 CEDU. IUS Penale.
Kant I (1987) Critique of judgment. Transl. by W.S. Pluhar. Orig. Ed. 1790. Hackett Publishing Company, Indianapolis/Cambridge
Lo Giudice A (2023) Il dramma del giudizio. Mimesis, Sesto San Giovanni
Lucchini L (1899) Elementi di procedura penale, 2nd edn. Barbera, Firenze
Malino E (2021) Completezza delle indagini preliminari e *ne bis in idem*: i risvolti applicativi dell'interazione dei principi della giustizia penale: https://www.rivistaoidu.net/wp-content/uploads/2023/08/Speciale-Ne-bis-in-Idem-impaginato.pdf, pp 81–98
Mazza O (2020) La riforma dei due orologi: la prescrizione fra miti populisti e realtà costituzionale. https://www.sistemapenale.it/it/opinioni/mazza-prescrizione-riforma-dei-due-orologi-populismo-costituzione
Negri (2014) L'imputato presente al processo. Una ricostruzione sistematica. Giappichelli, Torino
Neroni Rezende I (2022) Facial recognition for preventive purposes: the human rights implications of detecting emotions in public spaces. In: Bachmaier Winter L, Ruggeri S (eds) Investigating and preventing crime in the digital era. Springer, Cham, pp 67–98
Orlando C (2022) The use of drones and the new procedural safeguards in crime control and criminal investigation. In: Bachmaier Winter L, Ruggeri S (eds) Investigating and preventing crime in the digital era. Springer, Cham, pp 101–118
Quattrocolo S (2011) Riqualificazione del fatto nella sentenza penale e tutela del contraddittorio. Jovene, Napoli
Quattrocolo S, Ruggeri S (eds) (2019) Personal participation in criminal proceedings. A comparative study of participatory safeguards and in absentia trials in Europe. Springer, Cham
Satta S (1949) Il mistero del processo. Rivista di diritto processuale I:273–288
Scalfati A (ed) (2019) Le indagini atipiche. Giappichelli, Torino

Format for Domestic Law Comparison[1]

A. Introduction. General features of domestic criminal justice
   a. Formal participants in criminal proceedings[2]
   b. Third parties to criminal proceedings[3]

[1] Both the authors of the country reports and of the Chapter on the comparative-law analysis of domestic jurisdictions were asked to follow the current format in carrying out their contributions.

[2] The authors of the national reports were asked to explain which natural or legal persons hold the formal status of parties to criminal proceedings in the relevant domestic jurisdiction.

[3] For the purpose of the present research, authors of the national reports were asked to deal with a broad concept of 'third parties'. More precisely, in a strict sense, the were informed that term relates to specific natural or legal persons other than formal participants in criminal process, who, however, are granted some procedural powers which are equivalent or similar to those of formal participants (access to the materials of the case, *ius postulandi*, etc.): for instance, the owner of the assets seized, or the holder of rights *in rem*. In some jurisdictions, such persons are sometimes treated as substantial parties to the proceedings. Furthermore, 'third parties' are also those people who are called upon or even compelled to take part in procedural acts (e.g., witnesses). In a broader sense still, authors were made aware that 'third parties' are those people who undergo procedural measures, that is, all those persons against whom procedural measures can be addressed without being formal participants (e.g., the addressee of wiretaps, surveillance, cyber investigations, etc.). Moreover, adopting a human rights perspective, i.e., a viewpoint oriented towards the degree of intrusiveness of procedural measures in the sphere of fundamental rights, further broadens the notion of 'third parties' by extending it to people that, even though criminal investigations are not addressed against them, may be indirectly affected by procedural activities (e.g., the family members of undercover agents or people under a special protection programme). Furthermore, some borderline categories may deserve special references depending on their classification in the relevant domestic jurisdiction (co-accused, victims, damaged party, etc.). Furthermore, a specific examination may be useful by dealing with third parties in particular situations (vulnerable witnesses, minors etc.)

For the purpose of the present research, authors were also informed that the concept of 'third persons' does not apply to general categories of people. However, a discussion on the relationship between the dynamics of criminal investigations or judicial proceedings, and the public opinion or

S. Ruggeri et al. (eds.), *Third Parties in Criminal Proceedings*, Legal Studies in International, European and Comparative Criminal Law 10,
https://doi.org/10.1007/978-3-031-73970-5

B. Fundamental rights and safeguards of third parties

   a. Constitutional law
   b. Domestication of international law
   c. Implementation of EU law

C. Third parties in criminal inquiries

   a. Police and law enforcement investigations
   b. Prosecutorial inquiry
   c. If relevant, judicial investigation

D. Scientific developments, new technologies and the safeguards of third parties[4]
E. Pre-trial measures and the protection of fundamental rights of third parties[5]
F. Third parties and the decision to charge (or to terminate the proceedings)
G. Third parties in court proceedings

   a. The right of third parties to be heard fairly
   b. The right of third parties not to be questioned
   c. The protection of non-parties in court activities involving formal participants[6]
   d. Can third parties take part in court activities?

H. The protection of third parties in decision-making processes[7]

---

the media, was requested whenever necessary to properly examine specific issues from the viewpoint of domestic law.

[4]The authors were invited to focus on the rapid developments occurred in science and technologies that have led to the use of ever new investigative measures interfering with fundamental rights of an increasing number of people other than formal participants in criminal proceedings. With this regard, for instance, several of such means of investigation may not have a clear legal basis in domestic law and could therefore be treated as 'atypical investigations'. This has called for enhanced controls of the justification and need for technological measures scientific evidence, while requiring a stronger protection of individual rights of 'third parties', starting with the protection of the personal data collected through these investigations. These points were specifically dealt with the national reports' authors. The authors of the reports were called upon to shed light on these thorny aspects affecting third parties.

[5]The discussion on this issue relates to pre-trial detention and its alternatives, as well as to further pre-trial measures aimed at restricting other fundamental freedoms (free movement, free availability of assets, etc.).

[6]This specific point has required to address any possible repercussions of the court activities on third parties, and on the ways the relevant jurisdictions grant them proper protection. For instance, authors of the national reports were given at least two types of repercussions, that is to say, those depending on whether they regard the same person involved in the procedural activity (a vulnerable or a minor witness) or other people (family members of the person examined in a special position, e.g., an undercover agent).

[7]Authors were asked to specify whether or not, in their jurisdiction, judicial bodies can take into consideration (or are even called upon to satisfy) the interests of persons other than formal participants in decision-making.

I. Third parties in appeal proceedings[8]
J. *Res judicata* and the effects of criminal judgments upon third parties[9]

[8] Authors were invited to clarify whether or not natural or legal persons other than formal parties can lodge legal remedies, and/or which role, if any, they can play in higher instances, whether special safeguards are provided for in appeal proceedings, etc., according to domestic law.

[9] Authors were asked to specify whether and to what extent domestic law provides for specific implications of the *ne bis in idem* principle on natural or legal persons other than defendants in the event of the institution of a new process for the same facts. They were also invited to examine whether or not final criminal judgments can produce binding or not binding effects in non-criminal proceedings linked with the facts ascertained in the criminal process, in favour or against natural or legal persons other than those who have been formal participants in criminal proceedings.

The manufacturer's authorised representative in the EU is Springer Nature Customer Service Centre GmbH, Europaplatz 3, 69115 Heidelberg, Germany. If you have any concerns regarding our products, please contact ProductSafety@springernature.com

Printed and bound by CPI Group (UK) Ltd, Croydon, CR0 4YY

01/10/2026

02225909-0014